SECOND EDITION

Programming Google App Engine

Dan Sanderson

O'REILLY®

Beijing • Cambridge • Farnham • Köln • Sebastopol • Tokyo

Programming Google App Engine, Second Edition
by Dan Sanderson

Printed in the United States of America.

Published by O'Reilly Media, Inc., 1005 Gravenstein Highway North, Sebastopol, CA 95472.

O'Reilly books may be purchased for educational, business, or sales promotional use. Online editions are also available for most titles (*http://my.safaribooksonline.com*). For more information, contact our corporate/institutional sales department: 800-998-9938 or *corporate@oreilly.com*.

Editors: Mike Loukides and Meghan Blanchette
Production Editor: Rachel Steely
Copyeditor: Nancy Reinhardt
Proofreader: Kiel Van Horn
Indexer: Aaron Hazelton, BIM
Cover Designer: Karen Montgomery
Interior Designer: David Futato
Illustrator: Rebecca Demarest

October 2012: Second Edition.

Revision History for the Second Edition:
2012-10-04 First release
See *http://oreilly.com/catalog/errata.csp?isbn=9781449398262* for release details.

ISBN: 978-1-449-39826-2

[LSI]

1349377222

For Lisa, Sophia, and Maxwell

Table of Contents

Preface

On the Internet, popularity is swift and fleeting. A mention of your website on a popular blog can bring 300,000 potential customers your way at once, all expecting to find out who you are and what you have to offer. But if you're a small company just starting out, your hardware and software aren't likely to be able to handle that kind of traffic. Chances are, you've sensibly built your site to handle the 30,000 visits per hour you're actually expecting in your first 6 months. Under heavy load, such a system would be incapable of showing even your company logo to the 270,000 others that showed up to look around. And those potential customers are not likely to come back after the traffic has subsided.

The answer is *not* to spend time and money building a system to serve millions of visitors on the first day, when those same systems are only expected to serve mere thousands per day for the subsequent months. If you delay your launch to build big, you miss the opportunity to improve your product by using feedback from your customers. Building big before allowing customers to use the product risks building something your customers don't want.

Small companies usually don't have access to large systems of servers on day one. The best they can do is to build small and hope meltdowns don't damage their reputation as they try to grow. The lucky ones find their audience, get another round of funding, and halt feature development to rebuild their product for larger capacity. The unlucky ones, well, don't.

But these days, there are other options. Large Internet companies such as Amazon.com, Google, and Microsoft are leasing parts of their high-capacity systems by using a pay-per-use model. Your website is served from those large systems, which are plenty capable of handling sudden surges in traffic and ongoing success. And since you pay only for what you use, there is no up-front investment that goes to waste when traffic is low. As your customer base grows, the costs grow proportionally.

Google App Engine, Google's application hosting service, does more than just provide access to hardware. It provides a model for building applications that grow automatically. App Engine runs your application so that each user who accesses it gets the same experience as every other user, whether there are dozens of simultaneous users or thousands. The application uses the same large-scale services that power Google's applications for data storage and retrieval, caching, and network access. App Engine takes care of the tasks of large-scale computing, such as load balancing, data replication, and fault tolerance, automatically.

The App Engine model really kicks in at the point where a traditional system would outgrow its first database server. With such a system, adding load-balanced web servers and caching layers can get you pretty far, but when your application needs to write data to more than one place, you have a hard problem. This problem is made harder when development up to that point has relied on features of database software that were never intended for data distributed across multiple machines. By thinking about your data in terms of App Engine's model up front, you save yourself from having to rebuild the whole thing later.

Often overlooked as an advantage, App Engine's execution model helps to distribute computation as well as data. App Engine excels at allocating computing resources to small tasks quickly. This was originally designed for handling web requests from users, where generating a response for the client is the top priority. With App Engine's task queue service, medium-to-large computational tasks can be broken into chunks that are executed in parallel. Tasks are retried until they succeed, making tasks resilient in the face of service failures. The App Engine execution model encourages designs optimized for the parallelization and robustness provided by the platform.

Running on Google's infrastructure means you never have to set up a server, replace a failed hard drive, or troubleshoot a network card. And you don't have to be woken up in the middle of the night by a screaming pager because an ISP hiccup confused a service alarm. And with automatic scaling, you don't have to scramble to set up new hardware as traffic increases.

Google App Engine lets you focus on your application's functionality and user experience. You can launch early, enjoy the flood of attention, retain customers, and start improving your product with the help of your users. Your app grows with the size of your audience—up to Google-sized proportions—without having to rebuild for a new architecture. Meanwhile, your competitors are still putting out fires and configuring databases.

With this book, you will learn how to develop applications that run on Google App Engine, and how to get the most out of the scalable model. A significant portion of the book discusses the App Engine scalable datastore, which does not behave like the relational databases that have been a staple of web development for the past decade. The application model and the datastore together represent a new way of thinking about web applications that, while being almost as simple as the model we've known, requires reconsidering a few principles we often take for granted.

This book introduces the major features of App Engine, including the scalable services (such as for sending email and manipulating images), tools for deploying and managing applications, and features for integrating your application with Google Accounts and

Google Apps using your own domain name. The book also discusses techniques for optimizing your application, using task queues and offline processes, and otherwise getting the most out of Google App Engine.

Using This Book

App Engine supports three technology stacks for building web applications: Java, Python, and Go (a new programming language invented at Google). The Java technology stack lets you develop web applications by using the Java programming language (or most other languages that compile to Java bytecode or have a JVM-based interpreter) and Java web technologies such as servlets and JSPs. The Python technology stack provides a fast interpreter for the Python programming language, and is compatible with several major open source web application frameworks such as Django. The Go runtime environment compiles your Go code on the server and executes it at native CPU speeds.

This book covers concepts that apply to all three technology stacks, as well as important language-specific subjects for Java and Python. If you've already decided which language you're going to use, you probably won't be interested in information that doesn't apply to that language. This poses a challenge for a printed book: how should the text be organized so information about one technology doesn't interfere with information about the other?

Foremost, we've tried to organize the chapters by the major concepts that apply to all App Engine applications. Where necessary, chapters split into separate sections to talk about specifics for Python and Java. In cases where an example in one language illustrates a concept equally well for other languages, the example is given in Python. If Python is not your language of choice, hopefully you'll be able to glean the equivalent information from other parts of the book or from the official App Engine documentation on Google's website.

As of this writing, the Go runtime environment is released as an "experimental" feature, and the API may be changing rapidly. The language has stabilized at version 1, so if you're interested in Go, I highly recommend visiting the Go website (*http://golang.org/*) and the Go App Engine documentation (*https://developers.google.com/appengine/docs/go/overview*). We are figuring out how to best add material on Go to a future edition of this book.

The datastore is a large enough subject that it gets multiple chapters to itself. Starting with Chapter 5, datastore concepts are introduced alongside Python and Java APIs related to those concepts. Python examples use the `ext.db` data modeling library, and Java examples use the Java datastore API, both provided in the App Engine SDK. Some Java developers may prefer a higher-level data modeling library such as the Java Persistence API, which supports fewer features of the datastore but can be adapted to run on other database solutions. We discuss data modeling libraries separately, in Chapter 9 for Python, and in Chapter 10 for Java.

This book has the following chapters:

Chapter 1, *Introducing Google App Engine*
: A high-level overview of Google App Engine and its components, tools, and major features.

Chapter 2, *Creating an Application*
: An introductory tutorial for both Python and Java, including instructions on setting up a development environment, using template engines to build web pages, setting up accounts and domain names, and deploying the application to App Engine. The tutorial application demonstrates the use of several App Engine features—Google Accounts, the datastore, and memcache—to implement a pattern common to many web applications: storing and retrieving user preferences.

Chapter 3, *Configuring an Application*
: A description of how App Engine handles incoming requests, and how to configure this behavior. This introduces App Engine's architecture, the various features of the frontend, app servers, and static file servers. The frontend routes requests to the app servers and the static file servers, and manages secure connections and Google Accounts authentication and authorization. This chapter also discusses quotas and limits, and how to raise them by setting a budget.

Chapter 4, *Request Handlers and Instances*
: A closer examination of how App Engine runs your code. App Engine routes incoming web requests to request handlers. Request handlers run in long-lived containers called instances. App Engine creates and destroys instances to accommodate the needs of your traffic. You can make better use of your instances by writing threadsafe code and enabling the multithreading feature.

Chapter 5, *Datastore Entities*
: The first of several chapters on the App Engine datastore, a scalable object data storage system with support for local transactions and two modes of consistency guarantees (strong and eventual). This chapter introduces data entities, keys and properties, and Python and Java APIs for creating, updating, and deleting entities.

Chapter 6, *Datastore Queries*
: An introduction to datastore queries and indexes, and the Python and Java APIs for queries. The App Engine datastore's query engine uses prebuilt indexes for all queries. This chapter describes the features of the query engine in detail, and how each feature uses indexes. The chapter also discusses how to define and manage indexes for your application's queries. Recent features like query cursors and projection queries are also covered.

Chapter 7, *Datastore Transactions*
: How to use transactions to keep your data consistent. The App Engine datastore uses local transactions in a scalable environment. Your app arranges its entities in

units of transactionality known as entity groups. This chapter attempts to provide a complete explanation of how the datastore updates data, and how to design your data and your app to best take advantage of these features. This edition contains updated material on the "High Replication" datastore infrastructure, and new features such as cross-group transactions.

Chapter 8, *Datastore Administration*
: Managing and evolving your app's datastore data. The Administration Console, AppCfg tools, and administrative APIs provide a myriad of views of your data, and information about your data (metadata and statistics). You can access much of this information programmatically, so you can build your own administration panels. This chapter also discusses how to use the Remote API, a proxy for building administrative tools that run on your local computer but access the live services for your app.

Chapter 9, *Data Modeling with Python*
: How to use the Python `ext.db` data modeling API to enforce invariants in your data schema. The datastore itself is schemaless, a fundamental aspect of its scalability. You can automate the enforcement of data schemas by using App Engine's data modeling interface. This chapter covers Python exclusively, though Java developers may wish to skim it for advice related to data modeling.

Chapter 10, *The Java Persistence API*
: A brief introduction to the Java Persistence API (JPA), how its concepts translate to the datastore, how to use it to model data schemas, and how using it makes your application easier to port to other environments. JPA is a Java EE standard interface. App Engine also supports another standard interface known as Java Data Objects (JDO), although JDO is not covered in this book. This chapter covers Java exclusively.

Chapter 11, *The Memory Cache*
: App Engine's memory cache service ("memcache"), and its Python and Java APIs. Aggressive caching is essential for high-performance web applications.

Chapter 12, *Large Data and the Blobstore*
: How to use App Engine's Blobstore service to accept and serve amounts of data of unlimited size—or at least, as large as your budget allows. The Blobstore can accept large file uploads from users, and serve large values as responses. An app can also create, append to, and read byte ranges from these very large values, opening up possibilities beyond serving files.

Chapter 13, *Fetching URLs and Web Resources*
: How to access other resources on the Internet via HTTP by using the URL Fetch service. This chapter covers the Python and Java interfaces, including implementations of standard URL fetching libraries. It also describes how to call the URL Fetch service asynchronously, in Python and in Java.

Chapter 14, *Sending and Receiving Email Messages*
: How to use App Engine services to send email. This chapter covers receiving email relayed by App Engine by using request handlers. It also discusses creating and processing messages by using tools in the API.

Chapter 15, *Sending and Receiving Instant Messages with XMPP*
: How to use App Engine services to send instant messages to XMPP-compatible services (such as Google Talk), and receive XMPP messages via request handlers. This chapter discusses several major XMPP activities, including managing presence.

Chapter 16, *Task Queues and Scheduled Tasks*
: How to perform work outside of user requests by using task queues. Task queues perform tasks in parallel by running your code on multiple application servers. You control the processing rate with configuration. Tasks can also be executed on a regular schedule with no user interaction.

Chapter 17, *Optimizing Service Calls*
: A summary of optimization techniques, plus detailed information on how to make asynchronous service calls, so your app can continue doing work while services process data in the background. This chapter also describes AppStats, an important tool for visualizing your app's service call behavior and finding performance bottlenecks.

Chapter 18, *The Django Web Application Framework*
: How to use the Django web application framework with the Python runtime environment. This chapter discusses setting up a project by using the Django 1.3 library included in the runtime environment, and using Django features such as component composition, URL mapping, views, and templating. With a little help from an App Engine library, you can even use Django forms with App Engine datastore models. The chapter ends with a brief discussion of django-nonrel, an open source project to connect more pieces of Django to App Engine.

Chapter 19, *Managing Request Logs*
: Everything you need to know about logging messages, browsing and searching log data in the Administration Console, and managing and downloading log data. This chapter also introduces the Logs API, which lets you manage logs programmatically within the app itself.

Chapter 20, *Deploying and Managing Applications*
: How to upload and run your app on App Engine, how to update and test an application using app versions, and how to manage and inspect the running application. This chapter also introduces other maintenance features of the Administration Console, including billing. The chapter concludes with a list of places to go for help and further reading.

Conventions Used in This Book

The following typographical conventions are used in this book:

Italic
: Indicates new terms, URLs, email addresses, filenames, and file extensions.

`Constant width`
: Used for program listings, as well as within paragraphs to refer to program elements such as variable or function names, databases, data types, environment variables, statements, and keywords.

`Constant width bold`
: Shows commands or other text that should be typed literally by the user.

`Constant width italic`
: Shows text that should be replaced with user-supplied values or by values determined by context.

This icon signifies a tip, suggestion, or general note.

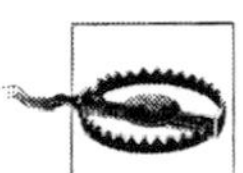

This icon indicates a warning or caution.

Using Code Samples

This book is here to help you get your job done. In general, you may use the code in this book in your programs and documentation. You do not need to contact us for permission unless you're reproducing a significant portion of the code. For example, writing a program that uses several chunks of code from this book does not require permission. Selling or distributing a CD-ROM of examples from O'Reilly books does require permission. Answering a question by citing this book and quoting example code does not require permission. Incorporating a significant amount of example code from this book into your product's documentation does require permission.

We appreciate, but do not require, attribution. An attribution usually includes the title, author, publisher, and ISBN. For example: "*Programming Google App Engine*, 2nd edition, by Dan Sanderson. Copyright 2013 Dan Sanderson, 978-1-449-39826-2."

If you feel your use of code examples falls outside fair use or the permission given above, feel free to contact us at *permissions@oreilly.com*.

Safari® Books Online

Safari Books Online (*www.safaribooksonline.com*) is an on-demand digital library that delivers expert content in both book and video form from the world's leading authors in technology and business.

Technology professionals, software developers, web designers, and business and creative professionals use Safari Books Online as their primary resource for research, problem solving, learning, and certification training.

Safari Books Online offers a range of product mixes and pricing programs for organizations, government agencies, and individuals. Subscribers have access to thousands of books, training videos, and prepublication manuscripts in one fully searchable database from publishers like O'Reilly Media, Prentice Hall Professional, Addison-Wesley Professional, Microsoft Press, Sams, Que, Peachpit Press, Focal Press, Cisco Press, John Wiley & Sons, Syngress, Morgan Kaufmann, IBM Redbooks, Packt, Adobe Press, FT Press, Apress, Manning, New Riders, McGraw-Hill, Jones & Bartlett, Course Technology, and dozens more. For more information about Safari Books Online, please visit us online.

How to Contact Us

Please address comments and questions concerning this book to the publisher:

O'Reilly Media, Inc.
1005 Gravenstein Highway North
Sebastopol, CA 95472
800-998-9938 (in the United States or Canada)
707-829-0515 (international or local)
707-829-0104 (fax)

We have a web page for this book, where we list errata, examples, and any additional information. You can access this page at *http://bit.ly/Programming_GoogleApp_Engine*.

You can download extensive sample code and other extras from the author's website at *http://www.dansanderson.com/appengine*.

To comment or ask technical questions about this book, send email to *bookquestions@oreilly.com*.

For more information about our books, courses, conferences, and news, see our website at *http://www.oreilly.com*.

Find us on Facebook: *http://facebook.com/oreilly*

Follow us on Twitter: *http://twitter.com/oreillymedia*

Watch us on YouTube: *http://www.youtube.com/oreillymedia*

Acknowledgments

I am indebted to the App Engine team for their constant support of this book since its inception in 2008. The number of contributors to App Engine has grown too large for me to list them individually, but I'm grateful to them all for their vision, their creativity, and their work, and for letting me be a part of it. I especially want to thank Kevin Gibbs, who was App Engine's tech lead through both the first and second editions.

The first edition of the book was developed under the leadership of Paul McDonald and Pete Koomen. Ryan Barrett provided many hours of conversation and detailed technical review. Max Ross and Rafe Kaplan contributed material and extensive review to the datastore chapters. Thanks to Matthew Blain, Michael Davidson, Alex Gaysinsky, Peter McKenzie, Don Schwarz, and Jeffrey Scudder for reviewing portions of the first edition in detail, as well as Sean Lynch, Brett Slatkin, Mike Repass, and Guido van Rossum for their support. For the second edition, I want to thank Peter Magnusson, Greg D'alesandre, Tom Van Waardhuizen, Mike Aizatsky, Wesley Chun, Johan Euphrosine, Alfred Fuller, Andrew Gerrand, Sebastian Kreft, Moishe Lettvin, John Mulhausen, Robert Schuppenies, David Symonds, and Eric Willigers.

Thanks also to Steven Hines, David McLaughlin, Mike Winton, Andres Ferrate, Dan Morrill, Mark Pilgrim, Steffi Wu, Karen Wickre, Jane Penner, Jon Murchinson, Tom Stocky, Vic Gundotra, Bill Coughran, and Alan Eustace.

At O'Reilly, I'd like to thank Michael Loukides and Meghan Blanchette for giving me this opportunity and helping me see it through to the end, twice.

I dedicate this book to Google's site-reliability engineers. It is they who carry the pagers, so we don't have to. We are forever grateful.

CHAPTER 1

Introducing Google App Engine

Google App Engine is a web application hosting service. By "web application," we mean an application or service accessed over the Web, usually with a web browser: storefronts with shopping carts, social networking sites, multiplayer games, mobile applications, survey applications, project management, collaboration, publishing, and all the other things we're discovering are good uses for the Web. App Engine can serve traditional website content too, such as documents and images, but the environment is especially designed for real-time dynamic applications.

In particular, Google App Engine is designed to host applications with many simultaneous users. When an application can serve many simultaneous users without degrading performance, we say it *scales*. Applications written for App Engine scale automatically. As more people use the application, App Engine allocates more resources for the application and manages the use of those resources. The application itself does not need to know anything about the resources it is using.

Unlike traditional web hosting or self-managed servers, with Google App Engine, you only pay for the resources you use. These resources are measured down to the gigabyte. Billed resources include CPU usage, storage per month, incoming and outgoing bandwidth, and several resources specific to App Engine services. To help you get started, every developer gets a certain amount of resources for free, enough for small applications with low traffic.

App Engine can be described as three parts: application instances, scalable data storage, and scalable services. In this chapter, we look at each of these parts at a high level. We also discuss features of App Engine for deploying and managing web applications, and for building websites integrated with other Google offerings such as Google Apps, Google Accounts, and Google Cloud Storage.

The Runtime Environment

An App Engine application responds to web requests. A web request begins when a client, typically a user's web browser, contacts the application with an HTTP request, such as to fetch a web page at a URL. When App Engine receives the request, it identifies the application from the domain name of the address, either an *.appspot.com* subdomain (provided for free with every app) or a subdomain of a custom domain name you have registered and set up with Google Apps. App Engine selects a server from many possible servers to handle the request, making its selection based on which server is most likely to provide a fast response. It then calls the application with the content of the HTTP request, receives the response data from the application, and returns the response to the client.

From the application's perspective, the runtime environment springs into existence when the request handler begins, and disappears when it ends. App Engine provides several methods for storing data that persists between requests, but these mechanisms live outside of the runtime environment. By not retaining state in the runtime environment between requests—or at least, by not expecting that state will be retained between requests—App Engine can distribute traffic among as many servers as it needs to give every request the same treatment, regardless of how much traffic it is handling at one time.

In the complete picture, App Engine allows runtime environments to outlive request handlers, and will reuse environments as much as possible to avoid unnecessary initialization. Each instance of your application has local memory for caching imported code and initialized data structures. App Engine creates and destroys instances as needed to accommodate your app's traffic. If you enable the multithreading feature, a single instance can handle multiple requests concurrently, further utilizing its resources.

Application code cannot access the server on which it is running in the traditional sense. An application can read its own files from the filesystem, but it cannot write to files, and it cannot read files that belong to other applications. An application can see environment variables set by App Engine, but manipulations of these variables do not necessarily persist between requests. An application cannot access the networking facilities of the server hardware, although it can perform networking operations by using services.

In short, each request lives in its own "sandbox." This allows App Engine to handle a request with the server that would, in its estimation, provide the fastest response. For web requests to the app, there is no way to guarantee that the same app instance will handle two requests, even if the requests come from the same client and arrive relatively quickly.

Sandboxing also allows App Engine to run multiple applications on the same server without the behavior of one application affecting another. In addition to limiting access to the operating system, the runtime environment also limits the amount of clock time and memory a single request can take. App Engine keeps these limits flexible, and applies stricter limits to applications that use up more resources to protect shared resources from "runaway" applications.

A request handler has up to 60 seconds to return a response to the client. While that may seem like a comfortably large amount for a web app, App Engine is optimized for applications that respond in less than a second. Also, if an application uses many CPU cycles, App Engine may slow it down so the app isn't hogging the processor on a machine serving multiple apps. A CPU-intensive request handler may take more clock time to complete than it would if it had exclusive use of the processor, and clock time may vary as App Engine detects patterns in CPU usage and allocates accordingly.

Google App Engine provides three possible runtime environments for applications: a Java environment, a Python environment, and an environment based on the Go language (a new systems language developed at Google). The environment you choose depends on the language and related technologies you want to use for developing the application.

The Java environment runs applications built for the Java 6 Virtual Machine (JVM). An app can be developed using the Java programming language, or most other languages that compile to or otherwise run in the JVM, such as PHP (using Quercus), Ruby (using JRuby), JavaScript (using the Rhino interpreter), Scala, Groovy, and Clojure. The app accesses the environment and services by using interfaces based on web industry standards, including Java servlets and the Java Persistence API (JPA). Any Java technology that functions within the sandbox restrictions can run on App Engine, making it suitable for many existing frameworks and libraries. Notably, App Engine fully supports Google Web Toolkit (GWT), a framework for rich web applications that lets you write all the app's code—including the user interface that runs in the browser—in the Java language, and have your rich graphical app work with all major browsers without plug-ins.

The Python environment runs apps written in the Python 2.7 programming language, using a custom version of CPython, the official Python interpreter. App Engine invokes a Python app using WSGI, a widely supported application interface standard. An application can use most of Python's large and excellent standard library, as well as rich APIs and libraries for accessing services and modeling data. Many open source Python web application frameworks work with App Engine, such as Django, web2py, Pyramid, and Flask. App Engine even includes a lightweight framework of its own, called webapp.

All three runtime environments use the same application server model: a request is routed to an app server, an application instance is initialized (if necessary), application code is invoked to handle the request and produce a response, and the response is returned to the client. Each environment runs application code within sandbox restrictions, such that any attempt to use a feature of the language or a library that would require access outside of the sandbox returns an error.

You can configure many aspects of how instances are created, destroyed, and initialized. How you configure your app depends on your need to balance monetary cost against performance. If you prefer performance to cost, you can configure your app to run many instances and start new ones aggressively to handle demand. If you have a limited budget, you can adjust the limits that control how requests queue up to use a minimum number of instances.

I haven't said anything about which operating system or hardware configuration App Engine uses. There are ways to figure out what operating system or hardware a server is using, but in the end it doesn't matter: the runtime environment is an abstraction *above* the operating system that allows App Engine to manage resource allocation, computation, request handling, scaling, and load distribution without the application's involvement. Features that typically require knowledge of the operating system are either provided by services outside of the runtime environment, provided or emulated using standard library calls, or restricted in sensible ways within the definition of the sandbox.

Everything stated above describes how App Engine allocates application instances dynamically to scale with your application's traffic. You can also run code on specialized instances that you allocate and deallocate manually, known as "backends" (or simply, "servers"). These specialized instances are well-suited to background jobs and custom services, and have their own parameters for how they execute code. They do not, however, scale automatically: once you reach the capacity of a server, it's up to your code to decide what happens next. Backends are a relatively new feature of App Engine, and this architecture is still evolving. We do not cover this feature in detail in this edition of this book.

The Static File Servers

Most websites have resources they deliver to browsers that do not change during the regular operation of the site. The images and CSS files that describe the appearance of the site, the JavaScript code that runs in the browser, and HTML files for pages without dynamic components are examples of these resources, collectively known as *static files*. Since the delivery of these files doesn't involve application code, it's unnecessary and inefficient to serve them from the application servers.

Instead, App Engine provides a separate set of servers dedicated to delivering static files. These servers are optimized for both internal architecture and network topology to handle requests for static resources. To the client, static files look like any other resource served by your app.

You upload the static files of your application right alongside the application code. You can configure several aspects of how static files are served, including the URLs for static files, content types, and instructions for browsers to keep copies of the files in a cache for a given amount of time to reduce traffic and speed up rendering of the page.

The Datastore

Most useful web applications need to store information during the handling of a request for retrieval during a later request. A typical arrangement for a small website involves a single database server for the entire site, and one or more web servers that connect to the database to store or retrieve data. Using a single central database server makes it easy to have one canonical representation of the data, so multiple users accessing multiple web servers all see the same and most recent information. But a central server is difficult to scale once it reaches its capacity for simultaneous connections.

By far the most popular kind of data storage system for web applications in the past two decades has been the relational database, with tables of rows and columns arranged for space efficiency and concision, and with indexes and raw computing power for performing queries, especially "join" queries that can treat multiple related records as a queryable unit. Other kinds of data storage systems include hierarchical datastores (filesystems, XML databases) and object databases. Each kind of database has pros and cons, and which type is best suited for an application depends on the nature of the application's data and how it is accessed. And each kind of database has its own techniques for growing past the first server.

Google App Engine's database system most closely resembles an object database. It is not a join-query relational database, and if you come from the world of relational-database-backed web applications (as I did), this will probably require changing the way you think about your application's data. As with the runtime environment, the design of the App Engine datastore is an abstraction that allows App Engine to handle the details of distributing and scaling the application, so your code can focus on other things.

Entities and Properties

An App Engine application stores its data as one or more datastore *entities*. An entity has one or more *properties*, each of which has a name, and a value that is of one of several primitive value types. Each entity is of a named *kind*, which categorizes the entity for the purpose of queries.

At first glance, this seems similar to a relational database: entities of a kind are like rows in a table, and properties are like columns (fields). However, there are two major differences between entities and rows. First, an entity of a given kind is not required to have the same properties as other entities of the same kind. Second, an entity can have a property of the same name as another entity has, but with a different type of value. In this way, datastore entities are "schemaless." As you'll soon see, this design provides both powerful flexibility as well as some maintenance challenges.

Another difference between an entity and a table row is that an entity can have multiple values for a single property. This feature is a bit quirky, but can be quite useful once understood.

Every datastore entity has a unique key that is either provided by the application or generated by App Engine (your choice). Unlike a relational database, the key is not a "field" or property, but an independent aspect of the entity. You can fetch an entity quickly if you know its key, and you can perform queries on key values.

An entity's key *cannot* be changed after the entity has been created. Neither can its kind. App Engine uses the entity's kind and key to help determine where the entity is stored in a large collection of servers—although neither the key nor the kind ensure that two entities are stored on the same server.

Queries and Indexes

A datastore query returns zero or more entities of a single kind. It can also return just the keys of entities that would be returned for a query. A query can filter based on conditions that must be met by the values of an entity's properties, and can return entities ordered by property values. A query can also filter and sort using keys.

In a typical relational database, queries are planned and executed in real time against the data tables, which are stored just as they were designed by the developer. The developer can also tell the database to produce and maintain indexes on certain columns to speed up certain queries.

App Engine does something dramatically different. With App Engine, *every* query has a corresponding index maintained by the datastore. When the application performs a query, the datastore finds the index for that query, scans down to the first row that matches the query, then returns the entity for each consecutive row in the index until the first row that doesn't match the query.

Of course, this requires that App Engine know ahead of time which queries the application is going to perform. It doesn't need to know the values of the filters in advance, but it does need to know the kind of entity to query, the properties being filtered or sorted, and the operators of the filters and the orders of the sorts.

App Engine provides a set of indexes for simple queries by default, based on which properties exist on entities of a kind. For more complex queries, an app must include index specifications in its configuration. The App Engine SDK helps produce this configuration file by watching which queries are performed as you test your application with the provided development web server on your computer. When you upload your app, the datastore knows to make indexes for every query the app performed during testing. You can also edit the index configuration manually.

When your application creates new entities and updates existing ones, the datastore updates every corresponding index. This makes queries very fast (each query is a simple table scan) at the expense of entity updates (possibly many tables may need updating for a single change). In fact, the performance of an index-backed query is not affected by the number of entities in the datastore, only the size of the result set.

It's worth paying attention to indexes, as they take up space and increase the time it takes to update entities. We discuss indexes in detail in Chapter 6.

Transactions

When an application has many clients attempting to read or write the same data simultaneously, it is imperative that the data always be in a consistent state. One user should never see half-written data or data that doesn't make sense because another user's action hasn't completed.

When an application updates the properties of a single entity, App Engine ensures that either every update to the entity succeeds all at once, or the entire update fails and the entity remains the way it was prior to the beginning of the update. Other users do not see any effects of the change until the change succeeds.

In other words, an update of a single entity occurs in a *transaction*. Each transaction is *atomic*: the transaction either succeeds completely or fails completely, and cannot succeed or fail in smaller pieces.

An application can read or update multiple entities in a single transaction, but it must tell App Engine which entities will be updated together when it creates the entities. The application does this by creating entities in *entity groups*. App Engine uses entity groups to control how entities are distributed across servers, so it can guarantee a transaction on a group succeeds or fails completely. In database terms, the App Engine datastore natively supports *local transactions*.

When an application calls the datastore API to update an entity, the call returns only after the transaction succeeds or fails, and it returns with knowledge of success or failure. For updates, this means the service waits for all entities to be updated before returning a result. The application can call the datastore asynchronously, such that the app code can continue executing while the datastore is preparing a result. But the update itself does not return until it has confirmed the change.

If a user tries to update an entity while another user's update of the entity is in progress, the datastore returns immediately with a contention failure exception. Imagine the two users "contending" for a single piece of data; the first user to commit an update wins. The other user must try her operation again, possibly rereading values and calculating the update from fresh data. Contention is expected, so retries are common. In database terms, App Engine uses *optimistic concurrency control*: each user is "optimistic" that her commit will succeed, so she does so without placing a lock on the data.

Reading the entity never fails due to contention. The application just sees the entity in its most recent stable state. You can also read multiple entities from the same entity group by using a transaction to ensure that all the data in the group is current and consistent with itself.

In most cases, retrying a transaction on a contested entity will succeed. But if an application is designed such that many users might update a single entity, the more popular the application gets, the more likely users will get contention failures. It is important to design entity groups to avoid a high rate of contention failures even with a large number of users.

It is often important to read and write data in the same transaction. For example, the application can start a transaction, read an entity, update a property value based on the last read value, save the entity, and then commit the transaction. In this case, the save action does not occur unless the entire transaction succeeds without conflict with another transaction. If there is a conflict and the app wants to try again, the app should retry the entire transaction: read the (possibly updated) entity again, use the new value for the calculation, and attempt the update again. By including the read operation in the transaction, the datastore can assume that related writes and reads from multiple simultaneous requests do not interleave and produce inconsistent results.

With indexes and optimistic concurrency control, the App Engine datastore is designed for applications that need to read data quickly, ensure that the data it sees is in a consistent form, and scale the number of users and the size of the data automatically. While these goals are somewhat different from those of a relational database, they are especially well suited to web applications.

The Services

The datastore's relationship with the runtime environment is that of a service: the application uses an API to access a separate system that manages all its own scaling needs separately from application instances. Google App Engine includes several other self-scaling services useful for web applications.

The memory cache (or *memcache*) service is a short-term key-value storage service. Its main advantage over the datastore is that it is fast, much faster than the datastore for simple storage and retrieval. The memcache stores values in memory instead of on disk for faster access. It is distributed like the datastore, so every request sees the same set of keys and values. However, it is not persistent like the datastore: if a server goes down, such as during a power failure, memory is erased. It also has a more limited sense of atomicity and transactionality than the datastore. As the name implies, the memcache service is best used as a cache for the results of frequently performed queries or calculations. The application checks for a cached value, and if the value isn't there, it performs the query or calculation and stores the value in the cache for future use.

App Engine provides a storage system for large values called the Blobstore. Your app can use the Blobstore to store, manage, and serve large files, such as images, videos, or file downloads. The Blobstore can also accept large files uploaded by users and offline processes. This service is distinct from the datastore to work around infrastructure limits on request and response sizes between users, application servers, and services.

Application code can read values from the Blobstore in chunks that fit within these limits. Code can also query for metadata about Blobstore values.

App Engine applications can access other web resources using the URL Fetch service. The service makes HTTP requests to other servers on the Internet, such as to retrieve pages or interact with web services. Since remote servers can be slow to respond, the URL Fetch API supports fetching URLs in the background while a request handler does other things, but in all cases the fetch must start and finish within the request handler's lifetime. The application can also set a deadline, after which the call is canceled if the remote host hasn't responded.

App Engine applications can send messages using the Mail service. Messages can be sent on behalf of the application or on behalf of the user who made the request that is sending the email (if the message is from the user). Many web applications use email to notify users, confirm user actions, and validate contact information.

An application can also receive email messages. If an app is configured to receive email, a message sent to the app's address is routed to the Mail service, which delivers the message to the app in the form of an HTTP request to a request handler.

App Engine applications can send and receive instant messages to and from chat services that support the XMPP protocol, including Google Talk. An app sends an XMPP chat message by calling the XMPP service. As with incoming email, when someone sends a message to the app's address, the XMPP service delivers it to the app by calling a request handler.

You can accomplish real-time two-way communication directly with a web browser using the Channel service, a clever implementation of the Comet model of browser app communication. Channels allow browsers to keep a network connection open with a remote host to receive real-time messages long after a web page has finished loading. App Engine fits this into its request-based processing model by using a service: browsers do not connect directly to application servers, but instead connect to "channels" via a service. When an application decides to send a message to a client (or set of clients) during its normal processing, it calls the Channel service with the message. The service handles broadcasting the message to clients, and manages open connections. Paired with web requests for messages from clients to apps, the Channel service provides real-time browser messaging without expensive polling. App Engine includes a JavaScript client so your code in the browser can connect to channels.

The image processing service can do lightweight transformations of image data, such as to make thumbnail images of uploaded photos. The image processing tasks are performed using the same infrastructure Google uses to process images with some of its other products, so the results come back quickly. This service includes special support for interacting with large data objects stored in the Blobstore, so it can operate on large image files uploaded by users.

Neither the Channel service nor the Images service are discussed in this book. See the official App Engine website for more information about these services.

As of the printing of this edition, App Engine has several compelling new services under development, some available for public beta testing. The Search service in particular may prove to be a major part of document-oriented websites and apps in the near future. Because these services are still being developed and may change, they too have been omitted from this edition. Again, see the official site for the latest.

Namespaces

The datastore, Blobstore, and memcache together store data for an app. It's often useful to partition an app's data on a global scale. For example, an app may be serving multiple companies, where each company is to see its own isolated instance of the application, and no company should see any data that belongs to any other company. You could implement this partitioning in the application code, using a company ID as the prefix to every key. But this is prone to error: a bug in the code may expose or modify data from another partition.

To better serve this case, App Engine provides this partitioning feature at the infrastructure level. An app can declare it is acting in a *namespace* by calling an API. All subsequent uses of any of the data services will restrict itself to the namespace automatically. The app does not need to keep track of which namespace it is in after the initial declaration.

The default namespace has a name equal to the empty string. This namespace is distinct from other namespaces. (There is no "global" namespace.) All data belongs to a namespace.

See the official documentation for more information on the namespace feature.

Google Accounts, OpenID, and OAuth

App Engine features integration with Google Accounts, the user account system used by Google applications such as Google Mail, Google Docs, and Google Calendar. You can use Google Accounts as your app's account system, so you don't have to build your own. And if your users already have Google accounts, they can sign in to your app using their existing accounts, with no need to create new accounts just for your app.

Google Accounts is especially useful for developing applications for your company or organization using Google Apps. With Google Apps, your organization's members can use the same account to access your custom applications as well as their email, calendar, and documents.

Of course, there is no obligation to use Google Accounts. You can always build your own account system, or use an OpenID provider. App Engine includes special support for using OpenID providers in some of the same ways you can use Google Accounts. This is useful when building applications for the Google Apps Marketplace, which uses OpenID to integrate with enterprise single sign-on services.

App Engine includes built-in support for OAuth, a protocol that makes it possible for users to grant permission to third-party applications to access personal data in another service, without having to share her account credentials with the third party. For instance, a user might grant a mobile phone application access to her Google Calendar account, to read appointment data and create new appointments on her behalf. App Engine's OAuth support makes it straightforward to implement an OAuth service for other apps to use. Note that the built-in OAuth feature only works when using Google Accounts, not OpenID or a proprietary identity mechanism.

There is no custom support for implementing an OAuth client in an App Engine app, but there are OAuth client libraries for Python and Java that work fine with App Engine.

Task Queues and Cron Jobs

A web application has to respond to web requests very quickly, usually in less than a second and preferably in just a few dozen milliseconds, to provide a smooth experience to the user sitting in front of the browser. This doesn't give the application much time to do work. Sometimes, there is more work to do than there is time to do it. In such cases it's usually OK if the work gets done within a few seconds, minutes, or hours, instead of right away, as the user is waiting for a response from the server. But the user needs a guarantee that the work will get done.

For this kind of work, an App Engine app uses task queues. Task queues let you describe work to be done at a later time, outside the scope of the web request. Queues ensure that every task gets done eventually. If a task fails, the queue retries the task until it succeeds.

There are two kinds of task queues: push queues, and pull queues. With push queues, each task record represents an HTTP request to a request handler. App Engine issues these requests itself as it processes a push queue. You can configure the rate at which push queues are processed to spread the workload throughout the day. With pull queues, you provide the mechanism, such as a custom computational engine, that takes task records off the queue and does the work. App Engine manages the queuing aspect of pull queues.

A push queue performs a task by calling a request handler. It can include a data payload provided by the code that created the task, delivered to the task's handler as an HTTP request. The task's handler is subject to the same limits as other request handlers, with one important exception: a single task handler can take as long as 10 minutes to perform a task, instead of the 60 second limit applied to user requests. It's still useful to divide work into small tasks to take advantage of parallelization and queue throughput, but the higher time limit makes tasks easier to write in straightforward cases.

An especially powerful feature of task queues is the ability to enqueue a task within a datastore transaction. This ensures that the task will be enqueued only if the rest of the datastore transaction succeeds. You can use transactional tasks to perform additional datastore operations that must be consistent with the transaction eventually, but that do not need the strong consistency guarantees of the datastore's local transactions.

App Engine has another service for executing tasks at specific times of the day, called the scheduled tasks service. Scheduled tasks are also known as "cron jobs," a name borrowed from a similar feature of the Unix operating system. The scheduled tasks service can invoke a request handler at a specified time of the day, week, or month, based on a schedule you provide when you upload your application. Scheduled tasks are useful for doing regular maintenance or sending periodic notification messages.

We'll look at task queues and scheduling and some powerful uses for them in Chapter 16.

Developer Tools

Google provides free tools for developing App Engine applications in Java or Python. You can download the software development kit (SDK) for your chosen language and your computer's operating system from Google's website. Java users can get the Java SDK in the form of a plug-in for the Eclipse integrated development environment. Python developers using Windows or Mac OS X can get the Python SDK in the form of a GUI application. Both SDKs are also available as ZIP archives of command-line tools, for using directly or integrating into your development environment or build system.

Each SDK includes a development web server that runs your application on your local computer and simulates the runtime environment, the datastore, the services, and task queues. The development server automatically detects changes in your source files and reloads them as needed, so you can keep the server running while you develop the application.

If you're using Eclipse, you can run the Java development server in the interactive debugger, and can set breakpoints in your application code. You can also use Eclipse for Python app development by using PyDev, an Eclipse extension that includes an interactive Python debugger. (Using PyDev is not covered in this book, but there are instructions on Google's site. Also check out my webcast of June 14, 2012, entitled "Python for Google App Engine," linked from the book's website.)

The development version of the datastore can automatically generate configuration for query indexes as the application performs queries, which App Engine will use to prebuild indexes for those queries. You can turn this feature off for testing whether queries have appropriate indexes in the configuration.

The development web server includes a built-in web application for inspecting the contents of the (simulated) datastore. You can also create new datastore entities using this interface for testing purposes.

Each SDK also includes a tool for interacting with the application running on App Engine. Primarily, you use this tool to upload your application code to App Engine. You can also use this tool to download log data from your live application, or manage the live application's datastore indexes and service configuration.

The Python and Java SDKs include a feature you can install in your app for secure remote programmatic access to your live application. The Python SDK includes tools that use this feature for bulk data operations, such as uploading new data from a text file and downloading large amounts of data for backup or migration purposes. The SDK also includes a Python interactive command-line shell for testing, debugging, and manually manipulating live data. These tools are in the Python SDK, but also work with Java apps by using the Java version of the remote access feature. You can write your own scripts and programs that use the remote access feature for large-scale data transformations or other maintenance.

But wait, there's more! The SDKs also include libraries for automated testing, and gathering reports on application performance. We'll cover one such tool, AppStats, in Chapter 17. (For Python unit testing, see again the aforementioned "Python for Google App Engine" webcast.)

The Administration Console

When your application is ready for its public debut, you create an administrator account and set up the application on App Engine. You use your administrator account to create and manage the application, view its resource usage statistics and message logs, and more, all with a web-based interface called the Administration Console.

You sign in to the Administration Console by using your Google account. You can use your current Google account if you have one. You may also want to create a Google account just for your application, which you might use as the "from" address on email messages. Once you have created an application by using the Administration Console, you can add additional Google accounts as administrators. Any administrator can access the Console and upload new versions of the application.

The Console gives you access to real-time performance data about how your application is being used, as well as access to log data emitted by your application. You can also query the datastore for the live application by using a web interface, and check on the status of datastore indexes. (Newly created indexes with large data sets take time to build.)

When you upload new code for your application, the uploaded version is assigned a version identifier, which you specify in the application's configuration file. The version used for the live application is whichever major version is selected as the "default." You control which version is the "default" by using the Administration Console. You can access nondefault versions by using a special URL containing the version identifier. This allows you to test a new version of an app running on App Engine before making it official.

You use the Console to set up and manage the billing account for your application. When you're ready for your application to consume more resources beyond the free amounts, you set up a billing account using a credit card and Google Accounts. The owner of the billing account sets a budget, a maximum amount of money that can be charged per calendar day. Your application can consume resources until your budget is exhausted, and you are only charged for what the application actually uses beyond the free amounts.

Things App Engine Doesn't Do...Yet

When people first start using App Engine, there are several things they ask about that App Engine doesn't do. Some of these are things Google may implement in the near future, and others run against the grain of the App Engine design and aren't likely to be added. Listing such features in a book is difficult, because by the time you read this, Google may have already implemented them. (Indeed, this list has gotten substantially shorter since the first edition of this book.) But it's worth noting these features here, especially to note workaround techniques.

An app can receive incoming email and XMPP chat messages at several addresses. As of this writing, none of these addresses can use a custom domain name. See Chapter 14 and Chapter 15 for more information on incoming email and XMPP addresses.

An app can accept web requests on a custom domain using Google Apps. Google Apps associates a subdomain of your custom domain to an app, and this subdomain can be `www` if you choose (*http://www.example.com/*). Requests for this domain, and all subdomains (*http://foo.www.example.com*), are routed to your application. Google Apps does not yet support requests for "naked" domains, such as *http://example.com/*.

App Engine does not support streaming or long-term connections directly to application servers. Apps can use the Channel service to push messages to browsers in real-time. XMPP is also an option for messaging in some cases, using an XMPP service (such as Google Talk). These mechanisms are preferred to a polling technique, where the client asks the application for updates on a regular basis. Polling is difficult to scale (5,000 simultaneous users polling every 5 seconds = 1,000 queries per second), and is not appropriate for all applications. Also note that request handlers cannot communicate with the client while performing other calculations. The server sends a response to the client's request only after the handler has returned control to the server.

App Engine only supports web requests via HTTP or HTTPS, and email and XMPP messages via the services. It does not support other kinds of network connections. For instance, a client cannot connect to an App Engine application via FTP.

The App Engine datastore does not support full-text search queries, such as for implementing a search engine for a content management system. The Search service, which as of this writing is in beta testing, will provide powerful document-based search functionality with good datastore integration. But full-text search is not an inherent ability of the datastore's query engine.

Getting Started

You can start developing applications for Google App Engine without creating an account. All you need to get started is the App Engine SDK appropriate for your choice of language, which is a free download from the App Engine website:

http://developers.google.com/appengine/

While you're there, check out the official "Getting Started Guide" for your language, which demonstrates how to create an application and use several of App Engine's features.

In the next chapter, we'll describe how to create a new project from start to finish, including how to create an account, upload the application, and run it on App Engine.

CHAPTER 2

Creating an Application

The App Engine development model is as simple as it gets:

1. Create the application.
2. Test the application on your own computer by using the web server software included with the App Engine development kit.
3. Upload the finished application to App Engine.

In this chapter, we walk through the process of creating a new application, testing it with the development server, registering a new application ID and setting up a domain name, and uploading the app to App Engine. We look at some of the features of the Python and Java software development kits (SDKs) and the App Engine Administration Console. We also discuss the workflow for developing and deploying an app.

We will take this opportunity to demonstrate a common pattern in web applications: managing user preferences data. This pattern uses several App Engine services and features.

Setting Up the SDK

All the tools and libraries you need to develop an application are included in the App Engine SDK. There are separate SDKs for Python and Java, each with features useful for developing with each language. The SDKs work on any platform, including Windows, Mac OS X, and Linux.

The Python and Java SDKs each include a web server that runs your app in a simulated runtime environment on your computer. The development server enforces the sandbox restrictions of the full runtime environment and simulates each of the App Engine services. You can start the development server and leave it running while you build your app, reloading pages in your browser to see your changes in effect.

Both SDKs include a multifunction tool for interacting with the app running on App Engine. You use this tool to upload your app's code, static files, and configuration. The tool can also manage datastore indexes, task queues, scheduled tasks, and service configuration, and can download messages logged by the live application so you can analyze your app's traffic and behavior.

The Python SDK has a few tools not available in the Java SDK, mostly because the tools are written in Python (and so require that Python be installed). Notably, the Python SDK includes tools for uploading and downloading data to and from the datastore. This is useful for making backups, changing the structure of existing data, and for processing data offline. This tool and others work fine with Java applications, and if you're using Java, you should consider installing Python and the App Engine Python SDK.

The Python SDKs for Windows and Mac OS X include a "launcher" application that makes it especially easy to create, edit, test, and upload an app, using a simple graphical interface. Paired with a good programming text editor (such as Notepad++ for Windows, or Sublime Text for Mac OS X), the launcher provides a fast and intuitive Python development experience.

For Java developers, Google provides a plug-in for the Eclipse integrated development environment that implements a complete App Engine development workflow. The plug-in includes a template for creating new App Engine Java apps, as well as a debugging profile for running the app and the development web server in the Eclipse debugger. To deploy a project to App Engine, you just click a button on the Eclipse toolbar.

Both SDKs also have cross-platform command-line tools that provide these features. You can use these tools from a command prompt, or otherwise integrate them into your development environment as you see fit. The Java SDK also includes an Apache Ant plug-in that makes it easy to integrate these tasks into an Ant-based workflow.

We discuss the Python SDK first, then the Java SDK in "Installing the Java SDK" on page 22. Feel free to skip the section that does not apply to your chosen language.

Installing the Python SDK

App Engine includes two Python runtime environments: a legacy environment based on Python 2.5, and a newer environment running Python 2.7. The newer environment has more than just a slightly newer version of the Python interpreter. In particular, the newer environment can serve multiple requests simultaneously from a single application instance, a performance-related feature that'll prove useful when you start to get large amounts of traffic. If you're creating a new app, there is no reason not to use Python 2.7, and if you have an existing app using the 2.5 runtime environment, you should consider upgrading. We assume the 2.7 environment for this tutorial and the rest of this book.

The App Engine SDK for the Python runtime environment runs on any computer that runs Python 2.7. If you are using Mac OS X or Linux, or if you have used Python previously, you may already have Python on your system. You can test whether Python is installed on your system and check which version is installed by running the following command at a command prompt (in Windows, Command Prompt; in Mac OS X, Terminal):

```
python -V
```

(That's a capital "V.") If Python is installed, it prints its version number, like so:

```
Python 2.7.1
```

You can download and install Python 2.7 for your platform from the Python website:

http://www.python.org/

Be sure to get Python version 2.7 (such as 2.7.2) from the "Download" section of the site. As of this writing, the latest major version of Python is 3.2, and the latest 2.x-compatible release is 2.7.

App Engine Python does not yet support Python 3. Python 3 includes several new language and library features that are not backward compatible with earlier versions. When App Engine adds support for Python 3, it will likely be in the form of a new runtime environment, in addition to the Python 2.5 and 2.7 environments. You control which runtime environment your application uses with a setting in the app's configuration file, so your application will continue to run as intended when new runtime environments are released.

You can download the App Engine Python SDK bundle for your operating system from the Google App Engine website:

http://developers.google.com/appengine/downloads

Download and install the file appropriate for your operating system:

- For Windows, the Python SDK is an *.msi* (Microsoft Installer) file. Click on the appropriate link to download it, then double-click on the file to start the installation process. This installs the Google App Engine Launcher application, adds an icon to your Start menu, and adds the command-line tools to the command path.
- For Mac OS X, the Python SDK is a Mac application in a *.dmg* (disk image) file. Click on the link to download it, then double-click on the file to mount the disk image. Drag the GoogleAppEngineLauncher icon to your Applications folder. To install the command-line tools, double-click the icon to start the Launcher, then allow the Launcher to create the "symlinks" when prompted.
- If you are using Linux or another platform, the Python SDK is available as a *.zip* archive. Download and unpack it (typically with the `unzip` command) to create a directory named *google_appengine*. The command-line tools all reside in this directory. Adjust your command path as needed.

To test that the App Engine Python SDK is installed, run the following command at a command prompt:

```
dev_appserver.py --help
```

The command prints a helpful message and exits. If instead you see a message about the command not being found, check that the installer completed successfully, and that the location of the `dev_appserver.py` command is on your command path.

Windows users, if when you run this command, a dialog box opens with the message "Windows cannot open this file... To open this file, Windows needs to know what program created it," you must tell Windows to use Python to open the file. In the dialog box, choose "Select the program from a list," and click OK. Click Browse, then locate your Python installation (such as *C:\Python27*). Select *python* from this folder, then click Open. Select "Always use the selected program to open this kind of file." Click OK. A window will open and attempt to run the command, then immediately close. You can now run the command from the Command Prompt.

Before proceeding, you will want to make sure that the Launcher is using your Python 2.7 installation, and not another version of Python that may be on your system. In particular, the Mac version of the Launcher will use `/usr/bin/python2.6` by default, even if `/usr/bin/python` is Python 2.7.

To change the version of Python used by the Launcher, select Preferences from the appropriate menu, then specify a "Python Path" value of `/usr/bin/python`. Close the window to store this preference. If you already have a development server running, stop it, then start it again for the change to take effect.

You can confirm that the Launcher is using the correct version of Python by starting the server, then clicking the Logs button. Scroll up to the top, and look for the line that says: `Python command: /usr/bin/python`. If the path setting did not take effect, close the Launcher application, then start it and try again.

A brief tour of the Launcher

The Windows and Mac OS X versions of the Python SDK include an application called the Google App Engine Launcher (hereafter, just "Launcher"). With the Launcher, you can create and manage multiple App Engine Python projects using a graphical interface. Figure 2-1 shows an example of the Launcher window in Mac OS X.

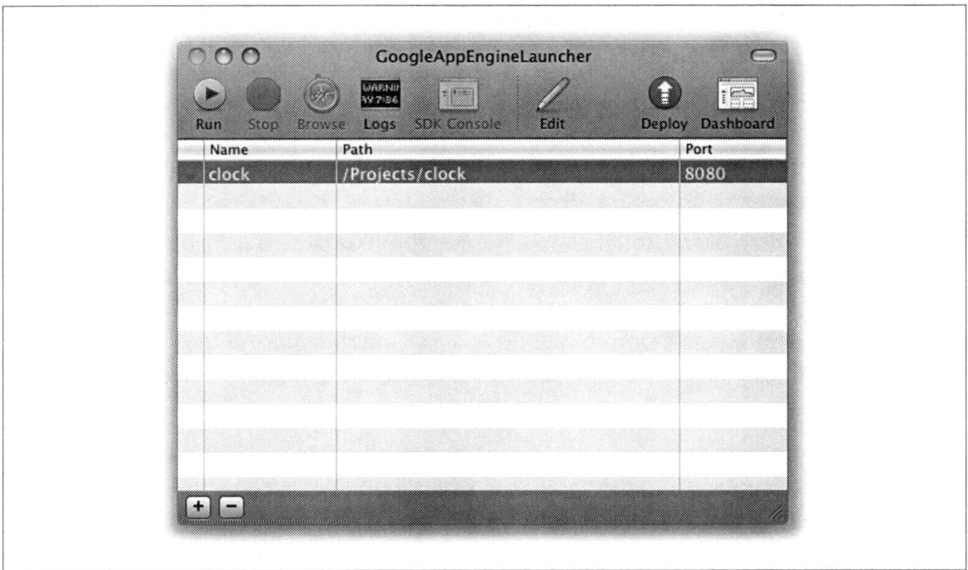

Figure 2-1. The Google App Engine Launcher for Mac OS X main window, with a project selected

To create a new project, select New Application from the File menu (or click the plus-sign button at the bottom of the window). Browse to where you want to keep your application files, then enter a name for the application. The Launcher creates a new directory at that location, named after the application, to hold the app's files, and creates several starter files. The app appears in the application list in the main launcher window.

To start the development web server, make sure the application is selected, then click the Run button. You can stop the server with the Stop button. To open the home page of the running app in a browser, click the Browse button. The Logs button displays messages logged by the app in the development server.

The SDK Console button opens a web interface for the development server with several features for inspecting the running application, including tools to inspect the contents of the (simulated) datastore and memory cache, and an interactive console that executes Python statements and displays the results.

The Edit button opens the app's files in your default text editor. In the Mac OS X version, this is especially useful with text editors that can open a directory's worth of files, such as TextMate or Emacs. In the Windows version, this just opens *app.yaml* for editing.

The Deploy button uploads the application to App Engine. Before you can deploy an application, you must register an application ID with App Engine and edit the application's configuration file with the registered ID. The Dashboard button opens a browser window with the App Engine Administration Console for the deployed app.

We'll look at the configuration file, the registration process, and the Administration Console later in this chapter.

The complete App Engine Python SDK, including the command-line tools, resides in the Launcher's application directory. In the Windows version, the installer adds the appropriate directory to the command path, so you can run these tools from a Command Prompt.

In Mac OS X, when you start the Launcher for the first time it asks for permission to create "symlinks." This creates symbolic links in the directory */usr/local/bin/* that refer to the command-line tools in the application bundle. With the links in this directory, you can type just the name of a command at a Terminal prompt to run it. If you didn't create the symlinks, you can do so later by selecting the Make Symlinks item from the GoogleAppEngineLauncher menu.

You can set command-line flags for the development server within the Launcher. To do so, select the application, then go to the Edit menu and select Application Settings. Add the desired command-line options to the Extra Flags field, then click Update.

The Mac OS X version of the Launcher installs Google's software update facility to check for new versions of the App Engine SDK. When a new version is released, this feature notifies you and offers to upgrade.

Immediately after you upgrade, you'll notice the symlinks stop working. To fix the symlinks, reopen the Launcher app and follow the prompts. The upgrade can't do this automatically because it needs your permission to create new symlinks.

Installing the Java SDK

The App Engine SDK for the Java runtime environment runs on any computer that runs the Java SE Development Kit (JDK). The App Engine for Java SDK supports JDK 6, and when running on App Engine, the Java runtime environment uses the Java 6 JVM and JRE. (JDK 5 support is limited and deprecated.)

If you don't already have it, you can download and install the Java 6 JDK for most platforms from Oracle's website (Mac users, see the next section):

http://www.oracle.com/technetwork/java/javase/downloads/index.html

You can test whether the Java development kit is installed on your system and check which version it is by running the following command at a command prompt (in Windows, Command Prompt; in Mac OS X, Terminal):

```
javac -version
```

If you have the Java 6 JDK installed, the command will print a version number similar to `javac 1.6.0`. The actual output varies depending on which specific version you have.

App Engine Java apps use interfaces and features from Java Enterprise Edition (Java EE). The App Engine SDK includes implementations for the relevant Java EE features. You do not need to install a separate Java EE implementation.

The steps for installing the App Engine SDK for Java depend on whether you wish to use the Google Plugin for the Eclipse IDE. We'll cover these situations separately.

Java on Mac OS X

Mac OS X versions 10.8 (Mountain Lion) and 10.7 (Lion) do not include the Java 6 runtime environment by default. If you are running Mac OS X 10.8, you may be prompted to download and install Java 6 when you first run Eclipse. If you are running Mac OS X 10.7, and you did not upgrade from a previous major version of the operating system, you may have to download and install Java for OS X Lion from Apple's website:

> *http://support.apple.com/kb/DL1421*

If you are running Mac OS X 10.6 (Snow Leopard), or have upgraded to 10.7 from 10.6, you should already have Java 6 installed. You may want to run Apple's Software Update (from the Apple menu) to ensure you have the latest minor version.

If you are using Mac OS X 10.5 (Leopard) and a 64-bit processor, Java 6 is installed, but you must explicitly change the default version of Java to be Java 6 by using the Java Preferences Utility. You can find this under */Applications/Utilities/*. In the Java Applications list, drag the desired version (such as "Java SE 6, 64-bit") to the top of the list. OS X uses the topmost version in the list that is compatible with your system. Leopard's version of Java 6 only works with 64-bit processors.

If you have a 32-bit Mac running Leopard, you're stuck using Java 5. Java 5 support in the App Engine SDK is deprecated. Consider upgrading to Mac OS X 10.6 Snow Leopard, which includes a 32-bit version of Java 6. (Mac OS X 10.7 does not work with 32-bit processors.)

If you are using Eclipse, make sure you get the version that corresponds with your processor. Separate versions of the "Eclipse IDE for Java EE Developers" bundle are available for 32-bit and 64-bit processors.

For more information about Java and Mac OS X, see Apple's developer website:

> *http://developer.apple.com/java/*

Installing the Java SDK with the Google Plugin for Eclipse

One of the easiest ways to develop App Engine applications in Java is to use the Eclipse IDE and the Google Plugin for Eclipse. The plug-in works with all versions of Eclipse from Eclipse 3.3 (Europa) to the Eclipse 4.2 (Juno). You can get Eclipse for your platform for free at the Eclipse website:

> *http://www.eclipse.org/*

If you're getting Eclipse specifically for App Engine development, get the "Eclipse IDE for Java EE Developers" bundle. This bundle includes several useful components for developing web applications, including the Eclipse Web Tools Platform (WTP) package.

You can tell Eclipse to use the JDK you have installed in the Preferences window. In Eclipse 4.2, select Preferences (Windows and Linux, in the Window menu; Mac OS X, in the Eclipse menu). In the Java category, select "Installed JREs." If necessary, add the location of the SDK to the list, and make sure the checkbox is checked.

To install the App Engine Java SDK and the Google Plugin, use the software installation feature of Eclipse. In Eclipse 4.2, select Install New Software from the Help menu, then type the following URL in the "Work with" field and click the Add button:

```
http://dl.google.com/eclipse/plugin/4.2
```

(This URL does not work in a browser; it only works with the Eclipse software installer.)

In the dialog box that opens, enter "Google" for the name, then click OK. Several items are added to the list. For a minimal App Engine development environment, select Google Plugin for Eclipse, then expand the SDKs category and select Google App Engine Java SDK. Figure 2-2 shows the Install Software window with these items selected.

There's other good stuff in here, all free of charge. Google Web Toolkit (GWT) is a development suite for making rich web user interfaces using Java, without having to write a single line of JavaScript. The Eclipse plug-in makes it easy to create GWT apps that run on App Engine. There's also a set of tools for making apps for Android devices that use App Engine as a networked backend. If that's of interest, you'll also want to get the Android Development Toolkit from developer.android.com (*http://developer.android.com*).

Check the boxes for the desired items, then click the Next button and follow the prompts.

For more information on installing the Google Plugin for Eclipse, including instructions for Eclipse 3.3 through 3.7, see the website for the plug-in:

http://developers.google.com/eclipse/

After installation, the Eclipse toolbar has a new drop-down menu button. The notifications bar at the bottom may also include a prompt to sign in with your Google account. These additions are shown in Figure 2-3.

The plug-in adds several features to the Eclipse interface:

- The drop-down menu button, with shortcuts for creating a new web application project, deploying to App Engine, and other features
- A Web Application Project item under New in the File menu
- A Web Application debug profile, for running an app in the development web server under the Eclipse debugger

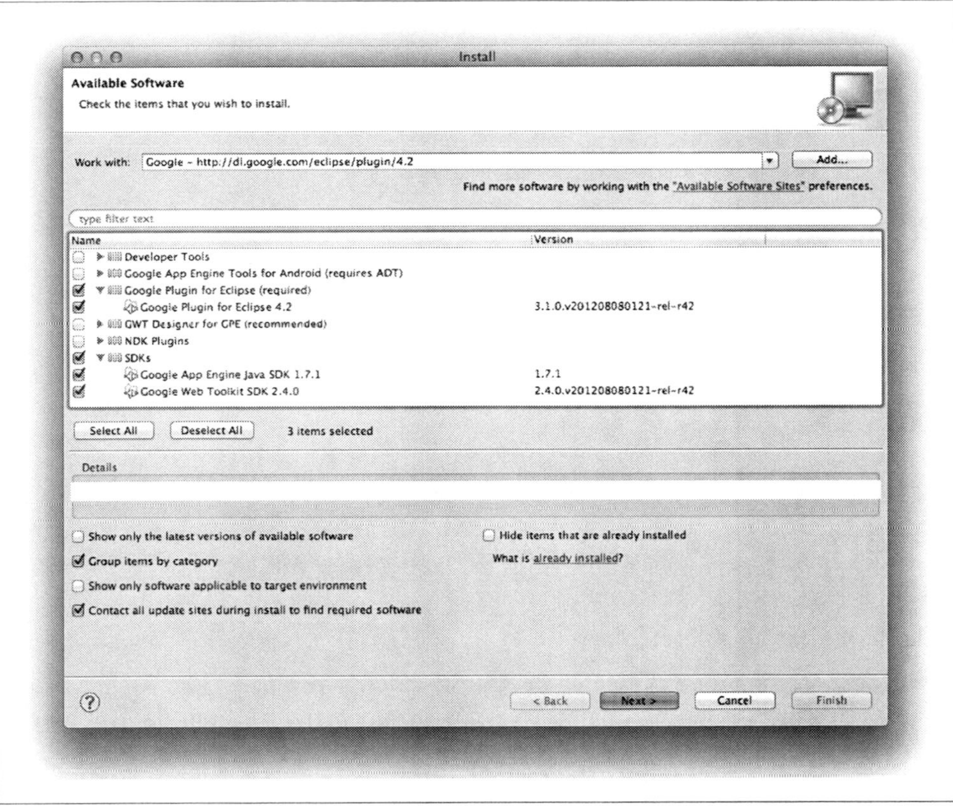

Figure 2-2. The Eclipse 4.2 (Juno) Install Software window, with the Google Plugin selected

You can use Eclipse to develop your application, and to deploy it to App Engine. To use other features of the SDK, like downloading log data, you must use the command-line tools from the App Engine SDK. Eclipse installs the SDK in your Eclipse application directory, under *eclipse/plugins/*. The actual directory name depends on the specific version of the SDK installed, but it looks something like this:

```
com.google.appengine.eclipse.sdkbundle_1.7.1/appengine-java-sdk-1.7.1/
```

This directory contains command-line tools in a subdirectory named *bin/*. In Mac OS X or Linux, you may need to change the permissions of these files to be executable in order to use the tools from the command line:

```
chmod 755 bin/*
```

You can add the *bin/* directory to your command path, but keep in mind that the path will change each time you update the SDK.

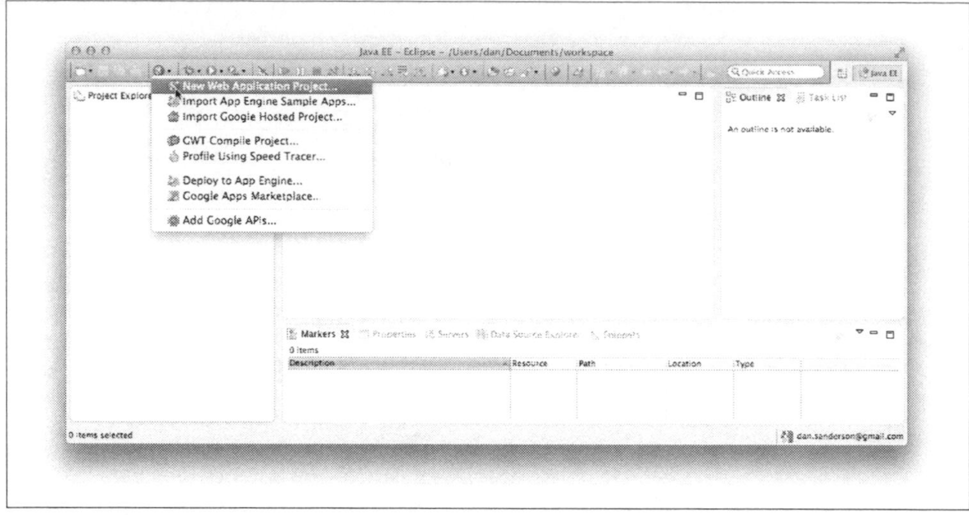

Figure 2-3. The Eclipse 4.2 window with the Google Plugin installed, with the drop-down menu button open

Installing the Java SDK without Eclipse

If you are not using the Eclipse IDE or otherwise don't wish to use the Google Plugin, you can download the App Engine Java SDK as a *.zip* archive from the App Engine website:

> *http://developers.google.com/appengine/downloads*

The archive unpacks to a directory with a name like *appengine-java-sdk-1.7.1*.

The SDK contains command-line launch scripts in the *bin/* subdirectory. You can add this directory to your command path to make the commands easier to run.

> Both the AppCfg tool and the development web server execute Java classes to perform their functions. You can integrate these tools into your IDE or build scripts by calling the launch scripts, or by calling the Java classes directly. Look at the contents of the launch scripts to see the syntax.
>
> The App Engine SDK includes a plug-in for Apache Ant that lets you perform functions of the SDK from an Ant build script. See the App Engine documentation for more information about using Ant with App Engine.

Test that the App Engine Java SDK is installed properly by running the following command at a command prompt:

```
dev_appserver --help
```

Mac OS X and Linux users, use `dev_appserver.sh` as the command name.

The command prints a helpful message and exits. If instead you see a message about the command not being found, check that the archive unpacked successfully, and that the SDK's *bin/* directory is on your command path.

Developing the Application

An App Engine application responds to web requests. It does so by calling *request handlers*, routines that accept request parameters and return responses. App Engine determines which request handler to use for a given request from the request's URL, using a configuration file included with the app that maps URLs to handlers.

An app can also include static files, such as images, CSS stylesheets, and browser JavaScript. App Engine serves these files directly to clients in response to requests for corresponding URLs without invoking any code. The app's configuration specifies which of its files are static, and which URLs to use for those files.

The application configuration includes metadata about the app, such as its application ID and version number. When you deploy the app to App Engine, all the app's files, including the code, configuration files, and static files, are uploaded and associated with the application ID and version number mentioned in the configuration. An app can also have configuration files specific to the services, such as for datastore indexes, task queues, and scheduled tasks. These files are associated with the app in general, not a specific version of the app.

The structure and format of the code and configuration files differ for Python apps and for Java apps, but the concepts are similar. In the next few sections, we create the files needed for a simple application in Python and Java, and look at how to use the tools and libraries included with each SDK.

The User Preferences Pattern

The application we create in this section is a simple clock. When a user visits the site, the app displays the current time of day according to the server's system clock. By default, the app shows the current time in the Coordinated Universal Time (UTC) time zone. The user can customize the time zone by signing in using Google Accounts and setting a preference.

This app demonstrates three App Engine features:

- The datastore, primary storage for data that is persistent, reliable, and scalable
- The memory cache (or *memcache*), secondary storage that is faster than the datastore, but is not necessarily persistent in the long term
- Google Accounts, the ability to use Google's user account system for authenticating and identifying users

Google Accounts works similarly to most user account systems. If the user is not signed in to the clock application, she sees a generic view with default settings (the UTC time zone) and a link to sign in or create a new account. If the user chooses to sign in or register, the application directs her to a sign-in form managed by Google Accounts. Signing in or creating an account redirects the user back to the application.

Of course, you can implement your own account mechanism instead of using Google Accounts. You can also use an OpenID provider (or a provider of the user's choosing) with App Engine's built-in OpenID support. Using Google Accounts or OpenID has advantages and disadvantages—the chief advantage being that you don't have to implement your own account mechanism. If a user of your app already has a Google account, the user can sign in with that account without creating a new account for your app.

If the user accesses the application while signed in, the app loads the user's preferences data and uses it to render the page. The app retrieves the preferences data in two steps. First, it attempts to get the data from the fast secondary storage, the memory cache. If the data is not present in the memory cache, the app attempts to retrieve it from the primary storage (the datastore), and if successful, it puts it into the memory cache to be found by future requests.

This means that for most requests, the application can get the user's preferences from the memcache without accessing the datastore. While reading from the datastore is reasonably fast, reading from the memcache is much faster and avoids the cost of a datastore call. The difference is substantial when the same data must be accessed every time the user visits a page.

Our clock application has two request handlers. One handler displays the current time of day, along with links for signing in and out. It also displays a web form for adjusting the time zone when the user is signed in. The second request handler processes the time zone form when it is submitted. When the user submits the preferences form, the app saves the changes and redirects the browser back to the main page.

The application gets the current time from the application server's system clock. It's worth noting that App Engine makes no guarantees that the system clocks of all its web servers are synchronized. Since two requests for this app may be handled by different servers, different requests may see different clocks. The server clock is not consistent enough as a source of time data for a real-world application, but it's good enough for this example.

In the next section, we implement this app using Python. We do the same thing with Java in the section "Developing a Java App" on page 44. As before, feel free to skip the section that doesn't apply to you.

Developing a Python App

The simplest Python application for App Engine is a single directory with two files: a configuration file named *app.yaml*, and a file of Python code for a request handler. The directory containing the *app.yaml* file is the application root directory. You'll refer to this directory often when using the tools.

If you are using the Launcher, you can start a new project by selecting the File menu, New Application. The Launcher creates a new project with several files, which you may wish to edit to follow along with the example. Alternatively, you can create the project directory and files by hand, then add the project to the Launcher by clicking the File menu, and then Add Existing Application.

Create a directory named *clock* to contain the project. Using your favorite text editor, create a file inside this directory named *app.yaml* similar to Example 2-1.

Example 2-1. The app.yaml configuration file for a simple application, using the Python 2.7 runtime environment

```
application: clock
version: 1
runtime: python27
api_version: 1
threadsafe: true

handlers:
- url: .*
  script: main.application

libraries:
- name: webapp2
  version: "2.5.1"
```

This configuration file is in a format called YAML, an open format for configuration files and network messages. You don't need to know much about the format beyond what you see here.

In this example, the configuration file tells App Engine that this is version 1 of an application called `clock`, which uses version 1 (`api_version`) of the Python 2.7 runtime environment. Every request for this application (every URL that matches the regular expression `.*`, which is all of them) is to be handled by an application object defined in the `application` variable of a Python module named `main`.

In the Python 2.5 runtime environment, URLs are mapped to the names of source files, which are executed as CGI scripts. While this is still supported with Python 2.7, concurrent requests (multithreading) require this new way of referring to the WSGI instance global variable in the *app.yaml* configuration.

Create a file named *main.py* similar to Example 2-2, in the same directory as *app.yaml*.

Example 2-2. A simple Python web application, using the webapp2 framework

```
import datetime
import webapp2

class MainPage(webapp2.RequestHandler):
    def get(self):
        message = '<p>The time is: %s</p>' % datetime.datetime.now()
        self.response.out.write(message)

application = webapp2.WSGIApplication([('/', MainPage)],
                                      debug=True)
```

This simple Python web application uses a web application framework called "webapp2," which is included with App Engine. This framework conforms to a common standard for Python web application frameworks known as the Web Server Gateway Interface (WSGI). You don't need to know much about WSGI, except that it's a Python standard, there are many useful frameworks to choose from, and it's easy to port a WSGI application to other application hosting environments using various adapters (such as a WSGI-to-CGI adapter). webapp2 is a simple example of a WSGI framework. Django, a popular open source web app framework for Python that's also included with App Engine, is another.

We'll walk through this example in a moment, but first, let's get it running. If you are using the Launcher app, start the development web server by clicking the Run button. The icon next to the project turns green when the server starts successfully.

Open a browser to view the project by clicking the Browse button. The browser displays a page similar to Figure 2-4.

You can leave the web server running while you develop your application. The web server notices when you make changes to your files, and reloads them automatically as needed.

If you are not using the Launcher, you can start the development server from a command prompt by running the `dev_appserver.py` command, specifying the path to the project directory (*clock*) as an argument:

```
dev_appserver.py clock
```

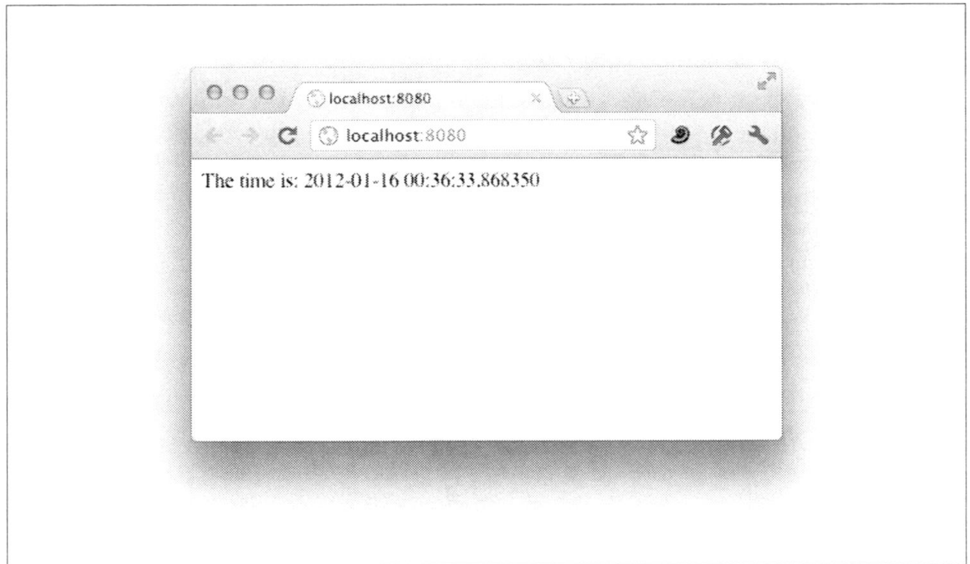

Figure 2-4. The first version of the clock application viewed in a browser

If your current working directory is the *clock* directory you just created, you can run the command using a dot (`.`) as the path to the project:

```
dev_appserver.py .
```

The server starts up and prints several messages to the console. If this is the first time you're running the server from the command line, it may ask whether you want it to check for updates; type your answer, then hit Enter. You can safely ignore warnings that say "Could not read datastore data" and "Could not initialize images API." These are expected if you have followed the installation steps so far. The last message should look something like this:

```
INFO ... Running application dev-clock on port 8080: http://localhost:8080
INFO ... Admin console is available at: http://localhost:8080/_ah/admin
```

This message indicates the server started successfully. If you do not see this message, check the other messages for hints, and double-check that the syntax of your *app.yaml* file is correct.

Test your application by visiting the server's URL in a web browser:

http://localhost:8080/

Introducing the webapp framework

App Engine's Python 2.7 runtime environment uses WSGI as the interface between your application and the server instance running the application. Typically, you would not write the code that implements this interface. Instead, you would use a *frame-*

work, a suite of libraries and tools that form an easy way to think about building web applications and perform common web tasks.

There are dozens of web frameworks written in Python, and several are mature, well documented, and have active developer communities. Django, web2py, and Pylons are examples of well-established Python web frameworks. But not every Python web application framework works completely with the App Engine Python runtime environment. Constraints imposed by App Engine's sandboxing logic limit which frameworks work out of the box. In addition to App Engine's own webapp2 framework, Django (*http://www.djangoproject.com/*) is known to work well and is included with App Engine. web2py (*http://web2py.com/*) includes special support for App Engine. Others have been adapted for App Engine with additional software. We'll discuss how to use Django with App Engine in Chapter 18.

The webapp2 framework (the successor to "webapp," the framework included with the legacy Python 2.5 environment) is intended to be small and easy to use. It doesn't have the features of more established frameworks, but it's good enough for small projects. For simplicity, most of the Python examples in this book use the webapp2 framework. We'll introduce some of its features here.

Let's take a closer look at our simple web application, line by line:

```
import datetime
import webapp2
```

This loads the libraries we intend to use in the `main` module. We use `datetime` to get the system time for our clock. The webapp2 framework is in the `webapp2` module:

```
class MainPage(webapp2.RequestHandler):
    def get(self):
        message = '<p>The time is: %s</p>' % datetime.datetime.now()
        self.response.out.write(message)
```

webapp2 applications consist of one or more *request handlers*, units of code mapped to URLs or URL patterns that are executed when a client (or other process) requests a URL. As we saw earlier, the first URL mapping takes place in *app.yaml*, which associates the request URL with its WSGI application object in a Python module. The webapp2 application maps this to a `RequestHandler` class.

To produce the response, webapp2 instantiates the class and then calls a method of the class that corresponds to the HTTP method of the request. When you type a URL into your browser's address bar, the browser uses the HTTP GET method with the request, so webapp2 calls the `get()` method of the request handler. Similarly, when you submit a web form, the browser uses the HTTP POST method, which would attempt to call a `post()` method.

The code can access the request data and produce the response data, using attributes of the instance. In this case, we prepared a response string (`message`), then used the output stream of the `response` attribute to write the message. You can also use the `response` attribute to set response headers, such as to change the content type. (Here, we leave the content type at its default of `text/html`.)

```
application = webapp2.WSGIApplication([('/', MainPage)],
                                      debug=True)
```

The `application` module global variable contains the object that represents the WSGI application. This value is created when the `main` module is imported for the first time, and stays in memory for the lifetime of the application instance. (App Engine creates and destroys application instances as needed to serve your app's traffic. More on that later.) App Engine knows which module and variable to use from the mapping in the *app.yaml* file.

The application object is an instance of the `WSGIApplication` class provided by the `webapp2` module. The constructor is called with two values. The first is a list of URL pattern and `RequestHandler` class pairs. When the application is called to handle a request, the URL is tested against each pattern in the order it appears in the list. The first to match wins. The URL pattern is a regular expression.

In this case, our application simply maps the root URL path (/) to `MainPage`. If the application is asked to handle any other URL path (any path that doesn't match), webapp2 serves an HTTP 404 error page. Notice that the *app.yaml* file maps all URL paths to this application, effectively putting webapp2 in charge of serving 404 errors. (If a URL does not match any pattern in *app.yaml*, App Engine serves its own 404 error.)

The `WSGIApplication` constructor is also given a `debug=True` parameter. This tells webapp2 to print detailed error messages to the browser when things go wrong. webapp2 knows to only use this in the development server, and disable this feature when it is running on App Engine, so you can just leave it turned on.

A single `WSGIApplication` instance can handle multiple URLs, routing the request to different `RequestHandler` classes based on the URL pattern. But we've already seen that the *app.yaml* file maps URL patterns to handler scripts. So which URL patterns should appear in *app.yaml*, and which should appear in the `WSGIApplication`? Many web frameworks include their own URL dispatcher logic, and it's common to route all dynamic URLs to the framework's dispatcher in *app.yaml*. With webapp2, the answer mostly depends on how you'd like to organize your code. For the clock application, we will create a second request handler as a separate script to take advantage of a feature of *app.yaml* for user authentication, but we could also put this logic in *main.py* and route the URL with the `WSGIApplication` object.

Users and Google Accounts

So far, our clock shows the same display for every user. To allow each user to customize the display and save her preferences for future sessions, we need a way to identify the user making a request. An easy way to do this is with Google Accounts, a.k.a. the Users service.

Before we make the user interface of our app more elaborate, let's introduce a templating system to manage our HTML. User-facing web applications have a browser-based user interface, consisting of HTML, CSS, and sometimes JavaScript. Mixing markup and code for the browser in your server-side code gets messy fast. It's nearly always better to use a library that can represent the user interface code separately from your app code, using templates. The app code calls the templating system to fill in the blanks with dynamic data and render the result.

For this example, we'll use the Jinja2 templating system. Jinja2 is an open source templating system written in Python, based on the templating system included with the Django web application framework. App Engine will provide this library to your app if you request it in the *app.yaml* file.

Edit *app.yaml*, and add these lines to the `libraries:` section near the bottom:

```
libraries:
# ...
- name: jinja2
  version: latest
- name: markupsafe
  version: latest
```

While libraries such as Jinja2 are available to your app when it is running on App Engine, you must install the library yourself on your own computer. (App Engine does not include every library in the SDK because it would have to include every supported version of every library, and that could get large.) To install Jinja2, use the *easy_install* command included with Python. For example, on Mac OS X:

```
sudo easy_install jinja2 markupsafe
```

(Enter your administrator password when prompted.)

Make sure to use the same version of Python to install the library as the version of Python you're using to run the development server! See the tip back in "Installing the Python SDK" on page 18 on setting up the Launcher.

Let's add something to our app's home page that indicates whether the user is signed in, and provides links for signing in and signing out of the application. Edit *main.py* to resemble Example 2-3.

Example 2-3. A version of main.py that invites the user to sign in with Google Accounts, using a Jinja2 template

```
import datetime
import jinja2
import os
import webapp2

from google.appengine.api import users
```

```
template_env = jinja2.Environment(
    loader=jinja2.FileSystemLoader(os.getcwd()))

class MainPage(webapp2.RequestHandler):
    def get(self):
        current_time = datetime.datetime.now()
        user = users.get_current_user()
        login_url = users.create_login_url(self.request.path)
        logout_url = users.create_logout_url(self.request.path)

        template = template_env.get_template('home.html')
        context = {
            'current_time': current_time,
            'user': user,
            'login_url': login_url,
            'logout_url': logout_url,
        }
        self.response.out.write(template.render(context))

application = webapp2.WSGIApplication([('/', MainPage)],
                                      debug=True)
```

Next, create a new file in the same directory named *home.html*, and edit it to resemble Example 2-4. This is the Jinja2 template.

Example 2-4. The HTML template for the home page, using the Jinja2 template system

```
<html>
  <head>
    <title>The Time Is...</title>
  </head>
  <body>
  {% if user %}
    <p>
      Welcome, {{ user.email() }}!
      You can <a href="{{ logout_url }}">sign out</a>.
    </p>
  {% else %}
    <p>
      Welcome!
      <a href="{{ login_url }}">Sign in or register</a> to customize.
    </p>
  {% endif %}
    <p>The time is: {{ current_time }}</p>
  </body>
</html>
```

Reload the page in your browser. The new page resembles Figure 2-5.

We've added a few new things to *main.py*:

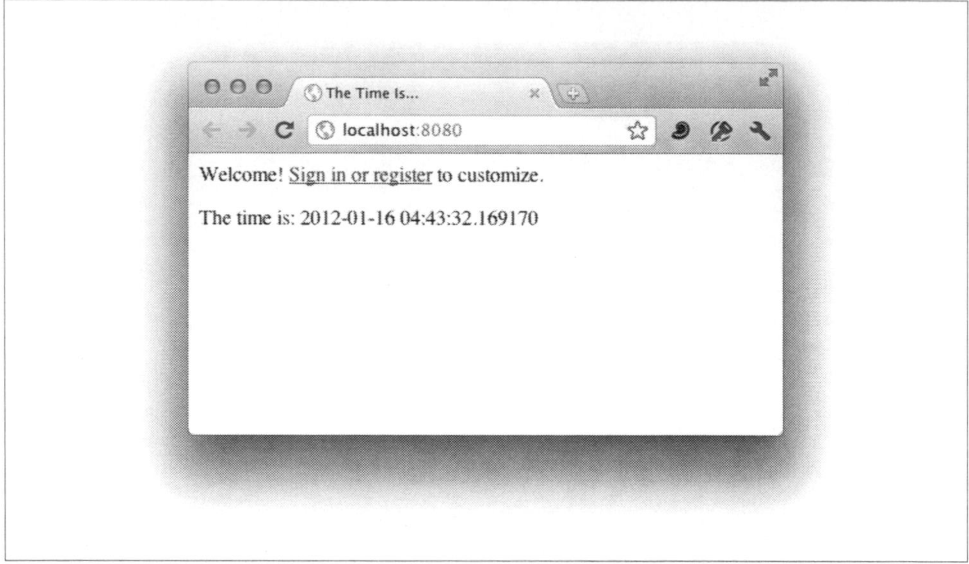

Figure 2-5. The clock app with a link to Google Accounts when the user is not signed in

```
import jinja2
import os

# ...

from google.appengine.api import users
```

You import the Jinja2 library the same way you would with a typical installation on your computer. The `libraries:` section of *app.yaml* puts Jinja2 on the library search path when running on App Engine.

We also import the `os` module to use in the next part, as well as the API for the Users service:

```
template_env = jinja2.Environment(
    loader=jinja2.FileSystemLoader(os.getcwd()))
```

One way to configure Jinja2 is with an `Environment` object. This object maintains aspects of the template system that are common across your app. In this case, we use the `Environment` to declare that our template files are loaded from the file system, using the `FileSystemLoader`.

We store the Jinja2 `Environment` object in a module global variable because we only need to create this object once in the lifetime of the application instance. As with the `WSGIApplication` object, the constructor is called when the module is imported, and the object stays resident in memory.

Remember that we've turned on concurrent requests using the `threadsafe: true` line in *app.yaml*. This tells App Engine to use one instance to process multiple requests simultaneously. These requests will share global module variables, and may interleave instructions. This is fine for most common read-only uses of global variables, such as configuration data and compiled regular expressions.

The `os.getcwd()` value passed to the `FileSystemLoader` constructor tells it to find templates in the current working directory. When the request handler is called, the current working directory is the application root directory. If you move your templates into a subdirectory (and that's probably a good idea), this value needs to be modified accordingly:

```
current_time = datetime.datetime.now()
user = users.get_current_user()
login_url = users.create_login_url(self.request.path)
logout_url = users.create_logout_url(self.request.path)
```

The request handler code calls the Users service API by using functions in the module `users`, from the package `google.appengine.api`. `users.get_current_user()` returns an object of class `users.User` that represents the user making the request if the user is signed in, or `None` (Python's null value) if the user is not signed in. You can use this value to access the user's email address, which our application does from within the template.

To allow a user to sign in or sign out, you direct the user's browser to the Google Accounts system "login" or "logout" URLs. The app gets these URLs using the `users.create_login_url()` and `users.create_logout_url()`, respectively. These functions take a URL path for your application as an argument. Once the user has signed in or signed out successfully, Google Accounts redirects the user back to your app using that URL path. For this app, we direct the user to sign in or sign out by presenting her with links to click. (In other situations, redirecting the user might be more appropriate.)

```
template = template_env.get_template('home.html')
context = {
    'current_time': current_time,
    'user': user,
    'login_url': login_url,
    'logout_url': logout_url
}
self.response.out.write(template.render(context))
```

Here, we load the *home.html* template, set the dynamic data in the template's "context," render the template with the context values into the text of the page, and finally write it to the response.

Within the template, we use a conditional section to display a different welcome message depending on whether the user is signed in or not. `{% if user %}` is true if the context value we set to `'user'` is considered true in Python, which it would be if `users.get_current_user()` returned a `User` object. The `{% else %}` and `{% endif %}` directives delimit the sections of the template to render, based on the condition. `{{ user.email() }}` calls the `email()` method of the object, and interpolates its return value into the template as a string. Similarly, `{{ logout_url }}`, `{{ login_url }}`, and `{{ current_time }}` interpolate the generated URLs we set in the context.

For more information about Jinja2 template syntax and features, see the Jinja2 website:

http://jinja.pocoo.org/

If you click on the "Sign in or register" link with the app running in the development server, the link goes to the development server's simulated version of the Google Accounts sign-in screen, as shown in Figure 2-6. At this screen, you can enter any email address, and the development server will proceed as if you are signed in with an account that has that address.

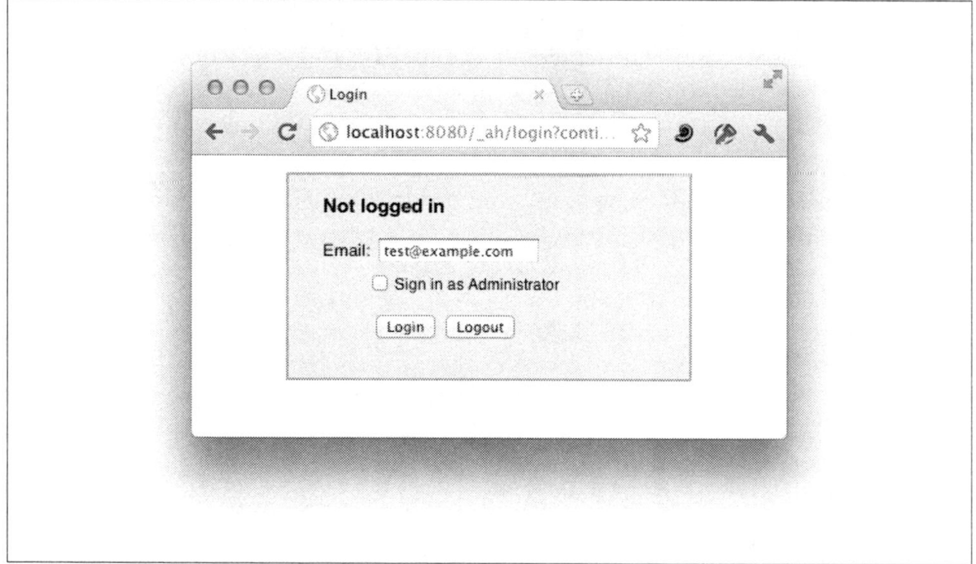

Figure 2-6. The development server's simulated Google Accounts sign-in screen

If this app were running on App Engine, the login and logout URLs would go to the actual Google Accounts locations. Once signed in or out, Google Accounts redirects back to the given URL path for the live application.

Click on "Sign in or register," then click on the Login button on the simulated Google Accounts screen, using the default test email address (*`test@example.com`*). The clock app now looks like Figure 2-7. To sign out again, click the "sign out" link.

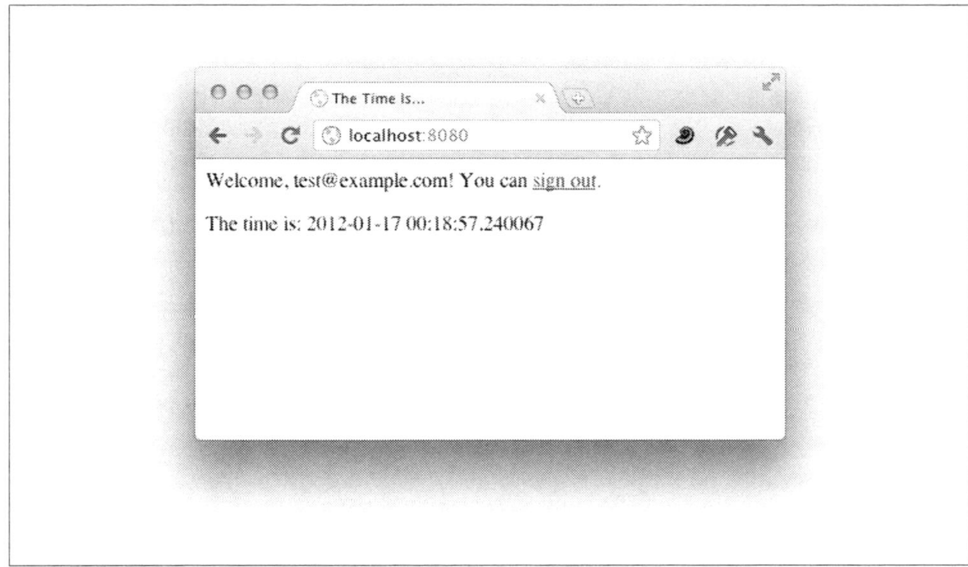

Figure 2-7. The clock app, with the user signed in

Web forms and the datastore

Now that we know who the user is, we can ask her for her preferred time zone, remember her preference, and use it on future visits.

First, we need a way to remember the user's preferences so future requests can access them. The App Engine datastore provides reliable, scalable storage for this purpose. The Python API includes a data modeling interface that maps Python objects to datastore entities. We can use it to write a `UserPrefs` class.

Create a new file named *models.py*, as shown in Example 2-5.

Example 2-5. The file models.py, with a class for storing user preferences in the datastore

```
from google.appengine.api import users
from google.appengine.ext import db

class UserPrefs(db.Model):
    tz_offset = db.IntegerProperty(default=0)
    user = db.UserProperty(auto_current_user_add=True)

def get_userprefs(user_id=None):
    if not user_id:
        user = users.get_current_user()
        if not user:
            return None
        user_id = user.user_id()

    key = db.Key.from_path('UserPrefs', user_id)
    userprefs = db.get(key)
    if not userprefs:
```

```
        userprefs = UserPrefs(key_name=user_id)
    return userprefs
```

The Python data modeling interface is provided by the module `db` in the package `google.appengine.ext`. A data model is a class whose base class is `db.Model`. The model subclass defines the structure of the data in each object by using class properties. This structure is enforced by `db.Model` when values are assigned to instance properties. For our `UserPrefs` class, we define two properties: `tz_offset`, an integer, and `user`, a `User` object returned by the Google Accounts API.

Every datastore entity has a primary key. Unlike a primary key in a relational database table, an entity key is permanent and can only be set when the entity is created. A key is unique across all entities in the system, and consists of several parts, including the entity's kind (in this case `'UserPrefs'`). An app can set one component of the key to an arbitrary value, known in the API as the *key name*.

The clock application uses the user's unique ID, provided by the `user_id()` method of the `User` object, as the key name of a `UserPrefs` entity. This allows the app to fetch the entity by key, since it knows the user's ID from the Google Accounts API. Fetching the entity by key is faster than performing a datastore query.

In *models.py*, we define a function named `get_userprefs()` that gets the `UserPrefs` object for the user. After determining the user ID, the function constructs a datastore key for an entity of the kind `'UserPrefs'` with a key name equivalent to the user ID. If the entity exists in the datastore, the function returns the `UserPrefs` object.

If the entity does not exist in the datastore, the function creates a new `UserPrefs` object with default settings and a key name that corresponds to the user. The new object is *not* saved to the datastore automatically. The caller must invoke the `put()` method on the `UserPrefs` instance to save it.

Now that we have a mechanism for getting a `UserPrefs` object, we can make two upgrades to the main page. If the user is signed in, we can get the user's preferences (if any) and adjust the clock's time zone.

Edit *main.py*. With the other `import` statements, import the `models` module we just created:

```
import models
```

In the request handler code, call the `models.get_userprefs()` function, and use the return value to adjust the `current_time` value. Also, add the `userprefs` value to the template context:

```
class MainPage(webapp2.RequestHandler):
    def get(self):
        # ...
        userprefs = models.get_userprefs()

        if userprefs:
            current_time += datetime.timedelta(
```

```
                0, 0, 0, 0, 0, userprefs.tz_offset)

        template = template_env.get_template('home.html')
        context = {
            # ...
            'userprefs': userprefs,
        }
        self.response.out.write(template.render(context))
```

Let's also add a web form to the template so the user can set a time zone preference. Edit *home.html*, and add the following near the bottom of the template, above the `</body>`:

```
{% if user %}
  <form action="/prefs" method="post">
    <label for="tz_offset">
      Timezone offset from UTC (can be negative):
    </label>
    <input name="tz_offset" id="tz_offset" type="text"
      size="4" value="{{ userprefs.tz_offset }}" />
    <input type="submit" value="Set" />
  </form>
{% endif %}
```

To enable the preferences form, we need a new request handler to parse the form data and update the datastore. Let's implement this as a new request handler module. (We'll see why in a moment.)

Create a file named *prefs.py* with the contents shown in Example 2-6.

Example 2-6. A new handler module, prefs.py, for the preferences form

```
import webapp2

import models

class PrefsPage(webapp2.RequestHandler):
    def post(self):
        userprefs = models.get_userprefs()
        try:
            tz_offset = int(self.request.get('tz_offset'))
            userprefs.tz_offset = tz_offset
            userprefs.put()
        except ValueError:
            # User entered a value that wasn't an integer.  Ignore for now.
            pass

        self.redirect('/')

application = webapp2.WSGIApplication([('/prefs', PrefsPage)],
                                      debug=True)
```

This request handler handles HTTP POST requests to the URL `/prefs`, which is the URL ("action") and HTTP method used by the form. Because it's an HTTP POST action, the code goes in the `post()` method (instead of the `get()` method used in *main.py*). The handler code calls the `get_userprefs()` function from *models.py* to get the `UserPrefs` object for the current user, which is either a new unsaved object with default values, or the object for an existing entity. The handler parses the `tz_offset` parameter from the form data as an integer, sets the property of the `UserPrefs` object, then saves the object to the datastore by calling its `put()` method. The `put()` method creates the object if it doesn't exist, or updates the existing object.

If the user enters something other than an integer in the form field, we don't do anything. It'd be appropriate to return an error message, but we'll leave this as is to keep the example simple.

The form handler redirects the user's browser to the / URL. In webapp2, the `self.redirect()` method takes care of setting the appropriate response headers for redirecting the browser.

Finally, edit *app.yaml* to map the handler module to the URL `/prefs` in the `handlers:` section, as shown in Example 2-7.

Example 2-7. A new version of app.yaml mapping the URL /prefs, with login required

```
application: clock
version: 1
runtime: python27
api_version: 1
threadsafe: true

handlers:
- url: /prefs
  script: prefs.application
  login: required

- url: .*
  script: main.application

libraries:
- name: webapp2
  version: "2.5.1"
- name: jinja2
  version: latest
- name: markupsafe
  version: latest
```

The `login: required` line says that the user must be signed in to Google Accounts to access the `/prefs` URL. If the user accesses the URL while not signed in, App Engine automatically directs the user to the Google Accounts sign-in page, then redirects her back to this URL afterward. This makes it easy to require sign-in for sections of your site, and to ensure that the user is signed in before the request handler is called.

Be sure to put the `/prefs` URL mapping before the `/.*` mapping. URL patterns are tried in order, and the first pattern to match determines the handler used for the request. Since the pattern `/.*` matches all URLs, `/prefs` must come first or it will be ignored.

Reload the page to see the customizable clock in action. Try changing the time zone by submitting the form. Also try signing out, then signing in again using the same email address, and again with a different email address. The app remembers the time zone preference for each user.

Caching with memcache

The code that gets user preferences data in Example 2-5 fetches an entity from the datastore every time a signed-in user visits the site. User preferences are often read and seldom changed, so getting a `UserPrefs` object from the datastore with every request is more expensive than it needs to be. We can mitigate the cost of reading from primary storage by using a caching layer.

We can use the memcache service as secondary storage for user preferences data. Because of the way we wrote *models.py*, adding caching requires just a few minor changes. Edit this file as shown in Example 2-8.

Example 2-8. A new version of models.py that caches UserPrefs objects in memcache

```
from google.appengine.api import memcache
from google.appengine.api import users
from google.appengine.ext import db

class UserPrefs(db.Model):
    tz_offset = db.IntegerProperty(default=0)
    user = db.UserProperty(auto_current_user_add=True)

    def cache_set(self):
        memcache.set('UserPrefs:' + self.key().name(), self)

    def put(self):
        super(UserPrefs, self).put()
        self.cache_set()

def get_userprefs(user_id=None):
    if not user_id:
        user = users.get_current_user()
        if not user:
            return None
        user_id = user.user_id()

    userprefs = memcache.get('UserPrefs:' + user_id)
    if not userprefs:
        key = db.Key.from_path('UserPrefs', user_id)
        userprefs = db.get(key)
        if userprefs:
            userprefs.cache_set()
        else:
            userprefs = UserPrefs(key_name=user_id)

    return userprefs
```

The Python API for the memcache service is provided by the module memcache in the package google.appengine.api. The memcache stores key-value pairs. The value can be of any type that can be converted to and from a flat data representation (*serialized*), using the Python pickle module, including most data objects.

The new version of the UserPrefs class overrides the put() method. When the put() method is called on an instance, the instance is saved to the datastore by using the superclass's put() method, then it is saved to the memcache.

A new UserPrefs method called cache_set() makes the call to memcache.set(). memcache.set() takes a key and a value. Here, we use the string 'UserPrefs:' followed by the entity's key name as the memcache key, and the full object (self) as the value. The API takes care of serializing the UserPrefs object, so we can put in and take out fully formed objects.

The new version of get_userprefs() checks the memcache for the UserPrefs object before going to the datastore. If it finds it in the cache, it uses it. If it doesn't, it checks the datastore, and if it finds it there, it stores it in the cache and uses it. If the object is in neither the memcache nor the datastore, get_userprefs() returns a fresh UserPrefs object with default values.

Reload the page to see the new version work. To make the caching behavior more visible, you can add logging statements in the appropriate places in *models.py*, like so:

```
import logging

class UserPrefs(db.Model):
    # ...
    def cache_set(self):
        logging.info('cache set')
        # ...
```

The development server prints logging output to the console. If you are using the Launcher, you can open a window of development server output by clicking the Logs button.

That's it for our Python app. Next, we'll take a look at the same example using the Java runtime environment. If you're not interested in Java, you can skip ahead to "Registering the Application" on page 63.

Developing a Java App

Java web applications for App Engine use the Java Servlet standard interface for interacting with the application server. An application consists of one or more servlet classes, each extending a servlet base class. Servlets are mapped to URLs using a standard configuration file called a "deployment descriptor," also known as *web.xml*. When App Engine receives a request for a Java application, it determines which servlet class to use based on the URL and the deployment descriptor, instantiates the class, and then calls an appropriate method on the servlet object.

All the files for a Java application, including the compiled Java classes, configuration files, and static files, are organized in a standard directory structure called a Web Application Archive, or "WAR." Everything in the WAR directory gets deployed to App Engine. It's common to have your development workflow build the contents of the WAR from a set of source files, either using an automated build process or WAR-aware development tools.

If you are using the Eclipse IDE with the Google Plugin, you can create a new project by using the Web Application wizard. Click the Google drop-down menu button, then select New Web Application Project. (Alternately, from the File menu, select New, then Web Application Project.) In the window that opens, enter a project name (such as `Clock`) and package name (such as `clock`).

Uncheck the "Use Google Web Toolkit" checkbox, and make sure the "Use Google App Engine" checkbox is checked. (If you leave the GWT checkbox checked, the new project will be created with GWT starter files. This is cool, but it's outside the scope of this chapter.) Figure 2-8 shows the completed dialog box for the `Clock` application. Click Finish to create the project.

If you are not using the Google Plugin for Eclipse, you will need to create the directories and files another way. If you are already familiar with Java web development, you can use your existing tools and processes to produce the final WAR. For the rest of this section, we assume you are using the directory structure that is created by the Eclipse plug-in.

Figure 2-9 shows the project file structure, as depicted in the Eclipse Package Explorer.

The project root directory (*Clock*) contains two major subdirectories: *src* and *war*. The *src/* directory contains all the project's class files in the usual Java package structure. With a package path of `clock`, Eclipse created source code for a servlet class named `ClockServlet` in the file *clock/ClockServlet.java*.

The *war/* directory contains the complete final contents of the application. Eclipse compiles source code from *src/* automatically and puts the compiled class files in *war/WEB-INF/classes/*, which is hidden from Eclipse's Package Explorer by default. Eclipse copies the contents of *src/META-INF/* to *war/WEB-INF/classes/META-INF/* automatically, as well. Everything else, such as CSS or browser JavaScript files, must be created in the *war/* directory in its intended location.

Let's start our clock application with a simple servlet that displays the current time. Open the file *src/clock/ClockServlet.java* for editing (creating it if necessary), and give it contents similar to Example 2-9.

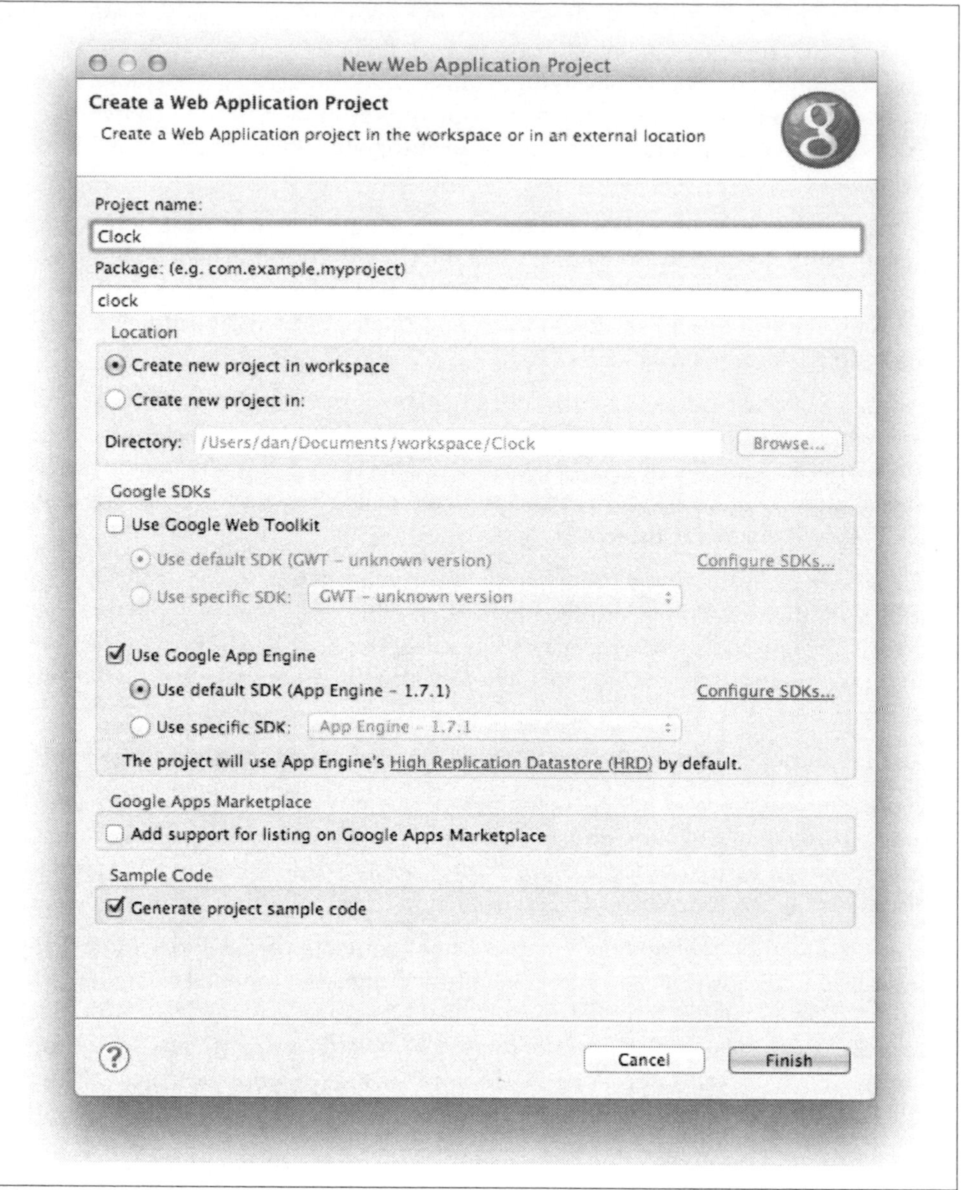

Figure 2-8. The Google Plugin for Eclipse New Web Application Project dialog, with values for the Clock application

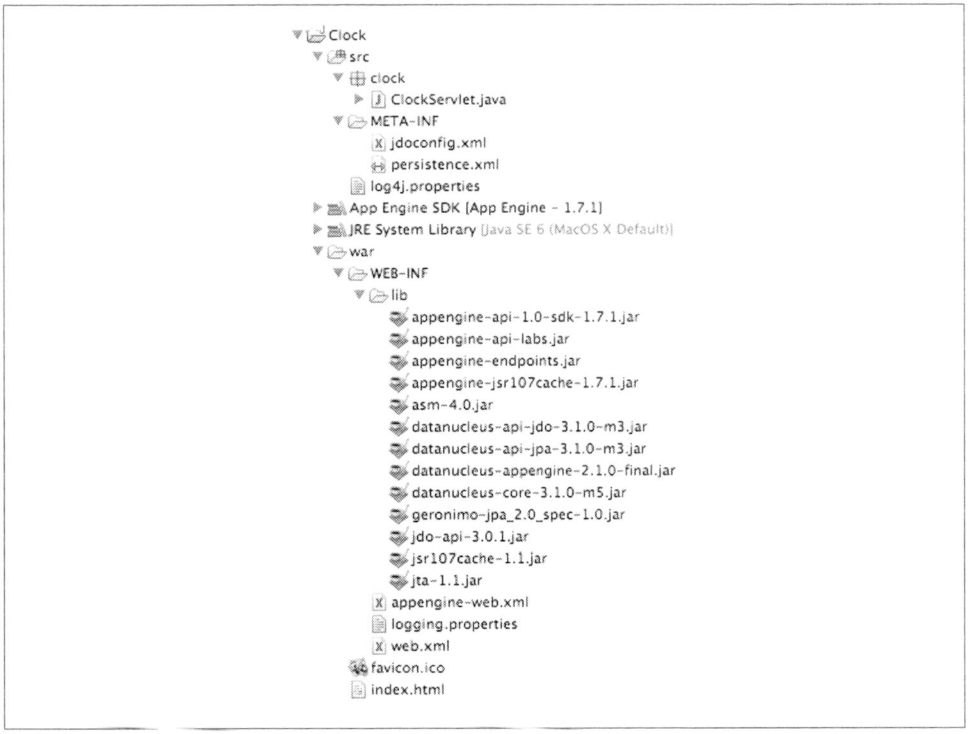

Figure 2-9. A new Java project structure, as shown in the Eclipse Package Explorer

Example 2-9. A simple Java servlet

```
package clock;

import java.io.IOException;
import java.io.PrintWriter;
import java.text.SimpleDateFormat;
import java.util.Date;
import java.util.SimpleTimeZone;
import javax.servlet.http.*;

@SuppressWarnings("serial")
public class ClockServlet extends HttpServlet {
    public void doGet(HttpServletRequest req,
                      HttpServletResponse resp)
          throws IOException {
        SimpleDateFormat fmt = new SimpleDateFormat("yyyy-MM-dd hh:mm:ss.SSSSSS");
        fmt.setTimeZone(new SimpleTimeZone(0, ""));

        resp.setContentType("text/html");
        PrintWriter out = resp.getWriter();
        out.println("<p>The time is: " + fmt.format(new Date()) + "</p>");
    }
}
```

The servlet class extends `javax.servlet.http.HttpServlet`, and overrides methods for each of the HTTP methods it intends to support. This servlet overrides the `doGet()` method to handle HTTP GET requests. The server calls the method with an `HttpServletRequest` object and an `HttpServletResponse` object as parameters. The `HttpServletRequest` contains information about the request, such as the URL, form parameters, and cookies. The method prepares the response, using methods on the `HttpServletResponse`, such as `setContentType()` and `getWriter()`. App Engine sends the response when the servlet method exits.

To tell App Engine to invoke this servlet for requests, we need a deployment descriptor: an XML configuration file that describes which URLs invoke which servlet classes, among other things. The deployment descriptor is part of the servlet standard. Open or create the file *war/WEB-INF/web.xml*, and give it contents similar to Example 2-10.

Example 2-10. The web.xml file, also known as the deployment descriptor, mapping all URLs to ClockServlet

```
<?xml version="1.0" encoding="utf-8"?>
<web-app xmlns:xsi="http://www.w3.org/2001/XMLSchema-instance"
  xmlns="http://java.sun.com/xml/ns/javaee"
  xmlns:web="http://java.sun.com/xml/ns/javaee/web-app_2_5.xsd"
  xsi:schemaLocation="http://java.sun.com/xml/ns/javaee
    http://java.sun.com/xml/ns/javaee/web-app_2_5.xsd" version="2.5">
  <servlet>
    <servlet-name>clock</servlet-name>
    <servlet-class>clock.ClockServlet</servlet-class>
  </servlet>
  <servlet-mapping>
    <servlet-name>clock</servlet-name>
    <url-pattern>/</url-pattern>
  </servlet-mapping>
</web-app>
```

Eclipse may open this file in its XML Design view, a table-like view of the elements and values. Select the Source tab at the bottom of the editor pane to edit the XML source.

web.xml is an XML file with a root element of `<web-app>`. To map URL patterns to servlets, you declare each servlet with a `<servlet>` element, then declare the mapping with a `<servlet-mapping>` element. The `<url-pattern>` of a servlet mapping can be a full URL path, or a URL path with a * at the beginning or end to represent a part of a path. In this case, the URL pattern / matches just the root URL path.

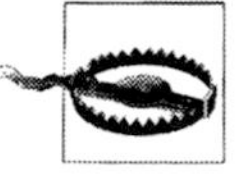

Be sure that each of your `<url-pattern>` values starts with a forward slash (/). Omitting the starting slash may have the intended behavior on the development web server but unintended behavior on App Engine.

App Engine needs one additional configuration file that isn't part of the servlet standard. Open or create the file *war/WEB-INF/appengine-web.xml*, and give it contents similar to Example 2-11.

Example 2-11. The appengine-web.xml file, with App Engine-specific configuration for the Java app

```
<?xml version="1.0" encoding="utf-8"?>
<appengine-web-app xmlns="http://appengine.google.com/ns/1.0">
  <application>clock</application>
  <version>1</version>
  <threadsafe>true</threadsafe>
</appengine-web-app>
```

In this example, the configuration file tells App Engine that this is version 1 of an application called `clock`. We also declare the app to be thread-safe, authorizing App Engine to reuse an application instance to serve multiple requests simultaneously. (Of course, we must also make sure our code is thread-safe when we do this.) You can also use this configuration file to control other behaviors, such as static files and sessions. For more information, see Chapter 3.

The WAR for the application must include several JARs from the App Engine SDK: the Java EE implementation JARs, and the App Engine API JAR. The Eclipse plug-in installs these JARs in the WAR automatically. If you are not using the Eclipse plug-in, you must copy these JARs manually. Look in the SDK directory in the *lib/user/* and *lib/shared/* subdirectories. Copy every *.jar* file from these directories to the *war/WEB-INF/lib/* directory in your project.

Finally, the servlet class must be compiled. Eclipse compiles all your classes automatically, as needed. If you are not using Eclipse, you probably want to use a build tool such as Apache Ant to compile source code and perform other build tasks. See the official App Engine documentation for information on using Apache Ant to build App Engine projects.

I suppose it's traditional to explain how to compile a Java project from the command line using the `javac` command. You can do so by putting each of the JARs from *war/WEB-INF/lib/* and the *war/WEB-INF/classes/* directory in the classpath, and making sure the compiled classes end up in the *classes/* directory. But in the real world, you want your IDE or an Ant script to take care of this for you.

One more thing for Eclipse users: the Eclipse new-project wizard created a static file named *war/index.html*. Delete it by right-clicking on it in the Project Explorer, selecting Delete, then clicking OK. (If you don't delete it, this static file will take precedence over the servlet mapping we just created.)

It's time to test this application with the development web server. The Eclipse plug-in can run the application and the development server inside the Eclipse debugger. To start it, select the Run menu, Debug As, and Web Application. The server starts, and prints the following message to the Console panel:

```
The server is running at http://localhost:8888/
```

If you are not using Eclipse, you can start the development server, using the `dev_appserver` command (`dev_appserver.sh` for Mac OS X or Linux). The command takes the path to the WAR directory as an argument, like so:

```
dev_appserver war
```

The command-line tool uses a different default port than the Eclipse plug-in uses (8080 instead of 8888). You can change the port used by the command-line tool with the `--port` argument, such as `--port=8888`.

Test your application by visiting the server's URL in a web browser:

http://localhost:8888

The browser displays a page similar to the Python example, shown earlier in Figure 2-4.

Introducing JSPs, JSTL, and EL

Right now, our clock displays the time in the UTC time zone. We'd like for our application to let the user customize the time zone, and to remember the user's preference for future visits. To do that, we use Google Accounts to identify which user is using the application.

Before we go any further, we should introduce a way to keep our HTML separate from our servlet code. This allows us to maintain the "business logic"—the code that implements the main purpose of our app—separately from the appearance of the app, making our logic easier to test and our appearance easier to change. Typically, you would use a templating system to define the appearance of the app in files that contain the HTML, CSS, and JavaScript, and leave blanks where the dynamic data should go. There are many fine templating systems to choose from in Java, such as Apache Velocity.

For this example, we use Java Servlet Pages, or JSPs. JSPs are a standard part of J2EE, which means you do not have to install anything else to use them. A JSP contains a mix of text (HTML) and Java code that defines the logic of the page. The JSP compiles to a servlet, just like the `ClockServlet` we already defined, that's equivalent to writing out the HTML portions, and evaluating the Java portions. In a sense, JSPs are just another way of writing servlet code.

JSPs are often criticized for being too powerful. Since the full Java language is available from within a JSP, there is a risk that business logic may creep into the templates, and you no longer have a useful separation. To mitigate this, later versions of the JSP specification included new ways of describing template logic that are intentionally less powerful than full Java code: the Java Servlet Templating Language (JSTL) and the JSP Expression Language (EL). We use these features for this example, and other places in the book where templated output is required.

Edit *ClockServlet.java* to resemble Example 2-12.

Example 2-12. Code for ClockServlet.java that displays Google Accounts information and links

```
package clock;

import java.io.IOException;
import java.text.SimpleDateFormat;
import java.util.Date;
import java.util.SimpleTimeZone;
import javax.servlet.RequestDispatcher;
import javax.servlet.ServletException;
import javax.servlet.http.*;

import com.google.appengine.api.users.User;
import com.google.appengine.api.users.UserService;
import com.google.appengine.api.users.UserServiceFactory;

@SuppressWarnings("serial")
public class ClockServlet extends HttpServlet {
    public void doGet(HttpServletRequest req,
                      HttpServletResponse resp)
          throws IOException, ServletException {
        SimpleDateFormat fmt = new SimpleDateFormat("yyyy-MM-dd hh:mm:ss.SSSSSS");
        fmt.setTimeZone(new SimpleTimeZone(0, ""));

        UserService userService = UserServiceFactory.getUserService();
        User user = userService.getCurrentUser();
        String loginUrl = userService.createLoginURL("/");
        String logoutUrl = userService.createLogoutURL("/");

        req.setAttribute("user", user);
        req.setAttribute("loginUrl", loginUrl);
        req.setAttribute("logoutUrl", logoutUrl);
        req.setAttribute("currentTime", fmt.format(new Date()));

        resp.setContentType("text/html");

        RequestDispatcher jsp = req.getRequestDispatcher("/WEB-INF/home.jsp");
        jsp.forward(req, resp);
    }
}
```

Next, create a new file named *home.jsp* in the *war/WEB-INF/* directory of your project, and give it contents similar to Example 2-13.

Example 2-13. Code for ClockServlet.java that displays Google Accounts information and links

```
<%@ taglib uri="http://java.sun.com/jsp/jstl/core" prefix="c" %>
<html>
  <head>
    <title>The Time Is...</title>
  </head>
  <body>
    <c:choose>
      <c:when test="${user != null}">
        <p>
```

```
          Welcome, ${user.email}!
          You can <a href="${logoutUrl}">sign out</a>.
        </p>
      </c:when>
      <c:otherwise>
        <p>
          Welcome!
          <a href="${loginUrl}">Sign in or register</a> to customize.
        </p>
      </c:otherwise>
    </c:choose>
    <p>The time is: ${currentTime}</p>
  </body>
</html>
```

Using Eclipse, you can leave the development web server running while you edit code. When you save changes to code, Eclipse compiles the class, and if it compiles successfully, Eclipse injects the new class into the already-running server. In most cases, you can simply reload the page in your browser, and it will use the new code.

If you are not using Eclipse, shut down the development server by hitting Ctrl-C. Recompile your project, then start the server again.

Reload the new version of the clock app in your browser. The new page resembles the Python example, shown previously in Figure 2-5.

Here's everything we're going to say about JSPs, JSTL, and EL in this book:

- Remember that *home.jsp* represents a servlet. In this case, it's one that expects certain attributes to be set in its context. `ClockServlet` invokes *home.jsp* by setting attributes on the `HttpServletRequest` object via its `setAttribute()` method, then forwarding the request and response to the *home.jsp* servlet.
- The forwarding takes place via a `RequestDispatcher` set up for the *home.jsp* servlet. In this case, we keep *home.jsp* inside the */WEB-INF/* directory, so that the servlet container doesn't map it to a URL. If the JSP resided outside of */WEB-INF/*, a URL to that path (from the WAR root) would map to the JSP servlet, and the servlet container would invoke it directly (assuming no explicit URL pattern matched the URL).
- The `getRequestDispatcher()` method of the request instance takes a path to a JSP and returns its `RequestDispatcher`. Make sure the path starts with a forward slash (*/*).
- To invoke the JSP, `ClockServlet` calls the `forward()` method of the `RequestDispatcher`, passing the `HttpServletRequest` and `HttpServletResponse` objects as arguments. The `forward()` method may throw the `ServletException`; in this example, we just add a `throws` clause to `doGet()`.
- A JSP contains text (HTML) and specially formatted directives. This example contains one directive, `<%@ taglib ... %>`, which loads a JSTL tag library. You might also see `<% ... %>`, which contains Java code that becomes part of the servlet, and

`<%= ... %>`, which contains a Java expression whose string form is printed to the page.

- `<c:choose>...</c:choose>`, `<c:when>...</c:when>`, and `<c:otherwise>...</c:otherwise>` are examples of JSTL tags. These come from the `/jsp/jstl/core` tag library imported by `taglib` import directive in the first line. The `c:` is the prefix associated with the library in the import directive. Here, the `<c:choose>` structure renders the `<c:when>` block when the user is signed in, and the `<c:otherwise>` block otherwise.
- `${user != null}` is an example of an EL expression. An EL expression can appear in the text of the document, where its value is rendered into the text, or in a JSTL tag attribute, where its value is used by the tag. The expression `${logoutUrl}` renders the `String` value of the `logoutUrl` attribute set by `ClockServlet`. `${user.email}` is an example of accessing a JavaBean property of a value: the result is equivalent to calling the `getEmail()` method of the `User` object value. `${user != null}` shows how an EL expression can use simple operators, in this case producing a `boolean` value used by the `<c:when test="...">`.

For this book, we'll stick to simple features of JSPs, JSTL, and EL, and not provide additional explanation. For more information about these J2EE features, see *Head First Servlets and JSP* by Brian Basham et al. (O'Reilly).

Be careful when mapping the URL pattern /* to a servlet in your deployment descriptor when using request dispatchers in this way. Explicit URL mappings override the default JSP path mapping, and the request dispatcher will honor it when determining the servlet for the path. If you have a /* URL mapping that might match a JSP path, you must have an explicit JSP URL mapping in the deployment descriptor that overrides it:

```
<servlet>
  <servlet-name>home-jsp</servlet-name>
  <jsp-file>/WEB-INF/home.jsp</jsp-file>
</servlet>
<servlet-mapping>
  <servlet-name>home-jsp</servlet-name>
  <url-pattern>/WEB-INF/home.jsp</url-pattern>
</servlet-mapping>

<servlet>
  <servlet-name>clock</servlet-name>
  <servlet-class>clock.ClockServlet</servlet-class>
</servlet>
<servlet-mapping>
  <servlet-name>clock</servlet-name>
  <url-pattern>/*</url-pattern>
</servlet-mapping>
```

Note that a mapping in */WEB-INF/* is still hidden from clients. A request for */WEB-INF/home.jsp* will return a 404 Not Found error, and will not invoke the JSP servlet.

Users and Google Accounts

The `ClockServlet` in Example 2-12 calls the Users API to get information about the user who may or may not be signed in with a Google Account. This interface is provided by the `com.google.appengine.api.users` package. The app gets a `UserService` instance by calling the `getUserService()` method of the `UserServiceFactory` class. Then it calls the `getCurrentUser()` method of the `UserService`, which returns a `User` object, or `null` if the current user is not signed in. The `getEmail()` method of the `User` object returns the email address for the user.

The `createLoginURL()` and `createLogoutURL()` methods of the `UserService` generate URLs that go to Google Accounts. Each of these methods takes a URL path for the app where the user should be redirected after performing the desired task. The login URL goes to the Google Accounts page where the user can sign in or register for a new account. The logout URL visits Google Accounts to sign out the current user, and then immediately redirects back to the given application URL without displaying anything.

If you click on the "Sign in or register" link with the app running in the development server, the link goes to the development server's simulated version of the Google Accounts sign-in screen, similar to the Python version shown earlier in Figure 2-6. At this screen, you can enter any email address, and the development server will proceed as if you are signed in with an account that has that address.

If this app were running on App Engine, the login and logout URLs would go to the actual Google Accounts locations. Once signed in or out, Google Accounts redirects back to the given URL path for the live application.

Click on "Sign in or register," then enter an email address (such as *test@example.com*) and click on the Login button on the simulated Google Accounts screen. The clock app now looks like Figure 2-7 (shown earlier). To sign out again, click the "sign out" link.

In addition to the `UserService` API, an app can also get information about the current user with the servlet "user principal" interface. The app can call the `getUserPrincipal()` method on the `HttpServletRequest` object to get a `java.security.Principal` object, or `null` if the user is not signed in. This object has a `getName()` method, which in App Engine is equivalent to calling the `getEmail()` method of a `User` object.

The main advantage to getting user information from the servlet interface is that the servlet interface is a standard. Coding an app to use standard interfaces makes the app easier to port to alternate implementations, such as other servlet-based web application environments or private servers. As much as possible, App Engine implements standard interfaces for its services and features.

The disadvantage to the standard interfaces is that not all standard interfaces represent all of App Engine's features, and in some cases the App Engine services don't implement every feature of an interface. All services include a nonstandard "low-level" API, which you can use directly or use to implement adapters to other interfaces.

Web forms and the datastore

Now that we can identify the user, we can prompt for the user's preferences and remember them for future requests. We can store preferences data in the App Engine datastore.

There are several ways to use the datastore from Java. The simplest way is to call the datastore API directly. This API lets you create and manipulate entities (records) in the datastore by using instances of an `Entity` class. Entities have named properties, which you can get and set using `getProperty()` and `setProperty()` methods. The API is easy to understand, and has a direct correspondence with the concepts of the datastore. We'll use the datastore API for this tutorial and the next few chapters.

The datastore API is sufficient for many uses, but it's not particularly Java-like to represent to data objects as instances of a generic `Entity` class. It'd be better if data objects could be represented by real Java objects, with classes, fields, and accessor methods that describe the role of the data in your code.

The App Engine SDK includes support for two major standard interfaces for manipulating data in this way: Java Data Objects (JDO) and the Java Persistence API (JPA). With JDO and JPA, you use regular Java classes to describe the structure of data, and include annotations that tell the interface how to save the data to the datastore and re-create the objects when the data is fetched. We discuss JPA in detail in Chapter 10.

You may also want to consider Objectify (*http://bit.ly/QVMneT*), a third-party open source library with many of these benefits. Objectify is easier to use than JDO and JPA, although it is specific to App Engine.

First, let's set up a way for a signed-in user to set a time zone preference. Edit *home.jsp* and add the following, just above the closing `</body>` tag:

```
<c:if test="${user != null}">
  <form action="/prefs" method="post">
    <label for="tz_offset">
      Timezone offset from UTC (can be negative):
    </label>
    <input name="tz_offset" id="tz_offset" type="text"
      size="4" value="${tzOffset}" />
    <input type="submit" value="Set" />
  </form>
</c:if>
```

(We will populate the `tzOffset` attribute in a moment. If you'd like to test the form now, remove the `${tzOffset}` reference temporarily.)

This web form includes a text field for the user's time zone preference, and a button that submits the form. When the user submits the form, the browser issues an HTTP

POST request (specified by the `method` attribute) to the URL `/prefs` (the `action` attribute), with a request body containing the form field data.

Naturally, we need a new servlet to handle these requests. Create a new servlet class `PrefsServlet` (*PrefsServlet.java*) with the code shown in Example 2-14.

Example 2-14. The PrefsServlet class, a servlet that handles the user preferences form

```
package clock;

import java.io.IOException;

import javax.servlet.http.HttpServlet;
import javax.servlet.http.HttpServletRequest;
import javax.servlet.http.HttpServletResponse;

import com.google.appengine.api.datastore.DatastoreService;
import com.google.appengine.api.datastore.DatastoreServiceFactory;
import com.google.appengine.api.datastore.Entity;
import com.google.appengine.api.datastore.Key;
import com.google.appengine.api.datastore.KeyFactory;
import com.google.appengine.api.users.User;
import com.google.appengine.api.users.UserService;
import com.google.appengine.api.users.UserServiceFactory;

@SuppressWarnings("serial")
public class PrefsServlet extends HttpServlet {
    public void doPost(HttpServletRequest req,
            HttpServletResponse resp)
          throws IOException {

        UserService userService = UserServiceFactory.getUserService();
        User user = userService.getCurrentUser();

        DatastoreService ds = DatastoreServiceFactory.getDatastoreService();
        Key userKey = KeyFactory.createKey("UserPrefs", user.getUserId());
        Entity userPrefs = new Entity(userKey);

        try {
            int tzOffset = new Integer(req.getParameter("tz_offset")).intValue();

            userPrefs.setProperty("tz_offset", tzOffset);
            userPrefs.setProperty("user", user);
            ds.put(userPrefs);

        } catch (NumberFormatException nfe) {
            // User entered a value that wasn't an integer.  Ignore for now.
        }

        resp.sendRedirect("/");
    }
}
```

A datastore entity has a *kind*, which groups related entities together for the purpose of queries. Here, the user's time zone preference is stored in an entity of the kind `"User`

Prefs". This entity has two properties. The first is named "tzOffset", and its value is the user's time zone offset, an integer. The second is "user", which contains a representation of the User value that represents the currently signed-in user.

Each datastore entity has a key that is unique across all entities. A simple key contains the kind, and either an app-assigned string (the *key name*) or a system-assigned number (referred to in the API as an *ID*). In this case, we provide a key name equal to the user ID from the User value.

The entity is saved to the datastore by the call to the ds.put() method. If an entity with the given key does not exist, the put() method creates a new one. If the entity does exist, put() replaces it. In a more typical case involving more properties, you would fetch the entity by key or with a query, update properties, then save it back to the datastore. But for PrefsServlet, it is sufficient to replace the entity without reading the old data.

When we are done updating the datastore, we respond with a redirect back to the main page (/). It is a best practice to reply to the posting of a web form with a redirect, to prevent the user from accidentally resubmitting the form by using the "back" button of the browser. It'd be better to offer more visual feedback for this action, but this will do for now.

Edit *web.xml* to map the new servlet to the /prefs URL used by the form. Add these lines just before the closing </web-app> tag:

```
<servlet>
  <servlet-name>Prefs</servlet-name>
  <servlet-class>clock.PrefsServlet</servlet-class>
</servlet>
<servlet-mapping>
  <servlet-name>Prefs</servlet-name>
  <url-pattern>/prefs</url-pattern>
</servlet-mapping>

<security-constraint>
  <web-resource-collection>
    <web-resource-name>prefs</web-resource-name>
    <url-pattern>/prefs</url-pattern>
  </web-resource-collection>
  <auth-constraint>
    <role-name>*</role-name>
  </auth-constraint>
</security-constraint>
```

The order in which the URL mappings appear in the file does not matter. Longer patterns (not counting wildcards) match before shorter ones.

The <security-constraint> block tells App Engine that only users signed in with a Google Account can access the URL /prefs. If a user who is not signed in attempts to access this URL, App Engine redirects the user to Google Accounts to sign in. When the user signs in, she is directed back to the URL she attempted to access. A security constraint is a convenient way to implement Google Accounts authentication for a set of URLs. In this case, it means that `PrefsServlet` does not need to handle the case where someone tries to submit data to the URL without being signed in.

Finally, edit the `doGet()` method in the `ClockServlet` class to fetch the `UserPrefs` entity and use its value, if one exists. Add this code prior to where the `"currentTime"` attribute is set, with the imports in the appropriate place:

```
import com.google.appengine.api.datastore.DatastoreService;
import com.google.appengine.api.datastore.DatastoreServiceFactory;
import com.google.appengine.api.datastore.Entity;
import com.google.appengine.api.datastore.EntityNotFoundException;
import com.google.appengine.api.datastore.Key;
import com.google.appengine.api.datastore.KeyFactory;

// ...
        Entity userPrefs = null;
        if (user != null) {
            DatastoreService ds = DatastoreServiceFactory.getDatastoreService();
            Key userKey = KeyFactory.createKey("UserPrefs", user.getUserId());
            try {
                userPrefs = ds.get(userKey);
            } catch (EntityNotFoundException e) {
                // No user preferences stored.
            }
        }
        if (userPrefs != null) {
            int tzOffset = ((Long) userPrefs.getProperty("tz_offset")).intValue();
            fmt.setTimeZone(new SimpleTimeZone(tzOffset * 60 * 60 * 1000, ""));
            req.setAttribute("tzOffset", tzOffset);
        } else {
            req.setAttribute("tzOffset", 0);
        }
```

This code retrieves the `UserPrefs` entity by reconstructing its key, then calling the `get()` method of the `DatastoreService`. This either returns the `Entity`, or throws `EntityNotFoundException`. In this case, if it's not found, we fall back on the default setting of 0 for the time zone offset. If it is found, we update the `SimpleDateFormat` to use the setting. In either case, we populate the `"tzOffset"` attribute with a value, which is displayed in the form.

Notice the casting of the property value in this example. When we set the property in the `PrefsServlet` class, we used an `int` value. The datastore only has a long integer value type internally, so it upgraded the value before storing it. When we retrieve the property with `getProperty()`, it comes out as a `Long`. (This value is `null` if the entity has no property of that name.) We must cast the value to a `Long`, then call its `intValue()` method to get our `int`.

This is where a data framework like JPA or Objectify comes in handy. Such a framework handles the marshaling of values and casting of types automatically, and can provide a degree of protection for type consistency. The datastore itself is "schemaless," which is important to understand as you modify your data model over the lifetime of your application.

Restart your development server, then reload the page to see the customizable clock in action. Try changing the time zone by submitting the form. Also try signing out, then signing in again using the same email address, and again with a different email address. The app remembers the time zone preference for each user.

Caching with memcache

So far, our application fetches the object from the datastore every time a signed-in user visits the site. Since user preferences data doesn't change very often, we can speed up the per-request data access using the memory cache (*memcache*) as secondary storage.

We need to make two changes to our app to achieve this. The first is to update `ClockServlet` to check the cache. If the value is found in the cache, `ClockServlet` uses it. If it is not found, it falls back on reading from the datastore as before. If the value is found in the datastore but not in the cache, it stores the value in the cache for use by future requests.

The second change we need is to `PrefsServlet`. When the user updates her preference, we must invalidate (delete) the value in the cache. The next attempt to read the value—likely the redirect to `ClockServlet` that immediately follows the form submission—will see the cache does not have the value, get it from the datastore, and update the cache.

We could have `PrefsServlet` update the cache itself, but we *must* have `ClockServlet` populate the cache as needed. Memcache is not durable storage, and could delete any value at any time. That's what makes it fast. If `ClockServlet` did not update the cache, the value could go missing, and performance would degrade until the next time the user updates her preference. To keep things simple, we make `ClockServlet` responsible for all cache updates, and simply delete the value from the cache when it changes in the datastore in `PrefsServlet`.

Edit the lines we just added to ClockServlet to use the cache, putting the new imports in the appropriate place:

```
import com.google.appengine.api.memcache.MemcacheService;
import com.google.appengine.api.memcache.MemcacheServiceFactory;

// ...
        Entity userPrefs = null;
        if (user != null) {
            DatastoreService ds = DatastoreServiceFactory.getDatastoreService();
            MemcacheService memcache = MemcacheServiceFactory.getMemcacheService();

            String cacheKey = "UserPrefs:" + user.getUserId();
            userPrefs = (Entity) memcache.get(cacheKey);
            if (userPrefs == null) {
                Key userKey = KeyFactory.createKey("UserPrefs", user.getUserId());
                try {
                    userPrefs = ds.get(userKey);
                    memcache.put(cacheKey, userPrefs);
                } catch (EntityNotFoundException e) {
                    // No user preferences stored.
                }
            }
        }

        if (userPrefs != null) {
            int tzOffset = ((Long) userPrefs.getProperty("tz_offset")).intValue();
            fmt.setTimeZone(new SimpleTimeZone(tzOffset * 60 * 60 * 1000, ""));
            req.setAttribute("tzOffset", tzOffset);
        } else {
            req.setAttribute("tzOffset", 0);
        }
```

Similarly, edit the doPost() method of PrefsServlet to delete the cached value (if any) when performing an update:

```
import com.google.appengine.api.memcache.MemcacheService;
import com.google.appengine.api.memcache.MemcacheServiceFactory;

// ...
        MemcacheService memcache = MemcacheServiceFactory.getMemcacheService();
        String cacheKey = "UserPrefs:" + user.getUserId();

        try {
            int tzOffset = new Integer(req.getParameter("tz_offset")).intValue();

            userPrefs.setProperty("tz_offset", tzOffset);
            userPrefs.setProperty("user", user);
            ds.put(userPrefs);
            memcache.delete(cacheKey);

        } catch (NumberFormatException nfe) {
            // User entered a value that wasn't an integer.  Ignore for now.
        }
```

Any object you store in the memcache must be serializable. That is, it must implement the `Serializable` interface from the `java.io` package. The `Entity` class is serializable. You can also use any serializable object as the key for a cache value; in this case we just use a `String`.

Reload the page to see the new version work. To make the caching behavior more visible, you can add logging statements to `ClockServlet`, like so:

```
import java.util.logging.*;

// ...
public class ClockServlet extends HttpServlet {
    private static final Logger log = Logger.getLogger(ClockServlet.class.getName());

    public void doGet(HttpServletRequest req,
                      HttpServletResponse resp)
        throws IOException, ServletException {

        // ...
            userPrefs = (Entity) memcache.get(cacheKey);
            if (userPrefs == null) {
                log.warning("CACHE MISS");
            } else {
                log.warning("CACHE HIT");
            }

        // ...
    }
}
```

The development server prints logging output to the console. If you are using Eclipse, these messages appear in the Console pane.

The Development Console

Both the Python and Java development web servers include a handy feature for inspecting and debugging your application while testing on your local machine: a web-based development console. With your development server running, visit the following URL in a browser to access the console:

http://localhost:8080/_ah/admin

(Java Eclipse users, remember that your default port number is 8888.)

In the Python Launcher, you can also click the SDK Console button to open the console in a browser window.

Figure 2-10 shows the Datastore Viewer in the Python console. The Java Development Console has most of the same features as the Python version, but not all.

The Development Console's Datastore Viewer lets you list and inspect entities by kind, edit entities, and create new ones. You can edit the values for existing properties, but you cannot delete properties or add new ones, nor can you change the type of the value.

Figure 2-10. The Development Console's Datastore Viewer, Python version

For new entities, the console makes a guess as to which properties belong on the entity based on existing entities of that kind, and displays a form to fill in those properties. Similarly, you can only create new entities of existing kinds, and cannot create new kinds from the console.

You can use the console to inspect the application's task queues, to see tasks currently on the queue (in the local instance of the app), run them ahead of schedule, and flush them. By default, the development server drives task queues in the background. You can disable this behavior for debugging purposes. See Chapter 16.

You can test how your app receives email and XMPP messages by sending it mock messages through the console. Simply select the Inbound Mail or XMPP section of the console, then fill out a form with the message data.

Some features are exclusive to the Python development server. An "interactive console" lets you type Python code directly in the browser, execute it in the (local) server environment, and see the result. In addition to the datastore viewer, the Python console has a memcache viewer for inspecting and manipulating cache values. The Python console also makes it easy to inspect task queue and scheduled task ("cron job") configuration.

The Java development server includes a way to simulate conditions of the Capabilities API. This API lets Java apps interrogate service status programmatically, so the app can respond automatically to scheduled or unplanned maintenance outages. You can tell the development server to simulate various conditions to test your app.

The Python Interactive Console

An especially powerful feature of the Python console is the "Interactive Console." This feature lets you type arbitrary Python code directly into a web form and see the results displayed in the browser. You can use this to write ad hoc Python code to test and manipulate the datastore, memcache, and global data within the local development server.

Here's an example: run your clock application, sign in with an email address, and then set a time zone preference, such as `-8`. Now open the Python development console, then select Interactive Console. In the lefthand text box, enter the following, where `-8` is the time zone preference you used:

```
from google.appengine.ext import db
import models

q = models.UserPrefs.gql("WHERE tz_offset = -8")

for prefs in q:
    print prefs.user
```

Click the Run Program button. The code runs, and the email address you used appears in the righthand box.

Code run in the development console behaves just like application code. If you perform a datastore query that needs a custom index, the development server adds configuration for that index to the application's *index.yaml* configuration file. Datastore index configuration is discussed in Chapter 6.

Registering the Application

Before you can upload your application to App Engine and share it with the world, you must first create a developer account, then register an application ID. If you intend to use a custom domain name (instead of the free *appspot.com* domain name included with every app), you must also set up the Google Apps service for the domain. You can do all of this from the App Engine Administration Console.

To access the Administration Console, visit the following URL in your browser:

https://appengine.google.com/

Sign in using the Google account you intend to use as your developer account. If you don't already have a Google account (such as a Gmail account), you can create one using any email address.

Once you have signed in, the Console displays a list of applications you have created, if any, and a button to "Create an Application," similar to Figure 2-11. From this screen, you can create and manage multiple applications, each with its own URL, configuration, and resource limits.

When you register your first application ID, the Administration Console prompts you to verify your developer account, using an SMS message sent to your mobile phone. After you enter your mobile phone number, Google sends an SMS to your phone with a confirmation code. Enter this code to continue the registration process. You can verify

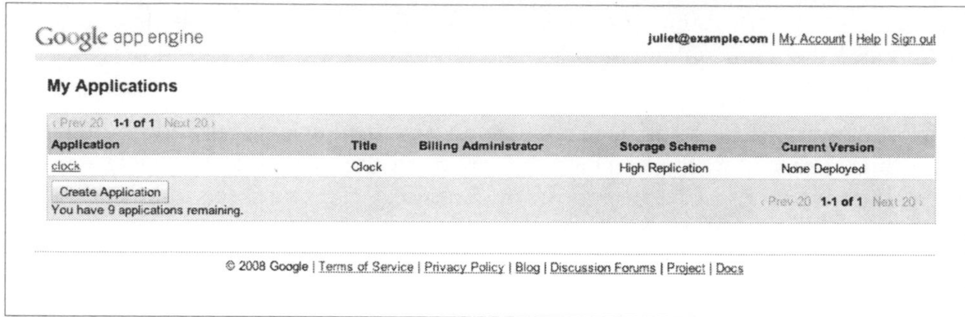

Figure 2-11. The Administration Console application list, with one app

only one account per phone number, so if you have only one mobile number (like most people), be sure to use it with the account you intend to use with App Engine.

If you don't have a mobile phone number, you can apply to Google for manual verification by filling out a web form. This process takes about a week. For information on applying for manual verification, see the official App Engine website.

You can have up to 10 active applications created by a given developer account. You can disable an application to reclaim a slot.

You have four decisions to make when creating a new application:

- The application ID
- The application title
- Authentication options
- Storage options

Of these, only the application title can be changed later.

The Application ID and Title

When you click the "Create an Application" button, the Console prompts for an application identifier. The application ID must be unique across all App Engine applications, just like an account username.

The application ID identifies your application when you interact with App Engine using the developer tools. The tools get the application ID from the application configuration file. For Python applications, you specify the app ID in the *app.yaml* file, on the `application:` line. For Java applications, you enter it in the `<application>` element of the *appengine-web.xml* file.

In the example earlier in this chapter, we chose the application ID "clock" arbitrarily. If you'd like to try uploading this application to App Engine, remember to edit the app's configuration file (*app.yaml* for Python, *appengine-web.xml* for Java) after you register the application to change the application ID to the one you chose.

The application ID is part of the domain name you can use to test the application running on App Engine. Every application gets a free domain name that looks like this:

```
app-id.appspot.com
```

The application ID is also part of email and XMPP addresses the app can use to receive incoming messages. See Chapter 14 and Chapter 15.

Because the application ID is used in the domain name, an ID can contain only lowercase letters, numbers, or hyphens, and must be shorter than 32 characters. Additionally, Google reserves every Gmail username as an application ID that only the corresponding Gmail user can register. As with usernames on most popular websites, a user-friendly application ID may be hard to come by.

When you register a new application, the Console also prompts for an "application title." This title is used to represent your application throughout the Console and the rest of the system. In particular, it is displayed to a user when the application directs the user to sign in with a Google account. Make sure the title is what you want your users to see.

Once you have registered an application, its ID cannot be changed, although you can delete the application and create a new one. You can change the title for an app at any time from the Administration Console.

Registering an application ID makes it permanently unavailable for others to register, or for you to reregister later, even if you disable or delete the app.

Setting Up a Domain Name

If you are developing a professional or commercial application, you probably want to use your own domain name instead of the *appspot.com* domain as the official location of your application. You can set up a custom domain name for your App Engine app by using Google's "software as a service," Google Apps.

Google Apps provides hosted applications for your business or organization, including email (with Gmail and POP/IMAP interfaces); calendaring (Google Calendar); chat (Google Talk); hosted word processing, spreadsheets, and presentations (Google Docs); easy-to-edit websites (Google Sites); video hosting; and so forth. You can also purchase access to third-party applications for your domain at the Google Apps Marketplace. You associate these services with your organization's domain name by mapping the domain to Google's servers in its DNS record, either by letting Google manage the DNS for the domain or by pointing subdomains to Google in your own DNS configuration. Your organization's members access the hosted services by using your domain name.

With App Engine, you can add your own applications to subdomains of your domain. Even if you do not intend to use the other Google Apps services, you can use Google Apps to associate your own domain with your App Engine application.

The website for Google Apps indicates that Standard Edition accounts are "ad-supported." This refers to ads that appear on Google products such as Gmail. It does not refer to App Engine: Google does not place ads on the pages of App Engine applications, even those using free accounts. Of course, you can put ads on your own sites, but that's your choice—and your ad revenue.

If you have not set up Google Apps for your domain already, you can do so during the application ID registration process. You can also set up Google Apps from the Administration Console after you have registered the app ID. If you haven't yet purchased a domain name, you can do so while setting up Google Apps, and you can host the domain on Google's name servers for free. To use a domain you purchased previously, follow the instructions on the website to point the domain to Google's servers.

Once you have set up Google Apps for a domain, you can access the Google Apps dashboard at a URL similar to the following:

```
http://www.google.com/a/example.com
```

To add an App Engine application as a service, click the "Add more services" link, then find Google App Engine in the list. Enter the application ID for your app, then click "Add it now." On the following settings screen, you can configure a subdomain of your domain name for the application. All web traffic to this subdomain will go to the application.

Google Apps does not support routing web traffic for the top-level domain (such as ***http://example.com/***) directly to an App Engine app. If you set up Google Apps to manage the DNS for the full domain name, an HTTP request to the top-level domain will redirect to ***http://www.example.com***, and you can assign the *www* subdomain to your App Engine app. If Google does not maintain the DNS record for your domain, you will need to set up the redirect yourself using a web server associated with the top-level domain.

By default, the subdomain *www* is assigned to Google Sites, even if you do not have the Sites app activated. To release this subdomain for use with App Engine, first enable the Sites service, then edit the settings for Sites and remove the *www* subdomain.

Google Apps and Authentication

The authentication options section of the new application form controls the behavior of the app's use of Google Accounts. By default, any Google account is allowed to sign in, and it's up to the app to decide which accounts can proceed. The alternative is to automatically restrict sign-in to accounts on the Google Apps domain. You would pick the latter option if you are using Google Apps to manage accounts on your domain, and wish to restrict access to the app to just those accounts.

Google Apps allows your organization's members (employees, contractors, volunteers) to create user accounts with email addresses that use your domain name (such as *juliet@example.com*). Members can sign in with these accounts to access services that are private to your organization, such as email or word processing. Using Apps accounts, you can restrict access to certain documents and services to members of the organization. It's like a hosted intranet that members can access from anywhere.

Similarly, you can limit access to your App Engine applications to just those users with accounts on the domain. This lets you use App Engine for internal applications such as project management or sales reporting. When an App Engine application is restricted to an organization's domain, only members of the organization can sign in to the application's Google Accounts prompt. Other Google accounts are denied access.

This authentication restriction must be set when the application is registered, in the Authentication Options section of the registration form. The default setting allows any user with a Google account to sign in to the application, leaving it up to the application to decide how to respond to each user. When the app is restricted to a Google Apps domain, only users with Google accounts on the domain can sign in.

After the application ID has been registered, the authentication options cannot be changed. If you want different authentication options for your application, you must register a new application ID.

The restriction applies only to the application's use of Google Accounts. If the application has any URLs that can be accessed without signing in to Google Accounts (such as a welcome page), those URLs will still be accessible by everyone. One of the simplest ways to restrict access to a URL is with application configuration. For example, a Python application can require sign-in for all URLs with the following in the *app.yaml* file:

```
handlers:
- url: /.*
  script: main.application
  login: required
```

A Java app can do something similar in the application's deployment descriptor (*web.xml*). See Chapter 3.

The sign-in restriction applies even when the user accesses the app, using the *appspot.com* domain. The user does not need to be accessing the app with the Apps domain for the authentication restriction to be enforced.

If you or other members of your organization want to use Google Apps accounts as developer accounts, you must access the Administration Console by using a special URL. For example, if your Apps domain is *example.com*, you would use the following URL to access the Administration Console:

```
https://appengine.google.com/a/example.com
```

You sign in to the domain's Console with your Apps account (for instance, *juliet@example.com*).

If you create an app by using a non-Apps account and restrict its authentication to the domain, you will still be able to access the Administration Console by using the non-Apps account. However, you will not be able to sign in to the app itself with that account, including when accessing URLs restricted to administrators.

Uploading the Application

In a traditional web application environment, releasing an application to the world can be a laborious process. Getting the latest software and configuration to multiple web servers and backend services in the right order and at the right time to minimize downtime and prevent breakage is often difficult and delicate. With App Engine, deployment is as simple as uploading the files with a single click or command. You can upload and test multiple versions of your application, and set any uploaded version to be the current public version.

For Python apps, you can upload an app from the Launcher, or from a command prompt. From the Launcher, select the app to deploy, then click the Deploy button. From a command prompt, run the `appcfg.py` command as follows, substituting the path to your application directory for *clock*:

```
appcfg.py update clock
```

As with `dev_appserver.py`, `clock` is just the path to the directory. If the current working directory is the *clock/* directory, you can use the relative path, a dot (`.`).

For Java apps, you can upload from Eclipse using the Google plug-in, or from a command prompt. In Eclipse, click the "Deploy to App Engine" button (the little App Engine logo) in the Eclipse toolbar. Or from a command prompt, run the `appcfg` (or `appcfg.sh`) command from the SDK's *bin/* directory as follows, using the path to your application's WAR directory for `war`:

```
appcfg update war
```

When prompted by these tools, enter your developer account's email address and password. The tools remember your credentials for subsequent runs so you don't have to enter them every time. (If your developer account uses two-step authentication, see the next section.)

The upload process determines the application ID and version number from the app configuration file—*app.yaml* for Python apps, *appengine-web.xml* for Java apps—then uploads and installs the files and configuration as the given version of the app. After you upload an application for the first time, you can access the application immediately using either the *.appspot.com* subdomain or the custom Google Apps domain you set up earlier. For example, if the application ID is `clock`, you can access the application with the following URL:

```
http://clock.appspot.com/
```

If your app is written in Python, a Python developer can download all files for an app she uploaded, including Python code. Only the developer that uploaded the app can download the files. This feature can be disabled, and once it is disabled, it cannot be reenabled. You can only do this with Python apps. See the official documentation for the `appcfg.py download_app` command.

This feature is not a substitute for proper file management practices. Make sure you are retaining copies of your application files, such as with a revision control system and regular backups.

Using Two-Step Verification

All Google accounts have an optional security feature called *two-step verification*. With this feature enabled, when you sign in to a Google web application, you are prompted for two things: your account password, and a temporary security code that Google sends to your mobile phone number via text message (or a recorded voice message) when you try to sign in. This protects your account by requiring something you know (your password) and something you have (your phone).

Two-step verification is an all-around good idea, and if you have a mobile phone, you should enable it for your Google account. To enable two-step verification, visit your Google account settings:

https://www.google.com/settings/

In the Security section, find "2-step verification." If this is "off," click Edit, then follow the prompts. The set-up process involves registering your phone number and receiving a test code.

For web applications and applications that can use browser-based sign-in (OAuth), two-step verification works as expected. When you sign in to the Google Plugin for Eclipse, for example, the plug-in opens a browser-like window to display the sign-in prompts on Google's website. The process grants Eclipse a token that it can use to interact with App Engine, without needing to know or store your Google account password. The token stays valid indefinitely: Eclipse will not prompt you again until the next time you sign out then sign back in again.

The Python command-line tool *appcfg.py/appcfg* can also use browser-based sign-in. If you provide the `--oauth2` flag, the command will attempt to open a web browser for you to sign in with your Google account and grant access to the account for the tool:

```
appcfg.py update --oauth2 clock
```

Some applications can't use, or don't yet know how to use, browser-based authentication. This includes the Python launcher, the Java `appcfg.sh` tool, and the Python `appcfg.py` tool when run without the `--oauth2` flag. With two-step authentication enabled, your regular Google account password will not work with these applications. Instead, you generate an *application-specific password*, and use it in that application where you previously used your account password.

To generate an application-specific password, go to your Google account settings, Security, find "Authorizing applications and sites," and click Edit. Enter your account password when prompted. Scroll down to "Application-specific passwords," then type a name you can use to remember what this password is for. (This name can be anything, such as "App Engine." It is only used in the list of generated passwords for when you wish to revoke it later.) Click "Generate password." Google generates the password and displays it.

You do not need to memorize this password. But you shouldn't write it down, either: it otherwise acts like an old-fashioned (one-step) password. The Python Launcher on the Mac can store this password in your OS X keychain. The command-line tools will attempt to remember this password for your current session. If any of these tools needs a password again, open your account settings in a browser, revoke the old password, then generate a new one. There is no way to retrieve a previously generated password.

You can revoke access for both kinds of applications from the "Authorizing applications and sites" screen. It's always safe to revoke access for apps you aren't currently using. You can reauthorize an application later by signing in again, either with two-step verification or with a new application-specific password.

Introducing the Administration Console

You manage your live application from your browser, using the App Engine Administration Console. You saw the Console when you registered the application, but as a reminder, you can access the Console at the following URL:

https://appengine.google.com/

If your app uses a Google Apps domain name and you are using an Apps account on the domain as your developer account, you must use the Apps address of the Administration Console:

```
https://appengine.google.com/a/example.com
```

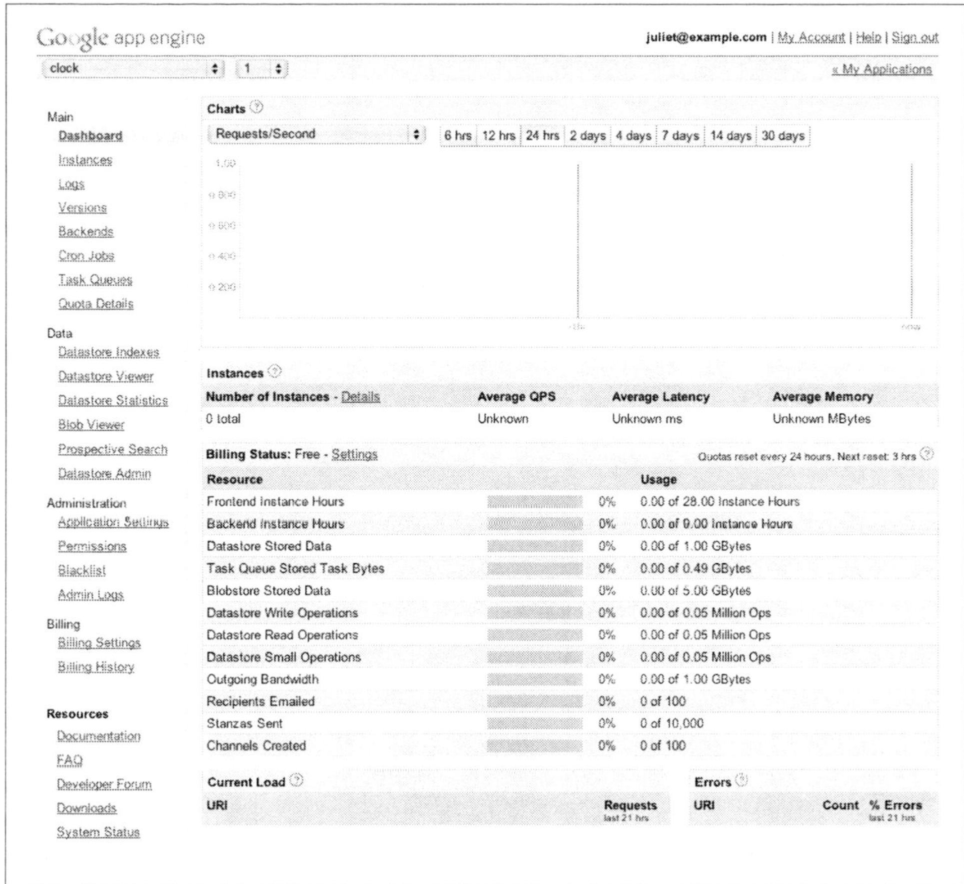

Figure 2-12. The Administration Console dashboard for a new app

Select your application (click its ID) to go to the Console for the app.

The first screen you see is the Dashboard, shown in Figure 2-12. The Dashboard summarizes the current and past status of your application, including traffic and load, resource usage, and error rates. You can view charts for the request rate, the amount of time spent on each request, error rates, bandwidth and CPU usage, and whether your application is hitting its resource limits.

If you've already tested your new application, you should see a spike in the requests-per-second chart. The scale of the chart goes up to the highest point in the chart, so the spike reaches the top of the graph even though you have only accessed the application a few times.

The Administration Console is your home base for managing your live application. From here, you can examine how the app is using resources, browse the application's request and message logs, and query the datastore and check the status of its indexes.

You can also manage multiple versions of your app, so you can test a newly uploaded version before making it the live "default" version. You can invite other people to be developers of the app, allowing them to access the Administration Console and upload new files. And when you're ready to take on large amounts of traffic, you can establish a billing account, set a daily budget, and monitor expenses.

Take a moment to browse the Console, especially the Dashboard, Logs, and Data sections. Throughout this book, we discuss how an application consumes system resources, and how you can optimize an app for speed and cost effectiveness. You will use the Administration Console to track resource consumption and diagnose problems.

CHAPTER 3

Configuring an Application

A web application is an application that responds to requests over the Web. Typically, these requests come from a user's web browser, when the user types the URL of your app or visits a link or bookmark, or when your app's JavaScript client code makes requests of its own. Requests could also come from other clients on the network, such as mobile or desktop applications, or systems accessing your app as a service.

To build an App Engine application, you write code for one or more *request handlers*, and describe to App Engine which requests go to which handlers, using configuration. The life of a request handler begins when a single request arrives, and ends when the handler has done the necessary work and calculated the response.

App Engine does all the heavy lifting of accepting incoming TCP/IP connections, reading HTTP request data, ensuring that an instance of your app is running on an application server, routing the request to an available instance, calling the appropriate request handler code in your app, and collecting the response from the handler and sending it back over the connection to the client.

The system that manages and routes requests is known generally as the *frontend*. You can configure the frontend to handle different requests in different ways. For instance, you can tell the frontend to route requests for some URLs to App Engine's static file servers instead of the application servers, for efficient delivery of your app's images, CSS, or JavaScript code. If your app takes advantage of Google Accounts for its users, you can tell the frontend to route requests from signed-in users to your application's request handlers, and to redirect all other requests to the Google Accounts sign-in screen. The frontend is also responsible for handling requests over secure connections, using HTTP over SSL (sometimes called "HTTPS," the URL scheme for such requests). Your app code only sees the request after it has been decoded, and the frontend takes care of encoding the response.

In this chapter, we take a look at App Engine's request handling architecture, and follow the path of a web request through the system. We discuss how to configure the system to handle different kinds of requests, including requests for static content, requests for the application to perform work, and requests over secure connections. We also cover

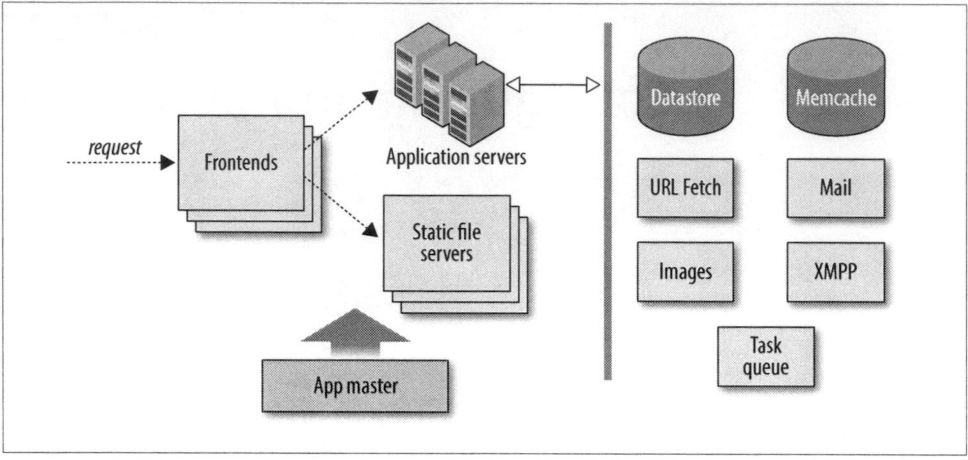

Figure 3-1. The App Engine request handling architecture

other frontend features such as custom error pages, and application features you can activate called "built-ins."

The App Engine Architecture

The architecture of App Engine—and therefore an App Engine application—can be summarized as shown in Figure 3-1. (There are some lines missing from this simplified diagram. For instance, frontends have direct access to the Blobstore. We'll take a closer look at these in later chapters.)

The first stop for an incoming request is the App Engine frontend. A load balancer, a dedicated system for distributing requests optimally across multiple machines, routes the request to one of many frontend servers. The frontend determines the app for which the request is intended from the request's domain name, either the Google Apps domain and subdomain or the *appspot.com* subdomain. It then consults the app's configuration to determine the next step.

The app's configuration describes how the frontends should treat requests based on their URL paths. A URL path may map to a static file that should be served to the client directly, such as an image or a file of JavaScript code. Or, a URL path may map to a request handler, application code that is invoked to determine the response for the request. You upload this configuration data along with the rest of your application.

If the URL path for a request does not match anything in the app's configuration, the frontends return an HTTP 404 Not Found error response to the client. By default, the frontends return a generic error response. If you want clients to receive a custom response when accessing your app (such as a friendly HTML message along with the error code), you can configure the frontend to serve a static HTML file. (In the case of

Not Found errors, you can also just map all unmatched URL paths to an application handler, and respond any way you like.)

If the URL path of the request matches the path of one of the app's static files, the frontend routes the request to the static file servers. These servers are dedicated to the task of serving static files, with network topology and caching behavior optimized for fast delivery of resources that do not change often. You tell App Engine about your app's static files in the app's configuration. When you upload the app, these files are pushed to the static file servers.

If the URL path of the request matches a pattern mapped to one of the application's request handlers, the frontend sends the request to the app servers. The app server pool starts up an instance of the application on a server, or reuses an existing instance if there is one already running. The server invokes the app by calling the request handler that corresponds with the URL path of the request, according to the app configuration.

A request handler runs in an *application instance*, a copy of your application in the memory of an application server. The instance is in a portion of the server isolated from whatever else is on the machine, set up to perform equivalently to a dedicated machine with certain hardware characteristics. The code itself executes in a *runtime environment* prepared with everything the request handler needs to inspect the request data, call services, and evaluate the app's code. There's enough to say about instances and the runtime environment that we'll give the subject its own chapter (Chapter 4).

You can configure the frontend to authenticate the user with Google Accounts. The frontend can restrict access to URL paths with several levels of authorization: all users, users who have signed in, and users who are application administrators. With a Google Apps domain, you can also set your application to allow only users on the domain to access URLs, such as for an employee-only website or school campus. The frontend checks whether the user is signed in, and redirects the user to the Google Accounts sign-in screen if needed.

The frontend takes the opportunity to tailor the response to the client. Most notably, the frontend compresses the response data, using the gzip format, if the client gives some indication that it supports compressed responses. This applies to both app responses and static file responses, and is done automatically. The frontend uses several techniques to determine when it is appropriate to compress responses, based on web standards and known browser behaviors. If you are using a custom client that does not support compressed content, simply omit the "Accept-Encoding" request header to disable the automatic gzip behavior.

The frontends, app servers, and static file servers are governed by an "app master." Among other things, the app master is responsible for deploying new versions of application software and configuration, and updating the "default" version served on an app's user-facing domain. Updates to an app propagate quickly, but are not atomic in the sense that only code from one version of an app is running at any one time. If you switch the default version to new software, all requests that started before the switch are allowed to complete using their version of the software. (An app that makes an HTTP request to itself might find itself in a situation where an older version is calling a newer version or vice versa, but you can manage that situation in your own code, if you really need to.)

Configuring a Python App

The files for a Python application include Python code for request handlers and libraries, static files, and configuration files. On your computer, these files reside in the application root directory. Static files and application code may reside in the root directory or in subdirectories. Configuration files always reside in fixed locations in the root directory.

You configure the frontend for a Python application, using a file named *app.yaml* in the application root directory. This file is in a format called YAML, a concise human-readable data format with support for nested structures like sequences and mappings.

Example 3-1 shows an example of a simple *app.yaml* file. We'll discuss these features in the following sections. For now, notice a few things about the structure of the file:

- The file is a mapping of values to names. For instance, the value `python` is associated with the name `runtime`.
- Values can be scalars (`python`, `1`), sequences of other values, or mappings of values to names. The value of `handlers` in Example 3-1 is a sequence of two values, each of which is a mapping containing two name-value pairs.
- Order is significant in sequences, but not mappings.
- YAML uses indentation to indicate scope.
- YAML supports all characters in the Unicode character set. The encoding is assumed to be UTF-8 unless the file uses a byte order mark signifying UTF-16.
- A YAML file can contain comments. All characters on a line after a # character are ignored, unless the # is in a quoted string value.

Example 3-1. An example of an app.yaml configuration file

```
application: ae-book
version: 1
runtime: python27
api_version: 1
threadsafe: true

handlers:
- url: /css
  static_dir: css

- url: /.*
  script: main.application
```

```
libraries:
- name: webapp2
  version: "2.5.1"
```

Runtime Versions

Among other things, this configuration file declares that this application (or, specifically, this version of this application) uses the Python 2.7 runtime environment. It also declares which version of the Python 2.7 runtime environment to use. Currently, there is only one version of this environment, so `api_version` is always `1`. If Google ever makes changes to the runtime environment that may be incompatible with existing applications, the changes may be released using a new version number. Your app will continue to use the version of the runtime environment specified in your configuration file, giving you a chance to test your code with the new runtime version before upgrading your live application.

You specify the name and version of the runtime environment in *app.yaml*, using the `runtime` and `api_version` elements, like so:

```
runtime: python27
api_version: 1
```

Google originally launched App Engine with a runtime environment based on Python 2.5. You can use this older environment by specifying a `runtime` of `python`. Note that this book mostly covers the newer Python 2.7 environment. You'll want to use Python 2.7 for new apps, as many recent features only work with the newer environment.

Configuring a Java App

A Java application consists of files bundled in a standard format called WAR (short for "web application archive"). The WAR standard specifies the layout of a directory structure for a Java web application, including the locations of several standard configuration files, compiled Java classes, JAR files, static files, and other auxiliary files. Some tools that manipulate WARs support compressing the directory structure into a single file similar to a JAR. App Engine's tools generally expect the WAR to be a directory on your computer's filesystem.

Java servlet applications use a file called a "deployment descriptor" to specify how the server invokes the application. This file uses an XML format, and is part of the servlet standard specification. In a WAR, the deployment descriptor is a file named *web.xml* that resides in a directory named *WEB-INF/*, which itself is in the WAR's root directory. Example 3-2 shows a very simple deployment descriptor.

Example 3-2. An example of a web.xml deployment descriptor file

```
<?xml version="1.0" encoding="utf-8"?>
<web-app xmlns="http://java.sun.com/xml/ns/javaee" version="2.5">
  <servlet>
```

```
    <servlet-name>ae-book</servlet-name>
    <servlet-class>aebook.MainServlet</servlet-class>
  </servlet>
  <servlet-mapping>
    <servlet-name>ae-book</servlet-name>
    <url-pattern>/*</url-pattern>
  </servlet-mapping>
</web-app>
```

The deployment descriptor tells the App Engine frontend most of what it needs to know, but not all. For the rest, App Engine uses a file named *appengine-web.xml*, also in the *WEB-INF/* directory and also using XML syntax. If your code editor supports XML validation, you can find the schema definition for this file in the App Engine Java SDK. Example 3-3 shows a brief example.

Example 3-3. An example of an appengine-web.xml configuration file

```
<?xml version="1.0" encoding="utf-8"?>
<appengine-web-app xmlns="http://appengine.google.com/ns/1.0">
  <application>ae-book</application>
  <version>1</version>
  <threadsafe>true</threadsafe>
</appengine-web-app>
```

The development server may add elements to this file with some default values the first time it is run.

When Google releases major new features for the Java API, the release includes a new version of the SDK with an updated *appengine-api-... .jar* file. App Engine knows which version of the API the app is expecting by examining the API JAR included in the app's WAR. The server may replace the JAR with a different but compatible implementation when the app is run.

Configuring a Java App with YAML Files

Deployment descriptors are part of the Java servlet standard, and together with App Engine's XML configuration files, they're a good choice for a typical servlet-based application, especially if you may need to port your app to another servlet container in the future. The App Engine Java SDK also supports configuring a Java app by using the YAML syntax, similar to that used by the Python SDK (described in "Configuring a Python App" on page 76, above). You might use YAML files instead of XML files if your app is written in a language other than Java that uses the JVM (such as JRuby), or to take advantage of the more convenient syntax for features like access control.

To use YAML configuration files with the Java runtime environment, create a file named *app.yaml* in your *WEB-INF/* directory. If the App Engine SDK finds this file, the development server will rewrite it as *web.xml* and *appengine-web.xml* files, overwriting any already present. The *app.yaml* file must contain values for `application` (the application ID), `version` (the application version), and `runtime` (`java` instead of `python`), and one or more `handlers`. For example:

```
application: clock
version: 1
runtime: java

handlers:
- url: /prefs
  servlet: clock.PrefsServlet
  login: required

- url: /*
  servlet: clock.ClockServlet
```

Java YAML configuration files bear only a partial resemblance to the Python configuration syntax. Some important differences:

- You do not specify a version number for the runtime environment for Java (`api_version` in Python). As when using a deployment descriptor, the runtime version is determined by the App Engine JARs in the app's WAR.
- URL patterns are not full regular expressions. Instead, they are similar to URL patterns in deployment descriptors. You can use a * wildcard at the beginning or end of a URL pattern to represent zero or more characters, and you can only use one wildcard in a pattern.
- Static file configuration does not use the same syntax as in Python. Instead, you configure static files and resources in a manner similar to *appengine-web.xml*, using top-level `static_files:` and `resource_files:` elements in the YAML file.

YAML configuration for Java supports the same access control (`login:`) and secure connection (`secure:`) attributes for servlet configuration as Python does for script handlers. Features such as inbound services, warm-up requests, Admin Console pages, and custom error pages also have app configuration similar to Python. The separate configuration files for services, such as datastore indexes and task queues, can also be specified using YAML files (e.g., *index.yaml* and *queue.yaml*) with syntax identical to that used with Python; these files reside in your *WEB-INF/* directory.

Java YAML configuration also supports features specific to deployment descriptors, including servlet parameters, servlet filters, context listeners, JSPs, system properties, and environment variables, using YAML syntax. You can even include a set of deployment descriptor XML in the *app.yaml* file by using the `web_xml` element. Features specific to *appengine-web.xml* (such as sessions) also have YAML equivalents (e.g., `sessions_enabled: true`).

We describe all of these features throughout this book, but we will not make additional asides to describe Java YAML configuration. See the official App Engine documentation for a complete description of using YAML configuration with Java.

Domain Names

Every app gets a free domain name on *appspot.com*, based on the application ID:

```
app-id.appspot.com
```

Requests for URLs that use your domain name are routed to your app by the frontend:

```
http://app-id.appspot.com/url/path...
```

You can register your own domain name (such as *example.com*) and set it up with Google Apps to point to your app. Once your domain is set up with Google Apps, you assign a subdomain of your top-level domain to point to the app. For instance, if your registered domain is *example.com* and you assign the *www* subdomain, the domain name for the app is:

```
www.example.com
```

To set up a domain name, visit the App Engine Administration Console and select your app, then select Application Settings. Scroll down to Domain Setup. If you've already registered a domain and set up Google Apps, enter your domain name and click the Add Domain... button. Otherwise, click the "Sign up for Google Apps" link to go through the sign-up process. You can sign up for Google Apps with a domain you've already registered, or you can register a new domain at that time. (Google Apps is free, but domain registration costs money.)

Google Apps does not support routing requests for the top-level domain without a subdomain. If you want users to see something when they visit *http://example.com/*, you must use your own domain name service (DNS) and web server to handle traffic to that domain name, and point subdomains to Google Apps in the DNS record. If you use the Google Apps DNS service for the domain, Google Apps will automatically redirect web requests for the bare domain to the `www` subdomain.

The `appspot.com` domain has a couple of useful features. One such feature is the ability to accept an additional domain name part:

```
anything.app-id.appspot.com
```

Requests for domain names of this form, where *anything* is any valid single domain name part (that cannot contain a dot, `.`), are routed to the application. This is useful for accepting different kinds of traffic on different domain names, such as for allowing your users to serve content from their own subdomains. Only `appspot.com` domains support the additional part. Google Apps domains do not.

You can determine which domain name was used for the request in your application code by checking the `Host` header on the request. Here's how you check this header using Python and webapp:

```
class MainHandler(webapp2.RequestHandler):
    def get(self):
        host = self.request.headers['Host']

        self.response.out.write('Host: %s' % host)
```

App IDs and Versions

Every App Engine application has an application ID that uniquely distinguishes the app from all other applications. As described in Chapter 2, you can register an ID for a new application using the Administration Console. Once you have an ID, you add it to the app's configuration so the developer tools know that the files in the app root directory belong to the app with that ID. This ID appears in the `appspot.com` domain name.

The app's configuration also includes a version identifier. Like the app ID, the version identifier is associated with the app's files when the app is uploaded. App Engine retains one set of files and frontend configuration for each distinct version identifier used during an upload. If you do not change the app version in the configuration before you upload files, the upload replaces the existing files for that version.

Each distinct version of the app is accessible at its own domain name, of the following form:

```
version-id.app-id.appspot.com
```

When you have multiple versions of an app uploaded to App Engine, you can use the Administration Console to select which version is the one you want the public to access. The Console calls this the "default" version. When a user visits your Google Apps domain (and configured subdomain), or the `appspot.com` domain without the version ID, she sees the default version.

The `appspot.com` domain containing the version ID supports an additional domain part, just like the default `appspot.com` domain:

```
anything.version-id.app-id.appspot.com
```

Unless you explicitly prevent it, anyone who knows your application ID and version identifiers can access any uploaded version of your application using the `appspot.com` URLs. You can restrict access to nondefault versions of the application by using code that checks the domain of the request and only allows authorized users to access the versioned domains. You can't restrict access to static files this way.

Another way to restrict access to nondefault versions is to use Google Accounts authorization, described later in this chapter. You can restrict access to app administrators while a version is in development, then replace the configuration to remove the restriction just before making that version the default version.

All versions of an app access the same datastore, memcache, and other services, and all versions share the same set of resources. Later on, we'll discuss other configuration files that control these backend services. These files are separate from the configuration files that control the frontend because they are not specific to each app version.

There are several ways to use app versions. For instance, you can have just one version, and always update it in place. Or you can have a "dev" version for testing and a "live" version that is always the public version, and do separate uploads for each. Some developers generate a new app version identifier for each upload based on the version numbers used by a source code revision control system.

You can have up to 10 active versions. You can delete previous versions, using the Administration Console.

Application IDs and version identifiers can contain numbers, lowercase letters, and hyphens.

App IDs and Versions in Python

For a Python app, the application ID and version identifier appear in the *app.yaml* file. The app ID is specified with the name `application`. The version ID is specified as `version`.

Here is an example of *app.yaml* using `dev` as the version identifier:

```
application: ae-book
version: dev
```

This would be accessible using this domain name:

```
http://dev.ae-book.appspot.com
```

App IDs and Versions in Java

The app ID and version identifier of a Java app appear in the *appengine-web.xml* file. The app ID is specified with the XML element `<application>`, and the version identifier is specified with `<version>`. For example:

```
<?xml version="1.0" encoding="utf-8"?>
<appengine-web-app xmlns="http://appengine.google.com/ns/1.0">
  <application>ae-book</application>
  <version>dev</version>
</appengine-web-app>
```

As in the Python example, this version of this app would be accessible using this domain name:

```
http://dev.ae-book.appspot.com
```

Multithreading

The Python 2.7 and Java runtime environments support handling multiple requests concurrently within each instance. This is a significant way to make the most of your instances, and is recommended. However, your code must be written with the knowledge that it will be run concurrently, and take the appropriate precautions with shared data. You must declare whether your code is "threadsafe" in your application configuration.

In Python, you specify the `threadsafe` value in *app.yaml*, either `true` or `false`:

```
threadsafe: true
```

In Java, you specify the `<threadsafe>` element in *appengine-web.xml*:

```
<threadsafe>true</threadsafe>
```

Request Handlers

The app configuration tells the frontend what to do with each request, routing it to either the application servers or the static file servers. The destination is determined by the URL path of the request. For instance, an app might send all requests whose URL paths start with `/images/` to the static file server, and all requests for the site's home page (the path /) to the app servers. The configuration specifies a list of patterns that match URL paths, with instructions for each pattern.

For requests intended for the app servers, the configuration also specifies the request handler responsible for specific URL paths. A request handler is an entry point into the application code. In Python, a request handler is a script of Python code. In Java, a request handler is a servlet class. Each runtime environment has its own interface for invoking the application.

The URL `/form` is reserved by App Engine and cannot be used by the app. The explanation for this is historical and internal to App Engine, and unfortunately this is easy to stumble upon by accident. This URL will always return a 404 Not Found error.

All URL paths under `/_ah/` are reserved for use by App Engine libraries and tools.

Request Handlers in Python

All URL paths for Python apps are described in the *app.yaml* file, using the `handlers` element. The value of this element is a sequence of mappings, where each item includes a pattern that matches a set of URL paths and instructions on how to handle requests for those paths. Here is an example with four URL patterns:

```
handlers:
- url: /profile/.*
  script: userprofile.application

- url: /css
  static_dir: css

- url: /info/(.*\.xml)
```

```
  static_files: datafiles/\1
  upload: datafiles/.*\.xml

- url: /.*
  script: main.application
```

The `url` element in a handler description is a regular expression that matches URL paths. Every path begins with a forward slash (/), so a pattern can match the beginning of a path by also starting with this character. This URL pattern matches all paths:

```
url: /.*
```

If you are new to regular expressions, here is the briefest of tutorials: the `.` character matches any single character, and the * character says the previous symbol, in this case any character, can occur zero or more times. There are several other characters with special status in regular expressions. All other characters, like `/`, match literally. So this pattern matches any URL that begins with a / followed by zero or more of any character.

If a special character is preceded by a backslash (\), it is treated as a literal character in the pattern. Here is a pattern that matches the exact path `/home.html`:

```
- url: /home\.html
```

See the Python documentation for the `re` module for an excellent introduction to regular expressions. The actual regular expression engine used for URL patterns is not Python's, but it's similar.

App Engine attempts to match the URL path of a request to each handler pattern in the order the handlers appear in the configuration file. The first pattern that matches determines the handler to use. If you use the catchall pattern `/.*`, make sure it's the last one in the list, since a later pattern will never match.

To map a URL path pattern to application code, you provide a `script` element. The value is the Python import path (with dots) to a global variable containing a WSGI application instance. The application root directory is in the lookup path, so in the example above, `main.application` could refer to the `application` variable in a Python source file named *main.py*:

```
import webapp2

class MainPage(webapp2.RequestHandler):
    def get(self):
        # ...

application = webapp2.WSGIApplication([('/', MainPage)], debug=True)
```

The `script` value can also be a filesystem path (with slashes) from the application root directory to a Python source file whose name ends in *.py*. The script must conform to the Common Gateway Interface standard, which describes how the request data is available on the standard input stream and environment variables, and how the code should emit the response headers and body to the standard output stream. This kind of script is supported for backward compatibility with components designed for the older Python 2.5 App Engine runtime environment, which didn't have the option of a WSGI import path.

If the frontend gets a request whose path matches a script handler, it routes the request to an application server to invoke the script and produce the response.

In the previous example, the following handler definition routes all URL paths that begin with `/profile/` to the `application` defined in a source file named *userprofile.py*:

```
- url: /profile/.*
  script: userprofile.application
```

The URL pattern can use regular expression groups to determine other values, such as the script path. A group is a portion of a regular expression inside parentheses, and the group's value is the portion of the request URL that matches the characters within (not including the parentheses). Groups are numbered starting with `1` from left to right in the pattern. You can insert the value of a matched group into a `script` path or other values with a backslash followed by the group number (`\1`). For example:

```
- url: /project/(.*?)/home
  script: apps.project_code.\1.app
```

With this pattern, a request for `/project/registration/home` would be handled by the WSGI application at `apps.project_code.registration.app`.

Request Handlers in Java

A Java web application maps URL patterns to servlets in the deployment descriptor (*web.xml*). You set up a servlet in two steps: the servlet declaration, and the servlet mapping.

The `<servlet>` element declares a servlet. It includes a `<servlet-name>`, a name for the purposes of referring to the servlet elsewhere in the file, and the `<servlet-class>`, the name of the class that implements the servlet. Here's a simple example:

```
<servlet>
  <servlet-name>ae-book</servlet-name>
  <servlet-class>aebook.MainServlet</servlet-class>
</servlet>
```

The servlet declaration can also define initialization parameters for the servlet. This is useful if you want to use the same servlet class in multiple servlet declarations, with different parameters for each one. For example:

```
<servlet>
  <servlet-name>ae-book</servlet-name>
  <servlet-class>aebook.MainServlet</servlet-class>
  <init-param>
    <param-name>colorscheme</param-name>
    <param-value>monochrome</param-value>
  </init-param>
  <init-param>
    <param-name>background</param-name>
```

```
    <param-value>dark</param-value>
  </init-param>
</servlet>
```

To map a servlet to a URL path pattern, you use the `<servlet-mapping>` element. A mapping includes the `<servlet-name>` that matches a servlet declaration, and a `<url-pattern>`:

```
<servlet-mapping>
  <servlet-name>ae-book</servlet-name>
  <url-mapping>/home/*</url-mapping>
</servlet-mapping>
```

The URL pattern matches the URL path. It can use a * character at the beginning or end of the pattern to represent zero or more of any character. Note that this wildcard can only appear at the beginning or end of the pattern, and you can only use one wildcard per pattern.

The order in which URL mappings appear is not significant. The "most specific" matching pattern wins, determined by the number of nonwildcard characters in the pattern. The pattern `/*` matches all URLs, but will only match if none of the other patterns in the deployment descriptor match the URL.

JSPs are supported, as servlets invoked from other servlets, as servlets named explicitly in the descriptor, and as standalone servlets mapped to URL paths that resemble their file paths. If a request path does not match an explicit URL pattern in the deployment descriptor but does match the path to a *.jsp* file from the root of the WAR (and the *.jsp* file is not under *WEB-INF/*), the JSP servlet will be compiled and invoked.

Static Files and Resource Files

Most web applications have a set of files that are served verbatim to all users, and do not change as the application is used. These can be media assets like images used for site decoration, CSS stylesheets that describe how the site should be drawn to the screen, JavaScript code to be downloaded and executed by a web browser, or HTML for full pages with no dynamic content. To speed up the delivery of these files and improve page rendering time, App Engine uses dedicated servers for static content. Using dedicated servers also means the app servers don't have to spend resources on requests for static files.

Both the deployment process and the frontend must be told which of the application's files are static files. The deployment process delivers static files to the dedicated servers. The frontend remembers which URL paths refer to static files, so it can route requests for those paths to the appropriate servers.

The static file configuration can also include a recommendation for a cache expiration interval. App Engine returns the cache instructions to the client in the HTTP header along with the file. If the client chooses to heed the recommendation (and most web browsers do), it will retain the file for up to that amount of time, and use its local copy instead of asking for it again. This reduces the amount of bandwidth used, but at the expense of clients retaining old copies of files that may have changed.

To save space and reduce the amount of data involved when setting up new app instances, static files are not pushed to the application servers. This means application code cannot access the contents of static files by using the filesystem.

The files that do get pushed to the application servers are known as "resource files." These can include app-specific configuration files, web page templates, or other static data that is read by the app but not served directly to clients. Application code can access these files by reading them from the filesystem. The code itself is also accessible this way.

There are ways to specify that a file is both a resource file and a static file, depending on which runtime environment you are using.

Static Files in Python

We've seen how request handlers defined in the *app.yaml* file can direct requests to scripts that run on the app servers. Handler definitions can also direct requests to the static file servers.

There are two ways to specify static file handlers. The easiest is to declare a directory of files as static, and map the entire directory to a URL path. You do this with the `static_dir` element, as follows:

```
handlers:
- url: /images
  static_dir: myimgs
```

This says that all the files in the directory *myimgs/* are static files, and the URL path for each of these files is `/images/` followed by the directory path and filename of the file. If the app has a file at the path *myimgs/people/frank.jpg*, App Engine pushes this file to the static file servers, and serves it whenever someone requests the URL path `/images/people/frank.jpg`.

Notice that with `static_dir` handlers, the `url` pattern does not include a regular expression to match the subpath or filename. The subpath is implied: whatever appears in the URL path after the URL pattern becomes the subpath to the file in the directory.

The other way to specify static files is with the `static_files` element. With `static_files`, you use a full regular expression for the `url`. The URL pattern can use regular expression groups to match pieces of the path, then use those matched pieces in the path to the file. The following is equivalent to the `static_dir` handler above:

```
- url: /images/(.*)
  static_files: myimgs/\1
  upload: myimgs/.*
```

The parentheses in the regular expression identify which characters are members of the group. The `\1` in the file path is replaced with the contents of the group when looking for the file. You can have multiple groups in a pattern, and refer to each group by number in the file path. Groups are numbered in the order they appear in the pattern from left to right, where `\1` is the leftmost pattern, `\2` is the next, and so on.

When using `static_files`, you must also specify an `upload` element. This is a regular expression that matches paths to files in the application directory on your computer. App Engine needs this pattern to know which files to upload as static files, since it cannot determine this from the `static_files` pattern alone (as it can with `static_dir`).

While developing a Python app, you keep the app's static files in the application directory along with the code and configuration files. When you upload the app, App Engine determines which files are static files from the handler definitions in *app.yaml*. Files mentioned in static file handler definitions are pushed to the static file servers. All other files in the application directory are considered resource files, and are pushed to the application servers. As such, static files are not accessible to the application code via the filesystem.

The Python SDK treats every file as either a resource file or a static file. If you have a file that you want treated as both a resource file (available to the app via the filesystem) and a static file (served verbatim from the static file servers), you can create a symbolic link in the project directory to make the file appear twice to the deployment tool under two separate names. The file will be uploaded twice, and count as two files toward the file count limit.

MIME types

When the data of an HTTP response is of a particular type, such as a JPEG image, and the web server knows the type of the data, the server can tell the client the type of the data by using an HTTP header in the response. The type can be any from a long list of standard type names, known as MIME types. If the server doesn't say what the type of the data is, the client has to guess, and may guess incorrectly.

By default, for static files, App Engine makes its own guess of the file type based on the last few characters of the filename (such as *.jpeg*). If the filename does not end in one of several known extensions, App Engine serves the file as the MIME type `application/octet-stream`, a generic type most web browsers treat as generic binary data.

If this is not sufficient, you can specify the MIME type of a set of static files by using the `mime_type` element in the static file handler configuration. For example:

```
- url: docs/(.*)\.ps
  static_files: psoutput/\1.dat
  upload: psoutput/.*\.dat
  mime_type: application/postscript
```

This says that the application has a set of datafiles in a directory named *psoutput/* whose filenames end in *.dat*, and these should be served using URL paths that consist of docs/, followed by the filename with the *.dat* replaced with *.ps*. When App Engine serves one of these files, it declares that the file is a PostScript document.

You can also specify mime_type with a static_dir handler. All files in the directory are served with the declared type.

Cache expiration

It's common for a static file to be used on multiple web pages of a site. Since static files seldom change, it would be wasteful for a web browser to download the file every time the user visits a page. Instead, browsers can retain static files in a cache on the user's hard drive, and reuse the files when they are needed.

To do this, the browser needs to know how long it can safely retain the file. The server can suggest a maximum cache expiration in the HTTP response. You can configure the cache expiration period App Engine suggests to the client.

To set a default cache expiration period for all static files for an app, you specify a default_expiration value. This value applies to all static file handlers, and belongs at the top level of the *app.yaml* file, like so:

```
application: ae-book
version: 1
runtime: python
api_version: 1

default_expiration: "5d 12h"

handlers:
  # ...
```

The value is a string that specifies a number of days, hours, minutes, and seconds. As shown here, each number is followed by a unit (d, h, m, or s), and values are separated by spaces.

You can also specify an expiration value for static_dir and static_files handlers individually, using an expiration element in the handler definition. This value overrides the default_expiration value, if any. For example:

```
handlers:
- url: /docs/latest
  static_dir: /docs
  expiration: "12h"
```

If the configuration does not suggest a cache expiration period for a set of static files, App Engine does not give an expiration period when serving the files. Browsers will use their own caching behavior in this case, and may not cache the files at all.

Sometimes you want a static file to be cached in the browser as long as possible, but then replaced immediately when the static file changes. A common technique is to add a version number for the file to the URL, then use a new version number from the app's

HTML when the file changes. The browser sees a new URL, assumes it is a new resource, and fetches the new version.

You can put the version number of the resource in a fake URL parameter, such as `/js/code.js?v=19`, which gets ignored by the static file server. Alternatively, in Python, you can use regular expression matching to match all versions of the URL and route them to the same file in the static file server, like so:

```
- handlers:
  url: /js/(.*)/code.js
  static_files: js/code.js
  expiration: "90d"
```

This handler serves the static file `js/code.js` for all URLs such as `/js/v19/code.js`, using a cache expiration of 90 days.

If you'd like browsers to reload a static file resource automatically every time you launch a new major version of the app, you can use the multiversion URL handler just discussed, then use the `CURRENT_VERSION_ID` environment variable as the "version" in the static file URLs:

```
self.response.out('<script src="/js/' +
                  os.environ['CURRENT_VERSION_ID'] +
                  '/code.js" />')
```

Static Files in Java

As we saw earlier, the WAR directory structure for a Java web application keeps all application code, JARs, and configuration in a subdirectory named *WEB-INF/*. Typically, files outside of *WEB-INF/* represent resources that the user can access directly, including static files and JSPs. The URL paths to these resources are equivalent to the paths to these files within the WAR.

Say an app's WAR has the following files:

```
main.jsp
forum/home.jsp
images/logo.png
images/cancelbutton.png
images/okbutton.png
terms.html
WEB-INF/classes/com/example/Forum.class
WEB-INF/classes/com/example/MainServlet.class
WEB-INF/classes/com/example/Message.class
WEB-INF/classes/com/example/UserPrefs.class
WEB-INF/lib/appengine-api.jar
```

This app has four static files: three PNG images and an HTML file named *terms.html*. When the app is uploaded, these four files are pushed to the static file servers. The frontends know to route requests for URL paths equivalent to these file paths (such as `/images/logo.png`) to the static file servers.

The two *.jsp* files are assumed to be JSPs, and are compiled to servlet classes and mapped to the URL paths equivalent to their file paths. Since these are application code, they are handled by the application servers. The JSP source files themselves are not pushed to the static file servers.

By default, *all* files in the WAR are pushed to the application servers, and are accessible by the application code via the filesystem. This includes the files that are identified as static files and pushed to the static file servers. In other words, all files are considered resource files, and all files except for JSPs and the *WEB-INF/* directory are considered static files.

You can change which files are considered resource files and which are considered static files by using the *appengine-web.xml* file, with the `<resource-files>` and `<static-files>` elements, respectively. These elements can contain an `<include>` element and an `<exclude>` element that modify the default behavior of including all files. For example:

```
<resource-files>
  <exclude path="/images/**" />
</resource-files>
```

This example excludes the contents of the *images/* directory and all subdirectories from the set of resource files. This reduces the amount of data that is pushed to the application servers when starting up a new application instance, at the expense of not being able to access those files from within the application (probably fine for site images). The ** pattern matches any number of characters in file and directory names, including subdirectories.

Another example:

```
<static-files>
  <exclude path="/**.xml" />
  <include path="/sitemap.xml" />
</static-files>
```

This excludes all files with names ending in *.xml* from the set of static files, except for *sitemap.xml*. Perhaps the XML files are intended for the application's eyes only, but we want to make sure search engines can see the site map.

Files in the *WEB-INF/* directory are always considered resource files. They cannot be included as static files or excluded from the set of resource files.

Browsers rely on the web server to tell them the type of the file being served. The static file server determines the MIME content type of a file from the extension on the filename. For instance, a file whose name ends in *.jpeg* is served with a MIME type of `image/jpeg`. The server has a built-in set of mappings from filename extensions to MIME types. You can specify additional mappings using `<mime-mapping>` elements in the deployment descriptor (*web.xml*). See a *web.xml* reference or the App Engine documentation for more information.

Browsers also need to know if a file is safe to cache, and for how long. The static file server can suggest a cache expiration duration when it serves a file (although a browser is not obligated to honor it). You can specify that a set of static files should be cached for a particular duration by including an `expiration` attribute on the `<include>` element in *appengine-web.xml*:

```
<static-files>
  <include path="images/**" expiration="30d" />
</static-files>
```

The value of `expiration` is a duration specified as numbers and units, where `d` is days, `h` is hours, `m` is minutes, and `s` is seconds. You can add values of multiple units by specifying them separated with spaces: `3d 12h`.

Secure Connections

When a client requests and retrieves a web page over an HTTP connection, every aspect of the interaction is transmitted over the network in its final intended form, including the URL path, request parameters, uploaded data, and the complete content of the server's response. For web pages, this usually means human-readable text is flying across the wire, or through the air if the user is using a wireless connection. Anyone else privy to the network traffic can capture and analyze this data, and possibly glean sensitive information about the user and the service.

Websites that deal in sensitive information, such as banks and online retailers, can use a secure alternative for web traffic. With servers that support it, the client can make an HTTPS connection (HTTP over the Secure Socket Layer, or SSL). All data sent in either direction over the connection is encrypted by the sender and decrypted by the recipient, so only the participants can understand what is being transmitted even if the encrypted messages are intercepted. Web browsers usually have an indicator that tells the user when a connection is secure.

App Engine supports secure connections for incoming web requests. By default, App Engine accepts HTTPS connections for all URLs, and otherwise treats them like HTTP requests. You can configure the frontend to reject or redirect HTTP or HTTPS requests for some or all URL paths, such as to ensure that all requests not using a secure connection are redirected to their HTTPS equivalents. The application code itself doesn't need to know the difference between a secure connection and a standard connection: it just consumes the decrypted request and provides a response that is encrypted by App Engine.

All URL paths can be configured to use secure connections, including those mapped to application code and those mapped to static files. The frontend takes care of the secure connection on behalf of the app servers and static file servers.

App Engine only supports secure connections over TCP port 443, the standard port used by browsers for `https://` URLs. Similarly, App Engine only supports standard connections over port 80. The App Engine frontend returns an error for URLs that specify a port other than the standard port for the given connection method.

The development server does not support secure connections, and ignores the security settings in the configuration. You can test these URLs during development by using the nonsecure equivalent URLs.

Because HTTPS uses the domain name to validate the secure connection, requests to versioned `appspot.com` URLs, such as `https://3.ae-book.appspot.com/`, will display a security warning in the browser saying that the domain does not match the security certificate. To prevent this, App Engine has a trick up its sleeve: replace the dots (`.`) between the version and app IDs with `-dot-` (that's hyphen, the word "dot," and another hyphen), like this:

```
https://3-dot-ae-book.appspot.com/
```

A request to this domain uses the certificate for `appspot.com`, and avoids the security warning.

Secure Connections and Custom Domains

App Engine supports secure connections to custom domains. You can choose between two implementations: Server Name Indication (SNI) and Virtual IP addressing (VIP). Each costs additional money. SNI is less expensive, but is only supported by modern browsers. VIP is more expensive, but is supported by all clients that support secure connections.

Both methods specify how the server proves to the client that it is who it says it is, and not an impostor. Site identification is based on the domain name of the site and the security certificate returned by the App Engine frontend. The difference between SNI and VIP is based on when in the connection process the server identifies the app being accessed, so it can send the appropriate certificate. With VIP, the app has its own IP address, and the server knows which app is being accessed as soon as the connection is made. SNI relies on the ability of the client and server to communicate the domain name of the request after the initial connection is made.

See the official App Engine website for pricing and setup information for secure connections with SNI and VIP. SSL support for `appspot.com` domains is provided free of charge.

Secure Connections in Python

To configure secure connections for a URL handler in a Python application, add a `secure` element to the handler's properties in the *app.yaml* file:

```
handler:
- url: /profile/.*
  script: userprofile.py
  secure: always
```

The value of the `secure` element can be `always`, `never`, or `optional`:

- `always` says that requests to this URL path should always use a secure connection. If a user attempts to request the URL path over a nonsecure connection, the App Engine frontend issues an HTTP redirect code telling it to try again using a secure HTTP connection. Browsers follow this redirect automatically.
- `never` says that requests to this URL path should never use a secure connection, and requests for an HTTPS URL should be redirected to the HTTP equivalent. Note that browsers often display a warning when a user follows a link from a secure page to a nonsecure page.
- `optional` allows either connection method for the URL path, without redirects. The app can use the `HTTPS` environment variable to determine which method was used for the request, and produce a custom response.

If you don't specify a `secure` element for a URL path, the default is `optional`.

Secure Connections in Java

With a Java application, you can use the deployment descriptor to require secure connections for certain URL paths. In the *web.xml* file, you declare a security constraint for a URL path or set of URL paths as follows:

```
<security-constraint>
  <web-resource-collection>
    <web-resource-name>home</web-resource-name>
    <url-pattern>/home/*</url-pattern>
  </web-resource-collection>
  <user-data-constraint>
    <transport-guarantee>CONFIDENTIAL</transport-guarantee>
  </user-data-constraint>
</security-constraint>
```

A security constraint, indicated by the `<security-constraint>` element, describes the minimum security requirements a request must meet to access a resource. You identify the resource by using a URL pattern in a `<web-resource-collection>` element containing a `<url-pattern>` element. (According to the spec, `<web-resource-collection>` must have a `<web-resource-name>`, although this name is not used for anything.) As with URL patterns in servlet mappings, the URL pattern can be a single URL path, or a partial URL path with a * wildcard at the beginning or at the end.

You specify a security constraint requiring a secure connection with a `<user-data-constraint>` element containing a `<transport-guarantee>` element, itself containing the value `CONFIDENTIAL`. (The transport guarantee `INTEGRAL` is also supported as a synonym for `CONFIDENTIAL`.) App Engine does not support other transport guarantee constraints.

If you do not want users accessing your app with HTTPS, you can disable secure connections by adding this to your *appengine-web.xml* configuration file:

```
<ssl-enabled>false</ssl-enabled>
```

Using the deployment descriptor and *appengine-web.xml*, you can only enable or disable SSL for the entire application. The deployment descriptor standard does not have a concept of accepting secure connections for some URL paths and not others. You can configure SSL for specific URL paths using YAML configuration files with the Java runtime environment. See "Configuring a Java App with YAML Files" on page 78.

Authorization with Google Accounts

Back in Chapter 2, we discussed how an App Engine application can integrate with Google Accounts to identify and authenticate users. We saw how an app can use library calls to check whether the user making a request is signed in, access the user's email address, and calculate the sign-in and sign-out URLs of the Google Accounts system. With this API, application code can perform fine-grained access control and customize displays.

Another way to do access control is to leave it to the frontend. With just a little configuration, you can instruct the frontend to protect access to specific URL handlers such that only signed-in users can request them. If a user who is not signed in requests such a URL, the frontend redirects the user to the Google Accounts sign-in and registration screen. Upon successfully signing in or registering a new account, the user is redirected back to the URL.

You can also tell the frontend that only the registered developers of the application can access certain URL handlers. This makes it easy to build administrator-only sections of your website, with no need for code that confirms the user is an administrator. You can manage which accounts have developer status in the Administration Console, in the "Developers" section. If you revoke an account's developer status, that user is no longer able to access administrator-only resources, effective immediately.

Later on, we will discuss App Engine services that call your application in response to events. For example, the scheduled tasks service (the "cron" service) can be configured to trigger a request to a URL at certain times of the day. Typically, you want to restrict access to these URLs so not just anybody can call them. For the purposes of access control enforced by the frontend, these services act as app administrators, so restricting these URLs to administrators effectively locks out meddling outsiders while allowing the services to call the app.

If your app runs on a Google Apps domain for the purposes of serving your organization's members, you can set an access policy for the app such that only Google Apps accounts on the domain can sign in to the app. You set this policy when you register the application ID; it cannot be changed after the app ID has been registered.

This coarse-grained access control is easy to set up in the frontend configuration. And unlike access control in the application code, frontend authentication can restrict access to static files as well as application request handlers.

Authorization in Python

For a Python app, you establish frontend access control for a URL handler with the `login` element in *app.yaml*, like so:

```
handlers:
- url: /myaccount/.*
  script: account.py
  login: required
```

The `login` element has two possible values: `required` and `admin`.

If `login` is `required`, then the user must be signed in to access URLs for this handler. If the user is not signed in, the frontend returns an HTTP redirect code to send the user to the Google Accounts sign-in and registration form.

If `login` is `admin`, then the user must be signed in *and* must be a registered developer for the application.

If no `login` is provided, the default policy is to allow anyone to access the resource, whether or not the client represents a signed-in user, and whether or not the app is set to use a members-only access policy.

You can use the `login` element with both script handlers and static file handlers.

Authorization in Java

For Java, you establish a frontend access control policy, using a security constraint in the deployment descriptor. We introduced security constraints earlier when we discussed secure connections. Authentication constraints are similar: they specify the minimum level of a condition required to access a resource.

Here's what an authentication constraint looks like in *web.xml*:

```
<security-constraint>
  <web-resource-collection>
    <web-resource-name>myaccount</web-resource-name>
    <url-pattern>/myaccount/*</url-pattern>
  </web-resource-collection>
  <auth-constraint>
    <role-name>*</role-name>
  </auth-constraint>
</security-constraint>
```

As before, the security constraint identifies a resource with a URL pattern, then specifies the constraint to apply. An `<auth-constraint>` element contains a `<role-name>` element that specifies the minimum level of authentication.

<role-name> can be one of two values: * (a single asterisk) or admin. If the role name is *, then any user that has signed in can access the resource. If the user is not signed in, the frontend sends an HTTP redirect code with the Google Accounts sign-in and registration page as the destination. If the role name is admin, then only a user who is both signed in and a registered developer for the application can access the resource.

If a URL does not have an authentication constraint, then anyone can access the URL, whether or not the client represents a signed-in user, and whether or not the app is set to use a members-only access policy.

Environment Variables

You can use app configuration to specify a list of environment variables to be set prior to calling any request handlers. This is useful to control components that depend on environment variables, without having to resort to hacks in your code to set them.

In Python, you set env_variables in *app.yaml* to a mapping value:

```
env_variables:
  DJANGO_SETTINGS_MODULE: 'gnero.prod.settings'
```

In Java, you can set both environment variables and system properties in *appengine-web.xml*. You set environment variables with a <env-variables> element containing one or more <env-var> elements, each with a name and a value. You set system properties with a <system-properties> element containing one or more <property> elements. Like so:

```
<system-properties>
  <property name="com.gnero.new-player-strength" value="1000" />
  <property name="com.gnero.beta-shield" value="true" />
</system-properties>

<env-variables>
  <env-var name="ZOMBIE_APOCALYPSE" value="false" />
</env-variables>
```

Inbound Services

Some App Engine services call an application's request handlers in response to external events. For example, the Mail service can call a request handler at a fixed URL when it receives an email message at an email address associated with the app. This is a common design theme in App Engine: all application code is in the form of request handlers, and services that need the app to respond to an event invoke request handlers to do it.

Each service capable of creating inbound traffic must be enabled in app configuration, to confirm that the app is expecting traffic from those services on the corresponding URL paths. For a Python app, you enable these services with the inbound_services element in *app.yaml*:

```
inbound_services:
- mail
- warmup
```

For a Java app, you enable inbound services with the `<inbound-services>` element in *appengine-web.xml*:

```
<inbound-services>
  <service>mail</service>
  <service>warmup</service>
</inbound-services>
```

Table 3-1 lists the services that can be enabled this way, and where to find more information about each service.

Table 3-1. Services that create in-bound traffic for an app, which must be enabled in service configuration

Service	Description	Name	Handler URLs
Channel Presence	Receive channel connection notifications.	`channel_presence`	`/_ah/channel/.*`
Mail	Receive email at a set of addresses. See Chapter 14.	`mail`	`/_ah/mail/.*`
XMPP Messages	Receive XMPP chat messages. For all XMPP services, see Chapter 15.	`xmpp_message`	`/_ah/xmpp/message/chat/`
XMPP Presence	Receive XMPP presence notifications.	`xmpp_presence`	`/_ah/xmpp/presence/.*`
XMPP Subscribe	Receive XMPP subscription notifications.	`xmpp_subscribe`	`/_ah/xmpp/subscription/.*`
XMPP Error	Receive XMPP error messages.	`xmpp_error`	`/_ah/xmpp/error/`
Warm-up Requests	Initialize an instance, with warm-up requests enabled. See "Warm-up Requests" on page 123.	`warmup`	`/_ah/warmup`

Custom Error Responses

When your application serves an status code that represents an error (such as 403 Forbidden or 500 Internal Server Error) in a response to a browser, it can also include an HTML page in the body of the response. The browser typically shows this HTML to the user if the browser expected to render a full page for the request. Serving an error page can help prevent the user from being disoriented by a generic error message—or no message at all.

There are cases when an error condition occurs before App Engine can invoke your application code, and must return an error response. For example, if none of the request handler mappings in the app's configuration match the request URL, App Engine has no request handler to call and must return a 404 Not Found message. By default, App Engine adds its own generic HTML page to its error responses.

You can configure custom error content to be used instead of App Engine's error page. You provide the response body in a file included with your app, and mention the file in your application configuration.

In Python, add an `error_handlers` element to your *app.yaml*. Its value is a list of mappings, one per error file:

```
error_handlers:
- file: error.html
- error_code: over_quota
  file: busy_error.html
- error_code: dos_api_denial
  file: dos_denial.txt
  mime_type: text/plain
```

In Java, add a `<static-error-handler>` element to your *appengine-web.xml*. The element contains a `<handler>` element for each error file:

```
<static-error-handlers>
  <handler file="error.html" />
  <handler error-code="over_quota" file="busy_error.html" />
  <handler error-code="dos_api_denial" file="dos_denial.txt" mime-type="text/plain" />
</static-error-handlers>
```

The `file` value specifies the path from the application root directory to the error file. The optional `mime_type` (or `mime-type`) specifies the MIME content type for the file, which defaults to `text/html`.

The `error_code` (or `error-code`) value associates the error file with a specific error condition. If omitted, the file is associated with every error condition that doesn't have a specific error file of its own. Error codes include the following:

- `over_quota`: the request cannot be fulfilled because the app has temporarily exceeded a resource quota or limit.
- `dos_api_denial`: the origin of the request is blocked by the app's denial of service protection configuration. See the App Engine documentation for more information about this feature.
- `timeout`: the request handler did not return a response before the request deadline.

Be careful not to map your custom error files to static file handlers elsewhere in your application configuration. They must be application files.

Administration Console Custom Pages

As an application administrator, you're likely to spend a lot of time in the Administration Console. You're also likely to build your own administrative functionality into your app, for performing special maintenance tasks or datastore inspections. You can add your own administration pages to the Administration Console interface with application configuration. Links to your administrative pages appear in the Administrative Console sidebar. When you click a link, the page is rendered in an iframe, with the Console header, sidebar, and footer around it.

In Python, you use the `admin_console` element in *app.yaml*. This element value is a mapping to leave room for future Administration Console configuration; for now, `pages` is the only key. The value of `pages` is a list of your administration pages, each with a `name` and a `url`, like so:

```
admin_console:
  pages:
  - name: Title
    url: /url
```

In Java, you use the `<admin-console>` element in *appengine-web.xml*, containing one or more `<page>` elements. Each `<page>` has a `name` attribute and a `url` attribute:

```
  <admin-console>
    <page name="Title" url="/url" />
  </admin-console>
```

You are responsible for providing the administration features themselves, at request handlers mapped to their URLs. Don't forget to restrict access to these URLs to administrators only, such as with authorization configuration; see "Authorization with Google Accounts" on page 95.

Because administrative pages are configured in *app.yaml* or *appengine-web.xml*, they are specific to the application version described in the file. The sidebar links for an app version only appear in the Console when the app version is selected in the Console's version drop-down menu. Naturally, the link will render the administrative page from the corresponding version of the app, even if that version is not the default.

More Python Features

To complete this discussion of configuring Python applications, we must mention several additional features specific to *app.yaml* and the Python runtime environment: using Python libraries, using built-in features with request handlers, and including app configuration from other files.

Python Libraries

On your own computer, Python programs run in an environment with access to many libraries of modules. Some of these modules—quite a few, actually—come with Python itself, in the Python standard library. Others you may have installed separately, such as with `pip install` or `easy_install`. Perhaps you use `virtualenv` to create multiple isolated Python environments, each with its own set of available libraries. A Python program can import any module within its environment, and a module must be available in this environment (or elsewhere on the Python library load path) to be importable.

On App Engine, a Python app also runs in an environment with access to libraries. This environment includes a slightly modified version of the Python 2.7 standard library. (The modifications account for restrictions of the App Engine runtime environment, which we'll discuss in Chapter 4.) App Engine adds to this the libraries and tools included with the App Engine SDK, such as APIs for accessing the services (such as `google.appengine.api.urlfetch`), and utilities such as the data modeling libraries (`google.appengine.ext.ndb`).

Naturally, the environment also includes any Python modules you provide in your application directory. In addition to your own code, you might add a copy of a third-party library your app uses to your app directory, where it is uploaded as part of your app. Note that this method only works for "pure Python" libraries, and not libraries that have portions written in C.

For convenience, the Python runtime environment includes several third-party libraries popular for web development. We've already seen Jinja, the templating library. The Django web application framework is also included. You can use NumPy for data processing and numerical analysis. The Python Cryptography Toolkit (PyCrypto) provides strong encryption capabilities.

To use one of the provided third-party libraries, you must declare it in the *app.yaml* file for the app, like so:

```
libraries:
- name: django
  version: "1.3"
```

This declaration is necessary to select the version of the library your app will use. When a new version of a third-party library becomes available, your app will continue to use the declared version until you change it. You'll want to test your app to make sure it's compatible with the new version before making the switch with your live app. With this declaration in place, `import django` will load the requested version of the library. (Without it, the import will fail with an `ImportError`.)

For more information about using Django with App Engine, see Chapter 18.

You can specify a `version` of `latest` to always request the latest major version of the library. This may be desired for small libraries, where new versions are typically backward compatible. For larger packages like Django, you almost certainly want to select a specific version, and upgrade carefully when a new version is added:

```
libraries:
- name: jinja2
  version: latest
- name: markupsafe
  version: latest
```

While the App Engine runtime environment provides these libraries, the Python SDK does not. You must install third-party libraries in your local Python environment yourself, and make sure your version matches the one requested in your *app.yaml*. Installation instructions are specific to each library.

Table 3-2 lists third-party libraries available as of SDK version 1.6.6. Check the official documentation for an up-to-date list.

Table 3-2. Third-party Python libraries available by request in the runtime environment

Library	Description	Name	Versions
Django	A web application framework. See the Django website (*http://bit.ly/OBQNvy*) for installation.	`django`	`1.3`, `1.2`
Jinja2	A templating library. MarkupSafe is recommended with Jinja2. To install: `sudo easy_install jinja2`	`jinja2`	`2.6`
lxml	An XML parsing and production toolkit. See the lxml website (*http://lxml.de/*) for installation, including the `libxml2` and `libxslt` libraries.	`lxml`	`2.3`
MarkupSafe	Fast HTML-aware string handler. To install: `sudo easy_install markupsafe`	`markupsafe`	`0.15`
NumPy	Data processing and numerical analysis. See the SciPy website (*http://www.scipy.org/*) for installation.	`numpy`	`1.6.1`
Python Imaging Library (PIL)	Image manipulation toolkit. See the PIL website (*http://www.pythonware.com/products/pil/index.htm*) for installation.	`pil`	`1.1.7`
Python Cryptography Toolkit (PyCrypto)	Cryptographic routines. See the PyCrypto website (*https://www.dlitz.net/software/pycrypto/*) for installation. Export restrictions may apply.	`pycrypto`	`2.3`
WebOb	An object-oriented interface to HTTP requests and responses. Used by (and included automatically with) the webapp framework. Included in the SDK.	`webob`	`1.1.1`
YAML	Library for parsing the YAML message serialization format. Used by the SDK for the config files. Included in the SDK.	`yaml`	`3.10`

Built-in Handlers

Some of the utilities included with the Python runtime environment use their own request handlers to provide functionality, such as a web-based administrative UI or web service endpoints. Typically, these handlers map to URLs with paths beginning with /_ah/, which are reserved for App Engine use. Because this code runs within your application, you must enable this functionality by setting up these request handlers.

To make it easy to do (and difficult to do incorrectly), many of these tools are available as "built-ins." You enable a built-in feature by naming it in your *app.yaml* file, in a mapping named `builtins`:

```
builtins:
- appstats: on
- remote_api: on
```

Table 3-3 lists the built-ins available as of SDK version 1.6.6. As usual, check the official documentation for an up-to-date list.

Table 3-3. Built-in features that must be enabled using the built-ins directive in app.yaml

Feature	Description	Name
Admin console redirect	Redirects all requests for /_ah/admin to the app's Administration Console if it is live, or the development console if it is running in the development server, so you can link to /_ah/admin from your own administrative pages.	`admin_redirect`
AppStats	Sets up the AppStats control panel at /_ah/stats. See "Visualizing Calls with AppStats" on page 442.	`appstats`
Deferred work	Sets up the task queue handler for the `deferred` library. See "Deferring Work" on page 420.	`deferred`
Remote API	Establishes the web service endpoint for remote API access. See "Remote Controls" on page 239.	`remote_api`

Includes

An *app.yaml* file can get rather large, especially if you use it to route your app's URLs to multiple handlers. You can organize your app's configuration into separate component files by using the `includes` directive. This also makes it easy to write App Engine components that can be installed in other apps, regardless of which frameworks the apps are using.

The `includes` value is a list of file or directory paths, like so:

```
includes:
- lib/component/ae_config.yaml
```

The path can be an absolute path, a path relative to the app root directory, or a path relative to the file that contains the `includes`. If the path is to a file, the file is parsed as a YAML file. If the path is to a directory, the filename is assumed to be *include.yaml* in the given directory.

An included file can contain `builtins`, `includes`, `handlers`, and `admin_console` values. These list values are *prepended* to the list that appears in the current file.

For `handlers`, this means that handler URL patterns from includes are tested before those in the current file. If your main *app.yaml* file has a handler mapped to the URL pattern `/.*`, handlers from includes will be tested first, and only those that don't match will fall to the catch-all handler. Notice that if an included file maps a handler to `/.*`, none of the handlers in the current file (or any file that includes the current file) will ever match a request! So don't do that.

Includes are aggregated in the order they appear in the list. For example, given this *app.yaml*:

```
handlers:
- url: /.*
  script: main.app

includes:
- lib/component_one
- lib/component_two
```

A request URL will try to match each of the `handlers` in *lib/component_one/include.yaml* in the order they appear in that file, followed by each of the `handlers` in *lib/componenttwo/include.yaml*, followed by the `/.*` handler in *app.yaml*.

Java Servlet Sessions

The Java runtime environment includes an implementation of the J2EE HTTP session interface. With sessions enabled, a new visitor to your application is issued a session ID, which is stored in a cookie in the visitor's browser and recalled on all subsequent requests. You can set attributes on the user's session, and these attributes are available during subsequent requests from the same user. The App Engine implementation uses the datastore and memcache to provide this functionality.

To use sessions, you must first enable this functionality in application configuration. In your *appengine-web.xml*, add the `<sessions-enabled>` element:

```
<sessions-enabled>true</sessions-enabled>
```

Session data is written to both the memcache and the datastore, and read from the memcache whenever possible. By default, if session attributes are modified during a request, the request handler updates both the memcache and the datastore before returning the response. You can configure this behavior so the (slower) datastore update is deferred out of the request handler using a task queue. This improves the response time of your request handlers in exchange for a modest risk of temporary session data inconsistency. (We'll discuss the datastore, memcache, and task queues in great detail later in this book, so you may want to refer to those chapters, then reread this paragraph.) In general, it's a good idea to enable this feature.

To enable asynchronous writing of session data to durable storage, add the following element to *appengine-web.xml*:

```
<async-session-persistence enabled="true" />
```

By default, the asynchronous write feature uses the default queue. To use a specific named queue (for example, to configure a more aggressive queue-processing rate), add the `queue-name="..."` attribute to `<async-session-persistence>`.

You access the `HttpSession` object by calling the `getSession()` method on the `HttpServletRequest`. This object has `getAttribute()` and `setAttribute()` methods for manipulating session attributes. With App Engine's implementation, all attribute values must be serializable, so they can be stored in the memcache and datastore.

Here's a simple example of using a session attribute. It prints the value of a session attribute on every request, along with a form that updates the value. When you update the value, it changes. When you reload the page, the previous value persists:

```
import java.io.IOException;
import javax.servlet.http.*;

@SuppressWarnings("serial")
public class TestServlet extends HttpServlet {
    public void doGet(HttpServletRequest req, HttpServletResponse resp)
            throws IOException {
        resp.setContentType("text/html");

        String v = (String) req.getSession().getAttribute("v");
        if (v != null) {
            // Normally you would HTML-escape this.
            resp.getWriter().println(
                    "<p>v is: " + v + "</p>");
        } else {
            resp.getWriter().println(
                    "<p>v is not set.</p>");
        }

        resp.getWriter().println(
                "<form action=\"/\" method=\"post\">" +
                "<input type=\"text\" name=\"v\" />" +
                "<input type=\"submit\" />" +
                "</form>");
    }

    public void doPost(HttpServletRequest req, HttpServletResponse resp)
            throws IOException {
        String newV = req.getParameter("v");
        if (newV != null) {
            req.getSession().setAttribute("v", newV);
        }
        resp.sendRedirect("/");
    }
}
```

(This assumes `TestServlet` is mapped to the URL path /.)

CHAPTER 4
Request Handlers and Instances

When a request arrives intended for your application code, the frontend routes it to the application servers. If an instance of your app is running and available to receive a user request, App Engine sends the request to the instance, and the instance invokes the request handler that corresponds with the URL of the request. If none of the running instances of the app are available, App Engine starts up a new one automatically. App Engine will also shut down instances it no longer needs.

The *instance* is your app's unit of computing power. It provides memory and a processor, isolated from other instances for both data security and performance. Your application's code and data stay in the instance's memory until the instance is shut down, providing an opportunity for local storage that persists between requests.

Within the instance, your application code runs in a *runtime environment*. The environment includes the language interpreter, libraries, and other environment features you selected in your app's configuration. Your app can also access a read-only filesystem containing its files (those that you did not send exclusively to the static file servers). The environment manages all the inputs and outputs for the request handler, setting up the request at the beginning, recording log messages during, and collecting the response at the end.

If you have multithreading enabled, an instance can handle multiple requests concurrently, with all request handlers sharing the same environment. With multithreading disabled, each instance handles one request at a time. Multithreading is one of the best ways to utilize the resources of your instances and keep your costs low. But it's up to you to make sure your request handler code runs correctly when handling multiple requests concurrently.

The runtime environment and the instance are abstractions. They rest above, and take the place of, the operating system and the hardware. It is these abstractions that allow your app to scale seamlessly and automatically on App Engine's infrastructure. At no point must you write code to start or stop instances, load balance requests, or monitor resource utilization. This is provided for you.

In fact, you could almost ignore instances entirely and just focus on request handlers: a request comes in, a request handler comes to life, a response goes out. During its brief lifetime, the request handler makes a few decisions and calls a few services, and leaves no mark behind. The instance only comes into play to give you more control over efficiency: local memory caching, multithreading, and warm-up initialization. You can also configure the hardware profile and parameters of instance allocation, which involve trade-offs of performance and cost.

In this chapter, we discuss the features of the runtime environments. We introduce a way of thinking about request handlers, and how they fit into the larger notion of instances and the App Engine architecture. We also cover how to tune your instances for performance and resource utilization.

The Runtime Environment

All code execution occurs in the runtime environment you have selected for your app. There are four major runtime environments: Java, Python 2.5, Python 2.7, and Go. For this edition of this book, we're focusing on the Python 2.7 and Java environments.

The runtime environment manages all the interaction between the application code and the rest of App Engine. To invoke an application to handle a request, App Engine prepares the runtime environment with the request data, calls the appropriate request handler code within the environment, then collects and returns the response. The application code uses features of the environment to read inputs, call services, and calculate the response data.

The environment isolates and protects your app to guarantee consistent performance. Regardless of what else is happening on the physical hardware that's running the instance, your app sees consistent performance as if it is running on a server all by itself. To do this, the environment must restrict the capabilities normally provided by a traditional server operating system, such as the ability to write to the local filesystem.

An environment like this is called a "sandbox": what's yours is yours, and no other app can intrude. This sandbox effect also applies to your code and your data. If a piece of physical hardware happens to be running instances for two different applications, the applications cannot read each other's code, files, or network traffic.

App Engine's services are similarly partitioned on an app-by-app basis, so each app sees an isolated view of the service and its data. The runtime environment includes APIs for calling these services in the form of language-specific libraries. In a few cases, portions of standard libraries have been replaced with implementations that make service calls.

The Sandbox

The runtime environment does not expose the complete operating system to the application. Some functions, such as the ability to create arbitrary network connections, are restricted. This "sandbox" is necessary to prevent other applications running on the same server from interfering with your application (and vice versa). Instead, an app can perform some of these functions using App Engine's scalable services, such as the URL Fetch service.

The most notable sandbox restrictions include the following:

- An app cannot spawn additional processes. All processing for a request must be performed by the request handler's process. Multiple threads within the process are allowed, but a request handler is not considered finished (and does not return a response) until all threads have exited.
- An app cannot make arbitrary network connections. Networking features are provided by the App Engine services, such as URL Fetch and Mail.
- The app does not manipulate the socket connection with the client directly. Instead, the app prepares the response data, then exits. App Engine takes care of returning the response. This isolates apps from the network infrastructre, at the expense of preventing some niceties like streaming partial results data.
- An app can only read from the filesystem, and can only read its own code and resource files. It cannot create or modify files. Instead of files, an app can use the datastore to save data.
- An app cannot see or otherwise know about other applications or processes that may be running on the server. This includes other request handlers from the same application that may be running simultaneously.
- An app cannot read another app's data from any service that stores data. More generally, an app cannot pretend to be another app when calling a service, and all services partition data between apps.

These restrictions are implemented on multiple levels, both to ensure that the restrictions are enforced and to make it easier to troubleshoot problems that may be related to the sandbox. For example, some standard library calls have been replaced with behaviors more appropriate to the sandbox.

Quotas and Limits

The sandboxed runtime environment monitors the system resources used by the application and limits how much the app can consume. For the resources you pay for, such as running time and storage, you can lift these limits by allocating a daily resource budget in the Administration Console. App Engine also enforces several system-wide limits that protect the integrity of the servers and their ability to serve multiple apps.

In App Engine parlance, "quotas" are resource limits that refresh at the beginning of each calendar day (at midnight, Pacific Time). You can monitor your application's daily consumption of quotas using the Administration Console, in the Quota Details section.

Since Google may change how the limits are set as the system is tuned for performance, we won't state some of the specific values of these limits in this book. You can find the actual values of these limits in the official App Engine documentation. Google has said it will give 90 days' notice before changing limits in a way that would affect existing apps.

Request limits

Several system-wide limits specify how requests can behave. These include the size and number of requests over a period of time, and the bandwidth consumed by inbound and outbound network traffic.

One important request limit is the request timer. An application has 60 seconds to respond to a user request.

Near the end of the 60 seconds, the server raises an exception that the application can catch for the purposes of exiting cleanly or returning a user-friendly error message. For Python, the request timer raises a `google.appengine.runtime.DeadlineExceededError`. For Java, the request timer throws a `com.google.apphosting.api.DeadlineExceededException`.

If the request handler has not returned a response or otherwise exited after 60 seconds, the server terminates the process and returns a generic system error (HTTP code 500) to the client.

The 60-second limit applies to user web requests, as well as requests for web hooks such as incoming XMPP and email requests. A request handler invoked by a task queue or scheduled task can run for up to 10 minutes in duration. Tasks are a convenient and powerful tool for performing large amounts of work in the background. We'll discuss tasks in Chapter 16.

The size of a request is limited to 32 megabytes, as is the size of the request handler's response.

Service limits

Each App Engine service has its own set of quotas and limits. As with system-wide limits, some can be raised using a billing account and a budget, such as the number of recipients the application has sent emails to. Other limits are there to protect the integrity of the service, such as the maximum size of a response to the URL Fetch service.

In Python, when an app exceeds a service-specific limit or quota, the runtime environment raises a `...runtime.apiproxy_errors.OverQuotaError`.

In Java, the service call throws a `com.google.apphosting.api.ApiProxy.OverQuotaException` when a service limit is exceeded. (Note the `apphosting` package name here, not `appengine`.)

With a few notable exceptions, the size of a service call and the size of the service response are each limited to 1 megabyte. This imposes an inherent limit on the size of datastore entities and memcache values. Even though an incoming user request can contain up to 32 megabytes, only 1 megabyte of that data can be stored using a single datastore entity or memcache value.

The datastore has a "batch" API that allows you to store or fetch multiple data objects in a single service call. The total size of a batch request to the datastore is unlimited: you can attempt to store or fetch as many entities as can be processed within an internal timing limit for datastore service calls. Each entity is still limited to 1 megabyte in size.

The memcache also has a batch API. The total size of the request of a batch call to the memcache, or its response, can be up to 32 megabytes. As with the datastore, each memcache value cannot exceed 1 megabyte in size.

The URL Fetch service, which your app can use to connect to remote hosts using HTTP, can issue requests up to 5 megabytes, and receive responses up to 32 megabytes.

We won't list all the service limits here. Google raises limits as improvements are made to the infrastructure, and numbers printed here may be out-of-date. See the official documentation for a complete list, including the latest values.

Deployment limits

Two limits affect the size and structure of your application's files. A single application file cannot be larger than 32 megabytes. This applies to resource files (code, configuration) as well as static files. Also, the total number of files for an application cannot be larger than 10,000, including resource files and static files. The total size of all files must not exceed 150 megabytes.

These limits aren't likely to cause problems in most cases, but some common tasks can approach these numbers. Some third-party libraries or frameworks can be many hundreds of files. Sites consisting of many pages of text or images (not otherwise stored in the datastore) can reach the file count limit. A site offering video or software for download might have difficulty with the 32-megabyte limit.

The Python runtime offers two ways to mitigate the application file count limit. If you have many files of Python code, you can store the code files in a ZIP archive file, then add the path to the ZIP archive to `sys.path` at the top of your request handler scripts. The request handler scripts themselves must not be in a ZIP archive. Thanks to `zipimport`, a feature built into Python, the Python interpreter recognizes the ZIP file automatically and unpacks it as needed when importing modules. Unpacking takes additional CPU time, but since imports are cached, the app only incurs this cost the first time the module is imported in a given app instance:

```
import sys
sys.path.insert(0, 'locales.zip')

import locales.es
```

The Python App Engine runtime includes a similar mechanism for serving static files from a ZIP archive file, called `zipserve`. Unlike `zipimport`, this feature is specific to App Engine. To serve static files from a ZIP archive, add the `zipserve` request handler to your *app.yaml*, associated with a URL path that represents the path to the ZIP file:

```
- url: /static/images/.*
  script: $PYTHON_LIB/google/appengine/ext/zipserve
```

This declares that all requests for a URL starting with `/static/images/` should resolve to a path in the ZIP file `/static/images.zip`.

The string `$PYTHON_LIB` in the script path refers to the location of the App Engine libraries, and is the only such substitution available. It's useful precisely for this purpose, to set up a request handler whose code is in the App Engine Python modules included with the runtime environment. (`zipserve` is not a configurable built-in because it needs you to specify the URL mapping.)

When using `zipserve`, keep in mind that the ZIP archive is uploaded as a resource file, not a static file. Files are served by application code, not the static file infrastructure. By default, the handler advises browsers to cache the files for 20 minutes. You can customize the handler's cache duration using the wrapper `WSGIApplication`. See the source code for `google/appengine/ext/zipserve/__init__.py` in the SDK for details.

Java applications have a common solution for reducing the file count for application code: JARs. If your app has too many *.class* files, simply put them in a JAR file by using the `jar` utility included with the Java development kit. As with Python, app caching reduces the overhead of unpacking JARs. There is no equivalent to `zipserve` for static files in Java included with the SDK, but it's easy to write something that behaves similarly using JAR files.

Also, with Java, make sure to use `<static-files>` and `<resource-files>` directives in your *appengine-web.xml* file to exclude the appropriate files. By default, all files outside of *WEB-INF/* belong to both groups, and so are counted *twice*, once for each group. The file count limit is the total count for both groups.

An application can only be uploaded a limited number of times per day, currently 1,000. You may not notice this limit during normal application development. If you are using app deployments to upload data to the application on a regular schedule, you may want to keep this limit in mind.

Billable quotas

Every application gets a limited amount of computing resources for free, so you can start developing and testing your application right away. You can purchase additional computing resources at competitive rates. You only pay for what you actually use, and you specify the maximum amount of money you want to spend.

You can create an app by using the free limits without setting up a billing account. Free apps never incur charges, but are constrained by the free quotas. When you are ready for your app to accept live traffic or otherwise exceed the free quotas, you enable billing for the app, and set a resource budget.

There are two categories of billing accounts: standard, and Premier. Standard account holders pay a minimum weekly charge for each app with billing enabled, in addition to resource charges. (Apps without billing enabled never incur a charge.) Standard accounts are paid via Google Wallet, which uses a credit card or a signature debit card. Premier account holders pay a flat monthly rate for unlimited apps, and only pay additionally for resource charges. Premier accounts are also eligible for monthly invoicing, a service-level agreement, and technical support from Google staff. See the App Engine website for information on pricing and Premier accounts.

Each app gets its own maximum daily resource budget. To enable billing and set the budget for an app, sign in to the Administration Console with the developer account that is to be the billing account. Select Billing Settings from the sidebar. Click the Enable Billing button, and follow the prompts.

For standard accounts, when you set a budget, you are prompted to go through Google Checkout to approve the maximum charge. Setting a budget does not apply a charge to your account, it only sets the maximum.

The budget specifies the amount of money App Engine can "spend" on resources, at the posted rates, over the course of a day. This budget is in addition to the free quotas: the budget is not consumed until after a resource has exceeded its free quota. After the budget for the calendar day is exhausted, service calls that would require more resources raise an exception. If there are not enough resources remaining to invoke a request handler, App Engine will respond to requests with a generic error message. The budget resets at the beginning of each calendar day (Pacific Time).

It's worth repeating: you are only charged for the resources your app uses. If you set a high daily resource budget and App Engine only uses a portion of it, you are only charged for that portion. Typically, you would test your app to estimate resource consumption, then set the budget generously so every day comes in under the budget. The budget maximum is there to prevent unexpected surges in resource usage from draining your bank account—a monetary surge protector, if you will. If you're expecting a spike in traffic (such as for a product launch), you may want to raise your budget in advance of the event.

The owner of the billing account can change the budget and the resource allocations for the app at any time using the Administration Console. A change to your budget takes about 10 minutes to complete, and you will not be able to change the setting again during those 10 minutes.

The official documentation includes a complete list of the free quota limits, the increased free quota limits with billing enabled, the maximum allocation amounts, and the latest billing rates.

The Python Runtime Environment

When an app instance receives a request intended for a Python application, it compares the URL path of the request to the URL patterns in the app's *app.yaml* file. As we saw in "Configuring a Python App" on page 76, each URL pattern is associated with either the Python import path for a WSGI application instance, or a file of Python code (a "script"). The first pattern to match the path identifies the code that will handle the request.

If the handler is a WSGI instance, the runtime environment prepares the request and invokes the handler according to the WSGI standard. The handler returns the response in kind.

If the handler is a file of Python code, the runtime environment uses the Common Gateway Interface (CGI) standard to exchange request and response data with the code. The CGI standard uses a combination of environment variables and the application process's input and output streams to handle this communication.

You're unlikely to write code that uses the WSGI and CGI interfaces directly. Instead, you're better off using an established web application framework. Python developers have many web frameworks to choose from. Django, Pyramid (of the Pylons Project), Flask, and web2py are several "full-stack" frameworks that work well with App Engine. For convenience, App Engine includes Django as part of the runtime environment. You can include other frameworks and libraries with your application simply by adding them to your application directory. As we saw in Chapter 2, App Engine also includes a simple framework of its own, called webapp2.

By the time an app instance receives the request, it has already fired up the Python interpreter, ready to handle requests. If the instance has served a request for the application since it was initialized, it may have the application in memory as well, but if it hasn't, it imports the appropriate Python module for the request. The instance invokes the handler code with the data for the request, and returns the handler's response to the client.

When you run a Python program loaded from a *.py* file on your computer, the Python interpreter compiles the Python code to a compact bytecode format, which you might see on your computer as a *.pyc* file. If you edit your *.py* source, the interpreter will recompile it the next time it needs it. Since application code does not change after you've uploaded your app, App Engine precompiles all Python code to bytecode one time when you upload the app. This saves time when a module or script is imported for the first time in each instance of the app.

The Python interpreter remains in the instance memory for the lifetime of the instance. The interpreter loads your code according to Python's module import semantics. Typically, this means that once a module is imported for the first time on an instance, subsequent attempts to import it do nothing, since the module is already loaded. This is true across multiple requests handled by the same instance.

The Python 2.7 runtime environment uses a modified version of the official Python 2.7 interpreter, sometimes referred to as "CPython" to distinguish it from other Python interpreters. The application code must run entirely within the Python interpreter. That is, the code must be purely Python code, and cannot include or depend upon extensions to the interpreter. Python modules that include extensions written in C cannot be uploaded with your app or otherwise added to the runtime environment. The "pure Python" requirement can be problematic for some third-party libraries, so be sure that libraries you want to use operate without extensions.

A few popular Python libraries, including some that depend on C code, are available within the runtime environment. Refer back to "Python Libraries" on page 100 for more information.

App Engine sets the following environment variables at the beginning of each request, which you can access using `os.environ`:

`APPLICATION_ID`
: The ID of the application. The ID is preceded by `s~` when running on App Engine, and `dev~` when running in a development server.

`CURRENT_VERSION_ID`
: The ID of the version of the app serving this request.

`AUTH_DOMAIN`
: This is set to `gmail.com` if the user is signed in using a Google Account, or the domain of the app if signed in with a Google Apps account; not set otherwise.

`SERVER_SOFTWARE`
: The version of the runtime environment; starts with the word `Development` when running on the development server.

For example:

```
import os

# ...
        if os.environ['SERVER_SOFTWARE'].startswith('Development'):
            # ... only executed in the development server ...
```

The Python interpreter prevents the app from accessing illegal system resources at a low level. Since a Python app can consist only of Python code, an app must perform all processing within the Python interpreter.

For convenience, portions of the Python standard library whose only use is to access restricted system resources have been disabled. If you attempt to import a disabled module or call a disabled function, the interpreter raises an `ImportError`. The Python development server enforces the standard module import restrictions, so you can test imports on your computer.

Some standard library modules have been replaced with alternate versions for speed or compatibility. Other modules have custom implementations, such as `zipimport`.

The Java Runtime Environment

The Java runtime environment behaves like a J2EE servlet container. When the app instance receives a request, it determines the servlet class to call by comparing the URL path to the servlet mappings in the deployment descriptor. The server uses the standard servlet interface to invoke the servlet, passing it a populated request object and an empty response object. The application's servlet code populates the response object and exits, and App Engine returns the response to the client.

The Java runtime environment uses the Java 6 virtual machine (JVM). The JVM runs Java bytecode, which is what you get from passing Java code to a Java compiler. It's also what you get from compilers for other languages that produce Java bytecode, such as Scala, and from interpreters for other languages implemented in Java bytecode, such as JRuby (Ruby), Rhino (JavaScript), Groovy, and even Jython (a Python interpreter implemented in Java). You can use any language that compiles to or has an interpreter for the JVM to write applications for App Engine, as long as the result implements a servlet interface.

Having a complete JVM also means you can use many third-party libraries with your application. Some restrictions apply—we'll look at a few in a moment—but in most cases, using a library is a simple matter of including the JAR or class files in the application's WAR.

An app can ask for information about the current environment by using the `SystemProperty` API, in the `com.google.appengine.api.utils` package. App Engine sets static fields of this class to the application ID (`applicationId`), the application version (`applicationVersion`), the version of the runtime environment (`version`), and whether the app is running in the development environment or on App Engine (`environment`):

```
import com.google.appengine.api.utils.SystemProperty;

// ...
        String applicationId = SystemProperty.applicationId.get();

        if (SystemProperty.environment.value() ==
            SystemProperty.Environment.Value.Development) {
            // ... only executed in the development server ...
        }
```

In the Java runtime environment, sandbox restrictions are enforced within the JVM. These restrictions are implemented using a combination of JVM permissions, a Java Runtime Environment (JRE) class whitelist, and alternate implementations for specific functions. This fine-grained approach allows more third-party libraries to work and makes other code easier to port than relying on JVM permissions alone.

The Java runtime environment includes a subset of the JRE classes. You can find a complete list of supported JRE classes in the official documentation. The development server enforces this list, so if your code (or some library code) crosses a line, the development server throws an exception.

Reflection is supported for all the app's own classes. Custom class loaders are supported, but with all classes granted the same permissions. Native JNI code is not supported.

The Request Handler Abstraction

Let's review what we know so far about request handlers. A request handler is an entry point into the application code, mapped to a URL pattern in the application configuration. Here is a section of configuration for a request handler in a Python app, which would appear in the *app.yaml* file:

```
handlers:
- url: /profile/.*
  script: users.profile.app
```

A Python source file named *users/profile.py* contains a WSGI application instance in a variable named `app`. This code knows how to invoke the webapp2 framework to handle the request, which in turn calls our code:

```
import jinja2
import os
import webapp2

from google.appengine.api import users
from google.appengine.ext import db

class UserProfile(db.Model):
    user = db.UserProperty()

template_env = jinja2.Environment(
    loader=jinja2.FileSystemLoader(os.path.dirname(__file__)))

class ProfileHandler(webapp2.RequestHandler):
    def get(self):
        # Call the Users service to identify the user making the request,
        # if the user is signed in.
        current_user = users.get_current_user()

        # Call the Datastore service to retrieve the user's profile data.
        profile = None
```

```
        if current_user:
            profile = UserProfile.all().filter('user', current_user).fetch(1)

        # Render a response page using a template.
        template = template_env.get_template('profile.html')
        self.response.out.write(template.render({'profile': profile}))

app = webapp2.WSGIApplication([('/profile/?', ProfileHandler)], debug=True)
```

When a user visits the URL path `/profile/` on this application's domain, App Engine matches the request to `users.profile.app` via the application configuration, and then invokes it to produce the response. The `WSGIApplication` creates an object of the `ProfileHandler` class with the request data, then calls its `get()` method. The method code makes use of two App Engine services, the Users service and the Datastore service, to access resources outside of the app code. It uses that data to make a web page, then exits.

In theory, the application process only needs to exist long enough to handle the request. When the request arrives, App Engine figures out which request handler it needs, makes room for it in its computation infrastructure, and creates it in a runtime environment. Once the request handler has created the response, the show is over, and App Engine is free to purge the request handler from memory. If the application needs data to live on between requests, it stores it by using a service like the datastore. The application itself does not live long enough to remember anything on its own.

Figure 4-1 illustrates this abstract lifecycle of a request handler.

On App Engine, a web application can handle many requests simultaneously. There could be many request handlers active at any given moment, in any stage of its lifecycle. As shown in Figure 4-2, all these request handlers access the same services.

Each service has its own specification for managing concurrent access from multiple request handlers, and for the most part, a request handler doesn't have to think about the fact that other request handlers are in play. The big exception here is datastore transactions, which we'll discuss in detail in Chapter 7.

The request handler abstraction is useful for thinking about how to design your app, and how the service-oriented architecture is justified. App Engine can create an arbitrary number of request handlers to handle an arbitrary number of requests simultaneously, and your code barely has to know anything about it. This is how your app scales with traffic automatically.

Introducing Instances

The idea of a web application being a big pot of bubbling request handlers is satisfying, but in practice, this abstraction fails to capture an important aspect of real-world system software. Starting a program for the first time on a fresh system can be expensive: code is read into RAM from disk, memory is allocated, data structures are set up with starting values, and configuration files are read and parsed. App Engine initializes new runtime

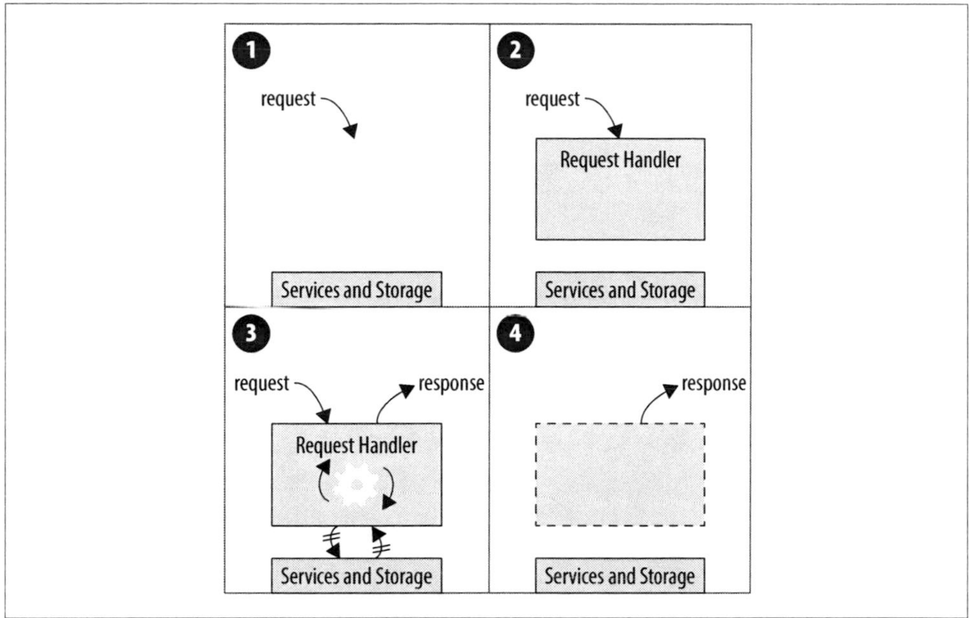

Figure 4-1. Request handlers in the abstract: 1. A request arrives; 2. A request handler is created; 3. The request handler calls services and computes the response; 4. The request handler terminates, the response is returned

environments prior to using them to execute request handlers, so the environment initialization cost is not incurred during the handler execution. But application code often needs to perform its own initialization that App Engine can't do on its own ahead of time. The JVM and Python interpreters are designed to exploit local memory, and many web application frameworks perform initialization, expecting the investment to pay off over multiple requests. It's wasteful and impractical to do this at the beginning of every request handler, while the user is waiting.

App Engine solves this problem with *instances*, long-lived containers for request handlers that retain local memory. At any given moment, an application has a pool of zero or more instances allocated for handling requests. App Engine routes new requests to available instances. It creates new instances as needed, and shuts down instances that are excessively idle. When a request arrives at an instance that has already handled previous requests, the instance is likely to have already done the necessary preparatory work, and can serve the response more quickly than a fresh instance.

The picture now looks something like Figure 4-3. The request handler still only lives as long as it takes to return the response, but its actions can now affect instance memory. This instance memory remains available to the next request handler that executes inside the instance.

Keep in mind that instances are created and destroyed dynamically, and requests are routed to instances based purely on availability. While instances are meant to live longer

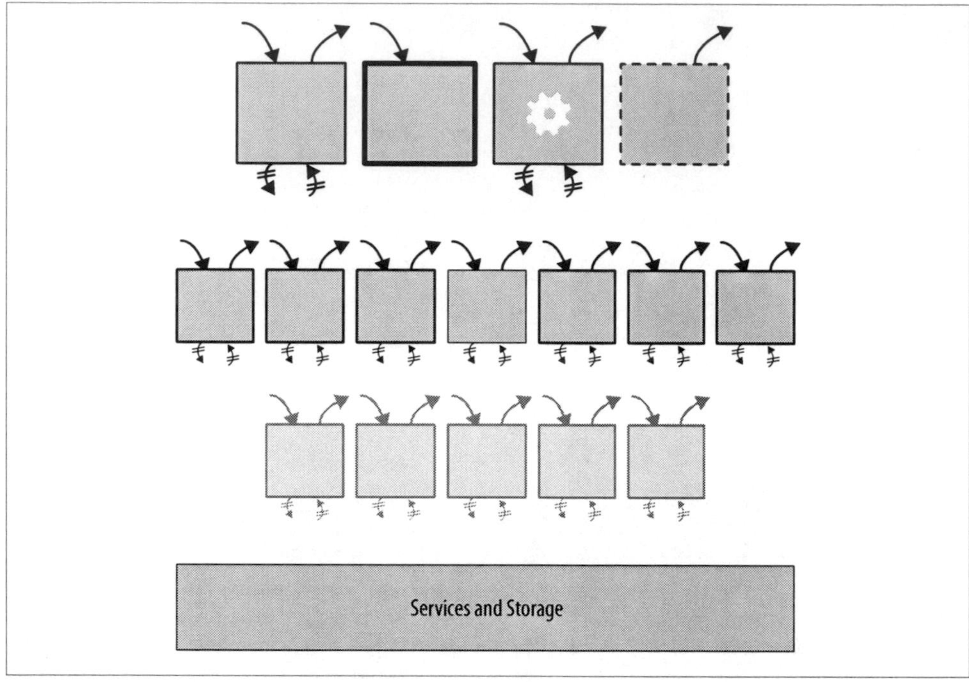

Figure 4-2. A web application handles many requests simultaneously; all request handlers access the same services

than request handlers, they are as ephemeral as request handlers, and any given request may be handled by a new instance. There is no guarantee that requests of a particular sort will always be handled by the same instance, nor is it assured that an instance will still be around after a given request is handled. Outside of a request handler, the application is not given the opportunity to rescue data from local memory prior to an instance being shut down. If you need to store user-specific information (such as session data), you must use a storage service. Instance memory is only suitable for local caching.

Instances can provide another crucial performance benefit: multithreading. With multithreading enabled in your application configuration, an instance will start additional request handlers in separate threads as local resources allow, and execute them concurrently. All threads share the same instance memory just like any other multithreaded application—which means your code must take care to protect shared memory during critical sections of code. Java, Python, and Go have language and library features for synchronizing access to shared memory.

Figure 4-4 illustrates an instance with multithreading enabled. Refer to "Multithreading" on page 82 for information on how to enable or disable multithreading in application configuration.

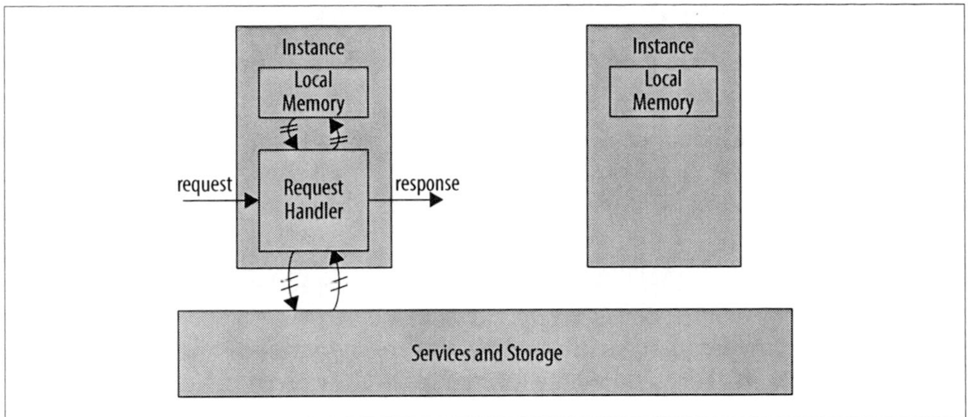

Figure 4-3. An instance handles a request, while another instance sits idle

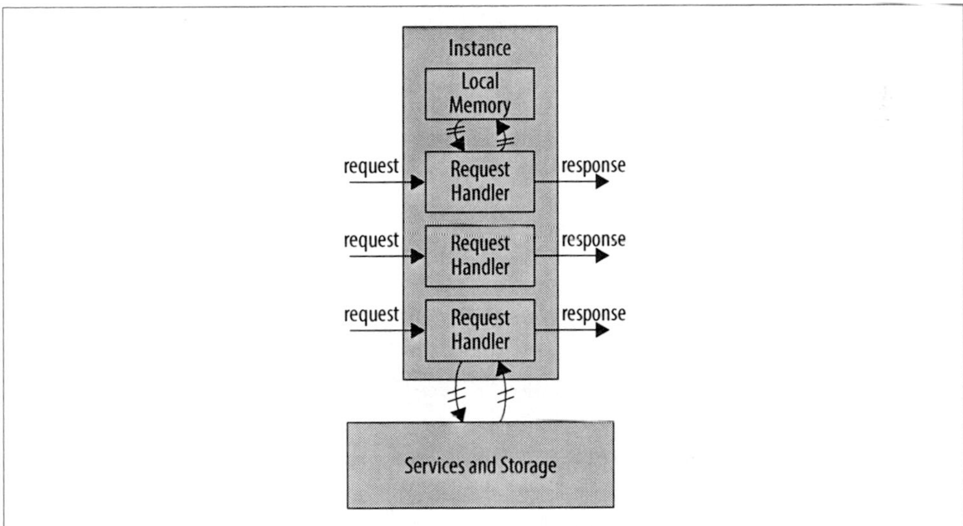

Figure 4-4. A multithreaded instance handles multiple requests concurrently

Instance uptime is App Engine's billable unit for computation, measured in fractions of an *instance hour*. This makes multithreading an important technique for maximizing throughput and minimizing costs. Most request handlers will spend a significant amount of time waiting for service calls, and a multithreaded instance can use the CPU for other handlers during that time.

Request Scheduling and Pending Latency

App Engine routes each request to an available instance. If all instances are busy, App Engine starts a new instance.

App Engine considers an instance to be "available" for a request if it believes the instance can handle the request in a reasonable amount of time. With multithreading disabled, this definition is simple: an instance is available if it is not presently busy handling a request.

With multithreading enabled, App Engine decides whether an instance is available based on several factors. It considers the current load on the instance (CPU and memory) from its active request handlers, and its capacity. It also considers historical knowledge of the load caused by previous requests to the given URL path. If it seems likely that the new request can be handled effectively in the capacity of an existing instance, the request is scheduled to that instance.

Incoming requests are put on a *pending queue* in preparation for scheduling. App Engine will leave requests on the queue for a bit of time while it waits for existing instances to become available, before deciding it needs to create new instances. This waiting time is called the *pending latency*.

You can configure a maximum pending latency and a minimum pending latency for your app. By default, App Engine will determine appropriate latency bounds automatically.

The *maximum pending latency* is the most amount of time a request will wait on the pending queue before App Engine decides more instances are needed to handle the current level of traffic. Lowering the maximum pending latency potentially reduces the average wait time, at the expense of activating more instances. Conversely, raising the maximum favors reusing existing instances, at the expense of potentially making the user wait a bit longer for a response.

The *minimum pending latency* specifies a minimum amount of time a request must be on the pending queue before App Engine can conclude a new instance needs to be started. Raising the minimum encourages App Engine to be more conservative about creating new instances. (This minimum only refers to creating new instances. Naturally, if an existing instance is available for a pending request, the request is scheduled immediately.)

To adjust the pending latency bounds for your app, go to the Administration Console. Select the Application Settings panel, then scroll down to the Performance heading to find the Pending Latency widget (pictured in Figure 4-5). Adjust the minimum and maximum sliders as needed, and then click the Save Settings button.

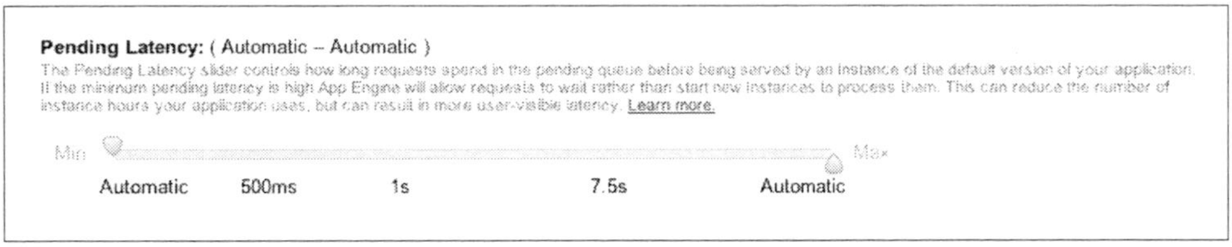

Figure 4-5. The Pending Latency control in the Administration Console, under Application Settings

Warm-up Requests

There is a period of time between the moment App Engine decides it needs a new instance and the moment the instance is available to handle the next request off the request queue. During this time, App Engine initializes the instance on the server hardware, sets up the runtime environment, and makes the app files available to the instance. App Engine takes this preparation period into account when scheduling request handlers and instance creation.

The goal is to make the instance as ready as possible prior to handling the first request, so when the request handler begins, the user only waits on the request handler logic, not the initialization. But App Engine can only do so much on its own. Many initialization tasks are specific to your application code. For instance, App Engine can't automatically import every module in a Python app, because imports execute code, and an app may need to import modules selectively.

App-specific initialization potentially puts undue burden on the first request handler to execute on a fresh instance. A "loading request" typically takes longer to execute than subsequent requests handled by the same instance. This is common enough that App Engine will add a log message automatically when a request is the first request for an instance, so you can detect a correlation between performance issues and app initialization.

You can mitigate the impact of app initialization with a feature called *warm-up requests*. With warm-up requests enabled, App Engine will attempt to issue a request to a specific warm-up URL immediately following the creation of a new instance. You can associate a warm-up request handler with this URL to perform initialization tasks that are better performed outside of a user-facing request handler.

To enable warm-up requests, activate the `warmup` inbound service in your app configuration. (Refer to "Inbound Services" on page 97.) In Python, set this in your *app.yaml* file:

```
inbound_services:
- warmup
```

In Java, set this in your *appengine-web.xml* file:

```
<inbound-services>
  <service>warmup</service>
</inbound-services>
```

Warm-up requests are issued to this URL path:

```
/_ah/warmup
```

You bind your warm-up request handler to this URL path in the usual way.

There are a few rare cases where an instance will not receive a warm-up request prior to the first user request even with warm-up requests enabled. Make sure your user request handler code does not depend on the warm-up request handler having already been called on the instance.

Resident Instances

Instances stick around for a while after finishing their work, in case they can be reused to handle more requests. If App Engine decides it's no longer useful to keep an instance around, it shuts down the instance. An instance that is allocated but is not handling any requests is considered an *idle instance*.

Instances that App Engine creates and destroys as needed by traffic demands are known as *dynamic instances*. App Engine uses historical knowledge about your app's traffic to tune its algorithm for dynamic instance allocation to find a balance between instance availability and efficient use of resources.

You can adjust how App Engine allocates instances by using two settings: minimum idle instances and maximum idle instances.

The *minimum idle instances* setting ensures that a number of instances are always available. The actual number of idle instances will still fluctuate with traffic, but increasing this number will cause App Engine to be more aggressive about starting new instances as it tries to ensure the minimum.

Setting a nonzero minimum for idle instances also ensures that at least this many instances are never terminated due to low traffic. Because App Engine does not start and stop these instances due to traffic fluctuations, these instances are not dynamic; instead, they are known as *resident instances*.

You *must* enable warm-up instances to set the minimum idle instances to a nonzero value.

Reserving resident instances can help your app handle sharp increases in traffic. For example, you may want to increase the resident instances prior to launching your product or announcing a new feature. You can reduce them again as traffic fluctuations return to normal. You might also reserve instances prior to executing a large batch job, or keep instances available for task queues, so spikes in load are less likely to affect end users.

App Engine only maintains resident instances for the default version of your app. While you can make requests to nondefault versions, only dynamic instances will be created to handle those requests. When you change the default version (in the Versions panel of the Administration Console), the previous resident instances are allowed to finish their current request handlers, then they are shut down and new resident instances running the new default version are created.

Resident instances are billed at the same rate as dynamic instances. Be sure you want to pay for 24 instance hours per day per resident instance before changing this setting.

The *maximum idle instances* setting adjusts how aggressively App Engine terminates idle instances above the minimum. Increasing the maximum causes idle dynamic instances to live longer; decreasing the maximum causes them to die more quickly. A larger maximum is useful for keeping more dynamic instances available for rapid fluctuations in traffic, at the expense of greater unused (dynamic) capacity. The name "maximum idle instances" is not entirely intuitive, but it opposes "minimum idle instances" in an obvious way: the maximum can't be lower than the minimum.

To adjust the minimum and maximum idle instances settings for your app, go to the Administration Console. Select the Application Settings panel, then scroll down to the Performance heading to find the Idle Instances widget (pictured in Figure 4-6). Adjust the minimum and maximum sliders as needed, and then click the Save Settings button.

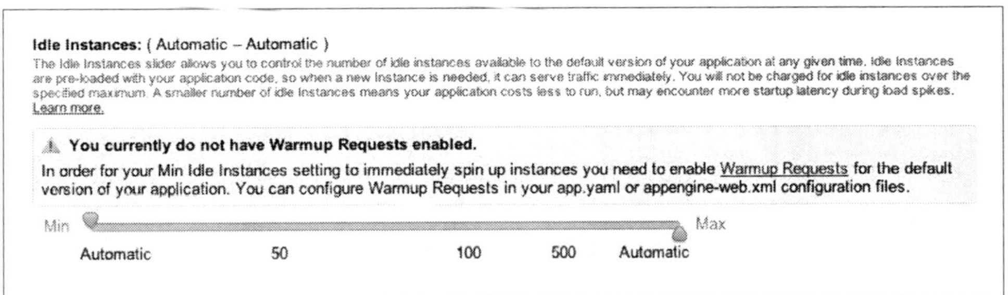

Figure 4-6. The Idle Instances control in the Administration Console, under Application Settings; the Console warns that warm-up requests must be enabled before setting a minimum

The Instances Console

The Administration Console includes a panel for inspecting your app's currently active instances. A portion of such a panel is shown in Figure 4-7.

You can use this panel to inspect the general behavior of your application code running in an instance. This includes summary information about the number of instances, and averages for QPS, latency, and memory usage per instance over the last minute of activity. Each active instance is also itemized, with its own QPS and latency averages,

Main
Dashboard
Instances
Logs
Versions
Backends
Cron Jobs
Task Queues
Quota Details

Data
Datastore Indexes
Datastore Viewer

Total number of instances	Average QPS*	Average Latency*	Average Memory
78 total (10 Resident)	1.661	138.2 ms	115.5 MBytes

Instances

QPS*	Latency*	Requests	Errors	Age	Memory	Logs	Availability	Shutdown
0.100	267.0 ms	38566	1	1 day, 20:03:48	167.5 MBytes	View Logs	Resident	Shutdown
0.233	112.6 ms	22215	0	1 day, 1:38:26	157.6 MBytes	View Logs	Resident	Shutdown
0.350	102.9 ms	7603	0	7:17:35	132.1 MBytes	View Logs	Resident	Shutdown
1.750	130.1 ms	582	0	0:09:04	98.2 MBytes	View Logs	Dynamic	Shutdown
0.833	219.6 ms	399	0	0:05:26	86.0 MBytes	View Logs	Dynamic	Shutdown
1.817	123.7 ms	1781	0	0:23:32	115.2 MBytes	View Logs	Dynamic	Shutdown

Figure 4-7. An excerpt of the Instances panel of the Administration Console

total request and error counts over the lifetime of the instance, the age of the instance, current memory usage, and whether the instance is resident or dynamic. You can query the logs for requests handled by the individual instance.

You can also shut down an instance manually from this panel. If you shut down a resident instance, a new resident instance will be started in its place, effectively like restarting the instance. If you shut down a dynamic instance, a new instance may or may not be created as per App Engine's algorithm and the app's idle instance settings.

As with several other Console panels, the Instances panel is specific to the selected version of your app. If you want to inspect instances handling requests for a specific app version, be sure to select it from the Console's app version drop-down at the top of the screen.

Instance Hours and Billing

Instance use is a resource measured in instance hours. An instance hour corresponds to an hour of clock time that an instance is alive. An instance is on the clock regardless of whether it is actively serving traffic or is idle, or whether it is resident or dynamic.

Each instance incurs a mandatory charge of 15 minutes, added to the end of the instance's lifespan. This accounts for the computational cost of instance creation and other related resources. This is one reason why you might adjust the minimum pending latency and maximum idle instances settings to avoid excess instance creation.

The free quotas include a set of instance hours for dynamic instances. The free quota for dynamic instances is enough to power one instance of the most basic class ("F1") continuously, plus a few extra hours per day.

When you set a resource budget for your app, you can also set up a plan to prepurchase instance hours at a discounted rate on a weekly basis. Once your app is up and receiving live traffic, you may be able to establish a lower bound for the number of instance hours your app consumes on a regular basis. You can save money by prepurchasing these hours at the discounted rate.

Instance Classes

Each instance gets a fixed amount of memory and CPU resources. You can select from one of several configurations of memory and CPU, called the *instance class*. The most basic instance class, the "F1" class, provides the equivalent of a 600 MHz CPU with 128 megabytes of memory.

Each class is defined as a multiple of the "F1" class, and is billed accordingly. An instance of the "F2" class provides a 1,200 MHz CPU and 256 megabytes of memory, twice as much of each resource as an "F1" instance. An instance hour of the "F2" class costs twice as much as an instance hour of the "F1" class. There's also an "F4" class, which is twice as powerful, and twice as expensive, as the "F2" class. (As usual, see the official App Engine website for the latest prices.)

The free quota and prepurchased discount hours are measured in the units of the "F1" class. Instances of higher classes consume these resources at multiplied rates.

You can select the instance class for user requests in the Administration Console: select the Application Settings screen, and scroll down to Performance. Select the desired Frontend Instance Class from the drop-down menu, then click the Save Settings button. When you change this setting, all resident instances are restarted to use the new class, and all new dynamic instances are created using this class.

CHAPTER 5

Datastore Entities

Most scalable web applications use separate systems for handling web requests and for storing data. The request handling system routes each request to one of many servers. The server handles the request without knowledge of other requests going to other servers. Each request handler behaves as if it is *stateless*, acting solely on the content of the request to produce the response. But most web applications need to maintain state, whether it's remembering that a customer ordered a product, or just remembering that the user who made the current request is the same user who made an earlier request handled by another server. For this, request handlers must interact with a central database to fetch and update the latest information about the state of the application.

Just as the request handling system distributes web requests across many machines for scaling and robustness, so does the database. But unlike the request handlers, databases are by definition *stateful*, and this poses a variety of questions. Which server remembers which piece of data? How does the system route a data query to the server or servers that can answer the query? When a client updates data, how long does it take for all servers that know that data to get the latest version, and what does the system return for queries about that data in the meantime? What happens when two clients try to update the same data at the same time? What happens when a server goes down?

As with request handling, Google App Engine manages the scaling and maintenance of data storage automatically. Your application interacts with an abstract model that hides the details of managing and growing a pool of data servers. This model and the service behind it provide answers to the questions of scalable data storage specifically designed for web applications.

App Engine's abstraction for data is easy to understand, but it is not obvious how to best take advantage of its features. In particular, it is surprisingly different from the kind of database with which most of us are most familiar, the relational database. It's different enough, in fact, that Google doesn't call it a "database," but a "datastore."

The App Engine datastore is a robust, scalable data storage solution. Your app's data is stored in several locations by using a best-of-breed consensus protocol (similar to the

"Paxos" protocol), making your app's access to this data resilient to most service failures and all planned downtime. When we discuss queries and transactions, we'll see how this affects how data is updated. For now, just know that it's a good thing.

We dedicate the next several chapters to this important subject.

In 2011–2012, App Engine transitioned from an older datastore infrastructure, known as the "master/slave" (M/S) datastore, to the current one, known as the "high replication" datastore (HR datastore, or HRD). The two architectures differ in how data is updated, but the biggest difference is that the M/S datastore requires scheduled maintenance periods during which data cannot be updated, and is prone to unexpected failures. The HR datastore stays available during scheduled maintenance, and is far more resistant to system failure.

All new App Engine applications use the HR datastore, and the M/S datastore is no longer an option. I only mention it because you'll read about it in older articles, and may see occasional announcements about maintenance of the M/S datastore. You may also see mentions of a datastore migration tool, which old apps still using the M/S datastore can use to switch to the new HR datastore. In this book, "the datastore" always refers to the HR datastore.

Entities, Keys, and Properties

The App Engine datastore is best understood as an object database. An object in the datastore is known as an *entity*.

An entity has a *key* that uniquely identifies the object across the entire system. If you have a key, you can fetch the entity for the key quickly. Keys can be stored as data in entities, such as to create a reference from one entity to another. A key has several parts, some of which we'll discuss here and some of which we'll cover later.

One part of the key is the application's ID, which ensures that nothing else about the key can collide with the entities of any other application. It also ensures that no other app can access your app's data, and that your app cannot access data for other apps. This feature of keys is automatic.

An important part of the key is the *kind*. An entity's kind categorizes the entity for the purposes of queries, and for ensuring the uniqueness of the rest of the key. For example, a shopping cart application might represent each customer order with an entity of the kind "Order." The application specifies the kind when it creates the entity.

The key also contains an *entity ID*. This can be an arbitrary string specified by the app, or it can be generated automatically by the datastore. The API calls an entity ID given by the app a *key name*, and an entity ID generated by the datastore an *ID*. An entity has either a key name or an ID, but not both.

App-assigned key names are strings, while system-assigned IDs are integers. System-assigned IDs are generally increasing, although they are not guaranteed to be monotonically increasing. If you want a strictly increasing ID, you must maintain this yourself in a transaction. (See Chapter 7.) If you purposefully do not want an increasing ID, such as to avoid exposing data sizes to users, you can either generate your own key name, or allow the system to generate a numeric ID, then encrypt and store it with other data.

Once an entity has been created, its key cannot be changed. This applies to all parts of its key, including the kind and the key name or ID.

The data for the entity is stored in one or more *properties*. Each property has a name and at least one value. Each value is of one of several supported data types, such as a string, an integer, a date-time, or a null value. We'll look at property value types in detail later in this chapter.

A property can have multiple values, and each value can be of a different type. As you will see in "Multivalued Properties" on page 140, multivalued properties have unusual behavior, but are quite useful for modeling some kinds of data, and surprisingly efficient.

It's tempting to compare these concepts with similar concepts in relational databases: kinds are tables; entities are rows; properties are fields or columns. That's a useful comparison, but watch out for differences.

Unlike a table in a relational database, there is no relationship between an entity's kind and its properties. Two entities of the same kind can have different properties set or not set, and can each have a property of the same name but with values of different types. You can (and often will) enforce a data schema in your own code, and App Engine includes libraries to make this easy, but this is not required by the datastore.

Also unlike relational databases, keys are not properties. You can perform queries on key names just like properties, but you cannot change a key name after the entity has been created.

A relational database cannot store multiple values in a single cell, while an App Engine property can have multiple values.

Introducing the Python Datastore API

In the Python API for the App Engine datastore, Python objects represent datastore entities. The class of the object corresponds to the entity's kind, where the name of the class is the name of the kind. You define kinds by creating classes that extend one of the provided base classes.

Each attribute of the object corresponds with a property of the entity. To create a new entity in the datastore, you call the class constructor, set attributes on the object, then call a method to save it. To update an existing entity, you call a method that returns the object for the entity (such as via a query), modify its attributes, and then save it.

Example 5-1 defines a class named Book to represent entities of the kind Book. It creates an object of this class by calling the class constructor, and then sets several property values. Finally, it calls the put() method to save the new entity to the datastore. The entity does not exist in the datastore until it is put() for the first time.

Example 5-1. Python code to create an entity of the kind Book

```
from google.appengine.ext import db
import datetime

class Book(db.Expando):
    pass

obj = Book()
obj.title = 'The Grapes of Wrath'
obj.author = 'John Steinbeck'
obj.copyright_year = 1939
obj.author_birthdate = datetime.datetime(1902, 2, 27)

obj.put()
```

The Book class inherits from the class Expando in App Engine's db package. The Expando base class says Book objects can have any of their properties assigned any value. The entity "expands" to accommodate new properties as they are assigned to attributes of the object. Python does not require that an object's member variables be declared in a class definition, and this example takes advantage of this by using an empty class definition—the pass keyword indicates the empty definition—and assigns values to attributes of the object after it is created. The Expando base class knows to use the object's attributes as the values of the corresponding entity's properties.

The Expando class has a funny name because this isn't the way the API's designers expect us to create new classes in most cases. Instead, you're more likely to use the Model base class with a class definition that ensures each instance conforms to a structure, so a mistake in the code doesn't accidentally create entities with malformed properties. Here is how we might implement the Book class using Model:

```
class Book(db.Model):
    title = db.StringProperty()
    author = db.StringProperty()
    copyright_year = db.IntegerProperty()
    author_birthdate = db.DateTimeProperty()
```

The Model version of Book specifies a structure for Book objects that is enforced while the object is being manipulated. It ensures that values assigned to an object's properties are of appropriate types, such as string values for title and author properties, and raises a runtime error if the app attempts to assign a value of the wrong type to a property. With Model as the base class, the object does not "expand" to accommodate other entities: an attempt to assign a value to a property not mentioned in the class definition raises a runtime error. `Model` and the various `Property` definitions also provide other features for managing the structure of your data, such as automatic values, required values, and the ability to add your own validation and serialization logic.

It's important to notice that these validation features are provided by the `Model` class and your application code, *not* the datastore. Even if part of your app uses a `Model` class to ensure a property's value meets certain conditions, another part of your app can still retrieve the entity without using the class and do whatever it likes to that value. The bad value won't raise an error until the app tries to load the changed entity into a new instance of the `Model` class. This is both a feature and a burden: your app can manage entities flexibly and enforce structure where needed, but it must also be careful when those structures need to change. Data modeling and the `Model` class are discussed in detail in Chapter 9.

The `Book` constructor accepts initial values for the object's properties as keyword arguments. The constructor code earlier could also be written like this:

```
obj = Book(title='The Grapes of Wrath',
           author='John Steinbeck',
           copyright_year=1939,
           author_birthdate=datetime.datetime(1902, 2, 27))
```

As written, this code does not set a key name for the new entity. Without a key name, the datastore generates a unique ID when the object is saved for the first time. If you prefer to use a key name generated by the app, you call the constructor with the `key_name` parameter:

```
obj = Book(key_name='0143039431',
           title='The Grapes of Wrath',
           author='John Steinbeck',
           copyright_year=1939,
           author_birthdate=datetime.datetime(1902, 2, 27))
```

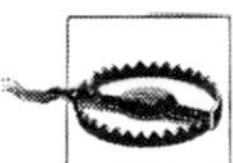

Because the Python API uses keyword arguments, object attributes, and object methods for purposes besides entity properties, there are several property names that are off-limits. For instance, you cannot use the Python API to set a property named `key_name`, because this could get confused with the `key_name` parameter for the object constructor. Names reserved by the Python API are enforced in the API, but *not* in the datastore itself. Google's official documentation lists the reserved property names.

The datastore reserves all property names beginning and ending with two underscores (such as `__internal__`). This is true for the Python API and the Java API, and will be true for future APIs as well.

The Python API ignores all object attributes whose names begin with a single underscore (such as `_counter`). You can use such attributes to attach data and functionality to an object that should not be saved as properties for the entity.

The complete key of an entity, including the key name and kind, must be unique. (We'll discuss another part to keys that contributes to a key's uniqueness, called ancestors, in Chapter 7.) If you build a new object with a key that is already in use, and then try to save it, the save will replace the existing object. When you don't want to overwrite existing data, you can use a system-assigned ID in the key, or you can use a transaction to test for the existence of an entity with a given key and create it if it doesn't exist.

The Python API provides a shortcut for creating entities with app-assigned key names. The `get_or_insert()` class method takes a key name and either returns an existing entity with that key name, or creates a new entity with that key name and no properties and returns it. Either way, the method is guaranteed to return an object that represents an entity in the datastore:

```
obj = Book.get_or_insert('0143039431')

if obj.title:
    # Book already exists.
    # ...
else:
    obj.title = 'The Grapes of Wrath'
    obj.author = 'John Steinbeck'
    obj.copyright_year = 1939
    obj.author_birthdate = datetime.datetime(1902, 2, 27)

    obj.put()
```

The Python datastore code shown in this book uses the `ext.db` library, provided in the App Engine SDK. The App Engine team recently added a new Python datastore library to the SDK, called NDB (`ext.ndb`). NDB is similar to `ext.db`, but adds powerful features for structured data, automatic caching, and efficient use of service calls. See the App Engine website for more information on NDB.

Introducing the Java Datastore API

App Engine for Java includes support for two major standard interfaces for databases: Java Data Objects (JDO) and the Java Persistence API (JPA). Like the other standards-based interfaces in the App Engine Java API, using one of these interfaces makes it easier to move your application from and to another platform. JDO and JPA support different kinds of databases, including object databases and relational databases. They provide an object-oriented interface to your data, even if the underlying database is not an object store.

Many of the concepts of these interfaces translate directly to App Engine datastore concepts: classes are kinds, objects are entities, fields are properties. App Engine's implementation also supports several advanced features of these interfaces, such as object relationships. Inevitably, some concepts do not translate directly and have behaviors that are specific to App Engine.

We'll discuss one of these interfaces, JPA, in Chapter 10. For now, here is a simple example of a data class using JPA:

```
import java.util.Date;
import javax.persistence.Entity;
import javax.persistence.GeneratedValue;
import javax.persistence.GenerationType;
import javax.persistence.Id;

@Entity
public class Book {
    @Id
    @GeneratedValue(strategy = GenerationType.IDENTITY)
    private Long id;

    private String title;
    private String author;
    private int copyrightYear;
    private Date authorBirthdate;

    public Long getId() {
        return id;
    }

    public String getTitle() {
        return title;
    }
    public void setTitle(String title) {
        this.title = title;
    }

    public String getAuthor() {
        return author;
    }
    public void setAuthor(String author) {
        this.author = author;
    }

    public int getCopyrightYear() {
        return copyrightYear;
    }
    public void setCopyrightYear(int copyrightYear) {
        this.copyrightYear = copyrightYear;
    }

    public Date getAuthorBirthdate() {
        return authorBirthdate;
    }
    public void setAuthorBirthdate(Date authorBirthdate) {
        this.authorBirthdate = authorBirthdate;
    }
}
```

The JDO and JPA implementations are built on top of a low-level API for the App Engine datastore. The low-level API exposes all of the datastore's features, and corresponds directly to datastore concepts. For instance, you must use the low-level API to manipulate entities with properties of unknown names or value types. You can also use the low-level API directly in your applications, or use it to implement your own data management layer.

The following code creates a Book entity by using the low-level API:

```
import java.io.IOException;
import java.util.Calendar;
import java.util.Date;
import java.util.GregorianCalendar;

import javax.servlet.http.HttpServlet;
import javax.servlet.http.HttpServletRequest;
import javax.servlet.http.HttpServletResponse;

import com.google.appengine.api.datastore.DatastoreService;
import com.google.appengine.api.datastore.DatastoreServiceFactory;
import com.google.appengine.api.datastore.Entity;

// ...
        DatastoreService ds = DatastoreServiceFactory.getDatastoreService();

        Entity book = new Entity("Book");

        book.setProperty("title", "The Grapes of Wrath");
        book.setProperty("author", "John Steinbeck");
        book.setProperty("copyrightYear", 1939);
        Date authorBirthdate =
            new GregorianCalendar(1902, Calendar.FEBRUARY, 27).getTime();
        book.setProperty("authorBirthdate", authorBirthdate);

        ds.put(book);

        // ...
```

Notice that the application code, not the datastore, is responsible for managing the structure of the data. JDO and JPA impose this structure by using classes whose fields are persisted to the datastore behind the scenes. This can be both a benefit and a burden when you need to change the structure of existing data.

To illustrate the datastore concepts, we will use the low-level API for Java examples in the next few chapters. In Chapter 10, we reintroduce JPA, and discuss how JPA concepts correspond with App Engine concepts. For more information on the Java Data Objects interface, see the official App Engine documentation.

If you'd prefer object-oriented management of datastore entities but do not need to use JPA for portability purposes, consider Objectify, a third-party open source project. Objectify is specific to App Engine, and supports most of the features of the low-level API. See the Objectify website for more information:

http://code.google.com/p/objectify-appengine/

Property Values

Each value data type supported by the datastore is represented by a primitive type in the language for the runtime or a class provided by the API. The data types and their language-specific equivalents are listed in Table 5-1. In this table, `db` is the Python package `google.appengine.ext.db`, and `datastore` is the Java package `com.google.appengine.api.datastore`.

Table 5-1. Datastore property value types and equivalent language types

Data type	Python type	Java type
Unicode text string (up to 500 bytes, indexed)	`unicode` or `str` (converted to `unicode` as ASCII)	`java.lang.String`
Long Unicode text string (not indexed)	`db.Text`	`datastore.Text`
Short byte string (up to 500 bytes, indexed)	`db.ByteString`	`datastore.ShortBlob`
Long byte string (not indexed)	`db.Blob`	`datastore.Blob`
Boolean	`bool`	`boolean`
Integer (64-bit)	`int` or `long` (converted to 64-bit `long`)	`byte`, `short`, `int`, or `long` (converted to `long`)
Float (double precision)	`float`	`float` or `double` (converted to `double`)
Date-time	`datetime.datetime`	`java.util.Date`
Null value	`None`	`null`
Entity key	`db.Key`	`datastore.Key`
A Google account	`users.User`	`...api.users.User`
A category (GD)	`db.Category`	`datastore.Category`
A URL (GD)	`db.Link`	`datastore.Link`
An email address (GD)	`db.Email`	`datastore.Email`
A geographical point (GD)	`db.GeoPt`	`datastore.GeoPt`
An instant messaging handle (GD)	`db.IM`	`datastore.IMHandle`
A phone number (GD)	`db.PhoneNumber`	`datastore.PhoneNumber`

Data type	Python type	Java type
A postal address (GD)	`db.PostalAddress`	`datastore.PostalAddress`
A user rating (GD)	`db.Rating`	`datastore.Rating`
A Blobstore key	`ext.blobstore.BlobKey`	`blobstore.BlobKey`

The datastore types in this table labeled "(GD)" are types borrowed from the Google Data protocol. These are supported as distinct native data types in the datastore, although most of them are implemented as text strings. Notable exceptions are `GeoPt`, which is a pair of floating-point values for latitude (–90 to +90) and longitude (–180 to +180), and `Rating`, which is an integer between 1 and 100.

Blobstore keys refer to values in the Blobstore. See Chapter 12 for more information.

Example 5-2 demonstrates the use of several of these data types in Python.

Example 5-2. Python code to set property values of various types

```
from google.appengine.ext import webapp
from google.appengine.ext import db
from google.appengine.api import users
import datetime

class Comment(db.Expando):
    pass

class CommentHandler(webapp.RequestHandler):
    def post(self):
        c = Comment()
        c.commenter = users.get_current_user()  # returns a users.User object
        c.message = db.Text(self.request.get('message'))
        c.date = datetime.datetime.now()
        c.put()

        # Display the result page...
```

When you use Python's `db.Expando` or Java's low-level datastore API, types that are widened to other types when stored come back as the wider datastore types when you retrieve the entity. For instance, a Java `Integer` comes back as a `Long`. If you use these APIs in your app, it's best to use the native datastore types, so the value types stay consistent.

The data modeling interfaces offer a way to store values in these alternate types and convert them back automatically when retrieving the entity. See Chapters 9 and 10.

Strings, Text, and Blobs

The datastore has two distinct data types for storing strings of text: short strings and long strings. Short strings are indexed; that is, they can be the subject of queries, such as a search for every Person entity with a given value for a last_name property. Short string values must be less than 500 bytes in length. Long strings can be longer than 500 bytes, but are not indexed.

Text strings, short and long, are strings of characters from the Unicode character set. Internally, the datastore stores Unicode strings by using the UTF-8 encoding, which represents some characters using multiple bytes. This means that the 500-byte limit for short strings is not necessarily the same as 500 Unicode characters. The actual limit on the number of characters depends on which characters are in the string.

The Python API distinguishes between short strings and long strings, using Python data types. The Python built-in types unicode and str represent short string values. str values are assumed to be text encoded as ASCII, and are treated as UTF-8 (which is equivalent to ASCII for the first 128 characters in the character set). For long strings, the Python API includes a db.Text class, which takes a unicode or str value as an argument for its constructor:

```
# Short strings.
e.prop = "a short string, as an ASCII str"
e.prop = unicode("a short string, as a unicode value")

# A long string.
e.prop = db.Text("a long string, can be longer than 500 bytes")
```

The Java API makes a similar distinction, treating String values as short strings, and using the datastore.Text class to represent long text strings.

The datastore also supports two additional classes for strings of bytes, or "blobs." Blobs are not assumed to be of any particular format, and their bytes are preserved. This makes them good for nontext data, such as images, movies, or other media. As with text strings, the blob types come in indexed and nonindexed varieties. The Python API provides the db.Blob class to represent blob values, which takes a str value as an argument for its constructor:

```
# A blob. self.request.body is the body of the request in a
# webapp request handler, such as an uploaded file.
e.prop = db.Blob(self.request.body)
```

In Java, the blob types are datastore.ShortBlob and datastore.Blob.

Unset Versus the Null Value

One possible value of a property is the null value. In Python, the null value is represented by the Python built-in value None. In Java, this value is null.

A property with the null value is not the same as an unset property. Consider the following Python code:

```
class Entity(db.Expando):
    pass
```

```
a = Entity()
a.prop1 = 'abc'
a.prop2 = None
a.put()

b = Entity()
b.prop1 = 'def'
b.put()
```

This creates two entities of the kind `Entity`. Both entities have a property named `prop1`. The first entity has a property named `prop2`; the second does not.

Of course, an unset property can be set later:

```
b.prop2 = 123
b.put()

# b now has a property named "prop2."
```

Similarly, a set property can be made unset. In the Python API, you delete the property by deleting the attribute from the object, using the `del` keyword:

```
del b.prop2
b.put()

# b no longer has a property named "prop2."
```

In Java, the low-level datastore API's `Entity` class has methods to set properties (`setProperty()`) and unset properties (`removeProperty()`).

Multivalued Properties

As we mentioned earlier, a property can have multiple values. We'll discuss the more substantial aspects of multivalued properties when we talk about queries and data modeling. But for now, it's worth a brief mention.

A property can have one or more values. A property cannot have zero values; a property without a value is simply unset. Each value for a property can be of a different type, and can be the null value.

The datastore preserves the order of values as they are assigned. The Python API returns the values in the same order as they were set.

In Python, a property with multiple values is represented as a single Python `list` value:

```
e.prop = [1, 2, 'a', None, 'b']
```

Because a property must have at least one value, it is an error to assign an empty list (`[]` in Python) to a property on an entity whose Python class is based on the `Expando` class:

```
class Entity(db.Expando):
    pass
```

```
e = Entity()
e.prop = []  # ERROR
```

In contrast, the `Model` base class includes a feature that automatically translates between the empty list value and "no property set." You'll see this feature in Chapter 9.

In the Java low-level datastore API, you can store multiple values for a property by using a `Collection` type. The low-level API returns the values as a `java.util.List`. The items are stored in the order provided by the `Collection` type's iterator. For many types, such as `SortedSet` or `TreeSet`, this order is deterministic. For others, such as `HashSet`, it is not. If the app needs the original data structure, it must convert the `List` returned by the datastore to the appropriate type.

Keys and Key Objects

The key for an entity is a value that can be retrieved, passed around, and stored like any other value. If you have the key for an entity, you can retrieve the entity from the datastore quickly, much more quickly than with a datastore query. Keys can be stored as property values, as an easy way for one entity to refer to another.

The Python API represents an entity key value as an instance of the `Key` class, in the `db` package. To get the key for an entity, you call the entity object's `key()` method. The `Key` instance provides access to its several parts by using accessor methods, including the kind, key name (if any), and system-assigned ID (if the entity does not have a key name).

The Java low-level API is similar: the `getKey()` method of the `Entity` class returns an instance of the `Key` class.

When you construct a new entity object and do not provide a key name, the entity object has a key, but the key does not yet have an ID. The ID is populated when the entity object is saved to the datastore for the first time. You can get the key object prior to saving the object, but it will be incomplete:

```
e = Entity()
e.prop = 123

k = e.key()  # key is incomplete, has neither key name nor ID
kind = k.kind()  # 'Entity'

e.put()  # ID is assigned
k = e.key()  # key is complete, has ID
id = k.id()  # the system-assigned ID
```

If the entity object was constructed with a key name, the key is complete before the object is saved—although, if the entity has not been saved, the key name is not guaranteed to be unique. (In Python, the entity class method `get_or_insert()`, mentioned earlier, always returns a saved entity, either one that was saved previously or a new one created by the call.)

You can test whether a key is complete by using a method on the `Key` object. In Python, this is the `has_id_or_name()` method. The `id_or_name()` method returns either the object's key name or its ID, whichever one it has.

In Java, you can call `isComplete()` to test the `Key` for completeness, and `getId()` or `getName()` to get the numeric ID or the string name.

Once you have a complete key, you can assign it as a property value on another entity to create a reference:

```
e2 = Entity()
e2.ref = k
e2.put()
```

If you know the kind and either the key name or ID of an entity in the datastore, you can construct the key for that entity without its object. In Python, you use the `from_path()` class method of the `Key` class. A complete explanation of this feature involves another feature we haven't mentioned yet (ancestor paths), but the following suffices for the examples you've seen so far:

```
e = Entity(key_name='alphabeta')
e.prop = 123
e.put()

# ...

k = db.Key.from_path('Entity', 'alphabeta')
```

In Java, you can build a `Key` object from parts using `KeyFactory`. The static method `KeyFactory.createKey()` takes the kind and the ID or name as arguments:

```
Key k = KeyFactory.createKey("Entity", "alphabeta");
```

Ancestor paths are related to how the datastore does transactions. We'll get to them in Chapter 7. For the entities we have created so far, the path is just the kind followed by the ID or name.

Keys can be converted to string representations for the purposes of passing around as textual data, such as in a web form or cookie. The string representation avoids characters considered special in HTML or URLs, so it is safe to use without escaping characters. The encoding of the value to a string is simple and easily reversed, so if you expose the string value to users, be sure to encrypt it, or make sure all key parts (such as kind names) are not secret. When accepting an encoded key string from a client, always validate the key before using it.

To convert between a key object and an encoded key string in Python:

```
k_str = str(k)

# ...
```

```
k = db.Key(k_str)
```

And in Java:

```
String k_str = KeyFactory.keyToString(k);

// ...

Key k = KeyFactory.stringToKey(k_str);
```

The Java `Key` class's `toString()` method does not return the key's string encoding. You must use `KeyFactory.keyToString()` to get the string encoding of a key.

Using Entities

Let's look briefly at how to retrieve entities from the datastore by using keys, how to inspect the contents of entities, and how to update and delete entities. The API methods for these features are straightforward.

Getting Entities Using Keys

Given a complete key for an entity, you can retrieve the entity from the datastore.

In the Python API, you can call the `get()` function in the `db` package with the `Key` object as an argument:

```
from google.appengine.ext import db

k = db.Key.from_path('Entity', 'alphabeta')

e = db.get(k)
```

If you know the kind of the entity you are fetching, you can also use the `get()` class method on the appropriate entity class. This does a bit of type checking, ensuring that the key you provide is of the appropriate kind:

```
class Entity(db.Expando):
    pass

e = Entity.get(k)
```

To fetch multiple entities in a batch, you can pass the keys to `get()` as a list. Given a list, the method returns a list containing entity objects, with `None` values for keys that do not have a corresponding entity in the datastore:

```
entities = db.get([k1, k2, k3])
```

Getting a batch of entities in this way performs a single service call to the datastore for the entire batch. This is faster than getting each entity in a separate call. The result of a batch get is unlimited.

For convenience, entity classes include methods that take just the IDs or key names and retrieve the corresponding entities, inferring the kind from the class name. See `get_by_id()` and `get_by_key_name()` in the official reference documentation.

In the Java low-level API, you get an entity by its key, using a `DatastoreService` instance (returned by `DatastoreServiceFactory.getDatastoreService()`). The instance provides a `get()` method that takes a `Key` for a single entity get, or an `Iterable<Key>` for a batch get. If given an iterable of keys, `get()` returns a `Map` of `Key` to `Entity`:

```
DatastoreService ds = DatastoreServiceFactory.getDatastoreService();

Map<Key, Entity> entities = ds.get(new ArrayList(Arrays.asList(k1, k2, k3)));

Entity e1 = entities.get(k1);
```

Of course, you won't always have the keys for the entities you want to fetch from the datastore. To retrieve entities that meet other criteria, you use datastore queries. Queries are discussed in Chapter 6.

Inspecting Entity Objects

Entity objects have methods for inspecting various aspects of the entity.

In the Java API, the methods of the `Entity` class provide straightforward access to the key (`getKey()`) and kind (`getKind()`) of the entity. The `getProperty()` method returns the value of a property given its name. The `hasProperty()` method tests whether a property is set. `setProperty()` takes a name and a value and sets the property, replacing any existing value.

The Python API has several features for inspecting entities worth mentioning here. You've already seen the `key()` method of an entity object, which returns the `db.Key`.

The `is_saved()` method returns `False` if the object has not been saved to the datastore since the object was constructed. If the object has been saved since it was constructed, or if the object was retrieved from the datastore, the method returns `True`. The method continues to return `True` even if the object's properties have been modified, so do not rely on this method to track changes to properties of previously saved entities:

```
e = Entity()
# e.is_saved() == False

e.put()
# e.is_saved() == True
```

In Java, you can tell if an entity with a system-assigned ID has been saved by calling the `isComplete()` method of its `Key` (`entity.getKey().isComplete()`). A key is complete if it has either a name or a system-assigned ID. A new entity created without a key name has an incomplete key if it has not been saved; saving it populates the system ID and completes the key.

In Python, entity properties can be accessed and modified just like object attributes:

```
e.prop1 = 1
e.prop2 = 'two'

print 'prop2 has the value ' + e.prop2
```

You can use Python built-in functions for accessing object attributes to access entity properties. For instance, to test that an entity has a property with a given name, use the `hasattr()` built-in:

```
if hasattr(e, 'prop1'):
    # ...
```

To get or set a property whose name is defined in a string, use **`getattr()`** and `setattr()`, respectively:

```
# Set prop1, prop2, ..., prop9.
for n in range(1, 10):
    value = n * n
    setattr(e, 'prop' + str(n), value)

value = getattr(e, 'prop' + str(7))
```

While entity objects support accessing properties by using these methods, the objects do not actually store property values as object attributes. For instance, you cannot use Python's **`dir()`** built-in to get a list of an entity's properties. Instead, entity objects provide their own method, **`instance_properties()`**, for this purpose:

```
for name in e.instance_properties():
    value = getattr(e, name)
```

Saving Entities

In Python, calling the `put()` method on an entity object saves the entity to the datastore. If the entity does not yet exist in the datastore, `put()` creates the entity. If the entity exists, `put()` updates the entity so that it matches the object:

```
e = Entity()
e.prop = 123

e.put()
```

When you update an entity, the app sends the complete contents of the entity to the datastore. The update is all or nothing: there is no way to send just the properties that have changed to the datastore. There is also no way to update a property on an entity without retrieving the complete entity, making the change, and then sending the new entity back.

You use the same API to create an entity as you do to update an entity. The datastore does not make a distinction between creates and updates. If you save an entity with a complete key (such as a key with a kind and a key name) and an entity already exists with that key, the datastore replaces the existing entity with the new one.

If you want to test that an entity with a given key does not exist before you create it, you can do so using a transaction. You must use a transaction to ensure that another process doesn't create an entity with that key after you test for it and before you create it. For more information on transactions, see Chapter 7.

If you have several entity objects to save, you can save them all in one call using the `put()` function in the `db` package. The `put()` function can also take a single entity object:

```
db.put(e)
db.put([e1, e2, e3])
```

In Java, you can save entities by using the `put()` method of a `DatastoreService` instance. As with `get()`, the method takes a single `Entity` for a single put, or an `Iterable<Entity>` for a batch put.

When the call to `put()` returns, the datastore is up-to-date, and all future queries in the current request handler and other handlers will see the new data. The specifics of how the datastore gets updated are discussed in detail in Chapter 7.

Deleting Entities

Deleting entities works similarly to putting entities. In Python, you can call the `delete()` method on the entity object, or you can pass entity objects or `Key` objects to the `delete()` function:

```
e = db.get('Entity', 'alphabeta')
e.delete()

db.delete(e)
db.delete([e1, e2, e3])

# Deleting without first fetching the entity:
k = db.Key('Entity', 'alphabeta')
db.delete(k)
```

In Java, you call the `delete()` method of the `DatastoreService` with either a single `Key` or an `Iterable<Key>`.

As with gets and puts, a delete of multiple entities occurs in a single batch call to the service, and is faster than making multiple service calls. Delete calls only send the keys to the service, even if you pass entire entities to the function.

Allocating System IDs

When you create a new entity without specifying an explicit key name, the datastore assigns a numeric system ID to the entity. Your code can read this system ID from the entity's key after the entity has been created.

Sometimes you want the system to assign the ID, but you need to know what ID will be assigned before the entity is created. For example, say you are creating two entities, and the property of one entity must be set to the key of the other entity. One option is to save the first entity to the datastore, then read the key of the entity, set the property on the second entity, and then save the second entity:

```
class Entity(db.Expando):
    pass

e1 = Entity()
e1.put()

e2 = Entity()
e2.reference = e1.key()
e2.put()
```

This requires two separate calls to the datastore in sequence, which takes valuable clock time. It also requires a period of time where the first entity is in the datastore but the second entity isn't.

We can't read the key of the first entity before we save it, because it is incomplete: calling `e1.key()` before `e1.put()` would return an unusable value. We could use a key name instead of a system ID, giving us a complete key, but it's often the case that we can't easily calculate a unique key name, which is why we'd rather have a system-assigned ID.

To solve this problem, the datastore provides a method to allocate system IDs ahead of creating entities. You call the datastore to allocate an ID (or a range of IDs for multiple entities), then create the entity with an explicit ID. Note that this is not the same as using a key name string: you give the entity the allocated numeric ID, and it knows the ID came from the system.

In Python, you call the `db.allocate_ids()` function. The first argument is either a key or an instance of the corresponding (path and) kind for which the IDs are intended. The second argument is the number of IDs to allocate. The function returns a list of numeric IDs. After the IDs are allocated, the system will not assign those IDs to any entity of the given (path and) kind. To use an allocated ID, you construct a `Key` object with it, then construct the entity instance, using the `key` argument, like so:

```
# Allocate 1 system ID for entities of kind "Entity".
# The "0" in the representative key is ignored.
ids = db.allocate_ids(db.Key.from_path('Entity', 0), 1)

# Make a key of kind Entity with the allocated system ID.
e1_key = db.Key.from_path('Entity', ids[0])

e1 = Entity(key=e1_key)
e2 = Entity()
e2.reference = e1_key

db.put([e1, e2])
```

In Java, you call the `allocateIds()` service method. It takes a kind (as a `String`) and the number of IDs to allocate. If the new key will have an ancestor in its path, the parent `Key` must be the first argument. The method returns a `KeyRange`, an iterable object that generates `Key` objects in the allocated ID range. `KeyRange` also has a `getStart()` method, which returns the first `Key`. To create an entity with a given `Key`, you provide the `Key` as the sole argument to the `Entity` constructor:

```
import java.util.ArrayList;
import java.util.Arrays;
import com.google.appengine.api.datastore.DatastoreService;
import com.google.appengine.api.datastore.Entity;
import com.google.appengine.api.datastore.Key;
import com.google.appengine.api.datastore.KeyRange;

// ...
        // DatastoreService ds = ...;
        KeyRange range = ds.allocateIds("Entity", 1);
        Key e1Key = range.getStart();
        Entity e1 = new Entity(e1Key);
        Entity e2 = new Entity("Entity");
        e2.setProperty("reference", e1Key);

        ds.put(new ArrayList<Entity>(Arrays.asList(e1, e2)));
```

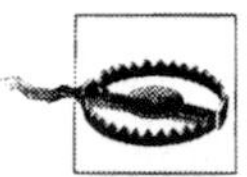

A batch put of two entities does not guarantee that both entities are saved together. If your app logic requires that either both entities are saved or neither are saved, you must use a transaction. See Chapter 7. (As you can probably tell by now, that's an important chapter.)

The Development Server and the Datastore

The development server simulates the datastore service on your local machine while you're testing your app. All datastore entities are saved to a local file. This file is associated with your app, and persists between runs of the development server, so your test data remains available until you delete it.

The Python development server stores datastore data in a file named *dev_appserver.datastore*, in a temporary location. You can tell the development server to reset this data when it starts. From the command line, you pass the `--clear_datastore` argument to `dev_appserver.py`:

```
dev_appserver.py --clear_datastore appdir
```

You can specify an explicit datastore file for the Python development server to use with the `--datastore_path=...` argument. To see the default location of this file, run `dev_appserver.py --help` and look for the description of this argument.

In the Python Launcher, you can specify this option in the Application Settings (in the Edit menu). Under Launch Settings, check the box labeled "Clear datastore on launch," then start the server. Remember to uncheck it again if you do not want it to clear the datastore every time.

The Java development server stores datastore data in a file named *local_db.bin* in your application's *war/WEB-INF/appengine-generated/* directory. To reset your development datastore, stop your server, delete this file, and then start the server again.

CHAPTER 6

Datastore Queries

Inevitably, an application that manages data must do more than store and retrieve that data one record at a time. It must also answer questions about that data: which records meet certain criteria, how records compare to one another, what a set of records represents in aggregate. Web applications in particular are expected not only to know the answers to questions about large amounts of data, but to provide them quickly in response to web requests.

Most database systems provide a mechanism for executing queries, and the App Engine datastore is no exception. But App Engine's technique differs significantly from that of traditional database systems. When the application asks a question, instead of rifling through the original records and performing calculations to determine the answer, App Engine simply finds the answer in a list of possible answers prepared in advance. App Engine can do this because it knows which questions are going to be asked.

This kind of list, or *index*, is common to many database technologies, and some relational databases can be told to maintain a limited set of indexes to speed up some kinds of queries. But App Engine is different: it maintains an index for *every* query the application is going to perform. Since the datastore only needs to do a simple scan of an index for every query, the application gets results back quickly. And for large amounts of data, App Engine can spread the data and the indexes across many machines, and get results back from all of them without an expensive aggregate operation.

This indexing strategy has significant drawbacks. The datastore's built-in query engine is downright weak compared to some relational databases, and is not suited to sophisticated data processing applications that would prefer slow but powerful runtime queries to fast simple ones. But most web applications need fast results, and the dirty secret about those powerful query engines is that they can't perform at web speeds with large amounts of data distributed across many machines. App Engine uses a model suited to scalable web applications: calculate the answers to known questions when the data is written, so reading is fast.

In this chapter, we explain how queries and indexes work, how the developer tools help you configure indexes automatically, and how to manage indexes as your application evolves. We also discuss several powerful features of the query engine, including cursors and projection queries. By understanding indexes, you will have an intuition for how to design your application and your data to make the most of the scalable datastore.

Queries and Kinds

You've seen how to retrieve an entity from the datastore given its key. But in most cases, the application does not know the keys of the entities it needs; it has only a general idea that it needs entities that meet certain criteria. For example, a leaderboard for the game app would need to retrieve the 10 `Player` entities with the highest `score` property values.

To retrieve entities this way, the app performs a *query*. A query includes:

- The kind of the entities to query
- Zero or more *filters*, criteria that property values must meet for an entity to be returned by the query
- Zero or more *sort orders* that determine the order in which results are returned based on property values

A query based on property values can only return entities of a single kind. This is the primary purpose of kinds: to determine which entities are considered together as possible results for a query. In practice, kinds correspond to the intuitive notion that each entity of the same nominal kind represents the same kind of data. But unlike other database systems, it's up to the app to enforce this consistency if it is desired, and the app can diverge from it if it's useful.

It is also possible to perform a limited set of queries on entities regardless of kind. Kindless queries can use a filter on the ID or key name, or on ancestors. We'll discuss ancestors and kindless queries in Chapter 7.

Query Results and Keys

When retrieving results for an entity query, the datastore returns the full entity for each result to the application.

For large entities, this may mean more data is transmitted between the datastore and the app than is needed. It's possible to fetch only a subset of properties under certain circumstances (we'll see this in "Projection Queries" on page 197), but these are not full entities. Another option is to store frequently accessed properties on one entity, and less popular properties on a separate related entity. The first entity stores the key of the second entity as a property, so when the app needs the less popular data, it queries for the first entity, then follows the reference to the second entity.

The datastore can return just the keys for the entities that match your query instead of fetching the full entities. A keys-only query is useful for determining the entities that match query criteria separately from when the entities are used. Keys can be remembered in the memcache or in a datastore property, and vivified as full entities when needed. We'll look at keys-only queries when we discuss each query API.

GQL

The Python and Java runtime environments provide several ways to formulate queries. They all do the same thing: they ask the datastore to return the entities whose keys and properties meet the given filter criteria, returned in an order determined by sorting the given properties.

One way to formulate a query is with *GQL*. GQL is a text-based query language that is intended to resemble SQL, the query language of relational databases. It supports only the features of the datastore's query engine, and therefore lacks many features common to SQL. But it is expressive and concise enough to be useful for datastore queries.

Say we have entities of the kind `Player` representing players in an online role-playing game. The following GQL query retrieves all `Player` entities whose "level" property is an integer between 5 and 20, sorted by level in ascending order, then by score in descending order:

```
SELECT * FROM Player
       WHERE level >= 5
         AND level <= 20
    ORDER BY level ASC, score DESC
```

You can use GQL to browse the contents of the datastore of your live application by using the Administration Console. To do this, select Data Viewer from the sidebar. You can browse entities by kind, or enter a GQL query. You can also create new entities through the Console, although new entities are limited to the kinds, properties, and value types of existing entities. You can also edit the properties of an entity by clicking on its ID. Figure 6-1 shows the results of running a GQL query in the Console.

You can only perform a query in the Administration Console if the query does not require a custom index, or if the app already has the requisite index for the query. We discuss indexes in depth later in this chapter.

Python apps can also perform queries using GQL from code. We'll look at this API in a moment. The Java datastore API does not yet support GQL. Java apps using JDO or JPA have other textual query languages at their disposal.

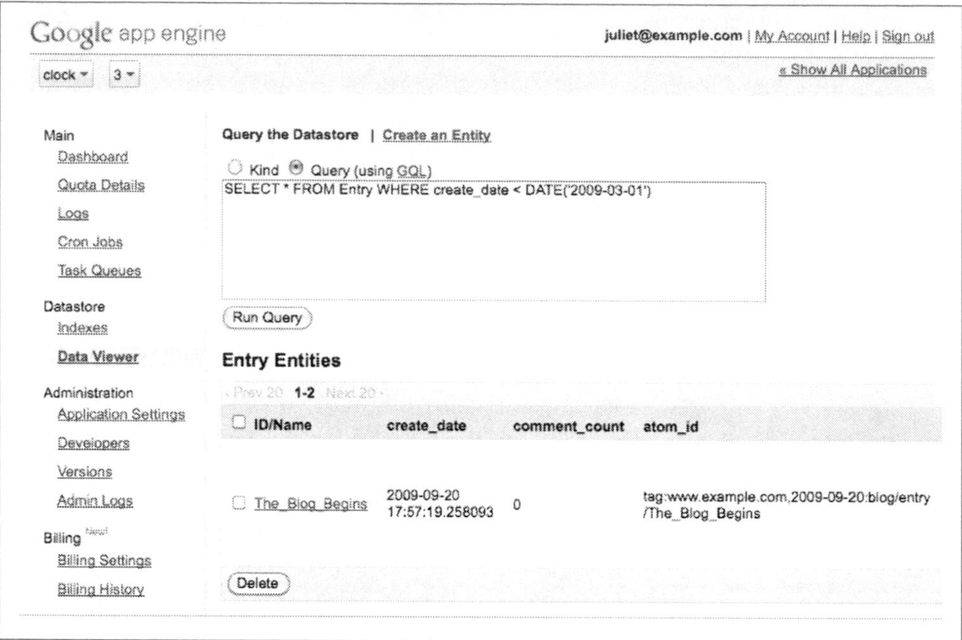

Figure 6-1. The Data Viewer panel of the Administration Console

The first part of the SQL-like syntax in the preceding GQL query, `SELECT * FROM Player`, says that the datastore should return complete entities as results, and that it should only consider entities of the kind `Player`. This is the most common kind of query. Unlike a SQL database, the datastore cannot "join" properties from entities of multiple kinds into a single set of results. Only one kind can appear after the `FROM`.

Despite its similarity with SQL, GQL can only represent queries, and cannot perform updates, inserts, or deletes. In other words, every GQL query begins with `SELECT`.

The rest of the query syntax also resembles SQL, and translates directly to filters and sort orders. The `WHERE` clause, if present, represents one or more filter conditions, separated by `AND`. The `ORDER BY` clause, if present, represents one or more sort orders, separated by commas, applied from left to right.

Each condition in a `WHERE` clause consists of the name of a property, a comparison operator, and a value. You can also specify a condition that matches an entity's ID or key name by using the reserved name `__key__` like a property name. (That's two underscores, the word "key," and two underscores.)

The datastore query engine supports five comparison operators for filters: `=`, `<`, `<=`, `>`, and `>=`. GQL also supports two additional operators: `!=`, meaning "not equal to," and `IN`, which tests that the value equals any in a set of values.

For `IN`, the values are represented by a comma-delimited list of values surrounded by parentheses:

```
SELECT * FROM Player WHERE level IN (5, 6, 7)
```

Internally, GQL translates the `!=` and `IN` operators into multiple datastore queries that have the same effect. If a query contains an `IN` clause, the query is evaluated once for each value in the clause, using an `=` filter. The results of all the queries are aggregated. The `!=` operator performs the query once using a `<` filter and once using a `>`, then aggregates the results. Using these operators more than once in a GQL statement requires a query for each combination of the required queries, so be judicious in their use.

The `WHERE` clause is equivalent to one or more filters. It is not like SQL's `WHERE` clause, and does not support arbitrary logical expressions. In particular, it does not support testing the logical-OR of two conditions.

The value on the righthand side of a condition can be a literal value that appears inside the query string. Seven of the datastore value types have string literal representations, as shown in Table 6-1.

Table 6-1. GQL value literals for datastore types

Type	Literal syntax	Examples
String	Single-quoted string; escape the quote by doubling it	`'Haven''t You Heard'`
Integer or float	Sign, digits; float uses decimal point	`-7 3.14`
Boolean	True or false keywords	`TRUE FALSE`

Date-time, date or time	Type, and value as numbers or a string
	`DATETIME(year, month, day, hour, minute, second)`
	`DATETIME('YYYY-MM-DD HH:MM:SS')`
	`DATE(year, month, day)`
	`DATE('YYYY-MM-DD')`
	`TIME(hour, minute, second)`
	`TIME('HH:MM:SS')`
		`DATETIME(1999, 12, 31, 23, 59, 59)`
		`DATETIME('1999-12-31 23:59:59')`
		`DATE(1999, 12, 31)`
		`DATE('1999-12-31')`
		`TIME(23, 59, 59)`
		`TIME('23:59:59')`

Entity key	Entity kind, and name or ID; can be a path
	`KEY('kind', 'name'/id)`
	`KEY('kind', 'name'/id, 'kind', 'name'/id, ...)`
		`KEY('Player', 1287)`

User object	`User('email-address')`	`User('edward@example.com')`
GeoPt object	`GEOPT(lat, long)`	`GEOPT(37.4219, -122.0846)`

The type of a filter's value is significant in a datastore query. If you use the wrong type for a value, such as by specifying a `'string_key'` when you meant to specify a `KEY('kind', 'key_name')`, your query may not return the results you intend, or may unexpectedly return no results.

A GQL query can specify a `LIMIT`, a maximum number of results to return. A query can also specify an `OFFSET`, a number of results to skip before returning the remaining results. The following example returns the third, fourth, and fifth results, and may return fewer if the query has fewer than five results:

```
SELECT * FROM Player LIMIT 3 OFFSET 2
```

GQL keywords, shown here in uppercase as is traditional with SQL, are case-insensitive. Kind and property names, however, are case-sensitive.

The Python Query API

Recall that the Python datastore API represents entities using objects of classes named after kinds. Example 6-1 shows Python code that creates three `Player` entities for an online role-playing game.

Example 6-1. Python code to create several entities of the kind Player

```
from google.appengine.ext import db
import datetime

class Player(db.Expando):
    pass

player1 = Player(name='wizard612',
                 level=1,
                 score=32,
                 charclass='mage',
                 create_date=datetime.datetime.now())
player1.put()

player2 = Player(name='druidjane',
                 level=10,
                 score=896,
                 charclass='druid',
                 create_date=datetime.datetime.now())
player2.put()

player3 = Player(name='TheHulk',
                 level=7,
                 score=500,
                 charclass='warrior',
                 create_date=datetime.datetime.now())
player3.put()
```

Once again, we'll use `Expando` to keep the examples simple. As we start talking about queries, the importance of using a consistent layout, or *schema*, for entities of a kind will become apparent.

The Python API provides two ways to formulate queries, one using an object-oriented interface and one based on GQL.

The Query Class

The first way to formulate a query is with an instance of the `Query` class. A `Query` object can be constructed in one of two ways, with equivalent results:

```
q = db.Query(Player)
```

```
q = Player.all()
```

In both cases, `q` is assigned a new `Query` instance that represents all entities of the kind `Player`. The query is not executed right away; right now it's just a question waiting to be asked. Without filters or sort orders, the object represents a query for all objects of the given kind.

To apply a filter to the query, you call the `filter()` method on the `Query` object. It takes two arguments. The first argument is a string containing the name of a property, a space character, and a comparison operator. The second argument is the value for the comparison, of a type appropriate for the situation:

```
q.filter('level >', 5)
```

You specify multiple filters by calling the `filter()` method multiple times. An entity must meet all filter criteria in order to be a result for the query. That is, filters have a logical-AND relationship with one another:

```
q.filter('level >', 5)
q.filter('level <', 20)
```

For convenience, the `filter()` method returns the `Query` object, so you can chain multiple calls to `filter()` in a single line:

```
q.filter('level >', 5).filter('level <', 20)
```

The `filter()` method supports the equality (`=`) operator, and the four inequality operators (`<`, `<=`, `>`, and `>=`). The `Query` class also supports the `!=` (not-equal) and `IN` operators from GQL, and does so in the same way, using multiple datastore queries and aggregating the results.

To apply a sort order, you call the `order()` method. This method takes one argument, a string containing the name of a property to sort by. If the string begins with a hyphen character (`-`), the sort will be in descending order; otherwise, the sort will be in ascending order. Like `filter()`, `order()` returns the `Query` object, for chaining:

```
q.order('-score')
```

The datastore can sort query results by multiple properties. First, it sorts by the property and order from the first call to `order()`, then it sorts entities with equal values for the first property, using the second order, and so on. For example, the following sorts first by `level` ascending, then by `score` descending:

```
q.order('level').order('-score')
```

The query engine supports limiting the number of results returned, and skipping ahead a number of results. You specify the limit and offset when you retrieve the results, described later.

GQL in Python

The Python environment includes a rich API for preparing queries, using GQL. In addition to the pure textual syntax, the Python API supports additional syntax for parameterized substitution of filter values.

To use GQL from Python, you instantiate an instance of the `GqlQuery` class with the text of the query:

```
q = db.GqlQuery("""SELECT * FROM Player
                    WHERE level > 5
                      AND level < 20
                 ORDER BY level ASC, score DESC""")
```

You can also instantiate a `GqlQuery` from the kind class directly, using its `gql()` class method. When using this method, omit the `SELECT * FROM Kind` from the string, since this is implied by the use of the method:

```
q = Player.gql("""WHERE level > 5
                    AND level < 20
               ORDER BY level ASC, score DESC""")
```

You can specify values for conditions by using parameter substitution. With parameter substitution, the query string contains a placeholder with either a number or a name, and the actual value is passed to `GqlQuery()` or `gql()` as either a positional argument or a keyword argument. The number or name appears in the query string preceded by a colon (`:1` or `:argname`):

```
q = db.GqlQuery("""SELECT * FROM Player
                    WHERE level > :1
                      AND level < :2""",
                5, 20)

q = db.GqlQuery("""SELECT * FROM Player
                    WHERE level > :min_level
                      AND level < :max_level""",
                min_level=5, max_level=20)
```

One advantage to parameter substitution is that each argument value is of the appropriate datastore type, so you don't need to bother with the string syntax for specifying typed values. For the datastore types that do not have string literal syntax (mostly the Google Data value types mentioned in Table 5-1), parameter substitution is the only way to use values of those types in a GQL query.

You can rebind new values to a GQL query by using parameter substitution after the `GqlQuery` object has been instantiated using the `bind()` method. This means you can reuse the `GqlQuery` object for multiple queries that have the same structure but different values. This saves time because the query string only needs to be parsed once. The `bind()` method takes the new values as either positional arguments or keyword arguments.

You can save more time by caching parameterized GqlQuery objects in global variables. This way, the query string is parsed only when a server loads the application for the first time, and the application reuses the object for all subsequent calls handled by that server:

```
_LEADERBOARD_QUERY = db.GqlQuery(
    """SELECT * FROM Player
          WHERE level > :min_level
            AND level < :max_level
       ORDER BY level ASC, score DESC""")

class LeaderboardHandler(webapp.RequestHandler):
    def get(self):
        _LEADERBOARD_QUERY.bind(min_level=5, max_level=20)
        # ...
```

Retrieving Results

Once you have a Query or GqlQuery object configured with filters, sort orders, and value bindings (in the case of GqlQuery), you can execute the query, using one of several methods. The query is not executed until you call one of these methods, and you can call these methods repeatedly on the same query object to re-execute the query and get new results.

The fetch() method returns a number of results, up to a specified limit. fetch() returns a list of entity objects, which are instances of the kind class:

```
q = db.Query(Player).order('-score')

results = q.fetch(10)
```

When serving web requests, it's always good to limit the amount of data the datastore might return, so an unexpectedly large result set doesn't cause the request handler to exceed its deadline. The fetch() method requires an argument specifying the number of results to fetch (the limit argument).

The fetch() method also accepts an optional offset parameter. If provided, the method skips that many results, then returns subsequent results, up to the specified limit:

```
q = db.Query(Player).order('-score')

results = q.fetch(10, offset=20)
```

For a GqlQuery, the fetch result limit and offset are equivalent to the LIMIT and OFFSET that can be specified in the query string itself. The arguments to fetch() override those specified in the GQL statement. The limit argument to fetch() is required, so it always overrides a GQL LIMIT clause.

In order to perform a fetch with an offset, the datastore must find the first result for the query and then scan down the index to the offset. The amount of time this takes is proportional to the size of the offset, and may not be suitable for large offsets.

If you just want to retrieve results in batches, such as for a paginated display, there's a better way: query cursors. See "Query Cursors" on page 192.

It's common for an app to perform a query expecting to get just one result, or nothing. You can do this with `fetch(1)`, and then test whether the list it returns is empty. For convenience, the query object also provides a `get()` method, which returns either the first result, or the Python value `None` if the query did not return any results:

```
q = db.Query(Player).filter('name =', 'django97')

player = q.get()
if player:
    # ...
```

The `count()` method executes the query, then returns the number of results that would be returned instead of the results themselves. `count()` must perform the query to count the results in the index, and so takes time proportional to what it is counting. `count()` accepts a limit as a parameter, and providing one causes the method to return immediately once that many results have been counted:

```
q = db.Query(Player).filter('level >', 10)
if q.count(100) == 100:
    # 100 or more players are above level 10.
```

To test whether a query would return a result, without retrieving any results:

```
if q.count(1) == 1:
    # The query has at least one result.
```

Query objects provide one other mechanism for retrieving results, and it's quite powerful. In the Python API, query objects are *iterable*. If you use the object in a context that accepts iterables, such as in a `for` loop, the object executes the query, then provides a Python standard iterator that returns each result one at a time, starting with the first result:

```
q = db.Query(Player).order('-score')

for player in q:
    # ...
```

As the app uses the iterator, the iterator fetches the results in small batches. The iterator will not stop until it reaches the last result. It's up to the app to stop requesting results from the iterator (to `break` from the `for` loop) when it has had enough.

Treating the query object as an iterable uses default options for the query. If you'd like to specify options but still use the iterable interface, call the `run()` method. This method takes the same options as `fetch()`, but returns the batch-loading iterator instead of the complete list of results.

Unlike `fetch()`, the `limit` argument is optional for `run()`. But it's useful! With the `limit` argument, results are fetched in batches with the iterator interface, but the query knows to stop fetching after reaching the limit:

```
for player in q.run(limit=100):
    # ...
```

This is especially useful for passing the iterator to a template, which may not have a way to stop the iteration on its own.

You can adjust the size of the batches fetched by the iterator interface by passing the `batch_size` argument to the `run()` method. The default is 20 results per batch.

When your application calls the `fetch()` method, your application must wait until all the results are retrieved before continuing. When using the iterator interface, results are retrieved in the background, as needed. This can make the overall running time of your request handler faster, because the datastore is working simultaneously with your app.

When using the query object as an iterator directly, the first call to the datastore does not happen until the first time the iterator is accessed, and the app must wait for the first batch of results before continuing. You can cause this first call to happen in the background by calling the `run()` method before using the iterator it returns:

```
player_iter = q.run()
# ... Do other things while the first batch is being fetched...

for player in player_iter:
    # ...
```

Keys-Only Queries

Instead of returning complete entities, the datastore can return just the keys of the entities that match the query. This can be useful in cases when a component only needs to know which entities are results, and doesn't need the results themselves. The component can store the keys for later retrieval of the entities, or pass the keys to other components, or perform further operations on the key list before fetching entities.

In the Python query API, you can query for keys by using either the `Query` interface or the `GqlQuery` interface. To request just the keys with `Query`, provide the `keys_only` argument set to `True` to the `Query` constructor:

```
q = db.Query(Player, keys_only=True)
```

To specify a keys-only query with GQL, begin the GQL query with SELECT __key__ (that's two underscores, the word key, and two more underscores) instead of SELECT *:

```
q = db.GqlQuery('SELECT __key__ FROM Player')
```

When performing a keys-only query, each result returned by the query object is a Key object instead of an instance of the model class:

```
q = db.Query(Player, keys_only=True)
for result_key in q:
    # result_key is a Key...
```

There is no way to perform keys-only queries by using the Model class methods all() and gql(). This makes sense: the return values of the Model methods represent collections of instances of the model class, not keys.

The Java Query API

If you are using the JPA interface or the JDO interface, you will use the query facilities of those interfaces to perform datastore queries: JPQL or JDOQL, respectively. The concepts of those interfaces map nicely to the concepts of datastore queries: a query has a kind (a class), filters, and sort orders. We'll look at the calling conventions for JPQL when we look at JPA in Chapter 10.

Naturally, the low-level Java datastore API includes a query interface as well, and it has more features. Here is a brief example:

```
import com.google.appengine.api.datastore.DatastoreService;
import com.google.appengine.api.datastore.DatastoreServiceFactory;
import com.google.appengine.api.datastore.Entity;
import com.google.appengine.api.datastore.PreparedQuery;
import com.google.appengine.api.datastore.Query;

// ...
        DatastoreService ds = DatastoreServiceFactory.getDatastoreService();

        Query q = new Query("Book");
        q.setFilter(
            new Query.FilterPredicate(
                "copyrightYear",
                Query.FilterOperator.LESS_THAN_OR_EQUAL,
                1950));
        q.addSort("title");

        PreparedQuery pq = ds.prepare(q);
        for (Entity result : pq.asIterable()) {
            String title = (String) result.getProperty("title");

            // ...
        }
```

To perform a query, you instantiate the Query class (from the com.google.appengine.api.datastore package), providing the name of the kind of the entities to query as an argument to the constructor. You call methods on the query object to add filters and sort orders. To perform the query, you pass the query object to a method of the `DatastoreService` instance. This method returns a `PreparedQuery` object, which you can manipulate to retrieve the results.

Let's take a closer look at building queries, and then fetching results.

Building the Query

You start a query by constructing a `Query` instance. To query entities of a kind, you provide the kind name as a constructor argument, as a string:

```
Query q = new Query("Book");
```

Without calling any additional methods, this represents a query for all entities of the kind `"Book"`.

You can tell the query to filter the results by calling the `setFilter()` method. A query has one filter, which can have one or more predicates. A predicate is a single property name, a comparison operator, and a value. If your query filter only has one predicate, you can construct a `Query.FilterPredicate`, and pass it directly to `setFilter()`:

```
q.setFilter(
    new Query.FilterPredicate(
        "copyrightYear",
        Query.FilterOperator.LESS_THAN_OR_EQUAL,
        1950));
```

Filter predicate operators include `LESS_THAN`, `LESS_THAN_OR_EQUAL`, `EQUAL`, `NOT_EQUAL`, `GREATER_THAN_OR_EQUAL`, `GREATER_THAN`, and `IN`.

To build a filter with more than one predicate, you use a `Query.CompositeFilter`. A composite filter is a collection of filters united by a logical operator, either "and" or "or." Each filter in the collection can be a filter predicate or another composite filter, allowing you to build complex filters.

The first argument to the `Query.CompositeFilter` constructor is the composite operator, either `Query.CompositeFilterOperator.AND` or `Query.CompositeFilterOperator.OR`. The second argument is a `Collection` of filters, each of which can be either a `Query.FilterPredicate` or a `Query.CompositeFilter` instance. The verbose object-oriented syntax looks like this:

```
q.setFilter(
    new Query.CompositeFilter(
        Query.CompositeFilterOperator.AND,
        new ArrayList<Query.Filter>(Arrays.asList(
            new Query.FilterPredicate(
                "copyrightYear",
                Query.FilterOperator.LESS_THAN_OR_EQUAL,
                1950),
            new Query.FilterPredicate(
                "category",
```

```
                                Query.FilterOperator.EQUAL,
                                "Science Fiction")))));
```

That can get a little unwieldy, so there's also a shortcut API using methods on the composite and predicate operator classes. `Query.CompositeFilterOperator.and()` and `Query.CompositeFilterOperator.or()` are static methods that take one or more filters and return a composite filter with the appropriate operator. Each filter predicate operator constant has an `of()` method that takes a property name and a value. The example above shortens to this:

```
q.setFilter(
    Query.CompositeFilterOperator.and(
        Query.FilterOperator.LESS_THAN_OR_EQUAL.of(
            "copyrightYear", 1950),
        Query.FilterOperator.EQUAL.of(
            "category", "Science Fiction")));
```

The filter predicate operators `IN` or `NOT_EQUAL` and the composite operator `OR` are not supported by the datastore natively. They are implemented by performing multiple datastore queries and processing the results. While it's possible to build arbitrarily complex query filters with the Java `Query` API, it's best to limit the use of these operators. See "Not-Equal and IN Filters" on page 181.

You can specify that the results of a query be sorted by calling the `addSort()` method for each sort order. The method takes a property name, and an optional `Query.SortDirection`, either `Query.SortDirection.ASCENDING` or `Query.SortDirection.DESCENDING`. The default is `ASCENDING`:

```
q.addSort("title");
```

Fetching Results with PreparedQuery

The query is not actually performed until you attempt to access results, using the `PreparedQuery` object. If you access the results by using an iterator via the `asIterable()` or `asIterator()` methods, the act of iterating causes the API to fetch the results in batches. When these methods are called without arguments, the resulting iterator keeps going until all results for the query have been returned. If a query has a large number of results, this may take longer than the time allowed for the request.

The `asIterable()` and `asIterator()` methods accept an optional argument, a `FetchOptions` object, that controls which results are returned. Options can include an *offset*, a number of results to skip prior to returning any, and a *limit*, a maximum number of results to return. `FetchOptions` uses a builder-style interface, as follows:

```
import com.google.appengine.api.datastore.Entity;
import com.google.appengine.api.datastore.FetchOptions;
import com.google.appengine.api.datastore.PreparedQuery;
import com.google.appengine.api.datastore.Query;
```

```
// ...
        // Query q = ...
        PreparedQuery pq = ds.prepare(q);

        Iterable<Entity> results =
            pq.asIterable(FetchOptions.Builder.withLimit(10).offset(20));

        for (Entity result : results) {
            String title = (String) result.getProperty("title");

            // ...
        }
```

This tells the datastore to skip the first 20 results, and return up to the next 10 results (if any).

In order to perform a fetch with an offset, the datastore must find the first result for the query and then scan down the index to the offset. The amount of time this takes is proportional to the size of the offset, and may not be suitable for large offsets.

If you just want to retrieve results in batches, such as for a paginated display, there's a better way: query cursors. See "Query Cursors" on page 192.

Instead of fetching results in batches, you can get all results in a list by calling the `asList()` method of the `PreparedQuery` class. The method returns a `List<Entity>`. Unlike the iterator interface, which gets results in batches, this method retrieves all results with a single service call. The method requires that a limit be specified using `FetchOptions`.

If a query is likely to have only one result, or if only the first result is desired, calling the `asSingleEntity()` method retrieves the result and returns an `Entity` object, or `null`.

If you just want a count of the results and not the entities themselves, you can call the `countEntities()` method of the `PreparedQuery`. Because the datastore has to perform the query to get the count, the speed of this call is proportional to the count, although faster than actually fetching the results.

To test whether a query would return a result without retrieving the result, call `countEntities()` with a limit of 1:

```
        if (pq.countEntities(FetchOptions.Builder.withLimit(1)) == 1) {
            // The query has at least one result.
        }
```

This is the fastest possible such test: it finds the first place in the index where there might be a result for the query, then attempts to count one result, and reports whether that count was successful.

Keys-Only Queries in Java

You can fetch just the keys for the entities that match a query instead of the full entities by using the low-level Java datastore API. To declare that a query should return just the keys, call the `setKeysOnly()` method on the `Query` object:

```
Query q = new Query("Book");

q.setKeysOnly();
```

When a query is set to return only keys, the results of the query are `Entity` objects without any properties set. You can get the key from these objects by using the `getKey()` method:

```
PreparedQuery pq = ds.prepare(q);
for (Entity result : pq.asIterable()) {
    Key k = result.getKey();

    // ...
}
```

You can also perform keys-only queries using the JDO and JPA interfaces. See Chapter 10.

Introducing Indexes

For every query an application performs, App Engine maintains an index, a single table of possible answers for the query. Specifically, it maintains an index for a set of queries that use the same filters and sort orders, possibly with different values for the filters. Consider the following simple query:

```
SELECT * FROM Player WHERE name = 'druidjane'
```

To perform this query, App Engine uses an index containing the keys of every `Player` entity and the value of each entity's `name` property, sorted by the `name` property values in ascending order. Such an index is illustrated in Figure 6-2.

To find all entities that meet the conditions of the query, App Engine finds the first row in the index that matches, then it scans down to the first row that doesn't match. It returns the entities mentioned on all rows in this range (not counting the nonmatching row), in the order they appear in the index. Because the index is sorted, all results for the query are guaranteed to be on consecutive rows in the table.

App Engine would use this same index to perform other queries with a similar structure but different values, such as the following query:

```
SELECT * FROM Player WHERE name = 'duran89'
```

This query mechanism is fast, even with a very large number of entities. Entities and indexes are distributed across multiple machines, and each machine scans its own index in parallel with the others. Each machine returns results to App Engine as it scans its

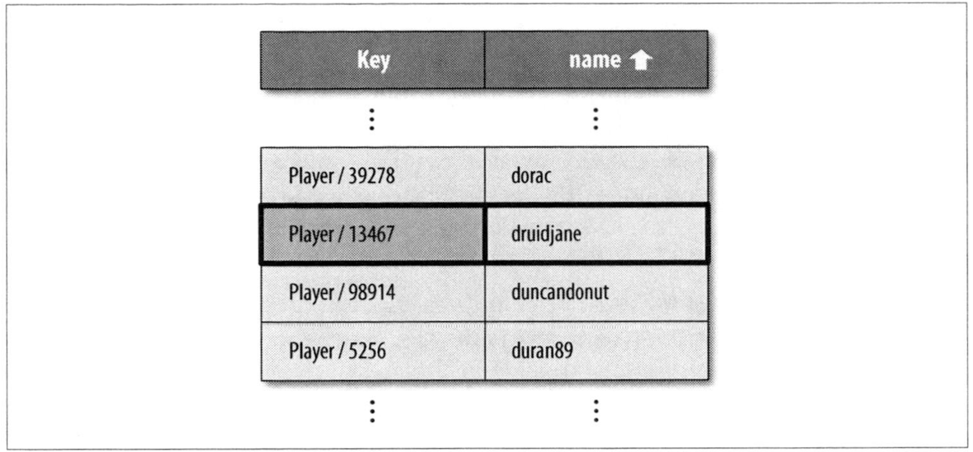

Figure 6-2. An index of Player entity keys and "name" property values, sorted by name in ascending order, with the result for WHERE name = 'druidjane'

own index, and App Engine delivers the final result set to the app, in order, as if all results were in one large index.

Another reason queries are fast has to do with how the datastore finds the first matching row. Because indexes are sorted, the datastore can use an efficient algorithm to find the first matching row. In the common case, finding the first row takes approximately the same amount of time regardless of the size of the index. In other words, the speed of a query is not affected by the size of the data set.

App Engine updates all relevant indexes when property values change. In this example, if an application retrieves a `Player` entity, changes the `name`, and then saves the entity with a call to the `put()` method, App Engine updates the appropriate row in the previous index. It also moves the row if necessary so the ordering of the index is preserved. The call to `put()` does not return until all appropriate indexes are updated.

Similarly, if the application creates a new `Player` entity with a `name` property, or deletes a `Player` entity with a `name` property, App Engine updates the index. In contrast, if the application updates a `Player` but does not change the `name` property, or creates or deletes a `Player` that does not have a `name` property, App Engine does not update the `name` index because no update is needed.

App Engine maintains two indexes like the previous example above for every property name and entity kind, one with the property values sorted in ascending order and one with values in descending order. App Engine also maintains an index of entities of each kind. These indexes satisfy some simple queries, and App Engine also uses them internally for bookkeeping purposes.

For other queries, you must tell App Engine which indexes to prepare. You do this using a configuration file, which gets uploaded along with your application's code. For

Python apps, this file is named *index.yaml*. For Java, this file is *WEB-INF/datastore-indexes.xml*.

It'd be a pain to write this file by hand, but thankfully you don't have to. While you're testing your application in the development web server from the SDK, when the app performs a datastore query, the server checks that the configuration file has an appropriate entry for the needed index. If it doesn't find one, it adds one. As long as the app performs each of its queries at least once during testing, the resulting configuration file will be complete.

The index configuration file must be complete, because when the app is running on App Engine, if the application performs a query for which there is no index, the query returns an error. You can tell the development web server to behave similarly if you want to test for these error conditions. (How to do this depends on which SDK you are using; see "Configuring Indexes" on page 200.)

Indexes require a bit of discipline to maintain. Although the development tools can help add index configuration, they cannot know when an index is unused and can be deleted from the file. Extra indexes consume storage space and slow down updates of properties mentioned in the index. And while the version of the app you're developing may not need a given index, the version of the app still running on App Engine may still need it. The App Engine SDK and the Administration Console include tools for inspecting and maintaining indexes. We'll look at these tools in Chapter 20.

Before we discuss index configuration, let's look more closely at how indexes support queries. We just saw an example where the results for a simple query appear on consecutive rows in a simple index. In fact, this is how most queries work: the results for every query that would use an index appear on consecutive rows in the index. This is both surprisingly powerful in some ways and surprisingly limited in others, and it's worth understanding why.

Automatic Indexes and Simple Queries

As we mentioned, App Engine maintains two indexes for every single property of every entity kind, one with values in ascending order and one with values in descending order. App Engine builds these indexes automatically, whether or not they are mentioned in the index configuration file. These automatic indexes satisfy the following kinds of queries using consecutive rows:

- A simple query for all entities of a given kind, no filters or sort orders
- One filter on a property using the equality (=) operator
- Filters using greater-than or less-than operators (>, >=, <, <=) on a single property
- One sort order, ascending or descending, and no filters, or with filters only on the same property used with the sort order
- Filters or a sort order on the entity key

- Kindless queries with or without key filters

Let's look at each of these in action.

All Entities of a Kind

The simplest datastore query asks for every entity of a given kind, in any order. Stated in GQL, a query for all entities of the kind `Player` looks like this:

```
SELECT * FROM Player
```

App Engine maintains an index mapping kinds to entity keys. This index is sorted using a deterministic ordering for entity keys, so this query returns results in "key order." The kind of an entity cannot be changed after it is created, so this index is updated only when entities are created and deleted.

Since a query can only refer to one kind at a time, you can imagine this index as simply a list of entity keys for each kind. Figure 6-3 illustrates an example of this index.

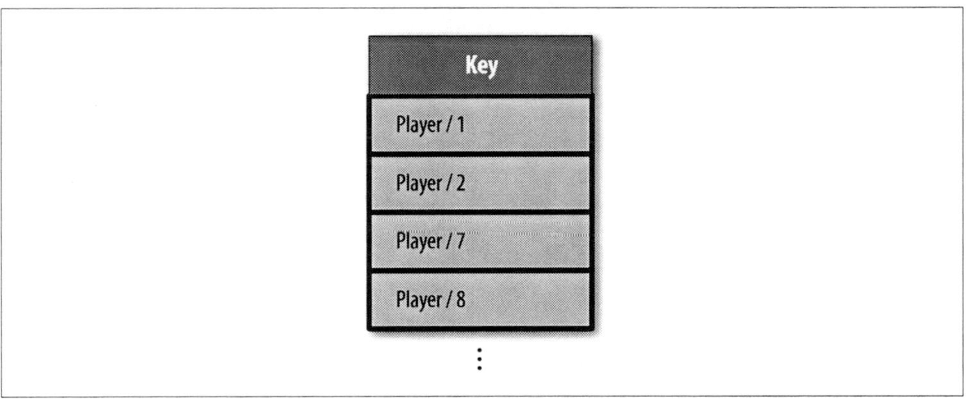

*Figure 6-3. An index of all Player entity keys, with results for SELECT * FROM Player*

When the query results are fetched, App Engine uses the entity keys in the index to find the corresponding entities, and returns the full entities to the application.

One Equality Filter

Consider the following query, which asks for every `Player` entity with a `level` property with a value of the integer 10:

```
SELECT * FROM Player WHERE level = 10
```

This query uses an index of `Player` entities with the `level` property, ascending—one of the automatic indexes. It uses an efficient algorithm to find the first row with a `level` equal to 10. Then it scans down the index until it finds the first row with a `level` not equal to 10. The consecutive rows from the first matching to the last matching represent

Key	level ⬆
⋮	⋮
Player / 9259	9
Player / 98914	9
Player / 5256	10
Player / 7289	10
Player / 13467	10
Player / 4751	11
⋮	⋮

Figure 6-4. An index of the Player entity "level" properties, sorted by level then by key, with results for WHERE level = 10

all the `Player` entities with a `level` property equal to the integer 10. This is illustrated in Figure 6-4.

Greater-Than and Less-Than Filters

The following query asks for every `Player` entity with a `score` property whose value is greater than the integer 500:

```
SELECT * FROM Player WHERE score > 500
```

This uses an index of `Player` entities with the `score` property, ascending, also an automatic index. As with the equality filter, it finds the first row in the index whose `score` is greater than 500. In the case of greater-than, since the table is sorted by `score` in ascending order, every row from this point to the bottom of the table is a result for the query. See Figure 6-5.

Similarly, consider a query that asks for every `Player` with a `score` less than 1,000:

```
SELECT * FROM Player WHERE score < 1000
```

App Engine uses the same index (`score`, ascending), and the same strategy: it finds the first row that matches the query, in this case the first row. Then it scans to the next row that doesn't match the query, the first row whose `score` is greater than or equal to `1000`. The results are represented by everything above that row.

Finally, consider a query for `score` values between 500 and 1,000:

```
SELECT * FROM Player WHERE score > 500 AND score < 1000
```

Key	score ⬆
⋮	⋮
Player / 10276	496
Player / 60126	500
Player / 9577	559
Player / 9259	590
Player / 8444	602
Player / 98914	642
⋮	⋮

Figure 6-5. An index of the Player entity "score" properties, sorted by "score" then by key, with results for WHERE score > 500

Once again, the same index and strategy prevail: App Engine scans from the top down, finding the first matching and next nonmatching rows, returning the entities represented by everything in between. This is shown in Figure 6-6.

If the values used with the filters do not represent a valid range, such as `score < 500 AND score > 1000`, the query planner notices this and doesn't bother performing a query, since it knows the query has no results.

One Sort Order

The following query asks for every `Player` entity, arranged in order by `level`, from lowest to highest:

```
SELECT * FROM Player ORDER BY level
```

As before, this uses an index of `Player` entities with `level` properties in ascending order. If both this query and the previous equality query were performed by the application, both queries would use the same index. This query uses the index to determine the order in which to return `Player` entities, starting at the top of the table and moving down until the application stops fetching results, or until the bottom of the table. Recall that every `Player` entity with a `level` property is mentioned in this table. See Figure 6-7.

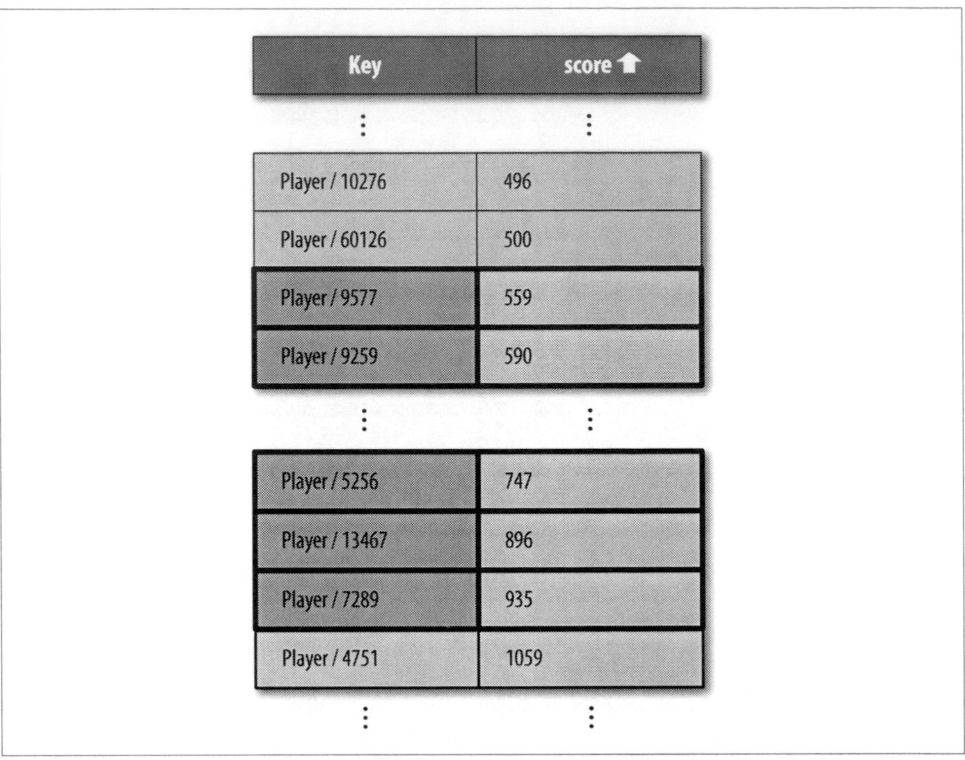

Figure 6-6. An index of the Player entity "score" properties, sorted by score, with results for WHERE score > 500 AND score < 1000

Key	level
Player / 39278	1
Player / 39320	1
Player / 40178	1
Player / 29911	2
Player / 84514	2

Figure 6-7. An index of the Player entity "level" properties sorted by level in ascending order, with results for ORDER BY level

The following query is similar to the previous one, but asks for the entities arranged by `level` from highest to lowest:

```
SELECT * FROM Player ORDER BY level DESC
```

This query cannot use the same index as before, because the results are in the wrong order. For this query, the results should start at the entity with the highest level, so the query needs an index where this result is in the first row. App Engine provides an automatic index for single properties in descending order for this purpose. See Figure 6-8.

Key	level ↓
Player / 3359	12
Player / 4751	11
Player / 7243	11
Player / 5256	10
Player / 7289	10
⋮	⋮

Figure 6-8. An index of the Player entity "level" properties sorted by level in descending order, with results for ORDER BY level DESC

If a query with a sort order on a single property also includes filters on that property, and no other filters, App Engine still needs only the one automatic index to fulfill the query. In fact, you may have noticed that for these simple queries, the results are returned sorted by the property in ascending order, whether or not the query specifies the sort order explicitly. In these cases, the ascending sort order is redundant.

Queries on Keys

In addition to filters and sort orders on properties, you can also perform queries with filters and sort orders on entity keys. You can refer to an entity's key in a filter or sort order using the special name `__key__`.

An equality filter on the key isn't much use. Only one entity can have a given key, and if the key is known, it's faster to perform a `get()` than a query. But an inequality filter on the key can be useful for fetching ranges of keys. (If you're fetching entities in batches, consider using query cursors. See "Query Cursors" on page 192.)

App Engine provides automatic indexes of kinds and keys, sorted by key in ascending order. The query returns the results sorted in key order. This order isn't useful for display purposes, but it's deterministic. A query that sorts keys in descending order requires a custom index.

App Engine uses indexes for filters on keys in the same way as filters on properties, with a minor twist: a query using a key filter in addition to other filters can use an automatic index if a similar query without the key filter could use an automatic index. Automatic indexes for properties already include the keys, so such queries can just use the same indexes. And of course, if the query has no other filters beyond the key filter, it can use the automatic key index.

Kindless Queries

In addition to performing queries on entities of a given kind, the datastore lets you perform a limited set of queries on entities of all kinds. Kindless queries cannot use filters or sort orders on properties. They can, however, use equality and inequality filters on keys (IDs or names).

Kindless queries are mostly useful in combination with ancestors, which we'll discuss in Chapter 7. They can also be used to get every entity in the datastore. (If you're querying a large number of entities, you'll probably want to fetch the results in batches. See "Query Cursors" on page 192.)

Using the Python `Query` class, you perform a kindless query by omitting the model class argument from the constructor:

```
q = db.Query()

q.filter('__key__ >', last_key)
```

Similarly in the Java low-level API, you perform a kindless query by instantiating the `Query` class using the no-argument constructor.

In GQL, you specify a kindless query by omitting the `FROM Kind` part of the statement:

```
q = db.GqlQuery('SELECT * WHERE __key__ > :1', last_key)
```

The results of a kindless query are returned in key order, ascending. Kindless queries use an automatic index.

The datastore maintains statistics about the apps data in a set of datastore entities. When the app performs a kindless query, these statistics entities are included in the results. The kind names for these entities all begin with the characters `__Stat_` (two underscores, `Stat`, and another underscore). Your app will need to filter these out if they are not desired.

The Python `ext.db` interface expects there to be a `db.Model` (or `db.Expando`) class defined or imported for each kind of each query result. When using kindless queries in Python, you must define or import all possible kinds. To load classes for the datastore statistics entity kinds, import the `db.stats` module:

```
from google.appengine.ext.db import stats
```

For more information about datastore statistics, see "Accessing Metadata from the App" on page 234.

Custom Indexes and Complex Queries

All queries not covered by the automatic indexes must have corresponding indexes defined in the app's index configuration file. We'll refer to these as "custom indexes," in contrast with "automatic indexes." App Engine needs these hints because building every possible index for every combination of property and sort order would take a gargantuan amount of space and time, and an app isn't likely to need more than a fraction of those possibilities.

In particular, the following queries require custom indexes:

- A query with multiple sort orders
- A query with an inequality filter on a property and filters on other properties
- Projection queries

A query that uses just equality filters on properties does not need a custom index in most cases thanks to a specialized query algorithm for this case, which we'll look at in a moment. Also, filters on keys do not require custom indexes; they can operate on whatever indexes are used to fulfill the rest of the query.

Let's examine these queries and the indexes they require. We'll cover projection queries in "Projection Queries" on page 197.

Multiple Sort Orders

The automatic single-property indexes provide enough information for one sort order. When two entities have the same value for the sorted property, the entities appear in the index in adjacent rows, ordered by their entity keys. If you want to order these entities with other criteria, you need an index with more information.

The following query asks for all `Player` entities, sorted first by the `level` property in descending order, then, in the case of ties, sorted by the `score` property in descending order:

```
SELECT * FROM Player ORDER BY level DESC, score DESC
```

The index this query needs is straightforward: a table of `Player` entity keys, `level` values, and `score` values, sorted according to the query. This is not one of the indexes provided by the datastore automatically, so it is a custom index, and must be mentioned in the index configuration file. If you performed this query in the Python development web server, the server would add the following lines to the *index.yaml* file:

```
- kind: Player
  properties:
  - name: level
    direction: desc
  - name: score
    direction: desc
```

The order the properties appear in the configuration file matters. This is the order in which the rows are sorted: first by `level` descending, then by `score` descending.

This configuration creates the index shown in Figure 6-9. The results appear in the table, and are returned for the query in the desired order.

Key	level ⬇	score ⬇
Player / 3359	12	1366
Player / 7243	11	1280
Player / 4751	11	1059
Player / 7289	10	935
Player / 13467	10	896
⋮	⋮	⋮

Figure 6-9. An index of the Player entity "level" and "score" properties, sorted by level descending, then score descending, then by key ascending

Filters on Multiple Properties

Consider the following query, which asks for every `Player` with a `level` greater than the integer `10` and a `charclass` of the string `'mage'`:

```
SELECT * FROM Player WHERE charclass='mage' AND level > 10
```

To be able to scan to a contiguous set of results meeting both filter criteria, the index must contain columns of values for these properties. The entities must be sorted first by `charclass`, then by `level`.

For Python, the index configuration for this query would appear as follows in the *index.yaml* file:

```
- kind: Player
  properties:
  - name: charclass
    direction: asc
  - name: level
    direction: asc
```

This index is illustrated in Figure 6-10.

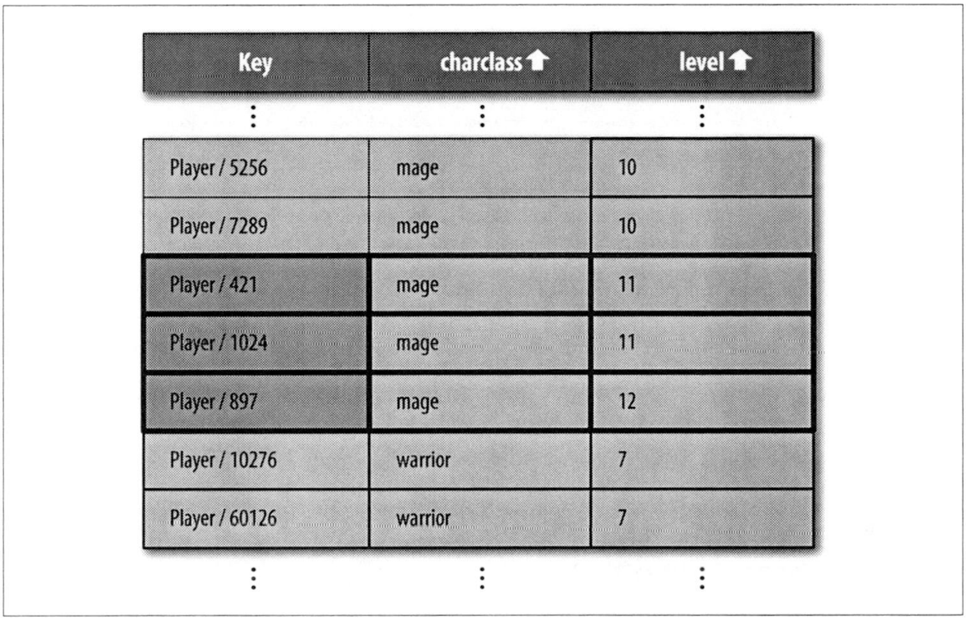

Key	charclass ↑	level ↑
⋮	⋮	⋮
Player / 5256	mage	10
Player / 7289	mage	10
Player / 421	mage	11
Player / 1024	mage	11
Player / 897	mage	12
Player / 10276	warrior	7
Player / 60126	warrior	7
⋮	⋮	⋮

Figure 6-10. An index of the Player entity "charclass" and "level" properties, sorted by charclass, then level, then key, with results for WHERE charclass = "mage" AND level > 10

The ordering sequence of these properties is important! Remember: the results for the query must all appear on adjacent rows in the index. If the index for this query were sorted first by `level` then by `charclass`, it would be possible for valid results to appear on nonadjacent rows. Figure 6-11 demonstrates this problem.

The index ordering requirement for combining inequality and equality filters has several implications that may seem unusual when compared to the query engines of other databases. Heck, they're downright weird. The first implication, illustrated previously, can be stated generally:

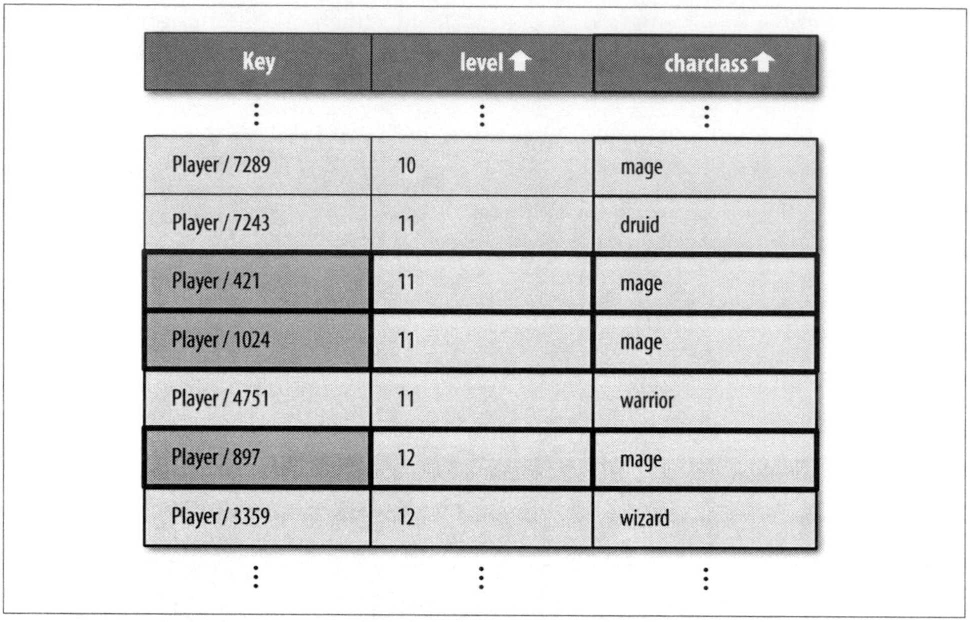

Key	level ↑	charclass ↑
⋮	⋮	⋮
Player / 7289	10	mage
Player / 7243	11	druid
Player / 421	11	mage
Player / 1024	11	mage
Player / 4751	11	warrior
Player / 897	12	mage
Player / 3359	12	wizard
⋮	⋮	⋮

Figure 6-11. An index of the Player entity "charclass" and "level" properties, sorted first by level then by charclass, which cannot satisfy WHERE charclass = "mage" AND level > 10 with consecutive rows

> **The First Rule of Inequality Filters:** If a query uses inequality filters on one property and equality filters on one or more other properties, the index must be ordered first by the properties used in equality filters, then by the property used in the inequality filters.

This rule has a corollary regarding queries with both an inequality filter and sort orders. Consider the following possible query:

```
SELECT * FROM Player WHERE level > 10 ORDER BY score DESC
```

What would the index for this query look like? For starters, it would have a column for the `level`, so it can select the rows that match the filter. It would also have a column for the `score`, to determine the order of the results. But which column is ordered first?

The First Rule implies that `level` must be ordered first. But the query requested that the results be returned sorted by `score`, descending. If the index were sorted by `score`, then by `level`, the rows may not be adjacent.

To avoid confusion, App Engine requires that the correct sort order be stated explicitly in the query:

```
SELECT * FROM Player WHERE level > 10 ORDER BY level, score DESC
```

In general:

> **The Second Rule of Inequality Filters:** If a query uses inequality filters on one property and sort orders of one or more other properties, the index must be ordered first by the property used in the inequality filters (in either direction), then by the other desired sort orders. To avoid confusion, the query must state all sort orders explicitly.

There's one last implication to consider with regard to inequality filters. The following possible query attempts to get all `Player` entities with a `level` less than 10 and a `score` less than 500:

```
SELECT * FROM Player WHERE level < 10 AND score < 500
```

Consider an index ordered first by `level`, then by `score`, as shown in Figure 6-12.

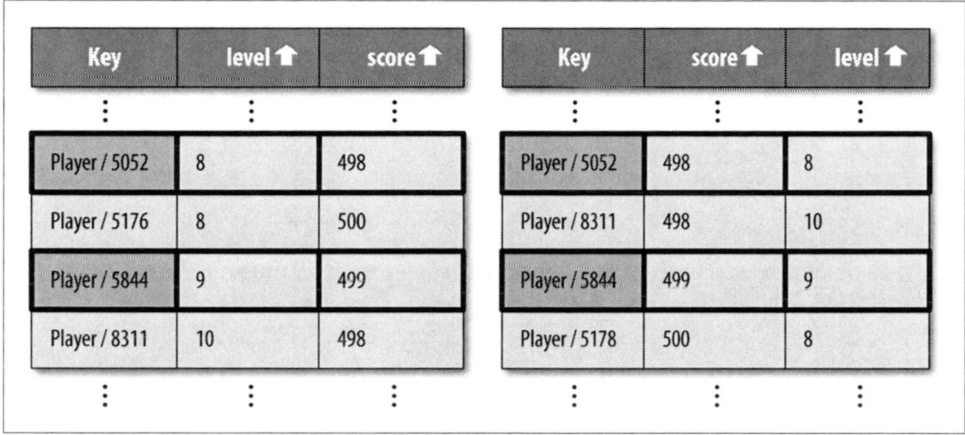

Figure 6-12. Neither possible index of the Player entity "level" and "score" properties can satisfy WHERE level < 10 AND score < 500 with consecutive rows

In fact, there is no possible index that could satisfy this query completely using consecutive rows. This is not a valid App Engine datastore query.

> **The Third Rule of Inequality Filters:** A query cannot use inequality filters on more than one property.

A query *can* use multiple inequality filters on the same property, such as to test for a range of values.

Multiple Equality Filters

For queries using just equality filters, it's easy to imagine custom indexes that satisfy them. For instance:

```
SELECT * FROM Player WHERE charclass='mage' AND level=10
```

A custom index containing these properties, ordered in any sequence and direction, would meet the query's requirements. But App Engine has another trick up its sleeve for this kind of query. For queries using just equality filters and no sort orders, instead of scanning a single table of all values, App Engine can scan the automatic single-property indexes for each property, and return the results as it finds them. App Engine can perform a "merge join" of the single-property indexes to satisfy this kind of query.

In other words, the datastore doesn't need a custom index to perform queries using just equality filters and no sort orders. If you add a suitable custom index to your configuration file, the datastore will use it. But a custom index is not required, and the development server's automatic index configuration feature will not add one if it doesn't exist.

Let's consider how the algorithm would perform the following query, using single-property indexes:

```
SELECT * FROM Kind WHERE a=1 AND b=2 AND c=3
```

Recall that each of these tables contains a row for each entity with the property set, with fields for the entity's key and the property's value. The table is sorted first by the value, then by the key. The algorithm takes advantage of the fact that rows with the same value are consecutive, and within that consecutive block, rows are sorted by key.

To perform the query, the datastore uses the following steps:

1. The datastore checks the `a` index for the first row with a value of `1`. The entity whose key is on this row is a candidate, but not yet a confirmed result.
2. It then checks the `b` index for the first row whose value is `2` *and* whose key is greater than or equal to the candidate's key. Other rows with a value of `2` may appear above this row in the `b` index, but the datastore knows those are not candidates because the first `a` scan determined the candidate with the smallest key.
3. If the datastore finds the candidate's key in the matching region of `b`, that key is still a candidate, and the datastore proceeds with a similar check in the index for `c`. If the datastore does not find the candidate in the `b` index but does find another larger key with a matching value, that key becomes the new candidate, and it proceeds to check for the new candidate in the `c` index. (It'll eventually go back to check `a` with the new candidate before deciding it is a result.) If it finds neither the candidate nor a matching row with a larger key, the query is complete.
4. If a candidate is found to match all criteria in all indexes, the candidate is returned as a result. The datastore starts the search for a new candidate, using the previous candidate's key as the minimum key.

Figure 6-13 illustrates this zigzag search across the single-property indexes, first with a failed candidate, then two successful candidates.

A key feature of this algorithm is that it finds results in the order in which they are to be returned: key order. The datastore does not need to compile a complete list of possible results for the query—possibly millions of entities—then sort them to determine which results ought to be first. Also, the datastore can stop scanning as soon as it has enough results to fulfill the query, which is always a limited number of entities.

Of course, this query could also use a custom index with all the filter properties in it. If you provide configuration for such an index, the query will use the custom index

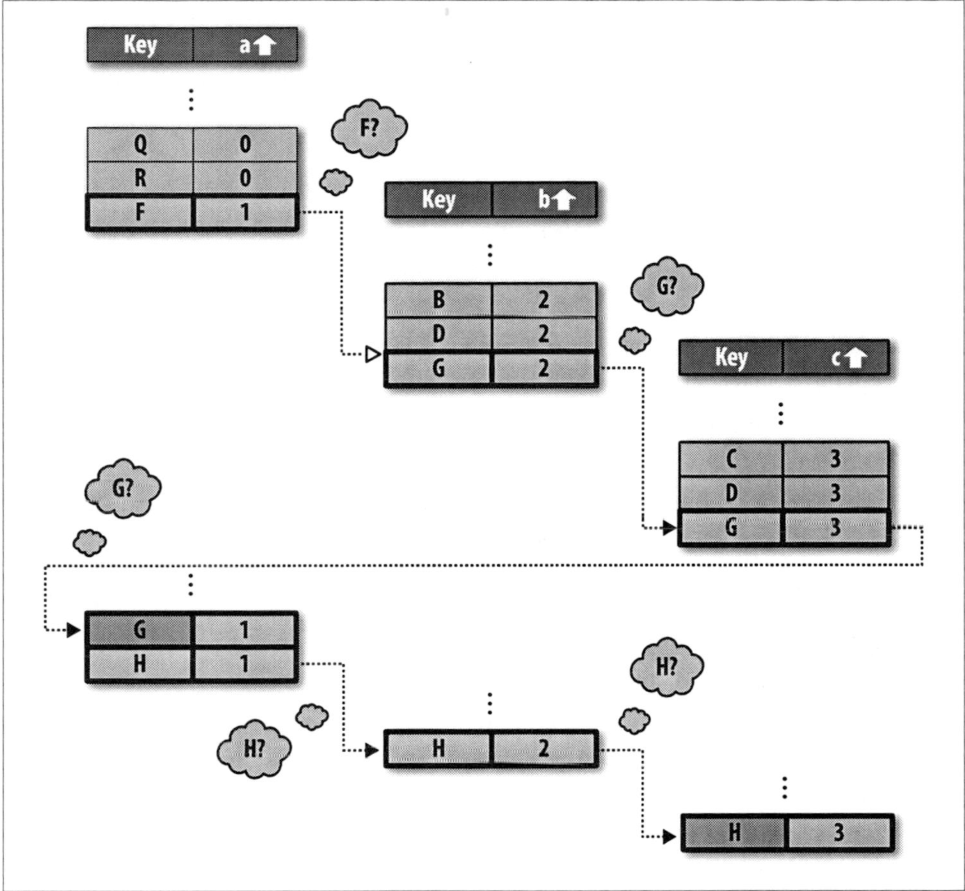

Figure 6-13. The merge join algorithm finding two entities WHERE a=1 AND b=2 AND c=3

instead of doing the zigzag join. This can result in a query faster than the zigzag join, at the expense of added time to update the indexed entities.

A zigzag-capable query using equality filters on properties can also use inequality filters on keys without needing a custom index. This is useful for fetching a large number of results in key ranges. (But if you're fetching batches, cursors might be more effective. See "Query Cursors" on page 192.)

Not-Equal and IN Filters

The Python and Java query APIs support two operators we haven't discussed yet: `!=` (not-equal) and `IN`. These operators are not actually supported by the datastore itself. Instead, they are implemented by the datastore API as multiple queries in terms of the other operators.

The filter `prop != value` matches every entity whose property does not equal the value. The datastore API determines the result set by performing two queries: one using `prop < value` in place of the not-equal filter, and one using `prop > value` in place of the filter. It returns both sets of results as one result set, which it can do reasonably quickly because the results are already in order.

Because not-equal is actually implemented in terms of the inequality operators, it is subject to the three rules of inequality operators:

1. The query's index must be ordered by the property used with the not-equal filter before other sort orders.
2. If the query uses other explicit sort orders, the not-equal filter's property must be explicitly ordered first.
3. And finally, any query using a not-equal filter cannot also use inequality or not-equal filters on other properties.

A not-equal filter will never return an entity that doesn't have the filtered property. This is true for all filters, but can be especially counterintuitive in the case of not-equal.

The filter `prop IN (value1, value2, value3)` matches every entity whose property equals any of the values. The datastore API implements this as a series of equality queries, one for each value to test. The more values that appear in the list, the longer the full set of queries will take to execute.

If a single query includes multiple `IN` filters on multiple properties, the datastore API must perform equality queries for every combination of values in all filters. `prop1 IN (value1, value2, value3, value4) AND prop2 IN (value5, value6, value7)` is equivalent to 12 queries using equality filters.

The `!=` and `IN` operators are useful shortcuts. But because they actually perform multiple queries, they take longer to execute than the other operators. It's worth understanding their performance implications before using them.

Unset and Nonindexed Properties

As you've seen, an index contains columns of property values. Typically, an app creates entities of the same kind with the same set of properties: every `Player` in our game has a name, a character class, a level, and a score. If every entity of a kind has a given property, then an index for that kind and property has a row corresponding to each entity of the kind.

But the datastore neither requires nor enforces a common layout of properties across entities of a kind. It's quite possible for an entity to not have a property that other entities of the same kind have. For instance, a `Player` entity might be created without a character class, and go without until the user chooses one.

It is possible to set a property with a null value (Python's `None`, Java's `null`), but a property set to the null value is distinct from the property not being set at all. This is different from a tabular database, which requires a value (possibly null) for every cell in a row.

If an entity does not have a property used in an index, the entity does not appear in the index. Stated conversely, an entity must have *every* property mentioned in an index to appear in the index. If a `Player` does not have a `charclass` property, it does not appear in any index with a `charclass` column.

If an entity is not mentioned in an index, it cannot be returned as a result for a query that uses the index. Remember that queries use indexes for both filters and sort orders. A query that uses a property for any kind of filter or any sort order can never return an entity that doesn't have that property. The `charclass`-less Player can never be a result for a `Player` query that sorts results by `charclass`.

In "Strings, Text, and Blobs" on page 138, we mentioned that text and blob values are not indexed. Another way of saying this is that, for the purposes of indexes, a property with a text or blob value is treated as if it is unset. If an app performs a query by using a filter or sort order on a property that is always set to a text or blob value, that query will always return no results.

It is sometimes useful to store property values of other types, and exempt them from indexes. This saves space in index tables, and reduces the amount of time it takes to save the entity.

In the Python API, the only way to declare a property as unindexed is with the `Model` API. There is currently no other way to set a specific property as unindexed in this API. We'll look at this feature when we discuss the modeling API in Chapter 9.

In the Java API, you can set a property as unindexed by using the `setUnindexedProperty()` method of the `Entity` object, instead of the `setProperty()` method. An entity can only have one property of a given name, so an unindexed property overwrites an indexed one, and vice versa. You can also declare properties as unindexed in the JDO and JPA interfaces; see Chapter 10.

If you need an entity to qualify as a result for a query, but it doesn't make sense in your data model to give the entity every property used in the query, use the null value to represent the "no value" case, and always set it. The Python modeling API and the Java JDO and JPA interfaces make it easy to ensure that properties always have values.

Sort Orders and Value Types

App Engine keeps the rows of an index sorted in an order that supports the corresponding query. Each type of property value has its own rules for comparing two values of the same type, and these rules are mostly intuitive: integers are sorted in numeric order, strings in Unicode order, and so forth.

Two entities can have values of different types for the same property, so App Engine also has rules for comparing such values, although these rules are not so intuitive. Values are ordered first by type, then within their type. For instance, all integers are sorted above all strings.

One effect of this that might be surprising is that all floats are sorted below all integers. The datastore treats floats and integers as separate value types, and so sorts them separately. If your app relies on the correct ordering of numbers, make sure all numbers are stored using the same type of value.

The datastore stores eight distinct types of values, not counting the nonindexed types (text and blob). The datastore supports several additional types by storing them as one of the eight types, then marshaling them between the internal representation and the value your app sees automatically. These additional types are sorted by their internal representation. For instance, a date-time value is actually stored as an integer, and will be sorted amongst other integer values in an index. (When comparing date-time values, this results in chronological order, which is what you would expect.)

Table 6-2 describes the eight indexable types supported by the datastore. The types are listed in their relative order, from first to last.

Table 6-2. How the datastore value types are sorted

Data type	Python type	Java type	Ordering
The null value	`None`	`null`	-
Integer and date-time	`long`, `datetime.datetime`, `db.Rating`	`long` (other integer types are widened), `java.util.Date`, `datastore.Rating`	Numeric (date-time is chronological)
Boolean	`bool` (`True` or `False`)	`boolean` (`true` or `false`)	False, then true
Byte string	`db.ByteString`	`datastore.ShortBlob`	Byte order
Unicode string	`unicode`, `db.Category`, `db.Email`, `db.IM`, `db.Link`, `db.PhoneNumber`, `db.PostalAddress`	`java.lang.String`, `datastore.Category`, `datastore.Email`, `datastore.IMHandle`, `datastore.Link`, `datastore.PhoneNumber`, `datastore.PostalAddress`	Unicode character order
Floating-point number	`float`	`double`	Numeric
Geographical point	`db.GeoPt`	`datastore.GeoPt`	By latitude, then longitude (floating-point numbers)
A Google account	`users.User`	`users.User`	By email address, Unicode order

Data type	Python type	Java type	Ordering
Entity key	`db.Key`	`datastore.Key`	Kind (byte string), then ID (numeric) or name (byte string)

Queries and Multivalued Properties

In a typical database, a field in a record stores a single value. A record represents a data object, and each field represents a single, simple aspect of the object. If a data object can have more than one of a particular thing, each of those things is typically represented by a separate record of an appropriate kind, associated with the data object by using the object's key as a field value. App Engine supports both of these uses of fields: a property can contain a simple value or the key of another entity.

But the App Engine datastore can do something most other databases can't: it can store more than one value for a single property. With multivalued properties (MVPs), you can represent a data object with more than one of something without resorting to creating a separate entity for each of those things, if each thing could be represented by a simple value.

One of the most useful features of multivalued properties is how they match an equality filter in a query. The datastore query engine considers a multivalued property equal to a filter value if any of the property's values is equal to the filter value. This ability to test for membership means MVPs are useful for representing sets.

Multivalued properties maintain the order of values, and can have repeated items. The values can be of any datastore type, and a single property can have values of different types.

A Simple Example

Consider the following example. The players of our online game can earn trophies for particular accomplishments. The app needs to display a list of all the trophies a player has won, and the app needs to display a list of all the players who have won a particular trophy. The app doesn't need to maintain any data about the trophies themselves; it's sufficient to just store the name of the trophy. (This could also be a list of keys for trophy entities.)

One option is to store the list of trophy names as a single delimited string value for each `Player` entity. This makes it easy to get the list of trophies for a particular player, but impossible to get the list of players for a particular trophy. (A query filter can't match patterns within string values.)

Another option is to record each trophy win in a separate property named after the trophy. To get the list of players with a trophy, you just query for the existence of the corresponding property. However, getting the list of trophies for a given player would require either coding the names of all the trophies in the display logic, or iterating over all the `Player` entity's properties looking for trophy names.

With multivalued properties, we can store each trophy name as a separate value for the `trophies` property. To access a list of all trophies for a player, we simply access the property of the entity. To get a list of all players with a trophy, we use a query with an equality filter on the property.

Here's what this example looks like in Python:

```
p = Player.get_by_key_name(user_id)
p.trophies = ['Lava Polo Champion',
              'World Building 2008, Bronze',
              'Glarcon Fighter, 2nd class']
p.put()

# List all trophies for a player.
for trophy in p.trophies:
    # ...

# Query all players that have a trophy.
q = Player.gql("WHERE trophies = 'Lava Polo Champion'")
for p in q:
    # ...
```

MVPs in Python

The Python API represents the values of a multivalued property as a Python list. Each member of the list must be of one of the supported datastore types:

```
class Entity(db.Expando):
  pass

e = Entity()

e.prop = [ 'value1', 123, users.get_current_user() ]
```

Remember that `list` is not a datastore type; it is only the mechanism for manipulating multivalued properties. A list cannot contain another list.

A property must have at least one value, otherwise the property does not exist. To enforce this, the Python API does not allow you to assign an empty list to a property. Notice that the API can't do otherwise: if a property doesn't exist, then the API cannot know to represent the missing property as an empty list when the entity is retrieved from the datastore. (This being Python, the API could return the empty list whenever a nonexistent property is accessed, but that might be more trouble than it's worth.)

Because it is often useful for lists to behave like lists, including the ability to contain zero items, the Python data modeling API provides a mechanism that supports assigning the empty list to a property. We'll look at this mechanism in Chapter 9.

MVPs in Java

The Java low-level datastore API represents multivalued properties as `java.util.List` objects, parameterized with a native datastore type. When you call `setProperty()` on an `Entity`, the value can be any `Collection` of a native type. The values are stored in iterator order. When you retrieve the property value with `getProperty()`, the values are returned in a `List`:

```
Entity trophyCase = new Entity("TrophyCase");

List<String> trophyNames = new ArrayList<String>();
trophyNames.add("Goblin Rush Bronze");
trophyNames.add("10-Hut! (built 10 huts)");
trophyNames.add("Moon Landing");
trophyCase.setProperty("trophyNames", trophyNames);

ds.put(trophyCase);

// ...

// Key tcKey = ...
Entity newTrophyCase = ds.get(tcKey);
@SuppressWarnings("unchecked")
List<String> newTrophyNames = (List<String>) trophyCase.getProperty("trophyNames");
```

To represent a multivalued property with diverse value types, use `List<Object>`. Storing an unsupported type in such a `List` is a runtime error.

A property must have at least one value, otherwise the property does not exist. To enforce this, the Java API throws a runtime error if you assign an empty collection to a property. When using the low-level datastore API, your code must handle this as a special case, and represent zero values by not setting (or by deleting) the property.

Remember that `List` (or `Collection`) is not a datastore type. It can only contain native types, and not another `Collection`.

MVPs and Equality Filters

As you've seen, when a multivalued property is the subject of an equality filter in a query, the entity matches if any of the property's values are equal to the filter value:

```
e1 = Entity()
e1.prop = [ 3.14, 'a', 'b' ]
e1.put()

e2 = Entity()
e2.prop = [ 'a', 1, 6 ]
e2.put()

# Returns e1 but not e2:
q = Entity.gql('WHERE prop = 3.14')

# Returns e2 but not e1:
```

```
q = Entity.gql('WHERE prop = 6')

# Returns both e1 and e2:
q = Entity.gql("WHERE prop = 'a'")
```

Recall that a query with a single equality filter uses an index that contains the keys of every entity of the given kind with the given property and the property values. If an entity has a single value for the property, the index contains one row that represents the entity and the value. If an entity has multiple values for the property, the index contains one row for each value. The index for this example is shown in Figure 6-14.

Key	prop ↑
e2	1
e2	6
e1	a
e2	a
e1	b
e1	3.14

Figure 6-14. An index of two entities with multiple values for the "prop" property, with results for WHERE prop='a'

This brings us to the first of several odd-looking queries that nonetheless make sense for multivalued properties. Since an equality filter is a membership test, it is possible for multiple equality filters to use the same property with different values and still return a result. An example in GQL:

```
SELECT * FROM Entity WHERE prop = 'a' AND prop = 'b'
```

App Engine uses the "merge join" algorithm, described in "Multiple Equality Filters" on page 179 for multiple equality filters, to satisfy this query, using the `prop` single-property index. This query returns the `e1` entity because the entity key appears in two places in the index, once for each value requested by the filters.

The way multivalued properties appear in an index gives us another way of thinking about multivalued properties: an entity has one or more properties, each with a name and a single value, and an entity can have multiple properties with the same name. The API represents the values of multiple properties with the same name as a list of values associated with that name.

The datastore does not have a way to query for the exact set of values in a multivalued property. You can use multiple equality filters to test that each of several values belongs to the list, but there is no filter that ensures that those are the only values that belong to the list, or that each value appears only once.

MVPs and Inequality Filters

Just as an equality filter tests that any value of the property is equal to the filter value, an inequality filter tests that any value of the property meets the filter criterion:

```
e1 = Entity()
e1.prop = [ 1, 3, 5 ]
e1.put()

e2 = Entity()
e2.prop = [ 4, 6, 8 ]
e2.put()

# Returns e1 but not e2:
q = Entity.gql("WHERE prop < 2")

# Returns e2 but not e1:
q = Entity.gql("WHERE prop > 7")

# Returns both e1 and e2:
q = Entity.gql("WHERE prop > 3")
```

Figure 6-15 shows the index for this example, with the results of `prop > 3` highlighted.

Key	prop ↑
e1	1
e1	3
e2	4
e1	5
e2	6
e2	8

Figure 6-15. An index of two entities with multiple values for the "prop" property, with results for WHERE prop > 3

In the case of an inequality filter, it's possible for the index scan to match rows for a single entity multiple times. When this happens, the first occurrence of each key in the index determines the order of the results. If the index used for the query sorts the property in ascending order, the first occurrence is the smallest matching value. For descending, it's the largest. In the example above, `prop > 3` returns `e2` before `e1` because `4` appears before `5` in the index.

MVPs and Sort Orders

To summarize things we know about how multivalued properties are indexed:

- A multivalued property appears in an index with one row per value.
- All rows in an index are sorted by the values, possibly distributing property values for a single entity across the index.
- The first occurrence of an entity in an index scan determines its place in the result set for a query.

Together, these facts explain what happens when a query orders its results by a multivalued property. When results are sorted by a multivalued property in ascending order, the smallest value for the property determines its location in the results. When results are sorted in descending order, the largest value for the property determines its location.

This has a counterintuitive—but consistent—consequence:

```
e1 = Entity()
e1.prop = [ 1, 3, 5 ]
e1.put()

e2 = Entity()
e2.prop = [ 2, 3, 4 ]
e2.put()

# Returns e1, e2:
q = Entity.gql("ORDER BY prop ASC")

# Also returns e1, e2:
q = Entity.gql("ORDER BY prop DESC")
```

Because `e1` has both the smallest value and the largest value, it appears first in the result set in ascending order *and* in descending order. See Figure 6-16.

Key	prop ↑
e1	1
e2	2
e1	3
e2	3
e2	4
e1	5

Key	prop ↓
e1	5
e2	4
e1	3
e2	3
e2	2
e1	1

Figure 6-16. Indexes of two entities with multiple values for the "prop" property, one ascending and one descending

MVPs and the Query Planner

The query planner tries to be smart by ignoring aspects of the query that are redundant or contradictory. For instance, `a = 3 AND a = 4` would normally return no results, so the query planner catches those cases and doesn't bother doing work it doesn't need to do. However, most of these normalization techniques don't apply to multivalued properties. In this case, the query could be asking, "Does this MVP have a value that is equal to 3 and another value equal to 4?" The datastore remembers which properties are MVPs (even those that end up with one or zero values), and never takes a shortcut that would produce incorrect results.

But there is one exception. A query that has both an equality filter and a sort order will drop the sort order. If a query asks for `a = 3 ORDER BY a DESC` and `a` is a single-value property, the sort order has no effect because all values in the result are identical. For an MVP, however, `a = 3` tests for membership, and two MVPs that meet that condition are not necessarily identical.

The datastore drops the sort order in this case anyway. To do otherwise would require too much index data and result in exploding indexes in cases that could otherwise survive. As always, the actual sort order is deterministic, but it won't be the requested order.

Exploding Indexes

There's one more thing to know about indexes when considering multivalued properties for your data model.

When an entity has multiple values for a property, each index that includes a column for the property must use multiple rows to represent the entity, one for each possible combination of values. In a single property index on the multivalued property, this is simply one row for each value, two columns each (the entity key and the property value).

In an index of multiple properties where the entity has multiple values for one of the indexed properties and a single value for each of the others, the index includes one row for each value of the multivalued property. Each row has a column for each indexed property, plus the key. The values for the single-value properties are repeated in each row.

Here's the kicker: if an entity has more than one property with multiple values, and more than one multivalued property appears in an index, the index must contain one row for each combination of values to represent the entity completely.

If you're not careful, the number of index rows that need to be updated when the entity changes could grow very large. It may be so large that the datastore cannot complete an update of the entity before it reaches its safety limits, and returns an error.

To help prevent "exploding indexes" from causing problems, App Engine limits the number of property values—that is, the number of rows times the number of columns—a single entity can occupy in an index. The limit is 5,000 property values, high enough for normal use, but low enough to prevent unusual index sizes from inhibiting updates.

If you do include a multivalued property in a custom index, be careful about the possibility of exploding indexes.

Query Cursors

A query often has more results than you want to process in a single action. A message board may have thousands of messages, but it isn't useful to show a user thousands of messages on one screen. Better would be to show the user a dozen messages at a time, and let the user decide when to look at more, such as by clicking a "next" link, or scrolling to the bottom of the display.

A *query cursor* is like a bookmark in a list of query results. After fetching some results, you can ask the query API for the cursor that represents the spot immediately after the last result you fetched. When you perform the query again at a later time, you can include the cursor value, and the next result fetched will be the one at the spot where the cursor was generated.

Cursors are fast. Unlike with the "offset" fetch parameter, the datastore does not have to scan from the beginning of the results to find the cursor location. The time to fetch results starting from a cursor is proportional to the number of results fetched. This makes cursors ideal for paginated displays of items.

The following is code for a simple paginated display, in Python:

```
import jinja2
import webapp2

from google.appengine.ext import db

template_env = jinja2.Environment(
    loader=jinja2.FileSystemLoader(os.getcwd()))

PAGE_SIZE = 10

class Message(db.Model):
    create_date = db.DateTimeProperty(auto_now_add=True)
    # ...

class ResultsPageHandler(webapp2.RequestHandler):
    def get(self):
        query = Message.all().order('-create_date')
        cursor = self.request.get('c', None)
        if cursor:
            query.with_cursor(cursor)
        results = query.fetch(PAGE_SIZE)

        new_cursor = query.cursor()
        query.with_cursor(new_cursor)
        has_more_results = query.count(1) == 1

        template = template_env.get_template('results.html')
        context = {
            'results': results,
        }
        if has_more_results:
            context['next_cursor'] = new_cursor
        self.response.out.write(template.render(context))

app = webapp2.WSGIApplication([
    ('/results', ResultsPageHandler),
    # ...
    ],
    debug=True)
```

The *results.html* template is as follows. Note the Next link in particular:

```
<html><body>

{% if results %}

<p>Messages:</p>
<ul>
{% for result in results %}
 <li>{{ result.key().id() }}: {{ result.create_date }}</li>
{% endfor %}
</ul>

{% if next_cursor %}
```

```
<p><a href="/results?c={{ next_cursor }}">Next</a></p>
{% endif %}

{% else %}
<p>There are no messages.</p>
{% endif %}

</body></html>
```

This example displays all of the `Message` entities in the datastore, in reverse chronological order, in pages of 10 messages per page. If there are more results after the last result displayed, the app shows a "Next" link back to the request handler with the `c` parameter set to the cursor pointing to the spot after the last-fetched result. This causes the next set of results fetched to start where the previous page left off.

A cursor is a base64-encoded string. It is safe to use as a query parameter this way: it cannot be corrupted by the user to fetch results outside of the expected query range. Note that, like the string form of datastore keys, the base64-encoded value can be decoded to reveal the names of kinds and properties, so you may wish to further encrypt or hide the value if these are sensitive.

The Python API shown here is simple: `c = q.cursor()` returns the cursor after the last-fetched result for the `Query` object. `q.with_cursor(c)` sets a parameter on the query to start fetching results at the given cursor. We'll review the complete Python and Java APIs in the next two sections.

This example uses a trick to determine whether there are any results after the cursor, so the template can hide the "Next" link if there are no further results. After establishing the cursor at the point after the last-fetched result, we immediately reinitialize the query with that cursor. Then we attempt to perform a count of one element after that point in the results:

```
new_cursor = query.cursor()
query.with_cursor(new_cursor)
has_more_results = query.count(1) == 1
```

This illustrates the "bookmark" nature of cursors: using a cursor does not move the cursor. The cursor just identifies a spot in the results.

This example shows how to use cursors to set up a "Next" link in a paginated display. Setting up a "Previous" link is left as an exercise for the reader. Hint: the cursor used to display the current page, if any, is the one the next page needs for the link.

A cursor is only valid for the query used to generate the cursor value. All query parameters, including kinds, filters, sort orders, and whether or not the query is keys-only, must be identical to the query used to generate the cursor.

A cursor remains valid over time, even if results are added or removed above or below the cursor in the index. A structural change to the indexes used to satisfy the query invalidates cursors for that query. This includes adding or removing fields of a custom index, or switching between built-in indexes and custom indexes for a query. These only occur as a result of your updating your index configuration. Rare internal changes to datastore indexes may also invalidate cursors. Using a cursor that is invalid for a given query (for whatever reason) will raise an exception.

Because a cursor stays valid even after the data changes, you can use cursors to watch for changes in some circumstances. For example, consider a query for entities with creation timestamps, ordered by timestamp. A process traverses the results to the end, and then stores the cursor for the end of the list (with no results after it). When new entities are created with later timestamps, those entities are added to the index after the cursor. Running the query with the cursor pick ups the new results.

The preceding example shows using a cursor to set the start position for fetching results. You can also use a cursor to set an end position for the fetch, instead of fetching a fixed number of results. We'll see how to do that in the next sections.

Conceptually, a cursor is a position in a list of results. Actually, a cursor is a position in the index (or path through multiple indexes) that represents the results for the query. This has a couple of implications.

You can't use a cursor on a query that uses not-equal (`!=`) or set membership (`IN`) queries. These queries are performed by multiple primitive queries behind the scenes, and therefore do not have all results in a single index (or index path).

A query with a cursor may result in a duplicate result if the query operates on a property with multiple values. Recall that an entity with multiple values for a property appears once for each value in the corresponding indexes. When a query gathers results, it ignores repeated results (which are consecutive in the index). Because a cursor represents a point in an index, it is possible for the same entity to appear both before and after the cursor. In this case, the query up to the cursor and the query after the cursor will both contain the entity in their results. It's a rare edge case—the entity would have to change after the cursor is created—but it's one to be aware of if you're using multivalued properties with queries and cursors.

Cursors in Python

To get a cursor for an executed query in Python, call the `cursor()` method of the `Query` (or `GqlQuery`) object. It returns the cursor value as a base64-encoded string:

```
query = Message.all().order('-create_date')
results = query.fetch(10)

cursor = query.cursor()
```

When you call cursor() on a query object whose results are being fetched by the iterator interface, this may invoke a datastore RPC call to get the cursor for the last result seen by the iterator. Behind the scenes, the iterator fetches results in batches, and only knows the cursor after the last result in the batch, which may not be the last result generated by the iterator.

There are several ways to fetch results for a query starting at a cursor. One way is to make the start cursor a parameter of the Query, by calling the with_cursor() method:

```
query.with_cursor(cursor)
```

You can use this method to set both a start cursor (the point before the first result to fetch) and an end cursor (the point after the last result to fetch), using the start_cursor and end_cursor keyword arguments. You can specify a start_cursor, an end_cursor, or both:

```
query.with_cursor(start_cursor=start)
query.with_cursor(end_cursor=end)

query.with_cursor(start_cursor=start, end_cursor=end)
```

You can also pass start_cursor and end_cursor arguments to any of the query execution methods: fetch(), get(), run(), and count():

```
start_cursor = self.request.get('start', None)
end_cursor = self.request.get('end', none)

results_iterable = query.run(
    limit=20,
    start_cursor=start_cursor,
    end_cursor=end_cursor)

template_context = {
    'results': results_iterable,
}
```

Cursors in Java

As we saw earlier, the Java PreparedQuery object has several methods that return results. The methods asQueryResultIterable(), asQueryResultIterator(), and asQueryResultList() return QueryResultIterable, QueryResultIterator, and QueryResultList instances, respectively. These three classes provide access to the cursor that points to the location after the last fetched result. The getCursor() method returns a Cursor instance:

```
import com.google.appengine.api.datastore.Cursor;
import com.google.appengine.api.datastore.Entity;
import com.google.appengine.api.datastore.FetchOptions;
import com.google.appengine.api.datastore.PreparedQuery;
import com.google.appengine.api.datastore.Query;
import com.google.appengine.api.datastore.QueryResultList;

// ...
        Query q = new Query("Message").addSort("create_date",
```

```
                                                Query.SortDirection.DESCENDING);
    PreparedQuery pq = ds.prepare(q);
    QueryResultList<Entity> results = pq.asQueryResultList(
        FetchOptions.Builder.withLimit(10));
    Cursor cursor = results.getCursor();
```

You can convert the `Cursor` to a web-safe string by using its `toWebSafeString()` method, and back again with the static class method `fromWebSafeString()` method:

```
    String cursorString = req.getParameter("c");
    Cursor cursor = null;
    if (cursorString != null) {
        cursor = Cursor.fromWebSafeString(cursorString);
    }

    // ...

    String newCursorString = cursor.toWebSafeString();
```

You use cursors with the query execution methods via `FetchOptions`. You can specify a `startCursor()`, an `endCursor()`, or both:

```
    QueryResultList<Entity> results = pq.asQueryResultList(
        FetchOptions.Builder.withLimit(10)
            .startCursor(cursor));
```

Projection Queries

We've described the datastore as an object store. You create an entity with all of its properties. When you fetch an entity by key, the entire entity and all its properties come back. When you want to update a property of an entity, you must fetch the complete entity, make the change to the object locally, then save the entire object back to the datastore.

The types of queries we've seen so far reflect this reality as well. You can either fetch entire entities that match query criteria:

```
SELECT * FROM Kind WHERE ...
```

Or you can fetch just the keys:

```
SELECT __key__ FROM Kind WHERE ...
```

And really, an entity query is just a key query that fetches the entities for those keys. The query criteria drive a scan of an index (or indexes) containing property values and keys, and the keys are returned by the scan.

But sometimes you only need to know one or two properties of an entity, and it's wasteful to retrieve an entire entity just to get at those properties. For times like these, App Engine has another trick up its sleeve: *projection queries*. Projection queries let you request specific properties of entities, instead of full entities, under certain conditions:

```
SELECT prop1, prop2 FROM Kind WHERE ...
```

The entity objects that come back have only the requested properties (known as the "projected properties") and their keys set. Only the requested data is returned by the datastore service.

The idea of projection queries is based on how indexes are used to resolve queries. While a normal query uses indexes of keys and property values to look up keys then fetch the corresponding entities, projection queries take the requested values directly from the indexes themselves.

Every projection query requires a custom index of the properties involved in the query. The development server adds index configuration for each combination of projected properties, kind, and other query criteria.

Projection queries tend to be faster than full queries, for several reasons. Result entities are not fetched separately after a key lookup. Instead, the result data comes directly from the index. And naturally, less data means less RPC communication. The entire procedure is to find the first row of the custom index and scan to the last row, returning the columns for the projected properties.

Several restrictions fall out of this trick, and they're fairly intuitive. Only indexed properties can be in a projection. Another way of saying this is, only entities with all the projected properties set to an indexable value can be a result for a projection query. A projection query needs a custom index even if the equivalent full-entity query does not.

There's another weird behavior we need to note here, and yes, once again it involves multivalued properties. As we saw earlier, if an entity contains multiple values for a property, an index containing that property contains a row for each value (and a row for each combination of values if you're indexing more than one multivalued property), repeating each of the single-valued properties in the index. Unlike an entity or key query, a projection query makes no attempt to de-duplicate the result list in this case. Instead, a projection on a multivalued property returns a separate result for each row in the index. Each result contains just the values of the properties on that row.

Each projection requires its own custom index. If you have two queries with the same kind and filter structures, but different projected properties, the queries require two custom indexes:

```
SELECT prop1, prop2 FROM Kind ...
SELECT prop1, prop3 FROM Kind ...
```

In this case, you can save space and time-to-update by using the same projection in both cases, and ignoring the unused properties:

```
SELECT prop1, prop2, prop3 FROM Kind ...
```

The SQL-like syntax we're using is indeed the GQL syntax for projection queries. You can perform projection queries in the Administration Console (for both Python and

Java apps). Remember that, as with other queries, the app must already have the appropriate index configured for the query to succeed in the Console.

Projection Queries in Python

In the Python interface, you request a projection query by listing the properties for the projection. In the `all()` model class method and the `db.Query()` constructor, you provide an iterable of property names as the `projection` argument:

```
q = MyModel.all(projection=('prop1', 'prop2'))

q = db.Query(MyModel, projection=('prop1', 'prop2'))
```

You can also use the GQL syntax for projection queries with the `db.GqlQuery()` constructor:

```
q = db.GqlQuery('SELECT prop1, prop2 FROM MyModel')
```

The `gql()` model class method only supports entity queries, and does not support projection queries.

The results of a projection query are instances of the model class with only the projected properties set. The model class is aware that the result is from a projection query, and alters its behavior slightly to accommodate. Specifically, it will allow a property modeled as `required=True` to be unset if it isn't one of the projected properties. (We'll cover property modeling in Chapter 9.) Also, it won't allow the partial instance to be `put()` back to the datastore, even if you set all of its properties to make it complete.

You can test whether a model instance is a projection result using the `db.model_is_projection(obj)` function. The function takes a model instance and returns `True` if it is the result of a projection query.

As sanity checks, the query API will not let you project a property and use it in an equality filter in the same query. It also won't allow you to project the same property more than once.

Projection Queries in Java

In Java, you request a projection query by calling the `addProjection()` method on the `Query` object for each property in the projection. (If you never call this method, the query is an entity query, and full entities are returned.) The `addProjection()` method takes a `PropertyProjection`, whose constructor takes the name of the property and an optional (but recommended) value type class:

```
import com.google.appengine.api.datastore.PropertyProjection;

// ...
        Query query = new Query("Message");
        query.addProjection(new PropertyProjection("prop1", String.class));
```

Each query result is an `Entity` with only the projected properties set. As usual, calling `getProperty()` will return the value as an `Object`, which you can then cast to the expected value type.

If projected properties may be of different types, you can pass `null` as the second argument of the `PropertyProjection` constructor. If you do this, the `getProperty()` method on the result will return the raw value wrapped in a `RawValue` instance. This wrapper provides several accessor methods with varying amounts of type control. `getValue()` returns the raw value as an `Object`; you can use introspection on the result to determine its type. `asType()` takes a `java.lang.Class` and returns a castable `Object`, as if you provided the class to the `PropertyProjection` constructor. And finally, `<T> asStrictType(java.lang.Class<T>)` provides an additional level of type control at compile time.

The Java Persistence API supports projection queries in its own query language, comparable to GQL or field selection in SQL. See Chapter 10 for more information on JPA.

Configuring Indexes

An application specifies the custom indexes it needs in a configuration file. Each index definition includes the kind, and the names and sort orders of the properties to include. A configuration file can contain zero or more index definitions.

Most of the time, you can leave the maintenance of this file to the development web server. The development server watches the queries the application makes, and if a query needs a custom index and that index is not defined in the configuration file, the server adds appropriate configuration automatically.

The development server will not remove index configuration. If you are sure your app no longer needs an index, you can edit the file manually and remove it.

You can disable the automatic index configuration feature. Doing so causes the development server to behave like App Engine: if a query doesn't have an index and needs one, the query fails. How to do this is particular to the runtime environment, so we'll get to that in a moment.

Index configuration is global to all versions of your application. All versions of an app share the same datastore, including indexes. If you deploy a version of the app and the index configuration has changed, App Engine will use the new index configuration for all versions.

Index Configuration for Python

For Python apps, the index configuration file is named *index.yaml*, and is in the YAML format (similar to *app.yaml*). It appears in the application root directory.

The structure is a single YAML list named `indexes`, with one element per index. Each index definition has a `kind` element (the kind name, a string) and a `properties` element. If the index supports queries with ancestor filters, it has an `ancestor` element with a value of `yes`.

`properties` is a list, one element per column in the index, where each column has a `name` and an optional `direction` that is either `asc` (ascending order, the default) or `desc` (descending order). The order of the properties list is significant: the index is sorted by the first column first, then by the second column, and so on.

Here's an example of an *index.yaml* file, using indexes from earlier in this chapter:

```
indexes:
- kind: Player
  properties:
  - name: charclass
  - name: level
    direction: desc

- kind: Player
  properties:
  - name: level
    direction: desc
  - name: score
    direction: desc
```

By default, the development server adds index configuration to this file as needed. When it does, it does so beneath this line, adding it (and a descriptive comment) if it doesn't find it:

```
# AUTOGENERATED
```

You can move index configuration above this line to take manual control over it. This isn't strictly necessary, since the development server will never delete index configuration, not even that which was added automatically.

To disable automatic index configuration in the development server, start the server with the `--require_indexes` command-line option. If you are using the Launcher, select the application, then go to the Edit menu and select Application Settings. Add the command-line option to the Extra Flags field and then click Update.

Index Configuration for Java

For Java apps, you add index configuration to a file named *datastore-indexes.xml*, in the directory *WEB-INF/* in the WAR. This is an XML file with a root element named

<datastore-indexes>. This contains zero or more <datastore-index> elements, one for each index.

Each <datastore-index> specifies the kind by using the `kind` attribute. It also has an `ancestor` attribute, which is `true` if the index supports queries with ancestor filters, and `false` otherwise.

A <datastore-index> contains one or more <property> elements, one for each column in the index. Each <property> has a `name` attribute (the name of the property) and a `direction` attribute (`asc` for ascending, `desc` for descending). The order of the <property> elements is significant: the index is sorted by the first column first, then by the second column, and so on.

An example:

```
<datastore-indexes autoGenerate="true">
  <datastore-index kind="Player" ancestor="false">
    <property name="charclass" direction="asc" />
    <property name="level" direction="desc" />
  </datastore-index>

  <datastore-index kind="Player" ancestor="false">
    <property name="level" direction="desc" />
    <property name="score" direction="desc" />
  </datastore-index>
</datastore-indexes>
```

The <datastore-indexes> root element has an attribute named `autoGenerate`. If it's `true`, or if the app does not have a *datastore-indexes.xml* file, the Java development server generates new index configuration when needed for a query. If it's `false`, the development server behaves like App Engine: if a query needs an index that is not defined, the query fails.

The development server does not modify *datastore-indexes.xml*. Instead, it generates a separate file named *datastore-indexes-auto.xml*, in the directory *WEB-INF/appengine-generated/*. The complete index configuration is the total of the two configuration files.

The Java server will never remove index configuration from the automatic file, so if you need to delete an index, you may need to remove it from the automatic file. You can move configuration from the automatic file to the manual file if that's easier to manage, such as to check it into a revision control repository.

CHAPTER 7

Datastore Transactions

With web applications, many users access and update data concurrently. Often, multiple users need to read or write to the same unit of data at the same time. This requires a data system that can give some assurances that simultaneous operations will not corrupt any user's view of the data. Most data systems guarantee that a single operation on a single unit of data maintains the integrity of the data, typically by scheduling operations that act on the same unit of data to be performed in a sequence, one at a time.

Many applications need similar data integrity guarantees when performing a set of multiple operations, possibly over multiple units of data. Such a set of operations is called a *transaction*. A data system that supports transactions guarantees that if a transaction succeeds, all the operations in the transaction are executed completely. If any step of the transaction fails, then none of its effects are applied to the data. The data remains in a consistent and predictable state before and after the transaction, even if other processes are attempting to modify the data concurrently.

For example, say you want to post a message to the bulletin board in the town square inviting other players to join your guild. The bulletin board maintains a count of how many messages have been posted to the board, so readers can see how many messages there are without reading every message object in the system. Posting a message requires three datastore operations: the app must read the old message count, update the message count with an incremented value, and create the new message object.

Without transactions, these operations may succeed or fail independently. The count may be updated but the message object may not be created. Or, if you create the message object first, the object may be created, but the count not updated. In either case, the resulting count is inaccurate. By performing these operations in a single transaction, if any step fails, none of the effects are applied, and the application can try the entire transaction again.

Also consider what happens when two players attempt to post to the message board at the same time. To increment the message count, each player process must read the old value, and then update it with a new value calculated from the old one. Without transactions, these operations may be interleaved: the first process reads the original count (say, 10), the second process reads the count (also 10), the first process adds 1 and updates the count with the new value (11), then finally the second process adds 1 to its value and updates the count (11). Because the second process doesn't know that the first process updated the value, the final count is 1 less than it ought to be (12). With transactions, the second process knows right away that the first process is updating the count and can do the right thing.

A scalable web application has several requirements that are at odds with transactions. For one, the application needs access to data to be fast, and not be affected by how much data is in the system or how it is distributed across multiple servers. The longer it takes for a transaction to complete, the longer other processes have to wait to access the data reserved by the transaction. The combined effect on how many transactions can be completed in a period of time is called *throughput*. For web apps, high throughput is important.

A web app usually needs transactions to finish completely and consistently, so it knows that the effects of the transaction can be relied upon by other processes for further calculations. The promise that all processes can see the changes once a transaction is complete is known as *strong consistency*.

An alternative policy known as *eventual consistency* trades this promise for greater flexibility in how changes are applied. With strong consistency, if a process wants to read a value, but a change for that value has been committed to the datastore but not yet saved to disk, the process waits until the save is complete, then reads the value. But if the process doesn't need the latest value, it can read the older value directly from the disk without waiting. Consistency is eventual because the impatient processes are not guaranteed to see the latest value, but will see it after the value is saved to disk.

The App Engine datastore provides transactions with strong consistency and low overhead. It does this by limiting the scope of transactions: a single transaction can only read or write to entities that belong to a single *entity group*. Every entity belongs to an entity group, by default a group of its own. The app assigns an entity to a group when the entity is created, and the assignment is permanent.

By having the app arrange entities into groups, the datastore can treat each group independently when applying concurrent transactions. Two transactions that use different groups can occur simultaneously without harm. With a bit of thought, an app can ensure that entities are arranged to minimize the likelihood that two processes will need to access the same group, and thereby maximize throughput.

Entity groups also come into play with queries and indexes. If a query only needs results from a single entity group, the query can return strongly consistent results, since the group's local index data is updated transactionally with the group's entities. The query requests this behavior by identifying the group as part of the query, using a part of the key path, or *ancestor*. (We're finally going to explain what key paths are: they form entity groups by arranging keys in a hierarchy.)

Whereas ancestor queries are strongly consistent, global queries are eventually consistent: global kind-based indexes are not guaranteed to be up-to-date by the time changes to entities are saved to disk. This makes ancestor queries—and good entity group design—a powerful weapon in your datastore arsenal.

An app can request more flexible behaviors, with their corresponding trade-offs. *Cross-group transactions* (sometimes called "XG" transactions) can act on up to five entity groups, in exchange for added latency and a greater risk of contention with other processes. An app can specify a *read policy* when reading data, which can request a faster eventually consistent read instead of a strongly consistent read that may have to wait on pending updates.

In this chapter, we discuss what happens when you update an entity group, how to create entities in entity groups, how to perform ancestor queries, and how to perform multiple operations on an entity group, using a transaction. We also discuss batch operations, how query indexes are built, and the consistency guarantees of the datastore.

Entities and Entity Groups

When you create, update, or delete a single entity, the change occurs in a transaction: either all your changes to the entity succeed, or none of them do. If you change two properties of an entity and save it, every request handler process that fetches the entity will see both changes. At no point during the save will a process see the new value for one property and the old value for the other. And if the update fails, the entity stays as it was before the save. In database terms, the act of updating an entity is *atomic*.

It is often useful to update multiple entities atomically, such that any process's view of the data is consistent across the entities. In the bulletin board example, the message count and each of the messages may be stored as separate entities, but the combined act of creating a new message entity and updating the count ought to be atomic. We need a way to combine multiple actions into a single transaction, so they all succeed or all fail.

To do this in a scalable way, App Engine must know in advance which entities may be involved in a single transaction. These entities are stored and updated together, so the datastore can keep them consistent and still access them quickly. You tell App Engine which entities may be involved in the same transaction by using entity groups.

Every entity belongs to an entity group, possibly a group containing just itself. An entity can only belong to one group. You assign an entity to a group when the entity is created. Group membership is permanent; an entity cannot be moved to another group once it has been created.

The datastore uses entity groups to determine what happens when two processes attempt to update data in the entity group at the same time. When this happens, the first update that completes "wins," and the other update is canceled. App Engine notifies the process whose update is canceled by raising an exception. In most cases, the process can just try the update again and succeed. But the app must decide for itself how to go about retrying, since important data may have changed between attempts.

This style of managing concurrent access is known as *optimistic concurrency control*. It's "optimistic" in the sense that the database tries to perform the operations without checking whether another process is working with the same data (such as with a "locking" mechanism), and only checks for collisions at the end, optimistic that the operations will succeed. The update is not guaranteed to succeed, and the app must reattempt the operations or take some other course of action if the data changes during the update.

Multiple processes vying for the opportunity to write to an entity group at the same time is known as *contention*. Two processes are contending for the write; the first to commit wins. A high rate of contention slows down your app, because it means many processes are getting their writes canceled and have to retry, possibly multiple times. In egregious cases, contention for a group may exclude a process to the point of the failure of that process. You can avoid high rates of contention with careful design of your entity groups.

Optimistic concurrency control is a good choice for web applications because reading data is fast—a typical reader never waits for updates—and almost always succeeds. If an update fails due to contention, it's usually easy to try again, or return an error message to the user. Most web applications have only a small number of users updating the same piece of data, so contention failures are rare.

Updating an entity in a group can potentially cancel updates to *any* other entity in the group by another process. You should design your data model so that entity groups do not need to be updated by many users simultaneously.

Be especially careful if the number of simultaneous updates to a single group grows as your application gets more users. In this case, you usually want to spread the load across multiple entity groups, and increase the number of entity groups automatically as the user base grows. Scalable division of a data resource like this is known as *sharding*.

Also be aware that some data modeling tasks may not be practical on a large scale. Incrementing a value in a single datastore entity every time any user visits the site's home page is not likely to work well with a distributed strong consistency data system.

Keys, Paths, and Ancestors

To create an entity in a group with other entities, you associate it with the key of another entity from that group. The existing entity becomes the new entity's *parent*, forming a path of ancestor relationships down to a *root* entity that does not have a parent. This path becomes part of the new entity's key. Every entity whose key begins with the same root is in the same group, including the root entity itself.

When you create an entity and do not specify a parent, the entity is created in a new group by itself. The new entity is the root of the new group.

We alluded to paths earlier when we discussed keys, so let's complete the picture. An entity's key consists of the path of ancestors in the entity's group, starting from the group's root. Each entity in the path is represented by the entity's kind followed by either the system-assigned numeric ID or the app-assigned string name. The full path is a sequence of kind and ID/name pairs.

The following keys represent entities in the same group, because they all have the same root ancestor:

```
MessageBoard, "The_Archonville_Times"

MessageBoard, "The_Archonville_Times" / Message, "first!"

MessageBoard, "The_Archonville_Times" / Message, "pk_fest_aug_21"

MessageBoard, "The_Archonville_Times" / Message, "first!" / Message, "keep_clean"
```

Here is Python code that creates four entities in the same group. The model class constructor accepts either an entity object or a `Key` object as the parent:

```
# Creating a new entity group with a root entity:
board = MessageBoard(key_name='The_Archonville_Times')
board.title = 'The Archonville Times'
board.put()

# Using the object for the "parent" argument:
msg1 = Message(parent=board, key_name='first!')
msg1.put()

# Using a Key for the "parent" argument:
p_key = board.key()
msg2 = Message(parent=p_key, key_name='pk_fest_aug_21')
msg2.put()

# Using an entity that isn't the root as the parent:
msg3 = Message(parent=msg1, key_name='keep_clean')
msg3.put()
```

When you're deriving the key of an entity with a parent, you must use the complete ancestor path. For example, in Python:

```
k = db.Key.from_path('MessageBoard', 'The_Archonville_Times',
                     'Message', 'first!',
                     'Message', 'keep_clean')
```

Similarly, GQL supports key literals with ancestors, as follows:

```
SELECT * FROM MessageAttachment
        WHERE message = KEY(MessageBoard, 'The_Archonville_Times',
```

```
                                 Message, 'first!',
                                 Message, 'keep_clean')
```

Notice that entities of different kinds can be in the same entity group. In the datastore, there is no relationship between kinds and entity groups. (You can enforce such a relationship in your app's code, if you like.)

Ancestors do not have to exist for a key to be valid. If you create an entity with a parent and then delete the parent, the key for the child is still valid and can still be assembled from its parts (such as with Python's `from_path()` method). This is true even for a group's root entity: the root can be deleted and other entities in the group remain in the group.

You can even use a made-up key for an entity that doesn't exist as the parent for a new entity. Neither the kind nor the name/ID of an ancestor needs to represent an actual entity. Group membership is defined by the first key part in the ancestor path, regardless of whether that part corresponds to an entity. Here is Python code that creates two entities in the same group without a root entity:

```
root = db.Key.from_path('MessageBoard', 'The_Baskinville_Post')

msg1 = Message(parent=root)
msg1.put()

msg2 = Message(parent=root)
msg2.put()
```

In the Java API, you create a new entity with a parent by specifying the parent key to the `Entity` constructor:

```
import com.google.appengine.api.datastore.Entity;
import com.google.appengine.api.datastore.Key;
import com.google.appengine.api.datastore.KeyFactory;

// ...
        Key parentKey = KeyFactory.createKey("MessageBoard", "The_Archonville_Times");
        Entity e = new Entity("Message", parentKey);
```

You can also build the complete key path by using the `KeyFactory.Builder`, then pass the entire key to the `Entity` constructor:

```
        Key entityKey = new KeyFactory.Builder("MessageBoard", "The_Archonville_Times")
            .addChild("Message", 0)
            .getKey();
        Entity e = new Entity(entityKey);
```

Ancestor Queries

The root ancestor in a key path determines group membership. Intermediate ancestors have no affect on group membership, which poses the question, what good are ancestor paths? One possible answer to that question: ancestor queries.

A datastore query can include a filter that limits the results to just those entities with a given ancestor. This can match any ancestor, not just the immediate parent. In other words, a query can match a sequence of key parts starting from the root.

Continuing the town square bulletin board example, where each `MessageBoard` is the root of an entity group containing things attached to the board, the following GQL query returns the 10 most recent `Message` entities attached to a specific board:

```
SELECT * FROM Message
         WHERE ANCESTOR IS KEY(MessageBoard,
                               'The_Archonville_Times')
         ORDER BY post_date DESC
         LIMIT 10
```

Most queries that use an ancestor filter need custom indexes. There is one unusual exception: a query does not need a custom index if the query also contains equality filters on properties (and no inequality filters or sort orders). In this exceptional case, the "merge join" algorithm can use a built-in index of keys along with the built-in property indexes. In cases where the query would need a custom index anyway, the query can match the ancestor to the keys in the custom index.

In Python, you can set an ancestor filter on a `Query` object by calling its `ancestor()` method. Its argument is the full key to the ancestor:

```
q = db.Query(Message)
q.ancestor(db.Key.from_path('MessageBoard',
                            'The_Archonville_Times'))
q.order('-post_date')
```

In Java, you create an ancestor query by passing the ancestor key to the `Query` constructor:

```
Key ancestorKey = KeyFactory.createKey("MessageBoard",
                                       "The_Archonville_Times");
Query query = Query("Message", ancestorKey);
query.addSort("post_date", Query.SortDirection.DESCENDING);
```

As we mentioned in Chapter 6, the datastore supports queries over entities of all kinds. Kindless queries are limited to key filters and ancestor filters. Since ancestors can have children of disparate kinds, kindless queries are useful for getting every child of a given ancestor, regardless of kind:

```
SELECT * WHERE ANCESTOR IS KEY('MessageBoard', 'The_Archonville_Times')
```

A kindless ancestor query in Python:

```
q = db.Query()
q.ancestor(db.Key.from_path('MessageBoard', 'The_Archonville_Times'))
```

A kindless ancestor query in Java:

```
Key ancestorKey = KeyFactory.createKey("MessageBoard",
                                       "The_Archonville_Times");
Query query = new Query(ancestorKey);
```

Although ancestor queries can be useful, don't get carried away building large ancestor trees. Remember that every entity with the same root belongs to the same entity group, and more simultaneous users that need to write to a group mean a greater likelihood of concurrency failures.

If you want to model hierarchical relationships between entities without the consequences of entity groups, consider using multivalued properties to store paths. For example, if there's an entity whose path in your hierarchy can be represented as `/A/B/C/D`, you can store this path as: `e.parents = ['/A', '/A/B', '/A/B/C']`. Then you can perform a query similar to an ancestor query on this property: `... WHERE parents = '/A/B'`.

What Can Happen in a Transaction

Entity groups ensure that the operations performed within a transaction see a consistent view of the entities in a group. For this to work, a single transaction must limit its operations to entities in a single group. The entity group determines the scope of the transaction.

Within a transaction, you can fetch, update, or delete an entity by using the entity's key. You can create a new entity that either is a root entity of a new group that becomes the subject of the transaction, or that has a member of the transaction's entity group as its parent. You can also create other entities in the same group.

You can perform queries over the entities of a single entity group in a transaction. A query in a transaction must have an ancestor filter that matches the transaction's entity group. The results of the query, including both the indexes that provide the results as well as the entities themselves, are guaranteed to be consistent with the rest of the transaction.

In the Python and Java APIs, you do not need to declare the entity group for a transaction explicitly. You simply perform datastore actions on entities of the same group. If you attempt to perform actions that involve different entity groups within a transaction, the API raises an exception. The API also raises an exception if you attempt to perform a query in a transaction that does not have an ancestor filter. (We'll see the specific exception that is raised in the next few sections.)

Transactions have a maximum size. A single transaction can write up to 10 megabytes of data.

Transactional Reads

Sometimes it is useful to fetch entities in a transaction even if the transaction does not update any data. Reading multiple entities in a transaction ensures that the entities are consistent with one another. As with updates, entities fetched in a transaction must be members of the same entity group.

A transaction that only reads entities never fails due to contention. As with reading a single entity, a read-only transaction sees the data as it appears at the beginning of the transaction, even if other processes make changes after the transaction starts and before it completes.

The same is true for ancestor-only queries within a transaction. If the transaction does not create, update, or delete data from the entity group, it will not fail due to contention.

The datastore can do this because it remembers previous versions of entities, using timestamps associated with the entity groups. The datastore notes the current time at the beginning of every operation and transaction, and this determines which version of the data the operation or transaction sees. This is known as *multiversion concurrency control*, a form of optimistic concurrency control. This mechanism is internal to the datastore; the application cannot access previous versions of data, nor can it see the timestamps.

This timestamp mechanism has a minor implication for reading data within transactions. When you read an entity in a transaction, the datastore returns the version of the entity most recent to the beginning of the transaction. If you update an entity and then refetch the same entity within the same transaction, the datastore returns the entity as it appeared *before* the update. In most cases, you can just reuse the in-memory object you modified (which has your changes) instead of refetching the entity.

Eventually Consistent Reads

As described above, transactional reads are strongly consistent. When the app fetches an entity by key, the datastore ensures that all changes committed prior to the beginning of the current transaction are written to disk—and are therefore returned by the read—before continuing. Occasionally, this can involve a slight delay as the datastore catches up with a backlog of committed changes. In a transaction, a strongly consistent read can only read entities within the transaction's entity group.

Similarly, when the app performs an ancestor query in a transaction, the query uses the group's local indexes in a strongly consistent fashion. The results of the index scans are guaranteed to be consistent with the contents of the entities returned by the query.

You can opt out of this protection by specifying a *read policy* that requests eventual consistency. With an eventually consistent read of an entity, your app gets the current known state of the entity being read, regardless of whether there are still committed changes to be applied. With an eventually consistent ancestor query, the indexes used for the query are consistent with the time the indexes are read from disk.

In other words, an eventual consistency read policy causes gets and queries to behave as if they are not a part of the current transaction. This may be faster in some cases, since the operations do not have to wait for committed changes to be written before returning a result.

Perhaps more importantly: an eventually consistent get operation can get an entity outside of the current transaction's entity group.

We'll look at the APIs for read policies in the next two sections.

Transactions in Python

The Python API uses function objects to handle transactions. To perform multiple operations in a transaction, you define a function that executes the operations by using the `@db.transactional()` decorator. When you call your function outside of a transaction, the function starts a new transaction, and all datastore operations that occur within the function are expected to comply with the transaction's requirements:

```
import datetime
from google.appengine.ext import db

class MessageBoard(db.Expando):
    pass

class Message(db.Expando):
    pass

@db.transactional()
def create_message_txn(board_name, message_name, message_title, message_text):
    board = db.get(db.Key.from_path('MessageBoard', board_name))
    if not board:
        board = MessageBoard(key_name=board_name)
        board.count = 0

    message = Message(key_name=message_name, parent=board)
    message.title = message_title
    message.text = message_text
    message.post_date = datetime.datetime.now()

    board.count += 1

    db.put([board, message])

# ...
        try:
            create_message_txn(
                board_name=board_name,
                message_name=message_title,
                message_title=message_title,
                message_text=message_text)

        except db.TransactionFailedError, e:
            # Report an error to the user.
            # ...
```

All calls to the datastore to create, update, or delete entities within the transaction function take effect when the transaction is committed. Typically, you would update an entity by fetching or creating the model object, modifying it, then saving it, and continue to use the local object to represent the entity. In the rare case where the transaction function fetches an entity after saving it, the fetch will see the entity as it was *before* the update, because the update has not yet been committed.

If the transaction function raises an exception, the transaction is aborted, and the exception is re-raised to the caller. If you need to abort the transaction but do not want the exception raised to the caller (just the function exited), raise the `db.Rollback` exception in the transaction function. This causes the function to abort the transaction, then return `None`.

If the transaction cannot be completed due to a concurrency failure, the function call is retried automatically. By default, it is retried three times. If all retries fail, the function raises a `db.TransactionFailedError`. You can configure the number of retries by providing the `retries` argument to the `@db.transactional` decorator:

```
@db.transactional(retries=10)
def create_message_txn(board_name, message_name, message_title, message_text):
    # ...
```

Make sure your transaction function can be called multiple times safely without undesirable side effects. If this is not possible, you can set `retries=0`, but know that the transaction will fail on the first incident of contention.

The default behavior of `@db.transactional` functions is to start a new transaction if one isn't already started, and join the started transaction otherwise. This behavior is controlled by the `propagation` argument to the decorator, whose default setting is `db.ALLOWED`. If the decorator sets `propagation=db.MANDATORY`, the function expects to be called during an already-started transaction, and throws `db.BadRequestError` if called outside a transaction. If the decorator sets `propagation=db.INDEPENDENT`, the function always starts a new transaction, pausing an already-started transaction, if any.

If a function should not be run in a transaction, you can use the `@db.non_transactional` decorator to isolate it. By default, calling a nontransactional function within a transaction pauses the transaction and does not start a new one, so datastore operations in the function do not participate in the transaction. If you specify `allow_existing=False` to the decorator, calling the nontransactional function during a transaction raises `db.BadRequestError`.

As an added convenience, you can test whether the code is currently being executed within a transaction by calling `db.is_in_transaction()`.

There's an older transactional function interface that you might see in older code, and it's still supported. With the older interface, you call the function `db.run_in_transaction()`, specifying as argument the transaction function and the arguments with which to call it. A variant, `db.run_in_transaction_custom_retries()`, allowed for setting the number of retries. Yet another variant, `db.run_in_transaction_options()`, takes a set of options as its first argument (a result of calling `db.create_transaction_options()`), followed by the transaction function, then the function's arguments.

The behavior of this old interface is largely the same, but this interface isn't as versatile. With the decorator, multiple transactional functions can call each other, and can specify how they join or create transactions.

Within a transaction, reading entities and fetching results from an ancestor query uses a read policy of strong consistency by default. To use an eventual consistency read policy, you specify the `read_policy=db.EVENTUAL_CONSISTENCY` keyword argument to `db.get()`, or the `Query` methods `run()`, `fetch()`, `get()`, or `count()`. The eventual consistency read policy causes these operations to behave as if they are not in a transaction:

```
@db.transactional()
def create_message_txn(board_name, message_name, message_title, message_text):
    # Read an entity in the group "GameVersion / 1" with eventual consistency.
    game_version = db.get(
        db.Key.from_path('GameVersion', 1),
        read_policy=db.EVENTUAL_CONSISTENCY)

    # Read an entity in the group "MessageBoard / [board_name]"
    # with strong consistency. All other transactional operations
    # in this function must use this group.
    board = db.get(db.Key.from_path('MessageBoard', board_name))
    if not board:
        board = MessageBoard(key_name=board_name)
        board.count = 0
        board.created_at_game_version = game_version.version_id

    # ...
```

Transactions in Java

The JDO and JPA interfaces provide their own mechanisms for formulating transactions. Google's online documentation describes JDO, and we'll cover the JPA interface in Chapter 10.

To perform multiple operations within a single transaction, you call the `beginTransaction()` method of the `DatastoreService` instance. This method returns a `Transaction` object that represents the transaction. You perform the datastore operations as you usually do, calling the `put()`, `get()`, and `delete()` methods of the

DatastoreService. Finally, you call the commit() method of the Transaction object to complete the transaction.

Updates (put() and delete()) do not take effect until you commit the transaction. Fetching an entity by using get() after it has been updated in the same transaction will return an Entity object that represents the state of the entity *before* the update.

If the transaction cannot be committed due to a concurrency failure (or other datastore error), the commit throws a DatastoreFailureException:

```
import com.google.appengine.api.datastore.DatastoreFailureException;
import com.google.appengine.api.datastore.EntityNotFoundException;
import com.google.appengine.api.datastore.Transaction;

// ...
        DatastoreService ds = DatastoreServiceFactory.getDatastoreService();

        Key boardKey;
        Entity messageBoard;

        try {
            Transaction txn = ds.beginTransaction();

            try {
                boardKey = KeyFactory.createKey("MessageBoard",
                                                "The_Archonville_Times");
                messageBoard = ds.get(boardKey);

            } catch (EntityNotFoundException e) {
                messageBoard = new Entity("MessageBoard", "The_Archonville_Times");
                messageBoard.setProperty("count", 0);
                boardKey = ds.put(messageBoard);
            }

            txn.commit();

        } catch (DatastoreFailureException e) {
            // Report an error...
        }
```

If you do not commit the transaction, the transaction is rolled back automatically after the servlet exits, and changes are not applied. You can roll back the transaction explicitly by calling the rollback() method of the Transaction object.

By default, each datastore operation is associated with the transaction started by the most recent call to beginTransaction(), known in the API as the "current" transaction. If you call beginTransaction() more than once, each Transaction is remembered in a stack. Calling commit() or rollback() removes the Transaction from the stack. If you commit or roll back the current transaction and there is another transaction on the stack, the next most recent transaction becomes the current transaction.

You can associate a datastore operation with a specific transaction explicitly by passing the Transaction object to the operation method:

```
Transaction txn = ds.beginTransaction();

ds.put(txn, messageBoard);

txn.commit();
```

If there is no current transaction on the stack, calling an operation method performs the operation without a transaction. Updates occur immediately. If there is a current transaction but you would like the operation performed immediately and outside of the transaction, provide `null` as the first argument to the operation:

```
Transaction txn = ds.beginTransaction();

// Add an update of entityOne to the transaction.
ds.put(txn, entityOne);

// Update entityTwo immediately, outside of the transaction.
ds.put(null, entityTwo);

// Commit the transaction, updating entityOne.
txn.commit();
```

Alternatively, you can disable the automatic behavior of these methods by setting the implicit transaction management policy when you create the `DatastoreService` instance:

```
import com.google.appengine.api.datastore.DatastoreServiceConfig;
import com.google.appengine.api.datastore.ImplicitTransactionManagementPolicy;

// ...
        DatastoreService datastore =
            DatastoreServiceFactory.getDatastoreService(
                DatastoreServiceConfig.Builder
                .withImplicitTransactionManagementPolicy(
                    ImplicitTransactionManagementPolicy.NONE));
```

The default policy is `ImplicitTransactionManagementPolicy.AUTO`: most operations (`put()`, `get()`, `delete()`) will join the most recently started transaction if you don't explicitly pass a `Transaction` to the method. If you set this policy to `ImplicitTransactionManagementPolicy.NONE`, calling a method without an explicit `Transaction` will cause it to start its own independent transaction for the operation.

Note that `ds.prepare()` never joins a transaction automatically. You must tell it which transaction to join. If omitted, it will always start its own transaction.

With optimistic concurrency control, it is usually appropriate for the application to try the transaction again in the event of a concurrency failure. The following example retries the transaction up to three times before reporting an error to the user:

```
import com.google.appengine.api.datastore.DatastoreFailureException;
import com.google.appengine.api.datastore.DatastoreService;
import com.google.appengine.api.datastore.DatastoreServiceFactory;
import com.google.appengine.api.datastore.Entity;
import com.google.appengine.api.datastore.EntityNotFoundException;
```

```java
import com.google.appengine.api.datastore.Key;
import com.google.appengine.api.datastore.KeyFactory;
import com.google.appengine.api.datastore.PreparedQuery;
import com.google.appengine.api.datastore.Query;
import com.google.appengine.api.datastore.Transaction;

// ...
        DatastoreService ds = DatastoreServiceFactory.getDatastoreService();

        int retries = 3;
        boolean success = false;
        while (!success && retries > 0) {
            --retries;
            try {
                Transaction txn = ds.beginTransaction();

                Key boardKey;
                Entity messageBoard;
                try {
                    boardKey = KeyFactory.createKey("MessageBoard", boardName);
                    messageBoard = ds.get(boardKey);

                } catch (EntityNotFoundException e) {
                    messageBoard = new Entity("MessageBoard", boardName);
                    messageBoard.setProperty("count", 0);
                    boardKey = ds.put(messageBoard);
                }

                Entity message = new Entity("Message", boardKey);
                message.setProperty("message_title", messageTitle);
                message.setProperty("message_text", messageText);
                message.setProperty("post_date", postDate);
                ds.put(message);

                long count = (Long) messageBoard.getProperty("count");
                ++count;
                messageBoard.setProperty("count", count);
                ds.put(messageBoard);

                log.info("Posting msg, updating count to " + count);

                txn.commit();

                // Break out of retry loop.
                success = true;

            } catch (DatastoreFailureException e) {
                // Allow retry to occur.
            }
        }
        if (!success) {
            // Tell the user it didn't work out...
            resp.getWriter().println
                ("<p>A new message could not be posted.  Try again later.</p>");
        }
```

```
// ...

Key boardKey = KeyFactory.createKey("MessageBoard", boardName);
try {
    Entity messageBoard = ds.get(boardKey);
    long count = (Long) messageBoard.getProperty("count");
    resp.getWriter().println("<p>Latest messages posted to
           " + boardName + " (" + count + " total):</p>");

    Query q = new Query("Message", boardKey);
    PreparedQuery pq = ds.prepare(q);
    for (Entity result : pq.asIterable()) {
        resp.getWriter().println("<h3>"
                + result.getProperty("message_title")
                + "</h3><p>"
                + result.getProperty("message_text")
                + "</p>");
    }
} catch (EntityNotFoundException e) {
    resp.getWriter().println("<p>No message board found.</p>");
}
```

Within a transaction, reading entities and fetching results from an ancestor query uses a read policy of strong consistency by default. To use an eventual consistency read policy, you use a separate instance of the `DatastoreService` configured with the eventual consistency read policy, like so:

```
import com.google.appengine.api.datastore.DatastoreService;
import com.google.appengine.api.datastore.DatastoreServiceConfig;
import com.google.appengine.api.datastore.DatastoreServiceFactory;
import com.google.appengine.api.datastore.ReadPolicy;

// ...
        // Create a datastore service instance with the default read policy.
        DatastoreService strongDatastore =
            DatastoreServiceFactory.getDatastoreService();

        // Create another datastore service instance with the eventual consistency
        // read policy.
        DatastoreServiceConfig datastoreServiceConfig =
            DatastoreServiceConfig.Builder.withReadPolicy(
                new ReadPolicy(ReadPolicy.Consistency.EVENTUAL));
        DatastoreService eventualDatastore =
            DatastoreServiceFactory.getDatastoreService(datastoreServiceConfig);

        // Start a datastore transaction for this thread.  (It doesn't matter
        // which service instance we use.)
        strongDatastore.beginTransaction();

        // Read an entity in the group "GameVersion / 1" with eventual consistency.
        Key gameVersionKey = KeyFactory.createKey("GameVersion", 1);
        Entity gameVersion = eventualDatastore.get(gameVersionKey);

        // Read an entity in the group "MessageBoard / [boardName]" with strong
```

```
// consistency.
// All other transactional operations in this function must use this group.
Key boardKey = KeyFactory.createKey("MessageBoard", boardName);
Entity board = strongDatastore.get(boardKey);
```

All reads and query result fetches made with this service instance will use the given read policy. Transactions are specific to the thread, not to the service instance, so you can use two service instances during the same transaction.

How Entities Are Updated

To fully understand how the datastore guarantees that your data stays consistent, it's worth discussing how transactions are performed behind the scenes. To do so, we must mention BigTable, Google's distributed data system that is the basis of the App Engine datastore. We won't go into the details of how entities, entity groups, and indexes are stored in BigTable, but we will refer to BigTable's own notion of atomic transactions in our explanation.

Figure 7-1 shows the phases of a successful transaction.

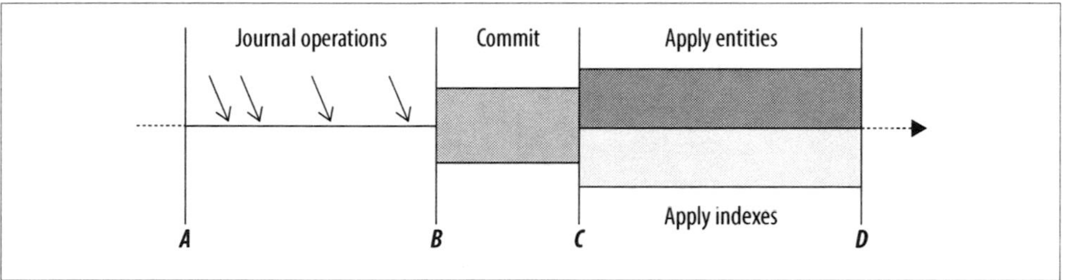

Figure 7-1. The timeline of a transaction: the operations, the commit phase, and the apply phase

The datastore uses a "journal" to keep track of changes that need to be applied to entities in an entity group. Each journal entry has a unique timestamp that indicates the order in which the changes were made. The datastore remembers the timestamp of the most recent change that has been committed, and guarantees that attempts to read the data will see all changes up to that point.

When an app begins a transaction for an entity group, the datastore makes a note of the current last-committed timestamp for the group (point A in Figure 7-1). As the app calls the datastore to update entities, the datastore writes the requested changes to the journal. Each change is marked as "uncommitted."

When the app finishes the transaction (point B), the datastore checks the group's last-committed timestamp again. If the timestamp hasn't changed since the transaction began, it marks all the transaction's changes as "committed" and then advances the group's timestamp. Otherwise, the timestamp was advanced by another request handler since the beginning of the transaction, so the datastore aborts the current transaction and reports a concurrency failure to the app.

Verifying the timestamp, committing the journal entries, and updating the timestamp all occur in an atomic BigTable operation. If another process attempts to commit a transaction to the same entity group while the first transaction's commit is in progress, the other process waits for the first commit to complete. This guarantees that if the first commit succeeds, the second process sees the updated timestamp and reports a concurrency failure. This is illustrated in Figure 7-2.

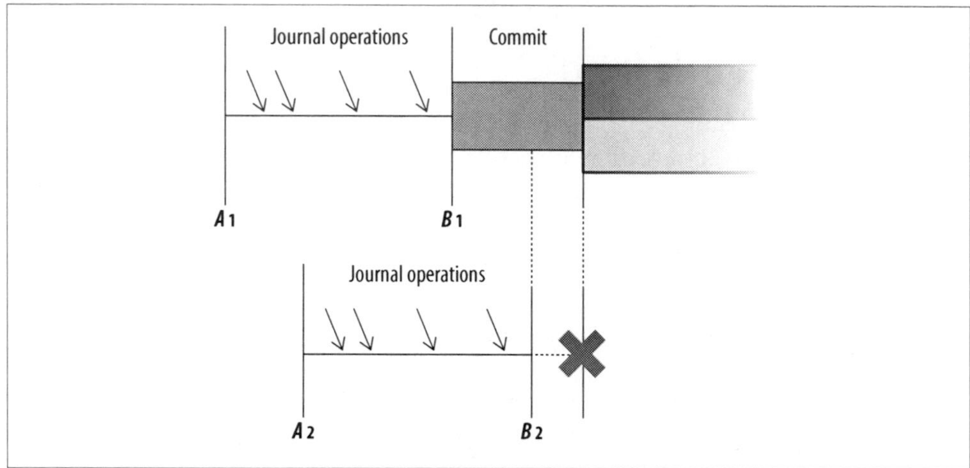

Figure 7-2. A timeline of two concurrent transactions; the first to commit "wins"

Once the journal entries have been committed (point C in Figure 7-1), the datastore applies each committed change to the appropriate entity and appropriate indexes, then marks the change as "applied." If there are multiple unapplied changes for an entity in the journal, they are applied in the order they were performed.

Here's the sneaky bit. If the apply phase fails for whatever reason (hard drive failure, power outage, meteorite), the committed transaction is still considered successful. If there are committed but unapplied changes the next time someone performs an operation on an entity in the entity group (within or without an explicit transaction), the datastore reruns the apply phase before performing the operation. This ensures that operations and transactions always see all changes that have been committed prior to the start of the operation or transaction. The datastore also uses background processes to roll forward unapplied operations, as well as purge old journal entries.

The roll-forward mechanism also ensures that subsequent operations can see all committed changes even if the apply phase is still in progress. At the beginning of an operation or transaction, the datastore notes the current time, then waits for all changes committed prior to that time to be applied before continuing.

Notice that the apply phase does not need to occur inside a BigTable transaction. Because of this, the datastore can spread multiple entities in the same group across multiple machines, and can allow an entity group to get arbitrarily large. Only the group's last-committed timestamp and journal need to be stored close enough together for a BigTable transaction. The datastore makes an effort to store entities of the same group "near" each other for performance reasons, but this does not limit the size or speed of entity groups.

When an app updates an entity outside of a transaction, the datastore performs the update with the same transactional mechanism, as if it were a transaction of just one operation. The datastore assumes that an update performed outside of a transaction is safe to perform at any time, and will retry the update automatically in the event of a concurrency failure. If several attempts fail, the datastore throws the concurrency exception. In contrast, an explicit transaction throws a concurrency exception on the first failure, because the datastore does not know if it is safe to commit the same changes. The app must retry the explicit transaction on its own. (The Python API's `@db.transactional` decorator knows how to rerun the function that performs the transaction, but this occurs as part of the application code.)

The App Engine datastore replicates all data to at least three places in each of at least two different data centers. The replication process uses a consensus algorithm based on "Paxos" to ensure that all sites agree that the change will be committed before proceeding. This level of replication ensures that your app's datastore remains available for both reads and writes during all planned outages—and most unplanned outages.

When an app calls the datastore to update data, the call does not return until the apply phase is complete. If an error occurs at any point in the process, the datastore call raises an exception in the application.

This is true even if the error occurs during the apply phase, after the commit phase is complete and the update is guaranteed to be applied before the next transaction. Because the application can't tell the difference between an error during the commit phase and an error during the apply phase, the application should react as if the update has not taken place.

In most cases, the app can simply retry the update. More care is needed if retrying the update relies on the previous attempt being unsuccessful, but these cases usually require testing the state of the data in a transaction, and the solution is simply to retry the entire transaction. If the transaction creates a new entity, one way to avoid creating a duplicate entity is to use a key name instead of a system-supplied numeric ID, precalculating and testing for the nonexistence of a global unique ID (GUID) if necessary.

Failures during the apply phase are very rare, and most errors represent a failure to commit. One of the most important principles in scalable app design is to be tolerant of the most rare kinds of faults.

How Entities Are Read

The timestamp mechanism explains what happens when two processes attempt to write to the same entity group at the same time. When one process commits, it updates the timestamp for the group. When the other process tries to commit, it notices the timestamp has changed, and aborts. The app can retry the transaction with fresh data, or give up.

The transaction is aborted only if the app attempted to update an entity during the transaction and another process has since committed changes. If the app only reads data in the transaction and does not make changes, the app simply sees the entities as they were at the beginning of the transaction. To support this, the datastore retains several old versions of each entity, marked with the timestamp of the most recently applied journal entry. Reading an entity in a transaction returns the version of the entity most recent to the timestamp at the beginning of the transaction.

Reading an entity outside of a transaction or with an eventual consistency read policy does not roll forward committed-but-unapplied changes. Instead, the read returns the entity as it appears on disk, as of the most recently applied changes. This is faster than waiting for pending changes to be applied, and usually not a concern for reads outside of transactions. But this means the entity may appear older or newer than other entities. If you need any consistency guarantees when reading multiple entities, use transactions and the strong consistency read policy.

Batch Updates

When you read, create, update, or delete an entity, the runtime environment makes a service call to the datastore. Each service call has some overhead, including serializing and deserializing parameters and transmitting them between machines in the data center. If you need to update multiple entities, you can save time by performing the updates together as a batch in one service call.

We introduced batch calls in Chapter 5. Here's a quick example of the Python batch API:

```
# Creating multiple entities:
e1 = Message(key_name='m1', text='...')
e2 = Message(key_name='m2', text='...')
e3 = Message(key_name='m3', text='...')
message_keys = db.put([e1, e2, e3])

# Getting multiple entities using keys:
message_keys = [db.Key('Message', 'm1'),
                db.Key('Message', 'm2'),
                db.Key('Message', 'm2')]
messages = db.get(message_keys)
for message in messages:
    # ...
```

```
# Deleting multiple entities:
db.delete(message_keys)
```

When the datastore receives a batch call, it bundles the keys or entities by their entity groups, which it can determine from the keys. Then it dispatches calls to the datastore machines responsible for each entity group. The datastore returns results to the app when it has received all results from all machines.

If the call includes changes for multiple entities in a single entity group, those changes are performed in a single transaction. There is no way to control this behavior, but there's no reason to do it any other way. It's faster to commit multiple changes to a group at once than to commit them individually, and no less likely to result in concurrency failures.

Each entity group involved in a batch update may fail to commit due to a concurrency failure. If a concurrency failure occurs for any update, the API raises the concurrency failure exception—even if updates to other groups were committed successfully.

Batch updates in disparate entity groups are performed in separate threads, possibly by separate datastore machines, executed in parallel to one another. This can make batch updates especially fast compared to performing each update one at a time.

Remember that if you use the batch API during a transaction, every entity or key in the batch must use the same entity group as the rest of the transaction.

How Indexes Are Updated

As we saw in Chapter 6, datastore queries are powered by indexes. The datastore updates these indexes as entities change, so results for queries can be determined without examining the entity properties directly. This includes an index of keys, an index for each kind and property, and custom indexes described by your app's configuration files that fulfill complex queries. When an entity is created, updated, or deleted, each relevant index is updated and sorted so subsequent queries match the new state of the data.

The datastore updates indexes after changes have been committed, during the apply phase. Changes are applied to indexes and entities in parallel. Updates of indexes are themselves performed in parallel, so the number of indexes to update doesn't necessarily affect how fast the update occurs.

As with entities, the datastore retains multiple versions of index data, labeled with timestamps. When you perform a query, the datastore notes the current time, then uses the index data that is most current up to that time. However, unless the query has an ancestor filter, the datastore has no way to know which entity groups are involved in the result set and so cannot wait for changes in progress to be applied.

This means that, for a brief period during an update, a query that doesn't have an ancestor filter (a nonancestor query, or global query) may return results that do not match the query criteria. While another process is updating an entity, the query may see the old version of its index but return the new version of the entity. And since changes to entities and changes to indexes are applied in parallel, it is possible for a query to see the new version of its index but return the old version of the entity.

Figure 7-3 illustrates one possibility of what nontransactional reads and queries may see while changes are being applied.

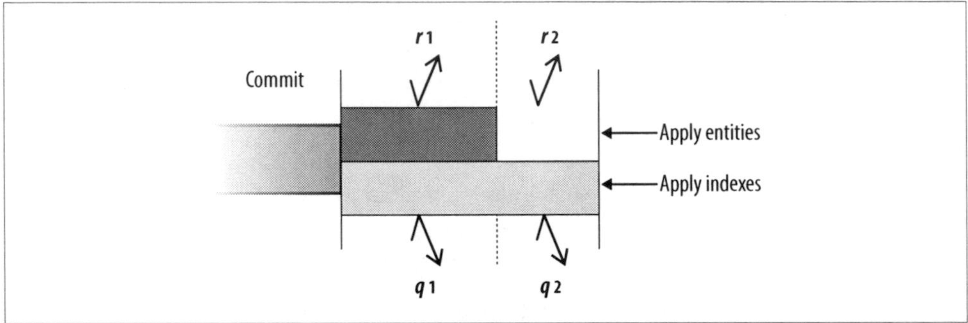

Figure 7-3. What nontransactional fetches and queries may see while changes are applied

Even though both fetches *r1* and *r2* occur after the commit, because they do not occur within transactions, they see different data: *r1* fetches the entity as it is before the update, and *r2* fetches the entity as it is after the update has been applied. Queries *q1* and *q2* may use the same (preupdate) index data to produce a list of results, but they return different entity data depending on whether changes have been applied to the entities.

In rare cases, it's also possible for changes to indexes to be applied prior to changes to entities, and for the apply phase to fail and leave committed changes unapplied until the next transaction on the entity group. If you need stronger guarantees, fetch or query entities within transactions to ensure all committed changes are applied before the data is used.

A query with an ancestor filter knows its entity group, and can therefore offer the same strong consistency guarantees within transactions as fetches. But many useful queries span entity groups, and therefore cannot be performed in transactions. If it is important to your application that a result for a nontransactional query match the criteria exactly, verify the result in the application code before using it.

Cross-Group Transactions

Transactions and entity groups present a fundamental tension in designing data for the App Engine datastore. If all we cared about was data consistency, we'd put all our data in a single entity group, and every transaction would have a consistent and current view of the entire world—and would be battling with every other simultaneous transaction to commit a change. Conversely, if we wanted to avoid contention as much as possible, we'd keep every entity in its own group and never perform more than one operation in a transaction.

Entity groups are a middle ground. They allow us to define limited sets of data that demand strongly consistent transactional updates, and with some thought we can organize these boundaries so an increase in traffic does not result in an increase in simultaneous updates to a single group. For example, if a user only ever updates an entity group dedicated to that user, then an increase in users will never increase the number of users writing to a given group simultaneously.

But real-world data patterns are not always so clean. Most useful applications involve sharing data between users. At another extreme, it's possible all users can view and modify the same set of data. At that point, we need to make some sacrifices to operate at scale, using techniques like sharding and eventually consistent data structures updated by background tasks to spread the updates over time and space.

There are many common scenarios where it'd be convenient if we could just operate on a few entity groups in a transaction, when one group is too constraining but we don't need to update the world. Sometimes we need to operate on several disparate sets of data at once, but it'd make our data model too complex to try and manage them in groups. For these cases, App Engine has a feature: *cross-group transactions*.

A cross-group transaction (or an "XG transaction") is simply a transaction that's allowed to operate on up to five entity groups transactionally. The datastore uses a slightly different—and slightly slower—mechanism for this, so to use more than one group transactionally, you must declare that your transaction is of the cross-group variety. The cross-group mechanism is built on top of the existing single-group mechanism in BigTable. It manages the updates so all groups commit or fail completely.

The important idea here is that you do not need to say ahead of time which groups will be involved in a transaction. Any given cross-group transaction can pick any entity groups on which to operate, up to five.

As with a single group transaction, a cross-group transaction can read from, write to, and perform ancestor queries on any of the groups in the transaction. If any group in a given cross-group transaction is updated after the transaction is started but before it tries to commit, the entire transaction fails and must be retried. Whether failure due to contention is more likely with more groups depends entirely on the design of your app.

In Python, you declare a transaction as a cross-group transaction by setting the `xg=True` argument in the `@db.transactional` decorator for the transaction function. If a transactional function is XG, or calls a transactional function that is XG, the entire transaction becomes an XG transaction:

```
@db.transactional(xg=True):
def update_win_tallies(winning_player, losing_player):
    # ...
```

In Java, you provide an appropriately configured `TransactionOptions` instance to the `beginTransaction()` method to make it a cross-group transaction:

```
import com.google.appengine.api.datastore.TransactionOptions;

// ...
        Transaction transaction = datastore.beginTransaction(
            TransactionOptions.Builder.withXG(true));
```

CHAPTER 8

Datastore Administration

Your data is the heart of your application, so you'll want to take good care of it. You'll want to watch it, and understand how it grows and how it affects your app's behavior. You'll want to help it evolve as your app's functionality changes. You'll probably want to make periodic backups, because nothing is perfect. You may even want up-to-date information about data types and sizes. And you'll want to poke at it, and prod it into shape using tools not necessarily built into your app.

App Engine provides a variety of administrative tools for learning about, testing, protecting, and fixing your datastore data. In this chapter, we look at a few of these tools, and their associated best practices.

Inspecting the Datastore

The first thing you might want to do with your app's datastore is see what's in it. Your app provides a natural barrier between you and how your data is stored physically in the datastore, so many data troubleshooting sessions start with pulling back the covers and seeing what's there.

The Datastore Viewer panel of the Administration Console (shown in Figure 8-1) is your main view of individual datastore entities. You can browse entities by kind, and you can perform queries using GQL by expanding the Options in the Query tab.

The GQL query you type into the datastore viewer is executed the same way it would be in an application running live. You can only perform queries for which there are indexes. If you enter a query that needs a custom index that isn't already in the uploaded index configuration, the query will return an error.

The GQL query parser is finicky in its syntax and strict typing of values. A few things to keep in mind, especially if your GQL queries are not returning the expected results:

- Quoted string values always use single quotes (`'...'`), never double quotes (`"..."`).
- Key values must always use the `KEY()` constructor. This constructor has two forms: `KEY('...')` with one argument takes a string-encoded key, like you might see

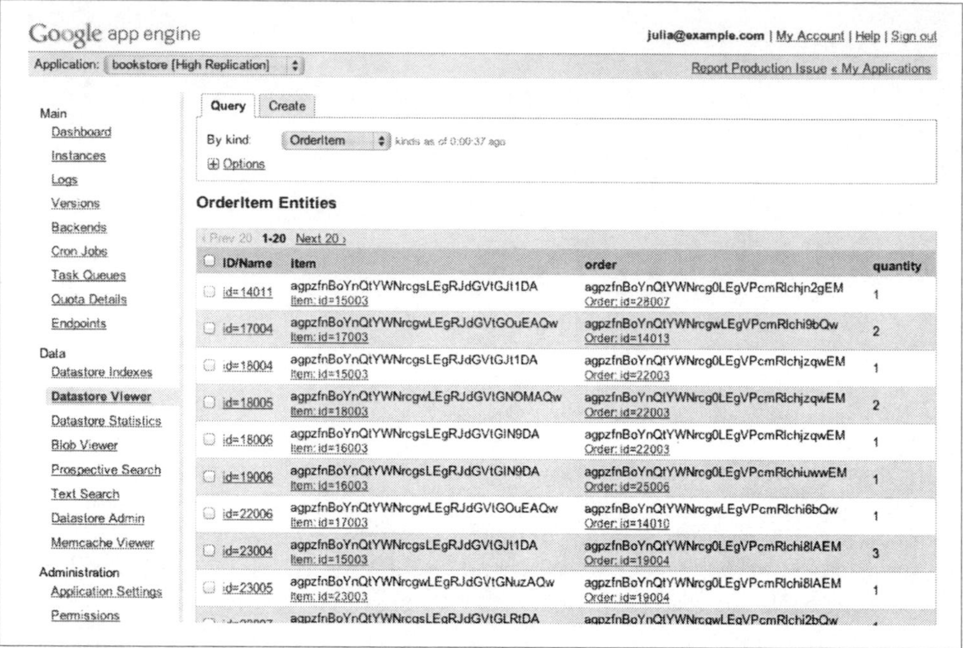

Figure 8-1. The Datastore Viewer panel of the Administration Console

elsewhere in the datastore viewer. `KEY('...', ...)` with an even number of arguments takes alternating pairs of a kind name (in single quotes) followed by either a string key name (in single quotes), or a numeric ID (no quotes). Only the full key, with the entire ancestor path, will match. `KEY('Foo', 897)` and `KEY('Bar', 123, 'Foo', 897)` are distinct keys.

- User values must always use the `USER()` constructor. Its sole argument is an email address (in single quotes). A query for just the email address string (`'foo@example.com'`) will not match a User value of that address.
- In general, all datastore values are typed, and most typed literals use a constructor form. The `DATETIME()`, `DATE()`, and `TIME()` types are all considered the same type when matching property values.

Refer to "GQL" on page 153 for more information on the GQL syntax.

You can click on any entity key in the results list to view the entity in detail, as in Figure 8-2.

You can change the value of the entity's properties directly from this screen, within a few limitations. You can update the value to another value of the same type by entering the new value in the field. Each datastore value type has a special syntax in this panel, such as `YYYY-MM-DD HH:MM:SS` for date-times. (The panel will provide instructions for the current type.)

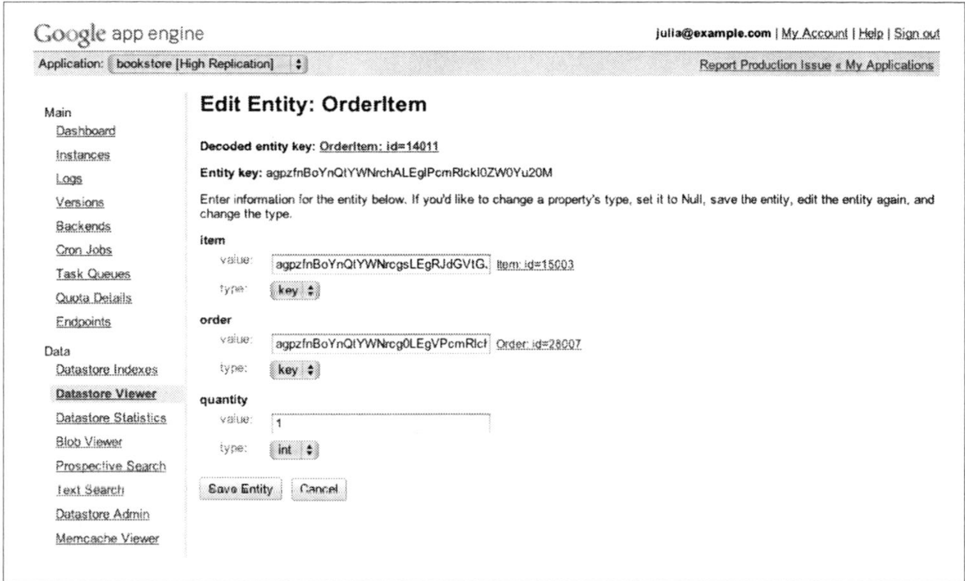

Figure 8-2. A single entity in the Datastore Viewer

You can set any property to the null value. When a property is null, you can update it to a value of any core datastore type. This allows you to change the type of a property in two steps: first set it to null, save it, and then select a new type.

You can't add or delete (unset) a property on an existing entity in the datastore viewer. You also can't convert an indexed property to an unindexed property, and vice versa. Multivalued properties are not supported.

On the main viewer screen, there is a Create tab next to the Query tab. From here, you can create a new entity of any kind that already exists in the datastore. The viewer determines which properties the entity ought to have and what their types ought to be based on properties of existing entities of that kind. If you have entities with varying property sets or multiple value types for a property, this is going to be a best guess, and you may have to create the entity with null values, then edit the entity to set the desired type. Again, multivalued properties and blob values are not supported in this interface. You can't create entities of a kind that does not already exist.

The Datastore Viewer is useful for inspecting entities and troubleshooting data issues, and may be sufficient for administrative purposes with simple data structures. However, you will probably want to build a custom administrative panel for browsing app-specific data structures and performing common administrative tasks.

The Datastore Statistics panel gives an overview of your data by type and size. This is especially useful for evaluating costs, and catching cases of excessive unused data. Statistics represent the cost of storing an entity and the cost of indexing an entity separately, so you can evaluate whether indexing a property is worth the storage cost. Metadata (information about each entity, such as keys and property names) is also measured separately. You can browse these statistics for all data, or for just entities of a given kind. Statistics are updated regularly, about once a day.

Figure 8-3 shows an example of the Datastore Statistics panel for entities of a kind.

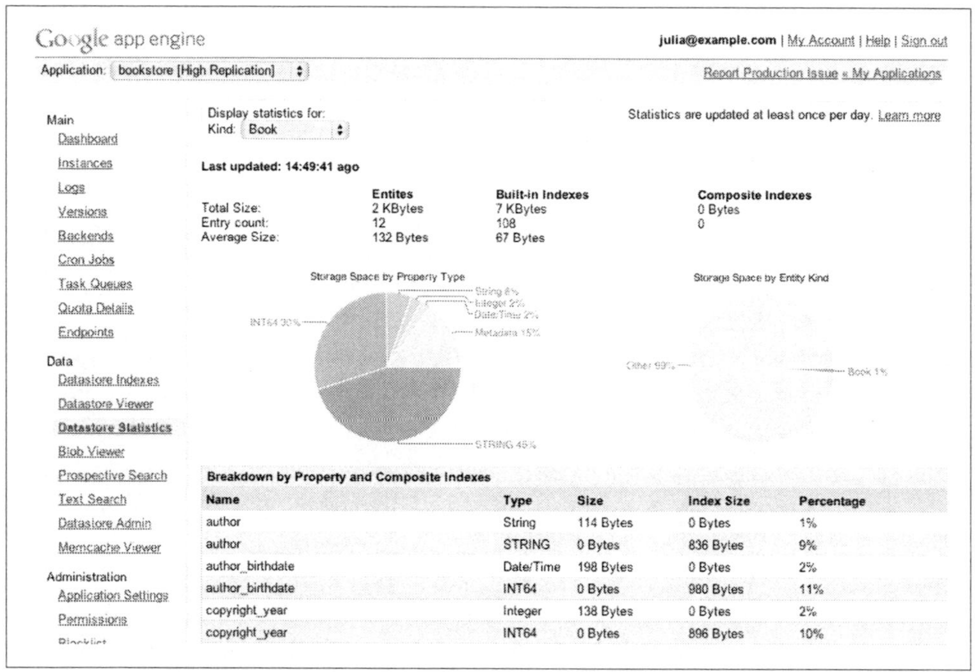

Figure 8-3. The Datastore Statistics panel of the Administration Console

Managing Indexes

When you upload the datastore index configuration for an app, the datastore begins building indexes that appear in the configuration but do not yet exist. This process is *not* instantaneous, and may take many minutes for new indexes that contain many rows. The datastore needs time to crawl all the entities to build the new indexes.

You can check on the build status of new indexes using the Administration Console, in the Indexes section. An index being built appears with a status of "Building." When it is ready, the status changes to "Serving." Figure 8-4 shows a simple example of the Indexes section.

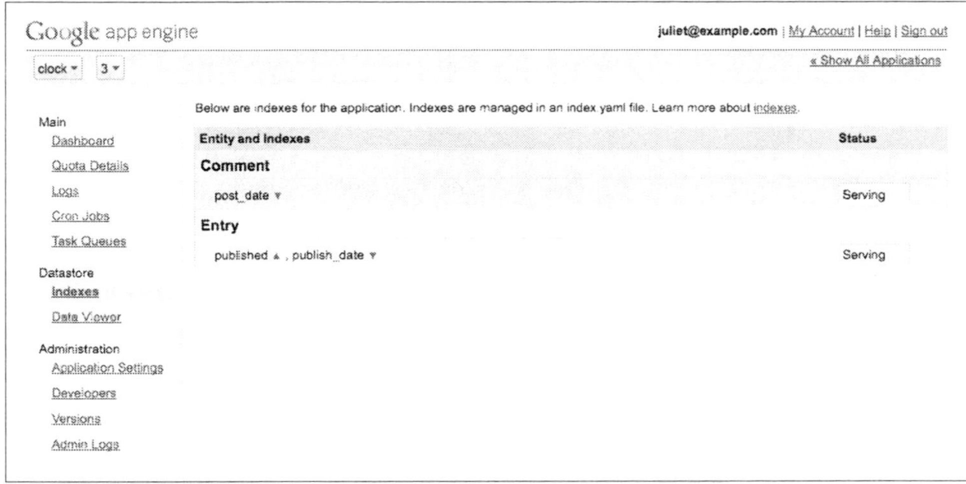

Figure 8-4. The Datastore Indexes panel of the Administration Console, with two indexes in the "Serving" status

If an index's build status is "Error," the index build failed. It's possible that the failure was due to a transient error. To clear this condition, you must first remove the index from your configuration and then upload the new configuration. It is also possible for an index build to fail due to an entity reaching its index property value limit. In these cases, you can delete the entities that are causing the problem. Once that is done, you can add the index configuration back and upload it again.

If your application performs a query while the index for the query is building, the query will fail. You can avoid this by uploading the index configuration, waiting until the index is built, and then making the app that uses that query available. The most convenient way to do this depends on whether you upload the new application in a new version:

- If you are uploading the new application with the version identifier that is currently the "default" version, upload the index configuration alone using the `appcfg.py update_indexes` command. When the indexes are built, upload the app.
- If you are uploading the application as a new version, or as a version that isn't the default and that nobody is actively using, you can safely upload the application and index configuration together (`appcfg.py update`). Wait until the indexes are built before making the new version the default.

If you upload index configuration that does not mention an index that has already been built, the datastore does not delete the unused index, since it might still be in use by an older version of the app. You must tell App Engine to purge unused indexes. To do this, run the AppCfg command with the `vacuum_indexes` option. For instance, in Python:

```
appcfg.py vacuum_indexes app-dir
```

App Engine will purge all custom indexes not mentioned in the index configuration uploaded most recently. This reclaims the storage space used by those indexes.

As we saw earlier, the development server tries to be helpful by creating new index configuration entries for queries that need them as you're testing your app. The development server will *never* delete an index configuration. As your app's queries change, this can result in unnecessary indexes being left in the file. You'll want to look through this file periodically, and confirm that each custom index is needed. Remove the unused index configuration, upload the file, and then vacuum indexes.

The Datastore Admin Panel

The fourth datastore-related panel of the Administration Console is the Datastore Admin panel. You can do three things from this panel: download a backup of all datastore entities or entities of a selected set of kinds, upload and restore data from a backup, and delete every entity of a given kind. For Python apps, the backup and restore feature can also be used to migrate large quantities of datastore data between two different apps. The panel also summarizes statistics about the sizes of entities, so you can estimate the scale of these operations before doing them. Figure 8-5 shows an example of this panel.

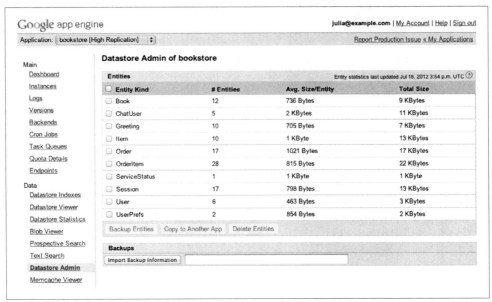

Datastore Admin of bookstore

Entities — Entity statistics last updated Jul 18, 2012 3:54 p.m. UTC

Entity Kind	# Entities	Avg. Size/Entity	Total Size
Book	12	736 Bytes	9 KBytes
ChatUser	5	2 KBytes	11 KBytes
Greeting	10	705 Bytes	7 KBytes
Item	10	1 KByte	13 KBytes
Order	17	1021 Bytes	17 KBytes
OrderItem	28	815 Bytes	22 KBytes
ServiceStatus	1	1 KByte	1 KByte
Session	17	798 Bytes	13 KBytes
User	6	463 Bytes	3 KBytes
UserPrefs	2	854 Bytes	2 KBytes

Figure 8-5. The Datastore Admin panel of the Administration Console (enabled)

Unlike other Administrator Console panels, this panel is implemented to run within your app, so major data operations are billed to your account. Because of this, you must enable the panel when you visit it for the first time. You can enable the panel by visiting it and following the prompt, or by enabling it in the Application Settings panel.

When you request a backup, the backup job crawls the datastore and aggregates the data in a Blobstore value (or, if you set it up when initiating the job, a Google Cloud Storage value). After it is finished, you can download the data, as prompted. The backup feature only downloads datastore data, it does not include Blobstore data in the backup.

Before doing a backup or restore, you may want to use another App Engine feature to prevent your application from writing to the datastore during the job and potentially corrupting data. To disable writing to the datastore, visit the Application Settings panel, then find the Disable Datastore Writes section and click the Disable Writes button. Confirm the prompt. With writes disabled, any attempt to write to the datastore by any version of your app will raise an exception. Reads and queries will still succeed. Note that the restore operation gets special permission to write to the datastore when writes are otherwise disabled. When the job is complete, you can re-enable writes from the Application Settings panel.

If you intend to disable writes for backups and restores, you may want to implement a "curtain" feature of your app that you activate prior to starting this process, to display a message to your users about the service interruption.

Backup, restore, and bulk delete are large jobs involving very many datastore operations. When you execute these jobs, the cost of the operations is charged to the app. You will want to do small tests before using these features with very large sets of data. These jobs also take a significant amount of time, scaling linearly with the size of your data. The jobs use task queues to throttle and parallelize the work running on your instances.

As of this writing, there's a bug that affects users with multiple active accounts and Google's multi-login feature. If you use multi-login and see a blank panel when trying to access Datastore Admin, the panel may be trying to display the multi-login selector, but failing because the panel is rendered in an iframe, and the multi-login selector uses a security policy that prevents login-related screens from displaying in frames. The workaround is to view the source of the Console page, get the iframe's URL, visit it in a separate window, and then acknowledge the multi-login selector. You can then reload the panel in the Administration Console.

I wouldn't normally mention a bug like this in a printed book (since it might get fixed before you read this), but as a multi-login user I run into it all the time, and it's good to know the workaround. It's also a good illustration of how the Datastore Admin panel works: it runs separately from the Administration Console so its resource usage gets billed to your app. The Datastore Admin panel is served from a reserved URL path in your app.

The Datastore Admin panel is currently described as an "experimental" feature, and its features or details of its implementation may change. See the official App Engine documentation for more information.

Accessing Metadata from the App

There are several ways to get information about the state of your datastore from within the application itself. The information visible in the Datastore Statistics panel of the Administration Console is also readable and queryable from entities in your app's datastore. Similarly, the facilities that allow the Datastore Viewer panel to determine the current kinds and property names are available to your app in the form of APIs and queryable metadata. You can also use APIs to get additional information about entity groups, index build status, and query planning.

We won't describe every metadata feature here. Instead, we'll look at a few representative examples. You can find the complete details in the official App Engine documentation.

Querying Statistics

App Engine gathers statistics about the contents of the datastore periodically, usually about once a day. It stores these statistics in datastore entities in your application. The Datastore Statistics panel of the Administration Console gets its information from these entities. Your app can also fetch and query these entities to access the statistics.

In Python, each statistic has an `ext.db` data model class, in the `google.appengine.ext.db.stats` module. You use these model classes to perform queries, like you would any other query. The actual kind name differs from the model class name.

In Java, you query statistics entities by setting up queries on the statistics entity kind names, just like any other datastore query. The query returns entities with statistics as property values.

Here's an example in Python that queries storage statistics for each entity kind:

```
import logging
from google.appengine.ext.db import stats

# ...
        kind_stats = stats.KindStat.all()
        for kind_stat in kind_stats:
            logging.info(
                'Stats for kind %s: %d entities, '
                'total %d bytes (%d entity bytes)',
                kind_stat.kind_name, kind_stat.count,
                kind_stat.bytes, kind_stat.entity_bytes)
```

Here's another example that reports the properties per kind taking up more than a terabyte of space:

```
import logging
from google.appengine.ext.db import stats

# ...
        q = stats.KindPropertyNameStat.all()
        q.filter('bytes >', 1024 * 1024 * 1024 * 1024)
        for kind_prop in q:
            logging.info(
                'Large property detected: %s:%s total size %d',
                kind_prop.kind_name, kind_prop.property_name,
                kind_prop.bytes)
```

Every statistic entity has a `count` property, a `bytes` property, and a `timestamp` property. `count` and `bytes` represent the total count and total size of the unit represented by the entity. As above, the statistic for a kind has a `bytes` property equal to the total amount of storage used by entities of the kind for properties and indexes. The `timestamp` property is the last time the statistic entity was updated. Statistic entity kinds have additional properties specific to the kind.

The `__Stat_Total__` kind (represented in Python by the `GlobalStat` class) represents the grand total for the entire app. The `count` and `bytes` properties represent the number of all entities, and the total size of all entities and indexes. These numbers are broken down further in several properties: `entity_bytes` is the storage for just the entities (not indexes), `builtin_index_bytes` and `builtin_index_count` are the total size and number of indexed properties in just the built-in indexes, and `composite_index_bytes` and `composite_index_count` are the same for just custom (composite) indexes. There is only one `__Stat_Total__` entity for the app.

The `__Stat_Kind__` kind (`KindStat`) represents statistics for each datastore kind individually, as existed at the time the statistics were last updated. There is one of these statistic entities for each kind. The `kind_name` property is set to the kind name, so you can query for a specific kind's statistics, or you can iterate over all kinds to determine which kinds there are. These entities have the same statistic properties as `__Stat_Total__`.

The `__Stat_PropertyName_Kind__` kind (`KindPropertyNameStat`) represents each named property of each kind. The `property_name` and `kind_name` properties identify the property and kind for the statistic. The statistic properties are `count`, `bytes`, `entity_bytes`, `builtin_index_bytes`, and `builtin_index_count`, defined as above.

For a complete list of the statistics entity kinds, see the official App Engine website.

Querying Metadata

The datastore always knows which namespaces, kinds, and property names are in use by an application. Unlike statistics, this metadata is available immediately. Querying this metadata can be slower than querying a normal entity, but the results reflect the current state of the data.

Each namespace has an entity of the kind `__namespace__`. Each kind is a `__kind__`, and each property name (regardless of kind) is a `__property__`. These entities have no properties: all information is stored in the key name. For example, a `__kind__` entity uses the kind name as its key name. (The full key is `__kind__ / KindName`.) A `__property__` entity has both the kind name and the property name encoded in its key name.

This information is derived entirely from the built-in indexes. As such, only indexed properties have corresponding `__property__` entities.

In Python, these all have `ext.db` model classes defined in the `google.appengine.ext.db.metadata` module. They are named `Namespace`, `Kind`, and `Property`. The classes include Python property methods for accessing names, as if they were datastore properties. The module also provides several convenience functions for common queries.

Here's a simple example in Python that lists all the kinds for which there is an entity, using a convenience function to get the list of kind names:

```
import logging
from google.appengine.ext.db import metadata

# ...
      kinds = metadata.get_kinds()
      for k in kinds:
          logging.info('Found a datastore kind: %s', k)
```

Index Status and Queries

The Datastore Indexes panel of the Administration Console reports on the indexes configured for the app, and the serving status of each. The app can get this same information by using the datastore API. A Python app can also ask the datastore which index was used to resolve a query, after the query has been executed.

In Python, you ask for the state of indexes by calling the `get_indexes()` function of the `google.appengine.ext.db` module. This function returns a list of tuples, each representing an index. Each tuple contains an index object, and a state value. The index object has the methods `kind()`, `has_ancestor()`, and `properties()`, representing the latest uploaded index configuration. The state value is one of several constants representing the index build states: `db.Index.BUILDING`, `db.Index.SERVING`, `db.Index.DELETING`, or `db.Index.ERROR`:

```
from google.appengine.ext import db

# ...
        for index, state in db.get_indexes():
            if state != db.Index.SERVING:
                kind = index.kind()
                ancestor_str = ' (ancestor)' if index.has_ancestor() else ''

                index_props = []
                for name, dir in index.properties():
```

```
            dir_str = 'ASC' if dir == db.Index.ASCENDING else 'DESC'
            index_props.append(name + ' ' + dir_str)
        index_property_spec = ', '.join(index_props)

        index_spec = '%s%s %s' % (kind, ancestor_str, index_property_spec)

        logging.info('Index is not serving: %s', index_spec)
```

A Python Query (or GqlQuery) instance has an `index_list()` method. This returns a list of index objects representing the indexes used to resolve the query. You must execute the query before calling this method.

In Java, the datastore service method `getIndexes()` returns a `Map<Index, Index.IndexState>`. An `Index` has accessor methods `getKind()`, `isAncestor()`, and `getProperties()`. `getProperties()` returns a `List<Index.Property>`, where each `Index.Property` provides `getName()` and `getDirection()` (a `Query.SortDirection`). The index state is one of `Index.IndexState.BUILDING`, `Index.IndexState.SERVING`, `Index.IndexState.DELETING`, or `Index.IndexState.ERROR`:

```
import java.util.Map;
import java.util.logging.Logger;
import com.google.appengine.api.datastore.DatastoreService;
import com.google.appengine.api.datastore.DatastoreServiceFactory;
import com.google.appengine.api.datastore.Index;
import com.google.appengine.api.datastore.Query;

public class MyServlet extends HttpServlet {
    private static final Logger log = Logger.getLogger(MyServlet.class.getName());

    public void doGet(HttpServletRequest req, HttpServletResponse resp)
            throws IOException {

        // ...

        DatastoreService datastore = DatastoreServiceFactory.getDatastoreService();

        Map<Index, Index.IndexState> indexes = datastore.getIndexes();
        for (Index index : indexes.keySet()) {
            if (indexes.get(index) != Index.IndexState.SERVING) {
                StringBuffer indexPropertySpec = new StringBuffer();
                for (Index.Property prop : index.getProperties()) {
                    indexPropertySpec.append(prop.getName());
                    indexPropertySpec.append(
                        prop.getDirection() == Query.SortDirection.ASCENDING ?
                        " ASC  " : " DESC  ");
                }

                log.info(
                    "Index is not serving: " +
                    index.getKind() +
                    (index.isAncestor() ? " (ancestor) " : " ") +
                    indexPropertySpec.toString());
            }
        }
```

```
        }
    }
```

There is not currently a way to inspect the indexes used by a query in the Java API.

Entity Group Versions

In Chapter 7, we described the datastore as using multiversioned optimistic concurrency control, with the entity group as the unit of transactionality. Each time any entity in an entity group is updated, the datastore creates a new version of the entity group. If any process reads an entity in the entity group before the new version is fully stored, the process simply sees the earlier version.

Each of these versions gets an ID number, and this number increases strictly and monotonically. You can use the metadata API to get the entity group version number for an entity.

In Python, this is the `get_entity_group_version()` function in the `google.appengine.ext.db.metadata` module. It takes an `ext.db` model instance or `db.Key` as an argument, and returns an integer, or `None` if the given entity group doesn't exist:

```
from google.appengine.ext import db
from google.appengine.ext.db import metadata

class MyKind(db.Expando):
    pass

# ...
        # Write to an entity group, and get its version number.
        parent = MyKind()
        parent.put()
        version = metadata.get_entity_group_version(parent)

        # Update the entity group by creating a child entity.
        child = MyKind(parent=parent)
        child.put()

        # The version number of the entire group has been incremented.
        version2 = metadata.get_entity_group_version(parent)
```

In Java, you get this information by fetching a fake entity with a specific key. You get the entity group key by calling the static method `Entities.createEntityGroupKey()`, passing it the `Key` of an entity in the group. The `Entity` that corresponds to the entity group key has a `__version__` property with an integer value:

```
import com.google.appengine.api.datastore.DatastoreService;
import com.google.appengine.api.datastore.DatastoreServiceFactory;
import com.google.appengine.api.datastore.Entities;
import com.google.appengine.api.datastore.Entity;

// ...
        DatastoreService datastore = DatastoreServiceFactory.getDatastoreService();
```

```
// Write to an entity group, and get its version number.
Entity parent = new Entity("MyKind");
datastore.put(parent);
Key groupKey = Entities.createEntityGroupKey(parent.getKey());
Long version = (Long) datastore.get(groupKey).getProperty("__version__");

// Update the entity group by creating a child entity.
Entity child = new Entity("MyKind", parent);
datastore.put(child);

// The version number of the entire group has been incremented.
Long version2 = (Long) datastore.get(groupKey).getProperty("__version__");
```

Remote Controls

One of the nice features of a relational database running in a typical hosting environment is the ability to connect directly to the database to perform queries and updates on a SQL command line or to run small administrative scripts. App Engine has a facility for doing something similar, and it works for more than just the datastore: you can call any live service on behalf of your application using tools running on your computer. The tools do this using a remote proxy API.

The proxy API is a request handler that you install in your app. It is restricted to administrators. You run a client tool that authenticates as an administrator, connects to the request handler, and issues service calls over the connection. The proxy performs the calls and returns the results.

App Engine includes versions of the proxy handler for Python and for Java. The client library and several tools that use it are implemented in Python only, but they can be used with Java apps. If you're primarily a Java developer, you will be installing the Python SDK to get the tools and client library.

The remote shell tool opens a Python command prompt, with the App Engine Python service libraries modified to use the remote API. You type Python statements as they would appear in app code, and all calls to App Engine services are routed to the live app automatically. This is especially useful in conjunction with Python apps, where you can import your app's own data models and request handler modules, and do interactive testing or data manipulation. You can also write your own tools in Python using the remote API, for repeated tasks.

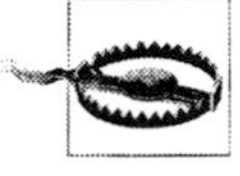

The remote API is clever and useful, but it's also slow: every service call is going over the network from your local computer to the app, then back. It is not suitable for running large jobs over arbitrary amounts of data. For large data transformation jobs, you're better off building something that runs within the app, using task queues.

Let's take a look at how to set up the proxy for Python and Java, how to use the remote Python shell, and how to write a Python tool that calls the API.

Setting Up the Remote API for Python

The Python remote API request handler is included in the runtime environment. To set it up, you activate a built-in in *app.yaml*, like so:

```
builtins:
- remote_api: on
```

This establishes a web service endpoint at the URL `/_ah/remote_api/`. Only clients authenticated using application administrator accounts can use this endpoint.

You can test this URL in a browser using the development server. Visit the URL (such as *http://localhost:8080/_ah/remote_api*), and make sure it redirects to the fake authentication form. Check the box to sign in as an administrator, and click Submit. You should see this message:

```
This request did not contain a necessary header.
```

The remote API expects an HTTP header identifying the remote API protocol version to use, which the browser does not provide. But this is sufficient to test that the handler is configured correctly.

Setting Up the Remote API for Java

To use the remote API tools with a Java application, you set up a URL path with a servlet provided by the SDK, namely `com.google.apphosting.utils.remoteapi.RemoteApiServlet`. You can choose any URL path; you will give this path to the remote API tools in a command-line argument. Be sure to restrict access to the URL path to administrators.

The following excerpt for your deployment descriptor (*web.xml*) associates the remote API servlet with the URL path `/_ah/remote_api`, and restricts it to administrator accounts:

```
<servlet>
  <servlet-name>remoteapi</servlet-name>
  <servlet-class>
    com.google.apphosting.utils.remoteapi.RemoteApiServlet
  </servlet-class>
</servlet>
<servlet-mapping>
  <servlet-name>remoteapi</servlet-name>
  <url-pattern>/_ah/remote_api</url-pattern>
</servlet-mapping>

<security-constraint>
  <web-resource-collection>
    <web-resource-name>remoteapi</web-resource-name>
    <url-pattern>/_ah/remote_api</url-pattern>
  </web-resource-collection>
  <auth-constraint>
    <role-name>admin</role-name>
```

```
    </auth-constraint>
  </security-constraint>
```

Using the Remote Shell Tool

With the remote API handler installed, you can use a tool included with the Python SDK to manipulate a live application's services from an interactive Python shell. You interact with the shell by using Python statements and the Python service APIs. This tool works with both Java and Python applications by using the remote API handler.

To start a shell session, run the `remote_api_shell.py` command. As with the other Python SDK commands, this command may already be in your command path:

```
remote_api_shell.py app-id
```

The tool prompts for your developer account email address and password. (Only registered developers for the app can run this tool, or any of the remote API tools.)

By default, the tool connects to the application via the domain name *app-id*`.appspot.com`, and assumes the remote API handler is installed with the URL path `/remote_api`. To use a different URL path, provide the path as an argument after the application ID:

```
remote_api_shell.py app-id /admin/util/remote_api
```

To use a different domain name, such as to use a specific application version, or to test the tool with the development server, give the domain name with the `-s ...` argument:

```
remote_api_shell.py -s dev.app-id.appspot.com app-id
```

The shell can use any service API that is supported by the remote API handler. This includes URL Fetch, memcache, Images, Mail, Google Accounts, and of course the datastore. (As of this writing, XMPP is not supported by the remote API handler.) Several of the API modules are imported by default for easy access.

The tool does not add the current working directory to the module load path by default, nor does it know about your application directory. You may need to adjust the load path (`sys.path`) to import your app's classes, such as your data models.

Here is an example of a short shell session:

```
% remote_api_shell.py clock
Email: juliet@example.com
Password:
App Engine remote_api shell
Python 2.5.1 (r251:54863, Feb  6 2009, 19:02:12)
[GCC 4.0.1 (Apple Inc. build 5465)]
The db, users, urlfetch, and memcache modules are imported.
clock> import os.path
clock> import sys
clock> sys.path.append(os.path.realpath('.'))
clock> import models
clock> books = models.Book.all().fetch(6)
```

```
clock> books
[<models.Book object at 0x7a2c30>, <models.Book object at 0x7a2bf0>,
<models.Book object at 0x7a2cd0>, <models.Book object at 0x7a2cb0>,
<models.Book object at 0x7a2d30>, <models.Book object at 0x7a2c90>]
clock> books[0].title
u'The Grapes of Wrath'
clock> from google.appengine.api import mail
clock> mail.send_mail('juliet@example.com', 'test@example.com',
'Test email', 'This is a test message.')
clock>
```

To exit the shell, press Ctrl-D.

Using the Remote API from a Script

You can call the remote API directly from your own Python scripts by using a library from the Python SDK. This configures the Python API to use the remote API handler for your application for all service calls, so you can use the service APIs as you would from a request handler directly in your scripts.

Here's a simple example script that prompts for a developer account email address and password, then accesses the datastore of a live application:

```
#!/usr/bin/python

import getpass
import sys

# Add the Python SDK to the package path.
# Adjust these paths accordingly.
sys.path.append('~/google_appengine')
sys.path.append('~/google_appengine/lib/yaml/lib')

from google.appengine.ext.remote_api import remote_api_stub

from google.appengine.ext import db
import models

# Your app ID and remote API URL path go here.
APP_ID = 'app_id'
REMOTE_API_PATH = '/remote_api'

def auth_func():
    email_address = raw_input('Email address: ')
    password = getpass.getpass('Password: ')
    return email_address, password

def initialize_remote_api(app_id=APP_ID,
                          path=REMOTE_API_PATH):
    remote_api_stub.ConfigureRemoteApi(
        app_id,
        path,
        auth_func)
    remote_api_stub.MaybeInvokeAuthentication()
```

```
def main(args):
    initialize_remote_api()

    books = models.Book.all().fetch(10)
    for book in books:
        print book.title

    return 0

if __name__ == '__main__':
    sys.exit(main(sys.argv[1:]))
```

The `ConfigureRemoteApi()` function (yes, it has a TitleCase name) sets up the remote API access. It takes as arguments the application ID, the remote API handler URL path, and a callable that returns a tuple containing the email address and password to use when connecting. In this example, we define a function that prompts for the email address and password, and pass the function to `ConfigureRemoteApi()`.

The function also accepts an optional fourth argument specifying an alternate domain name for the connection. By default, it uses *`app-id`*`.appspot.com`, where *`app-id`* is the application ID in the first argument.

The `MaybeInvokeAuthentication()` function sends an empty request to verify that the email address and password are correct, and raises an exception if they are not. (Without this, the script would wait until the first remote call to verify the authentication.)

Remember that every call to an App Engine library that performs a service call does so over the network via an HTTP request to the application. This is inevitably slower than running within the live application. It also consumes application resources like web requests do, including bandwidth and request counts, which are not normally consumed by service calls in the live app.

On the plus side, since your code runs on your local computer, it is not constrained by the App Engine runtime sandbox or the 30-second request deadline. You can run long jobs and interactive applications on your computer without restriction, using any Python modules you like—at the expense of consuming app resources to marshal service calls over HTTP.

CHAPTER 9

Data Modeling with Python

Data modeling is the process of translating the data requirements of your application to the features of your data storage technology. While the application deals in players, towns, weapons, potions, and gold, the datastore knows only entities, entity groups, keys, properties, and indexes. The data model describes how the data is stored and how it is manipulated. Entities represent players and game objects; properties describe the status of objects and the relationships between them. When an object changes location, the data is updated in a transaction, so the object cannot be in two places at once. When a player wants to know about the weapons in her inventory, the application performs a query for all weapon objects whose location is the player, possibly requiring an index.

In the last few chapters, we've been using the Python class `db.Expando` to create and manipulate entities and their properties. As we've been doing it, this class illustrates the flexible nature of the datastore. The datastore itself does not impose or enforce a structure on entities or their properties, giving the application control over how individual entities represent data objects. This flexibility is also an essential feature for scalability: changing the structure of millions of records is a large task, and the proper strategy for doing this is specific to the task and the application.

But structure is needed. Every player has a number of health points, and a `Player` entity without a `health` property, or with a `health` property whose value is not an integer, is likely to confuse the battle system. The data ought to conform to a structure, or *schema*, to meet the expectations of the code. Because the datastore does not enforce this schema itself—the datastore is *schemaless*—it is up to the application to ensure that entities are created and updated properly.

App Engine includes a data modeling library for defining and enforcing data schemas in Python. This library resides in the `google.appengine.ext.db` package. It includes several related classes for representing data objects, including `db.Model`, `db.Expando`, and `db.PolyModel`. To give structure to entities of a given kind, you create a subclass of one of these classes. The definition of the class specifies the properties for those objects, their allowed value types, and other requirements.

In this chapter, we introduce the Python data modeling library and discuss how to use it to enforce a schema for the otherwise schemaless datastore. We also discuss how the library works and how to extend it.

Models and Properties

The `db.Model` superclass lets you specify a structure for every entity of a kind. This structure can include the names of the properties, the types of the values allowed for those properties, whether the property is required or optional, and a default value. Here is a definition of a `Book` class similar to the one we created in Chapter 5:

```
from google.appengine.ext import db
import datetime

class Book(db.Model):
    title = db.StringProperty(required=True)
    author = db.StringProperty(required=True)
    copyright_year = db.IntegerProperty()
    author_birthdate = db.DateProperty()

obj = Book(title='The Grapes of Wrath',
           author='John Steinbeck')
obj.copyright_year = 1939
obj.author_birthdate = datetime.date(1902, 2, 27)

obj.put()
```

This `Book` class inherits from `db.Model`. In the class definition, we declare that all `Book` entities have four properties, and we declare their value types: `title` and `author` are strings, `copyright_year` is an integer, and `author_birthdate` is a date-time. If someone tries to assign a value of the wrong type to one of these properties, the assignment raises a `db.BadValueError`.

We also declare that `title` and `author` are required properties. If someone tries to create a `Book` without these properties set as arguments to the `Book` constructor, the attempt raises a `db.BadValueError`. `copyright_year` and `author_birthdate` are optional, so we can leave them unset on construction, and assign values to the properties later. If these properties are not set by the time the object is saved, the resulting entity will not have these properties—and that's allowed by this model.

A property declaration ensures that the entity created from the object has a value for the property, possibly `None`. As we'll see in the next section, you can further specify what values are considered valid using arguments to the property declaration.

A model class that inherits from `db.Model` ignores all attributes that are not declared as properties when it comes time to save the object to the datastore. In the resulting entity, all declared properties are set, and no others.

This is the sole difference between `db.Model` and `db.Expando`. A `db.Model` class ignores undeclared properties. A `db.Expando` class saves all attributes of the object as properties of the corresponding entity. That is, a model using a `db.Expando` class "expands" to accommodate assignments to undeclared properties.

You can use property declarations with `db.Expando` just as with `db.Model`. The result is a data object that validates the values of the declared properties, and accepts any values for additional undeclared properties.

The official documentation refers to properties with declarations as *static properties* and properties on a `db.Expando` without declarations as *dynamic properties*. These terms have a nice correspondence with the notions of static and dynamic typing in programming languages. Property declarations implement a sort of runtime validated static typing for model classes, on top of Python's own dynamic typing.

As we'll see, property declarations are even more powerful than static typing, because they can validate more than just the type of the value.

For both `db.Model` and `db.Expando`, object attributes whose names begin with an underscore (_) are always ignored. You can use these private attributes to attach transient data or functions to model objects. (It's possible to create an entity with a property whose name starts with an underscore; this convention only applies to object attributes in the modeling API.)

Because model objects also have attributes that are methods and other features, you cannot use certain names for properties in the Python model API. Some of the more pernicious reserved names are `key`, `kind`, and `parent`. The official documentation has a complete list of reserved names. In the next section, we'll see a way to use these reserved names for datastore properties even though they aren't allowed as attribute names in the API.

Beyond the model definition, `db.Model` and `db.Expando` have the same interface for saving, fetching, and deleting entities, and for performing queries and transactions. `db.Expando` is a subclass of `db.Model`.

Property Declarations

You declare a property for a model by assigning a property declaration object to an attribute of the model class. The name of the attribute is the name of the datastore property. The value is an object that describes the terms of the declaration. As discussed earlier, the `db.StringProperty` object assigned to the `title` class attribute says that the entity that an instance of the class represents can only have a string value for its `title` property. The `required=True` argument to the `db.StringProperty` constructor says that the object is not valid unless it has a value for the `title` property.

This can look a little confusing if you're expecting the class attribute to shine through as an attribute of an instance of the class, as it normally does in Python. Instead, the db.Model class hooks into the attribute assignment mechanism so it can use the property declaration to validate a value assigned to an attribute of the object. In Python terms, the model uses *property descriptors* to enhance the behavior of attribute assignment.

Property declarations act as intermediaries between the application and the datastore. They can ensure that only values that meet certain criteria are assigned to properties. They can assign default values when constructing an object. They can even convert values between a data type used by the application and one of the datastore's native value types, or otherwise customize how values are stored.

The db.StringProperty declaration has a feature that always trips me up, so I'm mentioning it here. By default, a string property value enforced by this declaration cannot contain newline characters. If you want to allow values with newline characters, specify the multiline=True argument to the declaration:

```
prop = db.StringProperty(multiline=True)
```

This feature corresponds with a similar feature in the Django web application framework, which is used to help ensure that text fields in forms don't accidentally contain newline characters. This is not a restriction of the App Engine datastore, it is merely the default behavior of db.StringProperty.

Property Value Types

db.StringProperty is an example of a property declaration class. There are several property declaration classes included with the Python SDK, one for each native datastore type. Each one ensures that the property can only be assigned a value of the corresponding type:

```
class Book(db.Model):
    title = db.StringProperty()

b = Book()

b.title = 99  # db.BadValueError, title must be a string

b.title = 'The Grapes of Wrath'  # OK
```

Table 9-1 lists the datastore native value types and their corresponding property declaration classes.

Table 9-1. Datastore property value types and the corresponding property declaration classes

Data type	Python type	Property class
Unicode text string (up to 500 bytes, indexed)	unicode or str (converted to unicode as ASCII)	db.StringProperty
Long Unicode text string (not indexed)	db.Text	db.TextProperty

Data type	Python type	Property class
Short byte string (up to 500 bytes, indexed)	db.ByteString	db.ByteStringProperty
Long byte string (not indexed)	db.Blob	db.BlobProperty
Boolean	bool	db.BooleanProperty
Integer (64-bit)	int or long (converted to 64-bit long)	db.IntegerProperty
Float (double precision)	float	db.FloatProperty
Date-time	datetime.date	db.DateProperty
	datetime.datetime	db.DateTimeProperty
	datetime.time	db.TimeProperty
Entity key	db.Key or a model instance	db.ReferenceProperty, db.SelfReferenceProperty
A Google account	users.User	db.UserProperty
A Blobstore key	blobstore.BlobKey	blobstore.BlobReferenceProperty

Property Validation

You can customize the behavior of a property declaration by passing arguments to the declaration's constructor. We've already seen one example: the `required` argument.

All property declaration classes support the `required` argument. If `True`, the property is required and must not be `None`. You must provide an initial value for each required property to the constructor when creating a new object. (You can provide an initial value for any property this way.)

```
class Book(db.Model):
    title = db.StringProperty(required=True)

b = Book()  # db.BadValueError, title is required

b = Book(title='The Grapes of Wrath')  # OK
```

The datastore makes a distinction between a property that is not set and a property that is set to the null value (`None`). Property declarations do not make this distinction, because all declared properties must be set (possibly to `None`). Unless you say otherwise, the default value for declared properties is `None`, so the `required` validator treats the `None` value as an unspecified property.

You can change the default value with the `default` argument. When you create an object without a value for a property that has a default value, the constructor assigns the default value to the property.

A property that is required and has a default value uses the default if constructed without an explicit value. The value can never be None:

```
class Book(db.Model):
    rating = db.IntegerProperty(default=1)

b = Book()  # b.rating == 1

b = Book(rating=5)  # b.rating == 5
```

By default, the name of the class attribute is used as the name of the datastore property. If you wish to use a different name for the datastore property than is used for the attribute, specify a name argument. This allows you to use names already taken by the API for class or instance attributes as datastore properties:

```
class Song(db.Model):
    song_key = db.StringProperty(name='key')

s = Song()
s.song_key = 'C# min'

# The song_key attribute is stored as the
# datastore property named 'key'.
s.put()
```

You can declare that a property should contain only one of a fixed set of values by providing a list of possible values as the choices argument. If None is not one of the choices, this acts as a more restrictive form of required, and therefore, the property must be set to one of the valid choices by using a keyword argument to the constructor:

```
_KEYS = ['C', 'C min', 'C 7',
         'C#', 'C# min', 'C# 7',
         # ...
        ]

class Song(db.Model):
    song_key = db.StringProperty(choices=_KEYS)

s = Song(song_key='H min')  # db.BadValueError

s = Song()  # db.BadValueError, None is not an option

s = Song(song_key='C# min')  # OK
```

All of these features validate the value assigned to a property, and raise a db.BadValueError if the value does not meet the appropriate conditions. For even greater control over value validation, you can define your own validation function and assign it to a property declaration as the validator argument. The function should take the value as an argument, and raise a db.BadValueError (or an exception of your choosing) if the value should not be allowed:

```
def is_recent_year(val):
    if val < 1923:
        raise db.BadValueError
```

```
class Book(db.Model):
    copyright_year = db.IntegerProperty(validator=is_recent_year)

b = Book(copyright_year=1922)  # db.BadValueError

b = Book(copyright_year=1924)  # OK
```

Nonindexed Properties

In Chapter 6, we mentioned that you can set properties of an entity in such a way that they are available on the entity, but are considered unset for the purposes of indexes. In the Python API, you establish a property as nonindexed by using a property declaration. If the property declaration is given an `indexed` argument of `False`, entities created with that model class will set that property as nonindexed:

```
class Book(db.Model):
    first_sentence = db.StringProperty(indexed=False)

b = Book()
b.first_sentence = "On the Internet, popularity is swift and fleeting."
b.put()

# Count the number of Book entities with
# an indexed first_sentence property...
c = Book.all().order('first_sentence').count(1000)

# c = 0
```

Automatic Values

Several property declaration classes include features for setting values automatically.

The `db.DateProperty`, `db.DateTimeProperty`, and `db.TimeProperty` classes can populate the value automatically with the current date and time. To enable this behavior, you provide the `auto_now` or `auto_now_add` arguments to the property declaration.

If you set `auto_now=True`, the declaration class overwrites the property value with the current date and time when you save the object. This is useful when you want to keep track of the last time an object was saved:

```
class Book(db.Model):
    last_updated = db.DateTimeProperty(auto_now=True)

b = Book()
b.put()  # last_updated is set to the current time

# ...

b.put()  # last_updated is set to the current time again
```

If you set auto_now_add=True, the property is set to the current time only when the object is saved for the first time. Subsequent saves do not overwrite the value:

```
class Book(db.Model):
    create_time = db.DateTimeProperty(auto_now_add=True)

b = Book()
b.put()  # create_time is set to the current time

# ...

b.put()  # create_time stays the same
```

The db.UserProperty declaration class also includes an automatic value feature. If you provide the argument auto_current_user=True, the value is set to the user accessing the current request handler if the user is signed in. However, if you provide auto_current_user_add=True, the value is only set to the current user when the entity is saved for the first time, and left untouched thereafter. If the current user is not signed in, the value is set to None:

```
class BookReview(db.Model):
    created_by_user = db.UserProperty(auto_current_user_add=True)
    last_edited_by_user = db.UserProperty(auto_current_user=True)

br = BookReview()
br.put()  # created_by_user and last_edited_by_user set

# ...

br.put()  # last_edited_by_user set again
```

At first glance, it might seem reasonable to set a default for a db.UserProperty this way:

```
from google.appengine.api import users

class BookReview(db.Model):
    created_by_user = db.UserProperty(
        default=users.get_current_user())
    # WRONG
```

This would set the default value to be the user who is signed in *when the class is imported*. Subsequent requests handled by the instance of the application will use a previous user instead of the current user as the default.

To guard against this mistake, db.UserProperty does not accept the default argument. You can use only auto_current_user or auto_current_user_add to set an automatic value.

List Properties

The data modeling API provides a property declaration class for multivalued properties, called `db.ListProperty`. This class ensures that every value for the property is of the same type. You pass this type to the property declaration, like so:

```
class Book(db.Model):
    tags = db.ListProperty(basestring)

b = Book()
b.tags = ['python', 'app engine', 'data']
```

The type argument to the `db.ListProperty` constructor must be the Python representation of one of the native datastore types. Refer back to Table 5-1 for a complete list.

The datastore does not distinguish between a multivalued property with no elements and no property at all. As such, an undeclared property on a `db.Expando` object can't store the empty list. If it did, when the entity is loaded back into an object, the property simply wouldn't be there, potentially confusing code that's expecting to find an empty list. To avoid confusion, `db.Expando` disallows assigning an empty list to an undeclared property.

The `db.ListProperty` declaration makes it possible to keep an empty list value on a multivalued property. The declaration interprets the state of an entity that doesn't have the declared property as the property being set to the empty list, and maintains that distinction on the object. This also means that you cannot assign `None` to a declared list property—but this isn't of the expected type for the property anyway.

The datastore *does* distinguish between a property with a single value and a multivalued property with a single value. An undeclared property on a `db.Expando` object can store a list with one element, and represent it as a list value the next time the entity is loaded.

The example above declares a list of string values. (`basestring` is the Python base type for `str` and `unicode`.) This case is so common that the API also provides `db.StringListProperty`.

You can provide a default value to `db.ListProperty`, using the `default` argument. If you specify a nonempty list as the default, a shallow copy of the list value is made for each new object that doesn't have an initial value for the property.

`db.ListProperty` does not support the `required` validator, since every list property technically has a list value (possibly empty). If you wish to disallow the empty list, you can provide your own `validator` function that does so:

```
def is_not_empty(lst):
    if len(lst) == 0:
        raise db.BadValueError

class Book(db.Model):
    tags = db.ListProperty(basestring, validator=is_not_empty)

b = Book(tags=[])  # db.BadValueError
```

```
b = Book()  # db.BadValueError, default "tags" is empty

b = Book(tags=['awesome'])  #  OK
```

`db.ListProperty` does not allow `None` as an element in the list because it doesn't match the required value type. It is possible to store `None` as an element in a list for an undeclared property.

Models and Schema Migration

Property declarations prevent the application from creating an invalid data object, or assigning an invalid value to a property. If the application always uses the same model classes to create and manipulate entities, then all entities in the datastore will be consistent with the rules you establish using property declarations.

In real life, it is possible for an entity that does not fit a model to exist in the datastore. When you change a model class—and you will change model classes in the lifetime of your application—you are making a change to your application code, not the datastore. Entities created from a previous version of a model stay the way they are.

If an existing entity does not comply with the validity requirements of a model class, you'll get a `db.BadValueError` when you try to fetch the entity from the datastore. Fetching an entity gets the entity's data, then calls the model class constructor with its values. This executes each property's validation routines on the data.

Some model changes are "backward compatible" such that old entities can be loaded into the new model class and be considered valid. Whether it is sufficient to make a backward-compatible change without updating existing entities depends on your application. Changing the type of a property declaration or adding a required property are almost always incompatible changes. Adding an optional property will not cause a `db.BadValueError` when an old entity is loaded, but if you have indexes on the new property, old entities will not appear in those indexes (and therefore won't be results for those queries) until the entities are loaded and then saved with the new property's default value.

The most straightforward way to migrate old entities to new schemas is to write a script that queries all the entities and applies the changes. We'll discuss how to implement this kind of batch operation in a scalable way using task queues, in "Task Chaining" on page 415.

Modeling Relationships

You can model relationships between entities by storing entity keys as property values. The Python data modeling interface includes several powerful features for managing relationships.

The db.ReferenceProperty declaration describes a relationship between one model class and another. It stores the key of an entity as the property value. The first argument to the db.ReferenceProperty constructor is the model class of the kind of entity referenced by the property. If someone creates a relationship to an entity that is not of the appropriate kind, the assignment raises a db.BadValueError.

You can assign a data object directly to the property. The property declaration stores the key of the object as the property's value to create the relationship. You can also assign a db.Key directly:

```
class Book(db.Model):
    title = db.StringProperty()
    author = db.StringProperty()

class BookReview(db.Model):
    book = db.ReferenceProperty(Book, collection_name='reviews')

b = Book()
b.put()

br = BookReview()

br.book = b        # sets br's 'book' property to b's key

br.book = b.key()  # same thing
```

We'll explain what collection_name does in a moment.

The referenced object must have a "complete" key before it can be assigned to a reference property. A key is complete when it has all its parts, including the string name or the system-assigned numeric ID. If you create a new object without a key name, the key is not complete until you save the object. When you save the object, the system completes the key with a numeric ID. If you create the object (or a db.Key) with a key name, the key is already complete, and you can use it for a reference without saving it first:

```
b = Book()
br = BookReview()
br.book = b  # db.BadValueError, b's key is not complete

b.put()
br.book = b  # OK, b's key has system ID

b = Book(key_name='The_Grapes_of_Wrath')
br = BookReview()
br.book = b  # OK, b's key has a name

db.put([b, br])
```

A model class must be defined before it can be the subject of a db.ReferenceProperty. To declare a reference property that can refer to another instance of the same class, you use a different declaration, db.SelfReferenceProperty:

```
class Book(db.Model):
    previous_edition = db.SelfReferenceProperty()

b1 = Book()
b2 = Book()
b2.previous_edition = b1
```

Reference properties have a powerful and intuitive syntax for accessing referenced objects. When you access the value of a reference property, the property fetches the entity from the datastore by using the stored key, then returns it as an instance of its model class. A referenced entity is loaded "lazily"; that is, it is not fetched from the datastore until the property is dereferenced:

```
br = db.get(book_review_key)
# br is a BookReview instance

title = br.book.title  # fetches book, gets its title property
```

This automatic dereferencing of reference properties occurs the first time you access the reference property. Subsequent uses of the property use the in-memory instance of the data object. This caching of the referenced entity is specific to the object with the property. If another object has a reference to the same entity, accessing its reference fetches the entity anew.

`db.ReferenceProperty` does another clever thing: it creates automatic back-references from a referenced object to the objects that refer to it. If a `BookReview` class has a reference property that refers to the `Book` class, the `Book` class gets a special property whose name is specified by the `collection_name` argument to the declaration (e.g., `reviews`). This property is special because it isn't actually a property stored on the entity. Instead, when you access the back-reference property, the API performs a datastore query for all `BookReview` entities whose reference property equals the key of the `Book`. Since this is a single-property query, it uses the built-in indexes, and never requires a custom index:

```
b = db.get(book_key)
# b is a Book instance

for review in b.reviews:
    # review is a BookReview instance
    # ...
```

If you don't specify a `collection_name`, the name of the back-reference property is the name of the referring class followed by `_set`. If a class has multiple reference properties that refer to the same class, you *must* provide a `collection_name` to disambiguate the back-reference properties:

```
class BookReview(db.Model):
     # Book gets a BookReview_set special property.
     book = db.ReferenceProperty(Book)

     # Book gets a recommended_book_set special property.
```

```
    recommended_book = db.ReferenceProperty(Book,
                                            collection_name='recommended_book_set')
```

Because the back-reference property is implemented as a query, it incurs no overhead if you don't use it.

As with storing db.Key values as properties, neither the datastore nor the property declaration requires that a reference property refer to an entity that exists. Dereferencing a reference property that points to an entity that does not exist raises a db.ReferencePropertyResolveError. Keys cannot change, so a relationship is only severed when the referenced entity is deleted from the datastore.

One-to-Many Relationships

A reference property and its corresponding back-reference represent a *one-to-many relationship* between classes in your data model. The reference property establishes a one-way relationship from one entity to another, and the declaration sets up the back-reference mechanism on the referenced class. The back-reference uses the built-in query index, so determining which objects refer to the referenced object is reasonably fast. It's not quite as fast as storing a list of keys on a property, but it's easier to maintain.

A common use of one-to-many relationships is to model ownership. In the previous example, each BookReview was related to a single Book, and a Book could have many BookReviews. The BookReviews belong to the Book.

One-to-One Relationships

You can also use a reference property to model a *one-to-one relationship*. The property declaration doesn't enforce that only one entity can refer to a given entity, but this is easy to maintain in the application code. Because the performance of queries scales with the size of the result set and not the size of the data set, it's usually sufficient to use the back-reference query to follow a one-to-one relationship back to the object with the reference.

If you'd prefer not to use a query to traverse the back-reference, you could also store a reference on the second object back to the first, at the expense of having to maintain the relationship in two places. This is tricky, because the class has to be defined before it can be the subject of a ReferenceProperty. One option is to use db.Expando and an undeclared property for one of the classes.

A one-to-one relationship can be used to model partnership. A good use of one-to-one relationships in App Engine is to split a large object into multiple entities to provide selective access to its properties. A player might have an avatar image up to 64 kilobytes in size, but the application probably doesn't need the 64 KB of image data every time it fetches the Player entity. You can create a separate PlayerAvatarImage entity to contain the image, and establish a one-to-one relationship by creating a reference property from the Player to the PlayerAvatarImage. The application must know to delete the related objects when deleting a Player:

```
class PlayerAvatarImage(db.Model):
    image_data = db.BlobProperty()
    mime_type = db.StringProperty()

class Player(db.Model):
    name = db.StringProperty()
    avatar = db.ReferenceProperty(PlayerAvatarImage)

# Fetch the name of the player (a string) a
# reference to the avatar image (a key).
p = db.get(player_key)

# Fetch the avatar image entity and access its
# image_data property.
image_data = p.avatar.image_data
```

Many-to-Many Relationships

A *many-to-many relationship* is a type of relationship between entities of two kinds where entities of either kind can have that relationship with many entities of the other kind, and vice versa. For instance, a player may be a member of one or more guilds, and a guild can have many members.

There are at least two ways to implement many-to-many relationships in the datastore. Let's consider two of these. The first method we'll call "the key list method," and the second we'll call "the link model method."

The key list method

With the key list method, you store a list of entity keys on one side of the relationship, using a db.ListProperty. Such a declaration does not have any of the features of a db.ReferenceProperty such as back-references or automatic dereferencing, because it does not involve that class. To model the relationship in the other direction, you can implement the back-reference feature by using a method and the Python annotation @property:

```
class Player(db.Model):
    name = db.StringProperty()
    guilds = db.ListProperty(db.Key)

class Guild(db.Model):
    name = db.StringProperty()

    @property
    def members(self):
        return Player.all().filter('guilds', self.key())

# Guilds to which a player belongs:
p = db.get(player_key)
```

```
guilds = db.get(p.guilds)  # batch get using list of keys
for guild in guilds:
    # ...

# Players that belong to a guild:
g = db.get(guild_key)
for player in g.members:
    # ...
```

Instead of manipulating the list of keys, you could implement automatic dereferencing using advanced Python techniques to extend how the values in the list property are accessed. A good way to do this is with a custom property declaration. We'll consider this in a later section.

The key list method is best suited for situations where there are fewer objects on one side of the relationship than on the other, and the short list is small enough to store directly on an entity. In this example, many players each belong to a few guilds; each player has a short list of guilds, while each guild may have a long list of players. We put the list property on the `Player` side of the relationship to keep the entity small, and use queries to produce the long list when it is needed.

The link model method

The link model method represents each relationship as an entity. The relationship entity has reference properties pointing to the related classes. You traverse the relationship by going through the relationship entity via the back-references:

```
class Player(db.Model):
    name = db.StringProperty()

class Guild(db.Model):
    name = db.StringProperty()

class GuildMembership(db.Model):
    player = db.ReferenceProperty(Player, collection_name='guild_memberships')
    guild = db.ReferenceProperty(Guild, collection_name='player_memberships')

p = Player()
g = Guild()
db.put([p, g])

gm = GuildMembership(player=p, guild=g)
db.put(gm)

# Guilds to which a player belongs:
for gm in p.guild_memberships:
    guild_name = gm.guild.name
    # ...

# Players that belong to a guild:
for gm in g.player_memberships:
    player_name = gm.player.name
    # ...
```

This technique is similar to how you'd use "join tables" in a SQL database. It's a good choice if either side of the relationship may get too large to store on the entity itself. You can also use the relationship entity to store metadata about the relationship (such as when the player joined the guild), or model more complex relationships between multiple classes.

The link model method is more expensive than the key list method. It requires fetching the relationship entity to access the related object.

Remember that App Engine doesn't support SQL-style join queries on these objects. You can achieve a limited sort of join by repeating information from the data objects on the link model objects, using code on the model classes to keep the values in sync. To do this with strong consistency, the link model object and the two related objects would need to be in the same entity group, which is not always possible or practical.

If eventual consistency would suffice, you could use task queues to propagate the information. See Chapter 16.

Model Inheritance

In data modeling, it's often useful to derive new kinds of objects from other kinds. The game world may contain many different kinds of carryable objects, with shared properties and features common to all objects you can carry. Since you implement classes from the data model as Python classes, you'd expect to be able to use inheritance in the implementation to represent inheritance in the model. And you can, sort of.

If you define a class based on either `db.Model` or `db.Expando`, you can create other classes that inherit from that data class, like so:

```
class CarryableObject(db.Model):
    weight = db.IntegerProperty()
    location = db.ReferenceProperty(Location)

class Bottle(CarryableObject):
    contents = db.StringProperty()
    amount = db.IntegerProperty()
    is_closed = db.BooleanProperty()
```

The subclass inherits the property declarations of the parent class. A `Bottle` has five property declarations: `weight`, `location`, `contents`, `amount`, and `is_closed`.

Objects based on the child class will be stored as entities whose kind is the name of the child class. The datastore has no notion of inheritance, and so by default will not treat `Bottle` entities as if they are `CarryableObject` entities. This is mostly significant for queries, and we have a solution for that in the next section.

If a child class declares a property already declared by a parent class, the class definition raises a `db.DuplicatePropertyError`. The data modeling API does not support overriding property declarations in subclasses.

A model class can inherit from multiple classes, using Python's own support for multiple inheritance:

```
class PourableObject(GameObject):
    contents = db.StringProperty()
    amount = db.IntegerProperty()

class Bottle(CarryableObject, PourableObject):
    is_closed = db.BooleanProperty()
```

Each parent class must not declare a property with the same name as declarations in the other parent classes, or the class definition raises a `db.DuplicatePropertyError`. However, the modeling API does the work to support "diamond inheritance," where two parent classes themselves share a parent class:

```
class GameObject(db.Model):
    name = db.StringProperty()
    location = db.ReferenceProperty(Location)

class CarryableObject(GameObject):
    weight = db.IntegerProperty()

class PourableObject(GameObject):
    contents = db.StringProperty()
    amount = db.IntegerProperty()

class Bottle(CarryableObject, PourableObject):
    is_closed = db.BooleanProperty()
```

In this example, both `CarryableObject` and `PourableObject` inherit two property declarations from `GameObject`, and are both used as parent classes to `Bottle`. The model API allows this because the two properties are defined in the same class, so there is no conflict. `Bottle` gets its `name` and `location` declarations from `GameObject`.

Queries and PolyModels

The datastore knows nothing of our modeling classes and inheritance. Instances of the `Bottle` class are stored as entities of the kind `'Bottle'`, with no inherent knowledge of the parent classes. It'd be nice to be able to perform a query for `CarryableObject` entities and get back `Bottle` entities and others. That is, it'd be nice if a query could treat `Bottle` entities as if they were instances of the parent classes, as Python does in our application code. We want *polymorphism* in our queries.

For this, the data modeling API provides a special base class: `db.PolyModel`. Model classes using this base class support polymorphic queries. Consider the `Bottle` class defined previously. Let's change the base class of `GameObject` to `db.PolyModel`, like so:

```
from google.appengine.ext.db import polymodel

class GameObject(polymodel.PolyModel):
    # ...
```

We can now perform queries for any kind in the hierarchy, and get the expected results:

```
here = db.get(location_key)

q = CarryableObject.all()
q.filter('location', here)
q.filter('weight >', 100)

for obj in q:
    # obj is a carryable object that is here
    # and weighs more than 100 kilos.
    # ...
```

This query can return any `CarryableObject`, including `Bottle` entities. The query can use filters on any property of the specified class (such as `weight` from `CarryableObject`) or parent classes (such as `location` from `GameObject`).

Behind the scenes, `db.PolyModel` does three clever things differently from its cousins:

- Objects of the class `GameObject` or any of its child classes are all stored as entities of the kind `'GameObject'`.
- All such objects are given a property named `class` that represents the inheritance hierarchy starting from the root class. This is a multivalued property, where each value is the name of an ancestor class, in order.
- Queries for objects of any kind in the hierarchy are translated by the `db.PolyModel` class into queries for the base class, with additional equality filters that compare the class being queried to the `class` property's values.

In short, `db.PolyModel` stores information about the inheritance hierarchy on the entities, then uses it for queries to support polymorphism.

Each model class that inherits directly from `db.PolyModel` is the root of a class hierarchy. All objects from the hierarchy are stored as entities whose kind is the name of the root class. As such, your data will be easier to maintain if you use many root classes to form many class hierarchies, as opposed to putting all classes in a single hierarchy. That way, the datastore viewer and bulk loading tools can still use the datastore's built-in notion of entity kinds to distinguish between kinds of objects.

Creating Your Own Property Classes

The property declaration classes serve several functions in your data model:

Value validation
: The model calls the class when a value is assigned to the property, and the class can raise an exception if the value does not meet its conditions.

Type conversion
: The model calls the class to convert from the value type used by the app to one of the core datastore types for storage, and back again.

Default behavior
: The model calls the class if no value was assigned to determine an appropriate default value.

Every property declaration class inherits from the `db.Property` base class. This class implements features common to all property declarations, including support for the common constructor arguments (such as `required`, `name`, and `indexed`). Declaration classes override methods and members to specialize the validation and type conversion routines.

Validating Property Values

Here is a very simple property declaration class. It accepts any string value, and stores it as a datastore short string (the default behavior for Python string values):

```
from google.appengine.ext import db

class PlayerNameProperty(db.Property):
    data_type = basestring

    def validate(self, value):
        value = super(PlayerNameProperty, self).validate(value)
        if value is not None and not isinstance(value, self.data_type):
            raise db.BadValueError('Property %s must be a %s.' %
                                   (self.name, self.data_type.__name__))
        return value
```

And here is how you would use the new property declaration:

```
class Player(db.Model):
    player_name = PlayerNameProperty()

p = Player()
p.player_name = 'Ned Nederlander'

p.player_name = 12345  # db.BadValueError
```

The `validate()` method takes the value as an argument, and either returns the value, returns a different value, or raises an exception. The value returned by the method becomes the application-facing value for the attribute, so you can use the `validate()` method for things like type coercion. In this example, the method raises a `db.BadValueError` if the value is not a string or `None`. The exception message can refer to the name of the property by using `self.name`.

The `data_type` member is used by the base class. It represents the core datastore type the property uses to store the value. For string values, this is `basestring`.

The `validate()` method should call the superclass's implementation before checking its own conditions. The base class's validator supports the `required`, `choices`, and `validator` arguments of the declaration constructor.

If the app does not provide a value for a property when it constructs the data object, the property starts out with a default value. This default value is passed to the `validate()` method during the object constructor. If it is appropriate for your property declaration to allow a default value of `None`, make sure your `validate()` method allows it.

So far, this example doesn't do much beyond `db.StringProperty`. This by itself can be useful to give the property type a class for future expansion. Let's add a requirement that player names be between 6 and 30 characters in length by extending the `validate()` method:

```
class PlayerNameProperty(db.Property):
    data_type = basestring

    def validate(self, value):
        value = super(PlayerNameProperty, self).validate(value)
        if value is not None:
            if not isinstance(value, self.data_type):
                raise db.BadValueError('Property %s must be a %s.' %
                                       (self.name, self.data_type.__name__))
            if (len(value) < 6 or len(value) > 30):
                raise db.BadValueError(('Property %s must be between 6 and ' +
                                        '30 characters.') % self.name)

        return value
```

The new validation logic disallows strings with an inappropriate length:

```
p = Player()
p.player_name = 'Ned'    # db.BadValueError
p.player_name = 'Ned Nederlander'    # OK

p = Player(player_name = 'Ned')  # db.BadValueError
```

Marshaling Value Types

The datastore supports a fixed set of core value types for properties, listed in Table 5-1. A property declaration can support the use of other types of values in the attributes of model instances by marshaling between the desired type and one of the core datastore types. For example, the `db.ListProperty` class converts between the empty list of the app side and the condition of being unset on the datastore side.

The `get_value_for_datastore()` method converts the application value to the datastore value. Its argument is the complete model object, so you can access other aspects of the model when doing the conversion.

The make_value_from_datastore() method takes the datastore value and converts it to the type to be used in the application. It takes the datastore value and returns the desired object attribute value.

Say we wanted to represent player name values within the application by using a PlayerName class instead of a simple string. Each player name has a surname and an optional first name. We can store this value as a single property, using the property declaration to convert between the application type (PlayerName) and a core datastore type (such as unicode):

```
class PlayerName(object):
    def __init__(self, first_name, surname):
        self.first_name = first_name
        self.surname = surname

    def is_valid(self):
        return (isinstance(self.first_name, unicode)
                and isinstance(self.surname, unicode)
                and len(self.surname) >= 6)

class PlayerNameProperty(db.Property):
    data_type = basestring

    def validate(self, value):
        value = super(PlayerNameProperty, self).validate(value)
        if value is not None:
            if not isinstance(value, PlayerName):
                raise db.BadValueError('Property %s must be a PlayerName.' %
                                       (self.name))

            # Let the data class have a say in validity.
            if not value.is_valid():
                raise db.BadValueError('Property %s must be a valid PlayerName.' %
                                       self.name)

            # Disallow the serialization delimiter in the first field.
            if value.surname.find('|') != -1:
                raise db.BadValueError(('PlayerName surname in property %s cannot ' +
                                        'contain a "|".') % self.name)
        return value

    def get_value_for_datastore(self, model_instance):
        # Convert the data object's PlayerName to a unicode.
        return (getattr(model_instance, self.name).surname + u'|'
                + getattr(model_instance, self.name).first_name)

    def make_value_for_datastore(self, value):
        # Convert a unicode to a PlayerName.
        i = value.find(u'|')
        return PlayerName(first_name=value[i+1:],
                          surname=value[:i])
```

And here's how you'd use it:

```
p = Player()
p.player_name = PlayerName(u'Ned', u'Nederlander')

p.player_name = PlayerName(u'Ned', u'Neder|lander')
    # db.BadValueError, surname contains serialization delimiter

p.player_name = PlayerName(u'Ned', u'Neder')
    # db.BadValueError, PlayerName.is_valid() == False, surname too short

p.player_name = PlayerName('Ned', u'Nederlander')
    # db.BadValueError, PlayerName.is_valid() == False, first_name is not unicode
```

Here, the application value type is a `PlayerName` instance, and the datastore value type is that value encoded as a Unicode string. The encoding format is the `surname` field, followed by a delimiter, followed by the `first_name` field. We disallow the delimiter character in the surname by using the `validate()` method. (Instead of disallowing it, we could also escape it in `get_value_for_datastore()` and unescape it in `make_value_for_datastore()`.)

In this example, `PlayerName(u'Ned', u'Nederlander')` is stored as this Unicode string:

```
Nederlander|Ned
```

The datastore value puts the surname first so that the datastore will sort `PlayerName` values first by surname, then by first name. In general, you choose a serialization format that has the desired ordering characteristics for your custom property type. (The core type you choose also impacts how your values are ordered when mixed with other types, although if you're modeling consistently this isn't usually an issue.)

If the conversion from the application type to the datastore type may fail, put a check for the conversion failure in the `validate()` method. This way, the error is caught when the bad value is assigned, instead of when the object is saved.

Customizing Default Values

When the app constructs a data object and does not provide a value for a declared property, the model calls the property declaration class to determine a default value. The base class implementation sets the default value to `None`, and allows the app to customize the default value in the model, using the `default` argument to the declaration.

A few of the built-in declaration classes provide more sophisticated default values. For instance, if a `db.DateTimeProperty` was set with `auto_now_add=True`, the default value is the current system date and time. (`db.DateTimeProperty` uses `get_value_for_datastore()` to implement `auto_now=True`, so the value is updated whether or not it has a value.)

The default value passes through the validation logic after it is set. This allows the app to customize the validation logic and disallow the default value. This is what happens when required=True: the base class's validation logic disallows the None value, which is the base class's default value.

To specify custom default behavior, override the default_value() method. This method takes no arguments and returns the desired default value.

Here's a simple implementation of default_value() for PlayerNameProperty:

```
class PlayerNameProperty(db.Property):
    # ...

    def default_value(self):
        default = super(PlayerNameProperty, self).default_value()
        if default is not None:
            return default

        return PlayerName(u'', u'Anonymous')
```

In this example, we call the superclass default() method to support the default argument to the constructor, which allows the app to override the default value in the model. If that returns None, we create a new PlayerName instance to be the default value.

Without further changes, this implementation breaks the required feature of the base class, because the value of the property is never None (unless the app explicitly assigns a None value). We can fix this by amending our validation logic to check self.required and disallow the anonymous PlayerName value if it's True.

Accepting Arguments

If you want the application to be able to control the behavior of your custom property declaration class, using arguments, you override the __init__() method. The method should call the superclass __init__() method to enable the features of the superclass that use arguments (like required). The Property API requires that the verbose_name property come first, but after that all __init__() arguments are keyword values:

```
class PlayerNameProperty(db.Property):
    # ...

    def __init__(self, verbose_name=None,
                 require_first_name=False, **kwds):
        super(PlayerNameProperty, self).__init__(verbose_name, **kwds)
        self.require_first_name = require_first_name

    def validate(self, value):
        value = super(PlayerNameProperty, self).validate(value)
        if value is not None:
            # ...

            if self.require_first_name and not value.first_name:
                raise db.BadValueError('Property %s PlayerName needs a first_name.' %
                                       self.name)

        # ...
```

You'd use this feature like this:

```
class Player(db.Model):
    player_name = PlayerNameProperty(require_first_name=True)

p = Player(player_name=PlayerName(u'Ned', u'Nederlander'))

p.player_name = PlayerName(u'', u'Charo')
# db.BadValueError, first name required

p = Player()
# db.BadValueError, default value PlayerName(u'', u'Anonymous') has empty first_name
```

CHAPTER 10

The Java Persistence API

The App Engine Java SDK includes implementations of two data access interface standards: the Java Persistence API (JPA) and Java Data Objects (JDO). These interfaces provide two essential features.

For one, these interfaces define a mechanism for describing the structure of data objects in terms of Java classes. You can use them to define and enforce consistent data schemas on top of App Engine's schemaless datastore, and take advantage of type safety in the Java language. These interfaces serve as a data modeling layer.

Because each interface is a standard supported by other popular data storage solutions, using a standard interface makes it easier to port an application to and from these other solutions. Different databases have varying degrees of support for these standards. Since the standards were developed with SQL-based relational databases in mind, the App Engine datastore can only be said to support a portion of the standard, and it is often easier to port away from App Engine than to it. But this alone adds value, as you can reserve the right to move your app to your company's own servers at any time. These interfaces are a portability layer.

The App Engine SDK uses an open source product called DataNucleus Access Platform as the basis for its implementations of JDO and JPA. Access Platform uses an adapter layer that translates both standards to an underlying implementation. The App Engine SDK includes an Access Platform adapter based on its low-level datastore API.

The JDO and JPA standards are similar, and share similar roots. The concepts that apply to the App Engine datastore have similar interfaces in both standards but with different terminology and minor behavioral differences. Which one you choose may depend on how familiar you are with it, or how well it is implemented for your most likely porting target, if you have one in mind.

In this chapter, we look at how to use JPA with App Engine. If you'd prefer to use JDO, check out the official documentation for App Engine, which includes a JDO tutorial.

A quick note on terminology: JPA refers to data objects as "entities." This similarity to datastore entities is convenient in some ways, and not so convenient in others. For this chapter, we'll refer to JPA entities as "data objects" (or just "objects") to avoid confusion with datastore entities.

Setting Up JPA

To use JPA, you must perform a few steps to set up the library.

JPA needs a configuration file that specifies that you want to use the App Engine implementation of the interface. This file is named *persistence.xml*, and should appear in your WAR's *WEB-INF/classes/META-INF/* directory. If you're using Eclipse, you can create this file in the *src/META-INF/* directory, and Eclipse will copy it to the final location automatically. It should look like this:

```
<?xml version="1.0" encoding="UTF-8" ?>
<persistence xmlns="http://java.sun.com/xml/ns/persistence"
  xmlns:xsi="http://www.w3.org/2001/XMLSchema-instance"
  xsi:schemaLocation="http://java.sun.com/xml/ns/persistence
      http://java.sun.com/xml/ns/persistence/persistence_1_0.xsd" version="1.0">
  <persistence-unit name="transactions-optional">
      <provider>
        org.datanucleus.api.jpa.PersistenceProviderImpl
      </provider>
      <properties>
          <property name="datanucleus.NontransactionalRead" value="true"/>
          <property name="datanucleus.NontransactionalWrite" value="true"/>
          <property name="datanucleus.ConnectionURL" value="appengine"/>
      </properties>
  </persistence-unit>
</persistence>
```

This configuration tells Access Platform to use the `"appengine"` adapter. It also says to allow reads and writes outside of transactions (`NontransactionalRead` and `NontransactionalWrite` are `true`), which fits the semantics of the datastore that we described earlier. We named this configuration set `"transactions-optional"` to match.

Your application uses an `EntityManager` object to perform a set of datastore operations. The application creates an `EntityManager`, using an `EntityManagerFactory`. The factory loads the configuration file and uses it for subsequent datastore interactions. You get an instance of the factory by calling a static method and passing it the name of the configuration set (`"transactions-optional"`):

```
import javax.persistence.EntityManagerFactory;
import javax.persistence.Persistence;

// ...
    EntityManagerFactory emfInstance =
        Persistence.createEntityManagerFactory("transactions-optional");
```

The `createEntityManagerFactory()` static method performs a nontrivial amount of work. You can think of the factory as a connection pool, and each `EntityManager` as an individual connection. Since you only need one factory for the entire existence of the application, a best practice is to call the method only once, store the factory in a static member, and reuse it for multiple web requests.

```
package myapp;  // where "myapp" is your app's package

import javax.persistence.EntityManagerFactory;
import javax.persistence.Persistence;

public final class EMF {
    private static final EntityManagerFactory emfInstance =
          Persistence.createEntityManagerFactory("transactions-optional");

    private EMF() {}

    public static EntityManagerFactory get() {
        return emfInstance;
    }
}
```

Access Platform hooks up the persistence plumbing to your JPA data classes in a post-compilation process that it calls "enhancement." If you are using Eclipse with the Google Plugin, the plug-in performs this step automatically. If you are not using Eclipse, you must add the enhancement step to your build process. See the official documentation for information about performing this build step with Apache Ant.

Entities and Keys

In JPA, you define data classes as plain old Java objects (POJOs). You use annotations to tell JPA which classes to persist to the datastore, and how to store its members. Defining your data exclusively in terms of the Java classes your application uses makes it easy to manipulate your persistent data. It also makes it easy to test your application, since you can create mock data objects directly from the classes.

JPA also lets you use an XML file instead of annotations to describe how to persist data classes. We'll only cover the annotation style here, but if you are familiar with the XML file mechanism, you can use it with Access Platform.

Here's a simple example of a data class:

```
import java.util.Date;
import javax.persistence.Entity;
import javax.persistence.Id;

@Entity(name = "Book")
public class Book {
    @Id
    private String isbn;

    private String title;
    private String author;
    private int copyrightYear;
    private Date authorBirthdate;
```

```
    // ... constructors, accessors ...
}
```

JPA knows instances of the Book class can be made persistent (saved to the datastore) because of the @Entity annotation. This annotation takes a name argument that specifies the name to be used in JPA queries for objects of this class. The name must be unique across all data classes in the application.

By default, the name of the datastore kind is derived from the name of the class. Specifically, this is the simple name of the class, without the package path (everything after the last ., e.g., "Book"). If you have two data classes with the same simple name in different packages, you can specify an alternate kind name by using the @Table annotation. (JPA was designed with tabular databases in mind, but the concept is equivalent.)

```
import javax.persistence.Entity;
import javax.persistence.Table;

@Entity(name = "Book")
@Table(name = "BookItem")
public class Book {
    // ...
}
```

The Book class has five members. Four of these members are stored as properties on the datastore entity: title, author, copyrightYear, and authorBirthdate. The fifth member, isbn, represents the key name for the entity. JPA knows this because the member has the @Id annotation, and because the type of the member is String.

Every data class needs a member that represents the object's primary key, annotated with @Id. If the type of this member is String and it has no other annotations, then the key has no ancestors, and the value of the member is the string key name. The application must set this field before saving the object for the first time.

To tell JPA to let the datastore assign a unique numeric ID instead of using an app-provided key name string, you declare the member with a type of Long and give it the annotation @GeneratedValue(strategy = GenerationType.IDENTITY), like so:

```
import javax.persistence.Entity;
import javax.persistence.GeneratedValue;
import javax.persistence.GenerationType;
import javax.persistence.Id;

@Entity(name = "Book")
public class Book {
    @Id
    @GeneratedValue(strategy = GenerationType.IDENTITY)
    private Long id;

    // ...
}
```

The member is set with the system-assigned ID when the object is saved to the datastore for the first time.

These simple key member types are sufficient for entities without ancestors. Together with the entity kind ("Book"), the member represents the complete key of a root entity. If an instance of the class may represent an entity with ancestors, the key member must be able to represent the full key path. There are two ways to do this.

One way is to declare the type of the key member to be the com.google.appengine.api.datastore.Key class:

```
import javax.persistence.Entity;
import javax.persistence.Id;
import com.google.appengine.api.datastore.Key;

@Entity(name = "Book")
public class Book {
    @Id
    private Key id;

    // ...
}
```

You can use this key member type to create a complete Key with a string name. You can also use system-assigned numeric IDs with ancestors by using the @GeneratedValue annotation, then assigning a Key value with neither the name nor the ID set.

If you'd prefer not to create a dependency on an App Engine–specific class, there is another way to implement a key with ancestors. Simply declare the ID field's type as String and use a DataNucleus JPA extension that encodes the complete key as a string value, like so:

```
import javax.persistence.Entity;
import javax.persistence.Id;
import org.datanucleus.api.jpa.annotations.Extension;
import com.google.appengine.api.datastore.Key;

@Entity(name = "Book")
public class Book {
    @Id
    @Extension(vendorName = "datanucleus",
               key = "gae.encoded-pk",
               value = "true")
    private String id;

    // ...
}
```

You can convert between a Key and a string-encoded key using the KeyFactory class's keyToString() and stringToKey() methods. (Note that the Key class's toString() method returns something else.)

You can use a `Key` ID field or a string-encoded ID field in combination with the `@GeneratedValue` annotation to produce keys with ancestors and system-assigned numeric IDs.

Entity Properties

The fields of the object become the properties of the corresponding entity. The name of a field is used as the name of the property. The `@Id` field is not stored as a property value, only as the key.

JPA and App Engine support many types of fields. Any of the types mentioned in Table 5-1 can be used as a field type. A field can contain a serializable object, stored as a single property. A field can also be a collection of one of the core datastore types or a serializable class, to be stored as a multivalued property. Additionally, App Engine supports JPA embedded data objects and relationships between entities using fields.

In some cases, JPA must be told which fields to save to the datastore. For the Java standard types (such as `Long` or `String` or `Date`), JPA assumes that fields of those types should be saved. For other types, especially the datastore-specific classes such as `datastore.ShortBlob`, you must tell JPA to save the field by giving it the `@Basic` annotation. If you have a field that should not be saved to the datastore, give it the `@Transient` annotation:

```
import java.util.List;
import javax.persistence.Basic;
import javax.persistence.Id;
import javax.persistence.Transient;
import com.google.appengine.api.datastore.ShortBlob;

@Entity(name = "Book")
public class Book {
    // ...

    private String title;     // saved

    @Basic                    // saved
    private ShortBlob coverIcon;

    @Basic                    // saved
    private List<String> tags;

    @Transient                // not saved
    private int debugAccessCount;
}
```

As with the low-level API, some types are widened before being stored. `int` and `Integer` are converted to `Long`, and `float` and `Float` become `Double`. With the JPA interface, these values are converted back to the declared field types when loaded into an object.

A `Serializable` class can be used as a field type, using the `@Lob` annotation. These values are stored in serialized form as `datastore.Blob` values. As such, these values are not indexed, and cannot be used in queries.

Collection types are stored as multivalued properties in iteration order. When loaded into the data class, multivalued properties are converted back into the specified collection type.

By default, the name of a field is used as the name of the corresponding property. You can override this by using the `@Column` annotation:

```
import javax.persistence.Column;
import javax.persistence.Entity;

@Entity(name = "Book")
public class Book {
    // ...

    @Column(name = "long_description")
    private String longDescription;
}
```

You can declare that the datastore property of a field should not be mentioned in indexes—the property of each entity should be created as a nonindexed property—using an `@Extension` annotation:

```
import org.datanucleus.api.jpa.annotations.Extension;

@Entity(name = "Book")
public class Book {
    // ...

    @Extension(vendorName = "datanucleus",
               key = "gae.unindexed",
               value = "true")
    private String firstSentence;
}
```

Embedded Objects

App Engine supports JPA embedded classes by storing the fields of the embedded class as properties on the same datastore entity as the fields of the primary class. You must declare the class to embed using the `@Embeddable` annotation:

```
import javax.persistence.Embeddable;

@Embeddable
public class Publisher {
    private String name;
    private String address;
    private String city;
    private String stateOrProvince;
    private String postalCode;
```

```
    // ...
}
```

To embed the class, simply use it as a field type:

```
import javax.persistence.Entity;
import Publisher;

@Entity(name = "Book")
public class Book {
    // ...

    private Publisher publisher;
}
```

Because fields of embedded classes are stored as separate properties, they are queryable just like other properties. You can refer to an embedded field in a property with the name of the outer field with a dot-notation, such as `publisher.name`. The actual property name is just the name of the inner field, and you can change this if needed, using an `@Column` annotation.

Saving, Fetching, and Deleting Objects

To start a session with the datastore, you use the `EntityManagerFactory` to create an `EntityManager`. You must create a new `EntityManager` for each request handler, and close it when you're done:

```
import javax.persistence.EntityManager;
import javax.persistence.EntityManagerFactory;
import myapp.EMF;  // where "myapp" is your app's package

// ...
        EntityManagerFactory emf = EMF.get();
        EntityManager em = null;
        try {
            em = emf.createEntityManager();
            // ... do datastore stuff ...
        } finally {
            if (em != null)
                em.close();
        }
```

To create a new data object, you construct the data class and then call the `EntityManager`'s `persist()` method with the object:

```
import myapp.Book;  // our data class

// ...
        EntityManager em = null;
        try {
            em = emf.createEntityManager();
            Book book = new Book();
            book.setTitle("The Grapes of Wrath");
```

```
        // ...
        em.persist(book);
    } finally {
        if (em != null)
            em.close();
    }
```

If you create an object with a complete key, and an entity with that key already exists in the datastore, saving the new object will overwrite the old one. In App Engine's implementation, JPA's `merge()` method is equivalent to `persist()` in this way. (Other implementations may do something different in this case.)

To fetch an entity with a known key, you use the `find()` method. This method takes the class of the object in which to load the entity, and the key of the object. The key can be any appropriate type: a string key name, a numeric ID, a `datastore.Key` object, or a string-encoded complete key. The method returns an object of the given class, or `null` if no object with that key is found:

```
    Book book = em.find(Book.class, "9780596156732");
    if (book == null) {
        // not found
    }
```

The ability of `find()` to accept all four key types is nonstandard. To make your code more portable, only call `find()`, using the type of key you used in the data class.

When you create or fetch an entity (or get an entity back from a query), the data object becomes "attached" to (or managed by) the entity manager. If you make changes to an attached object and do not save them by calling the `persist()` method explicitly, the object is saved automatically when you close the entity manager. As we'll see in the next section, if you need the entity to be updated in a transaction, you pass the updated object to the `persist()` method at the moment it needs to be saved.

To delete an entity, you call the `remove()` method. This method takes the data object as its sole argument. The object still exists in memory after it is removed from the datastore:

```
    em.remove(book);
```

The `remove()` method requires a loaded data object. There is no way to delete an entity with this method without fetching its object first. (You can delete entities without fetching them by using a JPQL delete query. See the section "Queries and JPQL" on page 279.)

Remember to close the EntityManager by calling its close() method. If you don't, changes to objects will not be saved to the datastore. The best way to do this is in a finally block, as shown previously, so the manager still gets closed in the event of an uncaught exception.

Transactions in JPA

The API for performing transactions in JPA is similar to the low-level datastore API. You call a method on the entity manager to create a Transaction object, then call methods on the object to begin and commit or roll back the transaction:

```
import javax.persistence.EntityTransaction;

// ...
        EntityTransaction txn = em.getTransaction();
        txn.begin();
        try {
            Book book = em.find(Book.class, "9780596156732");
            BookReview bookReview = new BookReview();
            bookReview.setRating(5);
            book.getBookReviews().add(bookReview);

            // Persist all updates and commit.
            txn.commit();
        } finally {
            if (txn.isActive()) {
                txn.rollback();
            }
        }
```

The JPA transaction interface was designed for databases that support global transactions, so it knows nothing of App Engine's local transactions and entity groups. It's up to the application to know which operations are appropriate to perform in a single transaction. You can manage entity groups and ancestors by using App Engine's extensions to JPA.

One way to set up a data class that can represent entities with parents is to use either a datastore.Key or a string-encoded key for the @Id field. When you create a new object, you can construct the complete key, including ancestors, and assign it to this field.

Alternatively, you can establish a second field to contain the parent key as either a Key or string-encoded key, using an extension:

```
import javax.persistence.Basic;
import javax.persistence.Entity;
import javax.persistence.GeneratedValue;
import javax.persistence.GenerationType;
import javax.persistence.Id;

import org.datanucleus.api.jpa.annotations.Extension;
```

```
@Entity
public class BookReview {
    @Id
    @GeneratedValue(strategy = GenerationType.IDENTITY)
    @Extension(vendorName = "datanucleus",
               key = "gae.encoded-pk",
               value = "true")
    private String keyString;

    @Basic
    @Extension(vendorName = "datanucleus",
               key = "gae.parent-pk",
               value = "true")
    private String bookKeyString;
}
```

The parent key field makes it easier to port your application to another database at a later time. It declares a slot in the data class for the ancestor relationship that is separate from the entity's key name.

The parent key field is required if you want to perform queries with ancestor filters. As we'll see in the next section, JPA queries must refer to fields on the data class.

The App Engine implementation of JPA includes features for managing entity groups automatically using object relationships. We'll discuss relationships later in this chapter.

Queries and JPQL

JPA includes a SQL-like query language called JPQL. JPQL provides access to the underlying database's query functionality at the level of abstraction of JPA data objects. You form queries for data objects in terms of the data classes, and get objects as results.

To perform a query, you call the entity manager's `createQuery()` method with the text of the JPQL query. This returns a `Query` object. To get the results, you call `getResultList()` on the `Query` object:

```
import java.util.List;
import javax.persistence.Query;

// ...

    Query query = em.createQuery("SELECT b FROM Book b");

    @SuppressWarnings("unchecked")
    List<Book> results = (List<Book>) query.getResultList();
```

In this example, the cast to `List<Book>` generates a compiler warning, so we suppress this warning by using an `@SuppressWarnings` annotation.

JPA knows which class to use for each result from the `@Entity(name = "...")` annotation on the class. You can also use the full package path of the class in the query.

You can use parameters in your JPQL query, and replace the parameters with values by calling `setParameter()`:

```
Query query = em.createQuery(
    "SELECT b FROM Book b WHERE copyrightYear >= :earliestYear");
query.setParameter("earliestYear", 1923);
```

`getResultList()` returns a special App Engine–specific implementation of `List` that knows how to fetch results in batches. If you iterate over the entire list, the `List` implementation may make multiple calls to the datastore to fetch results.

If you are only expecting one result, you can call `getSingleResult()` instead. This gets the first result if any, or `null` if there are no results:

```
Book book = (Book) query.getSingleResult();
```

You can fetch a range of results by setting an offset and a maximum number of results, using the `setFirstResult()` and `setMaxResults()` methods before calling `getResultList()`:

```
// Get results 5-15.
query.setFirstResult(4);
query.setMaxResults(10);

@SuppressWarnings("unchecked")
List<Book> results = (List<Book>) query.getResultList();
```

The syntax of JPQL is straightforward, and similar to SQL or the Python API's GQL. JPQL keywords can be all uppercase or all lowercase, and are shown as uppercase here, as is tradition. Class and field names are case-sensitive. The query begins by identifying the simple name of the class of objects to query, corresponding to the kind of the entities:

```
SELECT b FROM Book b
```

This query returns all `Book` data objects, where `Book` is the value of the `name` argument to the `@Entity` annotation on the data class (which happens to also be named `Book`). The class name is followed by an identifier (`b`); stating that identifier after the word `SELECT` tells JPA to return objects of that class as results.

To perform a keys-only query, give the name of the key field instead of the class identifier. The methods that return results return values of the type used for the `@Id` field in the data class:

```
Query query = em.createQuery("SELECT isbn FROM Book");

@SuppressWarnings("unchecked")
List<String> results = (List<String>) query.getResultList();
```

The App Engine implementation of JPQL supports queries for specific fields, although perhaps not in the way you'd expect. For a query for specific fields, the datastore returns the complete data for each entity to the application, and the interface implementation selects the requested fields and assembles the results. This is only true if one of the requested fields is a datastore property, and is not true if the only field is a key field (`@Id`).

If the query is for one field, each result is a value of the type of that field. If the query is for multiple fields, each result is an `Object[]` whose elements are the field values in the order specified in the query:

```
Query query = em.createQuery("SELECT isbn, title, author FROM Book");

// Fetch complete Book objects, then
// produce result objects from 3 fields
// of each result
@SuppressWarnings("unchecked")
List<Object[]> results = (List<Object[]>) query.getResultList();
for (Object[] result : results) {
    String isbn = (String) result[0];
    String title = (String) result[1];
    String author = (String) result[2];

    // ...
}
```

You specify filters on fields by using a `WHERE` clause and one or more conditions:

```
SELECT b FROM Book b WHERE author = "John Steinbeck"
                     AND copyrightYear >= 1940
```

To filter on the entity key, refer to the field that represents the key in the data class (the `@Id` field):

```
SELECT b FROM Book b WHERE author = "John Steinbeck"
                     AND isbn > :firstKeyToFetch
```

You can perform an ancestor filter by establishing a parent key field (as we did in the previous section) and referring to that field in the query:

```
SELECT br FROM BookReview br WHERE bookKey = :pk
```

As with `find()`, you can use any of the four key types with parameterized queries, but the most portable way is to use the type used in the class.

You specify sort orders by using an `ORDER BY` clause. Multiple sort orders are comma-delimited. Each sort order can have a direction of `ASC` (the default) or `DESC`.

```
SELECT b FROM Book b ORDER BY rating DESC title
```

The App Engine implementation of JPQL includes a couple of additional tricks that the datastore can support natively. One such trick is the string prefix trick:

```
SELECT b FROM Book b WHERE title LIKE 'The Grape%'
```

The implementation translates this to `WHERE title >= 'The Grape'`, which does the same thing: it returns all books with a title that begins with the string `The Grape`, including `"The Grape"`, `"The Grapefruit"`, and `"The Grapes of Wrath"`.

This trick only supports a single wildcard at the end of a string. It does not support a wildcard at the beginning of the string.

Another trick App Engine's JPQL implementation knows how to do is to translate queries on key fields into batch gets. For example:

```
SELECT b FROM Book b WHERE isbn IN (:i1, :i2, :i3)
```

This becomes a batch get of three keys, and does not perform a query at all.

In addition to these `SELECT` queries, App Engine's JPA implementation supports deleting entities that meet criteria with JPQL. A delete query can include filters on keys and properties to specify the entities to delete:

```
DELETE FROM Book b WHERE isbn >= "TEST_000" AND isbn <= "TEST_999"
```

To execute a `DELETE` query, call the `Query` object's `executeUpdate()` method. This method returns no results.

As with other mechanisms for modifying data, if you perform a delete query outside of a transaction, it is possible for a delete of one entity to fail while the others succeed. If you perform it inside a transaction, it'll be all or nothing, but all entities must be in the same entity group, and the delete query must use an ancestor filter.

The JPA specification supports many features of queries that are common to SQL databases, but are not supported natively in the App Engine datastore. With a SQL database, using one of these features calls the database directly, with all the performance implications (good and bad) of the datastore's implementation.

When an app uses a feature of JPQL that the underlying database does not support, DataNucleus Access Platform tries to make up the difference using its own in-memory query evaluator. It attempts to load all the information it needs to perform the query into memory, execute the nonnative operations itself, then return the result.

Because such features are potential scalability hazards—an `AVG()` query would require fetching every entity of the kind, for example—the App Engine implementation disables the Access Platform in-memory query evaluator.

Relationships

Most useful data models involve relationships between classes of data objects. Players are members of guilds, book reviews are about books, messages are posted to message boards, customers place orders, and orders have multiple line items. For logical reasons or architectural reasons, two concepts may be modeled as separate but related classes. Those relationships are as much a part of the data model as the data fields of the objects.

In the App Engine datastore (and most databases), one easy way to model a relationship between two objects is to store the entity key of one object as a property of the other, and (if needed) vice versa. The datastore supports `Key` values as a native property value type, and also provides a way to encode key values as strings. You don't need any help from JPA to model relationships this way.

But relationships are so important to data modeling that JPA has a family of features to support them. In JPA, you can define *owned relationships* in the data model that enforce constraints by managing changes. With owned relationships, you can say that a book has zero or more book reviews, and JPA ensures that you can't have a book review without a book. If you delete a `Book` object, JPA knows to also delete all its `BookReview` objects. In the Java code, the relationship is represented by a field whose type is of the related data class, ensuring that only the appropriate classes are used on either side of the relationship.

The App Engine implementation of JPA supports one-to-one and one-to-many relationships. It does not yet support JPA's notion of many-to-many relationships.

An *unowned relationship* is a relationship without these constraints. App Engine supports unowned relationships through the storing of literal key values, but does not yet support them through JPA. You can use multivalued properties of `Key` values to model unowned one-to-one, one-to-many, and many-to-many relationships.

To completely support the semantics of JPA owned relationships, App Engine stores objects with owned relationships in the same entity group. It's easy to see why this has to be the case. If one object is deleted within a transaction, the relationship says the related object must also be deleted. But to do that in the same transaction requires that both objects be in the same entity group. If one object is deleted outside of a transaction, then the other object must be deleted in a separate operation, and if one delete or the other fails, an object remains that doesn't meet the relationship requirement.

While the use of entity groups may sound constraining, it's also a powerful feature. You can use JPA owned relationships to perform transactions on related entities, and the JPA implementation will manage entity groups for you automatically.

You specify an owned one-to-one relationship by creating a field whose type is of the related class, and giving the field an `@OneToOne` annotation. For example, you could associate each book with a cover image, like so:

```
import javax.persistence.Entity;
import javax.persistence.OneToOne;
import bookstore.BookCoverImage;

@Entity(name = "Book")
public class Book {
    // ...

    @OneToOne(cascade=CascadeType.ALL)
    private BookCoverImage bookCoverImage;
}
```

This annotation declares a one-to-one relationship between the Book and BookCoverImage classes.

In every relationship, one class "owns" the relationship. The owner of a relationship is responsible for propagating changes to related objects. In this example, the Book class is the "owner" of the relationship.

The cascade=CascadeType.ALL argument annotation says that all kinds of changes should propagate to related objects (including PERSIST, REFRESH, REMOVE, and MERGE). For example:

```
// EntityManager em;
// ...

Book book = new Book();
book.setBookCoverImage(new BookCoverImage());

book.setTitle("The Grapes of Wrath");
book.bookCoverImage.setType("image/jpg");

EntityTransaction txn = em.getTransaction();
txn.begin();
try {
    em.persist(book);
    txn.commit();
} finally {
    if (txn.isActive()) {
        txn.rollback();
    }
}
em.close();
```

This code creates a Book and a related BookCoverImage. When it makes the Book persistent, the BookCoverImage is made persistent automatically (the PERSIST action cascades). Similarly, if we were to delete the Book, the BookCoverImage would also be deleted (the DELETE action cascades). Cascading actions follow all ownership paths from "owner" to "owned," and do the right thing if the objects they find have changed since they were loaded from the datastore.

You can have JPA populate a field on the "owned" class that points back to the owner automatically, like so:

```
import javax.persistence.Entity;
import javax.persistence.OneToOne;
import bookstore.Book;

@Entity(name = "BookCoverImage")
public class BookCoverImage {
    // ...

    @OneToOne(mappedBy="bookCoverImage")
    private Book book;
}
```

The mappedBy argument tells JPA that the book field refers to the Book object that is related to this object. This is managed from the "owner" side of the relationship: when the BookCoverImage is assigned to the Book's field, JPA knows that the back-reference refers to the Book object.

To specify a one-to-many relationship, you use a field type that is a List or Set of the related class, and use the @OneToMany annotation on the "one" class, with a mappedBy argument that refers to the property on the entities of the "many" class:

```
import java.util.List;
import javax.persistence.CascadeType;
import javax.persistence.Entity;
import javax.persistence.OneToMany;
import bookstore.BookReview;

@Entity(name = "Book")
public class Book {
    // ...

    @OneToMany(cascade=CascadeType.ALL, mappedBy="book")
    private List<BookReview> bookReviews = null;
}
```

To create a back-reference from the "many" class to the "one" class, you use a @ManyToOne annotation, with no arguments:

```
// BookReview.java
@Entity(name = "BookReview")
public class BookReview {
    // ...

    @ManyToOne()
    private Book book;
}

// Book.java
@Entity(name = "Book")
public class Book {
    // ...

    @OneToMany(cascade=CascadeType.ALL,
               mappedBy="book")
    private List<BookReview> bookReviews;
}
```

In a one-to-many relationship, the "one" is always the owner class, and the "many" is the owned class. In a one-to-one relationship, JPA knows which is the "owned" class by the absence of a back-reference field, or a back-reference field mentioned by a mappedBy annotation argument: the side with the mappedBy is the owned class.

When you fetch a data object that has a relationship field, JPA does not fetch the related objects right away. Instead, it waits until you access the field to fetch the object (or objects). This is called "lazy" fetching, and it saves your app from unnecessary datastore operations. The App Engine implementation of JPA only supports lazy fetching (FetchType.LAZY), and does not yet support its opposite, "eager" fetching (FetchType.EAGER). Note that you must access related objects prior to closing the EntityManager, so they are fetched into memory:

```
// Fetch a Book, but not its BookCoverImage.
Book book = em.find(Book.class, "9780596156732");
// ...

// The BookCoverImage is fetched when it is first accessed.
resp.setContentType(book.bookCoverImage.type);
```

In the datastore, the relationship is represented using ancestors. The owner object is the parent, and all owned objects are children. When you access the relationship field on the owner object, the interface uses an ancestor query to get the owned objects. When you access a back-reference to the owner from the owned object, the interface parses the owned object's key to get the parent.

Related objects are created in the same entity group, so they can all be updated within the same transaction if necessary. The owner's entity is created first (if necessary) and becomes the parent of the owned objects' entities. If you declare a back-reference by using mappedBy, no property is stored on the owned object's entity. Instead, when the field is dereferenced, the implementation uses the owned object's key path to determine the owner's key and fetches it.

The App Engine implementation does not support many-to-one relationships where the "many" is the owner. That is, it does not support a one-to-many relationship where actions cascade from the many to the one.

Creating new relationships between existing data classes can be tricky, because the entity group requirements must be met in the migrated data. Adding a relationship to the owner class is like adding a field: the entities that represent instances of the owner class must be updated to have appropriate key properties. The "owned" side is trickier: since an owned object's entity must have the owner as its parent, if the owned object already exists in the datastore, it must be deleted and re-created with the new parent. You can't change an entity's parent after the entity has been created.

This use of datastore ancestors means you cannot reassign an owned object to another owner after it has been saved to the datastore. This also means that one object cannot be on the "owned" side of more than one relationship, since the entity can have only one parent.

Relationships and cascading actions imply that an operation on a data object can translate to multiple datastore operations on multiple entities, all in the same entity group. If you want these operations to occur in a single transaction, you must perform the initial operation (such as em.merge(...)) within an explicit transaction.

If you perform a cascading action outside of an explicit transaction, each of the datastore operations performed by JPA occurs in a separate operation. Some of these operations may fail while others succeed. As such, it's a best practice to perform all JPA updates within explicit transactions, so there is no confusion as to what succeeded and what failed.

You can perform queries on relationship fields in JPQL by using key values. For a query on the owner class, the query is a simple key property query:

```
SELECT FROM Book b WHERE bookCoverImage = :bci AND publishDate > :pdate
```

For a query on an owned class, a query on the back-reference field becomes an ancestor filter:

```
SELECT FROM BookCoverImage bci WHERE book = :b
```

You cannot refer to properties of the related entity in the query filter. App Engine does not support join queries.

For More Information

The JDO and JPA interfaces have many useful features that work with the App Engine implementation. One excellent source of documentation on these interfaces is the DataNucleus Access Platform website:

http://www.datanucleus.org/products/accessplatform/

The App Engine implementation is an open source project hosted on Google Code. The source includes many unit tests that exercise and demonstrate many features of JDO and JPA. You can browse the source code at the project page:

http://code.google.com/p/datanucleus-appengine/

To read the unit tests, click the Source tab, then click Browse in the navigation bar. The path is *svn/trunk/tests/org/datanucleus/store/appengine/*.

CHAPTER 11

The Memory Cache

Durable data storage requires a storage medium that retains data through power loss and system restarts. Today's medium of choice is the hard drive, a storage device composed of circular platters coated with magnetic material on which data is encoded. The platters spin at a constant rate while a sensor moves along the radius, reading and writing bits on the platters as they travel past. Reading or writing a specific piece of data requires a *disk seek* to position the sensor at the proper radius and wait for the platter to rotate until the desired data is underneath. All things considered, hard drives are astonishingly fast, but for web applications, disk seeks can be costly. Fetching an entity from the datastore by key can take time on the order of tens of milliseconds.

Most high-performance web applications mitigate this cost with a *memory cache*. A memory cache uses a volatile storage medium, usually the RAM of the cache machines, for very fast read and write access to values. A *distributed memory cache* provides scalable, consistent temporary storage for distributed systems, so many processes on many machines can access the same data. Because memory is volatile—it gets erased during an outage—the cache is not useful for long-term storage, or even short-term primary storage for important data. But it's excellent as a secondary system for fast access to data also kept elsewhere, such as the datastore. It's also sufficient as global high-speed memory for some uses.

The App Engine distributed memory cache service, known as *memcache* in honor of the original `memcached` system that it resembles, stores key-value pairs. You can set a value with a key, and get the value given the key. A value can be up to a megabyte in size. A key is up to 250 bytes, and the API accepts larger keys and uses a hash algorithm to convert them to 250 bytes.

The memcache does not support transactions like the datastore does, but it does provide several atomic operations. Setting a single value in the cache is atomic: the key either gets the new value or retains the old one (or remains unset). You can tell memcache to set a value only if it hasn't changed since it was last fetched, a technique known as "compare and set" in the API. The App Engine memcache also includes the ability to increment and decrement numeric values as an atomic operation.

A common way to use the memcache with the datastore is to cache datastore entities by their keys. When you want to fetch an entity by key, you first check the memcache for a value with that key, and use it if found (known as a *cache hit*). If it's not in the memcache (a *cache miss*), you fetch it from the datastore, then put it in the memcache so future attempts to access it will find it there. At the expense of a small amount of overhead during the first fetch, subsequent fetches become much faster.

If the entity changes in the datastore, you can attempt to update the memcache when the entity is updated in the datastore, so subsequent requests can continue to go to the cache but see fresh data. This mostly works, but it has two minor problems. For one, it is possible that the memcache update will fail even if the datastore update succeeds, leaving old data in the cache. Also, if two processes update the same datastore entity, then update the memcache, the datastore will have correct data (thanks to datastore transactions), but the memcache update will have the value of whichever update occurs last. Because of this possibility, it's somewhat better to just delete the memcache key when the datastore changes, and let the next read attempt populate the cache with a current value. Naturally, the delete could also fail.

Because there is no way to update both the datastore and the memcache in a single transaction, there is no way to avoid the possibility that the cache may contain old data. To minimize the duration that the memcache will have a stale value, you can give the value an expiration time when you set it. When the expiration time elapses, the cache unsets the key, and a subsequent read results in a cache miss and triggers a fresh fetch from the datastore.

Of course, this caching pattern works for more than just datastore entities. You can use it for datastore queries, web service calls made with URL Fetch, expensive calculations, or any other data that can be replaced with a slow operation, where the benefits of fast access outweigh the possibility of staleness.

This is so often the case with web applications that a best practice is to cache aggressively. Look through your application for opportunities to make this trade-off, and implement caching whenever the same value is needed an arbitrary number of times, especially if that number increases with traffic. Site content such as an article on a news website often falls into this category. Caching speeds up requests and saves CPU time.

The APIs for the memcache service are straightforward. Let's look at each of the memcache features, in Python and Java.

Calling Memcache from Python

The Python API for the memcache service is provided by the `google.appengine.api.memcache` package. The API comes in two flavors: a set of simple functions (such as `set()` and `get`), and a `Client` class whose methods are equivalent to the corresponding functions.

This API is intended to be compatible with the Python memcached library, which existing code or third-party libraries might use. When a feature of this library does not apply to App Engine, the method or argument for the feature is supported, but does nothing. We won't discuss the compatibility aspects here, but see the official documentation for more information.

The Client class supports one feature that the simple functions do not: compare-and-set. This mechanism needs to store state between calls, and does so on the Client instance. This class is not threadsafe, so be sure to create a new Client instance for each request handler, and don't store it in a global variable.

Here's a simple example that fetches a web feed by using the URL Fetch service (via App Engine's version of the urllib2 library), stores it in the memcache, and uses the cached value until it expires five minutes (300 seconds) later. The key is the feed URL, and the value is the raw data returned by URL Fetch:

```
import urllib2
from google.appengine.api import memcache

def get_feed(feed_url):
    feed_data = memcache.get(feed_url)
    if not feed_data:
        feed_data = urllib2.urlopen(feed_url).read()
        memcache.set(feed_url, feed_data, time=300)
    return feed_data
```

Calling Memcache from Java

App Engine supports two Java APIs to memcache. The first is a proprietary interface, which will be the subject of the Java portions of this chapter. App Engine also includes an implementation of JSR 107, known as JCache, an interface standard for memcache services. You can find the JCache interface in the package net.sf.jsr107cache.

The Java API to the memcache service is in the com.google.appengine.api.memcache package. As with the other service APIs, you get a service implementation by calling a static method on the MemcacheServiceFactory class, then interact with the service by calling methods on this instance.

To make synchronous calls to the memcache service, you use an implementation of the MemcacheService interface, which you get by calling the getMemcacheService() method of the factory:

```
import com.google.appengine.api.memcache.MemcacheService;
import com.google.appengine.api.memcache.MemcacheServiceFactory;

// ...
        MemcacheService memcache = MemcacheServiceFactory.getMemcacheService();
```

To make asynchronous calls, you use an implementation of the AsyncMemcacheService interface, obtained by calling the getAsyncMemcacheService() method. For more information about asynchronous service calls, see "Calling Services Asynchronously" on page 430.

Memcache values can be partitioned into namespaces. To use a namespace, provide the namespace as a `String` argument to the factory method. All calls to the resulting service implementation will use the namespace.

Here's a simple example that fetches a web feed by using the URL Fetch service, stores it in the memcache, and uses the cached value until it expires five minutes (300 seconds) later. The key is the feed URL, and the value is the raw data returned by URL Fetch:

```
import java.net.URL;

import com.google.appengine.api.memcache.Expiration;
import com.google.appengine.api.memcache.MemcacheService;
import com.google.appengine.api.memcache.MemcacheServiceFactory;
import com.google.appengine.api.urlfetch.URLFetchService;
import com.google.appengine.api.urlfetch.URLFetchServiceFactory;

// ...
    public byte[] getFeed(URL feedUrl) {
        MemcacheService memcache = MemcacheServiceFactory.getMemcacheService();
        byte[] feedData = (byte[]) memcache.get(feedUrl);

        if (feedData == null) {
            URLFetchService urlFetch = URLFetchServiceFactory.getURLFetchService();
            try {
                feedData = urlFetch.fetch(feedUrl).getContent();
                memcache.put(feedUrl, feedData, Expiration.byDeltaSeconds(300));
            } catch (Exception e) {
                return null;
            }
        }
        return feedData;
    }
```

Keys and Values

The memcache service stores key-value pairs. To store a value, you provide both a key and a value. To get a value, you provide its key, and memcache returns the value.

Both the key and the value can be data of any type that can be serialized. In Python, the key and value are serialized using the `pickle` module in the standard library. In Java, the key and value can be of any class that implements the `java.io.Serializable` interface, which includes the (auto-boxed) primitive types.

The key can be of any size. App Engine converts the key data to 250 bytes by using a hash algorithm, which makes for a number of possible unique keys larger than a 1 followed by 600 zeroes. You generally don't have to think about the size of the key.

The value can be up to 1 megabyte in its serialized form. In practice, this means that pretty much anything that can fit in a datastore entity can also be a memcache value.

Setting Values

The simplest way to store a value in memcache is to set it. If no value exists for the given key, setting the value will create a new value in memcache for the key. If there is already a value for the key, it will be replaced with the new value.

In Python, you call either the `set()` function, or the equivalent method on a `Client` instance. The method returns `True` on success. It only returns `False` if there was an issue reaching the memcache service. Since memcache may evict (delete) values at any time, it is typical to ignore this return value:

```
success = memcache.set(key, value)

# Or:
memcache_client = memcache.Client()
success = memcache_client.set(key, value)

if not success:
    # There was a problem accessing memcache...
```

In Java, you call the `put()` method of the service implementation. When called with just the key and value, this method sets the key-value pair, and the method has no return value:

```
memcache.put(key, value)
```

Setting Values that Expire

By default, a memcache value stays in the memcache until it is deleted by the app with a service call, or until it is evicted by the memcache service. The memcache service will evict a value if it runs out of space, or if a machine holding a value goes down or is turned down for maintenance.

When you set a value, you can specify an optional expiration time. If provided, the memcache service will make an effort to evict the value when the expiration time is reached. The timing may not be exact, but it'll be close. Setting an expiration time encourages a cache-backed process to refresh its data periodically, without the app having to track the age of a cached value and forcibly delete it.

To set an expiration for a value in Python, you include a `time` argument to `set()`. Its value is either a number of seconds in the future relative to the current time up to one month (2,592,000 seconds), or it is an absolute date and time as a Unix epoch date:

```
success = memcache.set(key, value, time=300)
```

In Java, you set the expiration as an optional third argument to the `put()` method. This value is an instance of the `Expiration` class, which you construct by calling a static class method. To set an expiration time in the future relative to the current time, you call `Expiration.byDeltaSeconds(int)`. You can also specify this time in milliseconds using `Expiration.byDeltaMillis(int)`; this value will be rounded down to the nearest second.

To set an expiration time as an absolute date and time, you call `Expiration.onDate(java.util.Date)`:

```
memcache.put(key, value, Expiration.byDeltaSeconds(300));
```

A value's expiration date is updated every time the value is updated. If you replace a value with an expiration date, the new value does not inherit the old date. There is no way to query a key for "time until expiration."

Adding and Replacing Values

There are two subtle variations on setting a value: adding and replacing.

When you add a value with a given key, the value is created in memcache only if the key is not already set. If the key is set, adding the value will do nothing. This operation is atomic, so you can use the add operation to avoid a race condition between two request handlers doing related work.

Similarly, when you replace a value with a given key, the value is updated in memcache only if the key is set. If the key is not set, the replace operation does nothing, and the key remains unset. Replacing a value is useful if the absence of the value is meaningful to another process, such as to inspire a refresh after an expiration date. Note that, as with replacing values with set, the replaced value will need its own expiration date if the previous value had one, and there is no way to preserve the previous expiration after a replacement.

In Python, you invoke these variants using separate functions: `add()` and `replace()`. As with `set()`, these functions have equivalent methods on the `Client` class. Both of these methods accept the `time` argument for setting an expiration date on the added or replaced value. The return value is `True` on success—and unlike `set()`, the add or replace may fail due to the existence or absence of the key, so this might be useful to know:

```
success = memcache.add(key, value)
if not success:
    # The key is already set, or there was a problem accessing memcache...

success = memcache.replace(key, value)
if not success:
    # The key is not set, or there was a problem accessing memcache...
```

In Java, the distinction between set, add, and replace is made using a fourth argument to `put()`. This argument is from the enum `MemcacheService.SetPolicy`, and is either `SET_ALWAYS` (set, the default), `ADD_ONLY_IF_NOT_PRESENT` (add), or `REPLACE_ONLY_IF_PRESENT` (replace). If you want to add or replace but do not want to set an expiration, you can set the third argument to `null`. The four-argument form of `put()` returns `true` on success, so you can test whether the add or replace failed, possibly due to the existence or absence of the key:

```
boolean success = memcache.put(key, value, null,
    MemcacheService.SetPolicy.ADD_ONLY_IF_NOT_PRESENT);
```

Getting Values

You can get a value out of the memcache by using its key.

In Python, you call the `get()` function (or method). If the key is not set, it returns `None`:

```
value = memcache.get(key)
if value is None:
    # The key was not set...
```

In Java, you call the `get()` method of the service implementation. Its return value is of type `Object`, so you'll need to cast it back to its original type. If the key is not set, the method returns `null`:

```
String value = (String) memcache.get(key);
if (value == null) {
    // The key was not set...
}
```

Deleting Values

An app can force an eviction of a value by deleting its key. The deletion is immediate, and atomic.

In Python, you pass the key to the `delete()` function or method. This returns one of three values: `memcache.DELETE_SUCCESSFUL` if the key existed and was deleted successfully, `memcache.DELETE_ITEM_MISSING` if there was no value with the given key, or `memcache.DELETE_NETWORK_FAILURE` if the delete could not be completed due to a service failure. These constants are defined such that if you don't care about the distinction between a successful delete and a missing key, you can use the result as a conditional expression. (`DELETE_NETWORK_FAILURE` is 0.)

```
success = memcache.delete(key)
if not success:
    # There was a problem accessing memcache...
```

In Java, you call the `delete()` method with the key to delete. This method returns `true` if the key was deleted successfully or if it was already unset, or `false` if the service could not be reached:

```
boolean success = memcache.delete(key);
```

Locking a Deleted Key

When you delete a value, you can tell memcache to lock the key for a period of time. During this time, attempts to add the key will fail as if the key is set, while attempts to get the value will return nothing. This is sometimes useful to give mechanisms that rely on an add-only policy some breathing room, so an immediate reading of the key doesn't cause confusion.

Only the add operation is affected by a delete lock. The set operation will always succeed, and will cancel the delete lock. The replace operation will fail during the lock period as long as the key is not set; it otherwise ignores the lock.

To lock the key when deleting in Python, you specify the optional `seconds` argument. Its value is either a number of seconds in the future up to a month, or an absolute Unix epoch date-time. The default is 0, which says not to use a lock:

```
success = memcache.delete(key, seconds=20)
```

In Java, you lock the key with a second argument to `delete()`. Its value, a `long`, is a number of milliseconds in the future. (You can't set an absolute date and time for a delete lock in Java.)

```
boolean success = memcache.delete(key, 20000);
```

Atomic Increment and Decrement

Memcache includes special support for incrementing and decrementing numeric values as atomic operations. This allows for multiple processes to contribute to a shared value in the cache without interfering with each other. With just the get and set operations we've seen so far, this would be difficult: incrementing a value would involve reading then setting the value with separate operations, and two concurrent processes might interleave these operations and produce an incorrect result. The atomic increment operation does not have this problem.

When considering using memcache for counting, remember that memcache is nondurable storage. Your process must be resilient to the counter value being evicted at any time. But there are many forms this resilience can take. For instance, the app can periodically save the counter value to the datastore, and detect and recover if the increment fails due to the key being unset. In other cases, the counter may be helpful but not strictly necessary, and the work can proceed without it. In practice, unexpected cache evictions are rare, but it's best to code defensively.

You can use the increment and decrement operations on any unsigned integer value. Memcache integers are 64 bits in size. Incrementing beyond the maximum 64-bit integer causes the value to wrap around to 0, and decrementing has the same behavior in reverse. If the value being incremented is not an integer, nothing changes.

When you call the increment operation, you can specify an optional initial value. Normally, the increment does nothing if the key is not set. If you specify an initial value and the key being incremented is not set, the key is set to the initial value, and the initial value is returned as the result of the operation.

The Python API provides two functions: `incr()` and `decr()`. Given a key as its sole argument, the functions will increment or decrement the corresponding integer value by 1, respectively. You can specify a different amount of change with the optional `delta` argument, which must be a nonnegative integer. You can also specify an `ini` tial_value, which sets the value if the key is unset. Without an initial value, incrementing or decrementing an unset key has no effect. The function returns the new value, or None if the increment does not occur:

```
# Increment by 1, if key is set. v = v + 1
result = memcache.incr(key)
if result is None:
    # The key is not set, or another error occurred...

# Increment by 9, or initialize to 0 if not set.
result = memcache.incr(key, delta=9, initial_value=0)

# Decrement by 3, if key is set. v = v - 3
result = memcache.decr(key, delta=3)
```

In the Java API, there is only one method: increment(). It takes as arguments the key and the amount of change, which can be negative. An optional third argument specifies an initial value, which sets the value if the key is unset. The method returns a java.lang.Long equal to the new value, or null if the increment does not occur:

```
// Increment by 1, if key is set. v = v + 1
Long result = memcache.increment(key, 1);
if (result == null) {
    // The key is not set, or another error occurred...
}

// Increment by 9, or initialize to 0 if not set.
result = memcache.increment(key, 9, 0);

// Decrement by 3, if key is set. v = v + (-3)
result = memcache.increment(key, -3);
```

Compare and Set

While memcache does not support general purpose transactions across multiple values, it does have a feature that provides a modest amount of transactionality for single values. The "compare and set" primitive operation sets a value if and only if it has not been updated since the last time the caller read the value. If the value was updated by another process, the caller's update does not occur, and the operation reports this condition. The caller can retry its calculation for another chance at a consistent update.

This is a simpler version of the optimistic concurrency control we saw with datastore transactions, with some important differences. "Compare and set" can only operate on one memcache value at a time. Because the value is retained in fast nondurable storage, there is no replication delay. Read and write operations occur simply in the order they arrive at the service.

The API for this feature consists of two methods: a different get operation that returns both the value and a unique identifier (the compare-and-set ID, or CAS ID) for the value that is meaningful to the memcache, and the compare-and-set operation that sends the previous CAS ID with the updated value. The CAS ID for a key in memcache changes whenever the key is updated, even if it is updated to the same value as it had before the update. The memcache service uses the provided CAS ID to decide whether the compare-and-set operation should succeed. The Python and Java APIs represent this functionality in slightly different ways.

In Python, the CAS IDs of retrieved values are kept internal to the `Client` instance you use to interact with the service. You call a slightly different method for getting values, `gets()`, which knows to ask for and remember the CAS ID for the key. To update with "compare and set," you call the `cas()` method on a key previously retrieved using `gets()`. Arguments for these methods are similar to `get()` and `set()`. There are no function-style equivalents to these `Client` methods because the methods store the CAS IDs for keys in the client instance:

```
memcache_client = memcache.Client()

# Attempt to append a string to a memcache value.
retries = 3
while retries > 0:
    retries -= 1
    value = memcache_client.gets(key) or ''
    value += 'MORE DATA!\n'
    if memcache_client.cas(key, value):
        break
```

The `Client` instance keeps track of all CAS IDs returned by calls to the `gets()` method. You can reset the client's CAS ID store by calling the `cas_reset()` method.

In the Java API, the `getIdentifiable()` method accepts a key, and returns the value and its CAS ID wrapped in an instance of the `MemcacheService.IdentifiableValue` class. You can access the value with its `getValue()` method. To perform a compare-and-set update, you call the `putIfUntouched()` method with the key, the original `MemcacheService.IdentifiableValue` instance, the new value, and an optional `Expiration` value. This method returns `true` on success:

```
MemcacheService.IdentifiableValue idValue;
int retries = 3;

// Attempt to append a string to a memcache value.
while (retries-- > 0) {
    idValue = memcache.getIdentifiable(key);
    String value = "";
    if (idValue != null) {
        value = (String) idValue.getValue();
    }
    value += "MORE DATA!\n";
    if (memcache.putIfUntouched(key, idValue, value)) {
        break;
    }
}
```

Batching Calls to Memcache

The memcache service includes batching versions of its API methods, so you can combine operations in a single remote procedure call. As with the datastore's batch API, this can save time in cases where the app needs to perform the same operation on multiple independent values. And as with the datastore, batching is not transactional: some operations may succeed while others fail. The total size of the batch call parameters can be up to 32 megabytes, as can the total size of the return values.

The details of the batch API differ between Python and Java, so we'll consider them separately.

Memcache Batch Calls in Python

The Python API includes separate batch functions for each operation, both as standalone functions and as `Client` methods. The names of the batch methods all end with `_multi`.

`set_multi()` sets multiple values. It takes a mapping of keys and values as its first argument, and an optional expiration `time` argument that applies to all values set. The method returns a list of keys *not* set. An empty list indicates that all values were set successfully:

```
value_dict = {}
for result in results:
    value_dict[key_for_result(result)] = result

keys_not_set = memcache.set_multi(value_dict)
if keys_not_set:
    # Keys in keys_not_set were not set...
```

`add_multi()` and `replace_multi()` behave similarly. They take a mapping argument and the optional `time` argument, and return a list of keys not set. As with `add()` and `replace()`, these methods may fail to set keys because they are already set, or are not set, respectively.

`get_multi()` takes a list of keys, and returns a mapping of keys to values for all keys that are set in memcache. If a provided key is not set, it is omitted from the result mapping:

```
value_dict = memcache.get_multi(keys)
for key in keys:
    if key not in value_dict:
        # key is unset...
    else:
        value = value_dict[key]
        # ...
```

`delete_multi()` takes a list of keys, and an optional `seconds` argument to lock all the keys from adds for a period of time. The method returns `True` if all keys were deleted successfully or are already unset, or False if any of the keys could not be deleted. Unlike delete(), delete_multi() does not distinguish between a successful delete and an unset key:

```
success = memcache.delete_multi(keys)
```

Batch increments and decrements are handled by a single method, offset_multi(). This method takes a mapping of keys to delta values, where positive delta values are increments and negative delta values are decrements. You can also provide a single initial_value argument, which applies to all keys in the mapping. The return value is a mapping of keys to updated values. If a key could not be incremented, its value in the result mapping is None:

```
increments = {}
for key in keys:
    increments[key] = increment_for_key(key)

value_dict = memcache.offset_multi(increments, initial_value=0)
```

To get multiple values for later use with "compare and set," you call the get_multi() method with an additional argument: for_cas=True. This returns a mapping of results just as it would without this argument, but it also stores the CAS IDs in the Client:

```
memcache_client = memcache.Client()

value_dict = memcache_client.get_multi(keys, for_cas=True)
```

To batch "compare and set" multiple values, you call the cas_multi() method with a mapping of keys and their new values. As with the other methods that update values, this method returns a list of keys not set successfully, with an empty list indicating success for all keys. If a key was not updated because it was updated since it was last retrieved, the key appears in the result list:

```
keys_not_set = memcache_client.cas_multi(value_dict)
```

Each Python batch function takes an optional key_prefix argument, a bytestring value. If provided, this prefix is prepended to every key sent to the service, and removed from every key returned by the service. This is useful as an inexpensive way to partition values. Note that key prefixes are distinct from namespaces:

```
prefix = 'alphabeta:'

value_dict = {'key1': 'value1',
              'key2': 'value2',
              'key3': 'value3'}
# Set 'alphabeta:key1', 'alphabeta:key2', 'alphabeta:key3'.
memcache.set_multi(value_dict, key_prefix=prefix)

keys = ['key1', 'key2', 'key3']
value_dict = memcache.get_multi(keys, key_prefix=prefix)
# value_dict['key1'] == 'value1'
# ('alphabeta:' does not appear in the value_dict keys.)
```

Memcache Batch Calls in Java

The Java API includes methods to perform operations in batches.

The `<T> putAll()` method takes a `java.util.Map` of keys and values, where `T` is the key type. As with `put()`, other forms of this method accept optional `Expiration` and `SetPolicy` values. The three-argument form of this method returns a `java.util.Set<T>` containing all the keys *not* set by the call. If the set is empty, then all keys were set successfully. (Without both an `Expiration` and the `SetPolicy` arguments, the method's return type is `void`.)

```
import java.util.HashMap;
import java.util.Map;
import java.util.Set;

// ...
        Map<String, String> valueMap = new HashMap<String, String>();
        Set<String> keysNotSet = memcache.putAll(valueMap);
        if (!keysNotSet.isEmpty()) {
            // Keys in keysNotSet were not set...
        }
```

The `getAll()` method takes a `java.util.Collection<T>` of keys, and returns a `Map<T, Object>` of keys and values that are set. If a provided key is not set, then it is omitted from the result `Map`:

```
        Map<String, Object> values = memcache.getAll(keys);
```

The `incrementAll()` method takes a `java.util.Collection<T>` of keys and an amount to change each value (a positive or negative `long`). Another form of the method takes an initial value as a third argument, which is used for all keys. The method returns a `Map<T, Long>` containing keys and updated values for all keys set or incremented successfully:

```
        Map<String, Long> newValues = memcache.incrementAll(keys, 1);

        newValues = memcache.incrementAll(keys, 10L, 0L);
```

To get multiple values that can be used with "compare and set" in a batch, you call the `getIdentifiables()` method (with the plural s at the end of the method name). It takes a `Collection` of keys and returns a `Map` of keys to `MemcacheService.IdentifiableValue` instances:

```
        Map<String, MemcacheService.IdentifiableValue> values;
        values = memcache.getIdentifiables(keys);

        // Get a value for key k from the result map.
        String v = (String) (values.get(k).getValue());
```

The `putIfUntouched()` method has a batch calling form for performing a "compare and set" with multiple values. It takes a `Map` of keys to instances of the wrapper class `MemcacheService.CasValues`, each of which holds the original `MemcacheService.IdentifiableValue`, the new value, and an optional `Expiration`. You can also provide an optional

Expiration to putIfUntouched(), which applies to all values in the batch. The return value is the Set of keys that was stored successfully:

```
MemcacheService.IdentifiableValue oldIdentValue1;
// ...

Map<String, MemcacheService.CasValues> updateMap =
    new HashMap<String, MemcacheService.CasValues>();
updateMap.put(key1, new MemcacheService.CasValues(oldIdentValue1, newValue1));
// ...

Set<String> successKeys = memcache.putIfUntouched(updateMap);
```

Memcache and the Datastore

The most common use of the memcache on App Engine is as a fast access layer in front of the datastore. We've discussed the general pattern several times already: when the app needs to fetch an entity by key, it checks the cache first, and if it's not there, it fetches from the datastore and puts it in the cache for later. This exchanges potential update latency (cached data may be old) for access speed. The memcache is well suited for this purpose: it can use datastore entity keys as keys, and serialized datastore entity structures as values.

In Java, caching a datastore entity is a simple matter of making sure your entity class is Serializable. The Entity class of the low-level datastore API is already Serializable, as are all property value types. If you're using JPA, you can usually just declare that your model class implements Serializable. The resulting memcache value contains the data in the properties of your entity, or the fields of your model class.

In Python, using ext.db, you could just drop an instance of a db.Model subclass into the memcache. The memcache library will use pickle to convert the instance to a memcache value, and convert it back when you fetch it. This works, and this is what we did in Chapter 2. However, pickle will attempt to serialize the entire object, including temporary data structures internal to the db.Model class. This wastes space and risks the value being incompatible with future changes to the internal logic of the class.

One solution to this problem is to use the db.to_dict() function. This function takes a model instance and returns a mapping of property names to property values for the instance. You can reconstruct the model instance from this mapping by using your model's class constructor. Note that the mapping does not include the key, so you'll need to take care of that separately. The following code updates the example from Chapter 2 to use this technique:

```
from google.appengine.api import memcache
from google.appengine.ext import db

class UserPrefs(db.Model):
    tz_offset = db.IntegerProperty(default=0)
    user = db.UserProperty(auto_current_user_add=True)
```

```
def get_userprefs(user_id):
    userprefs = None
    userprefs_dict = memcache.get('UserPrefs:' + user_id)
    userprefs_key = db.Key.from_path('UserPrefs', user_id)
    if userprefs_dict:
        userprefs = UserPrefs(key=userprefs_key, **userprefs_dict)
    else:
        userprefs = db.get(userprefs_key)
        if userprefs:
            memcache.set(
                'UserPrefs:' + self.key().name(),
                db.to_dict(userprefs))
        else:
            userprefs = UserPrefs(key_name=user_id)

    return userprefs
```

Handling Memcache Errors

By default, if the memcache service is unavailable or there is an error accessing the service, the memcache API behaves as if keys do not exist. Attempts to set, add, or replace values report failure as if the put failed due to the set policy. Attempts to get values will behave as cache misses.

In the Java API, you can change this behavior by installing an alternate error handler. The `setErrorHandler()` method of `MemcacheService` takes an object that implements the `ErrorHandler` interface. Two such implementations are provided: `LogAndContinueErrorHandler` and `StrictErrorHandler`. The default is `LogAndContinueErrorHandler` with its log level set to `FINE` (the "debug" level in the Administration Console). `StrictErrorHandler` throws `MemcacheServiceException` for all transient service errors:

```
import com.google.appengine.api.memcache.StrictErrorHandler;

// ...
        memcache.setErrorHandler(new StrictErrorHandler());
```

Error handlers can have custom responses for invalid values and service errors. Other kinds of exceptions thrown by the API behave as usual.

Memcache Administration

With the memcache service playing such an important role in the health and wellbeing of your application, it's important to understand how your app is using it under real-world conditions. App Engine provides a Memcache Viewer in the Administration Console, which shows you up-to-date statistics about your app's memcache data, and lets you query values by key. You can also delete the entire contents of the cache from this panel, a drastic but sometimes necessary act.

The viewer displays the number of hits (successful attempts to get a value), the number of misses (attempts to get a value using a key that was unset), and the ratio of these numbers. The raw numbers are roughly over the lifetime of the app, but it's the ratio that's the more useful number: the higher the hit ratio, the more time is being saved by using a cached value instead of performing a slower query or calculation.

Also shown is the total number of items and the total size of all items. These numbers mostly serve as vague insight into the overall content of the cache. They don't apply to any fixed limits or billable quotas, and there's no need to worry if these numbers are large. Understanding the average item size might be useful if you're troubleshooting why small items used less frequently than very large items are getting evicted.

A particularly interesting statistic is the "oldest item age." This is a bit of a misnomer: it's actually the amount of time since the last access of the least recently accessed item, not the full age of that item. Under moderate load, this value approximates the amount of time a value can go without being accessed before it is evicted from the cache to make room for hotter items. You can think of it as a lower bound on the usefulness of the cache. Note that more popular cache items live longer than less popular ones, so this age refers to the least popular item in the cache.

You can use the Memcache Viewer to query, create, and modify a value in the memcache, if you have the key. The Python and Java APIs let you use any serializable data type for keys, and the Viewer can't support all possible types, so this feature is only good for some key types. String keys are supported for Python, Java, and Go apps. You can also query keys of several Java primitive types, such an integers. Similarly, updating values from the Viewer is limited to several data types, including bytestrings, Unicode text strings, Booleans, and integers.

Lastly, the Memcache Viewer has a big scary button to flush the cache, evicting (deleting) all of its values. Hopefully you've engineered your app to not depend on a value being available in the cache, and clicking this button would only inconvenience the app while it reloads values from primary storage or other computation. But for an app of significant size under moderate traffic with a heavy reliance on the cache, flushing the cache can be disruptive. You may need this button to clear out data inconsistencies caused by a bug after deploying a fix (for example), but you may want to schedule the flush during a period of low traffic.

The Python development server includes a version of the memcache viewer in the development console, so you can inspect statistics, query specific (string) keys, and flush the contents of the simulated memcache service. With your development server running, visit the development console (`/_ah/admin`), then select Memcache Viewer from the sidebar. As of version 1.7.0, the Java development server does not yet have a memcache viewer.

Cache Statistics

The memcache statistics shown in the Administration Console are also available to your app through a simple API.

In Python, you fetch memcache statistics with the `get_stats()` method. This method returns a dictionary containing the statistics:

```
import logging

stats = memcache.get_stats()

logging.info('Memcache statistics:')
for stat in stats.iteritems():
    logging.info('%s = %d' % stat)
```

In Java, you call the `getStatistics()` service method. This returns an instance of the `Stats` class, a read-only object with getters for each of the statistics.

Available statistics include the following:

`hits` / `getHitCount()`
: The number of cache hits counted.

`misses` / `getMissCount()`
: The number of cache misses counted.

`items` / `getItemCount()`
: The number of items currently in the cache.

`bytes` / `getTotalItemBytes()`
: The total size of items currently in the cache.

`byte_hits` / `getBytesReturnsForHits()`
: The total of bytes returned in response to cache hits, including keys and values.

`oldest_item_age` / `getMaxTimeWithoutAccess()`
: The amount of time since the last access of the least recently accessed item in the cache, in milliseconds.

Flushing the Memcache

You can delete every item in the memcache for your app, using a single API call. Just like the button in the Administration Console, this action is all or nothing: there is no way to flush a subset of keys, beyond deleting known keys individually or in a batch call.

If your app makes heavy use of memcache to front-load datastore entities, keep in mind that flushing the cache may cause a spike in datastore traffic and slower request handlers as your app reloads the cache.

To flush the cache in Python, you call the `flush_all()` function. It returns `True` on success:

```
memcache.flush_all()
```

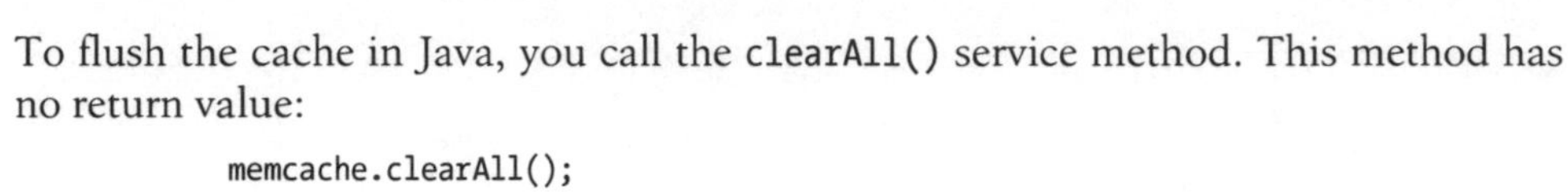

To flush the cache in Java, you call the `clearAll()` service method. This method has no return value:

```
memcache.clearAll();
```

CHAPTER 12

Large Data and the Blobstore

App Engine limits the sizes of chunks of data that can be passed between the clients, application instances, and services. Incoming requests and outgoing responses cannot exceed 32 megabytes, datastore entities and memcache values cannot contain more than 1 megabyte, and services limit API calls and responses to sizes ranging between 1 and 32 megabytes, depending on the service. These limits help App Engine maintain a responsive infrastructure at a large scale. Google has managed to increase some of these limits by improving and tuning its infrastructure, but the role of limits remains.

1 megabyte data entities and 32 megabyte requests and responses are generous for many purposes, but insufficient for others. Images, audio, video, and large data applications such as scientific computing often involve transmitting and manipulating larger units. Even if most of your user-oriented transactions are small, administrative tasks such as backups and data aggregation can get hefty.

The App Engine Blobstore is a specialized service for creating, manipulating, and serving very large amounts of data. The size of a single Blobstore value is unlimited. (Or rather, it's limited only by your budget.) Your app can accept a large file as a user upload, serve a Blobstore value in response to a request, create a new Blobstore value, or append to or delete an existing one. An app can also read from a Blobstore value, a portion at a time.

For the same reasons other services have limits, the way apps interact with the Blobstore is also limited. An app can only read 32 megabytes from a Blobstore value with a single API call. If it needs more, it must make multiple calls. Appending to values is similarly constrained.

However, the Blobstore has a special relationship with the frontend, such that much larger values can be served as responses to requests, or accepted from users as uploads. Your app manages these interactions, using a combination of response headers, Blobstore-specific upload URLs, and standard browser protocols. The app can serve a Blobstore value in response to any request by setting a response header. The frontend intercepts the header, and pipes the value directly from the Blobstore to the client. The data does not pass through the application instance.

An app can also accept a new Blobstore value by using a standard web form's file upload widget, or from any client that behaves similarly (using a PUT request with MIME multipart data). The app calls the Blobstore API to generate a unique short-lived upload URL for the form. When the user submits the form, the file upload fields are routed directly to the Blobstore to become large Blobstore values, and the rest of the form data becomes a request for the app itself. The app gets an opportunity to accept or reject the value, and can preemptively set certain limits on what the Blobstore will accept.

Blobstore values are simple, potentially large, chunks of data. They have no structure that is used by the service, and cannot be queried directly with a service call. Each value has a Blobstore key. For easier retrieval of keys, the Blobstore interacts with the datastore to store metadata about its values in datastore entities. These entities can be referred to in your own data models, and queried for metadata properties (such as size). They can even be deleted: deleting the datastore entity deletes the corresponding Blobstore value.

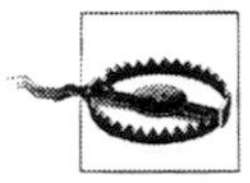

Careful not to confuse Blobstore values and the name for the bytestring value type in the datastore API ("blob"). These are not related. We'll try to use the term "Blobstore value" consistently, but be aware that the Blobstore API sometimes uses the word "blob" to mean "Blobstore value."

In this chapter, we walk through the features of the Blobstore, such as accepting large files from users with a web form, managing the values with the datastore, and serving them back to users. We also discuss creating, appending to, and reading byte ranges from values in application code. This chapter also presents a complete example app, in Python and Java, for a simple private file storage service. You can download the complete code for the example apps from the book's website (*http://www.dansanderson.com/appengine*).

Accepting User Uploads

The Blobstore was originally designed as a way to accept file uploads from users, such as for photo sharing or document management services. The mechanism for accepting large data in requests is compatible with how browsers submit file uploads from web forms, by using MIME multipart messages in a POST request. You can also implement this standard protocol in a custom client.

Because the POST request may exceed the request size limit for an application server, the request must go to a special URL known to the frontend as intended for the Blobstore. Your app creates this URL by calling the Blobstore API. When the frontend receives a request at this URL, it recognizes the file uploads and directs them to the Blobstore to become Blobstore values. If the data contains multiple such parts, multiple Blobstore values are created. Then the data portions of these parts are removed from the request, the parts are annotated with Blobstore information (such as the Blobstore key for the new value), and the annotated request is passed to a "success" request handler for further processing. You tell App Engine which request handler URL to use when you generate the Blobstore upload URL.

You can specify size limits on the expected user uploads when you call the API to create the upload URL. App Engine will reject a request with an individual value or total size exceeding the limits you set. If the request doesn't meet these requirements or is otherwise malformed, App Engine responds with a generic HTTP 500 server error status code. In this case, no Blobstore values are created, and the app's request handler is not invoked.

The upload URL is randomly generated and difficult to guess, it can only be used once, and it must be used within 10 minutes of when it is created. It otherwise has no restrictions. If the user is uploading private data that ought to be associated with her account, or if the user must otherwise be signed in to upload files, the request handler must check for these conditions, and delete inappropriate uploaded Blobstore values, if any. Cookies are preserved on the rewritten request. Note that merely restricting access to the upload request handler URL in *app.yaml* is not enough to prevent Blobstore values from being created.

The request handler can do whatever it wants in response to the posted form. A best practice is to reply to the client with an HTTP redirect, using status code 302 and a `Location` header of another URL. This prevents browsers from allowing the accidental resubmission of the form if the user navigates through their browser history (such as with the "back" button). This also prevents the rather weird-looking generated Blobstore URL from appearing in the browser's address bar.

Using the "back" button to return to a simple form whose action in a Blobstore upload URL can be problematic. A Blobstore upload URL expires after its first use, and a subsequent submission to that URL results in a 404 Not Found error response served by the Blobstore. If your users are likely to use the "back" button after submitting a form in order to submit the form again, you may want to use JavaScript to call the app and regenerate the form each time it is viewed. (The 302 Redirect only prevents the browser's "Do you want to resubmit?" message, it does not prevent the user from viewing the form again from the browser history.)

Blobstore values are created before your request handler is called. If your app decides it does not want the values, it must delete them. Furthermore, if there is an error during the execution of the request handler, the Blobstore values will remain.

Before we see the APIs for processing uploads in Python and Java, let's take a quick look at the underlying protocol. Understanding the protocol is useful when adapting these instructions to your web application framework of choice.

Web Forms and MIME Multipart Data

Here is HTML for a typical web form, with a file upload field:

```
<form action="/my-upload-url" method="post" enctype="multipart/form-data">
  <label for="title">Title:</label>
  <input type="text" id="title" name="title" /><br />
  <label for="upload">File:</label>
  <input type="file" id="upload" name="upload" /><br />
  <input type="submit" value="Upload File" />
</form>
```

This form describes three form widgets: a text field, a file upload field, and a submit button. Figure 12-1 shows what this form looks like in Chrome on a Mac.

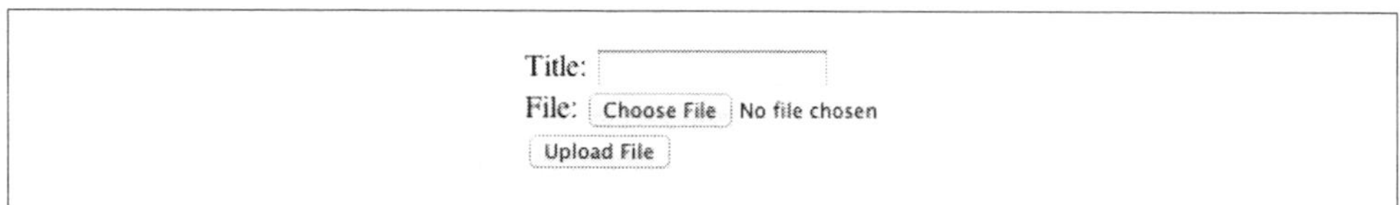

Figure 12-1. A simple web form, with a text field, a file upload field, and a submit button

When the user clicks the "Upload File" button, the browser assembles the data entered into the form fields (if any) into a request to the URL declared in the `action` attribute of the `<form>` element, in this case `/my-upload-url`. The request uses the HTTP method POST, which is set in the `method` attribute.

The request includes a `Content-Type` header that tells the server how to interpret the rest of the data. Its value has two parts: a declaration that the body of the request is a MIME multipart value, and the *boundary* string used to delimit the parts. The client generates a random boundary string that it knows does not appear in the data of any of the parts. For example:

```
Content-Type: multipart/form-data;
boundary=----WebKitFormBoundaryBv22aFA2OgESR2pT
```

(This would appear without a line break in the request header text.) The request also includes the header `Mime-Version: 1.0`, which allows for future revisions of the MIME message protocol.

> The `enctype="multipart/form-data"` attribute of the `<form>` element is required for forms with one or more file upload fields. Without it, the form data is sent with the simpler content type of `application/x-www-form-urlencoded`, and the value of the file upload field becomes just the filename, without the file contents.

The request body consists of one or more parts. Each part consists of two hyphens (`--`), the boundary string, an end-of-line sequence (a carriage return followed by a newline), zero or more header lines, a blank line, and the part body, followed by one more end-of-line sequence. The entire request body ends with two hyphens, the boundary string, and two more hyphens.

For example, the web form above might produce a request body like so:

```
------WebKitFormBoundaryBv22aFA20gESR2pT
Content-Type: text/plain
MIME-Version: 1.0
Content-Disposition: form-data; name="title"

The value of the title field
------WebKitFormBoundaryBv22aFA20gESR2pT
Content-Type: application/octet-stream
MIME-Version: 1.0
Content-Length: 12345
Content-MD5: NzgyMGRkYTRjNTVmOThjODAyY2U2M2M1Y2ZkNjA2NzA=
Content-Type: application/octet-stream
Content-Disposition: form-data; name="upload"; filename="filename"

The content of the file
------WebKitFormBoundaryBv22aFA20gESR2pT--
```

Each field in the form that has a value becomes a message part. The name of the field appears in the `Content-Disposition` header of the part, and the value of the field is the part's body.

Multiple parts can have the same name. This occurs if the form has multiple fields of the same name and the fields have values. For example, you might give a set of checkboxes (of `type="checkbox"`) all the same name, so the selected checkboxes are grouped when the app reads the form data. If a file upload field (of `type="file"`) has the attribute `multiple="true"`, the browser will allow the user to select more than one file, and each file will appear as a separate part, using the name of the field.

A form field must have a value to appear as a part. How this behaves depends on the field type. For example, a checkbox widget only contributes a part to the request if it is checked. A file upload field only contributes a part if there is a file selected.

File parts have a `Content-Disposition` header that includes the name of the field as well as the filename of the upload, as reported by the browser. The browser also provides a `Content-Type` header, which it either gets from the filesystem or derives from the filename extension. For example:

```
Content-Disposition: form-data; name="upload"; filename="mypic.jpg"
Content-Type: image/jpeg
```

The header and body are separated by a blank line. The body itself is a stream of bytes that represents the content of the file, followed by the end-of-line sequence and the next boundary string (either beginning the next part or ending the request body).

Blobstore Upload Requests

We just saw what the request looks like when it arrives at the frontend. If the request URL (the form's action URL) is a Blobstore upload URL, the frontend juggles the data such that file upload parts go to the Blobstore, and the rest of the request goes to your app.

When handling a request to a Blobstore upload URL, App Engine processes the MIME multipart data looking for file upload fields, specifically parts where a filename="..." appears in the Content-Disposition header and a Content-Type header is provided. For each of these, App Engine creates a Blobstore value whose content is the body of the part. It also remembers the filename, the content type, and the date and time the file was uploaded. The Blobstore value is assigned a unique, randomly generated key.

App Engine then rewrites the request. The result is still in the MIME multipart format, with one part for each field with a value. App Engine generates a new boundary string to make sure it does not collide with anything in the rewritten request. Parts without filenames are otherwise left intact.

Parts with filenames are replaced with new data that indicates the actual data for the part is now in the Blobstore. The new data includes the Blobstore key for the value, as well as everything else it knows about the value. For example:

```
--===============1986177482156009064==
Content-Type: message/external-body; blob-key="UKtO9ITADgRVeO_WZDdz2w==";
  access-type="X-AppEngine-BlobKey"
MIME-Version: 1.0
Content-Disposition: form-data; name="upload"; filename="mypic.jpg"

Content-Type: image/jpeg
MIME-Version: 1.0
Content-Length: 733
Content-MD5: ZjIyMzY3MDIyYTViMWEzYzZiNzYwNjhhZjMwMWI2YTQ=
content-type: image/jpeg
content-disposition: form-data; name="upload"; filename="mypic.jpg"
X-AppEngine-Upload-Creation: 2012-01-18 22:45:06.980751


--===============1986177482156009064==--
```

As shown, the Blobstore key appears in the Content-Type header for the part, as blob-key="...". The body of the part now includes more header-like information, such as the MD5 hash and creation date and time. This region ends with two blank lines, which any MIME message parser would recognize as an empty body. (The additional header information is actually in the body of this part, but you could further parse this body data as a MIME message.)

That's all you need to know about web forms and the Blobstore. Let's look at some common ways to implement the web form and upload request handler, first in Python, then in Java.

Handling Uploads in Python

To generate a Blobstore upload URL in Python, call the `create_upload_url()` function in the `blobstore` module, which is in the `google.appengine.ext` package. (Note the `ext` in the package path, not `api`. There is a `google.appengine.api.blobstore` module, but `ext` provides a few additional features, which we'll use later.)

Here's a simple request handler for rendering an upload form using a Jinja2 template. Since we know we'll need it in a moment, we'll also include the upload handler, which for now just redirects back to the main page without doing anything special with the Blobstore data:

```
import jinja2
import os
import webapp2
from google.appengine.ext import blobstore

template_env = jinja2.Environment(
    loader=jinja2.FileSystemLoader(os.getcwd()))

class MainPage(webapp2.RequestHandler):
    def get(self):
        upload_url = blobstore.create_upload_url('/upload')

        template = template_env.get_template('home.html')
        context = {
            'upload_url': upload_url,
        }
        self.response.write(template.render(context))

class UploadHandler(webapp2.RequestHandler):
    def post(self):
        self.redirect('/')

application = webapp2.WSGIApplication([('/', MainPage),
                                       ('/upload', UploadHandler)],
                                      debug=True)
```

The web form itself is defined in the template, which in this example is named *home.html*:

```
<html>
  <head>
    <title>Blobstore Demo</title>
  </head>
  <body>
     <form action="{{ upload_url }}" method="post" enctype="multipart/form-data">
      <label for="title">Title:</label>
      <input type="text" name="title" id="title" /><br />
      <label for="upload">File:</label>
      <input type="file" name="upload" id="upload" /><br />
      <input type="submit" value="Upload File" />
    </form>
```

```
    </body>
  </html>
```

The `create_upload_url()` function takes the URL path to a request handler as its first argument. Without additional arguments, the upload URL it generates accepts file uploads of any size. You can restrict the size of an individual file, or the total size of the upload request, using the `max_bytes_per_blob` and `max_bytes_total` arguments, respectively. A request that exceeds either of these amounts is rejected by App Engine, and no Blobstore values are created.

The details of parsing the request data in your upload request handler depend on the web application framework you are using. All major frameworks provide a way to access multipart form data. (If for some reason you're stuck having to parse the MIME multipart request body yourself, look at the Python standard library's `cgi` module and its `FieldStorage` class.) Check your framework's documentation.

The webapp2 framework provides request data on the request handler's `self.request` object. This object is an instance of the `Request` class, provided by the open source library WebOb, included with App Engine. WebOb parses the request data into `self.request.params`, an object that maps field names to values. This object has `dict`-like features, with extensions that support multiple values with the same key. For example:

```
title = self.request.params['title']
multiple_uploads = self.request.params.getall('upload')

for key, value in self.request.params.items():
    # This loop may see the same key more than once.
    # ...
```

A Blobstore file upload field has a value that is an instance of the `cgi.FieldStorage` class. This value must be parsed further to extrapolate the information about the Blobstore value, so the API provides a function for that: `blobstore.parse_blob_info()`. This function returns an instance of the `BlobInfo` class:

```
for value in multiple_uploads:
    blob_info = blobstore.parse_blob_info(value)
    filename = blob_info.filename
```

Every Blobstore value has a corresponding datastore entity of the kind `'BlobInfo'`. The `BlobInfo` class is the `db.Model`-like class for these entities. `blobstore.parse_blob_info()` creates a `BlobInfo` object based on the request data, without actually accessing the datastore. We'll discuss `BlobInfo` objects in the next section.

webapp (the original, compatible version of webapp2) provides a slightly more convenient way to access file uploads, in the form of a base class for the request handler. This class is called `BlobstoreUploadHandler`, in the `blobstore_handlers` module of the `google.appengine.ext.webapp` package. The `get_uploads()` method of this class returns a list of `BlobInfo` objects:

```
from google.appengine.ext.webapp import blobstore_handlers
# ...

class UploadHandler(blobstore_handlers.BlobstoreUploadHandler):
    def post(self):
        blob_info_objects = self.get_uploads('upload')
        # ...
```

When you call `blobstore.create_upload_url()` in the development server, the server creates a datastore entity of the kind `__BlobUploadSession__`, which you'll see in the datastore viewer of the Console. When your app is running on App Engine, the Blobstore itself tracks these values and does not use datastore entities.

The development server doesn't clean these up, but leaving them around doesn't interfere with anything. You can use the `--clear_datastore` flag when you start the development server to clear all persistent data, including these entities and the corresponding Blobstore values. (See "The Development Server and the Datastore" on page 148.)

Handling Uploads in Java

The Blobstore API in Java is in the package `com.google.appengine.api.blobstore`. As with other service APIs in Java, you access Blobstore functionality by calling methods on an object that implements the `BlobstoreService` interface. You get such an object by calling the static method `BlobstoreServiceFactory.getBlobstoreService()`:

```
import com.google.appengine.api.blobstore.BlobstoreService;
import com.google.appengine.api.blobstore.BlobstoreServiceFactory;

// ...
        BlobstoreService blobstoreService =
            BlobstoreServiceFactory.getBlobstoreService();
```

To generate a Blobstore upload URL, call the `createUploadUrl()` method. Its first argument is the URL path to a request handler, as a `String`:

```
        String uploadUrl = blobstoreService.createUploadUrl("/upload");
```

Without additional arguments, the upload URL it generates accepts file uploads of any size. You can restrict the size of an individual file, or the total size of the upload request, by passing an `UploadOptions` instance as a second argument. `UploadOptions` uses the Builder pattern, via `UploadOptions.Builder`, like so:

```
import com.google.appengine.api.blobstore.UploadOptions;

// ...
        UploadOptions uploadOptions = UploadOptions.Builder
                .withMaxUploadSizeBytesPerBlob(1024 * 1024 * 1024)
                .maxUploadSizeBytes(10 * 1024 * 1024 * 1024);
        String uploadUrl = blobstoreService.createUploadUrl("/upload", uploadOptions);
```

This example generates a Blobstore upload URL that accepts an upload request up to 10 gigabytes in size, where each file part can be at most 1 gigabyte in size. A request that exceeds either of these amounts is rejected by App Engine, and no Blobstore values are created.

The `HttpServletRequest` object itself doesn't offer much help for parsing multipart form data, but there are various libraries and frameworks that can help (such as Apache Struts). To keep things easy, the Blobstore API itself includes a request parser for extracting Blobstore keys from the processed upload request. The **`getUploads()`** method of `BlobstoreService` takes the `HttpServletRequest` and returns a `Map` of form field names to `List`s of `BlobKey` objects. (A form field may map to zero or more uploads, depending on whether the form accepts multiple files for a single upload field, and how the user completed the form.) Each `BlobKey` object wraps the string form of the key that appears in the `blob-key` part of the `Content-Type` header:

```
import java.util.List;
import java.util.Map;
import com.google.appengine.api.blobstore.BlobKey;

// ...
        Map<String, List<BlobKey>> blobFields = blobstoreService.getUploads(req);
        List<BlobKey> blobKeys = blobFields.get("upload");
        BlobKey blobKey = null;
        if (blobKeys != null && !blobKeys.isEmpty()) {
            // We're only expecting one, so take the first one.
            blobKey = blobKeys.get(0);
        }
```

When you call `blobstoreService.createUploadUrl(()` in the development server, the server creates a datastore entity of the kind `__BlobUploadSession__`, which you'll see in the datastore viewer of the Console. When your app is running on App Engine, the Blobstore itself tracks these values and does not use datastore entities. The development server doesn't clean these up, but leaving them around doesn't interfere with anything.

Using BlobInfo Entities

The Blobstore remembers a set of metadata properties about each value. These properties include the generated Blobstore key, the date and time the value was created, the content type and filename reported by the client, and the size and MD5 hash of the uploaded value.

The Blobstore maintains a read-only entity in the datastore for each value, known in the API as a BlobInfo entity. The datastore kind name for these entities is `__BlobInfo__` (that's two underscores before and after), and each entity's key name is the Blobstore key. An entity represents the metadata for a value with entity properties. You can perform queries for BlobInfo entities by using the metadata properties. You can refer to BlobInfo entities in properties of other datastore entities by using the BlobInfo entity's key, just like any other entity key.

Naturally, the BlobInfo entities do not pretend to contain the Blobstore values themselves, and you cannot perform queries on the data in the values. The result of a BlobInfo query is zero or more BlobInfo entities, which you can trace back to Blobstore values using Blobstore keys stored in the entities. And since these entities are read-only, you cannot modify the properties, or save BlobInfo entities back to the datastore.

We've already seen how to build a BlobInfo object in the upload request handler using just the request information. This action does not access the datastore, but it does build the same BlobInfo object that would be returned by the datastore for the value.

The development console (*http://localhost:8080/_ah/admin*, where 8080 is your development server's port) does not have an explicit "Blobstore viewer" feature. However, you can use the datastore viewer to inspect __BlobInfo__ entities. This entry kind appears in the datastore viewer after your app creates its first Blobstore value. Deleting a `__BlobInfo__` entity in this interface will also delete the Blobstore value.

When your app is running on App Engine, the kind `__BlobInfo__` does not appear in the list of kinds in the Datastore Viewer. But you can perform GQL queries on this kind in the Viewer. The Administration Console also features a Blob Viewer, which you can use to browse and delete Blobstore values.

Using BlobInfo Entities in Python

In Python, the `blobstore` module in the `google.appengine.ext` package provides a `BlobInfo` class. Instances of this class behave like a `db.Model` class, but disallow the updating of properties or saving of the entity. The class also manages the special kind name behind the scenes, and provides a couple of Blobstore-specific features.

The Blobstore metadata properties are simply attributes of the object:

content_type
: The MIME content type (a `str`).

creation
: The date and time the value was created (a `datetime.datetime`).

filename
: The filename provided with the upload.

size
: The size of the value, in bytes (an `int`).

The `key()` method of a `BlobInfo` instance returns the Blobstore key for the value, in the form of a `BlobKey` object. This class (also defined in `google.appengine.ext.blobstore`) can convert between the key value and a web-safe string. `str(key)` evaluates to the string, and BlobKey(key_str) makes a new BlobKey value for that key. This is the same key string that you see in the blob-key part of the upload request's Content-Type. We'll see this again in the next section on serving Blobstore values.

Because BlobInfo entities are read-only, if you want to associate additional data with a Blobstore value, you must use another datastore entity, and store the BlobKey object in one of its properties. BlobKey objects are fundamental value types in the datastore, and can be stored directly in a property.

You can model this property in a db.Model, using the blobstore.BlobReferenceProperty class. (Refer back to Chapter 9 for information about db.Model.) Similar to db.ReferenceProperty attributes, an attribute modeled as a BlobReferenceProperty can be treated as the BlobInfo object it represents. The BlobInfo object is fetched from the datastore when its attributes are accessed for the first time.

Here's an example of an upload handler that creates a UserUpload entity in the datastore that associates the signed-in user with the Blobstore value via the key. Another handler can render a page of the files the user has uploaded by querying the UserUpload entities:

```
import webapp2
from google.appengine.api import users
from google.appengine.ext import blobstore
from google.appengine.ext import db
from google.appengine.ext.webapp import blobstore_handlers
# ...

class UserUpload(db.Model):
    user = db.UserProperty()
    blob = blobstore.BlobReferenceProperty()

class UploadHandler(blobstore_handlers.BlobstoreUploadHandler):
    def post(self):
        for blob_info in self.get_uploads('upload'):
            upload = UserUpload(user=users.get_current_user(),
                                blob=blob_info.key())
            upload.put()
        self.redirect('/')

class MyUploadsPage(webapp2.RequestHandler):
    def get(self):
        user = users.get_current_user()
        for upload in UserUpload.all().filter('user =', user):
            filename = upload.blob.filename
            # ...
```

BlobInfo entities can be queried directly by using the same methods as with other db.Model classes. As we saw in Chapter 6, the all() returns a query object for all BlobInfo entities, and this query can be refined further using the query object's filter() and order() methods:

```
# Query for all Blobstore values > 1 gigabyte in size.
q = blobstore.BlobInfo.all().filter('size >',
                                    1024 * 1024 * 1024)
```

```
for result in q:
    filename = result.filename
    # ...
```

The gql() method lets you prepare a similar query, using GQL string syntax:

```
# Query for all Blobstore values > 1 gigabyte in size.
q = blobstore.BlobInfo.gql('WHERE size > 1073741824')
for result in q:
    filename = result.filename
    # ...
```

Using BlobInfo Entities in Java

In Java, the BlobInfo class in the com.google.appengine.api.blobstore package represents the metadata for a Blobstore value. You use accessors to get the fields:

getContentType()
: The MIME content type (a String).

getCreation()
: The date and time the value was created (a java.util.Date).

getFilename()
: The filename provided with the upload.

getSize()
: The size of the value, in bytes (a long).

You get BlobInfo objects with a BlobInfoFactory. This factory uses the datastore for querying BlobInfo data. If you have a custom implementation of the DatastoreService (such as in a stubbed testing environment), you can pass it to the BlobInfoFactory constructor. But typically you'd just use the default constructor, with no arguments:

```
BlobInfoFactory blobInfoFactory = new BlobInfoFactory();
```

You can get a BlobInfo instance given a BlobKey instance, such as those returned by blobstoreService.getUploads(req) in the upload request handler. The blobInfoFactory.loadBlobInfo() method takes a BlobKey and performs a datastore fetch to get the metadata for the value:

```
// BlobKey blobKey;
BlobInfo blobInfo = blobInfoFactory.loadBlobInfo(blobKey);
```

To perform a query of Blobstore value metadata, you perform a datastore query using the low-level datastore API. (See Chapter 6.) The kind and field names are available as constants in the BlobInfoFactory class: KIND, CONTENT_TYPE, CREATION, FILENAME, and SIZE. You can convert each Entity result to a BlobInfo instance using the blobInfoFactory.createBlobInfo() method:

```
// Query for all Blobstore values > 1 gigabyte in size.
DatastoreService ds = DatastoreServiceFactory.getDatastoreService();
Query q = new Query(BlobInfoFactory.KIND);
```

```
q.addFilter(BlobInfoFactory.SIZE,
  Query.FilterOperator.GREATER_THAN,
  1024L * 1024L * 1024L);

PreparedQuery pq = ds.prepare(q);
Iterable<Entity> results = pq.asIterable();
for (Entity result : results) {
    BlobInfo blobInfo = blobInfoFactory.createBlobInfo(result);

    // ...
}
```

Serving Blobstore Values

An application can serve a Blobstore value in response to any request. It does so by setting a special header on the response whose value is the Blobstore key. The frontend recognizes this header, and instead of the body set by the request handler, it streams the value directly out of the Blobstore to the client. As with uploads, the app code never sees a byte of the Blobstore value.

Note that the app can respond this way to any request. Unlike upload URLs, which are special URLs generated by the Blobstore API, the app can define its own scheme for when and where to serve Blobstore values. Combined with upload handlers that redirect immediately to an app URL, the user never sees an App Engine-generated URL in the address bar of the browser. Furthermore, the app can decide to not serve a Blobstore value but instead generate its own response for any URL, if the situation warrants it.

The header to set is named `X-AppEngine-BlobKey`. Its value is the string form of the Blobstore key, similar to the `blob-key` in the upload request header, and which the app can get from the BlobInfo entity.

The app is responsible for setting other headers that go with the content, especially `Content-Type`. While the Blobstore records the content type declared by the client that uploaded the value, it's up to the app to decide whether to trust it and serve it, or to use another type.

If you're serving a file that a browser ought to save as a file instead of attempt to view, set the `Content-Disposition` header on the response. This header can suggest a filename to the browser, which can be the filename used for the original upload, or another name:

```
Content-Disposition: attachment; filename=YourPhotos.zip
```

Without further information, the frontend serves the entire value. The app can instruct the frontend to serve only a range of bytes from the value in response to the request. This is useful when responding to requests that ask for a byte range with the `Range` header, or when it's otherwise needed to send parts of a value in separate requests. To send a partial value, the app sets the X-AppEngine-BlobRange header on the response. Its value is a starting index, an ending index, or both, separated by the hyphen, where the first byte of the value is 0. For example, 0-499 sends the first 500 bytes, as does -499. 500- sends all bytes starting with the 501st.

When serving a partial value, the frontend uses HTTP status code 206 Partial Content. If the range is invalid for the value, it serves HTTP status code 416 Requested Range Not Satisfiable.

Serving Blobstore Values in Python

Continuing the Python example from this chapter, here's a new request handler that takes the string form of the key for a UserUpload datastore entity as a query parameter, verifies that the user making the request is the user who uploaded the file, and then serves the Blobstore value. It serves the value with the same Content-Type that was declared with the upload, which we trust in this case because the user uploaded the file in the first place:

```
class ViewHandler(webapp2.RequestHandler):
    def get(self):
        user = users.get_current_user()
        upload_key_str = self.request.params.get('key')
        upload = None
        if upload_key_str:
            upload = db.get(upload_key_str)

        if (not user or not upload or upload.user != user):
            self.error(404)
            return

        self.response.headers['X-AppEngine-BlobKey'] = str(upload.blob.key())
        self.response.headers['Content-Type'] = str(upload.blob.content_type)
```

As written, this handler ignores the Range header in the request, if one was provided, and just serves the entire Blobstore value. You can implement this directly in the handler, checking self.request.headers['Range'] and setting self.response.headers['X-AppEngine-BlobRange'] appropriately. (Don't forget to validate the request data.)

Alternatively, webapp includes a handler base class that can take care of this automatically, named BlobstoreDownloadHandler in the blobstore_handlers module of the google.appengine.ext.webapp package. The handler also sets Content-Type from the BlobInfo automatically, if the app doesn't override it. To use it, simply subclass it, and then call the self.send_blob() method from your get() handler.

Here's an improved version of ViewHandler using BlobstoreDownloadHandler that supports Range requests:

```
from google.appengine.ext.webapp import blobstore_handlers
# ...

class ViewHandler(blobstore_handlers.BlobstoreDownloadHandler):
```

```
    def get(self):
        user = users.get_current_user()
        upload_key_str = self.request.params.get('key')
        upload = None
        if upload_key_str:
            upload = db.get(upload_key_str)

        if (not user or not upload or upload.user != user):
            self.error(404)
            return

        self.send_blob(upload.blob)
```

Serving Blobstore Values in Java

Given a `BlobKey` object or a Blobstore key string, a Java app can send the corresponding Blobstore value in response to any request by setting the `X-AppEngine-BlobKey` header in the response. The app can do this directly by calling the `setHeader()` method on the `HttpServletRequest`, but there's an easier way. The `BlobstoreService` instance provides a `serve()` method that modifies the response to serve a Blobstore value.

The `serve()` method takes a `BlobKey` and the `HttpServletResponse` object, and sets the appropriate headers on the response, including the `Content-Type`:

```
        blobstoreService.serve(blobKey, res);
```

You can tell the method to serve just a portion of the value. `serve()` can accept a properly formatted HTTP range string as its second argument (the `HttpServletResponse` is the third). It can also accept an instance of the `ByteRange` class, provided by the `blob store` package, and it'll handle the formatting of the `Content-Range` header itself:

```
import com.google.appengine.api.blobstore.ByteRange;

// ...
        // Serve the first 500 bytes.
        blobstoreService.serve(blobKey, "0-499", res);

        // Serve the first 500 bytes.
        ByteRange byteRange = new ByteRange(0, 499);
        blobstoreService.serve(blobKey, byteRange, res);

        // Serve all bytes after the first 500.
        ByteRange byteRange = new ByteRange(500);
        blobstoreService.serve(blobKey, byteRange, res);
```

A client can ask for a specific byte range (such as when resuming a large download) by specifying the `Range` header in the request. To honor this request, your app must validate the header and set the range in the response. The `BlobstoreService` includes another convenience method for this purpose: `getByteRange()` takes the `HttpServletRequest` and returns a `ByteRange` suitable for passing to `serve()`. (This can be `null`, but that's OK: `serve()` will serve the entire value if the range argument is `null`.)

```
blobstoreService.serve(
        blobKey,
        blobstoreService.getByteRange(req),
        res);
```

Deleting Blobstore Values

There are two ways to delete a value from the Blobstore. The first is to call a method of the Blobstore API with the Blobstore key to delete. The second is to use the datastore API to delete the BlobInfo entity.

The datastore method is useful for deleting Blobstore values and datastore entities together. BlobInfo entities cannot be created belonging to an existing entity group, but they *can* be the entity group parent of other entities you create. This allows you to delete a Blobstore value and other datastore entities (created with the BlobInfo entity as their parent) in a single datastore transaction. Even without a transaction, it's useful to delete BlobInfo entities and other entities in the same datastore batch call, to reduce the number of API calls made by the app.

Deleting a Blobstore value with the Blobstore API has the same effect as deleting the value in the datastore API. One consequence of this is you cannot delete using the Blobstore API in a datastore transaction where you could not also delete using the datastore API. The Blobstore API does not circumvent the entity group requirement of a transaction.

To delete a Blobstore value with the Blobstore API in Python, you can call the `blobstore.delete()` function with the `BlobKey` object. You can also call the `delete()` method of the `BlobInfo` object, which in turn uses the Blobstore API (not the datastore API) to delete the value:

```
# blob_key_str = ...
blob_key = blobstore.BlobKey(blob_key_str)
blobstore.delete(blob_key)

# Or:
blob_info = blobstore.BlobInfo.get(blob_key)
if blob_info:
    blob_info.delete()

# Deleting multiple Blobstore values in a batch:
blob_key_lst = [blob_key_1, blob_key_2, blob_key_3]
blobstore.delete(blob_key_lst)
```

As with some datastore functions in Python, the `blobstore.delete()` function accepts a singular `BlobKey` value, the `str` form of a Blobstore key, or a list of `BlobKey` or `str`. Given a list, the delete is performed with a single batch call to the service, which is faster than multiple serial calls with single arguments.

In Java, you call the `delete()` method of the `BlobstoreService`, with one or more `BlobKey` values:

```
// Deleting a single Blobstore value:
// BlobKey blobKey;
blobstoreService.delete(blobKey);

// Using the variable length parameter list:
blobstoreService.delete(blobKey1, blobKey2, blobKey3);

// Using an array of BlobKey:
// BlobKey[] blobKeyArray;
blobstoreService.delete(blobKeyArray);
```

You can reset the state of the development server datastore by starting the server with the `--clear_datastore` command-line flag. This also deletes all Blobstore values. As with datastore values, Blobstore values persist between runs of the development server, unless you specify this command-line flag. (See "The Development Server and the Datastore" on page 148.)

Reading Blobstore Values

The mechanisms we've seen so far go to great lengths to avoid passing Blobstore data through the application code. To accept an uploaded a value, the app facilitates a direct connection between the client and the Blobstore using an upload URL generated by the API. To serve a value, the app collaborates with the frontend to have the data streamed to the client directly from storage. These methods work around a constraint imposed by the service infrastructure that caps the amount of data that passes between services and application instances. (App Engine relies on such constraints to tune the performance of its infrastructure.)

Applications can read data from Blobstore values directly, as long as a single call to the Blobstore service fits within the size constraint. You can use the Blobstore API to read ranges of bytes from a value, up to the maximum size of 32 megabytes. The API also provides a streaming data abstraction that can access the entire value using multiple service calls. This abstraction can behave as a file-like object to interoperate with libraries that know how to read data from filesystems.

Because a Blobstore value can be arbitrarily large, it may take an arbitrary amount of time and computation to process an entire value. Depending on your use case, you may need to either limit the amount of data you process, or distribute your computation across multiple tasks. See Chapter 16 for more information.

Fetching Byte Ranges

To fetch a range of bytes in Python, call the `fetch_data()` method:

```
from google.appengine.ext import blobstore

# ...
```

```
        # blob = ...
        start_index = 0
        end_index = 1024
        bytes = blobstore.fetch_data(blob, start_index, end_index)
```

The `blob` parameter can be a `BlobKey` object, a string-ified blob key, or a `BlobInfo` entity.

The maximum fetch size (`end_index - start_index`) is available in the API as the constant `blobstore.MAX_BLOB_FETCH_SIZE`.

In Java, you call the `fetchData()` method of the `BlobstoreService` instance:

```
import com.google.appengine.api.blobstore.BlobKey;
import com.google.appengine.api.blobstore.BlobstoreService;
import com.google.appengine.api.blobstore.BlobstoreServiceFactory;

// ...
        BlobstoreService blobstore = BlobstoreServiceFactory.getBlobstoreService();
        // BlobKey blobKey = ...;

        long startIndex = 0;
        long endIndex = 1024;
        byte[] bytes = blobstore.fetchData(blobKey, startIndex, endIndex);
```

The maximum fetch size constant in Java is `BlobstoreService.MAX_BLOB_FETCH_SIZE`.

Reading Values with Streams

Fetching byte ranges is mostly useful as a building block for other access patterns. The Blobstore API provides such a pattern: a buffered streaming interface that fetches byte ranges as needed using multiple service calls.

In Python, you use a `BlobReader`, a read-only file-like object. You get a reader either by constructing it directly, or by calling the `open()` method of a `BlobInfo` instance:

```
from google.appengine.ext import blobstore

# ...
        # blob = ...
        reader = blobstore.BlobReader(blob)

        # Or:
        # blob_info = ...
        reader = blob_info.open()
```

As before, the constructor's `blob` argument can be a `BlobKey`, a string, or a `BlobInfo`. You can optionally configure the buffer size (in bytes) and starting byte position for the reader with the `buffer_size` and `position` arguments to the constructor. `blob_info.open()` returns a `BlobReader` with default settings.

Given a reader, you can access its `BlobInfo` object by accessing the `blob_info` property:

```
        blob_info = reader.blob_info
```

BlobReader instances support most of the file interface. For example, you can iterate over lines in textual data:

```
import re

# ...
        # MAX_LINE_COUNT = ...

        for i, line in enumerate(reader):
            if i >= MAX_LINE_COUNT:
                break
            words = re.sub(r'\W', ' ', line).lower().split()
            # ...
```

Or parse the data as a comma-separated values file exported from a spreadsheet:

```
import csv

# ...
        sheet = csv.DictReader(reader)
        total = 0
        for row in sheet:
            total += row['Price']
```

Or read compressed data from a ZIP archive:

```
import zipfile

# ...
        zip = zipfile.ZipFile(reader)
        file_list = zip.infolist()
        # ...
```

BlobReader objects can be serialized with pickle for storage, or passing between tasks (see Chapter 16).

The Java API provides the BlobstoreInputStream class, a proper subclass of java.io.InputStream. You can combine this with reader classes appropriate for the data you are reading. For example, you can read lines of text:

```
import java.io.BufferedReader;
import java.io.InputStreamReader;
import com.google.appengine.api.blobstore.BlobKey;
import com.google.appengine.api.blobstore.BlobstoreInputStream;

// ...
        // BlobKey blobKey = ...;
        // final long MAX_LINE_COUNT = ...;

        BufferedReader reader =
            BufferedReader(InputStreamReader(BlobstoreInputStream(blobKey)));
        int lineCount = 0;
        String line;
        while ((line = reader.readLine()) != null
              && lineCount++ < MAX_LINE_COUNT) {
            String[] words = line.replaceAll("\\W", " ").toLowerCase().split("\\s");
```

```
        // ...
    }
```

Or read compressed data from a ZIP archive:

```
import java.util.zip.ZipEntry;
import java.util.zip.ZipInputStream;
import com.google.appengine.api.blobstore.BlobKey;
import com.google.appengine.api.blobstore.BlobstoreInputStream;

// ...
        zipStream = ZipInputStream(BlobstoreInputStream(blobKey));
        ZipEntry entry;
        while ((entry = zipStream.getNextEntry()) != null) {
            // ...
        }
```

A Complete Example

Let's put the features of the Blobstore to use in a complete sample application. This application accepts uploads from a user, associates the upload with the user's account, shows the user a list of files she has uploaded, and offers to serve them back. In other words, it's a simple private file storage app.

We'll use the same structure for both the Python version and the Java version:

- The / URL displays a list of the (signed-in) user's files, with metadata (filename, size) and links. It also displays an upload form with a "description" text field and a file upload field. The form uses `multiple="true"` to allow the user to attach multiple files to the same description.
- The form action is a Blobstore upload URL, which passes through to the handler mapped to the `/upload` URL. The handler stores the Blobstore keys along with the description and the user ID, then redirects back to /.
- When the user clicks on a file in her file list, the app serves the file. The app uses the MIME content type and filename used for the upload to serve the file.
- The file list is also a form, with checkboxes next to each file. If the user checks one or more boxes and clicks the Delete Selected button, the form submits to the `/delete` URL. A handler at this URL deletes the Blobstore values and corresponding datastore entities, and redirects back to /.

Each user upload has a datastore entity of the kind `UserUpload`. This entity contains the user value (from the Users API) that identifies the user, the description the user entered into the form, and a reference to the `BlobInfo` entity for the Blobstore value.

You'll notice that each `UserUpload` entity is created with an entity group parent specific to the user. (The parent does not need to be an entity that exists. We just need to create and use a consistent parent key.) This lets us use an ancestor query to get the file list.

If we were to do this without an ancestor, the query would rely on a global index for the `UserUpload` kind. Global indexes in the HR datastore are eventually consistent, and may not update completely between the time we create the entity in the upload handler and the time we perform the global query on the main page. By using an entity group per user, we can perform a query on an index that is strongly consistent with the update, guaranteeing a complete result.

Of course, the trade-off is all the `UserUpload` entities for a user are in the same entity group. But a typical app can organize its datastore activity to minimize contention on data for a single user. See Chapter 7 for more information on entity groups.

This design also prevents us from using the technique of putting the `UserUpload` entity in the same entity group as the BlobInfo record, so they can be deleted together transactionally. A robust workaround would be to use a single transaction to delete the `UserUpload` entity and enqueue a task that deletes the Blobstore value. See Chapter 16.

Remember, you can download the complete application code for this and other chapters from the book's website:

http://www.dansanderson.com/appengine

A Blobstore Example in Python

The Python version of this app uses four request handlers, all defined in *main.py* (Example 12-1):

- / is handled by `MainPage`. This handler gets information about the currently signed-in user from the Users service, queries the datastore for all entities of the kind `UserUpload` belonging to that user, and generates URLs for sign in, sign out, and Blobstore uploading. It then renders the *home.html* Jinja2 template with all of this information.
- `/upload` is handled by `UploadHandler`. The `/upload` URL is used by `MainPage` as the target for the Blobstore upload URL. The `UploadHandler` class inherits from `blobstore_handlers.BlobstoreUploadHandler`, which provides the `self.get_uploads()` method that parses the form data after it has been modified by the Blobstore. The handler creates a new `UserUpload` entity for each upload, which associates the user's identity with each Blobstore key.
- `/view` is handled by `ViewHandler`. The parent class `blobstore_handlers.BlobstoreDownloadHandler` provides the `self.send_blob()` method, which this handler uses to serve the requested value. But first, it uses the entity key provided in the request to fetch the `UserUpload` value and confirm that the current user owns the file. If so, it passes the Blobstore key from the entity to `self.send_blob()`.
- `/delete` is handled by `DeleteHandler`. This processes the delete form containing the checkboxes and the Delete Selected button. The handler loads each `UserUpload`

entity, confirms that the current user owns them, then deletes both the datastore entities and the Blobstore values referred to by those entities.

The datastore entities are modeled by the `UserUpload` class, a `db.Model` with three modeled properties. The `blob` property uses `blobstore.BlobReferenceProperty` to manage the storage of Blobstore keys.

The only other files used by this application are *home.html* (Example 12-2), the Jinja2 template for the main page, and *app.yaml* (Example 12-3), which simply associates all URL paths with the WSGI application defined in `main.application` (in the *main.py* source file). The `WSGIApplication` instance itself maps the URL paths to the specific handler classes.

Example 12-1. A Blobstore example in Python, main.py

```
import jinja2
import os
import webapp2
from google.appengine.api import users
from google.appengine.ext import blobstore
from google.appengine.ext import db
from google.appengine.ext.webapp import blobstore_handlers

template_env = jinja2.Environment(
    loader=jinja2.FileSystemLoader(os.getcwd()))

class UserUpload(db.Model):
    user = db.UserProperty()
    description = db.StringProperty()
    blob = blobstore.BlobReferenceProperty()

class MainPage(webapp2.RequestHandler):
    def get(self):
        user = users.get_current_user()
        login_url = users.create_login_url(self.request.path)
        logout_url = users.create_logout_url(self.request.path)

        uploads = None
        if user:
            q = UserUpload.all()
            q.filter('user =', user)
            q.ancestor(db.Key.from_path('UserUploadGroup', user.email()))
            uploads = q.fetch(100)

        upload_url = blobstore.create_upload_url('/upload')

        template = template_env.get_template('home.html')
        context = {
            'user': user,
            'login_url': login_url,
            'logout_url': logout_url,
            'uploads': uploads,
            'upload_url': upload_url,
        }
```

```
        self.response.write(template.render(context))

class UploadHandler(blobstore_handlers.BlobstoreUploadHandler):
    def post(self):
        user = users.get_current_user()
        description = self.request.params['description']
        for blob_info in self.get_uploads('upload'):
            upload = UserUpload(
                parent=db.Key.from_path('UserUploadGroup', user.email()),
                user=user,
                description=description,
                blob=blob_info.key())
            upload.put()
        self.redirect('/')

class ViewHandler(blobstore_handlers.BlobstoreDownloadHandler):
    def get(self):
        user = users.get_current_user()
        upload_key_str = self.request.params.get('key')
        upload = None
        if upload_key_str:
            upload = db.get(upload_key_str)

        if (not user or not upload or upload.user != user):
            self.error(404)
            return

        self.send_blob(upload.blob)

class DeleteHandler(webapp2.RequestHandler):
    def post(self):
        user = users.get_current_user()
        if user:
            entities_to_delete = []
            for delete_key in self.request.params.getall('delete'):
                upload = db.get(delete_key)
                if upload.user != user:
                    continue
                entities_to_delete.append(upload.key())
                entities_to_delete.append(
                    db.Key.from_path('__BlobInfo__', str(upload.blob.key())))

            db.delete(entities_to_delete)

        self.redirect('/')

application = webapp2.WSGIApplication([('/', MainPage),
                                       ('/upload', UploadHandler),
                                       ('/view', ViewHandler),
                                       ('/delete', DeleteHandler)],
                                      debug=True)
```

Example 12-2. A Blobstore example in Python, home.html

```
<html>
  <head>
```

```
    <title>Blobstore Demo</title>
  </head>
  <body>
    {% if user %}
    <p>Welcome, {{ user.email() }}! You can <a href="{{ logout_url }}">sign out</a>.</p>

    {% if uploads %}
    <form action="/delete" method="post">
    <p>Your uploads:</p>
    <ul>
      {% for upload in uploads %}
      <li>
        <input type="checkbox" name="delete" value="{{ upload.key() }}" />
        {{ upload.description }}:
        <a href="/view?key={{ upload.key() }}">{{ upload.blob.filename }}</a>
      </li>
      {% endfor %}
    </ul>
    <input type="submit" value="Delete Selected" />
    </form>
    {% else %} {# User has no uploads. #}
    <p>You have no uploads.</p>
    {% endif %}

    <p>Upload files:</p>
    <form action="{{ upload_url }}" method="post" enctype="multipart/form-data">
      <label for="description">Description:</label>
        <input type="text" name="description" id="description" /><br />
      <label for="upload">File:</label>
        <input type="file" name="upload" id="upload" multiple="true" /><br />
      <input type="submit" value="Upload File" />
    </form>

    {% else %} {# User is not signed in. #}
    <p>Welcome! Please
    <a href="{{ login_url }}">sign in or register</a> to upload files.</p>
    {% endif %}
  </body>
</html>
```

Example 12-3. A Blobstore example in Python, app.yaml

```
application: blobstore
version: 1
runtime: python27
api_version: 1
threadsafe: yes

handlers:
- url: .*
  script: main.application

libraries:
- name: webapp2
  version: "2.5.1"
- name: jinja2
```

```
  version: latest
- name: markupsafe
  version: latest
```

A Blobstore Example in Java

The Java version of this app has four servlets mapped to URL paths:

- `/` calls `MainPageServlet` (Example 12-4). This servlet calls the Users service to get information about the signed-in user, performs a datastore query to get the user's `UserUpload` entities, and generates a Blobstore upload URL. It forwards all of this information to the *home.jsp* servlet (Example 12-5) to render the final page.
- `/upload` calls `UploadServlet` (Example 12-6). This is the forwarding target of the Blobstore upload URL. It receives an HTTP POST request when the user submits the upload form, after the Blobstore has consumed the uploaded data. The servlet creates `UserUpload` datastore entities as needed, and then redirects the user back to `/`.
- `/view` calls `ViewUploadServlet` (Example 12-7). It expects an HTTP GET request with the `key` parameter on the URL. The parameter's value is the string form of the datastore key for a `UserUpload` entity that belongs to the user. If the entity exists and belongs to the user, the servlet tells the Blobstore to serve the value. Otherwise, it serves a 404 Not Found error.
- `/delete` calls `DeleteUploadServlet` (Example 12-8). This is the form action for the Delete Selected feature of the file list on the main page. In an HTTP POST request, each `delete` parameter contains the key of a `UserUpload` entity. For each one, if the entity exists and is owned by the user, both the datastore entity and the corresponding Blobstore value are deleted. The servlet redirects the user back to `/`.

If you're following along at home, create each of the Java source files in the appropriate package in your *src/* directory. *home.jsp* and *web.xml* go in *war/WEB-INF/*.

Example 12-4. A Blobstore example in Java, MainPageServlet.java

```
package blobstoredemo;

import java.io.IOException;
import java.util.ArrayList;
import java.util.HashMap;
import java.util.List;
import java.util.Map;
import javax.servlet.RequestDispatcher;
import javax.servlet.ServletException;
import javax.servlet.http.*;

import com.google.appengine.api.blobstore.BlobInfoFactory;
import com.google.appengine.api.blobstore.BlobKey;
import com.google.appengine.api.blobstore.BlobstoreService;
import com.google.appengine.api.blobstore.BlobstoreServiceFactory;
import com.google.appengine.api.blobstore.UploadOptions;
```

```
import com.google.appengine.api.datastore.DatastoreService;
import com.google.appengine.api.datastore.DatastoreServiceFactory;
import com.google.appengine.api.datastore.Entity;
import com.google.appengine.api.datastore.Key;
import com.google.appengine.api.datastore.KeyFactory;
import com.google.appengine.api.datastore.PreparedQuery;
import com.google.appengine.api.datastore.Query;
import com.google.appengine.api.users.User;
import com.google.appengine.api.users.UserService;
import com.google.appengine.api.users.UserServiceFactory;

@SuppressWarnings("serial")
public class MainPageServlet extends HttpServlet {
    public void doGet(HttpServletRequest req,
                      HttpServletResponse resp)
        throws IOException, ServletException {

        UserService userService = UserServiceFactory.getUserService();
        User user = userService.getCurrentUser();
        String loginUrl = userService.createLoginURL("/");
        String logoutUrl = userService.createLogoutURL("/");

        BlobstoreService blobstoreService =
                BlobstoreServiceFactory.getBlobstoreService();
        UploadOptions uploadOptions = UploadOptions.Builder
                .withMaxUploadSizeBytesPerBlob(1024L * 1024L * 1024L)
                .maxUploadSizeBytes(10L * 1024L * 1024L * 1024L);
        String uploadUrl = blobstoreService.createUploadUrl("/upload", uploadOptions);

        DatastoreService ds = DatastoreServiceFactory.getDatastoreService();
        BlobInfoFactory blobInfoFactory = new BlobInfoFactory();
        List<Map<String, Object>> uploads = new ArrayList<Map<String, Object>>();

        Key userGroupKey = KeyFactory.createKey("UserUploadGroup", user.getEmail());
        Query q = new Query("UserUpload").setAncestor(userGroupKey);
        q.addFilter("user", Query.FilterOperator.EQUAL, user);
        PreparedQuery pq = ds.prepare(q);
        Iterable<Entity> results = pq.asIterable();
        for (Entity result : results) {
            Map<String, Object> upload = new HashMap<String, Object>();
            upload.put("description", (String) result.getProperty("description"));
            BlobKey blobKey = (BlobKey) result.getProperty("upload");
            upload.put("blob", blobInfoFactory.loadBlobInfo(blobKey));
            upload.put("uploadKey", KeyFactory.keyToString(result.getKey()));
            uploads.add(upload);
        }

        req.setAttribute("user", user);
        req.setAttribute("loginUrl", loginUrl);
        req.setAttribute("logoutUrl", logoutUrl);
        req.setAttribute("uploadUrl", uploadUrl);
        req.setAttribute("uploads", uploads);
        req.setAttribute("hasUploads", !uploads.isEmpty());

        resp.setContentType("text/html");
```

```
        RequestDispatcher jsp = req.getRequestDispatcher("/WEB-INF/home.jsp");
        jsp.forward(req, resp);
    }
}
```

Example 12-5. A Blobstore example in Java, home.jsp

```
<%@ taglib uri="http://java.sun.com/jsp/jstl/core" prefix="c" %>
<html>
  <head>
    <title>Blobstore Demo</title>
  </head>
  <body>
    <c:choose>
      <c:when test="${user != null}">
        <p>
          Welcome, ${user.email}!
          You can <a href="${logoutUrl}">sign out</a>.
        </p>

        <c:choose>
          <c:when test="${hasUploads}">
            <form action="/delete" method="post">
            <p>Your uploads:</p>
            <ul>
              <c:forEach var="upload" items="${uploads}">
                <li>
                  <input type="checkbox" name="delete" value="${upload.uploadKey}" />
                  ${upload.description}
                  <a href="/view?key=${upload.uploadKey}"
                    >${upload.blob.filename}</a>
                </li>
              </c:forEach>
            </ul>
            <input type="submit" value="Delete Selected" />
            </form>
          </c:when>
          <c:otherwise>
            <p>You have no uploads.</p>
          </c:otherwise>
        </c:choose>

        <form action="${uploadUrl}" method="post" enctype="multipart/form-data">
          <label for="description">Description:</label>
            <input type="text" name="description" id="description" /><br />
          <label for="upload">File:</label>
            <input type="file" name="upload" multiple="true" /><br />
          <input type="submit" value="Upload File" />
        </form>
      </c:when>
      <c:otherwise>
        <p>
          Welcome! Please
          <a href="${loginUrl}">sign in or register</a> to upload files.
        </p>
```

```
      </c:otherwise>
    </c:choose>
  </body>
</html>
```

Example 12-6. A Blobstore example in Java, UploadServlet.java

```
package blobstoredemo;

import java.io.IOException;
import java.util.List;
import java.util.Map;
import javax.servlet.http.HttpServlet;
import javax.servlet.http.HttpServletRequest;
import javax.servlet.http.HttpServletResponse;

import com.google.appengine.api.blobstore.BlobKey;
import com.google.appengine.api.blobstore.BlobstoreService;
import com.google.appengine.api.blobstore.BlobstoreServiceFactory;
import com.google.appengine.api.datastore.DatastoreService;
import com.google.appengine.api.datastore.DatastoreServiceFactory;
import com.google.appengine.api.datastore.Entity;
import com.google.appengine.api.datastore.Key;
import com.google.appengine.api.datastore.KeyFactory;
import com.google.appengine.api.users.User;
import com.google.appengine.api.users.UserService;
import com.google.appengine.api.users.UserServiceFactory;

@SuppressWarnings("serial")
public class UploadServlet extends HttpServlet {
 public void doPost(HttpServletRequest req,
                      HttpServletResponse resp)
        throws IOException {

        UserService userService = UserServiceFactory.getUserService();
        User user = userService.getCurrentUser();
        DatastoreService ds = DatastoreServiceFactory.getDatastoreService();
        BlobstoreService bs =
                BlobstoreServiceFactory.getBlobstoreService();

        Map<String, List<BlobKey>> blobFields = bs.getUploads(req);
        List<BlobKey> blobKeys = blobFields.get("upload");
        Key userGroupKey = KeyFactory.createKey("UserUploadGroup", user.getEmail());
        for (BlobKey blobKey : blobKeys) {
            Entity userUpload = new Entity("UserUpload", userGroupKey);
            userUpload.setProperty("user", user);
            userUpload.setProperty("description", req.getParameter("description"));
            userUpload.setProperty("upload", blobKey);
            ds.put(userUpload);
        }

        resp.sendRedirect("/");
    }
}
```

Example 12-7. A Blobstore example in Java, ViewUploadServlet.java

```
package blobstoredemo;

import java.io.IOException;

import javax.servlet.http.HttpServlet;
import javax.servlet.http.HttpServletRequest;
import javax.servlet.http.HttpServletResponse;

import com.google.appengine.api.blobstore.BlobKey;
import com.google.appengine.api.blobstore.BlobstoreService;
import com.google.appengine.api.blobstore.BlobstoreServiceFactory;
import com.google.appengine.api.datastore.DatastoreService;
import com.google.appengine.api.datastore.DatastoreServiceFactory;
import com.google.appengine.api.datastore.Entity;
import com.google.appengine.api.datastore.EntityNotFoundException;
import com.google.appengine.api.datastore.KeyFactory;
import com.google.appengine.api.users.User;
import com.google.appengine.api.users.UserService;
import com.google.appengine.api.users.UserServiceFactory;

@SuppressWarnings("serial")
public class ViewUploadServlet extends HttpServlet {
    public void doGet(HttpServletRequest req,
            HttpServletResponse resp)
            throws IOException {
        UserService userService = UserServiceFactory.getUserService();
        User user = userService.getCurrentUser();
        DatastoreService ds = DatastoreServiceFactory.getDatastoreService();
        BlobstoreService bs =
                BlobstoreServiceFactory.getBlobstoreService();

        String uploadKeyStr = req.getParameter("key");
        Entity userUpload = null;
        BlobKey blobKey = null;
        if (uploadKeyStr != null) {
            try {
                userUpload = ds.get(KeyFactory.stringToKey(uploadKeyStr));
                if (((User)userUpload.getProperty("user")).equals(user)) {
                    blobKey = (BlobKey)userUpload.getProperty("upload");
                }
            } catch (EntityNotFoundException e) {
                // Leave blobKey null.
            }
        }

        if (blobKey != null) {
            bs.serve(
                    blobKey,
                    bs.getByteRange(req),
                    resp);
        } else {
            resp.sendError(404);
        }
```

```
    }
}
```

Example 12-8. A Blobstore example in Java, DeleteUploadServlet.java

```
package blobstoredemo;

import java.io.IOException;
import java.util.ArrayList;
import java.util.List;

import javax.servlet.http.HttpServlet;
import javax.servlet.http.HttpServletRequest;
import javax.servlet.http.HttpServletResponse;

import com.google.appengine.api.blobstore.BlobInfoFactory;
import com.google.appengine.api.blobstore.BlobKey;
import com.google.appengine.api.datastore.DatastoreService;
import com.google.appengine.api.datastore.DatastoreServiceFactory;
import com.google.appengine.api.datastore.Entity;
import com.google.appengine.api.datastore.EntityNotFoundException;
import com.google.appengine.api.datastore.Key;
import com.google.appengine.api.datastore.KeyFactory;
import com.google.appengine.api.users.User;
import com.google.appengine.api.users.UserService;
import com.google.appengine.api.users.UserServiceFactory;

@SuppressWarnings("serial")
public class DeleteUploadServlet extends HttpServlet {
    public void doPost(HttpServletRequest req,
            HttpServletResponse resp)
            throws IOException {
        UserService userService = UserServiceFactory.getUserService();
        User user = userService.getCurrentUser();
        DatastoreService ds = DatastoreServiceFactory.getDatastoreService();
        BlobstoreService bs =
                BlobstoreServiceFactory.getBlobstoreService();

        String[] uploadKeyStrings = req.getParameterValues("delete");
        List<Key> keysToDelete = new ArrayList<Key>();
        if (uploadKeyStrings != null) {
         for (String uploadKeyStr : uploadKeyStrings) {
                try {
                    Entity userUpload = ds.get(KeyFactory.stringToKey(uploadKeyStr));
                    if (((User)userUpload.getProperty("user")).equals(user)) {
                        BlobKey blobKey = (BlobKey)userUpload.getProperty("upload");
                        Key blobInfoKey = KeyFactory.createKey(
                                BlobInfoFactory.KIND, blobKey.getKeyString());
                        keysToDelete.add(blobInfoKey);
                        keysToDelete.add(userUpload.getKey());
                    }
                } catch (EntityNotFoundException e) {
                    // Do nothing.
                }
            }
        }
```

```
        ds.delete(keysToDelete.toArray(new Key[0]));

        resp.sendRedirect("/");
    }
}
```

Example 12-9. A Blobstore example in Java, web.xml

```
<?xml version="1.0" encoding="utf-8"?>
<web-app xmlns:xsi="http://www.w3.org/2001/XMLSchema-instance"
  xmlns="http://java.sun.com/xml/ns/javaee"
  xmlns:web="http://java.sun.com/xml/ns/javaee/web-app_2_5.xsd"
  xsi:schemaLocation="http://java.sun.com/xml/ns/javaee
    http://java.sun.com/xml/ns/javaee/web-app_2_5.xsd" version="2.5">
  <servlet>
    <servlet-name>mainpage</servlet-name>
    <servlet-class>blobstoredemo.MainPageServlet</servlet-class>
  </servlet>
  <servlet-mapping>
    <servlet-name>mainpage</servlet-name>
    <url-pattern>/</url-pattern>
  </servlet-mapping>
  <servlet>
    <servlet-name>upload</servlet-name>
    <servlet-class>blobstoredemo.UploadServlet</servlet-class>
  </servlet>
  <servlet-mapping>
    <servlet-name>upload</servlet-name>
    <url-pattern>/upload</url-pattern>
  </servlet-mapping>
  <servlet>
    <servlet-name>viewupload</servlet-name>
    <servlet-class>blobstoredemo.ViewUploadServlet</servlet-class>
  </servlet>
  <servlet-mapping>
    <servlet-name>viewupload</servlet-name>
    <url-pattern>/view</url-pattern>
  </servlet-mapping>
  <servlet>
    <servlet-name>deleteupload</servlet-name>
    <servlet-class>blobstoredemo.DeleteUploadServlet</servlet-class>
  </servlet>
  <servlet-mapping>
    <servlet-name>deleteupload</servlet-name>
    <url-pattern>/delete</url-pattern>
  </servlet-mapping>
</web-app>
```

CHAPTER 13

Fetching URLs and Web Resources

An App Engine application can connect to other sites on the Internet to retrieve data and communicate with web services. It does this not by opening a connection to the remote host from the application server, but through a scalable service called the URL Fetch service. This takes the burden of maintaining connections away from the app servers, and ensures that resource fetching performs well regardless of how many request handlers are fetching resources simultaneously. As with other parts of the App Engine infrastructure, the URL Fetch service is used by other Google applications to fetch web pages.

The URL Fetch service supports fetching URLs by using the HTTP protocol, and using HTTP with SSL (HTTPS). Other methods sometimes associated with URLs (such as FTP) are not supported.

Because the URL Fetch service is based on Google infrastructure, the service inherits a few restrictions that were put in place in the original design of the underlying HTTP proxy. The service supports the five most common HTTP actions (GET, POST, PUT, HEAD, and DELETE) but does not allow for others or for using a nonstandard action. Also, it can only connect to TCP ports in several allowed ranges: 80–90, 440–450, and 1024–65535. By default, it uses port 80 for HTTP, and port 443 for HTTPS. The proxy uses HTTP 1.1 to connect to the remote host.

The outgoing request can contain URL parameters, a request body, and HTTP headers. A few headers cannot be modified for security reasons, which mostly means that an app cannot issue a malformed request, such as a request whose `Content-Length` header does not accurately reflect the actual content length of the request body. In these cases, the service uses the correct values, or does not include the header.

Request and response sizes are limited, but generous. A request can be up to 5 megabytes in size (including headers), and a response can be up to 32 megabytes in size.

The service waits for a response up to a time limit, or "deadline." The default fetch deadline is 5 seconds, but you can increase this on a per-request basis. The maximum deadline is 60 seconds during a user request, or 10 minutes during a task queue or scheduled task or from a backend. That is, the fetch deadline can be up to the request handler's own deadline, except for backends (which have none).

Both the Python and Java runtime environments offer implementations of standard libraries used for fetching URLs that call the URL Fetch service behind the scenes. For Python, these are the `urllib`, `httplib`, and `urllib2` modules. For Java, this is the `java.net.URLConnection` set of APIs, including `java.net.URL`. These implementations give you a reasonable degree of portability and interoperability with other libraries.

Naturally, the standard interfaces do not give you complete access to the service's features. When using the standard libraries, the service uses the following default behaviors:

- If the remote host doesn't respond within five seconds, the request is canceled and a service exception is raised.
- The service follows HTTP redirects up to five times before returning the response to the application.
- Responses from remote hosts that exceed 32 megabytes in size are truncated to 32 megabytes. The application is not told whether the response is truncated.
- HTTP over SSL (HTTPS) URLs will use SSL to make the connection, but the service will not validate the server's security certificate. (The App Engine team has said certificate validation will become the default for the standard libraries in a future release, so check the App Engine website.)

All of these behaviors can be customized when calling the service APIs directly. You can increase the fetch response deadline, disable the automatic following of redirects, cause an exception to be thrown for responses that exceed the maximum size, and enable validation of certificates for HTTPS connections.

The development server simulates the URL Fetch service by making HTTP connections directly from your computer. If the remote host might behave differently when your app connects from your computer rather than from Google's proxy servers, be sure to test your URL Fetch calls on App Engine.

In this chapter, we introduce the standard-library and direct interfaces to the URL Fetch service, in Python and in Java. We also examine several features of the service, and how to use them from the direct APIs.

Fetching resources from remote hosts can take quite a bit of time. Like several other services, the URL Fetch service offers a way to call the service asynchronously, so your application can issue fetch requests and do other things while remote servers take their time to respond. See Chapter 17 for more information.

Fetching URLs in Python

In Python, you can call the URL Fetch service by using the `google.appengine.api.urlfetch` module, or you can use Python standard libraries such as `urllib2`.

The Python runtime environment overrides portions of the `urllib`, `urllib2`, and `httplib` modules in the Python standard library so that HTTP and HTTPS connections made with these modules use the URL Fetch service. This allows existing software that depends on these libraries to function on App Engine, as long as the requests function within certain limitations. `urllib2` has rich extensible support for features of remote web servers such as HTTP authentication and cookies. We won't go into the details of this module here, but Example 13-1 shows a brief example using the module's `urlopen()` convenience function.

Example 13-1. A simple example of using the urllib2 module to access the URL Fetch service

```
import urllib2
from google.appengine.api import urlfetch

# ...
        try:
            newsfeed = urllib2.urlopen('http://ae-book.appspot.com/blog/atom.xml/')
            newsfeed_xml = newsfeed.read()
        except urllib2.URLError, e:
            # Handle urllib2 error...

        except urlfetch.Error, e:
            # Handle urlfetch error...
```

In this example, we catch both exceptions raised by `urllib2` and exceptions raised from the URL Fetch Python API, `google.appengine.api.urlfetch`. The service may throw one of its own exceptions for conditions that `urllib2` doesn't catch, such as a request exceeding its deadline.

Because the service follows redirect responses by default (up to five times) when using `urllib2`, a `urllib2` redirect handler will not see all redirects, only the final response.

If you use the service API directly, you can customize these behaviors. Example 13-2 shows a similar example using the `urlfetch` module, with several options changed.

Example 13-2. Customizing URL Fetch behaviors, using the urlfetch module

```
from google.appengine.api import urlfetch

# ...
        try:
            newsfeed = urlfetch.fetch('http://ae-book.appspot.com/blog/atom.xml/',
                                      allow_truncated=False,
                                      follow_redirects=False,
                                      deadline=10)
            newsfeed_xml = newsfeed.content
```

```
    except urlfetch.Error, e:
        # Handle urlfetch error...
```

We'll consider the direct URL Fetch API for the rest of this chapter.

Fetching URLs in Java

In Java, the direct URL Fetch service API is provided by the `com.google.appengine.api.urlfetch` package. You can also use standard `java.net` calls to fetch URLs. The Java runtime includes a custom implementation of the `URLConnection` class in the `java.net` package that calls the URL Fetch service instead of making a direct socket connection. As with the other standard interfaces, you can use this interface and rest assured that you can port your app to another platform easily.

Example 13-3 shows a simple example of using a convenience method in the `URL` class, which in turn uses the `URLConnection` class to fetch the contents of a web page. The `openStream()` method of the `URL` object returns an input stream of bytes. As shown, you can use an `InputStreamReader` (from `java.io`) to process the byte stream as a character stream. The `BufferedReader` class makes it easy to read lines of text from the `InputStreamReader`.

Example 13-3. Using java.net.URL to call the URL Fetch service

```
import java.net.URL;
import java.net.MalformedURLException;
import java.io.IOException;
import java.io.InputStream;
import java.io.InputStreamReader;
import java.io.BufferedReader;

// ...
        try {
            URL url = new URL("http://ae-book.appspot.com/blog/atom.xml/");
            InputStream inStream = url.openStream();

            InputStreamReader inStreamReader = new InputStreamReader(inStream);
            BufferedReader reader = new BufferedReader(inStreamReader);
            // ... read characters or lines with reader ...
            reader.close();

        } catch (MalformedURLException e) {
            // ...
        } catch (IOException e) {
            // ...
        }
```

Note that the URL Fetch service has already buffered the entire response into the application's memory by the time the app begins to read. The app reads the response data from memory, not from a network stream from the socket or the service.

You can use other features of the `URLConnection` interface, as long as they operate within the functionality of the service API. Notably, the URL Fetch service does not maintain a persistent connection with the remote host, so features that require such a connection will not work.

By default, the URL Fetch service waits up to five seconds for a response from the remote server. If the server does not respond by the deadline, the service throws an `IOException`. You can adjust the amount of time to wait using the `setConnectTimeout()` method of the `URLConnection`. (The `setReadTimeout()` method has the same effect; the service uses the greater of the two values.) The deadline can be up to 60 seconds during user requests, or up to 10 minutes (600 seconds) for task queue and scheduled tasks and when running on a backend.

When using the `URLConnection` interface, the URL Fetch service follows HTTP redirects automatically, up to five consecutive redirects. The app does not see the intermediate redirect responses, only the last one. If there are more than five redirects, the service returns the fifth redirect response to the app.

The low-level API for the URL Fetch service lets you customize several behaviors of the service. Example 13-4 demonstrates how to fetch a URL with this API with options specified. As shown, the `FetchOptions` object tells the service not to follow any redirects, and to throw a `ResponseTooLargeException` if the response exceeds the maximum size of 32 megabytes instead of truncating the data.

Example 13-4. Using the low-level API to call the URL Fetch service, with options

```
import java.net.URL;
import java.net.MalformedURLException;
import com.google.appengine.api.urlfetch.FetchOptions;
import com.google.appengine.api.urlfetch.HTTPMethod;
import com.google.appengine.api.urlfetch.HTTPRequest;
import com.google.appengine.api.urlfetch.HTTPResponse;
import com.google.appengine.api.urlfetch.ResponseTooLargeException;
import com.google.appengine.api.urlfetch.URLFetchService;
import com.google.appengine.api.urlfetch.URLFetchServiceFactory;

// ...
        try {
            URL url = new URL("http://ae-book.appspot.com/blog/atom.xml/");

            FetchOptions options = FetchOptions.Builder
                .doNotFollowRedirects()
                .disallowTruncate();
            HTTPRequest request = new HTTPRequest(url, HTTPMethod.GET, options);

            URLFetchService urlfetch = URLFetchServiceFactory.getURLFetchService();
            HTTPResponse response = urlfetch.fetch(request);
            // ... process response.getContent() ...

        } catch (ResponseTooLargeException e) {
            // ...
        } catch (MalformedURLException e) {
```

```
        // ...
    } catch (IOException e) {
        // ...
    }
```

You use the `FetchOptions` to adjust many of the service's features. You get an instance of this class by calling a static method of `FetchOptions.Builder`, and then set options by calling methods on the instance. For convenience, there is a static method for each option, and every method returns the instance, so your code can build the full set of options with a single statement of chained method calls.

We will use the direct `urlfetch` API for the remainder of this chapter.

Outgoing HTTP Requests

An HTTP request can consist of a URL, an HTTP method, request headers, and a payload. Only the URL and HTTP method are required, and the API assumes you mean the HTTP GET method if you only provide a URL.

In Python, you fetch a URL using HTTP GET by passing the URL to the `fetch()` function in the `google.appengine.api.urlfetch` module:

```
from google.appengine.api import urlfetch

# ...
        response = memcache.fetch('http://www.example.com/feed.xml')
```

In Java, you prepare an instance of the `HTTPRequest` class from the `com.google.appengine.api.urlfetch` package with the URL as a `java.net.URL` instance, then you pass the request object to the service's `fetch()` method. (Notice that this `HTTPRequest` class is different from the J2EE class you use with your request handler servlets.)

```
import java.net.URL;
import com.google.appengine.api.urlfetch.HTTPRequest;
import com.google.appengine.api.urlfetch.HTTPResponse;
import com.google.appengine.api.urlfetch.URLFetchService;
import com.google.appengine.api.urlfetch.URLFetchServiceFactory;

// ...
        HTTPRequest outRequest =
            new HTTPRequest(new URL("http://www.example.com/feed.xml"));

        URLFetchService urlfetch = URLFetchServiceFactory.getURLFetchService();
        HTTPResponse response = urlfetch.fetch(outRequest);
```

The URL

The URL consists of a scheme, a domain, an optional port, and a path. For example:

```
https://www.example.com:8081/private/feed.xml
```

In this example, `https` is the scheme, `www.example.com` is the domain, `8081` is the port, and `/private/feed.xml` is the path.

The URL Fetch service supports the `http` and `https` schemes. Other schemes, such as `ftp`, are not supported.

If no port is specified, the service will use the default port for the scheme: port 80 for HTTP, and port 443 for HTTPS. If you specify a port, it must be within 80–90, 440–450, or 1024–65535.

As a safety measure against accidental request loops in an application, the URL Fetch service will refuse to fetch the URL that maps to the request handler doing the fetching. An app can make connections to other URLs of its own, so request loops are still possible, but this restriction provides a simple sanity check.

As shown above, the Python API takes the URL as a string passed to the `fetch()` function as its first positional argument. The Java API accepts a `java.net.URL` object as an argument to the `HTTPRequest` constructor.

The HTTP Method and Payload

The HTTP method describes the general nature of the request, as codified by the HTTP standard. For example, the GET method asks for the data associated with the resource identified by the URL (such as a document or database record). The server is expected to verify that the request is allowed, then return the data in the response, without making changes to the resource. The POST method asks the server to modify records or perform an action, and the client usually includes a payload of data with the request.

The URL Fetch service can send requests using the GET, POST, PUT, HEAD, and DELETE methods. No other methods are supported.

In Python, you set the method by providing the `method` keyword argument to the `fetch()` function. The possible values are provided as constants by the `urlfetch` method. If the argument is omitted, it defaults to `urlfetch.GET`. To provide a payload, you set the `payload` keyword argument:

```
profile_data = profile.get_field_data()
response = urlfetch.fetch('http://www.example.com/profile/126542',
                          method=urlfetch.POST,
                          payload=new_profile_data)
```

In Java, the method is an optional second argument to the `HTTPRequest` constructor. Its value is from the enum `HTTPMethod`, whose values are named `GET`, `POST`, `PUT`, `HEAD`, and `DELETE`. To add a payload, you call the `setPayload()` method of the `HTTPRequest`, passing in a `byte[]`:

```
import com.google.appengine.api.urlfetch.HTTPMethod;

// ...
        byte[] profileData = profile.getFieldData();
```

```
HTTPRequest request = new HTTPRequest(url, HTTPMethod.POST);
request.setPayload(profileData);
```

Request Headers

Requests can include headers, a set of key-value pairs distinct from the payload that describe the client, the request, and the expected response. App Engine sets several headers automatically, such as `Content-Length`. Your app can provide additional headers that may be expected by the server.

In Python, the `fetch()` function accepts additional headers as the `headers` keyword argument. Its value is a mapping of header names to values:

```
response = urlfetch.fetch('http://www.example.com/article/roof_on_fire',
                          headers={'Accept-Charset': 'utf-8'},
                          payload=new_profile_data)
```

In Java, you set a request header by calling the `setHeader()` method on the `HTTPRequest`. Its sole argument is an instance of the `HTTPHeader` class, whose constructor takes the header name and value as strings:

```
import com.google.appengine.api.urlfetch.HTTPHeader;

// ...
        HTTPRequest request =
            new HTTPRequest(new URL("http://www.example.com/article/roof_on_fire"));
        request.setHeader(new HTTPHeader("Accept-Charset", "utf-8"));
```

Some headers cannot be set directly by the application. This is primarily to discourage request forgery or invalid requests that could be used as an attack on some servers. Disallowed headers include `Content-Length` (which is set by App Engine automatically to the actual size of the request), `Host`, `Vary`, `Via`, `X-Forwarded-For`, and `X-ProxyUser-IP`.

The `User-Agent` header, which most servers use to identify the software of the client, can be set by the app. However, App Engine will append a string to this value identifying the request as coming from App Engine. This string includes your application ID. This is usually enough to allow an app to coax a server into serving content intended for a specific type of client (such as a specific brand or version of web browser), but it won't be a complete impersonation of such a client.

HTTP Over SSL (HTTPS)

When the scheme of a URL is `https`, the URL Fetch service uses HTTP over SSL to connect to the remote server, encrypting both the request and the response.

The SSL protocol also allows the client to verify the identity of the remote host, to ensure it is talking directly to the host and traffic is not being intercepted by a malicious host (a "man in the middle" attack). This protocol involves security certificates and a process for clients to validate certificates.

By default, the URL Fetch service does *not* validate SSL certificates. With validation disabled, traffic is still encrypted, but the remote host's certificates are not validated before sending the request data. You can tell the URL Fetch service to enable validation of security certificates.

To enable certificate validation in Python, you provide the `validate_certificate=True` argument to `fetch()`:

```
response = urlfetch.fetch('https://secure.example.com/profile/126542',
                          validate_certificate=True)
```

In Java, you use a `FetchOptions` instance with the request, and call its `validateCertificate()` option. Its antonym is `doNotValidateCertificate()`, which is the default:

```
FetchOptions options = FetchOptions.Builder
    .validateCertificate();
HTTPRequest request = new HTTPRequest(
    new URL("https://secure.example.com/profile/126542"),
    HTTPMethod.GET, options);
```

The standard libraries use the default behavior and do not validate certificates. The App Engine team has said they will change this default for the standard libraries in a future release. See the official App Engine website for updates.

Request and Response Sizes

The request can be up to 5 megabytes in size, including the headers and payload. The response can be up to 32 megabytes in size.

The URL Fetch service can do one of two things if the remote host returns a response larger than 32 megabytes: it can truncate the response (delete everything after the first 32 megabytes), or it can raise an exception in your app. You control this behavior with an option.

In Python, the `fetch()` function accepts an `allow_truncated=True` keyword argument. The default is `False`, which tells the service to raise a `urlfetch.ResponseTooLargeError` if the response is too large:

```
response = memcache.fetch('http://www.example.com/firehose.dat',
                          allow_truncated=True)
```

In Java, the `FetchOptions` method `allowTruncate()` enables truncation, and `disallowTruncate()` tells the service to throw a `ResponseTooLargeException` if the response is too large:

```
FetchOptions options = FetchOptions.Builder
    .allowTruncate();
HTTPRequest request = new HTTPRequest(
    new URL("http://www.example.com/firehose.dat"),
    HTTPMethod.GET, options);
```

The standard libraries tell the URL Fetch service to allow truncation. This ensures that the standard libraries won't raise an unfamiliar exception when third-party code fetches a URL, at the expense of returning unexpectedly truncated data when responses are too large.

Request Deadlines

The URL Fetch service issues a request, waits for the remote host to respond, and then makes the response available to the app. But the service won't wait on the remote host forever. By default, the service will wait 5 seconds before terminating the connection and raising an exception with your app.

You can adjust the amount of time the service will wait (the "deadline") as an option to the fetch call. You can set a deadline up to 60 seconds for fetches made during user requests, and up to 10 minutes (600 seconds) for requests made during tasks. That is, you can wait up to the maximum amount of time your request handler can run. Typically, you'll want to set a fetch deadline shorter than your request handler's deadline, so it can react to a failed fetch.

To set the fetch deadline in Python, provide the `deadline` keyword argument, whose value is a number of seconds. If a fetch exceeds its deadline, the service raises a `urlfetch.DeadlineExceededError`:

```
response = memcache.fetch('http://www.example.com/users/ackermann',
                          deadline=30)
```

In Java, the `FetchOptions` class provides a `setDeadline()` method, which takes a `java.lang.Double`. The `Builder` static method is slightly different, named `withDeadline()` and taking a `double`. The value is a number of seconds:

```
FetchOptions options = FetchOptions.Builder
    .withDeadline(30);
HTTPRequest request = new HTTPRequest(
    new URL("http://www.example.com/users/ackermann"),
    HTTPMethod.GET, options);
```

Handling Redirects

You can tell the service to follow redirects automatically, if HTTP redirect requests are returned by the remote server. The server will follow up to five redirects, then return the last response to the app (regardless of whether the last response is a redirect or not).

In Python, `urlfetch.fetch()` accepts a `follow_redirects=True` keyword argument. The default is `False`, which means to return the first response even if it's a redirect. When using the `urllib2`, redirects are followed automatically, up to five times:

```
response = memcache.fetch('http://www.example.com/bounce',
                          follow_redirects=True)
```

In Java, the FetchOptions.Builder has a followRedirects() method, and its opposite doNotFollowRedirects(). The default is to not follow redirects. When using java.net.URLConnection, redirects are followed automatically, up to five times:

```
FetchOptions options = FetchOptions.Builder
    .followRedirects();
HTTPRequest request = new HTTPRequest(
    new URL("http://www.example.com/bounce"),
    HTTPMethod.GET, options);
```

When following redirects, the service does not retain or use cookies set in the responses of the intermediate steps. If you need requests to honor cookies during a redirect chain, you must disable the automatic redirect feature, and process redirects manually in your application code.

Response Objects

In Python, the fetch() function returns an object with response data available on several named properties. (The class name for response objects is _URLFetchResult, which implies that only the fetch() function should be constructing these objects—or relying on the class name.)

In Java, the fetch() service method returns an HTTPResponse instance, with getter methods for the response data.

The response fields are as follows:

content / getContent()
: The response body. A Python str or Java byte[].

status_code / getResponseCode()
: The HTTP status code. An int.

headers / getHeaders()
: The response headers. In Python, this value is a mapping of names to values. In Java, this is a List<HTTPHeader>, where each header has getName() and getValue() methods (returning strings).

final_url / getFinalUrl()
: The URL that corresponds to the response data. If automatic redirects were enabled and the server issued one or more redirects, this is the URL of the final destination, which may differ from the request URL. A Python str or a Java java.net.URL.

content_was_truncated *(Python only)*
: True if truncation was enabled and the response data was larger than 32 megabytes. (There is no Java equivalent.)

CHAPTER 14

Sending and Receiving Email Messages

While today's Internet offers many modes of communication, one of the oldest modes is still one of the most popular: email. People use email for correspondence, announcements, newsletters, and many other kinds of long-form, direct messages. Specific to web applications, email is the primary mechanism for representing and validating identity, and managing access to application-specific accounts. Email is how your app reaches out to your users when they are not on your website and signed in.

An App Engine app can send email messages by calling the Mail service API. An app might send email to notify users of system events or the actions of other users (such as to send social networking invitations), confirm user actions (such as to confirm an order), follow up on long-term user actions (such as to send a shipping notice for an order), or send system notifications to administrators. The app can send email on behalf of itself or the app's administrators. The app can also send email on behalf of the currently signed-in user, during the request handler.

Sending email messages is similar to initiating HTTP requests: the app calls a service by using an API, and the service takes care of making remote connections and managing the appropriate protocols. Unlike the URL Fetch service, the Mail service does not return a response immediately. Instead, messages are enqueued for delivery, and errors are reported via "bounce" email messages to the sender address.

An app can also receive email messages sent to specific addresses. This might allow an app to provide an email interface to the application, or to moderate or monitor email discussions. The app can reply to the email immediately, or set up work that causes a reply to be sent later.

Receiving email messages is also similar to receiving HTTP requests. In fact, this uses the same mechanism: request handlers. When a service receives an email message intended for your app, the Mail service sends an HTTP request to the app using a specified URL with the message in the HTTP payload. The app processes incoming messages, using request handlers mapped to the specified URLs. The service ignores the response for the request; if the app needs to reply to the user, it can send a message using the API.

Figure 14-1 illustrates the flow of incoming email messages.

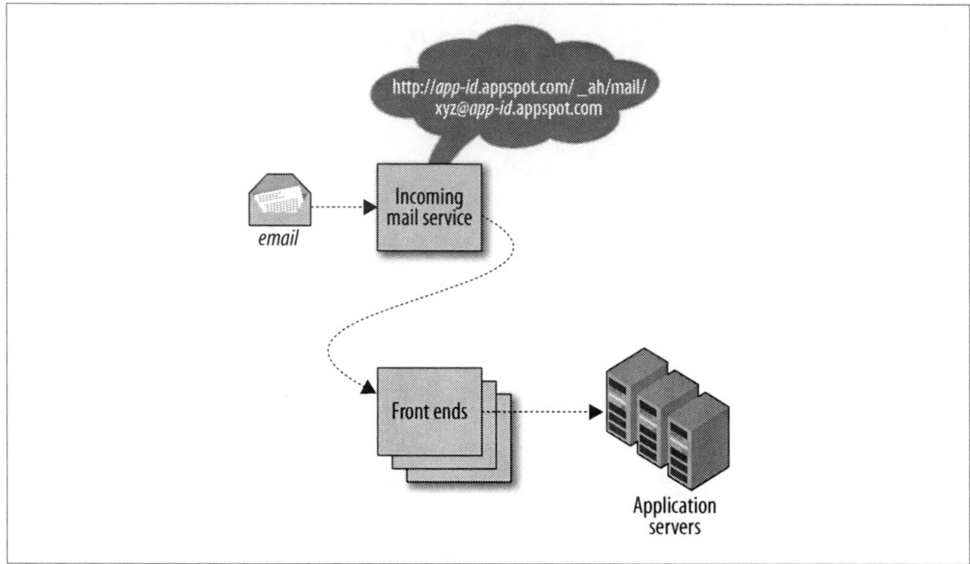

Figure 14-1. Architecture of incoming email messages, calling web hooks in response to incoming message events

Each app has its own set of incoming email addresses, based on its application ID. For email, the app can receive messages at addresses of these forms:

app-id@appspotmail.com

anything@*app-id*.appspotmail.com

App Engine does not support receiving email at an address on an app's custom (Google Apps) domain name. However, you can use an email address on your custom domain as a "From" address by setting it up as a Google account, and then making that account a "developer" of the app in the Administration Console. You can further configure automatic forwarding of replies to that address by using Gmail.

In this chapter, we discuss the APIs for sending and receiving email messages, and language-specific tools for creating and processing those messages.

Sending Email Messages

To send an email message, you call the API of the Mail service. The outgoing message has a sender address ("From"), one or more recipients ("To," "Cc," or "Bcc"), a subject, a message body, and optional file attachments.

An email message can contain a limited set of message headers, which are understood by mail servers and clients. The headers an app can set are restricted to prevent the service from being abused to send forged messages. (See the official documentation for the current list of allowed headers.) The Mail service attaches additional headers to the message, such as the date and time the message is sent.

You can specify a multipart message body, such as to include both plain text and HTML versions of the message, and to include attachments. The total size of the message, including all headers and attachments, cannot exceed 10 megabytes.

The call to the Mail service is asynchronous. When your application calls the Mail service to send a message, the message is enqueued for delivery, and the service call returns. If there is a problem delivering the message, such as if the remote mail server cannot be contacted or the remote server says the address is invalid, an error message is sent via email to the sender address. The app is not notified of the failure by the service directly. If the app must be notified of a message send failure, you can use an incoming email address for the app as the sender address. The app will have to parse the message sent by the remote server for an error.

When running on App Engine, outgoing email counts towards your outgoing bandwidth quota, as well as the quota for the total number of email recipients. You can increase these quota by adjusting your billing settings. Email messages sent to the application administrators use a separate limit (Admins Emailed in the Quotas display of the Administration Console) to allow for apps that send maintenance reports and alerts to administrators but do not need to send email to arbitrary recipients.

App Engine gives special treatment to the limit on email recipients to prevent abuse of the system, such as sending junk or scam email (which is against the terms of service and an all-around lousy thing to do). New apps are only allowed a small number of email recipients per month under the free plan. When you activate billing for an app for the first time, this limit is not raised until the first charge to your billing account succeeds. This is intended to discourage abusers from activating billing with invalid payment details just to temporarily raise the recipient limit.

If your app relies on sending email to many users (such as for registration confirmation), be sure to activate billing and test your email features two weeks in advance of launching your website.

Sending Email from the Development Server

When your app runs in the development server, sending a message causes the server to print information about the message to the logs, and no message is sent. In the Python development server only, you can configure the server to actually send email messages by using either Sendmail (if it's set up on your machine) or an SMTP server.

To configure the Python development server to use Sendmail to send email, give the server the `--enable_sendmail` flag:

```
dev_appserver.py --enable_sendmail appdir
```

To configure the Python development server to use an SMTP server to send email, use the `--smtp_host=...` (with optional `--smtp_port=...`), `--smtp_user=...`, and `--smtp_password=...` arguments:

```
dev_appserver.py \
    --smtp_host=smtp.example.com \
    --smtp_user=exmail \
    --smtp_password="t3!!t43w0r!d" \
    appdir
```

The Java development server does not support sending email; it just logs the message at the "info" log level. You can adjust the level at which outgoing mail messages are logged by running the development server with the `mail.log_mail_level` property set to a value such as `WARNING`. You can also tell the development server to log the body of the message by setting the `mail.log_mail_body` system property to `true`. From the command line:

```
dev_appserver.sh \
    --jvm_flag=-Dmail.log_mail_level=WARNING \
    --jvm_flag=-Dmail.log_message_body=true \
    appdir
```

From Eclipse, select the Run menu, Debug Configurations, and then select your app's configuration. Select the Arguments tab, then in the "VM arguments" section, set VM properties like this:

```
-Dmail.log_mail_level=WARNING -Dmail.log_mail_body=true
```

Sender Addresses

The sender ("From") address on an outgoing email message must be one of the allowed addresses:

- The Google Account address of one of the application administrators
- The address of the user currently signed in to the app with Google Accounts (during the request handler that is sending the message)
- A valid incoming email address for the application

Replies to messages sent by the app go to the sender address, as do error messages sent by the outgoing mail server (such as "Could not connect to remote host") or the remote mail server (such as "User not found").

You can use an application developer's Google Account address as the sender address. To add accounts as application administrators, go to the Developers section of the Administration Console. If you do not want to use the account of a specific developer as the sender address, you can create a new Google Account for a general purpose address, then add it as a developer for the app: in the Console, select Permissions, then invite the user account. Be sure to select the Viewer role, so if someone gets the account's password, that person cannot make changes to the app. You can use Gmail to monitor the account for replies, and you can set up automatic email forwarding in Gmail to relay replies to specific administrators or a mailing list (or Google Group) automatically.

A Google account can use a Gmail address or a Google Apps domain address. If your app has a custom domain, you can create a new Google account with an address on the domain (such as `support@example.com`), give the account Viewer permissions for the app, and use the address for outgoing mail.

If you don't have an Apps domain, you can create a Gmail account, using the application ID, and add *`app-id`*`@gmail.com` as a developer. Note that if you create the Gmail account before you register the application ID, you must be signed in using the Gmail account when you register the application ID. App Engine won't let you register an app ID that matches a Gmail account name unless you are signed in with that account.

Technically it's possible for someone else to register a Gmail account with your app ID after you have registered the app ID, although it's unlikely. If you'd like to claim your ID as a Gmail address, do it soon. Of course, the owner of the Gmail account can't administer your app unless you add the account as a developer.

You can use the email address of a user as the sender address if and only if the address is of a registered Google Account, the user is signed in, and the user initiated the request whose handler is sending the email. That is, you can send email on behalf of the "current" user. This is useful if the email is triggered by the user's action and if replies to the message ought to go to the user's email address. The Google Accounts API does not expose the user's human-readable name, so you won't be able to provide that unless you get it from the user yourself.

As we mentioned earlier, an application can receive email messages at addresses of the form *`app-id`*`@appspotmail.com` or *`anything`*`@`*`app-id`*`.appspotmail.com`, where *`app-id`* is your application ID and *`anything`* can be any string that's valid on the left side of the email address (it can't contain an `@` symbol). You can use an incoming email address as the sender of an email message to have replies routed to a request handler.

The "anything" lets you create custom sender addresses on the fly. For example, a customer support app could start an email conversation with a unique ID and include the ID in the email address (`support+`*`ID`*`@`*`app-id`*`.appspotmail.com`), and save replies for that conversation in the datastore so the entire thread can be viewed by customer service personnel.

Note that the sender address will also receive error ("bounce") messages. If you use an incoming mail address as the sender, you could have the app process error messages to remove invalid email addresses automatically. Note that different remote email servers may use different formatting for error messages.

Any email address can also have a human-friendly name, such as `"The Example Team <admin@example.com>"`. How you do this is specific to the interface; we'll look at the interfaces in a moment.

You can include a separate "Reply-to" address in addition to the sender ("From") address. Most mail readers and servers will use this address instead of the sender address for replies and error messages. The "Reply-to" address must meet the same requirements as the sender address.

The development server does not check that the sender address meets these conditions because it doesn't know who the app's developers are. Be sure to test features that send email while running on App Engine.

Recipients

An outgoing email message can use any address for a recipient, and can have multiple recipients.

A recipient can be a primary recipient (the "To" field), a secondary or "carbon-copied" recipient (the "Cc" field), or a "blind carbon-copied" recipient ("Bcc"). The "To" and "Cc" recipients are included in the content of the message, so a reply intended for all recipients can be sent to the visible addresses. The "Bcc" recipients receive the message, but their addresses are not included in the content of the message, and so are not included in replies.

The "Bcc" recipient type is especially useful if you want a single message to go to multiple recipients, but you do not want any recipient to know who received the message. You can use this technique to send an email newsletter to users without exposing the users' email addresses. A common technique for newsletters is to use the sender address as the sole "To" recipient, and make everyone else a "Bcc" recipient.

The number of recipients for an email message counts toward an email recipient quota. This quota is initially small to prevent unsolicited email advertisers from abusing the system. You can raise this quota by allocating part of your budget toward email recipients.

When you enable billing in your app for the first time, the email recipients quota will not increase from the free level until your first payment is processed. This is one of several measures to prevent spammers from abusing the service.

Attachments

An app can attach files to an email message. One good use of attachments is to include images for rich HTML email messages.

For security reasons (mostly having to do with insecure email clients), some file types are not allowed as email attachments. A file's type is determined by its filename extension. For example, files that represent executable programs (such as *.exe*, *.bat*, or *.sh*) are not allowed. Currently, common file archive types, like *.zip*, are also not allowed.

The MIME content type of each attachment is derived from the filename extension. If a filename extension is not recognized, the content type is set to `application/octet-stream`.

See the official documentation for the complete list of disallowed attachment types, as well as a list of mappings from extensions to MIME content types.

If you want to deliver files to users that are not allowed as attachments, one option is to send a link to a request handler that delivers the file through the browser. The link can be personalized with a temporary unique ID, or restricted using Google Accounts authentication.

Sending Email in Python

The Python API includes two ways of preparing and sending messages. One way is to call a function with the fields of the message as keyword arguments. Another is to prepare the message in an object, then call a method on the object to send the message. The Mail service API is provided by the `google.appengine.api.mail` package.

The `send_mail()` method takes the fields of the message as parameters:

```
from google.appengine.api import mail
from google.appengine.api import users

message_body = '''
Welcome to Example!  Your account has been created.
You can edit your user profile by clicking the
following link:

http://www.example.com/profile/

Let us know if you have any questions.

The Example Team
'''

# (admin@example.com is a Google Account that has
# been added as a developer for the app.)
mail.send_mail(
    sender='The Example Team <admin@example.com>',
    to=users.get_current_user().email(),
    subject='Welcome to Example.com!',
    body=message_body)
```

Alternatively, you can prepare the message using an EmailMessage object, then call its send() method. The EmailMessage constructor accepts the same arguments as the send_mail() function:

```
message = mail.EmailMessage(
    sender='The Example Team <admin@example.com>',
    to=users.get_current_user().email(),
    subject='Welcome to Example.com!',
    body=message_body)

message.send()
```

You can also set the fields of an EmailMessage using attributes of the object. This allows you to reuse the same object to send multiple messages with modified values.

The possible fields of a message are listed in Table 14-1.

Table 14-1. Fields of an email message in the Python interface

Field	Value	Required?
sender	The sender's email address. A string.	Required
to	A "To" recipient address as a string, or multiple "To" recipient addresses as a list of strings.	Required
subject	The subject of the message. A string.	Required
body	The plain-text body of the message. A string.	Required
cc	A "Cc" recipient address as a string, or multiple "Cc" recipient addresses as a list of strings.	Optional
bcc	A "Bcc" recipient address as a string, or multiple "Bcc" recipient addresses as a list of strings. "Bcc" recipients receive the message, but are not included in the content of the message.	Optional
reply_to	An alternate address to which clients should send replies instead of the sender address. A string.	Optional
html	An alternate HTML representation of the body of the message, displayed instead of body by HTML-capable email readers. A string.	Optional
attachments	File attachments for the message. A list of tuples, one per attachment, each containing the filename and the file data.	Optional
headers	A dict of additional message headers. See the official documentation for a list of allowed headers.	Optional

The value of an email address field (sender, to, cc, bcc, reply_to) can be a plain email address:

```
'juliet@example.com'
```

It can also be an address with a human-readable name, in the standard format (RFC 822):

```
'Juliet <juliet@example.com>'
```

When you call the send() method or the send_mail() function, the API checks the message to make sure it is valid. This includes testing the email addresses for validity, and making sure the message has all the required fields. You can call functions to perform these checks separately. The `is_email_valid(address)` function returns `True` if it considers an email address valid. The `is_initialized()` method of an `EmailAddress` object returns `True` if the object has all the fields necessary for sending.

The API includes a shortcut method that sends an email message to all administrators (developers) for the application. The `send_mail_to_admins()` function accepts the same arguments as `send_mail()`, but without the recipient fields. There is also an `AdminEmailMessage` class that is similar to the `EmailMessage` class, but with recipients set to be the app administrators automatically. When calling this function, the message size is limited to 16 kilobytes. (This is a safety limit that ensures delivery of important administrative messages.)

Example 14-1 shows a larger example using `EmailMessage`, with both plain text and HTML parts, and an attachment.

Example 14-1. An example of sending an email message in Python, using several features

```
from google.appengine.api import mail

def send_registration_key(user_addr, software_key_data):
    message_body = '''
    Thank you for purchasing The Example App, the best
    example on the market!  Your registration key is attached
    to this email.

    To install your key, download the attachment, then select
    "Register..." from the Help menu.  Select the key file, then
    click "Register".

    You can download the app at any time from:
      http://www.example.com/downloads/

    Thanks again!

    The Example Team
    '''

    html_message_body = '''
    <p>Thank you for purchasing The Example App, the best
    example on the market!  Your registration key is attached
    to this email.</p>

    <p>To install your key, download the attachment, then select
    <b>Register...</b> from the <b>Help</b> menu.  Select the key file, then
    click <b>Register</b>.</p>

    <p>You can download the app at any time from:</p>

    <p>
      <a href="http://www.example.com/downloads/">
        http://www.example.com/downloads/
      </a>
```

```
</p>

<p>Thanks again!</p>

<p>The Example Team<br />
<img src="http://www.example.com/images/logo_email.gif" /></p>
'''

message = mail.EmailMessage(
    sender='The Example Team <admin@example.com>',
    to=user_addr,
    subject='Your Example Registration Key',
    body=message_body,
    html=html_message_body,
    attachments=[('example_key.txt', software_key_data)])

message.send()
```

Sending Email in Java

The Java interface to the Mail service is the JavaMail standard interface (`javax.mail.*`). There is also a low-level interface, although you can access every feature of the service through the JavaMail implementation. (As such, we'll only discuss the JavaMail interface here.)

To use JavaMail, you first create a JavaMail "session." The `Session` object usually contains information needed to connect to a mail server, but with App Engine, no configuration is needed. You prepare the message as a `MimeMessage` object, then send it using the `send()` static method of the `Transport` class. The `Transport` class uses the most recently created session to send the message:

```
import java.util.Properties;
import javax.mail.Message;
import javax.mail.MessagingException;
import javax.mail.Session;
import javax.mail.Transport;
import javax.mail.internet.AddressException;
import javax.mail.internet.InternetAddress;
import javax.mail.internet.MimeMessage;

import com.google.appengine.api.users.User;
import com.google.appengine.api.users.UserServiceFactory;

// ...
        User user = UserServiceFactory.getUserService().getCurrentUser();
        String recipientAddress = user.getEmail();

        Properties props = new Properties();
        Session session = Session.getDefaultInstance(props, null);

        String messageBody =
            "Welcome to Example!  Your account has been created. " +
            "You can edit your user profile by clicking the " +
```

```
            "following link:\n\n" +
            "http://www.example.com/profile/\n\n" +
            "Let us know if you have any questions.\n\n" +
            "The Example Team\n";

        try {
            Message message = new MimeMessage(session);
            message.setFrom(new InternetAddress("admin@example.com",
                                               "The Example Team"));
            message.addRecipient(Message.RecipientType.TO,
                             new InternetAddress(recipientAddress));
            message.setSubject("Welcome to Example.com!");
            message.setText(messageBody);
            Transport.send(message);

        } catch (AddressException e) {
            // An email address was invalid.
            // ...
        } catch (MessagingException e) {
            // There was an error contacting the Mail service.
            // ...
        }
```

As shown here, you call methods on the `MimeMessage` to set fields and to add recipients and content. The simplest message has a sender (`setFrom()`), one "To" recipient (`addRecipient()`), a subject (`setSubject()`), and a plain-text message body (`setText()`).

The `setFrom()` method takes an `InternetAddress`. You can create an `InternetAddress` with just the email address (a `String`) or the address and a human-readable name as arguments to the constructor. The email address of the sender must meet the requirements described earlier. You can use any string for the human-readable name.

The `addRecipient()` method takes a recipient type and an `InternetAddress`. The allowed recipient types are `Message.RecipientType.TO` ("To," a primary recipient), `Message.RecipientType.CC` ("Cc" or "carbon-copy," a secondary recipient), and `Message.RecipientType.BCC` ("Bcc" or "blind carbon-copy," where the recipient is sent the message but the address does not appear in the message content). You can call `addRecipient()` multiple times to add multiple recipients of any type.

The `setText()` method sets the plain-text body for the message. To include an HTML version of the message body for mail readers that support HTML, you create a `MimeMultipart` object, then create a `MimeBodyPart` for the plain-text body and another for the HTML body and add them to the `MimeMultipart`. You then make the `MimeMultipart` the content of the `MimeMessage`:

```
import javax.mail.Multipart;
import javax.mail.internet.MimeBodyPart;
import javax.mail.internet.MimeMultipart;

// ...
            String textBody = "...text...";
            String htmlBody = "...HTML...";
```

```
Multipart multipart = new MimeMultipart();

MimeBodyPart textPart = new MimeBodyPart();
textPart.setContent(textBody, "text/plain");
multipart.addBodyPart(textPart);

MimeBodyPart htmlPart = new MimeBodyPart();
htmlPart.setContent(htmlBody, "text/html");
multipart.addBodyPart(htmlPart);

message.setContent(multipart);
```

You attach files to the email message in a similar way:

```
Multipart multipart = new MimeMultipart();
// ...

byte[] fileData = getBrochureData();
String fileName = "brochure.pdf";
String fileType = "application/pdf";

MimeBodyPart attachmentPart = new MimeBodyPart();
attachmentPart.setContent(fileData, fileType);
attachmentPart.setFileName(fileName);
multipart.addBodyPart(attachmentPart);

// ...
message.setContent(multipart);
```

You can add multiple `MimeBodyPart` objects to a single `MimeMultipart`. The plain-text body, the HTML body, and the file attachments are each part of a MIME multipart message.

When using a `MimeMultipart`, you must include a `text/plain` part to be the plain-text body of the message. The multipart object overrides any plain-text content set on the `MimeMessage` with `setText()`.

App Engine's implementation of the JavaMail interface includes a shortcut for sending an email message to all of the app's administrators. To send a message to all administrators, use a recipient address of `"admins"`, with no `@` symbol or domain name.

Receiving Email Messages

To receive incoming email messages, you must first enable the feature in your app's configuration. Incoming email is disabled by default, so unwanted messages are ignored and do not try to contact your app or incur costs.

To enable inbound services, you add a section to the app's configuration file. In Python, you add a section similar to the following in the *app.yaml* file:

```
inbound_services:
- mail
```

In Java, you add a similar section to the *appengine-web.xml* file, anywhere inside the root element:

```
<inbound-services>
  <service>mail</service>
</inbound-services>
```

Once your app is deployed, you can confirm that the incoming mail service is enabled from the Administration Console, under Application Settings. If your app does not appear to be receiving HTTP requests for incoming email messages, check the Console and update the configuration if necessary.

With the `mail` inbound service enabled in configuration, an application can receive email messages at any of several addresses. An incoming mail message is routed to the app in the form of an HTTP request.

Email sent to addresses of the following forms are routed to the default version of the app:

`app-id@appspotmail.com`

`anything@app-id.appspotmail.com`

The HTTP request uses the POST action, and is sent to the following URL path:

`/_ah/mail/to-address`

The recipient email address of the message is included at the end of the URL path, so the app can distinguish between different values of "anything."

The body content of the HTTP POST request is the complete MIME email message, including the mail headers and body. It can be parsed by any library capable of parsing MIME email messages. We'll look at examples in Python and Java in the next two sections.

The development server console (*http://localhost:8080/_ah/admin/*) includes a feature for simulating incoming email by submitting a web form. The development server cannot receive actual email messages.

If the app has the incoming mail service enabled but does not have a request handler for the appropriate URL, or if the request handler returns an HTTP response code other than 200 for the request, the message gets "bounced" and the sender receives an error email message.

Receiving Email in Python

To receive email in Python, you map the incoming email URL path to a script handler in *app.yaml* file:

```
handlers:
- url: /_ah/mail/.+
  script: handle_email.py
```

The app address used for the message is included in the URL path, so you can set up separate handlers for different addresses directly in the configuration:

```
handlers:
- url: /_ah/mail/support%40.*app-id\.appspotmail\.com
  script: support_contact.py
- url: /_ah/mail/.+
  script: handle_email.py
```

Email addresses are URL-encoded in the final URL, so this pattern uses `%40` to represent an `@` symbol. Also notice you must include a `.*` before the application ID when using this technique, so the pattern works for messages sent to version-specific addresses (such as `support@dev.`*`app-id`*`.appspotmail.com`).

The Python SDK includes a class for parsing the POST content into a convenient object, called `InboundEmailMessage` (in the `google.appengine.api.mail` package). It takes the multipart MIME data (the POST body) as an argument to its constructor. Here's an example using the webapp framework:

```
from google.appengine.api import mail
from google.appengine.ext import webapp2

class IncomingMailHandler(webapp2.RequestHandler):
    def post(self):
        message = mail.InboundEmailMessage(self.request.body)
        sender = message.sender
        recipients = message.to
        body = list(message.bodies(content_type='text/plain'))[0]
        # ...

application = webapp2.WSGIApplication([('/_ah/mail/.+', IncomingMailHandler)],
                                      debug=True)
```

The `InboundEmailMessage` object includes attributes for the fields of the message, similar to `EmailMessage`. `sender` is the sender's email address, possibly with a displayable name in the standard format (`Mr. Sender <sender@example.com>`). `to` is a list of primary recipient addresses, and `cc` is a list of secondary recipients. (There is no `bcc` on an incoming message, because blind-carbon-copied recipients are not included in the message content.) `subject` is the message's subject.

The `InboundEmailMessage` object may have more than one message body: an HTML body and a plain-text body. You can iterate over the MIME multipart parts of the types `text/html` and `text/plain`, using the `bodies()` method. Without arguments, this method returns an iterator that returns the HTML parts first, and then the plain-text parts. You can limit the parts returned to just the HTML or plain-text parts by setting the `content_type` parameter. For example, to get just the plain-text bodies:

```
for text_body in message.bodies(content_type='text/plain'):
    # ...
```

In the example earlier, we extracted the first plain-text body by passing the iterator to the `list()` type, then indexing its first argument (which assumes one exists):

```
text = list(message.bodies(content_type='text/plain'))[0]
```

If the incoming message has file attachments, then these are accessible on the `attachments` attribute. As with using `EmailMessage` for sending, this attribute is a list of tuples whose first element is the filename and whose second element is the data byte string. `InboundEmailMessage` allows all file types for incoming attachments, and does not require that the filename accurately represent the file type. *Be careful* when using files sent to the app by users, since they may not be what they say they are, and have not been scanned for viruses.

The Python SDK includes a convenient webapp handler base class for processing incoming email, called `InboundMailHandler` in the `google.appengine.ext.webapp.mail_handlers` package. You use the handler by creating a subclass that overrides the `receive()` method, then installing it like any other handler. When the handler receives an email message, the `receive()` method is called with an `InboundEmailMessage` object as its argument:

```
from google.appengine.ext.webapp import mail_handlers

class MyMailHandler(mail_handlers.InboundMailHandler):
    def receive(self, message):
        # ...

application = webapp2.WSGIApplication([('/_ah/mail/.+', MyMailHandler)],
                                      debug=True)
```

Receiving Email in Java

In Java, you map the incoming email URL path to a servlet with an entry in the deployment descriptor (*web.xml*):

```
<servlet>
  <servlet-name>mailreceiver</servlet-name>
  <servlet-class>myapp.MailReceiverServlet</servlet-class>
</servlet>
<servlet-mapping>
  <servlet-name>mailreceiver</servlet-name>
  <url-pattern>/_ah/mail/*</url-pattern>
</servlet-mapping>
```

The JavaMail and servlet APIs provide everything we need to parse the MIME multipart message in the HTTP POST request. The `MimeMessage` class (in the `javax.mail.internet` package) has a constructor that accepts a `java.io.InputStream`, which we can get from the `HttpServletRequest` by using its `getInputStream()` method. The `MimeMessage` constructor also needs a JavaMail `Session`, which, as with sending email, can use the default empty configuration:

```
import java.io.IOException;
import java.util.Properties;
import javax.mail.Session;
import javax.mail.MessagingException;
```

```
import javax.mail.Multipart;
import javax.mail.Part;
import javax.mail.internet.MimeMessage;
import javax.servlet.http.*;

public class MailReceiverServlet extends HttpServlet {
    public void doPost(HttpServletRequest req,
                       HttpServletResponse resp)
            throws IOException {
        Properties props = new Properties();
        Session session = Session.getDefaultInstance(props, null);

        try {
            MimeMessage message = new MimeMessage(session, req.getInputStream());
            String contentType = message.getContentType();
            Object content = message.getContent();
            if (content instanceof String) {
                // A plain text body.
                // ...

            } else if (content instanceof Multipart) {
                // A multipart body.
                for (int i = 0; i < ((Multipart) content).getCount(); i++) {
                    Part part = ((Multipart) content).getBodyPart(i);
                    // ...

                }
            }

        } catch (MessagingException e) {
            // Problem parsing the message data.
            // ...

        }
    }
}
```

If the incoming message is a MIME multipart message (such as a message with an HTML body, or attachments), the `getContent()` method of the `MimeMessage` returns an object that implements the `Multipart` interface. You can use this interface to get a count of the parts (`getCount()`) and select parts by index (`getBodyPart(int index)`, which returns a `BodyPart`).

CHAPTER 15

Sending and Receiving Instant Messages with XMPP

So far, we've seen two mechanisms an app can use to communicate with the outside world. The first and most prominent of these is HTTP: an app can receive and respond to HTTP requests, and can send HTTP requests to other hosts and receive responses with the URL Fetch service. The second is email: an app can send email messages by using the Mail service, and can receive messages via a proxy that calls a request handler for each incoming email message.

In this chapter, we introduce a third method of communication: XMPP, also known as "instant messages," or simply "chat." An app can participate in a chat dialogue with a user of any XMPP-compatible chat service, such as Google Talk or any Jabber server. The XMPP service is useful for chat interfaces, such as a chat-based query engine, or a customer service proxy. App Engine does not act as an XMPP service itself. Instead, it connects to Google Talk's infrastructure to participate as a chat user.

Sending and receiving XMPP messages works similarly to email messages. To send a message, an app calls the XMPP service API. To receive a message, the app declares that it accepts such messages in its configuration, and then handles HTTP requests sent by the XMPP service to special-purpose URLs. Figure 15-1 illustrates the flow of incoming XMPP messages.

Each participant in an XMPP communication has an address similar to an email address, known as a *JID*. (JID is short for "Jabber ID," named after the Jabber project, where XMPP originated.) A JID consists of a username, an "at" symbol (`@`), and the domain name of the XMPP server. A JID can also have an optional "resource" string, which is used to identify specific clients connected to the service with the username. A message sent to the ID without the resource goes to all connected clients:

```
username @ domain / resource
```

To send a message, a chat participant sends an XMPP message to its own XMPP server. The participant's chat service contacts the recipient service's host by using the domain

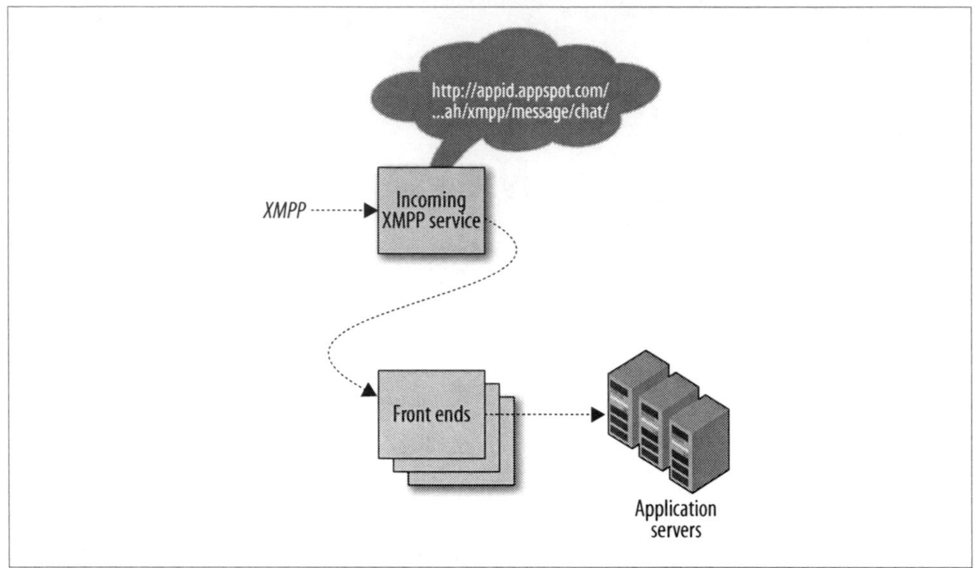

Figure 15-1. Architecture of incoming XMPP messages, calling web hooks in response to incoming message events

name of the JID and a standard port, then delivers the message. If the remote service accepts messages for the JID and someone is connected to the service with a chat client for that JID, the service delivers the message to the client.

As with email, each app has its own set of JIDs, based on its application ID. For XMPP chat, the app can receive messages at addresses of these forms:

`app-id@appspot.com`

`anything@app-id.appspotchat.com`

(Notice the differences in the domain names from the options available for incoming email.)

App Engine does not support XMPP addresses on a custom (Google Apps) domain. This is one of only a few cases where exposing your application ID to users cannot be avoided.

If your users have Google accounts, you can use the Google Talk API to build custom clients to interact with your app over XMPP. See the Google Talk API documentation (*http://developers.google.com/talk/*) for more information.

Let's take a look at the features and API of the XMPP service.

Inviting a User to Chat

Before a user of an XMPP-compatible instant messaging service will see any messages your app sends, the service needs to know that the user is expecting your messages. This can happen in two ways: either the user explicitly adds your app's JID to her contact list, or she accepts an invitation to chat sent by the app.

An app can send an invitation to chat by calling the XMPP service API. For apps, it's polite to get the user's permission to do this first, so the complete workflow looks something like this:

1. The user visits the website, and activates the chat-based feature of the service, providing a JID.
2. The app sends an invitation to chat to the user's JID.
3. The user accepts the invitation in her chat client.
4. The user and app exchange chat messages.

The alternative where the user adds the app's JID to her contact list is usually equivalent to sending an invitation to the app. App Engine accepts all such invitations automatically, even if the app does not accept chat messages.

An accepted invitation entitles both parties to know the other party's *presence* status, whether the party is connected and accepting messages. This includes the ability to know when an invitation is accepted. See "Managing Presence" on page 378.

In the development server, inviting a user to chat emits a log message, but otherwise does nothing.

Sending Invitations in Python

To invite a user to chat in Python, you call the `send_invite()` function in the `google.appengine.api.xmpp` module. It takes the recipient JID as its first argument, and an optional sender JID (`from_jid`) as its second argument. By default, it uses *`app-id`*`@appspot.com` as the sender JID:

```
from google.appengine.api import xmpp

jid = 'juliet@example.com'

xmpp.send_invite(jid)  # from app-id@appspot.com

xmpp.send_invite(jid, from_jid='support@app-id.appspotchat.com')  # from a custom JID
```

Sending Invitations in Java

In Java, each JID is represented by an instance of the `JID` class, in the package `com.google.appengine.api.xmpp`. You create this by passing the address as a string to the `JID` constructor. To send an invitation, you call the `sendInvitation()` method with either one or two arguments:

```
import com.google.appengine.api.xmpp.JID;
import com.google.appengine.api.xmpp.XMPPService;
import com.google.appengine.api.xmpp.XMPPServiceFactory;

// ...
        XMPPService xmpp = XMPPServiceFactory.getXMPPService();

        // From app-id@appspot.com:
        xmpp.sendInvitation(new JID("juliet@example.com"));

        // From a custom JID:
        xmpp.sendInvitation(new JID("juliet@example.com"),
                            new JID("support@app-id.appspotchat.com"));
```

Sending Chat Messages

An XMPP message includes a sender address, one or more recipient addresses, a message type, and a message body.

The sender address must be one of the app's incoming XMPP addresses. These are of the form *app-id*@`appspot.com` or *anything*@*app-id*.`appspotchat.com`, where *app-id* is your application ID and *anything* can be any string that's valid on the left side of a JID (it can't contain an `@` symbol). Unlike incoming email addresses, it's not as convenient to use the "anything" form for creating IDs on the fly, since the recipient needs to accept an invitation from that ID before receiving messages. But it can still be useful for sessions that begin with an invitation, or addresses that represent specific purposes or users of the app (`support@`*app-id*`.appspotchat.com`).

If the version of the app that is sending an XMPP message is not the default version, App Engine modifies the sender address to a version-specific address, so replies go directly to the correct version: either *anything*@*version*.*app-id*.`appspotchat.com` or *app-id*@*version*.*app-id*.`appspotchat.com`.

App Engine adds a "resource" to the end of the sender JID (after the domain name) that looks like this: `/bot`. This is mostly just to comply with the best practice of sending messages using JIDs with resources. It isn't noticed by chat users, and is not needed when a user wishes to send a message to the app. You'll see it in log messages.

The message type can be any of the types in the XMPP standard, including chat, error, groupchat, headline, and normal. An app can only receive messages of the types chat, normal, and error, and so cannot participate in group chats. For straightforward communication between an app and a chat user, you usually want to send chat messages. For an app and a custom client, you can do what you like.

Messages are sent asynchronously. The service call returns immediately, and reports success only if the XMPP service enqueued the message successfully. You can configure the app to receive error messages, such as to be notified if a sent message was not received because the user went offline. See "Handling Error Messages" on page 377.

When an app is running in the development server, sending an XMPP chat message or invitation causes the server to print the message to the console. The development server does not contact the XMPP service or send messages.

Sending Chat Messages in Python

To send a chat message in Python, you call the `send_message()` function in the `google.appengine.api.xmpp` module. The function takes a JID or list of JIDs, the body of the message, and an optional sender JID (`from_jid`). It returns a success code, or a list of success codes, one for each recipient JID:

```
result = xmpp.send_message(
    'juliet@example.com',
    'Your dog has reached level 12!')

if result != xmpp.NO_ERROR:
    # ...
```

By default, this sends a message of the "chat" type. You can send a message of a different type by setting the `message_type` parameter. Acceptable values include `xmpp.MESSAGE_TYPE_CHAT` (the default), `xmpp.MESSAGE_TYPE_ERROR`, `xmpp.MESSAGE_TYPE_GROUPCHAT`, `xmpp.MESSAGE_TYPE_HEADLINE`, and `xmpp.MESSAGE_TYPE_NORMAL`.

Complete XMPP messages are sent over the network as XML data. By default, `send_message()` treats the text of the message as plain text, and knows to escape XML characters. Instead of a text message, you can send an XML stanza. This is included verbatim (assuming the stanza is well formed) in the XMPP message, so you can send structured data to XMPP clients. To tell `send_message()` that the content is an XML stanza so it doesn't escape XML characters, provide the `raw_xml=True` parameter.

The `send_message()` function returns a status code for each recipient JID, as a single value if called with a single JID, or as a list of codes if called with a list of JIDs. The possible status values are `xmpp.NO_ERROR`, `xmpp.INVALID_JID`, and `xmpp.OTHER_ERROR`.

Sending Chat Messages in Java

In Java, each action is a method of an `XMPPService` object, which you get from `XMPPServiceFactory.getXMPPService()`. You send a message by calling the `sendMessage()` method. The method takes a `Message` object, which you build with a `MessageBuilder` object. `sendMessage()` returns a `SendResponse` object, which contains status codes for each intended recipient of the message:

```
import com.google.appengine.api.xmpp.JID;
import com.google.appengine.api.xmpp.Message;
import com.google.appengine.api.xmpp.MessageBuilder;
import com.google.appengine.api.xmpp.SendResponse;
```

```
import com.google.appengine.api.xmpp.XMPPService;
import com.google.appengine.api.xmpp.XMPPServiceFactory;

// ...
        XMPPService xmpp = XMPPServiceFactory.getXMPPService();

        JID recipient = new JID("juliet@example.com");
        Message message = new MessageBuilder()
            .withRecipientJids(recipient)
            .withBody("Your dog has reached level 12!")
            .build();

        SendResponse success = xmpp.sendMessage(message);
        if (success.getStatusMap().get(recipient) != SendResponse.Status.SUCCESS) {
            // ...
        }
```

You use the `MessageBuilder` class to assemble the (immutable) `Message` object. You can chain its methods to construct a complete message in a single statement. Relevant methods include:

`withBody(String body)`
: Sets the message body.

`asXml(boolean asXml)`
: Declares that the body contains a well-formed XML stanza (and not plain text).

`withFromJid(JID jid)`
: Sets the sender JID.

`withRecipientJids(JID jid1, ...)`
: Adds one or more recipient JIDs.

`withMessageType(MessageType type)`
: Sets the message type.

`build()`
: Returns the finished `Message`.

Message types are represented by the `MessageType` enum: `MessageType.CHAT`, `MessageType.ERROR`, `MessageType.GROUPCHAT`, `MessageType.HEADLINE`, and `MessageType.NORMAL`.

The `sendMessage()` method returns a `SendResponse` object. Calling this object's `getStatusMap()` method returns a `Map<JID, SendResponseStatus>`, a map of recipient JIDs to status codes. The possible status codes are `SendResponse.Status.SUCCESS`, `SendResponse.Status.INVALID_ID`, and `SendResponse.Status.OTHER_ERROR`.

Receiving Chat Messages

As with email, to receive incoming XMPP messages, you must first enable the feature by adding the XMPP inbound services to your app's configuration. In Python, you add a section similar to the following in the *app.yaml* file:

```
inbound_services:
- xmpp_message
```

In Java, you add a similar section to the *appengine-web.xml* file, anywhere inside the root element:

```
<inbound-services>
  <service>xmpp_message</service>
</inbound-services>
```

This is the same configuration list as the `mail` inbound service. If you're enabling both email and XMPP, you provide one list of inbound services with all the items.

Deploy your app, and confirm that incoming XMPP is enabled using the Administration Console, under Application Settings. If your app does not appear to be receiving HTTP requests for incoming XMPP messages, check the Console and update the configuration if necessary.

The `xmpp_message` inbound service routes incoming XMPP messages of the types chat and normal to your app.

An app receives XMPP messages at several addresses. Messages sent to addresses of these forms are routed to the default version of the app:

> *app-id*`@appspot.com`
>
> *anything*`@`*app-id*`.appspotchat.com`

Messages sent to addresses of this form are routed to the specified version of the app, useful for testing:

> *anything*`@`*version*`.`*app-id*`.appspotmail.com`

Each message is delivered to the app as an HTTP POST request to a fixed URL path. Chat messages (both chat and normal) become POST requests to this URL path:

```
/_ah/xmpp/message/chat/
```

(Unlike incoming email, the sender JID is not included in these URL paths.)

The body content of the HTTP POST request is a MIME multipart message, with a part for each field of the message:

`from`
: The sender's JID.

`to`
: The app JID to which this message was sent.

body
: The message body content (with characters as they were originally typed).

stanza
: The full XML stanza of the message, including the previous fields (with XML special characters escaped); useful for communicating with a custom client using XML.

The Python and Java SDKs include classes for parsing the request data into objects. (See the sections that follow.)

The development server console (*http://localhost:8080/_ah/admin/*) includes a feature for simulating incoming XMPP messages by submitting a web form. The development server cannot receive actual XMPP messages.

When using the development server console to simulate an incoming XMPP message, you must use a valid JID for the app in the "To:" field, with the application ID that appears in the app's configuration. Using any other "To:" address in the development server is an error.

Receiving Chat Messages in Python

In Python, you map the URL path to a script handler in the *app.yaml* file, as usual:

```
handlers:
- url: /_ah/xmpp/message/chat/
  script: handle_xmpp.py
  login: admin
```

As with all web hook URLs in App Engine, this URL handler can be restricted to `admin` to prevent anything other than the XMPP service from activating the request handler.

The Python library provides a `Message` class that can contain an incoming chat message. You can parse the incoming message into a `Message` object by passing a mapping of the POST parameters to its constructor. With the webapp2 framework, this is a simple matter of passing the parsed POST data (a mapping of the POST parameter names to values) in directly:

```
from google.appengine.api import xmpp
from google.appengine.ext import webapp2

class IncomingXMPPHandler(webapp2.RequestHandler):
    def post(self):
        message = xmpp.Message(self.request.POST)

        message.reply('I got your message! '
                      'It had %d characters.' % len(message.body))

application = webapp2.WSGIApplication([('/_ah/xmpp/message/chat/',
```

```
                                  IncomingXMPPHandler)],
                                debug=True)
```

The Message object has attributes for each message field: sender, to, and body. (The attribute for the "from" field is named sender because from is a Python keyword.) It also includes a convenience method for replying to the message, reply(), which takes the body of the reply as its first argument.

Handling Commands over Chat in Python

The Message class includes methods for parsing chat-style commands of this form:

```
/commandname args
```

If the chat message body is of this form, the command attribute of the Message is the command name (without the slash), and the arg attribute is everything that follows. If the message is not of this form, command is None.

webapp includes a request handler base class that makes it easy to implement chat interfaces that perform user-issued commands. Here's an example that responds to the commands /stats and /score username, and ignores all other messages:

```
from google.appengine.api import xmpp
from google.appengine.ext import webapp2
from google.appengine.ext.webapp import xmpp_handlers

def get_stats():
    # ...

def get_score_for_user(username):
    # ...

class UnknownUserError(Exception):
    pass

class ScoreBotHandler(xmpp_handlers.CommandHandler):
    def stats_command(self, message):
        stats = get_stats()
        if stats:
            message.reply('The latest stats: %s' % stats)
        else:
            message.reply('Stats are not available right now.')

    def score_command(self, message):
        try:
            score = get_score_for_user(message.arg)
            message.reply('Score for user %s: %d' % (message.arg, score))
        except UnknownUserError, e:
            message.reply('Unknown user %s' % message.arg)

application = webapp2.WSGIApplication([('/_ah/xmpp/message/chat/', ScoreBotHandler)],
                                      debug=True)
```

The `CommandHandler` base class, provided by the `google.appengine.ext.webapp.xmpp_handlers` package, parses the incoming message for a command. If the message contains such a command, the handler attempts to call a method named after the command. For example, when the app receives this chat message:

```
/score druidjane
```

The handler would call the `score_command()` method with a message where `message.arg` is `'druidjane'`.

If there is no method for the parsed command, the handler calls the `unhandled_command()` method, whose default implementation replies to the message with "Unknown command." You can override this method to customize its behavior.

The base handler calls the command method with the `Message` object as an argument. The method can use the `command` and `arg` properties to read the parsed command.

If the incoming message does not start with a `/commandname`-style command, the base handler calls the `text_message()` method with the `Message` as its argument. The default implementation does nothing, and you can override it to specify behavior in this case.

This package also contains a simpler handler class named `BaseHandler`, with several useful features. It parses incoming messages, and logs and ignores malformed messages. If a message is valid, it calls its `message_received()` method, which you override with the intended behavior. The class also overrides `webapp.RequestHandler`'s `handle_exception()` method to send an XMPP reply with a generic error message when an uncaught exception occurs, so the user isn't left to wonder whether the message was received. (`CommandHandler` extends `BaseHandler`, and so also has these features.)

Receiving Chat Messages in Java

In Java, you process incoming XMPP messages by mapping a servlet to the URL path called by the XMPP service, in the deployment descriptor. You can restrict the URL path by using a `<security-constraint>` to ensure only the XMPP service can access it:

```
<servlet>
  <servlet-name>xmppreceiver</servlet-name>
  <servlet-class>myapp.XMPPReceiverServlet</servlet-class>
</servlet>
<servlet-mapping>
  <servlet-name>xmppreceiver</servlet-name>
  <url-pattern>/_ah/xmpp/message/chat/</url-pattern>
</servlet-mapping>

<security-constraint>
  <web-resource-collection>
    <url-pattern>/_ah/xmpp/message/chat/</url-pattern>
  </web-resource-collection>
  <auth-constraint>
    <role-name>admin</role-name>
```

```
    </auth-constraint>
  </security-constraint>
```

The XMPPService object includes a parseMessage() method that knows how to parse the incoming request data into a Message object. You access the data by using the Message's methods:

```
import java.io.IOException;
import javax.servlet.http.*;

import com.google.appengine.api.xmpp.Message;
import com.google.appengine.api.xmpp.XMPPService;
import com.google.appengine.api.xmpp.XMPPServiceFactory;

public class XMPPReceiverServlet extends HttpServlet {
    public void doPost(HttpServletRequest req,
                       HttpServletResponse resp)
            throws IOException {
        XMPPService xmpp = XMPPServiceFactory.getXMPPService();
        Message message = xmpp.parseMessage(req);
        // ...
    }
}
```

You access the fields of a Message using methods:

getFromJid()
: The sender JID.

getMessageType()
: The MessageType of the message: MessageType.CHAT or MessageType.NORMAL.

getRecipientJids()
: The app JID used, as a single-element JID[].

getBody()
: The String content of the message.

getStanza()
: The String raw XML of the message.

Handling Error Messages

When an app calls the XMPP service to send a message, the message is queued for delivery and sent asynchronously with the call. The call will only return with an error if the message the app is sending is malformed. If the app wants to know about an error during delivery of the message (such as the inability to connect to a remote server), or an error returned by the remote XMPP server (such as a nonexistent user), it can listen for error messages.

Error messages are just another type of chat message, but the XMPP service separates incoming error messages into a separate inbound service. To enable this service, add the xmpp_error inbound service to the app's configuration.

In Python's *app.yaml*:

```
inbound_services:
- xmpp_message
- xmpp_error
```

In Java's *appengine-web.xml*:

```
<inbound-services>
  <service>xmpp_message</service>
  <service>xmpp_error</service>
</inbound-services>
```

Error messages arrive as POST requests at this URL path:

```
/_ah/xmpp/error/
```

You handle an error message just as you would a chat message: create a request handler, map it to the URL path, and parse the POST request for more information.

Neither the Python nor Java APIs provide any assistance parsing incoming error messages. While XMPP error messages are similar in structure to chat messages (with a type of `error`), minor differences are not recognized by the message parsers provided. You can examine the XML data structure in the POST message body, which conforms to the XMPP message standard. See the XMPP specification (*http://xmpp.org/*) for details.

Managing Presence

After the user accepts an app's invitation to chat, both parties are able to see whether the other party is available to receive chat messages. In XMPP RFC 3921 (*http://xmpp.org/rfcs/rfc3921.html*), this is known as *presence*. The process of asking for and granting permission to see presence is called *subscription*. For privacy reasons, one user must be successfully subscribed to the other before she can send messages, see presence information, or otherwise know the user exists.

When a user accepts an app's invitation to chat (subscription request), the user's client sends a "subscribed" message to the app, to confirm that the app is now subscribed. If, later, the user revokes this permission, the client sends an "unsubscribed" message. While the app is subscribed to a user, the user's client will send all changes in presence to the app as another kind of message.

Conversely, a user can also send "subscribe" and "unsubscribe" messages to the app. It's the app's responsibility to maintain a list of subscribed users to use when sending presence updates.

If you'd like to receive these new message types (and be billed for the bandwidth), you must enable these as separate inbound services. Subscription information (invitation responses and subscription requests) use the `xmpp_subscribe` service, and presence updates use the `xmpp_presence` service.

Here's the Python configuration for *app.yaml* that enables all four XMPP inbound message types:

```
inbound_services:
- xmpp_message
- xmpp_error
- xmpp_subscribe
- xmpp_presence
```

And here's Java configuration for *appengine-web.xml* that does the same:

```
<inbound-services>
  <service>xmpp_message</service>
  <service>xmpp_error</service>
  <service>xmpp_subscribe</service>
  <service>xmpp_presence</service>
</inbound-services>
```

If you want to know when a user accepts or revokes your app's chat invitation, but otherwise do not need to see the user's presence updates, enable the `xmpp_subscribe` service without the `xmpp_presence` service. This can save on costs associated with the incoming bandwidth of changes in the user's presence, which can be frequent.

As with chat messages, you can simulate incoming subscription and presence messages in the development server by using the development console. Outgoing subscription and presence messages in the development server are logged to the console, but not actually sent.

Managing Subscriptions

An app subscribes to a user when it sends an invitation to chat, with the `send_invite()` function (Python) or the `sendInvitation()` method (Java). An app cannot send an explicit "unsubscribe" message, only "subscribe."

When the user accepts the invitation, her chat client sends a `subscribed` message to the app. If the user later revokes the invitation, the client sends an `unsubscribed` message.

These messages arrive via the `xmpp_subscribe` inbound service as POST requests on the following URL paths:

```
/_ah/xmpp/subscription/subscribed/
/_ah/xmpp/subscription/unsubscribed/
```

A user can send an explicit subscription request (invitation to chat) to the app by sending a `subscribe` message. Similarly, the user can explicitly unsubscribe from presence updates by sending an `unsubscribe` message. These arrive at the following URL paths:

```
/_ah/xmpp/subscription/subscribe/
/_ah/xmpp/subscription/unsubscribe/
```

The subscription process typically happens just once in the lifetime of the relationship between two chat users. After the users are successfully subscribed, they remain subscribed until one party explicitly unsubscribes from the other (`unsubscribe`), or one party revokes the other party's invitation (`unsubscribed`).

If you intend for your app to have visible changes in presence, the app must maintain a roster of subscribers based on `subscribe` and `unsubscribe` messages, and send updates only to subscribed users.

Incoming subscription-related requests include form-style fields in the POST data, with the following fields:

`from`
: The sender's JID.

`to`
: The app JID to which this message was sent.

`stanza`
: The full XML stanza of the subscription message, including the previous fields.

Because the POST data for these requests does not contain a `body` field, you cannot use the SDK's `Message` class to parse the data. You access these fields simply as POST form fields in the request.

The app gets the subscription command from the URL path.

Subscriptions in Python

Here is an outline for a request handler that processes subscription-related messages, using Python and webapp2:

```
import webapp2
from google.appengine.api import xmpp

def truncate_jid(jid):
    # Remove the "resource" portion of a JID.
    if jid:
        i = jid.find('/')
        if i != -1:
            jid = jid[:i]
    return jid

class SubscriptionHandler(webapp2.RequestHandler):
    def post(self, command):
        user_jid = truncate_jid(self.request.POST.get('from'))

        if command == 'subscribed':
            # User accepted a chat invitation.
            # ...

        if command == 'unsubscribed':
            # User revoked a chat invitation.
```

```
        # ...

    if command == 'subscribe':
        # User wants presence updates from the app.
        # ...

    if command == 'unsubscribed':
        # User no longer wants presence updates from the app.
        # ...

application = webapp2.WSGIApplication(
    [('/_ah/xmpp/subscription/(.*)/', SubscriptionHandler)],
    debug=True)
```

As mentioned earlier, an app sends a subscription request (`'subscribe'`) to a user by calling the `xmpp.send_invite(jid)` function. There is no way to send an `'unsubscribe'` message from an app. If the app no longer cares about a user's presence messages, the only choice is to ignore the incoming presence updates from that user.

Subscriptions in Java

As with chat messages, the Java API's `XMPPService` includes a facility for parsing subscription messages out of the incoming HTTP request. The `parseSubscription()` method takes the `HttpServletRequest` and returns a `Subscription` object:

```
import com.google.appengine.api.xmpp.JID;
import com.google.appengine.api.xmpp.Subscription;
import com.google.appengine.api.xmpp.SubscriptionType;
import com.google.appengine.api.xmpp.XMPPService;
import com.google.appengine.api.xmpp.XMPPServiceFactory;

// ...
public class SubscriptionServlet extends HttpServlet {
    public void doPost(HttpServletRequest req,
                       HttpServletResponse resp)
        throws IOException, ServletException {

        XMPPService xmpp = XMPPServiceFactory.getXMPPService();
        Subscription sub = xmpp.parseSubscription(req);
        JID userJID = sub.getFromJid();

        if (sub.getSubscriptionType() == SubscriptionType.SUBSCRIBED) {
            // User accepted a chat invitation.
            // ...

        } else if (sub.getSubscriptionType() == SubscriptionType.UNSUBSCRIBED) {
            // User revoked a chat invitation.
            // ...

        } else if (sub.getSubscriptionType() == SubscriptionType.SUBSCRIBE) {
            // User wants presence updates from the app.
            // ...

        } else if (sub.getSubscriptionType() == SubscriptionType.UNSUBSCRIBE) {
```

```
                // User no longer wants presence updates from the app.
                // ...

            }
        }
    }
```

You can access the fields of a `Subscription` message, using methods:

`getFromJid()`
: The sender `JID`.

`getToJid()`
: The app's recipient `JID` used in the message.

`getSubscriptionType()`
: The type of the subscription message: `SubscriptionType.SUBSCRIBED`, `SubscriptionType.UNSUBSCRIBED`, `SubscriptionType.SUBSCRIBE`, or `SubscriptionType.UNSUBSCRIBE`.

`getStanza()`
: The `String` raw XML of the message.

An app sends a subscription request (`'subscribe'`) to a user by calling the `sendInvitation(jid)` method of the `XMPPService`. There is no way to send an `'unsubscribe'` message from an app. If the app no longer cares about a user's presence messages, the only choice is to ignore the incoming presence updates from that user.

Managing Presence Updates

While an app is subscribed to a user, the user sends changes in presence to the app. If the app is configured to receive inbound presence messages via the `xmpp_presence` service, these messages arrive as POST requests on one of these URL paths:

```
/_ah/xmpp/presence/available/
/_ah/xmpp/presence/unavailable/
```

Chat clients typically send an `available` message when connecting, and an `unavailable` message when disconnecting (or going "invisible").

A presence message can also contain additional status information: the *presence show* ("show me as") value and a *status message*. Most chat clients represent the show value as a colored dot or icon, and may display the status message as well. And of course, most chat clients allow the user to change the show value and the message. The possible show values, along with how they typically appear in chat clients, are as follows:

chat
: The user is available to chat. Green, "available."

away
: The user is away from her computer temporarily and not available to chat. Yellow, "away." A typical chat client switches to this presence show value automatically when the user is away from the keyboard.

dnd
: "Do not disturb": the user may be at her computer, but does not want to receive chat messages. Red, "busy."

xa
: "Extended away": the user is not available to chat and is away for an extended period. Red.

In XMPP, availability and the presence show value are distinct concepts. For a user to appear as "busy," the user must be available. For example, a red-colored "busy" user is available, with a show value of "dnd." Chat clients represent unavailable users either with a grey icon or by showing the user in another list.

An incoming presence update request includes form-style fields in the POST data, with the following fields:

`from`
: The sender's JID.

`to`
: The app JID to which this message was sent.

`show`
: One of several standard presence show values. If omitted, this implies the "chat" presence.

`status`
: A custom status message. Only present if the user has a custom status message set, or is changing her status message.

`stanza`
: The full XML stanza of the subscription message, including the previous fields.

An app can notify users of its own presence by sending a presence message. If the app's presence changes, it should attempt to send a presence message to every user known to be subscribed to the app. To support this, the app should listen for "subscribe" and "unsubscribe" messages, and keep a list of subscribed users, as described in "Managing Subscriptions" on page 379.

An app should also send a presence message to a user if it receives a *presence probe* message from that user. See "Probing for Presence" on page 386.

As with chat and subscription messages, the development server can simulate incoming presence messages. However, it cannot include presence show and status strings in these updates.

Presence in Python

Here is an outline for a request handler for processing incoming presence updates, using Python and webapp2:

```
import webapp2
from google.appengine.api import xmpp

def truncate_jid(jid):
    # Remove the "resource" portion of a JID.
    if jid:
        i = jid.find('/')
        if i != -1:
            jid = jid[:i]
    return jid

class PresenceHandler(webapp2.RequestHandler):
    def post(self, command):
        user_jid = truncate_jid(self.request.POST.get('from'))

        if command == 'available':
            # The user is available.

            show = self.request.POST.get('show')
            status_message = self.request.POST.get('status')
            # ...

        elif command == 'unavailable':
            # The user is unavailable (disconnected).
            # ...

application = webapp2.WSGIApplication(
    [('/_ah/xmpp/presence/(.*)/', PresenceHandler)],
    debug=True)
```

To send a presence update to a single user in Python, you call the `xmpp.send_presence()` method:

```
xmpp.send_presence(user_jid,
                   status="Doing fine.",
                   presence_type=xmpp.PRESENCE_TYPE_AVAILABLE,
                   presence_show=xmpp.PRESENCE_SHOW_CHAT)
```

The `send_presence()` function takes the `jid`, a `status` message (up to 1 kilobyte), the `presence_type`, and the `presence_show` as arguments. `presence_type` is either `xmpp.PRESENCE_TYPE_AVAILABLE` or `xmpp.PRESENCE_TYPE_UNAVAILABLE`. `presence_show` is one of the standard presence show values, which are also available as library constants: `xmpp.PRESENCE_SHOW_CHAT`, `xmpp.PRESENCE_SHOW_AWAY`, `xmpp.PRESENCE_SHOW_DND`, and `xmpp.PRESENCE_SHOW_XA`.

When the app wishes to broadcast a change in presence, it must call `send_presence()` once for each user currently subscribed to the app. Unlike `send_message()`, you can't pass a list of JIDs to `send_presence()` to send many updates in one API call. A best practice is to use task queues to query your data for subscribed users and send presence updates in batches. See Chapter 16 for more information on task queues.

Presence in Java

The Java API's `XMPPService` can also parse incoming presence update messages. The `parsePresence()` method takes the `HttpServletRequest` and returns a `Presence` object:

```
import com.google.appengine.api.xmpp.JID;
import com.google.appengine.api.xmpp.Presence;
import com.google.appengine.api.xmpp.PresenceShow;
import com.google.appengine.api.xmpp.PresenceType;
import com.google.appengine.api.xmpp.XMPPService;
import com.google.appengine.api.xmpp.XMPPServiceFactory;

// ...
public class PresenceServlet extends HttpServlet {
    public void doPost(HttpServletRequest req,
                       HttpServletResponse resp)
        throws IOException, ServletException {

        XMPPService xmpp = XMPPServiceFactory.getXMPPService();
        Presence presence = xmpp.parsePresence(req);
        JID userJID = presence.getFromJid();

        if (presence.getPresenceType() == PresenceType.AVAILABLE) {
            // The user is available.

            PresenceShow show = presence.getPresenceShow();
            String status = presence.getStatus();
            // ...

        } else if (presence.getPresenceType() == PresenceType.AVAILABLE) {
            // The user is not available (disconnected).
            // ...

        }
    }
}
```

You can access the fields of a `Presence` message, using methods:

`getFromJid()`
: The sender `JID`.

`getToJid()`
: The app's recipient `JID` used in the message.

`getPresenceType()`
: The type of the presence message: `PresenceType.AVAILABLE`, `PresenceType.UNAVAILABLE`, or `PresenceType.PROBE` (see later).

`isAvailable()`
: A convenience method for testing whether the presence type is "available." Returns `true` or `false`.

`getPresenceShow()`
: The presence show value: `PresenceShow.NONE`, `PresenceShow.AWAY`, `PresenceShow.CHAT`, `PresenceShow.DND`, or `PresenceShow.XA`. This returns `null` if no value was present in the message.

`getStatus()`
: A custom status message, if the user has one set.

`getStanza()`
: The `String` raw XML of the message.

To send a presence update to a single user, call the `sendPresence()` method of the `XMPPService`:

```
xmpp.sendPresence(new JID("arthur@example.com"),
                  PresenceType.AVAILABLE,
                  PresenceShow.CHAT,
                  null);
```

This takes as arguments a `JID`, a `PresenceType`, a `PresenceShow`, and a `String` custom status message. You can set the show value or status message to `null` if no value is appropriate.

When the app wishes to broadcast a change in presence, it must call `sendPresence()` once for each user currently subscribed to the app. Unlike `sendMessage()`, you can't pass a list of JIDs to `sendPresence()` to send many updates in one API call. A best practice is to use task queues to query your data for subscribed users and send presence updates in batches. See Chapter 16 for more information on task queues.

Probing for Presence

Chat services broadcast presence updates to subscribed users as a user's presence changes. But this is only useful while the subscribed users are online. When a user comes online after a period of being disconnected (such as if her computer was turned off or not on the Internet), the user's client must *probe* the users in her contact list to get updated presence information.

When a user sends a probe to an app, it comes in via the `xmpp_presence` inbound service, as a POST request to this URL path:

```
/_ah/xmpp/presence/probe/
```

The POST data contains the following fields:

`from`
: The sender's JID.

`to`
: The app JID to which this message was sent.

stanza
: The full XML stanza of the subscription message, including the previous fields.

If your app receives this message, it should respond immediately by sending a presence update just to that user.

An app can send a presence probe message to a user. If the app is subscribed to the user, the user will send a presence message to the app in the usual way.

In the development server, outgoing probe messages are logged to the console, and not actually sent. There is currently no way to simulate an incoming probe message in the development console.

Presence probes in Python

Here's how you would extend the `PresenceHandler` in the previous Python example to respond to presence probes:

```
class PresenceHandler(webapp2.RequestHandler):
    def post(self, command):
        user_jid = truncate_jid(self.request.POST.get('from'))

        if command == 'available':
            # ...
        elif command == 'unavailable':
            # ...

        elif command == 'probe':
            # The user is requesting the app's presence information.
            xmpp.send_presence(
                user_jid,
                presence_type=xmpp.PRESENCE_TYPE_AVAILABLE,
                presence_show=xmpp.PRESENCE_SHOW_CHAT)
```

To send a presence probe to a user, you call `xmpp.send_presence()` with a `presence_type` of `xmpp.PRESENCE_TYPE_PROBE`:

```
xmpp.send_presence(jid, presence_type=xmpp.PRESENCE_TYPE_PROBE)
```

The reply comes back as a presence update message.

Presence probes in Java

In Java, an incoming presence probe message is just another type of `Presence` message. You can map a separate servlet to the `/_ah/xmpp/presence/probe/` URL path, or just test the PresenceType of the parsed message in a servlet that handles all /_ah/xmpp/presence/* requests:

```
XMPPService xmpp = XMPPServiceFactory.getXMPPService();
Presence presence = xmpp.parsePresence(req);
JID userJID = presence.getFromJid();

if (presence.getPresenceType() == PresenceType.PROBE) {
    xmpp.sendPresence(userJID,
                      PresenceType.AVAILABLE,
                      PresenceShow.CHAT,
                      null);
}
```

Similarly, to send a presence probe to a user, you call the sendPresence() method with a presence type of PresenceType.PROBE:

```
xmpp.sendPresence(jid, PresenceType.PROBE, null, null);
```

The reply comes back as a presence update message.

Checking a Google Talk User's Status

By virtue of the fact that the XMPP service is using Google Talk's infrastructure, an app can check the presence of a Google Talk user with an immediate API call, without using a probe and waiting for a response.

For privacy reasons, a Google Talk user will only appear as available to an App Engine app if the app has an active subscription to the user (the user accepted an invitation from the app and has not revoked it). All other users appear as "not present."

To get the presence of a Google Talk user in Python, you call the get_presence() function with the user's JID and an optional custom sender JID (from_jid). The function returns True if the user is connected and can receive chat messages from the app:

```
if xmpp.get_presence('juliet@example.com'):
    # User can receive chat messages from the app.
    # ...
```

If you specify the argument get_show=True, instead of a Boolean value, get_presence() returns a tuple. The first value is the availability Boolean. The second value is one of the four presence show values: 'chat', 'away', 'dnd', or 'xa'. There is no way to get the custom status message with get_presence().

In Java, you call the getPresence() method of the XMPPService instance with the user's JID and an optional sender JID. The method returns a Presence object, which is populated as if parsed from a presence update message:

```
import com.google.appengine.api.xmpp.Presence;
import com.google.appengine.api.xmpp.PresenceShow;

// ...
        JID jid = new JID("juliet@example.com");
```

```
Presence presence = xmpp.getPresence(jid);
if (presence.isAvailable()) {
    PresenceShow presenceShow = presence.getPresenceShow();
    String status = presence.getStatus();
    // ...
}
```

When running in the development server, all user addresses are present, with a presence show value of chat. There is no way to change the return value of this API in the development server. (Simulating XMPP presence messages will not change it.)

CHAPTER 16

Task Queues and Scheduled Tasks

The App Engine architecture is well suited for handling web requests, small amounts of work that run in a stateless environment with the intent of returning a response to the user as fast as possible. But many web applications have other kinds of work that need to get done, work that doesn't fit in the fast response model. Instead of doing the work while the user waits, it's often acceptable to record what work needs to get done, respond to the user right away, then do the work later, within seconds or minutes. The ability to make this trade-off is especially useful with scalable web applications that use a read-optimized datastore, since updating an element of data may require several related but time-consuming updates, and it may not be essential for those updates to happen right away.

What we need is a way to do work outside of a user-facing request handler. By "outside," we mean code that is run separately from the code that evaluates a request from a user and returns a response to the user. This work can run in parallel to the user-facing request handler, or after the request handler has returned a response, or completely independently of user requests. We also need a way to request that this work be done.

App Engine has two major mechanisms for initiating this kind of work: *task queues* and *scheduled tasks*. A *task* is simply a request that a unit of work be performed separately from the code requesting the task. Any application code can call the task queue service to request a task, and the task queue manages the process of driving the task to completion. Scheduled tasks are tasks that are invoked on a schedule that you define in a configuration file, separately from any application code or queue (although a scheduled task is welcome to add other tasks to a queue, as is any other task running on App Engine).

In the terminology of task queues, a *producer* is a process that requests that work be done. The producer *enqueues* a task that represents the work onto a queue. A *consumer* is a process, separate from the producer, that *leases* tasks on the queue that it intends to perform. If the consumer performs a task successfully, it deletes the task from the queue so no other consumer tries to perform it. If the consumer fails to delete the task, the queue assumes the task was not completed successfully, and after an amount of time, the lease expires and becomes available again to other consumers. A consumer may also explicitly revoke the lease if it can't perform the task.

Task queues are a general category for two mechanisms for driving work to completion: *push queues* and *pull queues*. With push queues, App Engine is the consumer: it executes tasks on the queues at configurable rates, and retries tasks that return a failure code. With pull queues, you provide the consumer mechanism that leases task records off of a queue, does the work they represent, and then deletes them from the queue. Your custom mechanism can run on App Engine, or it can run on your own infrastructure and pull tasks, using a REST API.

To perform a task on a push queue, App Engine does what it does best: it invokes a request handler! You can configure a URL path in your app per queue, or specify a specific URL path when you enqueue a task. To implement the task, you simply implement a request handler for requests sent to that URL. Naturally, you can secure these URLs against outside requests, so only tasks can trigger that logic. This is why we've been making a distinction between "user-facing" request handlers and other handlers. All code on App Engine runs in a request handler, and typically code for handling user requests is distinct from code for performing tasks.

Scheduled tasks also run on App Engine, and also use request handlers. You configure a schedule of URL paths and times, and App Engine calls your application at those URL paths at the requested times. Scheduled tasks are not retried to completion, but you can achieve this effect by having a scheduled task enqueue a task on a queue.

All of these mechanisms support a major design goal for App Engine applications: do as much work outside of user-facing requests as possible, so user-facing requests are as fast as possible. Task queues allow your code to request that work be done separately from the current unit of work. Scheduled tasks initiate computation on a predefined schedule, independently of other code. The results of this work can be stored in the datastore, memcache, and Blobstore, so user-facing request handlers can retrieve and serve it quickly, without doing the work itself.

Enqueueing a task is fast, about three times faster than writing to the datastore. This makes tasks useful for pretty much anything whose success or failure doesn't need to be reported to the user in the response to the user request that initiates the work. For example, an app can write a value to the memcache, then enqueue a task to persist that value to the datastore. This saves time during the user request, and allows the task to do bookkeeping or make other time-consuming updates based on the change (assuming it meets the application's needs that the bookkeeping happens later than the initial update).

App Engine invokes a request handler for a push queue task or scheduled task in the same environment as it does a handler for a user request, with a few minor differences. Most notably, a task handler can run continuously for up to 10 minutes, instead of 60 seconds for user-facing request handlers. In some cases, it can be better to implement task handlers with short running times, then split a batch of work over multiple tasks, so the tasks can be executed in parallel in multiple threads or on multiple instances. But 10 minutes of head room let you simplify your code for work that can or must take its time on an instance.

Figure 16-1 illustrates how task queues and scheduled tasks take advantage of the request handler infrastructure.

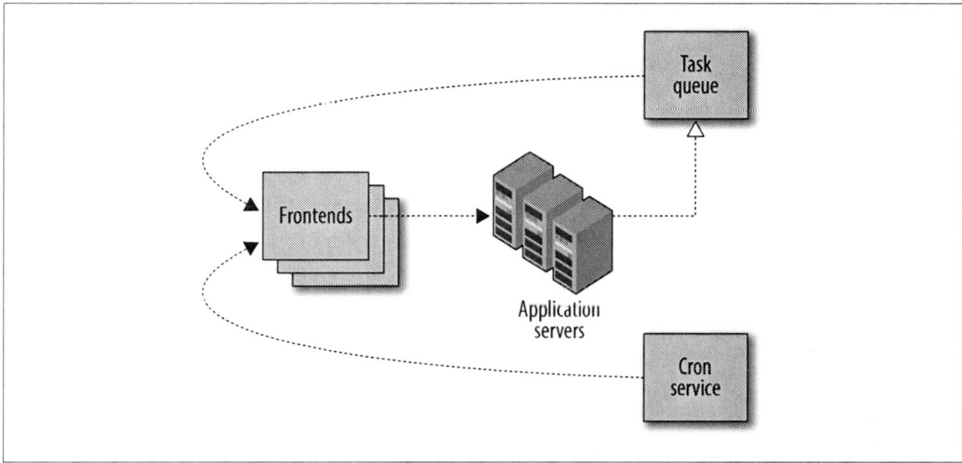

Figure 16-1. Architecture of push queues and scheduled tasks ("cron")

The development server maintains push and pull queues, and can run push queues in the background and simulate their timing and throttling behaviors. Of course, it won't be as fast as running on App Engine, but it's enough to test the behavior. You can use the development console web interface to inspect the configured queues, check their contents, and delete individual tasks or all tasks on a queue ("Purge Queue"). With push queues, you can also force a task to run from the console.

Task queues are an important part of App Engine, with several powerful features for structuring your work and optimizing your application's behavior. Not the least of these features is how task queues integrate with the App Engine datastore transactions. In this chapter, we describe the concepts of task queues and scheduled tasks, and how to use them in Python and Java applications. We take a brief look at pull queues and consider how they are useful. We cover using tasks and datastore transactions to achieve special effects, especially eventually consistent data operations and task chaining. And finally, we review the queue-related features of the Administrator Console.

Configuring Task Queues

Every app has one default push queue with default settings. You can use a configuration file to change the settings of the default push queue, create new named push and pull queues each with their own settings, and set global parameters for task queues in general.

In Python, you create a file named *queue.yaml*. This is a YAML file (same as *app.yaml*). Here is an example file that updates the rate of the default queue, and defines a new named push queue with its own configuration:

```
queue:
- name: default
  rate: 10/s
- name: attack_effects
  rate: 100/s
  bucket_size: 20
```

In Java, you create a file named *queue.xml* in your *war/WEB-INF/* directory. This is an XML file whose root element is `<queue-entries>`. The following example does the same thing as the Python example above:

```
<queue-entries>
  <queue>
    <name>default</name>
    <rate>10/s</rate>
  </queue>
  <queue>
    <name>attack_effects</name>
    <rate>100/s</rate>
    <bucket-size>20</bucket-size>
  </queue>
</queue-entries>
```

(We'll see what these settings do in a moment.)

Task queues contain durable data, and this storage counts towards your billable storage quota, just like data in the datastore. You can set a total limit for the amount of task queue data to store with configuration. In *queue.yaml*, this setting is named `total_storage_limit`:

```
total_storage_limit: 200M

queue:
# ...
```

In *queue.xml*, the element is named `total-storage-limit`:

```
<queue-entries>
  <total-storage-limit>200M</total-storage-limit>

  <!-- ... -->
</queue-entries>
```

Its value is a number followed by a unit of storage measurement, such as `M` for megabytes, `G` for gigabytes, or `T` for terabytes.

The default mode for a queue is to be a push queue. To declare a queue as a pull queue, you set the `mode` of the queue to `pull`. In *queue.yaml*:

```
queue:
- name: process_images
  mode: pull
```

In *queue.xml*:

```
<queue-entries>
  <queue>
    <name>process_images</name>
    <mode>pull</mode>
  </queue>
</queue-entries>
```

We'll mention additional configuration options when we discuss push queues and pull queues in more detail.

Task queue configuration is uploaded when you deploy your application. You can upload new task queue configuration separately from the rest of your app with the AppCfg tool's `update_queues` command:

```
appcfg.py update_queues appdir
```

Task queue configuration is distinct from application configuration (*app.yaml* or *appengine-web.xml*), and is kept in a separate file. Unlike application configuration, task queue configuration modifies the behavior of task queues for the entire application. All application versions use the same task queue configuration.

Enqueuing a Task

Your app adds a task to a queue (it *enqueues* the task) by calling the task queue service API with appropriate arguments. Some arguments are specific to push queues or pull queues, but the main API is the same for both.

We'll look at the Python task queue API, then the Java API, followed by a summary of options you can set for tasks.

Enqueuing a Task in Python

A Python application enqueues tasks by using the API provided by the `google.appengine.api.labs.taskqueue` module. The simplest way to enqueue a task is to call the `add()` function. Without arguments, the `add()` function enqueues a task to the `default` queue by using the default options for that queue:

```
from google.appengine.api import taskqueue

# ...
        taskqueue.add()
```

The default queue is a push queue, so App Engine will process this task by invoking a request handler at a URL path. The default URL path for the default queue is:

```
/_ah/queue/default
```

You map the URL to a request handler that performs the task in the *app.yaml* file. You can restrict the URL so that it can only be called by task queues and by the app's developers (for testing), using `login: admin`, like so:

```
handlers:
- url: /_ah/queue/default
  script: default_task.app
  login: admin
```

With this configuration, the no-argument call to the `add()` function enqueues the task on the default queue with the default URL and no arguments. When the task queue processes this task, it issues an HTTP POST request with default arguments to the URL path `/_ah/queue/default`, which invokes the *default_task.app* request handler.

The `add()` function returns immediately after the task is enqueued. The actual execution of the task happens separately from the rest of the code that called `add()`.

You can pass arguments to the `add()` function to specify aspects of the task or the queue. The Python API offers an object-oriented alternative with the `Task` and `Queue` classes. For example, here are several ways to add a task to a queue named `reward_players`:

```
# Add a task to the reward_players queue, using the add() function.
taskqueue.add(queue_name='reward_players')

# Construct a Task, and add it to the reward_players queue, using its add() method.
t = taskqueue.Task()
t.add(queue_name='reward_players')

# Construct a Queue for the reward_players queue, then add a Task to it.
t = taskqueue.Task()
q = taskqueue.Queue('reward_players')
q.add(t)
```

As shown, the `queue_name` argument to the `add()` function, the `Task` object's `add()` method, or the `Queue` constructor, specifies the queue name. This corresponds with the `name` queue configuration parameter in *queue.yaml*. If the queue name is anything other than `'default'`, the queue must appear in the configuration file with the `name` parameter for the queue to exist.

You set parameters of the task itself by passing keyword arguments to either the `add()` function or the `Task` constructor. We'll introduce these parameters in a moment.

You can add multiple tasks to a single queue in a single service call (a batch call). You must use the `Queue` object's `add()` method for this. To make a batch call, pass an iterable of `Task` objects as the first argument to `add()`:

```
# ...
        tasks = []
        for e in elems:
            tasks.append(Task(params=e.params))
```

```
        queue = Queue('process_elems')
        queue.add(tasks)
```

Enqueuing a Task in Java

The Java task queue API is provided by the `com.google.appengine.api.taskqueue` package. You manipulate a queue via a `Queue` instance, which you get from the `QueueFactory` static methods `getDefaultQueue()`, which returns the `default` queue, and `getQueue(name)`, which returns the queue of the given name:

```
import com.google.appengine.api.taskqueue.Queue;
import com.google.appengine.api.taskqueue.QueueFactory;

// ...
        Queue defaultQueue = QueueFactory.getDefaultQueue();
        Queue queue = QueueFactory.getQueue("reward_players");
```

To add a task to a queue, you call its `add()` method. With no arguments, `add()` puts a task onto the queue with default options. `add()` returns a `TaskHandle`, which describes the task just added, including fields filled in by the system (such as `getQueueName()`):

```
        TaskHandle handle = defaultQueue.add();
```

The default queue is a push queue, so App Engine will process this task by invoking a request handler at a URL path. The default URL path for the default queue is:

```
/_ah/queue/default
```

If you need them, the default queue name and URL path are available as the constants `Queue.DEFAULT_QUEUE` and `Queue.DEFAULT_QUEUE_PATH`.

You map a servlet to the URL in the usual way, with *web.xml*. You can restrict access to the URL so that only App Engine can call it (and outsiders can't), using a `security-constraint` with the `admin` role:

```
  <servlet>
    <servlet-name>defaultqueue</servlet-name>
    <servlet-class>app.DefaultQueueServlet</servlet-class>
  </servlet>
  <servlet-mapping>
    <servlet-name>defaultqueue</servlet-name>
    <url-mapping>/_ah/queue/default</url-mapping>
  </servlet-mapping>

  <security-constraint>
    <web-resource-collection>
      <web-resource-name>defaultqueue</web-resource-name>
      <url-pattern>/_ah/queue/default</url-pattern>
    </web-resource-collection>
    <auth-constraint>
      <role-name>admin</role-name>
    </auth-constraint>
  </security-constraint>
```

Adding an empty task record to a queue can be quite useful, since the task handler can do anything you want. You can further control the behavior of the task and how it interacts with the queue, using options. To set options for a task, you build and pass a `TaskOptions` instance to the `add()` method. This is a `Builder`-based API, where you can start a new instance with a static method and chain additional options to the same statement. `TaskOptions.Builder.withDefaults()` returns a `TaskOptions` with all default settings, which is useful in cases where a `TaskOptions` is required but no options need to be changed. (`add()` with no arguments is equivalent to `add(TaskOptions.Builder.withDefaults())`.)

```
queue.add(TaskOptions.Builder
        .withParam("player_id", playerId)
        .param("achievement", "paid_in_full"));
```

We'll discuss some of the available options in the next section and elsewhere in this chapter.

You can add multiple tasks to a single queue in a single service call (a batch call) by passing an `Iterable<TaskOptions>`. This form of the method returns a `List<TaskHandle>`, whose members correspond directly with the inputs:

```
TaskOptions t1, t2, t3;
// ...

List<TaskHandle> handle = queue.add(Arrays.asList(t1, t2, t3));
```

Task Parameters

A task record on a queue carries two kinds of parameters: parameters that are passed on to the code or system performing the task, and parameters that affect how the task is managed on the queue. You set these parameters when you enqueue the task. After the task is enqueued, the parameters can't be changed, although you can delete and re-create a task, as needed.

The following sections describe task parameters common to both push queues and pull queues. We'll look at mode-specific options later.

Payloads

A task's *payload* is a set of data intended for the system performing the task. You don't need a payload if the task handler already knows what to do, but it's useful to write task handling code in a general way, and parameterize its behavior with a payload.

For example, you could have a task that performs a transformation on a datastore entity, such as to update its property layout to a new schema. The task handler would take the ID of an entity to transform, and perform one transformation. You'd then have a process (possibly also managed with task queues) that traverses all the entities that need transformation with a datastore query, and it creates a task for each entity, using the task handler and a payload.

For convenience, the task API has two ways to set a payload: as a byte string, or as a set of named parameters with byte string values. When you set a payload as a set of parameters, the data is formatted like a web form (`application/x-www-form-urlencoded`), so the task handler can parse the payload into parameters, using typical web request handling code. Payloads and parameters are mutually exclusive: you set one or the other, not both.

To set a payload in Python, you specify either the `payload` argument as a `str`, or the `params` argument as a mapping of names to values. A parameter value may be a string, or a list of strings:

```
taskqueue.add(payload=img_data)

taskqueue.add(params={'entity_key': str(e.key()), 'version': '7'})

t = taskqueue.Task(payload=img_data)
q = taskqueue.Queue()
q.add(t)
```

In Java, you set a payload for a task by using the `payload()` method or the `param()` method of `TaskOptions`, or the corresponding starter methods `withPayload()` or `withParam()` of the `TaskOptions.Builder` class. `payload()` sets or overrides the payload. `param()` sets a named parameter, and can be called multiple times in a builder chain to set multiple parameters. A payload or parameter value can be a `String` or a `byte[]`:

```
// byte[] imgData = ...;
queue.add(TaskOptions.Builder.withPayload(imgData));

queue.add(TaskOptions.Builder
        .withParam("entity_key", KeyFactory.keyToString(entity.getKey()))
        .param("version", "7"));
```

The `payload(byte[])` form can take an optional second argument to specify the MIME content type of the data. The `payload(String)` form can take an optional second argument to specify a character set. These arguments affect how the payload is converted into an HTTP request when managed by a push queue.

Task Names

Every task has a unique name. By default, App Engine will generate a unique name for a task when it is added to a queue. You can also set the task name in the app. A task name can be up to 500 characters, and can contain letters, numbers, underscores, and hyphens.

If an app sets the name for a task and another task already exists for that name on a given queue, the API will raise an exception when the app adds the task to the queue. Task names prevent the app from enqueuing the same task more than once on the same queue. App Engine remembers in-use task names for a period of time after the task completes (on the order of days). (The remembered names are called *tombstones* or *tombstoned tasks*.)

This is especially useful when enqueuing a task from within a push task handler. Consider the datastore entity transformation example again. A master task performs a datastore query, then creates a transformation task for each entity in the results, like so (in Python):

```
class MasterTaskHandler(webapp2.RequestHandler):
    def post(self):
        for entity in models.MyEntity.all():
            taskqueue.add(queue_name='upgrade',
                          params={'entity_key': str(entity.key()),
                                  'version': '7'})
```

If there is a datastore error while the master task is fetching results, the datastore raises an exception, which bubbles up to webapp and the request handler returns an HTTP 500 server error. The push queue sees the error, then retries the master task from the beginning. If the first run of the master task successfully enqueued some tasks for entities to the `'upgrade'` queue, those entities will be added to the queue again, wasting work.

The master task handler can guard against this by using a task name for each task that uniquely represents the work. In the example above, a good task name might be the entity's key concatenated with the upgrade version (the two parameters to the task):

```
import re
import webapp2

from google.appengine.api import taskqueue

class MasterTaskHandler(webapp2.RequestHandler):
    def post(self):
        for entity in models.MyEntity.all():
            try:
                task_name = str(entity.key()) + '7'
                task_name = re.sub('[^a-zA-Z0-9_-]', '_', task_name)
                taskqueue.add(queue_name='upgrade',
                              name=task_name,
                              params={'entity_key': str(entity.key()),
                                      'version': '7'})
            except taskqueue.DuplicateTaskNameError, e:
                pass
```

As seen here, in Python you set the task name with the `name` parameter. An attempt to add a task with a name already in use raises a `DuplicateTaskNameError`. (In this example, we catch and ignore the exception because we can be confident that the task is enqueued and will be completed.)

In Java, you set the task name with the `taskName()` (`withTaskName()`) builder method of `TaskOptions`.

```
String taskName = KeyFactory.keyToString(entity.getKey()) + "7";
taskName = taskName.replaceAll("[^a-zA-Z0-9_-]", "_");
queue.add(TaskOptions.Builder
        .withName(taskName)
        .param("entity_key", KeyFactory.keyToString(entity.getKey()))
        .param("version", "7"));
```

Take care when using datastore keys, query cursors, and other values as parts of task names that the resulting name meets the requirements of task names. A task name can contain letters, numbers, underscores, and hyphens. Base64-encoded values (such as string-ified datastore keys) use this alphabet, but may use equal-sign (=) characters for padding. The examples above use a regular expression to substitute characters outside of this alphabet with underscores.

Countdowns and ETAs

By default, a task is made available to run immediately. A push queue can execute an available task whenever it is ready (subject to its rate limiting configuration, which we'll see later). The consumer of a pull queue sees only available tasks when it requests a lease.

You can delay the availability of a task when you add it, so it doesn't become available until a later time. You specify this as either a number of seconds into the future from the time of the enqueue operation (a countdown), or an explicit date and time in the future (an earliest time of availability, or ETA). Delaying the availability of a task can be a useful way to slow down a complex multistage process, such as to avoid hitting a remote server too often.

In Python, these are the `countdown` and `eta` options, respectively. A `countdown` is a number of seconds. An `eta` is a Unix epoch date-time in the future:

```
# Execute no earlier than 5 seconds from now.
taskqueue.add(params={'url': next_url}, countdown=5)

# Execute no earlier than December 31, 2012, midnight UTC.
taskqueue.add(params={'url': next_url}, eta=1356940800)
```

In Java, you use the `countdownMillis()` (`withCountdownMillis()`) or `etaMillis()` (`withEtaMillis()`) builder methods with `TaskOptions`. `countdownMillis()` takes a number of milliseconds in the future. `etaMillis()` takes a date and time in the future, as a Unix epoch date-time in milliseconds:

```
// Execute no earlier than 5 seconds from now.
queue.add(TaskOptions.Builder
    .withParam("url", nextUrl)
    .countdownMillis(5000));

// Execute no earlier than December 31, 2012, midnight UTC.
queue.add(TaskOptions.Builder
```

```
        .withParam("url", nextUrl)
        .etaMillis(1356940800000));
```

Countdowns and ETAs specify the earliest time the task will be available, not the exact time the task will be performed. Do not rely on ETAs as exact timers.

Push Queues

Push queues are queues of tasks that are performed automatically by App Engine at a configurable rate. App Engine performs a task by invoking a request handler of your app. It forms an HTTP request based on the contents of the task record, and issues the request to a URL path associated with the task. App Engine uses the HTTP status code of the response to decide whether the task was completed successfully and should be deleted from the queue. Unsuccessful tasks are retried again later.

Because tasks on push queues are just requests to your app, they use the same infrastructure as any other request handler. You implement tasks by implementing request handlers mapped to URLs, using your web application framework of choice. Tasks are executed in threads of instances, and use the same automatic scaling mechanism as user requests. A queue with multiple tasks will distribute the tasks to multiple threads and instances to be performed in parallel, based on the availability of instances and the processing rate of the queue.

You can control aspects of the HTTP request for task by setting task options. You can also configure aspects of how push queues process tasks, and how tasks are retried.

Task Requests

You can set various aspects of the HTTP request issued for a task using task options, including the URL, the HTTP method, and request headers. The payload for the task also becomes part of the request, depending on the method.

By default, the URL path for a task is based on the queue name, in this format:

`/_ah/queue/`*`queue_name`*

You can override the URL path for an individual task. In Python, this is the `url` option to `taskqueue.Task()` or `taskqueue.add()`:

```
taskqueue.add(url='/admin/tasks/persist_scores')
```

In Java, this is the `url()` (`withUrl()`) builder method on `TaskOptions`:

```
queue.add(TaskOptions.Builder
    .withUrl("/admin/tasks/persist_scores"));
```

If there is no request handler mapped to the URL for a task (or the task's queue, if no custom URL is specified), the invocation of the task will return a 404 status code. This is interpreted by the push queue as task failure, and the task is added back to the queue to be retried. You can delete these tasks by flushing the queue in the Administration Console, or by pushing a software version that supplies a successful handler for the task URL.

By default, the HTTP request uses the POST method. In Python, you can change this with the `method` option, with one of these string values: `'GET'`, `'POST'`, `'PUT'`, `'READ'`, or `'DELETE'`. In Java, this is the `method()` (`withMethod()`) `TaskOptions` builder method, which takes a value from the `TaskOptions.Method` enum: `GET`, `POST`, `PUT`, `READ`, or `DELETE`.

You can set HTTP headers on the task's request. In Python, you provide a `headers` argument, whose value is a mapping of header names to header string values. In Java, you can set an individual header with the `header()` (`withHeader()`) builder method of `TaskOptions`, passing it a string name and a string value. Alternatively, you can set multiple headers in one call with the `headers()` (`withHeaders()`) builder method, which takes a `Map<String, String>`.

Task queues have special behavior with regard to app versions. If the version of the app that enqueued a task was the default version, then the task uses the default version of the app when it executes—even if the default version has changed since the task was enqueued. If the version of the app that enqueued the task was not the default version at the time, then the task uses that version specifically when it executes. This allows you to test nondefault versions that use tasks before making them the default. You can set a specific version for a task by using the `target` option in Python, or the `target()` (`withTarget()`) builder method of `TaskOptions` in Java.

App Engine adds the following headers to the request automatically when invoking the request handler, so the handler can identify the task record:

- `X-AppEngine-QueueName`, the name of the queue issuing the task request.
- `X-AppEngine-TaskName`, the name of the task, either assigned by the app or assigned by the system.
- `X-AppEngine-TaskRetryCount`, the number of times this task has been retried.
- `X-AppEngine-TaskETA`, the time this task became available, as the number of microseconds since January 1, 1970. This is set when the app specifies a countdown or an ETA, or if the task was retried with a delay.

Incoming requests from outside App Engine are not allowed to set these headers, so a request handler can test for these headers to confirm the request is from a task queue.

Task requests are considered to be from an administrator user for the purposes of the URL access control in *app.yaml* or *web.xml*. You can restrict task URLs to be administrator-only, and then only task queues (and actual app administrators) can issue requests to the URL.

The body of a response from a task's request handler is ignored. If the task needs to store or communicate information, it must do so by using the appropriate services or by logging messages.

A call to a task handler appears in the request log, just like a user-initiated web request. You can monitor and analyze the performance of tasks just as you would user requests.

Processing Rates and Token Buckets

The processing rate for a queue is controlled using a "token bucket" algorithm. In this algorithm, a queue has a number of "tokens," and it spends a token for each task it executes. Tokens are replenished at a steady rate up to a maximum number of tokens (the "bucket size"). Both the replenishment rate and the bucket size are configurable for a queue.

If a queue contains a task and has a token, it usually executes the task immediately. If a queue has many tasks and many available tokens, it executes as many tasks as it can afford, immediately and in parallel. If there are tasks remaining, the queue must wait until a token is replenished before executing the next task. The token bucket algorithm gives a queue the flexibility to handle bursts of new tasks, while still remaining within acceptable limits. The larger the bucket, the more tasks an idle queue will execute immediately when the tasks are enqueued all at once.

I say it *usually* executes the tasks immediately because App Engine may adjust the method and rate of how it executes tasks based on the performance of the system. In general, task queue schedules are approximate, and may vary as App Engine balances resources.

A queue does not wait for one task to finish before executing the next task. Instead, it initiates the next task as soon as a token is available, in parallel with any currently running tasks. Tasks are not strictly ordered, but App Engine makes an effort to perform tasks in the order they are enqueued. Tasks must not rely on being executed serially or in a specific order.

Each task queue has a name and processing rate (token replenishment rate and bucket size). Every app has a queue named `default` that processes 5 tasks per second, with a bucket size of 5. If you don't specify a queue name when enqueueing a task, the task is added to the default queue. You can adjust the rate and bucket size of the default queue, and can set the rate to 0 to turn it off. Tasks enqueued to a paused queue remain on the queue until you upload the new configuration with a positive rate.

Task queues and token buckets help you control how tasks are executed so you can plan for maximizing throughput, making the most efficient use of system resources to execute tasks in parallel. Tasks inevitably share resources, even if the resource is just the pool of warmed-up application servers. Executing a bunch of tasks simultaneously may not be the fastest way to complete all the tasks, since App Engine may need to start up new instances of the application to handle the sudden load. If multiple tasks operate on the same entity groups in the datastore, it may be faster to perform only a few tasks at a time and let datastore retries sort out contention, instead of relying on task retries to drive in all the changes. Limiting the execution rate with token buckets can actually result in faster completion of multiple tasks.

Queue processing rates are configured using the queue configuration file (*queue.yaml* or *queue.xml*). You specify the rate of bucket replenishment using the `rate` option for a queue. Its value is a number, a slash (/), and a unit of time (`s` for seconds), such as `20/s` for twenty tokens per second.

You specify the size of the token bucket with the `bucket_size` (`bucket-size` for *queue.xml*) option. Its value is a number:

```
queue:
- name: fast_queue
  rate: 20/s
  bucket_size: 10
```

In addition to the rate and bucket size, you can set a maximum number of tasks from the queue that can be executed at the same time, with the `max_concurrent_requests` (`max-concurrent-requests`) option. Its value is the number of tasks. If this many task requests are in progress, the queue will wait to issue another task even if there are tokens in the bucket. This allows for large bucket sizes but still prevents bursts of new tasks from flooding instances. It also accommodates tasks that take a variable amount of time, so slow tasks don't take over your instances.

Together, these options control the flow of tasks from the push queue into the request queue for the application. If a given queue is processing tasks too quickly, you can upload a new temporary configuration for the queue that tells it to run at a slower rate, and the change will take effect immediately. You can experiment with different rates and token bucket sizes to improve task throughput.

Retrying Push Tasks

To ensure that tasks get completed in a way that is robust against system failure, a task queue will retry a task until it is satisfied the task is complete.

A push queue retries a task if the request handler it invokes returns an HTTP response with a status code other than a "success" code (in the range 200–299). It retries the task by putting it back on the queue with a countdown, so it'll wait a bit before trying again in the hopes that the error condition will subside. You can configure the retry behavior for every queue in a task by using the queue configuration, and you can override this configuration on a per-task basis with task options.

Under very rare circumstances, such as after a system failure, a task may be retried even if it completed successfully. This is a design trade-off that favors fast task creation over built-in, once-only fault tolerance. A task that can be executed multiple times without changing the end result is called *idempotent*. Whether a task's code must be strictly idempotent depends on what the task is doing and how important it is that the calculation it is performing be accurate. For instance, a task that deletes a datastore entity can be retried because the second delete fails harmlessly.

Because a task on a push queue is retried when its handler returns anything other than a successful HTTP status code, a buggy handler that always returns an error for a given input will be retried indefinitely, or until the retry limit is reached if a retry limit was specified.

If a task needs to abort without retrying, it must return a success code.

There are five parameters that control how push queues retry a given task. We'll define these parameters first. Then we'll see how to set defaults for these parameters in queue configuration, and how to override them for a specific task.

The `task_retry_limit` is the maximum number of times a failing task is retried before it is deleted from the queue. If you do not specify a retry limit, the task is retried indefinitely, or until you flush the cache or delete the task by some other means. A retry limit is a good guard against perpetual failure (such as a bug in a task), and in some cases it makes sense to abort a task in transient but long-lasting failure conditions. Be sure to set it high enough so that tasks can accommodate brief transient failures, which are to be expected in large distributed systems.

The `task_age_limit` calls for automatic deletion of an incomplete task after a period of time on the queue. If not specified, the task lives until it succeeds, hits its retry limit, or is deleted by other means. Its value is a number followed by a unit of time: `s` for seconds, `m` for minutes, `h` for hours, `d` for days. For example, `3d` is three days.

When a task fails, it is readded to the queue with a countdown. The duration of this countdown doubles each time the task is retried, a method called *exponential backoff*. (The queue is "backing off" the failing task by trying it less frequently with each failure.) Three settings control the backoff behavior. `min_backoff_seconds` is the minimum countdown, the countdown of the first retry. `max_backoff_seconds` is the maximum; retries will increase the countdown up to this amount. These values are an amount of time, as a number of seconds. Finally, the `max_doublings` setting lets you set the number of times the countdown doubles. After that many retries, the countdown stays constant for each subsequent retry.

To set any of these retry options as the default for all tasks added to a queue, you add them to the queue configuration file, in a `retry_parameters` subsection of the queue's configuration. Here's an example of retry configuration in *queue.yaml*:

```
queue:
- name: respawn_health
  rate: 2/s
  retry_parameters:
    task_retry_limit: 10
    max_doublings: 3
```

The same configuration in *queue.xml* is similar:

```
<queue-entries>
  <queue>
    <name>respawn_health</name>
    <rate>2/s</rate>
    <retry-parameters>
      <task-retry-limit>10</task-retry-limit>
      <max-doublings>3</max-doublings>
    </retry-parameters>
  </queue>
</queue-entries>
```

To override these settings for a task in Python, you set the `retry_options` argument to `taskqueue.Task()` or `taskqueue.add()` with an instance of the `TaskRetryOptions()` class. The class's constructor takes the retry options as keyword arguments, and validates them:

```
t = taskqueue.Task(
    retry_options=taskqueue.TaskRetryOptions(
        task_retry_limit=10,
        max_doublings=3))
q = taskqueue.Queue('respawn_health')
q.add(t)
```

In Java, the `TaskOptions` builder method `retryOptions()` (`withRetryOptions()`) takes an instance of the `RetryOptions` class. This class also uses the builder pattern with methods for each setting: `taskRetryLimit()`, `taskAgeLimitSeconds()`, `minBackoffSeconds()`, `maxBackoffSeconds()`, and `maxDoublings()` (and their `withXXX()` starter equivalents):

```
Queue queue = QueueFactory.getQueue("respawn_health");
queue.add(TaskOptions.Builder.withRetryOptions(
    RetryOptions.Builder
        .withTaskRetryLimit(10)
        .maxDoublings(3)));
```

Pull Queues

In our initial definition of a task queue, we said that a queue has a producer and a consumer. With push queues, the producer is application code running in an App Engine request handler, and the consumer is the App Engine push queue mechanism, which calls request handlers to do the actual work of the task. With pull queues, you provide the consumer logic. The consumer calls the pull queue to lease one or more tasks, and the queue ensures that a task is leased to only one consumer at a time. Typically, the consumer deletes the task from the queue after performing the corresponding work, so no other consumer sees it. If the consumer fails to delete it, eventually the lease expires and the pull queue makes the task available to consumers again.

A pull queue is useful when you want to customize the consumer logic. For example, the push queue driver consumes one task at a time, executing a separate request handler for each task. With a pull queue, a custom consumer can lease multiple related tasks at once, and perform them together as a batch. This might be faster or more productive than doing it one at a time. For example, each task might represent an update to an entity group in the datastore. If a pull queue consumer sees multiple updates in the queue, it can lease them all in a batch, and make a single transactional update to the entity group for all of them. This is likely to be faster than multiple push queue tasks each trying to make their own transactional update to the same data.

You can build pull queue consumers on App Engine, using request handlers (such as a scheduled task that processes the queue periodically), or using a long-running process on a backend that polls for new tasks on a recurring basis. You can also build a consumer that runs on a remote system, using the task queue web service REST API. With a remote consumer, your app can enqueue tasks that trigger behavior in separate systems. The REST API also allows you to build remote producers that add tasks to pull queues. (A remote producer can't add to push queues directly, but a local consumer running on App Engine could periodically convert remotely added tasks to push queue tasks.)

As of press time for this edition, the task queue REST API is released as an experimental feature. For more information about this feature, see the official App Engine website.

To create a pull queue, you add it to the queue configuration file. A pull queue must have a name, and must have its mode set to `pull`. In Python's *queue.yaml*:

```
queue:
- name: update_leaderboard
  mode: pull
```

In Java's *queue.xml*:

```
<queue-entries>
  <queue>
    <name>update_leaderboard</name>
    <mode>pull</mode>
  </queue>
</queue-entries>
```

Enqueuing Tasks to Pull Queues

You enqueue a task on a pull queue similarly to how you enqueue a task on a push queue, using a named queue whose mode is `pull`. As with push queues, a task on a pull queue can have a payload, a task name, and a countdown or ETA.

A task added to a pull queue must have a `method` set to `PULL`. This tells the queue that the task is only compatible with the queue when it is in the pull queue mode. In Python, this is the `method='PULL'` argument:

```
taskqueue.add(queue_name='update_leaderboard', method='PULL')
```

In Java, you call the `method()` (`withMethod()`) builder method on `TaskOptions` with the value `TaskOptions.Method.PULL`:

```
Queue queue = QueueFactory.getQueue("update_leaderboard");
queue.add(TaskOptions.Builder
    .withMethod(TaskOptions.Method.PULL));
```

Leasing and Deleting Tasks

A pull queue consumer running on App Engine can use the task queue service API to lease and delete tasks.

A lease is a guarantee that the consumer that acquired the lease has exclusive access to a task for a period of time. During that time, the consumer can do whatever work corresponds with that task record. The consumer is expected to delete the task at the end.

To lease tasks from a pull queue, you call a method of the queue specifying the duration of the lease and the maximum number of tasks. The service reserves up to that many tasks currently available on the queue for the requested amount of time, then returns identifiers for each of the successfully leased tasks. You can use these identifiers to delete the tasks, or update leases.

In Python, you construct the `Queue` object for the named pull queue, then call the `lease_tasks()` method. Its arguments are the lease duration as a number of seconds, and the maximum number of tasks to return. The method returns a list of `Task` objects, possibly empty if the queue has no available tasks:

```
# Lease 5 tasks from update_leaderboard for up to 20 seconds.
queue = Queue('update_leaderboard')
tasks = queue.lease_tasks(20, 5)

for task in tasks:
    # Read task.payload and do the corresponding work...
```

In Java, you construct the `Queue` object for the named pull queue, then call the `leaseTasks()` method. This method takes a `LeaseOptions` instance, built from `LeaseOptions.Builder` builder methods. The `leasePeriod()` (`withLeasePeriod()`) builder method takes a `long` and a `java.util.concurrent.TimeUnit`, which together specify the duration of the lease. The countLimit() (withCountLimit()) builder method sets the maximum number of tasks to lease. leaseTasks() returns a List<TaskHandle>, which may be empty:

```
import java.util.concurrent.TimeUnit;

// ...
        // Lease 5 tasks from update_leaderboard for up to 20 seconds.
        Queue queue = QueueFactory.getQueue("update_leaderboard");
        List<TaskHandle> tasks = queue.leaseTasks(
            LeaseOptions.Builder
                .withLeasePeriod(20, TimeUnit.SECONDS)
                .countLimit(5));

        for (TaskHandle task : tasks) {
            // Read task.getPayload() and do the corresponding work...
        }
```

Once the consumer has executed the work for a task successfully, it must delete the task to prevent it from being re-leased to another consumer. In Python, you call the delete_task() method of the Queue, passing it a Task object or a list of Task objects to delete:

```
        # ...
        queue.delete_task(tasks)
```

In Java, you call the deleteTask() method of the Queue. The single-task form takes either a TaskHandle or a String task name, and returns true on success. The batch form takes a List<TaskHandle>, and returns a corresponding List<Boolean>:

```
        // ...
        List<Boolean> success = queue.deleteTask(tasks);
```

Each of the examples shown here leases a batch of tasks, does the work for all the tasks, and then deletes them all with another batch call. When using this pattern, make sure the lease duration is long enough to accommodate all the work in the batch. Even if you delete each task as it finishes, the last task must wait for all of the others.

If the consumer needs more time, you can renew the lease without relinquishing it to another consumer. In Python, the Queue method modify_task_lease() takes the Task and a number of seconds for the new lease. In Java, the Queue method modifyTaskLease() takes a TaskHandle, a long, and a TimeUnit, and returns the new TaskHandle.

Retrying Pull Queue Tasks

When a lease duration on a task expires, the task becomes available on the pull queue. When another consumer leases tasks from the queue, it may obtain a lease on the task and start the work again. This is the pull queue equivalent of a "retry": if the first consumer failed to delete the task before the lease expired, then the task is assumed to have failed and needs to be tried again.

You can set a limit to the number of times a task is retried. This can be a default for all tasks added to a queue, in the queue configuration. You can also set this for an individual task, overriding the queue default. If the lease for a task is allowed to expire as many times as the limit for the task, the task is deleted automatically.

To configure a retry limit for a queue in *queue.yaml*, you provide a `retry_parameters` section in the queue's configuration, with a `task_retry_limit` value:

```
queue:
- name: update_leaderboard
  retry_parameters:
    task_retry_limit: 10
```

The same configuration in *queue.xml* is similar:

```
<queue-entries>
  <queue>
    <name>update_leaderboard</name>
    <retry-parameters>
      <task-retry-limit>10</task-retry-limit>
    </retry-parameters>
  </queue>
</queue-entries>
```

To set the limit for an individual task in Python, you provide the `retry_options` argument with a `TaskRetryOptions` instance as its value, passing the limit to the constructor:

```
t = taskqueue.Task(
    retry_options=taskqueue.TaskRetryOptions(
        task_retry_limit=10))
q = taskqueue.Queue('update_leaderboard')
q.add(t)
```

In Java, the `TaskOptions` builder method `retryOptions()` (`withRetryOptions()`) takes an instance of the `RetryOptions` class, using the `taskRetryLimit()` (`withTaskRetryLimit()`) builder method to set the limit:

```
Queue queue = QueueFactory.getQueue("update_leaderboard");
queue.add(TaskOptions.Builder.withRetryOptions(
    RetryOptions.Builder
        .withTaskRetryLimit(10)));
```

Transactional Task Enqueueing

Task queues are an essential reliability mechanism for App Engine applications. If a call to enqueue a task is successful, and the task can be completed, the task is guaranteed to be completed, even given the possibility of transient service failure. It is common to pair the reliability of task queues with the durability of the datastore: tasks can take datastore values, act on them, and then update the datastore.

To complete this picture, the task queue service includes an extremely useful feature: the ability to enqueue a task as part of a datastore transaction. A task enqueued within a transaction is only enqueued if the transaction succeeds. If the transaction fails, the task is not enqueued.

This opens up a world of possibilities for the datastore. Specifically, it enables easy transactions that operate across an arbitrary number of entity groups, with eventual consistency.

Consider the message board example from Chapter 7. To maintain an accurate count of every message in each conversation, we have to update the count each time a message is posted. To do this with strong consistency, the count and the message have to be updated in the same transaction, which means they have to be in the same entity group—and therefore every message in the thread has to be in the same entity group. This might be acceptable for a count of messages per conversation, since it's unlikely that many users will be posting to the same conversation simultaneously, and even so, the delay for resolving concurrency failures might not be noticed.

But what if we want a count of every message on the website? Putting every message in a single entity group would be impractical, as it would effectively serialize all updates to the entire site. We need a way to update the count reliably without keeping everything in one entity group.

Transactional task enqueueing lets us update the count reliably without concern for entity groups. To post a message, we use a transaction to create the message entity and enqueue a task that will update the count. If the transaction fails, the task is not enqueued, so the count remains accurate. The task is performed outside of the transaction, so the count does not need to be in the same entity group as the message, but transactional enqueueing and task retries ensure that the count is updated, but only under the proper circumstances.

Of course, this comes with a trade-off: it must be acceptable for the count to be inaccurate between the time the message entity is created and the time the count is updated. In other words, we must trade strong consistency for *eventual consistency*. Transactional task enqueueing gives us a simple way to implement eventually consistent global transactions.

You might think that eventual consistency is suitable for the global message count, because who cares if the message count is accurate? But eventual consistency is useful for important data as well. Say the user Alicandria posts a quest with a bounty of 10,000 gold, and a guild of 20 players completes the quest, claiming the bounty. Since any player can trade gold with any other player, it is impractical to put all players in the same entity group. A typical person-to-person exchange can use a cross-group transaction, but this can only involve up to five entity groups. So to distribute the bounty, we use transactional task enqueueing: the app deducts 10,000 gold pieces from Alicandria's inventory, then enqueues a task to give 500 gold pieces to each member of the guild, all in a transaction. We use task names and memcache locks to ensure the system doesn't accidentally create new gold pieces if it retries the task. Also, since the guild might get angry if they don't get their money quickly, we configure the gold transfer queue to execute at a fast rate and with a large token bucket.

You can enqueue up to five tasks transactionally. In a typical case, it's sufficient to start a master task within the transaction, then trigger additional tasks as needed, and let the queue-retry mechanism drive the completion of the work.

The API for transactional task enqueuing is simple, and typically just means calling the task queue API during an active transaction. Let's take a quick look at Python, then Java.

Only the task enqueuing action joins the datastore transaction. The task itself is executed outside of the transaction, either in its own request handler (push queues) or elsewhere (pull queues). Indeed, by definition, the task is not enqueued until the transaction is committed, so the task itself has no way to contribute further actions to the transaction.

Transactional Tasks in Python

Recall from Chapter 7 that we perform a transaction in Python and `ext.db` by calling a function that has the decorator `@db.transactional`. Every datastore call made between the start and end of the function participates in a single transaction, unless the call opts out of the current transaction (by joining or creating another transaction).

The `add()` function, the `add()` convenience method of a `Task`, and the `add()` method of a `Queue` all take an optional `transactional=True` argument. If provided, the task will be enqueued as part of the current transaction. If there is no current transaction, it raises a `taskqueue.BadTransactionStateError`. If the argument is not provided (or its value is `False`), the task is enqueued immediately, regardless of whether the transaction commits or aborts.

Here's an example of transferring gold from one player to many other players in a single transaction:

```
from google.appengine.api import taskqueue
from google.appengine.ext import db

@db.transactional
def pay_quest_bounty(quest_master_key, guild_member_keys, amount):
    quest_master = db.get(quest_master_key)
    assert quest_master is not None

    quest_master.gold -= amount
    db.put(quest_master)
    taskqueue.add(url='/actions/payment/bounty',
                  params={'user_key': guild_member_keys,  # repeated element
                          'total_amount': str(amount)})
```

The deduction and the task enqueue occur in the same transaction, so there's no risk of the deduction happening without enqueueing the task (gold disappears), nor is there a risk of the task getting enqueued without the deduction succeeding (gold is created). Assuming the bounty task is implemented correctly (and properly handles edge cases like a guild member's account being deleted), the transaction will complete with eventual consistency.

Transactional Tasks in Java

In the Java datastore API from Chapter 7, we saw that you start a datastore transaction with the `beginTransaction()` service method. This method returns a `Transaction` object. You perform a datastore operation within the transaction by passing the `Transaction` object to the operation's method. Alternatively, if you configured the service instance with `ImplicitTransactionManagementPolicy.AUTO`, you can call an operation's method without the transaction instance, and it will join the most recently created (and not committed) transaction.

The task queue API works the same way. The `add()` method of a `Queue` accepts an optional `Transaction` instance as its first argument. If you're using `ImplicitTransactionManagementPolicy.AUTO`, calling the `add()` method without this argument while an uncommitted transaction is open will cause the enqueue operation to join the transaction. The task is enqueued when the transaction is committed, if and only if the `txn.commit()` method is successful.

Here is a Java version of the previous Python example:

```
import java.util.List;
import com.google.appengine.api.datastore.DatastoreService;
import com.google.appengine.api.datastore.DatastoreServiceFactory;
import com.google.appengine.api.datastore.Entity;
import com.google.appengine.api.datastore.Key;
import com.google.appengine.api.datastore.Transaction;
import com.google.appengine.api.taskqueue.Queue;
import com.google.appengine.api.taskqueue.QueueFactory;
import com.google.appengine.api.taskqueue.TaskOptions;

// ...
    void payQuestBounty(Key questMasterKey,
                        List<String> guildMemberKeyStrs,
                        long amount) {
        DatastoreService datastore = DatastoreServiceFactory.getDatastoreService();
        Transaction txn = datastore.beginTransaction();

        Entity questMaster = datastore.get(questMasterKey);
        // ... Handle the case where questMaster == null...
        Long gold = (Long) questMaster.getProperty("gold");
        gold -= amount;
        questMaster.setProperty("gold", gold);
        datastore.put(questMaster);

        Queue queue = QueueFactory.getDefaultQueue();
        TaskOptions task = TaskOptions.Builder.withUrl("/actions/payment/bounty");
        for (userKeyStr : guildMemberKeyStrs) {
```

```
            task = task.param("user_key", userKeyStr);
        }
        task = task.param("total_amount", Long(amount).toString());
        queue.add(task);

        txn.commit();
    }
```

Task Chaining

A single task performed by a push queue can run for up to 10 minutes. There's a lot you can get done in 10 minutes, but the fact that there's a limit at all raises a red flag: a single task does not scale. If a job uses a single task and the amount of work it has to do scales with a growing factor of your app, the moment the amount of work exceeds 10 minutes, the task breaks.

One option is to use a master task, a task whose job is to figure out what work needs to be done, and then create an arbitrary number of tasks to do fixed-size units of the work. For example, the master task could fetch a feed URL from a remote host, and then create a task for each entry in the feed to process it. This goes a long way to doing more work within the 10 minute limit, and is useful to parallelize the units of work to complete the total job more quickly. But it's still a fixed capacity, limited to the number of child tasks the master task can create in 10 minutes.

For jobs of arbitrary size, another useful pattern is a *task chain*. The idea is straightforward: complete the job with an arbitrary number of tasks, where each task is responsible for creating the subsequent task, in addition to doing a fixed amount of work. Each task must be capable of performing its own amount of work in a fixed amount of time, as well as determining what the next unit of work ought to be.

Task chains are especially useful when combined with datastore query cursors, which meet these exact requirements. A task that ought to update every entity of a kind (possibly those that match other query criteria) can use the following steps:

1. Start a query for entities of the kind. If the task payload includes a cursor, set the query to start at the cursor location.
2. Read and process a fixed number of entities from the query results.
3. Take the cursor after the last query result. If there are any results after the cursor, create a new task with the new cursor as its payload.
4. Return a success code.

This produces the simple task chain shown in Figure 16-2. Each new task starts just as the previous task finishes.

If the work for the next task can be determined before performing the work for the current task, and the next task does not depend upon the completion of the current task, we can improve the performance of this job by creating the next task before we

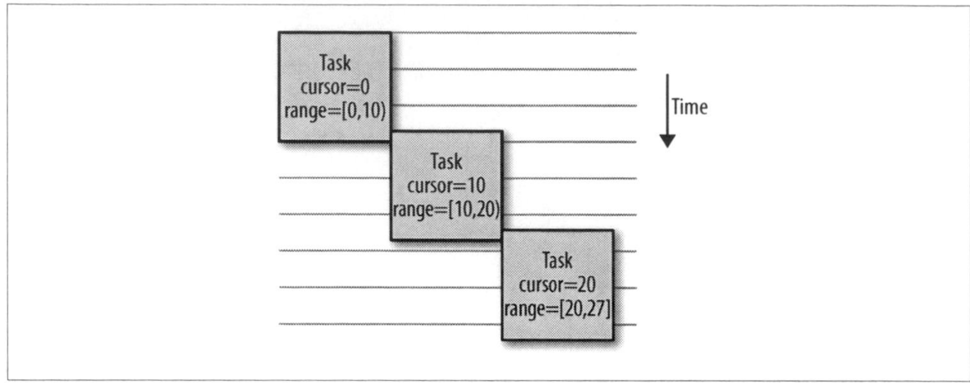

Figure 16-2. A simple task chain, where each task does a fixed amount of work, then creates the next task

begin the work. In the case of iterating over every result of a query, we can get the next cursor immediately after performing the query:

1. Start a query for entities of the kind. If the task payload includes a cursor, set the query to start at the cursor location.
2. Read a fixed number of entities from the query results.
3. Take the cursor after the last query result. If there are any results after the cursor, create a new task with the new cursor as its payload.
4. Process the results from the query.
5. Return a success code.

This technique compresses the timeline so the work of each task is performed concurrently. App Engine will perform the tasks up to the capacity of the queue, and will utilize instances based on your app's performance settings, so you can create tasks aggressively and throttle their execution to your taste. Figure 16-3 shows the timeline of the compressed behavior.

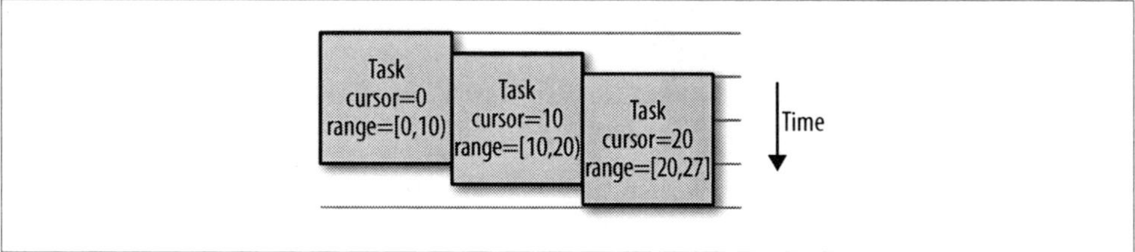

Figure 16-3. An improved task chain, where each task creates the next task before doing its own work

The last step of each task is to return a success code. This tells the push queue that the task was successful and can be deleted from the queue. If the task does not return a success code, such as due to a transient service error throwing an uncaught exception, the push queue puts the task back on the queue and tries it again. As we've described it so far, this is a problem for our task chain, because retrying one task will create another task for the next unit of work, and so on down the rest of the chain. We might end up with something like Figure 16-4, with a ton—potentially an exponential amount—of wasted work.

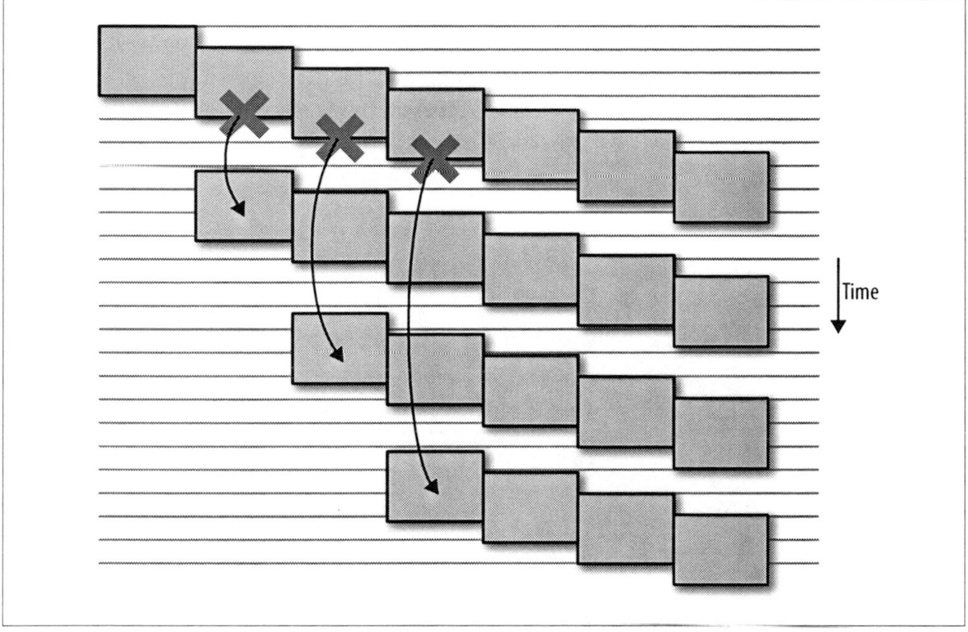

Figure 16-4. A transient error in a naive task chain explodes into many chains of wasted work, as links in the chain are retried

You might think the solution is to go back to the previous version of the task, where the work is performed before the next task is enqueued. This would reduce the likelihood that a transient service error occurs after the next link in the chain is created, but this doesn't eliminate the possibility. Even with no lines of code following the task enqueue operation in the handler, a failure on the app instance might still cause an error condition, and a fork in the chain.

The real solution is to use task names. As we saw earlier, every task has a unique name, either specified by the app or by the system. A given task name can only be used once (within a reasonably long period of time, on the order of days). When a named task finishes, it leaves behind a "tombstone" record to prevent the name from being reused right away.

A task name can be any string that identifies the next unit of work, and that the current task can calculate. In the datastore traversal example, we already have such a value: the query cursor. We can prepend a *nonce value* that identifies the job, to distinguish the query cursor for this job from a similar cursor of a job we might run later.

Our resilient task routine is as follows:

1. Start a query for entities of the kind. If the task payload includes a cursor, set the query to start at the cursor location.
2. Read a fixed number of entities from the query results.
3. Take the cursor after the last query result. If there are any results after the cursor, prepare to create a new task. If the task payload contains a nonce value for the job, use it, otherwise generate a new one. Generate the next task name based on the nonce value and the new query cursor. Create a new task with the task name, and the nonce value and the new cursor as its payload.
4. Process the results from the query.
5. Return a success code.

Transient errors no longer bother us, resulting in a pattern like Figure 16-5. Tasks that fail due to transient errors are retried and may cause their units of work to complete later, but they no longer cause the rest of the chain to be re-created for each failure.

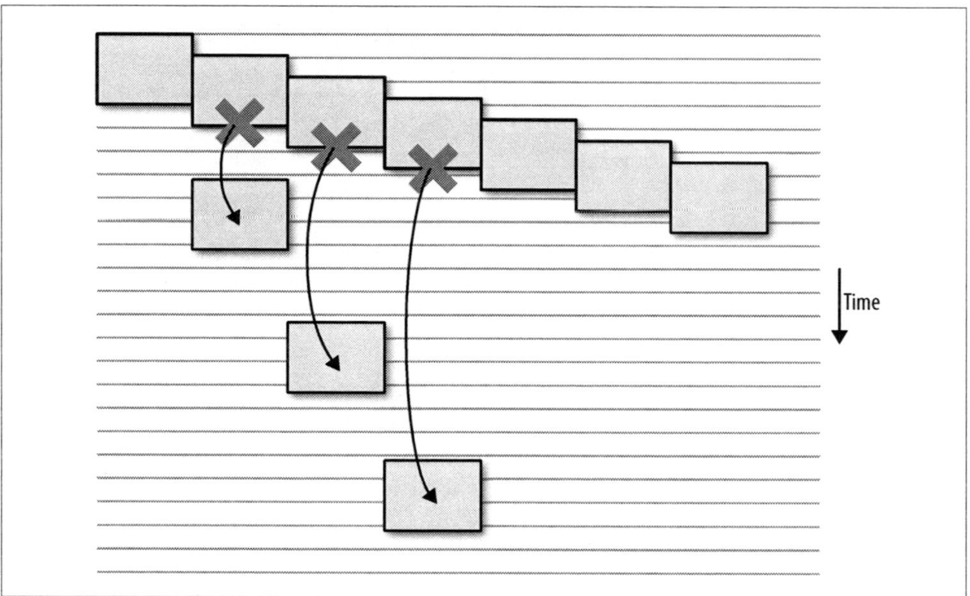

Figure 16-5. Named tasks prevent an exploding chain during a transient error

We close this discussion of task chains with an example implementation in Python. You can find the equivalent Java example in the sample code package on the website for this book:

```
import datetime
import re
import time
import urllib
```

```
import webapp2

from google.appengine.api import taskqueue
from google.appengine.ext import db

TASK_SIZE = 10

class Quest(db.Model):
    # ...
    end_timestamp = db.IntegerProperty()
    end_datetime = db.DateTimeProperty()

class UpgradeQuestEntitiesTaskHandler(webapp2.RequestHandler):
    def post(self):
        query = Quest.all()
        cursor = self.request.get('cursor', None)
        if cursor:
            query.with_cursor(cursor)

        results = query.fetch(TASK_SIZE)
        new_cursor = query.cursor()

        query.with_cursor(new_cursor)
        if query.count(1) == 1:
            job_id = self.request.get('job_id')
            task_name = job_id + '_' + new_cursor
            task_name = re.sub('[^a-zA-Z0-9_-]', '_', task_name)
            taskqueue.add(
                name=task_name,
                url='/admin/jobs/upgradequests/task',
                params={
                    'job_id': job_id,
                    'cursor': new_cursor })

        # Do the work.
        for quest in results:
            # Upgrade end_timestamp to end_datetime.
            quest.end_datetime = datetime.fromtimestamp(quest.end_timestamp)
        db.put(results)

class StartUpgradeQuestEntitiesJob(webapp2.RequestHandler):
    def get(self):
        started_job_id = self.request.get('job_id', None)
        if started_job_id is not None:
            self.response.out.write(
                '<p>Job started: %s</p>' % started_job_id)
        self.response.out.write("""
<form action="/admin/jobs/upgradequests/start" method="POST">
  <input type="submit" value="Start New Upgrade Quest Entities Job" />
</form>
""")

    def post(self):
        job_id = ('UpgradeQuestEntities_%s' % int(time.time()))
        taskqueue.add(
```

```
            name=job_id,
            url='/admin/jobs/upgradequests/task',
            params={ 'job_id': job_id })

        self.redirect('/admin/jobs/upgradequests/start?'
            + urllib.urlencode({ 'job_id': job_id }))

application = webapp2.WSGIApplication([
    ('/admin/jobs/upgradequests/task', UpgradeQuestEntitiesTaskHandler),
    ('/admin/jobs/upgradequests/start', StartUpgradeQuestEntitiesJob)],
    debug=True)
```

Task Queue Administration

The Administration Console provides a great deal of information about the current status of your task queues and their contents. The Task Queues panel lists all the queues you have configured, with their rate configurations and current running status. You can click on any queue to get more information about individual tasks, such as their calling parameters and how many times they have been retried. You can also delete tasks or force tasks to run, pause and restart the queue, or purge all tasks.

The features of this panel are intuitive, so we'll just add one comment on a common use of the panel: finding and deleting stuck tasks. If a queue has a task that is failing and being retried repeatedly, the Oldest Task column may have a suspiciously old date. Select the queue, then browse for a task with a large number in the Retries column. You can trace this back to logs from an individual attempt by copying the URL from the Method/URL column, then going to the Logs panel to do a search for that path. You may need to force a run of the task by clicking the Run Now button to get a recent entry to show up in the logs.

How you fix the problem depends on how important the data in the task record is. If the task is failing because of an error in the code that can be fixed, you can leave the task in the queue, fix the bug in the code, and then deploy new code to the target version of the task. When the task is retried, it'll use the new code, and proceed to completion. If the task is failing because the task record is incompatible with a recent change to the code, you can try to rescue the task record with a code change, or just delete the task record. It's often easier to delete old task records and re-create the activity they represent than to figure out how to usher them to completion.

Deferring Work

The Python and Java libraries each include a handy utility that makes it easy to throw work into a task without writing a custom task handler. The utility uses a prepackaged general purpose task handler to process deferred work.

Each utility is specific to the language. Let's see how to defer work in Python first, then in Java.

Deferring Work in Python

To defer work in Python, you create a Python function or other callable object that performs the work to be executed outside of the current request handler, then pass that callable object to the `defer()` function from the `google.appengine.ext.deferred` package. The `defer()` function takes the object to call within the task and arguments to pass to the callable object.

To use this feature, you must set up the deferred work task handler. This is a built-in for *app.yaml*:

```
builtins:
- deferred: on
```

Here's a simple example that spans two Python modules, one containing the deferred function, and one containing the request handler that defers it. First, here's the function, to appear in a module named *invitation.py*:

```
from google.appengine.api import mail
import logging

_INVITATION_MESSAGE_BODY = '''
You have been invited to join our community...
'''

def send_invitation(recipient):
    mail.send_mail('support@example.com',
                   recipient,
                   'You\'re invited!',
                   _INVITATION_MESSAGE_BODY)
    logging.info('Sent invitation to %s' % recipient)
```

And here's the request handler script:

```
from google.appengine.ext import webapp2
from google.appengine.ext import deferred
import invitation

class SendInvitationHandler(webapp2.RequestHandler):
    def get(self):
        # recipient = ...
        deferred.defer(invitation.send_invitation, recipient)

        # ...

application = webapp2.WSGIApplication([
    ('/sendinvite', SendInvitationHandler),
    ], debug=True)
```

The `defer()` function enqueues a task on the default queue that calls the given callable object with the given arguments. The arguments are serialized and deserialized using Python's `pickle` module; all argument values must be `pickle`-able.

Most Python callable objects can be used with defer(), including functions and classes defined at the top level of a module, methods of objects, class methods, instances of classes that implement __call__(), and built-in functions and methods. defer() does not work with lambda functions, nested functions, nested classes, or instances of nested classes. The task handler must be able to access the callable object by name, possibly via a serializable object, since it does not preserve the scope of the call to defer().

You also can't use a function or class in the same module as the request handler class from which you call defer(). This is because pickle believes the module of the request handler class to be __main__ while it is running, and so it doesn't save the correct package name. This is why the previous example keeps the deferred function in a separate module.

You can control the parameters of the task, such as the delay, by passing additional arguments to defer(). These are the same arguments you would pass to Task(), but with the argument names prepended with an underscore so they are not confused with arguments for the callable:

```
deferred.defer(invitation.send_invitation,
               'juliet@example.com',
               _countdown=86400)
```

To call the callable, the task handler determines the module location of the callable from the description saved by the defer() function, imports the required module, re-creates any required objects from their serialized forms, then calls the callable. If the module containing the callable imports other modules, those imports will occur during the task. If the deferred callable requires any additional setup, such as changes to the module import path, make sure this happens in the callable's module, or within the callable itself.

The task handler determines the success or failure of the task based on exceptions raised by the callable. If the callable raises a special exception called deferred.PermanentTaskFailure, the task handler logs the error, but returns a success code to the task queue so the task is not retried. If the callable raises any other exception, the exception is propagated to the Python runtime and the handler returns an error code, which causes the task queue to retry the task. If the callable does not raise an exception, the task is considered successful.

The deferred library is careful to raise deferred.PermanentTaskFailure for errors it knows will prevent the task from ever succeeding. Such errors log messages, then return success to flush the task from the queue.

Deferring Work in Java

The Java task queue library's mechanism for deferring work is based on the DeferredTask interface. This interface describes a class which is both java.lang.Runnable and java.io.Serializable. You provide an implementation of this interface, with a run()

method that does the work. To defer a call to this code, you add an instance of your class to a push queue, using a special form of the `withPayload()` builder method to `TaskOptions`. This method serializes the instance and puts it on the queue, to be executed by the deferred task handler provided by the runtime environment. No further setup is required, making this a convenient way to run code in the future:

```
import com.google.appengine.api.taskqueue.DeferredTask;
import com.google.appengine.api.taskqueue.Queue;
import com.google.appengine.api.taskqueue.QueueFactory;
import com.google.appengine.api.taskqueue.TaskOptions;

public class MyWork implements DeferredTask {
    String arg;

    public MyWork(String arg) {
        this.arg = arg;
    }

    void run() {
        // Do something with arg...
    }
}

// ...
        Queue queue = QueueFactory.getDefaultQueue();
        queue.add(TaskOptions.Builder.withPayload(new MyWork("my arg")));
```

Within the `run()` method, your deferred task can access basic information about the request handler in which it is running by using static methods of the `DeferredTaskContext` class. The `getCurrentServlet()` method returns the servlet, and `getCurrentRequest()` and `getCurrentResponse()` return the request and response, respectively.

By default, an unchecked exception thrown by the `run()` method causes the task to be retried. You can disable this behavior by calling the `DeferredTaskContext.setDoNotRetry(true)` method within the `run()` method. With retries disabled, any uncaught exception will be treated as a clean exit, and the task will be deleted from the queue.

The serialized version of the instance of your deferred task is stored as data in the task record. If you upload a new version of your application code and serialized data cannot be deserialized into an instance by using the new code, the task will fail perpetually. Take care to either clear deferred work from task queues before uploading new code, or only make serialization-compatible changes to the code while deferred work is in a task queue.

Scheduled Tasks

Applications do work in response to external stimuli: user requests, incoming email and XMPP messages, HTTP requests sent by a script on your computer. And while task queues can be used to trigger events across a period of time, a task must be enqueued by application code before anything happens.

Sometimes you want an application to do something "on its own." For instance, an app may need to send nightly email reports of the day's activity, or fetch news headlines from a news service. For this purpose, App Engine lets you specify a schedule of tasks to perform on a regular basis. In the App Engine API, scheduled tasks are also known as "cron jobs," named after a similar feature in the Unix operating system.

A scheduled task consists of a URL path to call and a description of the recurring times of the day, week, or month at which to call it. It can also include a textual description of the task, which is displayed in the Administration Console and other reports of the schedule.

To execute a scheduled task, App Engine calls the URL path by using an empty GET request. A scheduled task cannot be configured with parameters, headers, or a different HTTP method. If you need something more complicated, you can do it in the code for the request handler mapped to the scheduled task's URL path.

As with task queue handlers, you can secure the URL path by restricting it to application developers in the frontend configuration. The system can call such URL paths to execute scheduled tasks.

The HTTP request includes the header `X-AppEngine-Cron: true` to differentiate it from other App Engine–initiated requests. Only App Engine can set this header. If an external request tries to set it, App Engine removes it before it reaches your app. You can use the header to protect against outside requests triggering the job. Scheduled task requests are also treated like requests from administrator user (similarly to push queue tasks), so you can guard task URLs by using a login requirement in *app.yaml* or *web.xml*.

Just like tasks in push queues, scheduled tasks have a request deadline of 10 minutes, so you can do a significant amount of computation and service calls in a single request handler. Depending on how quickly the task needs to be completed, you may still wish to break work into small pieces and use task queues to execute them on multiple instances in parallel.

Unlike push queues, scheduled tasks that fail are not retried. If a failed schedule task should be retried immediately, the scheduled task should put the work onto a push queue.

The development console does not execute scheduled tasks automatically. If you need to test a scheduled task, you can visit the task URL path while signed in as an administrator. The Python version of the development console includes a Cron Jobs section that lists the URL paths in the configuration file for easy access.

If you have enabled billing for your application, your app can have up to 100 task schedules. At the free billing tier, an app can have up to 20 task schedules.

Configuring Scheduled Tasks

In Python, the schedule is a configuration file named *cron.yaml*. It contains a value named `cron`, which is a list of task schedules. Each task schedule has a `description`, a `url`, and a `schedule`. You can also specify a `timezone` for the schedule:

```
cron:
- description: Send nightly reports.
  url: /cron/reports
  schedule: every day 23:59
  timezone: America/Los_Angeles
- description: Refresh news.
  url: /cron/getnews
  schedule: every 1 hours
```

In Java, the corresponding file in the *WEB-INF/* directory is named *cron.xml*. A `<cronentries>` element contains zero or more `<cron>` elements, one for each schedule. The `<url>`, `<description>`, `<schedule>`, and `<timezone>` elements define the scheduled task:

```
<cronentries>
  <cron>
    <url>/cron/reports</url>
    <description>Send nightly reports.</description>
    <schedule>every day 23:59</schedule>
    <timezone>America/Los_Angeles</timezone>
  </cron>
  <cron>
    <url>/cron/getnews</url>
    <description>Refresh news.</description>
    <schedule>every 1 hours</schedule>
  </cron>
</cronentries>
```

As with other service configuration files, the scheduled task configuration file applies to the entire app, and is uploaded along with the application. You can also upload it separately. With the Python SDK:

```
appcfg.py update_cron app-dir
```

With the Java SDK (`appcfg.sh update_cron` on Mac OS X or Linux):

```
appcfg update_cron war
```

You can validate your task schedule and get a human-readable description of it by using `appcfg.py cron_info app-dir` (Python) or `appcfg cron_info war` (Java). The report includes the exact days and times of the next few runs, so you can make sure that the schedule is what you want.

These are the possible fields for each scheduled task:

`description`
: A textual description of the scheduled task, displayed in the Administration Console.

`url`
: The URL path of the request handler to call for this task.

`schedule`
: The schedule on which to execute this task.

`timezone`
: The time zone for the schedule, as a standard "zoneinfo" time zone descriptor (such as `America/Los_Angeles`). If omitted, the schedule times are interpreted as UTC time.

`target`
: The ID of the app version to use for the task. If omitted, App Engine calls the version that is the default at the time the task executes.

If you choose a time zone identifier where Daylight Saving Time (DST) is used and have a task scheduled during the DST hour, your task will be skipped when DST advances forward an hour, and run twice when DST retreats back an hour. Unless this is desired, pick a time zone that does not use DST, or do not schedule tasks during the DST hour. (The default time zone UTC does not use DST.)

Specifying Schedules

The value for the `schedule` element (in either Python or Java) uses a simplified English-like format for describing the recurrence of the task. It accepts simple recurrences, such as:

```
every 30 minutes
every 3 hours
```

The minimum interval is `every 1 minutes`. The parser's English isn't that good: it doesn't understand `every 1 minute` or `every minute`. It does understand `every day`, as an exception.

The interval `every day` accepts an optional time of day, as a 24-hour `hh:mm` time. This runs every day at 11:59 p.m.:

```
every day 23:59
```

You can have a task recur weekly using the name of a weekday, as in `every tuesday`, and can also include a time: `every tuesday 23:59`. In another English parsing foible, day names must use all lowercase letters. You can abbreviate day names using just the first three letters, such as `every tue 23:59`.

You can have a task recur monthly or on several days of a given month by specifying a comma-delimited list of ordinals (such as `2nd`, or `first,third`) and a comma-delimited list of weekday names (`monday,wednesday,friday` or `sat,sun`). You can also include a time of day, as earlier. This occurs on the second and fourth Sunday of each month:

```
2nd,4th sunday
```

You can have a task recur yearly by including the word "of" and a comma-delimited list of lowercase month names (`january,july`, or `oct,nov,dec`). This schedule executes at 6 p.m. on six specific days of the year:

```
3rd,4th tue,wed,thu of march 18:00
```

You can specify recurrences to occur between two times of the day. This executes the task every 15 minutes between 3 a.m. and 5 a.m. every day:

```
every 15 mins from 03:00 to 05:00
```

By default, when a schedule uses a time interval without an explicit start time, App Engine will wait for the previous task to complete before restarting the timer. If a task runs every 15 minutes and the task takes 5 minutes to complete, each task's start time begins 20 minutes apart. If you'd prefer the next task to start at a specific interval from the previous start time regardless of the time taken to complete the previous task (or whether the previous task has finished), use the `synchronized` keyword:

```
every 15 mins synchronized
```

CHAPTER 17

Optimizing Service Calls

Handlers for user-facing requests spend most of their time calling App Engine services, such as the datastore or memcache. As such, making user-facing requests fast requires understanding how your application calls services, and applying techniques to optimize the heaviest uses of calls.

We've seen three optimization techniques already, but they're worth reviewing:

- Store heavily used results of datastore queries, URL fetches, and large computations in memcache. This exchanges expensive operations (even simple datastore gets) for fast calls to the memcache in the vast majority of cases, at the expense of a potentially stale view of the data in rare cases.
- Defer work outside of the user-facing request by using task queues. When the work to prepare results for users occurs outside of the user-facing request, it's easy to see how user-facing requests are dominated by requests to the datastore or memcache.
- Use the datastore and memcache batch APIs when operating on many independent elements (when batch size limitations are not an issue). Every call to the service has remote procedure call overhead, so combining calls into batches saves overhead. It also reduces clock time spent on the call, because the services can perform the operations on the elements in parallel.

Another important optimization technique is to call services *asynchronously*. When you call a service asynchronously, the call returns immediately. Your request handler code can continue executing while the service does the requested work. When your code needs the result, it calls a method that waits for the service call to finish (if it hasn't finished already), and then returns the result. With asynchronous calls, you can get services and your app code doing multiple things at the same time, so the user response is ready sooner.

App Engine supports asynchronous service APIs to the datastore, memcache, and URL Fetch services in both Python and Java. Support for asynchronous calls is also currently supported in a few other places, specifically the Python Blobstore API and the Java Images API (not described in this book).

All of these optimization techniques require understanding your application's needs and recognizing where the benefits of the technique justify the added code complexity. App Engine includes a tool called AppStats to help you understand how your app calls services and where you may be able to optimize the call patterns. AppStats hooks into your application logic to collect timing data for service calls, and reports this data visually in a web-based interface.

In this chapter, we demonstrate how to call services using the asynchronous APIs. We also walk through the process of setting up and using AppStats, and see how it can help us understand our application's performance.

Calling Services Asynchronously

Consider the following call to the URL Fetch service, shown here in Python:

```
from google.appengine.api import urlfetch

# ...
        response = urlfetch.fetch('http://store.example.com/products/molasses')
        process_data(response)
```

When execution of the request handler reaches this line, a sequence of events takes place. The app issues a remote procedure call to the URL Fetch service. The service prepares the request, then opens a connection with the remote host and sends it. The remote host does whatever it needs to do to prepare a response, invoking handler logic, making local connections to database servers, performing queries, and formatting results. The response travels back over the network, and the URL Fetch service concludes its business and returns the response data to the app. Execution of the request handler continues with the next line.

From the point when it makes the service call to the point it receives the response data, the app is idle. If the app has multithreading enabled in its configuration, the handler's instance can use the spare CPU to handle other requests. But no further progress is made on this request handler.

In the preceding case, that's the best the request handler can do: it needs the response in order to proceed to the next line of execution. But consider this amended example:

```
        ingred1 = urlfetch.fetch('http://store.example.com/products/molasses')
        ingred2 = urlfetch.fetch('http://store.example.com/products/sugar')
        ingred3 = urlfetch.fetch('http://store.example.com/products/flour')

        combine(ingred1, ingred2, ingred3)
```

Here, the request handler issues the first request, then waits for the first response before issuing the second request. It waits again for the second response before issuing the third. The total running time of just these three lines is equal to the sum of the execution times of each call, and during that time the request handler is doing nothing but waiting. Most importantly, the code does not need the data in the first response in order to issue the second or third request. In fact, it doesn't need any of the responses until the fourth line.

These calls to the URL Fetch service are *synchronous*: each call waits for the requested action to be complete before proceeding. With synchronous calls, your code has complete results before it proceeds, which is sometimes necessary, but sometimes not. Our second example would benefit from service calls that are *asynchronous*, where the handler can do other things while the service prepares its results.

When your app makes an asynchronous service call, the call returns immediately. Its return value is not the result of the call (which is still in progress). Instead, the call returns a special kind of object called a *future*, which represents the call and provides access to the results when you need them later. A future is an I.O.U., a promise to return the result at a later time. Your app is free to perform additional work while the service does its job. When the app needs the promised result, it calls a method on the future. This call either returns the result if it's ready, or waits for the result.

A synchronous call can be thought of as an asynchronous call that waits on the future immediately. In fact, this is precisely how the App Engine synchronous APIs are implemented.

Here is the asynchronous version of the second example. Note that the Python URL Fetch API:

```
ingred1_rpc = urlfetch.make_fetch_call(
    urlfetch.create_rpc(), 'http://store.example.com/products/molasses')
ingred2_rpc = urlfetch.make_fetch_call(
    urlfetch.create_rpc(), 'http://store.example.com/products/sugar')
ingred3_rpc = urlfetch.make_fetch_call(
    urlfetch.create_rpc(), 'http://store.example.com/products/flour')

combine(
    ingred1_rpc.get_result(),
    ingred2_rpc.get_result(),
    ingred3_rpc.get_result())
```

The `make_fetch_call()` function calls each issue their request to the service, then return immediately. The requests execute in parallel. The total clock time of this code, including the `get_result()` calls, is equal to the longest of the three service calls, not the sum. This is a potentially dramatic speed increase for our code.

Figure 17-1 illustrates the difference between a synchronous and an asynchronous call, using the Python URL Fetch API as an example.

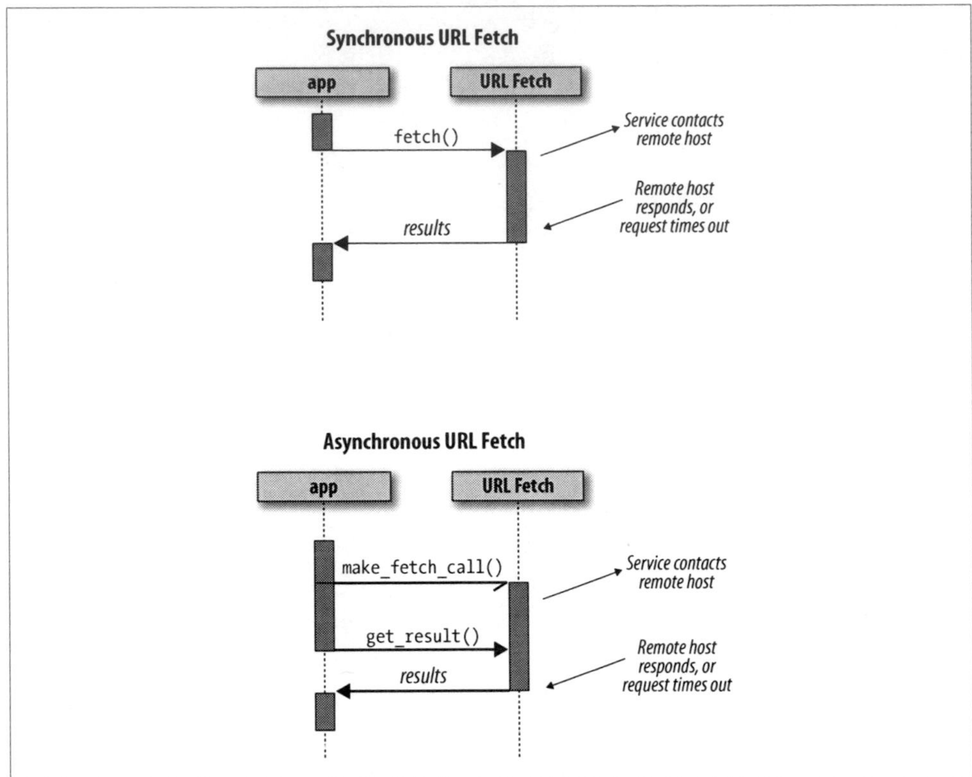

Figure 17-1. Sequence diagrams of a synchronous URL fetch and an asynchronous URL fetch

The example above was trivial: we could determine an obvious optimization just from looking at the code, and the change was not complicated. In a real app, reordering your code and data dependencies to best exploit asynchronous calls can add complexity. Like most optimization, it's an investment to gain performance.

The Python and Java service APIs have their own particular ways of making asynchronous calls. Furthermore, not every service has an official asynchronous API in every runtime environment. Let's take a look at what's available, first for Python, then for Java.

Asynchronous Calls in Python

The Python runtime environment has documented asynchronous calls for the datastore, memcache, Blobstore, and URL Fetch services. The calling syntax varies slightly between the URL Fetch service and the other services, but the general idea is the same.

All asynchronous calls in Python return an RPC (remote procedure call) object. You can call the `get_result()` method of this object to wait for results (if necessary), and either raise exceptions to report service errors, or return the result.

More specifically, the RPC object advances through four states during its lifetime:

1. Created. The object has been created, but has not been associated with a call.
2. In progress. The service call has been initiated and associated with the object.
3. Ready. The call has completed, either with results or with an error.
4. Checked. The status of the call has been reported to the application, such as by having raised an exception to represent an error.

When you call a service's asynchronous function, the service returns an RPC object in the "in progress" state. Calling the RPC object's `get_result()` method advances it through the "ready" state to the "checked" state. Calling `get_result()` on an RPC object in the "checked" state will return the result (if any) again, but will not reraise exceptions.

You can advance the RPC object through the last two states manually by using methods. The `wait()` method waits for the fetch to finish ("in progress" to "ready"). The `check_result()` method verifies and reports the final status ("ready" to "checked"). Calling any of these methods advances the object to the appropriate state, performing the tasks along the way. If the starting state for the method has already passed, such as calling `wait()` when in the "ready" state, the method does nothing.

Figure 17-2 illustrates the RPC object states and transitions.

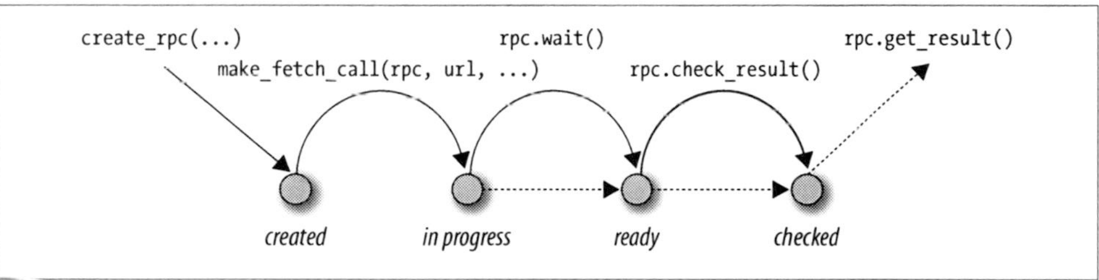

Figure 17-2. The RPC object states and transitions, using URL Fetch as an example

Datastore

The Python datastore API in the `google.appengine.ext.db` package has asynchronous equivalents for the major functions. The arguments are the same. Instead of returning a result, the asynchronous functions return an RPC object, whose `get_result()` method returns the expected result. Table 17-1 lists each function and its asynchronous equivalent.

Table 17-1. Python functions in ext.db and their asynchronous equivalents

Synchronous	Asynchronous
`db.get()`	`db.get_async()`
`db.put()`	`db.put_async()`
`db.delete()`	`db.delete_async()`

Synchronous	Asynchronous
db.allocate_ids()	db.allocate_ids_async()
db.get_indexes()	db.get_indexes_async()

A brief example:

```
from google.appengine.ext import db

# ...
        get_rpcs = {}
        for k in keys:
            get_rpcs[k] = db.get_async(k)
            # ...

        # ...
        v1 = get_rpcs[k1].get_result()
```

The asynchronous calls are only available as package functions. The methods of the `Model` class, such as `obj.put()`, do not have asynchronous versions. Of course, you can pass any model instance to the package functions.

A transaction function can contain asynchronous function calls. When the transaction function exits, any asynchronous calls made within the function that are not in the "checked" state are resolved before the transaction commits.

Queries can be performed asynchronously. Normally, a `Query` object doesn't make a service call until results are fetched. If you use the object as an iterable, the first few results are fetched immediately, and subsequent results are prefetched asynchronously, as needed. You can start the asynchronous prefetching process early by calling the `run()` method. `run()` returns an iterable of results just like the object. The only difference is the asynchronous prefetching process is started before the first use of the iterable:

```
from google.appengine.ext import db

class Player(db.Expando):
    pass

# ...
        # Prepare the query.  (No service calls.)
        query = Player.all().order('-score')

        # Call the service asynchronously to start prefetching results.
        results = query.run()

        # ...

        for player in results:
            # ...
```

In contrast, the `fetch()` method initiates synchronous service calls to perform the query and retrieve the requested number of result entities.

Memcache

The Python memcache API includes asynchronous versions of a set of the `Client` methods. All of the memcache's functionality is available with asynchronous calls, although only a subset of the calling syntax is supported. In particular, only methods of the `Client` class have asynchronous versions, not the package functions. For most methods, only the batch versions have asynchronous equivalents, but of course you can always call a batch method with a single element. Table 17-2 lists the methods.

Table 17-2. Python methods of api.memcache.Client and their asynchronous equivalents

Synchronous	Asynchronous
`client.get_multi()`	`client.get_multi_async()`
`client.set_multi()`	`client.set_multi_async()`
`client.add_multi()`	`client.add_multi_async()`
`client.replace_multi()`	`client.replace_multi_async()`
`client.cas_multi()`	`client.cas_multi_async()`
`client.incr()`	`client.incr_async()`
`client.decr()`	`client.decr_async()`
`client.offset_multi()`	`client.offset_multi_async()`
`client.flush_all()`	`client.flush_all_async()`
`client.get_stats()`	`client.get_stats_async()`

An example:

```
from google.appengine.api import memcache

# ...
        client = memcache.Client()

        add_rpc = client.add_multi_async(mapping)
        # ...

        if add_rpc.get_result().get(k, None) is None:
            # ...
```

Blobstore

The Python Blobstore API has asynchronous versions of the major functions. Table 17-3 lists the functions.

Table 17-3. Python functions in ext.blobstore and their asynchronous equivalents

Synchronous	Asynchronous
`blobstore.create_upload_url()`	`blobstore.create_upload_url_async()`
`blobstore.delete()`	`blobstore.delete_async()`

Synchronous	Asynchronous
`blobstore.fetch_data()`	`blobstore.fetch_data_async()`
`blobstore.create_gs_key()`	`blobstore.create_gs_key_async()`

The `BlobInfo` methods do no have asynchronous equivalents. To delete a Blobstore value asynchronously, use the **`blobstore`** function.

In this example, we call the Blobstore service asynchronously to create an upload URL, then pass the RPC object to the template engine rendering the page. This allows us to finish other work and fire up the template engine while the service call is in progress. The template itself blocks on the RPC object to get the result when it is needed at the last possible moment:

```
import jinja2
from google.appengine.ext import blobstore

template_env = jinja2.Environment(
    loader=jinja2.FileSystemLoader(os.getcwd()))

# ...
        template = template_env.get_template('form.html')
        context = {
            'upload_url_rpc': blobstore.create_upload_url_async('/formhandler'),
            'orig_data': load_orig_data(),
        }
        self.response.out.write(template.render(context))
```

The template calls the `get_result()` method of the RPC object to get the value it needs:

```
<!-- ... -->

  <form action="{{ upload_url_rpc.get_result() }}" method="post">
    <!-- ... -->
  </form>
```

URL Fetch

The Python URL Fetch asynchronous API uses a slightly different syntax from the others. The asynchronous equivalent of `urlfetch.fetch(...)` is `urlfetch.make_fetch_call(urlfetch.create_rpc(), ...)`. Like the `_async()` methods, it returns an RPC object. Unlike the others, you must create the RPC object first, and pass it in as the first argument. The function updates the RPC object, then returns it. The remaining arguments are equivalent to `urlfetch.fetch()`.

This style of passing an RPC object to a service call predates the _async-style methods in the other APIs. It appears inconsistently throughout the Python service APIs, so you might notice some other modules have it. The ext.blobstore module has a create_rpc() method, and many methods accept an rpc keyword argument. The api.memcache module also has a create_rpc() method, although only the _async methods of the Client class support it.

Asynchronous calling of the URL Fetch service is only available using the urlfetch API. The Python standard library urllib2 always calls the service synchronously.

Using callbacks

To make the most of the parallel execution of asynchronous calls, a request handler should initiate the call as soon as possible in the handler's lifetime. This can be as straightforward as calling asynchronous methods early in a routine, then calling the get_results() method at the point in the routine where the results are needed. If your handler uses multiple diverse components to perform tasks, and each component may require the results of asynchronous calls, you could have the main routine ask each component to initiate its service calls, then allow the components to get their own results as control reaches the appropriate points in the code.

The Python RPC object offers another way to organize the code that handles the results of fetches: callbacks. A callback is a function associated with the RPC object that is called at some point after the RPC is complete, when the app calls the wait(), check_results(), or get_results() method. Specifically, the callback is invoked when the object goes from the "in progress" state to the "ready" state. Since the RPC never reverts states, the callback is only called once, even if the app accesses results multiple times.

You can set a callback by setting the callback attribute of the RPC object. (Be sure to do this before calling wait(), check_results(), or get_results().)

```
rpc = db.get_async(k)
rpc.callback = some_func

# ...

# Wait for the call to finish, then calls some_func.
rpc.wait()
```

In the URL Fetch API, and other APIs that let you create an RPC object explicitly, you can also pass the callback function value as the callback keyword argument to create_rpc().

The callback function is called without arguments. This is odd, because a common use for a callback function is to process the results of the service call, so the function needs access to the RPC object. There are several ways to give the callback function access to the object.

One way is to use a *bound method*, a feature of Python that lets you refer to a method of an instance of a class as a callable object. Define a class with a method that processes the results of the call, using an RPC object stored as a member of the class. Create an instance of the class, then create the RPC object, assigning the bound method as the callback. Example 17-1 demonstrates this technique.

Example 17-1. Using an object method as a callback to access the RPC object

```
from google.appengine.api import urlfetch

# ...
class CatalogUpdater(object):
    def prepare_urlfetch_rpc(self):
        self.rpc = urlfetch.make_fetch_call(
            urlfetch.create_rpc(),
            'http://api.example.com/catalog_feed')
        self.rpc.callback = self.process_results
        return self.rpc

    def process_results(self):
        try:
            results = self.rpc.get_result()
            # Process results.content...

        except urlfetch.Error, e:
            # Handle urlfetch errors...

class MainHandler(webapp.RequestHandler):
    def get(self):
        rpcs = []

        catalog_updater = CatalogUpdater(self.response)
        rpcs.append(catalog_updater.prepare_urlfetch_rpc())

        # ...

        for rpc in rpcs:
            rpc.wait()
```

Another way to give the callback access to the RPC object is to use a *nested function* (sometimes called a *closure*). If the callback function is defined in the same scope as a variable whose value is the RPC object, the function can access the variable when it is called.

Example 17-2 demonstrates the use of a nested function as a callback. The `create_callback()` function creates a function object, a `lambda` expression, that calls another function with the RPC object as an argument. This function object is assigned to the `callback` property of the RPC object.

Example 17-2. Using a nested function as a callback to access the RPC object

```
from google.appengine.api import urlfetch

def process_results(rpc):
    try:
        results = self.rpc.get_result()
        # Process results.content...

    except urlfetch.Error, e:
        # Handle urlfetch errors...

def create_callback(rpc):
    # Use a function to define the scope for the lambda.
    return lambda: process_results(rpc)

# ...
        rpc = urlfetch.create_rpc()
        rpc.callback = create_callback(rpc)
        urlfetch.make_fetch_call(rpc, 'http://api.example.com/catalog_feed')

        # ...

        rpc.wait()
```

If you've used other programming languages that support function objects, the `create_callback()` function may seem unnecessary. Why not create the function object directly where it is used? In Python, the scope of an inner function is the outer function, including its variables. If the outer function redefines the variable containing the RPC object (`rpc`), when the inner function is called it will use that value. By wrapping the creation of the inner function in a dedicated outer function, the value of `rpc` in the scope of the callback is always set to the intended object.

Someone still needs to call the `wait()` method on the RPC object so the callback can be called. But herein lies the value of callbacks: the component that calls `wait()` does not have to know anything about what needs to be done with the results. The main routine can query its subcomponents to prepare and return RPC objects, then later it can call `wait()` on each of the objects. The callbacks assigned by the subcomponents are called to process each result.

If you have multiple asynchronous service calls in progress simultaneously, the callback for an RPC is invoked if the service call finishes during any call to `wait()`—even if the `wait()` is for a different RPC. Of course, the `wait()` doesn't return until the fetch for its own RPC object finishes and its callbacks are invoked. A callback is only invoked once: if you call `wait()` for an RPC whose callback has already been called, it does nothing and returns immediately.

If your code makes multiple simultaneous asynchronous calls, be sure not to rely on an RPC's callback being called only during its own `wait()`.

Asynchronous Calls in Java

The Java runtime environment includes asynchronous APIs for the datastore, memcache, URL Fetch, and Images services. (The Images service is not described here.) The location of these methods differs slightly from service to service, but they all use the same standard mechanism for representing results: `java.util.concurrent.Future<T>`.

For each synchronous method that returns a value of a particular type, the asynchronous equivalent for that method returns a `Future<T>` wrapper of that type. The method invokes the service call, then immediately returns the `Future<T>` to the app. The app can proceed with other work while the service call is in progress. When it needs the result, the app calls the `get()` method of the `Future<T>`, which waits for the call to complete (if needed) and then returns the result of type `T`:

```
import java.util.concurrent.Future;
import com.google.appengine.api.urlfetch.URLFetchService;
import com.google.appengine.api.urlfetch.URLFetchServiceFactory;
import com.google.appengine.api.urlfetch.HTTPResponse;

// ...
        URLFetchService urlfetch = URLFetchServiceFactory.getURLFetchService();
        Future<HTTPResponse> responseFuture =
            urlfetch.fetchAsync(new URL("http://store.example.com/products/molasses"));

        // ...
        HTTPResponse response = responseFuture.get();
```

The `get()` method accepts optional parameters that set a maximum amount of time for the app to wait for a pending result. This amount is specified as two arguments: a `long`, and a `java.util.concurrent.TimeUnit` (such as `TimeUnit.SECONDS`). This timeout is separate from any deadlines associated with the service itself; it's just how long the app will wait on the call.

The `Future<T>` has a `cancel()` method, which cancels the service call. This method returns `true` if the call was canceled successfully, or `false` if the call had already completed or was previously canceled. The `isCancelled()` method (note the spelling) returns `true` if the call has been canceled in the past. `isDone()` returns `true` if the call is not in progress, including if it succeeded, failed, or was canceled.

Service calls that don't return values normally have a `void` return type in the API. The asynchronous versions of these return a `Future<java.lang.Void>`, so you can still wait for the completion of the call. To do so, simply call the `get()` method in a void context.

Datastore

To call the datastore asynchronously in Java, you use a different service class: `AsyncDatastoreService`. You get an instance of this class by calling `DatastoreServiceFactory.getAsyncDatastoreService()`. Like its synchronous counterpart, this factory method can take an optional `DatastoreServiceConfig` value.

The methods of `AsyncDatastoreService` are identical to those of `DatastoreService`, except that return values are all wrapped in `Future<T>` objects.

There are no explicit asynchronous methods for fetching query results. Instead, the `PreparedQuery` methods `asIterable()`, `asIterator()`, and `asList()` always return immediately and begin prefetching results in the background. (This is true even when using the `DatastoreService` API.)

Committing a datastore transaction will wait for all previous asynchronous datastore calls since the most recent commit. You can commit a transaction asynchronously using the `commitAsync()` method of the `Transaction`. Calling `get()` on its `Future` will block similarly.

When using `AsyncDatastoreService` with transactions, you must provide the `Transaction` instance explicitly with each call. Setting the implicit transaction management policy to `AUTO` (in `DatastoreServiceConfig`) will have no effect. This is because the automatic policy sometimes has to commit transactions, and this would block on all unresolved calls, possibly unexpectedly. To avoid confusion, `AsyncDatastoreService` does not support implicit transactions.

The `cancel()` method of a datastore `Future<T>` may return `true` even if the service call has already modified data. Canceling a data change in progress does not roll back changes.

Memcache

To call the memcache asynchronously in Java, you use the `AsyncMemcacheService` service class. You get an instance of this class by calling `MemcacheServiceFactory.getAsyncMemcacheService()`. The methods of `AsyncMemcacheService` are identical to those of `MemcacheService`, except that return values are all wrapped in `Future<T>` objects.

URL Fetch

The Java URL Fetch API has one asynchronous method: `fetchAsync()`, of the `URLFetchService` class. This method is equivalent to the `fetch()` method, except it returns a `Future<HTTPResponse>`.

Visualizing Calls with AppStats

AppStats is a tool to help you understand how your code calls services. After you install the tool in your application, AppStats records timing data for requests, including when each service call started and ended relative to the request running time. You use the AppStats Console to view this data as a timeline of the request activity.

Let's take another look at our contrived URL Fetch example from earlier in this chapter:

```
ingred1 = urlfetch.fetch('http://store.example.com/products/molasses')
ingred2 = urlfetch.fetch('http://store.example.com/products/sugar')
ingred3 = urlfetch.fetch('http://store.example.com/products/flour')

combine(ingred1, ingred2, ingred3)
```

Figure 17-3 is the AppStats timeline for this code. It's clear from this graph how each individual call contributes to the total running time. In particular, notice that the "Grand Total" is as large as the "RPC Total."

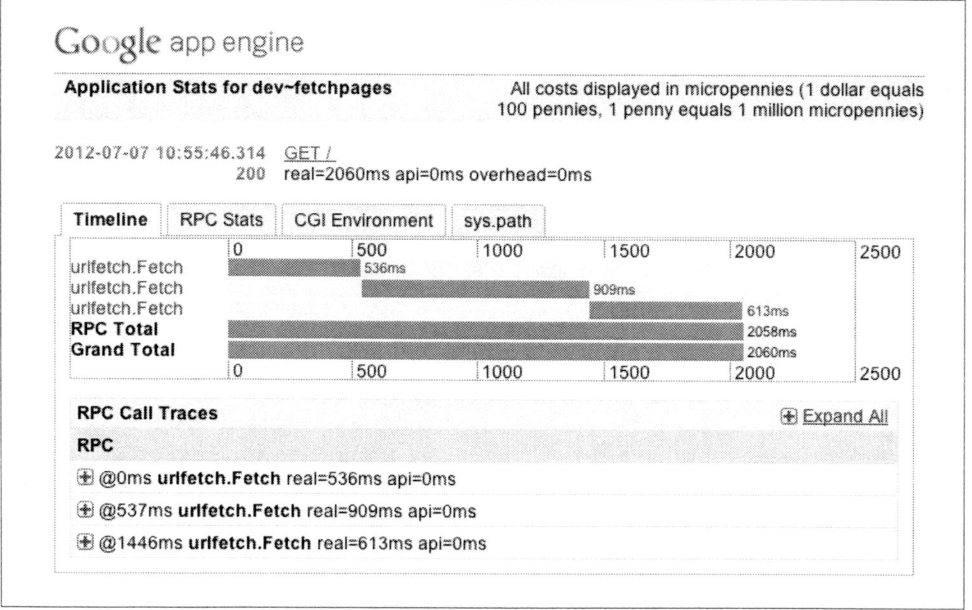

Figure 17-3. The AppStats Console illustrating three synchronous calls to urlfetch.Fetch

Here's the same example using asynchronous calls to the URL Fetch service:

```
ingred1_rpc = urlfetch.make_fetch_call(
    urlfetch.create_rpc(), 'http://store.example.com/products/molasses')
ingred2_rpc = urlfetch.make_fetch_call(
    urlfetch.create_rpc(), 'http://store.example.com/products/sugar')
ingred3_rpc = urlfetch.make_fetch_call(
    urlfetch.create_rpc(), 'http://store.example.com/products/flour')

combine(
    ingred1_rpc.get_result(),
    ingred2_rpc.get_result(),
    ingred3_rpc.get_result())
```

Figure 17-4 shows the new chart, and the difference is dramatic: the URL Fetch calls occur simultaneously, and the "Grand Total" is not much larger than the longest of the three fetches.

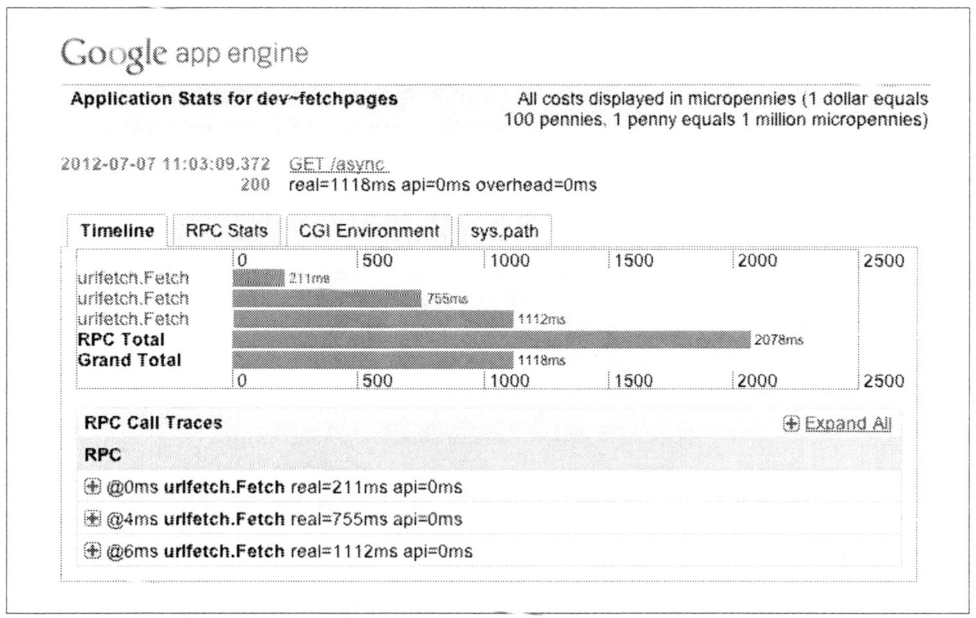

Figure 17-4. The AppStats Console illustrating three overlapping asynchronous calls to urlfetch.Fetch

AppStats is available for both Python and Java apps. The tool has two parts: the event recorder and the AppStats Console. Both parts live within your app, and are included in the runtime environment.

Once installed, you can use AppStats in both the development server and your live app. Running in the development server can give you a good idea of the call patterns, although naturally the timings will not match the live service.

The event recorder hooks into the serving infrastructure for your app to start recording at the beginning of each request, and store the results at the end. It records the start and end times of the request handler, and the start and end times of each remote procedure call (RPC) to the services. It also stores stack traces (and, for Python, local variables) at each call site.

The recorder uses memcache for storage, and does not use the datastore. It stores two values: a short record, and a long record. The short record is used by the AppStats Console to render a browsing interface for the long records. Only the most recent 1,000 records are retained. Of course, memcache values may be evicted more aggressively if your app uses memcache heavily. But in general, AppStats is able to show a representative sample of recent requests.

The performance overhead of the recorder is minimal. For typical user-facing requests, you can leave the recorder turned on for live traffic in a popular app. If necessary, you can limit the impact of the recorder by configuring it to only record a subset of traffic, or traffic to a subset of URLs. AppStats records and reports its own overhead.

AppStats accrues its timing data in instance memory during the request, and then stores the result in memcache at the end of the request handler's lifetime. This works well for user-facing requests, even those that last many seconds. For non-user-facing task handlers that last many minutes and make many RPC calls, App Engine may kill the task (and log a critical error) due to excess memory consumption. AppStats can be useful for optimizing batch jobs, but you may want to watch carefully for memory overruns, and disable it for large task handlers when you're not testing them actively.

In the next few sections, we'll walk through how to install the event recorder and the Console, for Python and Java. Then we'll take a closer look at the AppStats Console.

Installing AppStats for Python

AppStats for Python includes two versions of the event recorder, one specifically for the Django web application framework, and another general purpose WSGI recorder.

If you're using Django, edit your app's *settings.py*, and find `MIDDLEWARE_CLASSES`. Add the `AppStatsDjangoMiddleware` class, with an entry like this:

```
MIDDLEWARE_CLASSES = (
    'google.appengine.ext.appstats.recording.AppStatsDjangoMiddleware',
    # ...
    )
```

For all other Python applications, you install the WSGI middleware, using an *appengine_config.py* file. This file is used to configure parts of the App Engine libraries, including AppStats. If you don't have this file already, create it in your application root directory, and add the following Python function:

```
def webapp_add_wsgi_middleware(app):
    from google.appengine.ext.appstats import recording
    app = recording.appstats_wsgi_middleware(app)
    return app
```

App Engine uses this middleware function for all WSGI applications, including those running in the Python 2.7 runtime environment.

Regardless of which method you use to install the recorder, you can specify additional configuration in the *appengine_config.py* file.

Three settings control which handlers get recorded. The first is a global variable named `appstats_FILTER_LIST` that specifies patterns that match environment variables. For example, to disable recording for request handlers on a particular URL path:

```
appstats_FILTER_LIST = [
    {
        'PATH_INFO': '/batchjobs/.*',
    },
    ]
```

`appstats_FILTER_LIST` is a list of clauses. Each clause is a mapping of environment variable names to regular expressions. If the environment variables for a given request match all the regular expressions in a clause, then the request is recorded. Do a Google search for "WSGI environment variables" for more information on the variables you can match. Also note that the regular expression matches from the beginning of the environment variable (a "match"-style regular expression).

The `appstats_RECORD_FRACTION` configuration variable sets a percentage of requests not already filtered by `appstats_FILTER_LIST` that should be recorded. The default is 1.0 (100%). To only record a random sampling of 20 percent of the requests:

```
appstats_RECORD_FRACTION = 0.2
```

If you need more control over how requests are selected for recording, you can provide a function named `appstats_should_record()`. The function takes a mapping of environment variables and returns `True` if the request should be recorded. Note that defining this function overrides the `appstats_FILTER_LIST` and `appstats_RECORD_FRACTION` behaviors, so if you want to retain these, you'll need to copy the logic that uses them into your function.

The `appstats_normalize_path(path)` configuration function takes the request path and returns a normalized request path, so you can group related paths together in the reports. It's common for a single handler to handle all requests whose URL paths match a pattern, such as `/profile/13579`, where `13579` is a record ID. With `appstats_normalize_path()`, you can tell AppStats to treat all such URL paths as one, like so:

```
def appstats_normalize_path(path):
    if path.startswith('/profile/'):
        return '/profile/X'
    return path
```

Other settings let you control how AppStats uses memcache space, such as the number of retained events or how much stack trace data to retain. For a complete list of AppStats Python configuration variables, see the *sample_appengine_config.py* file in the SDK, in the *google/appengine/ext/appstats/* directory.

The last step is to install the AppStats Console. Edit *app.yaml*, and enable the `appstats` built-in:

```
builtins:
- appstats: on
```

The AppStats Console lives on the path `/_ah/stats/` in your application. The Console works in the development server as well as the live app, and is automatically restricted to administrative accounts.

You can add a link from the Administration Console sidebar to the AppStats Console using the Custom Pages feature (see "Administration Console Custom Pages" on page 99), with an entry like this in your *app.yaml*:

```
admin_console:
  pages:
  - name: AppStats
    url: /_ah/stats/
```

Installing AppStats for Java

The Java version of the AppStats event recorder is a servlet filter. You install the filter by editing your deployment descriptor (*web.xml*) and adding lines such as the following:

```
<filter>
    <filter-name>appstats</filter-name>
    <filter-class>com.google.appengine.tools.appstats.AppstatsFilter</filter-class>
</filter>

<filter-mapping>
    <filter-name>appstats</filter-name>
    <url-pattern>/*</url-pattern>
</filter-mapping>
```

The `url-pattern` controls which requests get recorded, based on the URL. As above, the `/*` pattern matches all requests. Adjust this pattern if needed.

The AppStats Console is a web servlet, like any other. Add the following lines to *web.xml* to install the Console at the path `/_ah/stats/`, restricted to app administrators:

```
<servlet>
    <servlet-name>appstats</servlet-name>
    <servlet-class>com.google.appengine.tools.appstats.AppstatsServlet</servlet-class>
</servlet>

<servlet-mapping>
    <servlet-name>appstats</servlet-name>
```

```
    <url-pattern>/_ah/stats/*</url-pattern>
</servlet-mapping>

<security-constraint>
    <web-resource-collection>
        <url-pattern>/_ah/stats/*</url-pattern>
    </web-resource-collection>
    <auth-constraint>
        <role-name>admin</role-name>
    </auth-constraint>
</security-constraint>
```

You can add a link from the Administration Console sidebar to the AppStats Console using the Custom Pages feature (see "Administration Console Custom Pages" on page 99), with an entry like this in your *appengine_web.xml* file:

```
<admin-console>
    <page name="AppStats" url="/_ah/stats" />
</admin-console>
```

Using the AppStats Console

The AppStats Console is your window to your app's service call behavior. To open the Console, visit `/_ah/stats/` in your app, or if you configured it, use the link you added to the Administration Console sidebar. AppStats works in your development server as well as your live app.

Figure 17-5 shows an example of the AppStats Console. (A very small app is shown, to limit the size of the example.)

The front page of the Console shows a summary of recent service calls. RPC Stats is a summary of calls by service, with the most popular service at the top. Click to expand a service to see which recent request URLs called the service. Path Stats shows the same information organized by path, with the URL with the heaviest total number of calls at the top. Click to expand a path to see a summary of the path's calls per service. The Most Recent Requests column references the Requests History table at the bottom of the screen.

The Requests History table at the bottom lists all recent requests for which AppStats has data, up to 1,000 recent requests, with the most recent request on top. Click the + to expand the tally of service calls made during the request.

To view the complete data for the request, click the blue request date and path in the Requests History table. Figure 17-6 shows an expanded version of an example we saw earlier.

The centerpiece of the request details page is the timeline. The timeline shows the history of the entire request, with a separate line for each service call. From this you can see when each service call began and ended in the lifetime of the request, the total (aggregate) time of all service calls (the "RPC Total"), and the actual amount of time

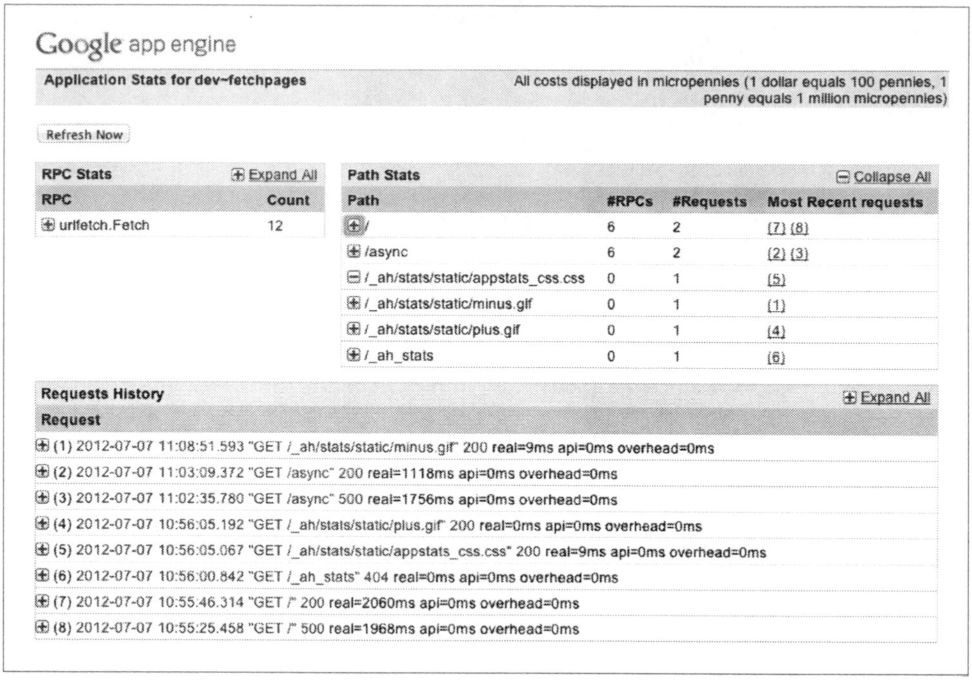

Figure 17-5. The AppStats Console front page for a small app

spent handling the request ("Grand Total"). As we saw earlier, the Grand Total can be less than the RPC Total if you use simultaneous asynchronous requests.

When running on App Engine (not the development server), the timeline also includes red bars on top of the blue ones. This represents an estimate of the monetary costs of the call, including API and bandwidth costs. (The unit, "API milliseconds," is not always useful, except in comparison to other red bars in the graph.)

The RPC Call Traces table below the timeline lets you examine each RPC call to find out where in the code it occurred. In the Python version, each element in the stack trace also includes the local variables at the call site at the time of the call.

The Python and Java request details pages include another tab that shows the service call tallies ("RPC Stats"). The Python version also has tabs for the environment variables as they were set at the beginning of the request ("CGI Environment"), and the Python package load path as it is currently set in the AppStats Console ("sys.path"). (The "sys.path" is not the exact load path of the request being viewed; it is determined directly from the AppStats Console environment itself.)

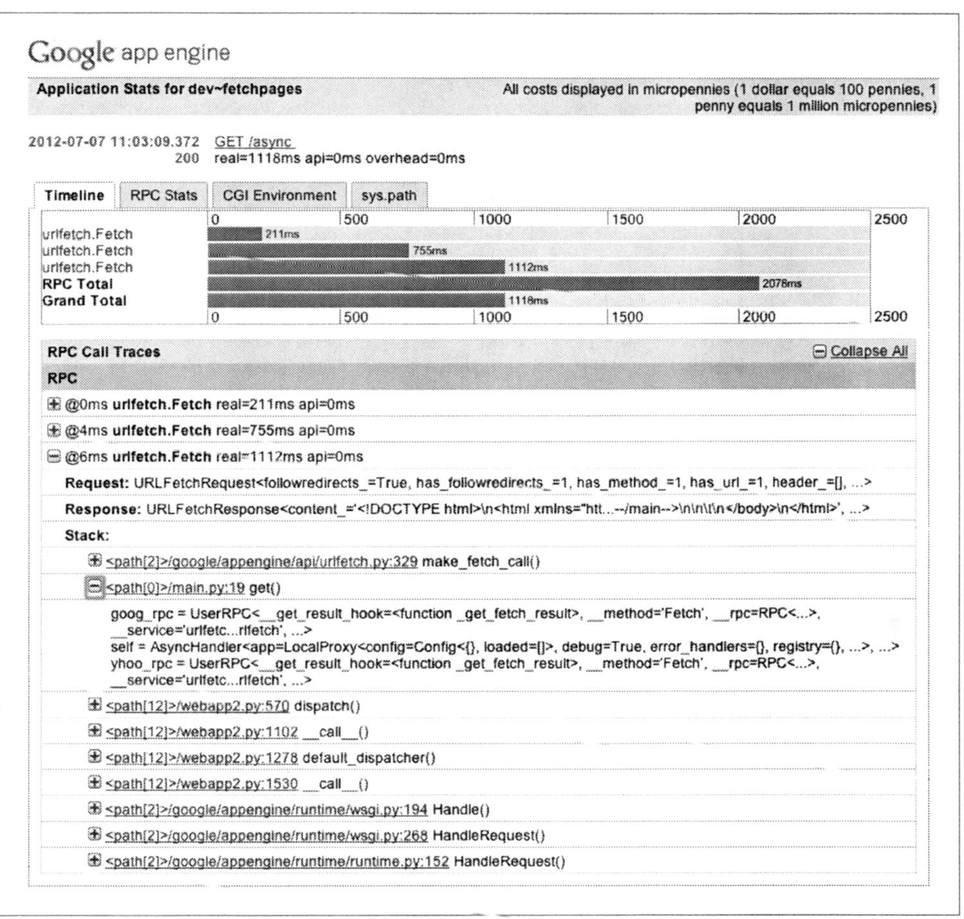

Figure 17-6. The AppStats Console request details page, Python version with stack trace

Both the Python and Java interfaces to the datastore are libraries built on top of a more rudimentary service interface. The correspondence between library calls and datastore RPCs are fairly intuitive, but you'll notice a few differences.

The most notable difference is how the datastore libraries fetch query results. Some features of the query APIs, such as the `!=` operator, use multiple datastore queries behind the scenes. Also, when results are fetched using iterator-based interfaces, the libraries use multiple datastore RPCs to fetch results as needed. These will appear as `RunQuery` and `Next` calls in AppStats.

Also, the local development server uses the RPC mechanism to update index configuration, so it'll sometimes show `CreateIndex` and `UpdateIndex` calls that do not occur when running on App Engine.

You can use stack traces to find where in the datastore library code each call is being made.

CHAPTER 18
The Django Web Application Framework

This chapter discusses how to use a major web application framework with the Python runtime environment. Java developers may be interested in the general discussion of frameworks that follows, but the rest of this chapter is specific to Python. Several frameworks for Java are known to work well with App Engine, and you can find information on these on the Web.

As with all major categories of software, web applications have a common set of problems that need to be solved in code. Most web apps need software to interface with the server's networking layer, communicate using the HTTP protocol, define the resources and actions of the application, describe and implement the persistent data objects, enforce site-wide policies such as access control, and describe the browser interface in a way that makes it easily built and modified by designers. Many of these components involve complex and detailed best practices for interoperating with remote clients and protecting against a variety of security vulnerabilities.

A *web application framework* is a collection of solutions and best practices that you assemble and extend to make an app. A framework provides the structure for an app, and most frameworks can be run without changes to demonstrate that the initial skeleton is functional. You use the toolkit provided by the framework to build the data model, business logic, and user interface for your app, and the framework takes care of the details. Frameworks are so useful that selecting one is often the first step when starting a new web app project.

Notice that App Engine isn't a web application framework, exactly. App Engine provides scaling infrastructure, services, and interfaces that solve many common problems, but these operate at a level of abstraction just below most web app frameworks. A better example of a framework is webapp2, a framework for Python included with the App Engine Python SDK that we've been using in examples throughout the book so far. webapp2 lets you implement request handlers as Python classes, and it takes care of the details of interfacing with the Python runtime environment and routing requests to handler classes.

Several major frameworks for Python work well with App Engine. Django, Pyramid, web2py, and Flask work well, and some frameworks have explicit support for App Engine. These frameworks are mature, robust, and widely used, and have large thriving support communities and substantial online documentation. You can buy books about some of these frameworks.

Not every feature of every framework works with App Engine. Most notably, many frameworks include a mechanism for defining data models, but these are usually implemented for relational databases, and don't work with the App Engine datastore. In some cases, you can just replace the framework's data modeling library with App Engine's `ext.db` library (or `ext.ndb`). Some features of frameworks also have issues running within App Engine's sandbox restrictions, such as by depending upon unsupported libraries. Developers have written adapter components that work around many of these issues.

In general, to use a framework, you add the framework's libraries to your application directory and then map all dynamic URLs (all URLs except those for static files) to a script that invokes the framework. Because the interface between the runtime environment and the app is WSGI, you can associate the framework's WSGI adapter with the URL pattern in *app.yaml*, just as we did with webapp2. Most frameworks have their own mechanism for associating URL paths with request handlers, and it's often easiest to send all dynamic requests to the framework and let it route them. You may still want to use *app.yaml* to institute Google Accounts–based access control for some URLs.

Django is a popular web application framework for Python, with a rich stack of features and pluggable components. It's also large, consisting of thousands of files. To make it easier to use Django on App Engine, the Python runtime environment includes the Django libraries, so you do not have to upload all of Django with your application files. The Python SDK bundles several versions of Django as well.

App Engine 1.7.0 provides Django 1.3. This version of Django does not include explicit support for App Engine, but many features work as documented with minimal setup. In this chapter, we discuss how to use Django via the provided libraries, and discuss which of Django's features work and which ones don't when using Django this way.

We also look at a third-party open source project called *django-nonrel*, a fork of Django 1.3 that enables most of Django's features for App Engine. In particular, it connects most of Django's own data modeling features to the App Engine datastore, so components and features that need a database can work with App Engine, without knowing it's App Engine behind the scenes. The data modeling layer also provides a layer of portability for your app, so your app code can run in environments that provide either a relational database or a nonrelational datastore (hence "nonrel").

The official documentation for Django is famously good, although it relies heavily on the data modeling features for examples. For more information about Django, see the Django project website:

> *http://www.djangoproject.com/*

> As of this writing, Google is testing a new service for hosting SQL databases, called Google Cloud SQL. The service provides a fully functional MySQL instance running on Google servers, which you can use with software like the Django application framework. However, a hosted SQL database does not scale automatically like the App Engine datastore. Check the Google Cloud website (*http://cloud.google.com/*) for updates on this feature. In this chapter, we'll assume your app will use the App Engine datastore for storage.

Using the Bundled Django Library

The App Engine 1.7.0 Python SDK provides Django 1.3 in its *lib/django_1_3/* subdirectory. With Django, you use a command-line tool to set up a new web application project. This tool expects *lib/django_1_3/* to be in the Python library load path, so it can load modules from the `django` package.

One way to set this up is to add it to the `PYTHONPATH` environment variable on your platform. For example, on the Mac OS X or Linux command line, using a bash-compatible shell, run this command to change the environment variable for the current session to load Django 1.3 from the Python SDK located at *~/google_appengine/*:

```
export PYTHONPATH=$PYTHONPATH:~/google_appengine/lib/django_1_3
```

The commands that follow will assume the SDK is in *~/google_appengine/*, and this `PYTHONPATH` is set.

The Django library is available in the runtime environment by using a `libraries:` directive in *app.yaml*, just like other libraries. We'll see an example of this in a moment.

Django 1.3 is the most recent version included with the Python runtime environment as of App Engine version 1.7.0. Later versions of Django are likely to be added to the runtime environment in future releases.

Instructions should be similar for later versions, although it isn't clear whether all future versions of Django will be added to the Python SDK. All previously included versions must remain in the SDK for compatibility, and the SDK might get a little large if it bundled every version. You may need to install Django on your local computer separately from the Python SDK in future versions. Django will likely be included in the runtime environment itself, similar to other third-party Python libraries. If you install Django yourself, you do not need to adjust the `PYTHONPATH`, and can run the Django commands without the library path.

Check the App Engine website for updates on the inclusion of future versions of Django in the runtime environment.

Creating a Django Project

For this tutorial, we will create an App Engine application that contains a Django project. In Django's terminology, a *project* is a collection of code, configuration, and static files. A project consists of one or more subcomponents called *apps*. The Django model encourages designing apps to be reusable, with behavior controlled by the project's configuration. The appearance of the overall website is also typically kept separate from apps by using a project-wide template directory.

To start, create the App Engine application root directory. From the Mac OS X or Linux command line, you would typically use these commands to make the directory and set it to be the current working directory:

```
mkdir myapp
cd myapp
```

You create a new Django project by running a command called `django-admin.py startproject`. Run this command to create a project named `myproject` in a subdirectory called *myproject/*:

```
python ~/google_appengine/lib/django_1_3/django/bin/django-admin.py \
    startproject myproject
```

This command creates the *myproject/* subdirectory with several starter files:

__init__.py
: A file that tells Python that code files in this directory can be imported as modules (this directory is a Python package).

manage.py
: A command-line utility you will use to build and manage this project, with many features.

settings.py
: Configuration for this project, in the form of a Python source file.

urls.py
: Mappings of URL paths to Python code, as a Python source file.

The `django-admin.py` tool has many features, but most of them are specific to managing SQL databases. This is the last time we'll use it here.

If you're following along with a Django tutorial or book, the next step is usually to start the Django development server by using the `manage.py` command. If you did so now, you would be running the Django server, but it would know nothing of App Engine. We want to run this application in the App Engine development server. To do that, we need a couple of additional pieces.

Hooking It Up to App Engine

To connect our Django project to App Engine, we need a short script that instantiates the Django WSGI adapter, and an *app.yaml* configuration file that maps all (nonstatic) URLs to the Django project.

Create a file named *main.py* in the application root directory with the following contents:

```
import os
os.environ['DJANGO_SETTINGS_MODULE'] = 'myproject.settings'

import django.core.handlers.wsgi

application = django.core.handlers.wsgi.WSGIHandler()
```

The first two lines tell Django where to find the project's `settings` module, which in this case is at the module path `myproject.settings` (the *myproject/settings.py* file). This must be set before importing any Django modules. The remaining two lines import the WSGI adapter, instantiate it, and store it in a global variable.

Next, create *app.yaml* in the application root directory, like so:

```
application: myapp
version: 1
runtime: python27
api_version: 1
threadsafe: yes

handlers:
- url: .*
  script: main.application

libraries:
- name: django
  version: "1.3"
```

This should be familiar by now, but to review, this tells App Engine this is an application with ID `myapp` and version ID `1` running in the Python 2.7 runtime environment, with multithreading enabled. All URLs are routed to the Django project we just created, via the WSGI adapter instantiated in *main.py*. The `libraries:` declaration selects Django 1.3 as the version to use when importing `django` modules.

Our directory structure so far looks like this:

```
myapp/
  app.yaml
  main.py
  myproject/
    __init__.py
    manage.py
    settings.py
    urls.py
```

We can now start this application in a development server. You can add this to the Python Launcher (File menu, Add Existing Application) and then start the server, or just start the development server from the command line, using the current working directory as the application root directory:

```
dev_appserver.py .
```

Load the development server URL (such as *http://localhost:8080/*) in a browser, and enjoy the welcome screen (Figure 18-1).

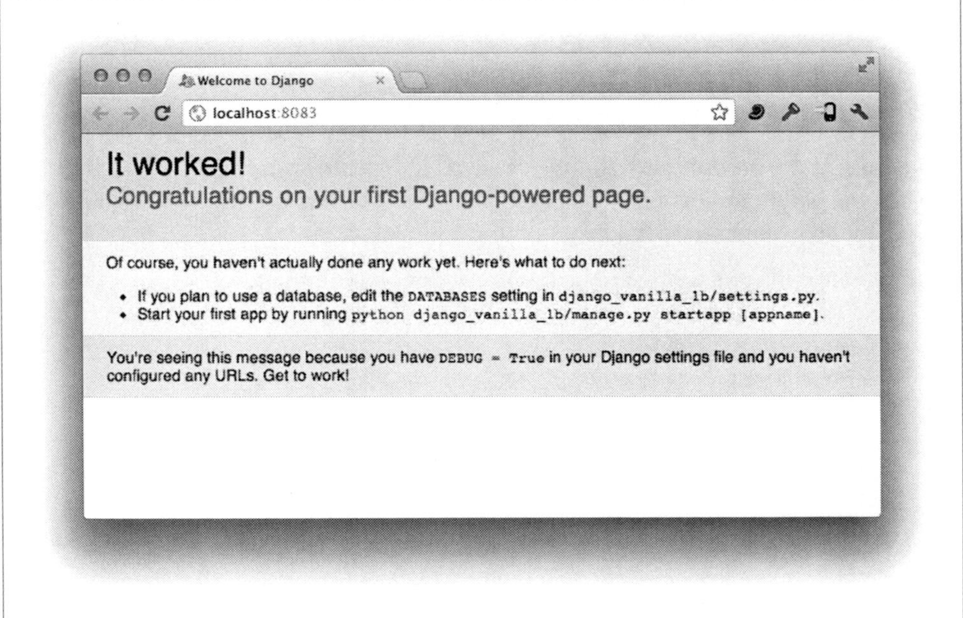

Figure 18-1. The Django welcome screen

Creating a Django App

The next step is to add a Django "app" to the Django project. You create new Django apps by using the project's `manage.py` script, which was generated when you created the project. (You can also use `django-admin.py` to create apps.)

With the current working directory still set to the application root, create a new app named `bookstore` for this project:

```
python myproject/manage.py startapp bookstore
```

This creates the subdirectory *myproject/bookstore*, with four new files:

__init__.py
: A file that tells Python that code files in this directory can be imported as modules (this directory is a Python package).

models.py
: A source file for data models common to this app.

tests.py
: A starter file illustrating how to set up automated tests in Django.

views.py
: A source file for Django views (request handlers).

This layout is Django's way of encouraging a design philosophy that separates data models and request handlers into separate, testable, reusable units of code. This philosophy comes naturally when using the App Engine datastore and `ext.db`. Django does not depend on this file layout directly, and you can change it as needed.

In addition to creating the app, it's useful to tell Django explicitly that this app will be used by this project. Edit *settings.py* in the project root directory, and find the `INSTALLED_APPS` value. Set it to a tuple containing the Python path to the app's package:

```
INSTALLED_APPS = (
    'myproject.bookstore',
)
```

(Be sure to include the trailing comma, which tells Python this is a one-element tuple.)

The *settings.py* file is a Python source file. It contains settings for the Django framework and related components, in the form of variables. The `INSTALLED_APPS` setting lists all apps in active use by the project, which enables some automatic features such as template loading. (It's primarily used by Django's data modeling tools, which we won't be using, in favor of App Engine's `ext.db`.)

Let's define our first custom response. Edit *bookstore/views.py*, and replace its contents with the following:

```
from django import http

def home(request):
    return http.HttpResponse('Welcome to the Book Store!')
```

In Django, a view is a function that is called with a `django.http.HttpRequest` object and returns an `django.http.HttpResponse` object. This view creates a simple response with some text. As you would expect, the `HttpRequest` provides access to request parameters and headers. You can set headers and other aspects of the `HttpResponse`. Django provides several useful ways to make `HttpResponse` objects, as well as specialized response classes for redirects and other return codes.

We still need to connect this view to a URL. URLs for views are set by the project, in the *urls.py* file in the project directory. This allows the project to control the URLs for all of the apps it uses. You can organize URLs such that each app specifies its own set of mappings of URL subpaths to views, and the project provides the path prefix for each app. For now, we'll keep it simple, and just refer to the app's view directly in the project's URL configuration.

Edit *urls.py* to contain the following:

```
from django.conf.urls.defaults import patterns, url

urlpatterns = patterns('myproject',
    url(r'^books/$', 'bookstore.views.home'),
)
```

Like *settings.py*, *urls.py* is a Python module. It defines a global variable named `urlpatterns` whose value is returned by the `patterns()` function from the `django.conf.urls.defaults` module. Its first argument is a Python path prefix that applies to all subsequent view paths; here, we set it to `'myproject'`, which is the first part of the Python path to every app in this project. Subsequent arguments are URL patterns, each returned by the `url()` function. In this case, we associate a regular expression matching a URL to the Python path for the view function we added.

With the development server still running, load the `/books/` URL in your browser. The app calls the view to display some text.

Using Django Templates

Django includes a templating system for building web pages and other displayable text. The Jinja2 templating library we've used throughout the book so far is based on the Django template system. Their syntax is mostly similar, but you'll notice minor differences between the two systems. As just one example, Jinja2 lets you call methods on template values with arguments, and so requires that you use parentheses after the method even when not using arguments: `{{ someval.method() }}`. In Django, templates can call methods of values but cannot pass arguments, and so the parentheses are omitted: `{{ someval.method }}`.

Django templates are baked into the Django framework, so they're easy to use. It's possible to use Jinja2 templates with a Django application, but Jinja2 does not automatically support some of the organizational features of Django.

Let's update the example to use a Django template. First, we need to set up a template directory. In the project directory, create a directory named `templates`, and a subdirectory in there named `bookstore`:

```
mkdir -p templates/bookstore
```

(The `-p` option to `mkdir` tells it to create the entire path of subdirectories, if any subdirectory does not exist.)

Edit *settings.py*. We're going to make two changes: adding an import statement at the top, and replacing the `TEMPLATE_DIRS` value. It should look something like this, with the rest of the file not shown:

```
import os

# ...

TEMPLATE_DIRS = (
    os.path.join(os.path.dirname(__file__), 'templates'),
)

# ...
```

The `TEMPLATE_DIRS` setting is a list (actually a tuple) of directory paths to check when a particular template file is requested. These paths must be absolute paths in the operating system, so we use `os.path.dirname(__file__)` to get the full path to the project directory (the directory containing the *settings.py* file), then `os.path.join(...)` to refer to the *templates/* subdirectory.

Inside the *templates/bookstore/* subdirectory, create the file *index.html* with the following template text:

```
<html>
  <body>
    <p>Welcome to The Book Store! {{ clock }}</p>
  </body>
</html>
```

Finally, edit *views.py* to look like this:

```
from django.shortcuts import render_to_response
import datetime

def home(request):
    return render_to_response(
        'bookstore/index.html',
        { 'clock': datetime.datetime.now() },
    )
```

Reload the page to see the template displayed by the new view.

The `render_to_response()` shortcut function takes as its first argument the path to the template file. This path is relative to one of the directories on the `TEMPLATE_DIRS` template lookup path. The second argument is a Python mapping that defines variables to be used within the template. In this example, we set a template variable named `clock` to be the current `datetime.datetime`. Within the template, `{{ code }}` interpolates this value as a string.

The behavior of the template engine can be extended in many ways. You can define custom tags and filters to use within templates. You can also change how templates are loaded, with template loader classes and the `TEMPLATE_LOADERS` setting variable. The filesystem-based behavior we're using now is provided by the `django.template.loaders.filesystem.Loader` class, which appears in the default settings file created by Django.

Using Django Forms

Django includes a powerful feature for building web forms based on data model definitions. The Django forms library can generate HTML for forms, validate that submitted data meets the requirements of the model, and redisplay the form to the user with error messages. The default appearance is useful, and you can customize the appearance extensively.

Django's data modeling library is similar to (and was the inspiration for) `ext.db`, but it was designed with SQL databases in mind. Django does not (yet) include its own adapter layer for using its modeling library with the App Engine datastore. (As we'll see later in this chapter, this is a primary goal of the django-nonrel project.) When using the Django library directly as we're doing now, we can't use its data modeling library, nor can we use any Django features that rely on it.

But there's good news for web forms: App Engine includes an adapter library so you can use the Django forms library with `ext.db` data models! This library is provided by the `google.appengine.ext.db.djangoforms` module.

We won't go into the details of how Django forms work—see the Django documentation for a complete explanation—but let's walk through a quick example to see how the pieces fit together. Our example will use the following behavior for creating and editing `Book` entities:

- An HTTP GET request to `/books/book/` displays an empty form for creating a new `Book`.
- An HTTP POST request to `/books/book/` processes the book creation form, and either creates the book and redirects to `/books` (the book listing page) or redisplays the form with errors, if any.
- An HTTP GET request to `/books/book/1234` displays the form to edit the `Book` entity, with the fields filled out with the current values.

- An HTTP POST request to /books/book/1234 updates the book with that ID, with the same error-handling behavior as the book creation form.

Edit *urls.py* to use a new view function named book_form() to handle these URLs:

```
from django.conf.urls.defaults import patterns, url

urlpatterns = patterns('myproject',
    url(r'^books/book/(\d*)', 'bookstore.views.book_form'),
    url(r'^books/', 'bookstore.views.home'),
)
```

The regular expression '^books/book/(\d*)' captures the book ID in the URL, if any, and passes it to the view function as an argument.

Edit *models.py* in the *bookstore/* app directory, and replace its contents with the following ext.db model definitions:

```
from google.appengine.ext import db

class Book(db.Model):
    title = db.StringProperty()
    author = db.StringProperty()
    copyright_year = db.IntegerProperty()
    author_birthdate = db.DateProperty()

class BookReview(db.Model):
    book = db.ReferenceProperty(Book, collection_name='reviews')
    review_author = db.UserProperty()
    review_text = db.TextProperty()
    rating = db.StringProperty(choices=['Poor', 'OK', 'Good', 'Very Good', 'Great'],
                               default='Great')
    create_date = db.DateTimeProperty(auto_now_add=True)
```

No surprises here; these are just ext.db models for datastore entities of the kinds Book and BookReview.

Now for the views. Edit *views.py*, and replace its contents with the following:

```
from django import template
from django.http import HttpResponseRedirect
from django.shortcuts import render_to_response
from google.appengine.ext import db
from google.appengine.ext.db import djangoforms

from bookstore import models

def home(request):
    q = models.Book.all().order('title')
    return render_to_response('bookstore/index.html',
                              { 'books': q })

class BookForm(djangoforms.ModelForm):
    class Meta:
        model = models.Book
```

```
def book_form(request, book_id=None):
    if request.method == 'POST':
        # The form was submitted.
        if book_id:
            # Fetch the existing Book and update it from the form.
            book = models.Book.get_by_id(int(book_id))
            form = BookForm(request.POST, instance=book)
        else:
            # Create a new Book based on the form.
            form = BookForm(request.POST)

        if form.is_valid():
            book = form.save(commit=False)
            book.put()
            return HttpResponseRedirect('/books/')
        # else fall through to redisplay the form with error messages

    else:
        # The user wants to see the form.
        if book_id:
            # Show the form to edit an existing Book.
            book = models.Book.get_by_id(int(book_id))
            form = BookForm(instance=book)
        else:
            # Show the form to create a new Book.
            form = BookForm()

    return render_to_response('bookstore/bookform.html', {
        'book_id': book_id,
        'form': form,
    }, template.RequestContext(request))
```

We've updated the home() view to set up a query for Book entities, and pass that query object to the template. Edit *templates/bookstore/index.html* to display this information:

```
<html>
  <body>
    <p>Welcome to The Book Store!</p>
    <p>Books in our catalog:</p>
    <ul>
    {% for book in books %}
      <li>{{ book.title }}, by {{ book.author }} ({{ book.copyright_year }})
      [<a href="/books/book/{{ book.key.id }}">edit</a>]</li>
    {% endfor %}
    </ul>
    <p>[<a href="/books/book/">add a book</a>]</p>
  </body>
</html>
```

Finally, create the template for the form used by the new book_form() view, named *templates/bookstore/bookform.html*:

```
<html>
  <body>

  {% if book_id %}
```

```
      <p>Edit book {{ book_id }}:</p>
      <form action="/books/book/{{ book_id }}" method="POST">
    {% else %}
      <p>Create book:</p>
      <form action="/books/book/" method="POST">
    {% endif %}
        {% csrf_token %}
        {{ form.as_p }}
        <input type="submit" />
      </form>

    </body>
  </html>
```

The BookForm class is a subclass of `google.appengine.ext.db.djangoforms.ModelForm`. It can examine an App Engine model class (a subclass of `db.Model`) and can render and process forms with fields based on the model's property declarations. It knows which model class to use from the `Meta` inner class, whose `model` class attribute is set to our `Book` class. The `ModelForm` has useful default rendering and processing behavior for each of the default property declaration types, and you can customize this extensively. For now, we'll use the defaults.

The `book_form()` view function takes the HTTP request object and the `book_id` captured by the regular expression in *urls.py* as arguments. If the request method is `'POST'`, then it processes the submitted form; otherwise it assumes the method is `'GET'` and just displays the form. In either case, the form is represented by an instance of the `BookForm` class.

If constructed without arguments, the `BookForm` represents an empty form for creating a new `Book` entity. If constructed with the `instance` argument set to a `Book` object, the form's fields are prepopulated with the object's property values.

To process a submitted form, you pass the dictionary of POST parameters (`request.POST`) to the `BookForm` constructor as its first positional argument. If you also provide the `instance` argument, the instance sets the initial values—including the entity key—and the form data overwrites everything else, as provided.

The `BookForm` object knows how to render the form based on the model class and the provided model instance (if any). It also knows how to validate data submitted by the user, and render the form with the user's input and any appropriate error messages included. The `is_valid()` method tells you if the submitted data is acceptable for saving to the datastore. If it isn't, you send the `BookForm` to the template just as you would when displaying the form for the first time.

If the data submitted by the user is valid, the `BookForm` knows how to produce the final entity object. The `save()` method saves the entity and returns it; if you set the `commit=False` argument, it just returns the entity and does not save it, so you can make further changes and save it yourself. In this example, a successful create or update redirects the user to `/books/` (which we've hardcoded in the view for simplicity) instead of rendering a template.

To display the form, we simply pass the BookForm object to a template. There are several methods on the object for rendering it in different ways; we'll use the as_p() method to display the form fields in <p> elements. The template is responsible for outputting the <form> tag and the Submit button. The BookForm does the rest.

Restart the development server, then load the book list URL (/books/) in the browser. Click "add a book" to show the book creation form. Enter some data for the book, then submit it to create it.

The default form widget for a date field is just a text field, and it's finicky about the format. In this case, the "author birthdate" field expects input in the form YYYY-MM-DD, such as 1902-02-27.

Continue the test by clicking the "edit" link next to one of the books listed. The form displays with that book's data. Edit some of the data and then submit the form to update the entity.

Also try entering invalid data for a field, such as nonnumeric data for the "copyright year" field, or a date that doesn't use the expected format. Notice that the form redisplays with your original input, and with error messages.

The main thing to notice about this example is that the data model class itself (in this case Book) completely describes the default form, including the display of its form fields and the validation logic. The default field names are based on the names of the properties. You can change a field's name by specifying a verbose_name argument to the property declaration on the model class:

```
class Book(db.Model):
    title = db.StringProperty(verbose_name="Book title")
    # ...
```

See the Django documentation for more information about customizing the display and handling of forms, and other best practices regarding form handling.

Cross-Site Request Forgery

Cross-site request forgery (CSRF) is a class of security issues with web forms where the attacker lures a victim into submitting a web form whose action is your web application, but the form is under the control of the attacker. The malicious form may intercept the victim's form values, or inject some of its own, and cause the form to be submitted to your app on behalf of the victim.

Django has a built-in feature for protecting against CSRF attacks, and it is enabled by default. The protection works by generating a token that is added to forms displayed by your app, and is submitted with the user's form fields. If the form is submitted without a valid token, Django rejects the request before it reaches the view code. The token is a digital signature, and is difficult to forge.

This requires the cooperation of our example code in two places. The *template/bookstore/bookform.html* template includes the `{% csrf_token %}` template tag somewhere inside the `<form>` element. Also, the `render_to_response()` function needs to pass the request to the template when rendering the form, with a third argument, `template.RequestContext(request)`.

The blocking magic happens in a component known as *middleware*. This architectural feature of Django lets you compose behaviors that act on some or all requests and responses, independently of an app's views. The `MIDDLEWARE_CLASSES` setting in *settings.py* activates middleware, and `django.middleware.csrf.CsrfViewMiddleware` is enabled by default. If you have a view that accepts POST requests and doesn't need CSRF protection (such as a web service endpoint), you can give the view the `@csrf_exempt` decorator, from the `django.views.decorators.csrf` module.

This feature of Django illustrates the power of a full-stack web application framework. Not only is it possible to implement a security feature like CSRF protection across an entire site with a single component, but this feature can be provided by a library of such components. (You could argue that this is a poor example, because it imposes requirements on views and templates that render forms. But the feature is useful enough to be worth it.)

See Django's CSRF documentation (*https://docs.djangoproject.com/en/1.3/ref/contrib/csrf/*) for more information.

The django-nonrel Project

What we've seen so far are just some of the features of the Django framework that are fully functional on App Engine. Django's component composition, URL mapping, templating, and middleware let you build, organize, and collaborate on large, complex apps. With a little help from an App Engine library, you can use App Engine datastore data models with Django's sophisticated form rendering features. And we've only scratched the surface.

The Achilles' heel of this setup is the datastore. Django was built first and foremost on top of a data management library. Its earliest claim to fame was its web-based data administration panel, from which you could manage a website like a content management system, or debug database issues without a SQL command line. Any Django component that needs to persist global data uses the data library. Just one example is Django's sessions feature, an important aspect of most modern websites.

This data library is built to work with any of several possible database backends, but as of Django 1.3, the App Engine datastore is not yet one of them. The django-nonrel project was founded to develop backends for the Django data library that work with several popular nonrelational datastores, including App Engine. The sister project `djangoappengine` also implements backend adapters for several other App Engine services, so Django library components can do things like send email via the email service.

`djangoappengine` also includes improved support for features of the Django app management tools.

django-nonrel is a fork of Django 1.3. To use it, you download and unpack several components, which together make up the entirety of Django 1.3, with the necessary modifications. These files become your application directory. When you upload your application, all of these files go with it; it ignores the version of Django included in the runtime environment.

As of this writing, management of the django-nonrel project is in transition. Even in it's current form, it's a useful addition to your toolkit. To download django-nonrel for App Engine, and to read more about its features and limitations, visit the `djangoappengine` project website:

> *http://www.allbuttonspressed.com/projects/djangoappengine*

CHAPTER 19
Managing Request Logs

Activity and message logs are an essential part of a web application. They are your view into what happens with your application over time as it is being used, who is using it and how, and what problems, if any, your users are having.

App Engine logs all incoming requests for your application, including application requests, static file requests, and requests for invalid URLs (so you can determine whether there is a bad link somewhere). For each request, App Engine logs the date and time, the IP address of the client, the URL requested (including the path and parameters), the domain name requested, the browser's identification string (the "user agent"), the referring URL if the user followed a link, and the HTTP status code in the response returned by the app or by the frontend.

App Engine also logs several important statistics about each request: the amount of time it took to handle each request, the amount of "CPU time" that was spent handling the request, and the size of the response. The CPU time measurement is particularly important to watch because requests that consistently consume a large amount of CPU may be throttled, such that the CPU use is spread over more clock time.

Your application code can log the occurrence of notable events and data by using a logging API. Logging a message associates a line of text with the request that emitted it, including all the data logged for the request. Each message has a *log level* indicating the severity of the message to make it easier to find important messages during analysis. App Engine supports five log levels: debug, info, warning, error, and critical.

You can browse your application's request and message logs, using the Administration Console, under Logs. You can also download your log data for offline analysis and recordkeeping. An app can query log data programmatically using the log service API.

In this brief but important chapter, we'll look at all of these features of the logging system.

If you're new to web programming, you can ignore the advanced features of the logging system for now. But be sure to read the first couple of sections right away. Writing log messages and finding them in the Administration Console are important methods for figuring out what's going on in a web application.

Writing to the Log

App Engine writes information about every request to the application log automatically. The app can write additional messages during the request to note application-specific details about what happened during the request handler.

An application log message has a *log level* that indicates the importance of the message. App Engine supports five levels: debug, info, warning, error, and critical. These are in order of "severity," where "debug" is the least severe. When you browse or query log data, you can filter for messages above a given log level, such as to see just the requests where an error condition occurred.

App Engine will occasionally write its own messages to the log for a request. Uncaught application exceptions are written to the log as errors, with traceback information. When a handler exceeds its request deadline, App Engine writes an explicit message stating this fact. App Engine may also write informational messages, such as to say that the request was the first request served from a newly started instance, and so may have taken more time than usual.

In the development server, log messages are printed to the terminal (if run in a terminal window), the Logs window (the Python Launcher), or the Console window (Eclipse). During development, you can use log messages to see what's going on inside your application, even if you decide not to keep those log messages in the live version of the app.

Logging in Python

Python applications can use the `logging` module from the standard library to log messages. App Engine hooks into this module to relay messages to the logging system, and to get the log level for each message. Example 19-1 shows this module in action.

Example 19-1. The use of the logging Python module to emit messages at different log levels

```
import logging

# ...
        logging.debug('debug level')
        logging.info('info level')
        logging.warning('warning level')
        logging.error('error level')
        logging.critical('critical level')
```

```
    sys.stderr.write('stderr write, logged at the error level\n')
```

In addition to messages logged with the logging module, each line of text written to the standard error stream (sys.stderr) is logged at the "error" level. (Because Python uses CGI, anything written to the standard output stream becomes part of the response data.)

In a traditional application using the logging module, you would configure the module to output only messages above a given level of severity. When running on App Engine, the level of the output is always the "debug" level, and it cannot be changed. You can filter messages by severity after the fact in the Administration Console, or when downloading logs with appcfg.py.

When running in the development web server, log messages are written to the Console, and data written to sys.stderr is written to the server's error stream. If you are running your server in the Launcher, you can open a window to view log messages by clicking the Logs button.

The development server sets its log level to INFO by default. You can change this to DEBUG by giving the server the command-line argument --debug.

Logging in Java

For Java applications, App Engine supports the java.util.logging library from the JRE. App Engine recognizes log levels of messages logged using this library. Example 19-2 illustrates the use of the Logger class and its convenience methods.

Example 19-2. The use of the java.util.logging package to emit messages at different log levels

```
import java.io.IOException;
import javax.servlet.http.*;

import java.util.logging.Logger;

public class LoggingServlet extends HttpServlet {

    private static final Logger log = Logger.getLogger(LoggingServlet.class.getName());

    public void doGet(HttpServletRequest req, HttpServletResponse resp)
            throws IOException {
        log.finest("finest level");    // DEBUG
        log.finer("finer level");      // DEBUG
        log.fine("fine level");        // DEBUG
        log.config("config level");    // DEBUG
        log.info("info level");        // INFO
        log.warning("warning level");  // WARNING
        log.severe("severe level");    // ERROR
```

```
        System.out.println("stdout level");  // INFO
        System.err.println("stderr level");  // WARNING
    }
}
```

The seven log levels of `java.util.logging` correspond to four of App Engine's log levels: "finest," "finer," "fine," and "config" all correspond to the App Engine debug level; "info" is info, "warning" is warning, and "severe" is error. The "critical" log level is reserved for exceptions that are not caught by the servlet; when this happens, the runtime environment logs a message at this level.

If the application writes any data to the standard output or error streams (`System.out` and `System.err`), App Engine adds that data to the log. Each line of text written to standard output becomes a log message at the "info" level, and each line written to standard error is logged at the "warning" level.

You can control which level of message should be written to the log by using configuration for `java.util.logging`. This allows you to leave detailed low-level logging statements in your code without having all that information clutter up the logs unnecessarily in a high-traffic app.

Configuring the log level requires two things: a configuration file and a system property that identifies the configuration file. For the configuration, create a resource file, such as *war/WEB-INF/logging.properties*, containing a line like this:

```
.level=INFO
```

You can configure the log level on a per-class basis by adding lines like this with the package path before the `.level`. This allows you to turn on fine-grained messaging for some components without turning it on for all components. For example, the Google Plugin for Eclipse creates a *logging.properties* configuration file with per-component settings for DataNucleus, the JDO/JPA interface package, so you can use verbose logging for your app code without cluttering up your output with messages from the DataNucleus component.

Be sure to use the `logging` level name (such as `FINEST`) and not the App Engine level name for values in *logging.properties*. App Engine log levels only affect how messages are represented in the Admin Console.

Next, set a system property telling the logging library where to find its configuration file. You do this by including a `<system-properties>` element in your *appengine-web.xml* file, like so:

```
<system-properties>
  <property name="java.util.logging.config.file"
            value="WEB-INF/logging.properties" />
</system-properties>
```

If you created your Java project using the Google Plugin for Eclipse, your app already has this configuration file and this system property. This configuration comes preloaded with log levels for the DataNucleus interface (an interface for the datastore), so you can leave those set to the "warning" level while the rest of your app uses another level.

The `java.util.logging` and the standard output and error streams are the only ways to log messages at specific log levels. If you or a component of your app prefers a different logging library, such as log4j, messages emitted by that library will work as long as the library can write to the standard streams. If you want to be able to use the Administration Console to filter logs by levels other than "info" and "warning," you will need an adapter of some kind that calls `java.util.logging` behind the scenes. You get complete log messages when you download log data, so you can always analyze alternate log formats in downloaded data.

When running in the development web server, log messages are written to the console, and text written to the standard streams is written to the corresponding streams for the server. In Eclipse, these messages appear in the Console pane.

Viewing Recent Logs

You can browse and search your application's request logs and messages from the Logs panel of the Administration Console. Figure 19-1 shows the Logs panel with a request opened to reveal the detailed request data.

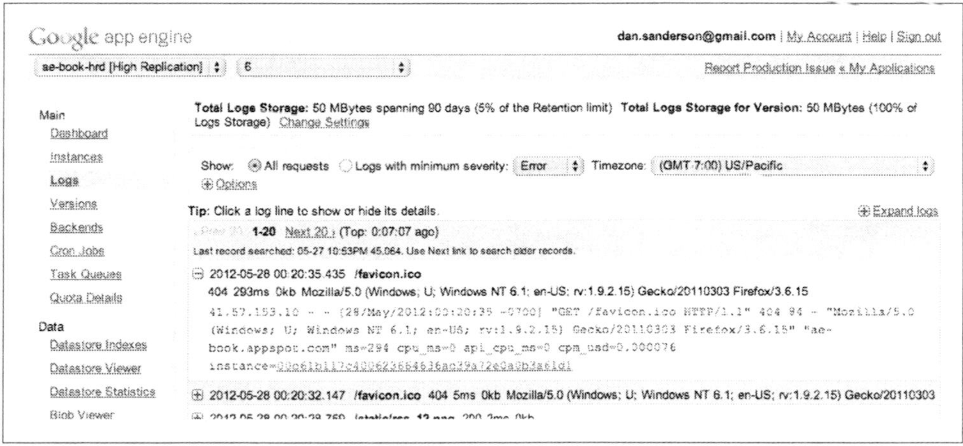

Figure 19-1. The Logs viewer in the Administration Console

The panel opens showing the 20 most recent requests. To filter this display to show only requests with messages above a particular log level, select the "Logs with minimum severity" radio button, then select the severity from the adjacent drop-down menu. The display updates automatically as soon as you change these settings.

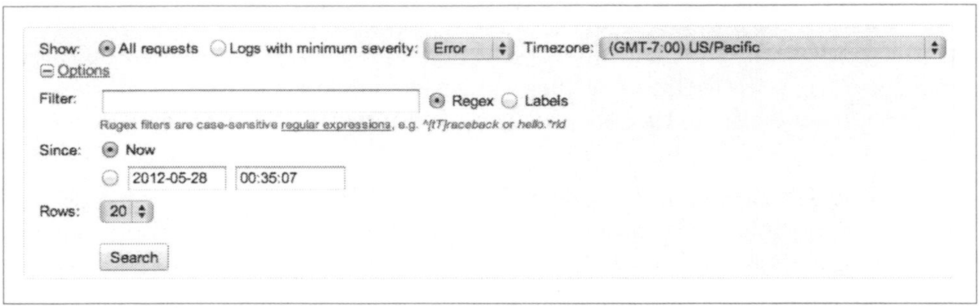

Figure 19-2. The search panel of the Logs viewer with expanded options

To perform a more specific search, expand the Options button. This panel looks like Figure 19-2.

You can specify a filter in one of two ways. The simplest is the Regex filter, where the filter value is a regular expression that matches against all request log fields and application log messages.

The other kind of filter is the Labels filter. This filter consists of one or more request log fields and patterns to match against the field values. Each field filter is the field name followed by a colon, then the regular expression for the pattern. Field filters are delimited by spaces. The valid field names are listed on the screen; some useful examples are `path` (the URL path, starting with a slash) and `user` (a user signed in with a Google Account; the pattern matches the Google username). For example, with Labels selected, this query shows requests by the user `dan.sanderson` for paths beginning with `/admin/`:

```
path:/admin/.* user:dan\.sanderson
```

The Logs panel shows log data for the application version currently selected in the Administration Console version drop-down menu. If you're having a problem with a live app, a useful technique is to deploy a separate version of the app with additional logging statements added to the code near the problem area, and then reproduce the issue using the version-specific URL (or temporarily make the new version the default, then switch it back). Then you can view and search the logs specific to the version with the added logging messages.

If a specific long-running instance appears to be having trouble, you can view logs just for that instance. Select the Instances panel, then click View Logs for the instance you wish to inspect.

The Logs panel is useful for digging up more information for problems with the application code. For broader analysis of traffic and user trends, you'll want to download the log data for offline processing, or use a web traffic analytics product like Google Analytics (*http://google.com/analytics/*).

For apps with a large amount of traffic, the Logs panel may return empty or incomplete results for some queries that otherwise have results. This is because the log retrieval service stops returning results after a period of time. The date and time of the oldest log record searched is displayed at the top of the results list. You can click Next Page to continue searching older log messages, even if the results page appears empty.

Downloading Logs

You can download log data for offline analysis and archiving by using the AppCfg command-line tool. (The Python Launcher and Google Plugin for Eclipse do not offer this feature.) To use it, run `appcfg.py` (Python) or `appcfg.sh` (Java) with the `request_logs` command, with the application directory and log output filename as arguments.

The following command downloads request logs for the app in the development directory *clock*, and saves them to a file named *logs.txt*:

```
appcfg.py request_logs clock logs.txt
```

This command takes many of the same arguments as `appcfg.py update`, such as those used for authentication.

The command fetches log data for the application ID and version described in the application config file. As with `appcfg.py update`, you can override these with the `--application=...` and `--version=...` arguments, respectively.

The command above downloads request data only. To download log messages emitted by the application, include a minimum severity level specified as a number, where `0` is all log messages ("debug" level and up) and `5` is only "critical" messages, using the `--severity` argument:

```
appcfg.py request_logs clock logs.txt --severity=1
```

Application messages appear in the file on separate lines immediately following the corresponding request. The format for this line is a tab, the severity of the message as a number, a colon, a numeric timestamp for the message, then the message:

```
	1:1246801590.938119 get_published_entries cache HIT
```

Log data is ordered chronologically by request, from earliest to latest. Application messages are ordered within each request by their timestamps.

Request data appears in the file in a common format known as the Apache Combined (or "NCSA Combined") logfile format, one request per line (shown here as two lines to fit on the page):

```
127.0.0.1 - - [05/Jul/2009:06:46:30 -0700] "GET /blog/ HTTP/1.1" 200 14598 -
"Mozilla/5.0 (Macintosh; U; Intel Mac OS X 10_5_8; en-us)...,gzip(gfe)"
```

From left to right, the fields are:

- The IP address of the client
- A - (an unused field retained for backward compatibility)
- The email address of the user who made the request, if the user is signed in using Google Accounts; - otherwise
- The date and time of the request
- The HTTP command string in double quotes, including the method and URL path
- The HTTP response code returned by the server
- The size of the response, as a number of bytes
- The "Referrer" header provided by the client, usually the URL of the page that linked to this URL
- The "User-Agent" header provided by the client, usually identifying the browser and its capabilities

By default, the command fetches the last calendar day's worth of logs, back to midnight, Pacific Time. You can change this with the `--num_days=...` argument. Set this to 0 to get all available log data. You can also specify an alternate end date with the `--end_date=...` option, whose value is of the form `YYYY-MM-DD` (such as `2009-11-04`).

You can specify the `--append` argument to extend the log data file with new data, if the logfile exists. By default, the command overwrites the file with the complete result of the query. The append feature is smart: it checks the data file for the date and time of the most recent log message, then only appends messages from after that time.

Logs Retention

By default, App Engine stores up to 1 gigabyte of log data, or up to 90 days worth of messages, whichever is less. Once the retention limit is reached, the oldest messages are dropped in favor of new ones.

You can increase the maximum amount and maximum age in the Application Settings panel of the Administration Console. Scroll down to Logs Retention, enter new values, and then click Save Settings.

The first gigabyte and 90 days of retention are included with the cost of your application. Additional storage and retention time is billed at a storage rate specific to logs. See the official website for the latest rates. If you're paying for log storage, you can retain logs for up to 365 days (one year).

Querying Logs from the App

App Engine provides a simple API for querying log data directly from the application. With this API, you can retrieve log data by date-time ranges, filter by log level and version ID, and page through results. You can use this API to build custom interactive log data inspectors for your app, or implement log-based alerts.

This is the same API that the Administration Console uses to power the Logs panel. You'll notice that the API does not include filters based on regular expressions. Instead, the Logs panel simply pages through unfiltered results, and only displays those that match a given pattern. Your app can use a similar technique.

The development server can retain log data in memory to help you test the use of this API. The Java server does this automatically. If you're using the Python development server, you must enable this feature with the `--persist_logs` flag:

```
dev_appserver.py --persist_logs
```

Querying Logs in Python

In Python, you fetch log data by calling the `fetch()` function in the `google.appengine.api.logservice` module. The function takes query parameters as arguments:

`include_app_logs`
: `True` if the log records returned should include application messages.

`minimum_log_level`
: The minimum severity a request's application log messages should have to be a result. The value is an integer from 0 (debug) to 4 (critical), represented by constants named like `logservice.LOG_LEVEL_INFO`. The default is to return all requests; specifying a log level limits the results to just those requests with application log messages at or above the specified level.

`start_time`
: The earliest timestamp to consider as a Unix epoch time. The default is `None`, no starting bound.

`end_time`
: The latest timestamp to consider as a Unix epoch time. The default is `None`, no ending bound.

`version_ids`
: A list of version IDs whose logs to fetch. The default is `None`, fetch the calling app's version.

`include_incomplete`
: If `True`, include incomplete requests in the results. (See "Flushing the Log Buffer" on page 478.)

`batch_size`
: The number of results to fetch per service call when iterating over results.

`offset`
: The offset of the last-seen result, for paging through results. The next result returned follows the last-seen result.

The function returns an iterable that acts as a stream of log results. Each result is an object with attributes for the fields of the request data, such as `method`, `resource`, and `end_time`. See the official documentation for the complete list of fields.

If application log messages are requested (`include_app_logs=True`), the `app_logs` attribute of a result is a list of zero or more objects, one for each log message. The attributes of this object are `time` (an epoch time), `level` (an integer), and `message`.

Here's a simple example:

```
import time
from google.appengine.api import logservice

# ...
        self.response.write('<pre>')

        count = 0
        for req_log in logservice.fetch(include_app_logs=True):
            # Stop after 20 results.
            count += 1
            if count > 20:
                break

            self.response.write(
                '%s %s %s\n' %
                (time.ctime(req_log.end_time),
                 req_log.method,
                 req_log.resource))

            for app_log in req_log.app_logs:
                self.response.write(
                    '   %s %s %s\n' %
                    (time.ctime(app_log.time),
                     ['DEBUG', 'INFO', 'WARNING',
                      'ERROR', 'CRITICAL'][app_log.level],
                     app_log.message))

        self.response.write('</pre>')
```

Each result includes an `offset` attribute, a web-safe string you can use to make a "next page" button in a paginated display. Simply pass the `offset` of the last result on a page to the `fetch()` function, and the first result returned will be the next result in the sequence.

Querying Logs in Java

In Java, you fetch log data by building a `LogQuery` object, then passing it to the `fetch()` method of a `LogService` instance. These classes are provided by the package `com.google.appengine.api.log`.

You get a LogQuery by calling LogQuery.Builder.withDefaults(). You can then call builder methods to specify the query parameters. Each method returns the LogQuery instance, so you can stack calls:

includeAppLogs(boolean)
: true if the log records returned should include application messages.

minLogLevel(LogService.LogLevel)
: The minimum severity a request's application log messages should have to be a result. The value is an enum constant from LogService.LogLevel, one of DEBUG, INFO, WARN, ERROR, or FATAL (critical). The default is to return all requests; specifying a log level limits the results to just those requests with application log messages at or above the specified level.

startTimeUsec(long)
: The earliest timestamp to consider as a Unix epoch time. If not specified, there is no starting bound.

endTimeUsec(long)
: The latest timestamp to consider as a Unix epoch time. If not specified, there is no ending bound.

majorVersionIds: a java.util.List<String>
: A list of version IDs whose logs to fetch. If not specified, this fetches the calling app's version.

includeIncomplete(boolean)
: If true, include incomplete requests in the results. (See "Flushing the Log Buffer" on page 478.)

batchSize(int)
: The number of results to fetch per service call when iterating over results.

offset(String)
: The offset of the last-seen result, for paging through results. The next result returned follows the last-seen result.

You get a LogService instance by calling LogServiceFactory.getLogService(). The instance's fetch() method takes the LogQuery as an argument, and returns an iterable of RequestLogs objects, one for each request that matches the query. RequestLogs has getters for each request data field, such as getMethod(), getResource(), and getEndTimeUsec(). See the official documentation for the complete list of fields.

If application log messages are requested (includeAppLogs(true)), the getAppLogLines() method of a RequestLogs returns a List of zero or more AppLogLine objects, one for each log message. AppLogLine has the getter methods getLogLevel() (returns a LogService.LogLevel), getLogMessage(), and getTimeUsec().

Here's a simple example:

```
import com.google.appengine.api.log.AppLogLine;
import com.google.appengine.api.log.LogQuery;
```

```
import com.google.appengine.api.log.LogService;
import com.google.appengine.api.log.LogServiceFactory;
import com.google.appengine.api.log.RequestLogs;
import java.util.Calendar;

// ...
        LogQuery query = LogQuery.Builder.withDefaults();
        query.includeAppLogs(true);

        Calendar cal = Calendar.getInstance();
        int count = 0;

        LogService logSvc = LogServiceFactory.getLogService();
        for (RequestLogs reqLog : logSvc.fetch(query)) {
            count++;
            if (count > 20) {
                break;
            }

            cal.setTimeInMillis(reqLog.getEndTimeUsec() / 1000);
            resp.getOutputStream().println(
                cal.getTime().toString() + " " +
                reqLog.getMethod() + " " +
                reqLog.getResource());

            for (AppLogLine appLog : reqLog.getAppLogLines()) {
                cal.setTimeInMillis(appLog.getTimeUsec() / 1000);
                resp.getOutputStream().println(
                    "  " +
                    cal.getTime().toString() + " " +
                    appLog.getLogLevel() + " " +
                    appLog.getLogMessage());
            }
        }
```

Each result includes a `getOffset()` method, which returns a web-safe string you can use to make a "next page" button in a paginated display. Simply add the offset string of the last result on a page as the `offset()` parameter of the query, and the first result returned will be the next result in the sequence.

Flushing the Log Buffer

In the log fetch API, an "incomplete request" is a request that has not yet finished, but may have written some messages to the log. The API lets you optionally fetch log data for incomplete requests, such as to include the logged activity of a long-running task in the log data.

In Python, application log messages accrue in a log buffer. Typically, the contents of the buffer are written to permanent log storage when the request handler exits. Since most request handlers are short-lived, this is sufficient for capturing log data in real time. For long-running request handlers (such as task handlers), you may wish to flush the log buffer periodically to make log messages available to the fetch API.

To flush the log buffer manually, call the `flush()` function in the `google.appengine.api.logservice` module:

```
from google.appengine.api import logservice

# ...
        logservice.flush()
```

You can also enable automatic log flushing for the duration of the request. To do this, you modify global variables in the `logservice` module. To flush the logs after a certain number of seconds:

```
        logservice.AUTOFLUSH_ENABLED = True
        logservice.AUTOFLUSH_EVERY_SECONDS = 10
```

To flush the logs after a certain number of bytes have been accrued in the buffer:

```
        logservice.AUTOFLUSH_ENABLED = True
        logservice.AUTOFLUSH_EVERY_BYTES = 4096
```

To flush the logs after a certain number of lines have been accrued in the buffer:

```
        logservice.AUTOFLUSH_ENABLED = True
        logservice.AUTOFLUSH_EVERY_LINES = 50
```

You can combine these settings. The flush occurs after any limit is reached. To disable a limit, set it to `None`.

Java apps write log data immediately, and do not use a log buffer.

CHAPTER 20

Deploying and Managing Applications

Uploading your application to App Engine is easy: just click a button or run a command, then enter your developer account email address and password. All your application's code, configuration, and static files are sent to App Engine, and seconds later your new app is running.

Easy deployment is one of App Engine's most useful features. You don't have to worry about which servers have which software, how servers connect to services, or whether machines need to be rebooted or processes restarted. Other than your developer account, there are no database passwords to remember, no secret keys to generate, and no need to administer and troubleshoot individual machines. Your application exists as a single logical entity, and running it on large-scale infrastructure is as easy as running it on your local computer.

App Engine includes features for testing a new version of an app before making it public, reverting to a previous version quickly in case of a problem, and migrating the datastore and service configuration for the app from one version to another. These features let you control how quickly changes are applied to your application: you can make a new version public immediately to fix small bugs, or you can test a new version for a while before making it the version everyone sees.

Service configuration is shared across all versions of an app, including datastore indexes, task queues, and scheduled tasks. When you upload the app, the service configuration files on your computer are uploaded as well, and take effect immediately for all app versions. You can also upload each configuration file separately. This is especially useful for datastore indexes, since new indexes based on existing entities take time to build before they are ready to serve datastore queries.

Notice that service configuration is separate from the application configuration, which includes URL mappings, runtime environment selection, and inbound service activation. Application configuration is bound to a specific app version.

App Engine provides rich facilities for inspecting the performance of an app while it is serving live traffic. Most of these features are available in the Administration Console, including analytic graphs of traffic and resource usage, and browsable request and message logs. You can also use the Console to inspect and make one-off changes to datastore entities.

You also use the Administration Console to perform maintenance tasks, such as giving other developers access to the Console, changing settings, and setting up a billing account.

In this chapter, we discuss how to upload a new app, how to update an existing app, and how to use App Engine's versioning feature to test a new version of an app on App Engine while your users continue to use the previous version. We look at how to migrate the datastore and service configuration from one version to another. We also look at features of the SDK and the Administration Console for inspecting, troubleshooting, and analyzing how your live application is running. And finally, we discuss other application maintenance tasks, billing, and where to get more information.

Uploading an Application

We introduced uploading an application way back in Chapter 2, but let's begin with a brief review.

If you're developing a Python app with the Launcher for Windows or Mac OS X, you can deploy your app by selecting it in the app list and then clicking the Deploy button. The Launcher prompts for your developer account email address and password. The Mac version can remember your account credentials on your Keychain, but it always prompts in case you want to specify a different account. The upload begins, and the Launcher opens a window to display status messages emitted by the uploader tool.

If you're developing a Java app with Eclipse and the Google Plugin, you can deploy your app by clicking on the Deploy App Engine Project button in the Eclipse toolbar (the one that looks like the App Engine logo, a gray airplane engine with blue wings). It prompts for your developer account email address and password. The upload begins, and an Eclipse progress window reports on the status.

You can also upload a Python or Java app with the AppCfg command-line tool from the SDK. For Python, the tool takes the `update` action and a path to your application root directory (the directory containing the *app.yaml* file):

```
appcfg.py update clock
```

For Java, the tool takes the `update` action and a path to the WAR directory:

```
appcfg update clock/war
```

(For Mac OS X or Linux and a Java app, use `appcfg.sh`.)

We said this earlier, but it's worth repeating: there is no way to download the app's files once they have been uploaded. We strongly advise that you keep backups and use a revision control system.

Using Versions

The upload tool determines the application ID from the appropriate configuration file. For Python, this is the `application` element in the *app.yaml* file. For Java, this is the `<application>` element in the *appengine-web.xml* file.

The tool also uses this file to determine the version ID to use for this upload, from the `version` element. If App Engine does not yet have a version of this app with this ID, then it creates a new version with the uploaded files. If App Engine does have such a version, then it replaces the existing version. The replacement is total: no remnants of the previous version's code or static files remain. The new app has only the files present in the project directory on your computer at the time of the upload. Of course, data stored by the services for the app remain, including the datastore, memcache, log data, and enqueued tasks.

The version of the app that is visible on your app's primary domain name—either *app-id*.`appspot.com` or your Google Apps domain—is known as the *default version*. When you upload your app for the first time, the initial version becomes the default version automatically. If you subsequently upload a version with a different version ID, the original version remains the default until you change the default using the Administration Console.

Recall from Chapter 3 that each version has its own `appspot.com` URL that includes the version ID as well as the application ID:

```
version-id.app-id.appspot.com
```

Remember that there are no special protections on the version URLs. If the app does not restrict access by using code or configuration, then anyone who knows an unrestricted URL can access it. If you don't want a user to be able to access a version other than the default, you can check the `Host` header in the app and respond accordingly. You can also upload the nondefault version with configuration that restricts all URLs to administrators. Be sure to upload it again with the real configuration before making it the default version.

When you replace an existing version by uploading the app with that version ID, App Engine starts using the uploaded app for requests for that version within seconds of the upload. It is not guaranteed that every request after a particular time will use the new code and static files, but it usually doesn't take more than a few seconds for the App Master to update all the frontend servers. The App Master ensures that all the files are in place on a frontend server before using the new files to handle requests.

Internally, App Engine maintains a "minor" version number for each version ID. When you upload the app, App Engine creates a new minor version for the app ID and version ID mentioned in the app's configuration file, and associates all code, static files, and frontend configuration with that minor version. When it is done creating the new minor version, it declares the new minor version the latest for the version ID, and the frontend starts to use it. Minor version numbers are an internal implementation detail, and are not exposed to the app or the Administration Console. You cannot access previous minor versions or the latest minor version number, and you cannot revert to previous minor versions. (This explains the word `latest` in the version URL, but you can't actually replace the word with a minor version number to access other minor versions.)

If you upload the app with the same version ID as that of the version that's currently the default, your users will start seeing the updated app within a few seconds of uploading. This is fine for small, low-risk changes that don't depend on changes to your data schemas or datastore indexes.

For larger changes, it's better to upload the app with a new version ID (in the application configuration file), test the app with the version URL, then switch the default version to direct traffic to the new version. To switch the default version, sign in to the Administration Console, and then select Versions from the sidebar. Select the radio button next to the desired version, and then click the Make Default button. This is shown in Figure 20-1.

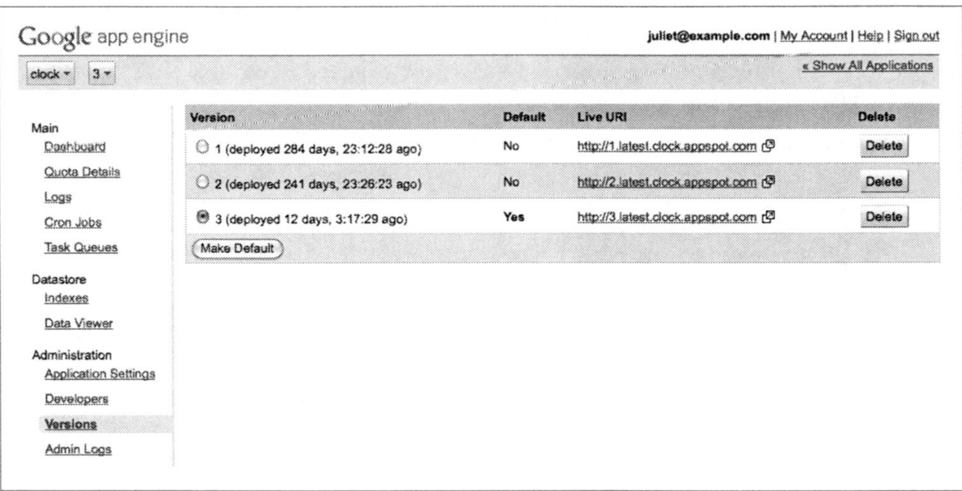

Figure 20-1. The Administration Console Versions panel

App Engine can host up to 10 different version IDs per app at one time. You can delete unused versions from the Administration Console by clicking the Delete button on the appropriate row.

Many actions in the Administration Console refer to a specific version of the app, including usage statistics and the log viewer. You can control which version you're looking at by selecting it from the drop-down menu in the top-left corner of the screen, next to the application ID. The version ID only appears as a drop-down menu if you have more than one version of the app. Similarly, the application ID appears as a drop-down menu if you have more than one app associated with your developer account.

Managing Service Configuration

All versions of an application use the same services. Service configuration and application data are shared across all versions of the app.

An app can have several service-related configuration files:

index.yaml or *datastore-indexes.xml*
: A description of all the required datastore indexes.

queue.yaml or *queue.xml*
: Configuration for task queues.

cron.yaml or *cron.xml*
: The schedule for scheduled tasks (cron jobs).

Whenever you upload the app, these configuration files are uploaded from your computer to the services and take effect for the entire app, replacing any configuration that was once there. This is true regardless of whether the app version ID is new or already exists, or whether the version ID is the default.

You can update the configuration for each service without uploading the entire app by using the AppCfg tool. To update just the index configuration, use the `update_indexes` action, with the project directory (e.g., `app-dir`):

```
appcfg.py update_indexes app-dir
```

To update just the task queue configuration, use `update_queues`:

```
appcfg.py update_queues app-dir
```

And to update just the pending task schedule, use `update_cron`:

```
appcfg.py update_cron app-dir
```

Application Settings

The Application Settings panel of the Administration Console lets you change or view several miscellaneous aspects of your application.

This panel lets you view the application ID and the authentication method (Google accounts or Google Apps) that you set when you registered the application ID. These cannot be changed. If you need different values, you must register a new application ID.

The application title is the user-visible name of your application. It appears on the Google Accounts sign-in screen. You set this when you created the application, and you can change it at any time from this panel.

The "cookie expiration" time is the amount of time a user signed in with a Google account will remain signed in. If the user signs in to your app, he will not have to sign in again from the computer he is using until the expiration time elapses.

Also on this screen, you can view which optional services are enabled for this application. Optional services are those that have passive behavior that affect the app, specifically the inbound services of incoming email and incoming XMPP. You can enable these for an app in the app's configuration file, as discussed in previous chapters.

This screen offers an alternate path for setting up a domain name for an app using Google Apps. Instead of adding the app as a service within Google Apps, you can use this setup procedure to associate the app with an Apps domain with default settings. Either setup procedure has the same effect, and you must still register the domain and create the Google Apps account separately. (There is a link to set up Google Apps on this screen.)

Managing Developers

When you register an application ID, you become a developer for the application automatically. You can invite other people to be developers for the application from the Developers section of the Administration Console.

To invite a developer, you enter the person's email address in the appropriate field and click Invite. App Engine sends an email to the developer inviting her to set up an account. If the email address you invited is for a Google account, the developer can use the existing account to access App Engine, although she must still accept the invitation by clicking on a link in the invitation email message. If the email address does not have a corresponding Google account, the developer can create a Google account for that address by following the instructions in the message. The developer cannot accept the invitation from a Google account with a different address; you must invite the alternate address explicitly.

An invited developer who has not yet accepted the invitation appears in the list with a status of "Pending." After the developer accepts the invitation, she appears with a status of "Active."

You can remove any developer from the list by clicking the Remove button for the developer. The developer loses all access immediately.

All developers of an application have the same rights and access. They can access the Administration Console, upload new application files, create and delete versions, change the default version, access logs, and inspect and tweak the datastore. They can even remove your administrator access, take over billing, and disable or delete the app. When a developer signs in to the application itself via Google Accounts, the app recognizes her as an administrator, allowing her to access URLs configured as administrator-only and telling the app about the administrator status when the app inquires via the API.

While you can only register up to 10 application IDs yourself, you can be a developer on as many applications as you like, assuming you can get invited. Of course, it's against the Terms of Service to create fake accounts just to be able to create more apps and invite your main account to them, so don't do that.

Every administrative action performed by a developer adds a corresponding entry in a special log. Any developer can view this log in the Admin Logs section of the Console. This log cannot be edited or erased. Activities that get logged include app updates, version changes, developer invites and removals, index changes, settings changes, and changes to datastore entities made from the Console.

Quotas and Billing

The first thing you see when you visit the Administration Console and select an app is the "dashboard." This handy screen provides a visual overview of your app's traffic, resource usage, and errors. For an example of the dashboard for a new app, refer back to Figure 2-12 in Chapter 2.

The topmost chart displays time-based data over the past 24 hours. You can select from several data sets to view via the drop-down menu, including requests per second, clock time or CPU time per request, bandwidth, errors, and quota denials. You can adjust the period for this chart by clicking on the buttons (such as "6 hr").

Below the chart is a graph showing how much of the billable quotas have been consumed for the calendar day, and how much of your daily budget has been spent for each quota. A message at the upper-right of the chart indicates how much of the calendar day is remaining. If any of the bars look like they might fill up before the next reset, you may need to increase your budget for that quota to avoid quota denials.

Near the bottom of the dashboard are lists of popular URL paths and URLs that are returning errors. You can click on a URL to view the detailed request logs for that URL path.

The dashboard's time-based chart and URL traffic lists show data for the version of the app selected by the drop-down menu in the upper-left corner of the screen. When you first sign in to the Console, the default version is selected. To view data for a different version of the app, select it from the drop-down menu.

You can view a more comprehensive chart of how the app is consuming resources with quotas from the Quota Details section of the Administration Console. This chart shows billable quotas as well as several fixed quotas, such as API calls and service bandwidth. If your app is having quota-denial errors, check this screen for information on how the app is consuming resources.

The resource usage chart on the dashboard and the quota details screen show the total of all resource usage for all versions of the app. All versions of an app share the same budget and quotas.

When your app is ready to outgrow the free quotas, you can set up billing and set a budget for additional resources. App Engine allocates more resources as needed according to the budget you establish, and you are only billed for the resources actually consumed. To set up billing for an application, you select the Billing Settings panel in the Administration Console and click the Enable Billing button. The developer account used to enable billing becomes the "billing account," and the owner of that account is solely responsible for setting the budget and paying for resources consumed.

When you enable billing, the Console prompts you for billing information and authorization to charge via Google Checkout, Google's payment service. The process looks as though you're making a purchase via Google Checkout, but no money is charged right away. You set the budget for the app, a maximum amount of money that can be charged to your account, then authorize Google Checkout to charge up to that amount. If you increase the budget at a later date, you must reauthorize the amount with Google Checkout. Figure 20-2 is an example of the budget settings screen.

You can view a history of charges made to the billing account, including a breakdown of the billed resource usage for each calendar day, in the Billing History panel.

Getting Help

If you have questions not answered by this book, you may find your answers in the official documentation on Google's website:

> *http://developers.google.com/appengine/*

The documentation includes complete references for the APIs and tools for both the Python and Java runtime environments; a list of frequently asked questions and answers (the FAQ); and a large collection of articles describing best practices, interesting features, and complete working examples.

You may also want to browse the contents of the SDK, as installed by either the Eclipse plug-in or the Python Launcher, and also available as a ZIP archive from the website. The source code for the Python SDK serves as supplementary documentation, and includes several undocumented (and unsupported) features and extensions. Both SDKs also include a set of functional example applications.

All App Engine developers should subscribe to Google's App Engine downtime mailing list. This low-traffic, announcement-only list is used by the App Engine team to announce scheduled times when services are taken down for maintenance, and also to report the status of unexpected problems:

> *http://groups.google.com/group/google-appengine-downtime-notify*

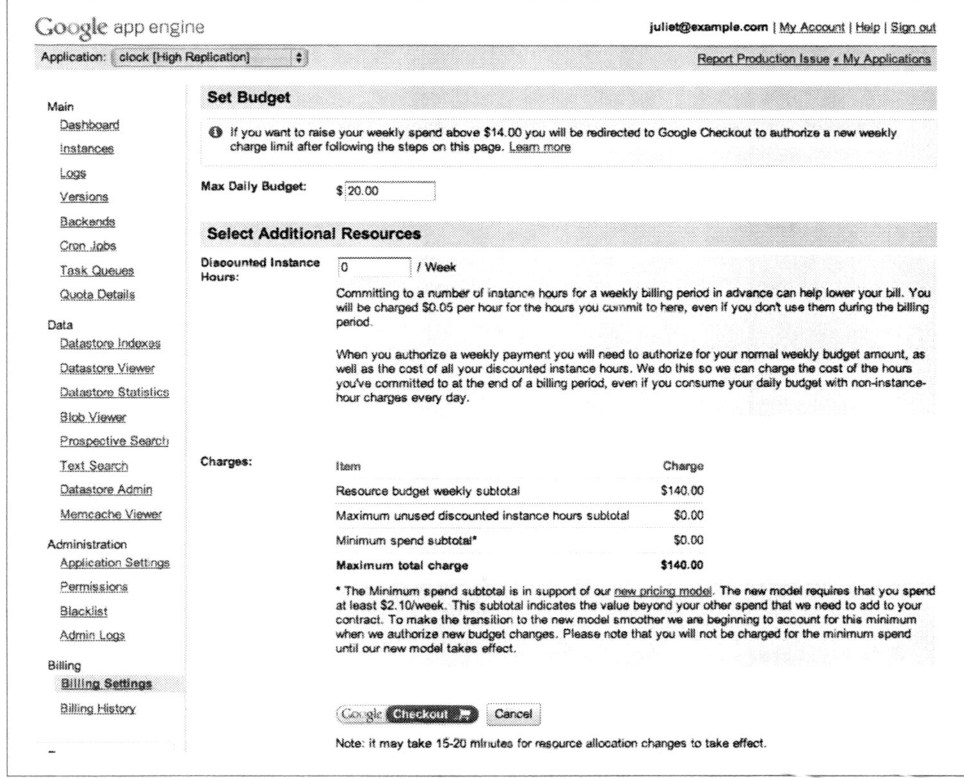

Figure 20-2. Setting the budget in the Administration Console

You can check the current and past health of App Engine and its services by consulting the system status site:

http://code.google.com/status/appengine

By far the best place to ask questions about Google App Engine is Stack Overflow. Post your question with the `google-app-engine` tag, and it'll be seen by the App Engine developer community, as well as the App Engine team at Google. As you learn more, you can answer other people's questions and build your reputation as an App Engine expert. Use Google to search past answers, which may have what you're looking for:

http://stackoverflow.com/questions/tagged/google-app-engine

If you believe you have found a bug in App Engine, the SDK, or the Administration Console, or if you have a feature you'd like to request, you can post to the App Engine issue tracker. You can also see features others have requested, and vote for your favorites. (The App Engine team does indeed consider the highly requested features in this list when determining the product road map.)

http://code.google.com/p/googleappengine/issues/list

Google has a general discussion group for App Engine developers and an IRC channel, and also does regular live-streamed video question-and-answer sessions with the team. This page has more information on community resources:

http://developers.google.com/appengine/community

Index

Symbols

A

We'd like to hear your suggestions for improving our indexes. Send email to *index@oreilly.com*.

D

G

H

K

L

M

N

O

P

Q

R

S

T

U

V

W

X

Y

Z

About the Author

Dan Sanderson is a technical writer and software engineer at Google, Inc. He has worked in the web industry for over 10 years as a software engineer and technical writer for Google, Amazon.com, and the Walt Disney Internet Group. He lives in Seattle, Washington. For more information about Dan Sanderson, visit his website at *http://www.dansanderson.com*.

Colophon

The animal on the cover of *Programming Google App Engine* is a waterbuck (*Kobus ellipsiprymnus*), a type of antelope found in western, eastern, and southern Africa. Waterbucks stand at about five feet at the shoulder and have reddish-brown coats that become darker in color as the animals age. Long, sinuous horns distinguish male waterbucks, while a ring of white hair around the tail distinguishes both genders from other antelopes.

Waterbucks live in savannas and other vegetative areas, where they graze on rough grass and leaves from trees and bushes. Contrary to its name, the waterbuck spends most of its time on land, but it will often take refuge in a body of water to avoid predators.

African myth claims that the meat of the waterbuck is inedible, but this isn't so. Although the waterbuck's sweat glands produce a strong odor reminiscent of turpentine in order to better protect itself from predators, the animal's meat—while not especially flavorful—is safe to consume.

Male waterbucks frequently use their horns as a means of defense against their enemies. As the males are polygamous and highly possessive of their mates, they are especially prone to fatally goring other male waterbucks who enter their territories and try to steal members of their harems.

The cover image is from Wood's *Animate Creations*. The cover font is Adobe ITC Garamond. The text font is Linotype Birka; the heading font is Adobe Myriad Condensed; and the code font is LucasFont's TheSansMonoCondensed.

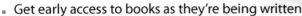

'SIA information can be obtained at www.ICGtesting.com
ted in the USA
W062354111012

57BV00001B/1/P